W9-BVZ-720

RICHARD HOFSTADTER, DeWitt Clinton Professor of History, Columbia University, is the author of *The Age of Reform,* which won the Pulitzer Prize for History in 1956. His other books include *The American Political Tradition,* and *The Development of Academic Freedom in the United States,* written with Walter P. Metzger.

WILSON SMITH, Associate Professor of History and Education, The Johns Hopkins University, has previously published *Professors & Public Ethics* (1956).

DISCARDED
JENKS LRC
GORDON COLLEGE

AMERICAN HIGHER EDUCATION: A DOCUMENTARY HISTORY

American Higher Education

A DOCUMENTARY HISTORY

Edited by RICHARD HOFSTADTER and WILSON SMITH

VOLUME II

 THE UNIVERSITY OF CHICAGO PRESS

378.73
H 677
vol. 2

Library of Congress Catalog Card Number: 61-15935

The University of Chicago Press, Chicago & London
The University of Toronto Press, Toronto 5, Canada

© 1961 by The University of Chicago. Published 1961
Composed and printed by The University of Chicago Press
Chicago, Illinois, U.S.A.

CONTENTS TO VOLUME II

P
ART SIX

THE DEMAND FOR A TRUE
UNIVERSITY

Part SEVEN

Part EIGHT

Part NINE

UNIVERSITY FACULTIES AND
UNIVERSITY CONTROL

Part TEN

ACADEMIC FREEDOM IN THE
UNIVERSITY

PART ELEVEN

HIGHER EDUCATION FOR THE

TWENTIETH-CENTURY WORLD

Part VI

THE DEMAND FOR A TRUE
UNIVERSITY

Tʜᴇ ᴏʟᴅ ᴄᴏʟʟᴇɢᴇ sʏsᴛᴇᴍ did not just suddenly give way to the university era in the decades following the Civil War. Years before, the demand for a true university was being pressed by a great many educators, and the modern American university was the final outcome of two generations of agitation, criticism, and hard work. Educational criticism quickened notably in the years between 1850 and the chartering of Cornell in 1865. President Francis Wayland of Brown was one of the leading figures in this agitation. In his famous 1850 report to the Corporation of his university (Doc. 1) he argued that the existing collegiate system was not serving the community's needs for scientific, practical, or advanced study, and recommended important revisions in the curriculum and in the scale of its operations. In the following year, Henry P. Tappan, writing on *University Education* (Doc. 2), agreed with Wayland that "education has become superficial by attempting too much in the short period allotted." "We inspire no general desire for higher education," he lamented, "and fail to attract college students, because we promise and do not perform." Strongly influenced by the German example, Tappan outlined the main features of a complete system of state-supported secular schools, extending from the elementary grades to the university. A student, adequately prepared in the succes-

475

sive stages of lower training, would, in Tappan's view, benefit from a true system of advanced study at the summit of the educational pyramid. Tappan found much resistance to his ideas in Michigan, but he gathered around him and profoundly influenced the educational thinking of a number of younger men, of whom the most important was Andrew D. White, through whose work (Doc. 5 and Part VII, Doc. 8) Tappan had an important effect on the university revolution of the postwar period. While Tappan projected ambitious plans and tried to educate the community to the true meaning of a university (Doc. 4), other critics, like F. A. P. Barnard (Doc. 3), criticized the cramped parochialism of the little American custodial college. If progress was to be made, he believed, the whole country must "abandon the cloister system entirely, and with it the attempt to do what is now done only in pretense; that is, the attempt to watch over the conduct and protect the morals of the student." What both men were calling for was an advance in maturity and the end of an era in which the college was thought of as merely an extension of the secondary school.

"Sordid" was the word Andrew D. White, the builder of Cornell, applied to most features of the old college, and even in his student days the idea of a real university had been growing (Doc. 6), fed by his visits to Oxford, Cambridge, Paris, and the German universities and his reading in the literature of educational criticism. In organizing Cornell (Doc. 7) White followed some of the lessons he had learned from Tappan—among them gathering the most competent faculty he could find and making the university attractive to them. "I did all in my power," he wrote, "to communicate to my colleagues something of my own enthusiasm for a university suitably endowed, free from sectarian trammels, centrally situated, and organized to meet fully the wants of the State as regarded advanced education, general and technical." The work of founding and establishing Cornell went on successfully despite harassments similar to those from which the ambitions of the organizers of the state universities had suffered since the time of Jefferson. It was necessary for Ezra Cornell, the institution's benefactor, to reply to charges that he was founding an "aristocratic" institution (Doc. 8). Sponsors of sectarian institutions and believers in the old fragmented collegiate system saw in the plans for Cornell a threat to their way of life and subjected the university to much attack (Doc. 9).

One of the major stimuli to the university, however, came from the technological needs of agriculture and business. The passing in 1862 of the Morrill Act (Doc. 11), giving federal aid to agricultural and mechanical colleges, was a recognition of these practical needs, for agricultural education had come to be regarded, at least by some, as a partial answer to the farmer's problem. Much of the funds set aside for education were used for small, struggling, ineffectual, excessively vocational schools; but the success of Cornell was made possible partly by the diversion to it of Morrill Act funds, and in states like Wisconsin, Minnesota, Missouri, Georgia, North Carolina, Tennessee, and Iowa, existing institutions were enlarged. It was not long before many who initially had been most enthusiastic about the "practical" intent of the land-grant colleges began to think of modifying the strictly vocational and technical nature of the schools (Doc. 14).

Another beneficiary of the Act was Yale's Sheffield Scientific School, then being formed. Excluded from the regular colleges, science had been entering the educational structure by the back door, in the form of separate technical schools, beginning with Rensselaer Polytechnic Institute in 1824, Harvard's Lawrence Scientific School and Sheffield in 1847, and Dartmouth's Chandler School of Science and Arts in 1851. The Massachusetts Institute of Technology was chartered in 1861. The new scientific schools not only entered into competition for students with the regular colleges, thus forcing them to reconsider what they were doing, but they also challenged the older educational philosophy. The governing board of the Sheffield School issued a call for new principles of education in 1868 (Doc. 13) that sounds like a direct answer to the philosophy of the Yale Report of 1828 (Part IV, Doc. 11).

For all the would-be architects of universities, the German university remained, as it had been for the generation of Ticknor, Bancroft, and Cogswell, the model toward which one should aspire. Moving through Tappan to Michigan and through White to New York, it had never ceased to have its appeal at Harvard where men like Frederick Henry Hedge, the professor of German literature who had gone to Germany with Bancroft as a boy of thirteen, kept the image of German achievement alive in the minds of his colleagues (Doc. 10). Another critic, James Morgan Hart, made an instructive and detailed comparison (Doc. 12) between the American college and the German university.

1. *Francis Wayland's Report to the Brown Corporation, 1850*

As a result of this proposal for a more flexible curriculum, Brown University liberalized its entrance requirements, introduced new subjects into the plan of studies, and inaugurated a limited elective system. For a brief period there was a rise in enrollment and endowment. Francis Wayland (1796–1865), however, did not live to see his plans mature as the next great step in the development of American higher education.

See Part IV, Doc. 21.

If it be the fact that our colleges cannot sustain themselves, but are obliged to make repeated calls upon the benevolence of the community, not because the community is poor and education inordinately expensive, but because, instead of attempting to furnish scientific and literary instruction to every class of our people, they have furnished it only to a single class, and that by far the least numerous; if they are furnishing an education for which there is no remunerative, but even at the present low prices, a decreasing demand; if they are, not by intention, but practically, excluding the vastly larger portion of the community from advantages in which they would willingly participate, and are thus accomplishing but a fraction of the good which is manifestly within their power, then it would seem that relief must be expected from a radical change of the system of collegiate instruction. We must carefully survey the wants of the various classes of the community in our own vicinity, and adapt our courses of instruction, not for the benefit of one class, but for the benefit of all classes. The demand for general education in our country is pressing and universal. The want of that science, which alone can lay the foundation of eminent success in the useful arts, is extensively felt. The proportion of our young men who are devoting themselves to the productive professions, is great and annually increasing. They all need such an education as our colleges, with some modifications in their present system, could very easily supply. Is there not reason to believe that, if such an education were furnished, they would cheerfully avail themselves of it?

Francis Wayland, *Report to the Corporation of Brown University, On Changes in the System of Collegiate Education, Read March 28, 1850* (Providence, R.I., 1850), pp. 50–63, 74–76.

Were an institution established with the intention of adapting its instruction to the wants of the whole community, its arrangements would be made in harmony with the following principles.

1. The present system of adjusting collegiate study to a fixed term of four years, or to any other term, must be abandoned, and every student be allowed, within limits to be determined by statute, to carry on, at the same time, a greater or less number of courses as he may choose.

2. The time allotted to each particular course of instruction would be determined by the nature of the course itself, and not by its supposed relation to the wants of any particular profession.

3. The various courses should be so arranged, that, in so far as it is practicable, every student might study what he chose, all that he chose, and nothing but what he chose. The Faculty, however, at the request of a parent or guardian, should have authority to assign to any student, such courses as they might deem for his advantage.

4. Every course of instruction, after it has been commenced, should be continued without interruption until it is completed.

5. In addition to the present courses of instruction, such should be established as the wants of the various classes of the community require.

6. Every student attending any particular course, should be at liberty to attend any other that he may desire.

7. It would be required that no student be admitted as a candidate for a degree, unless he had honorably sustained his examination in such studies as may be ordained by the corporation; but no student would be under any obligation to proceed to a degree, unless he chose.

8. Every student would be entitled to a certificate of such proficiency as he may have made in every course that he has pursued.

The courses of instruction to be pursued in this institution might be as follows:

1. A course of instruction in Latin, occupying two years.
2. A course of instruction in Greek, occupying two years.
3. A course of instruction in three Modern Languages.
4. A course of instruction in Pure Mathematics, two years.
5. A course of instruction in Mechanics, Optics, and Astronomy, either with or without Mathematical Demonstrations, $1\frac{1}{2}$ years.
6. A course of instruction in Chemistry, Physiology and Geology, $1\frac{1}{2}$ years.

7. A course of instruction in the English Language and Rhetoric, one year.

8. A course of instruction in Moral and Intellectual Philosophy, one year.

9. A course of instruction in Political Economy, one term.

10. A course of instruction in History, one term.

11. A course of instruction in the Science of Teaching.

12. A course of instruction on the Principles of Agriculture.

13. A course of instruction on the Application of Chemistry to the Arts.

14. A course of instruction on the Application of Science to the Arts.

15. A course of instruction in the Science of Law.

Some of these courses would require a lesson or lecture every working day of the week, others only two or three in the week. Any professor might be allowed to conduct the studies of more than one course, if he could do it with advantage to the institution.

Should this idea be adopted, and the instruction given in this college be arranged on these principles, it would be seen that opportunity would be afforded to modify it as as [sic] experience should prove desirable. Some courses may be abridged or abolished, and others added or extended. The object of the change would be to adapt the institution to the wants, not of a class, but of the whole community. It by no means is to be taken for granted, in a country like our own, that every college is to teach the same studies, and to the same extent. It would be far better that each should consult the wants of its own locality, and do that best, for which it possessed the greatest facilities. Here would arise opportunity for diversified forms of excellence; the knowledge most wanted would the more easily become diffused, and the general progress of science would receive an important impulse from every institution of learning in our land.

It may be proper here to indicate the manner in which, as your committee believes, the plan proposed would relieve the embarrassments of the institution.

In explaining their views on this part of the subject, it is not pretended, that with any plan that can be devised, in the present condition of New England, this can be wholly a self-supporting institution. Education is afforded at all our colleges so far below cost, that, at cost price, it is doubtful whether it could be disposed of. The college is far from supporting itself now. Unless it receives some aid, it cannot be carried on. The inquiry which we have felt it to be our duty to make, has been this: In what manner, at the least expense to its friends, can it be put in a condition to support itself? It has seemed to your committee, that in no other way can this result be arrived at, than by extending its advantages to every class of the community, and thus increasing the number of its pupils. The more it can do for itself, the less need its friends do for it.

That such a change as is here proposed, would add to the number of its pupils, seems to your committee probable, for several reasons.

1. The course of instruction will, it is hoped, present a better preparation for the learned professions, than that pursued at present. There is no reason, therefore, why this class of pupils should be diminished.

2. Opportunity would be afforded to those who wished to pursue a more generous course of professional education, to remain in college profitably for five or six years, instead of four, as at present.

3. Many young men who intend to enter the professions, are unwilling or unable to spend four years in the preparatory studies of college. They would, however, cheerfully spend one or two years in such study, if they were allowed to select such branches of science as they chose. This class would probably form an important addition to our numbers, and we should thus, in some degree, improve the education of a large portion of all the professions.

4. If we except the ancient languages, there are but few of the studies now pursued in college, which, if well taught, would not be attractive to young men preparing for any of the active departments of life. If these several courses were so arranged as to be easily accessible to intelligent young men of all classes, it may reasonably be expected that many will desire to spend a term, a year, or two years, under our instruction.

5. It is not probable that the courses of instruction in agriculture, or chemistry, or science applied to the arts, will, of necessity, occupy all the time of the student. Many of these persons will probably desire to avail themselves of the advantages so easily placed in their power. Another source of demand for the courses in general science would thus be created.

Should these expectations be realized, it will be perceived that the addition to our numbers will come from classes who now receive no benefit whatever from the college system, as it at present exists. Our numbers would thus be increased without diminishing the number of students in other colleges in New England; and we should be carrying the blessings of scientific and literary education to portions of society from which they have thus far been practically excluded.

Perhaps it may not be inappropriate to add, that if the above views be correct, any college in our country now able to support itself, might easily adopt, to a considerable extent, the system we have ventured to recommend. Its means now are, its funds and its fees for tuition. It is not supposed that the number of its students could be diminished by offering its advantages to vastly larger classes of the community. Supposing its numbers to be the same, it would have the same means of support as at present. There would seem, therefore, to be no particular risk in trying the experiment, since its resources will be increased by every student that it may attract from those classes of society that now yield it no income.

If reasons need be offered for attempting the changes in our collegiate system that have been here indicated, the following will readily suggest themselves.

1. IT IS JUST.—Every man who is willing to pay for them, has a right to all the means which other men enjoy, for cultivating his mind by discipline, and enriching it with science. It is therefore unjust, either practically or theoretically, to restrict the means of this cultivation and discipline to one class, and that the smallest class in the community.

If every man who is willing to pay for them, has an *equal* right to the benefits of education, every man has a *special* right to that *kind* of education which will be of the greatest value to him in the prosecution of useful industry. It is therefore eminently unjust, practically to exclude the largest classes of the community from an opportunity of acquiring that knowledge, the possession of which is of inestimable importance, both to national progress and individual success. And yet we have in this country, one hundred and twenty colleges, forty-two theological seminaries, and forty-seven law schools, and we have not a single institution designed to furnish the agriculturist, the manufacturer, the mechanic, or the merchant with the education that will prepare him for the profession to which his life is to be devoted.

Our institutions of learning have generally been endowed by the wealth of the productive classes of society. It is surely unjust that a system should be universally adopted, which, practically, excludes them from the benefits which they have conferred upon others.

2. IT IS EXPEDIENT.—The moral conditions being equal, the progress

of a nation in wealth, happiness, and refinement, is measured by the universality of its knowledge of the laws of nature, and its skill in adapting these laws to the purposes of man. Civilization is advancing, and it can only advance in the line of the useful arts. It is, therefore, of the greatest national importance to spread broadcast over the community, that knowledge, by which alone the useful arts can be multiplied and perfected. Every producer, who labors in his art scientifically, is the best of all experimenters; and he is, of all men, the most likely, by discovery, to add to our knowledge of the laws of nature. He is, also, specially the individual most likely to invent the means by which those laws shall be subjected to the service of man. Of the truth of these remarks, every one must be convinced, who will observe the success to which any artisan arrives, who, fortunately, by his own efforts, (for at present he could do it in no other way,) has attained to a knowledge of the principles which govern the process in which he is employed.

Suppose that, since the Revolution, as much capital and talent had been employed in diffusing among all classes of society, the knowledge of which every class stands in need, as has been employed in inculcating the knowledge needed in preparation for the professions, is it possible to estimate the benefits which would have been conferred upon our country? The untold millions that have been wasted by ignorance, would have been now actively employed in production. A knowledge universally diffused of the laws of vegetation, might have doubled our annual agricultural products. Probably no country on earth can boast of as intelligent a class of mechanics and manufacturers, as our own. Had a knowledge of the principles been generally diffused among them, we should already have outstripped Europe in all those arts which increase the comforts, or multiply the refinements of human life. Perhaps, in the earlier history of our country, such knowledge would not have been adequately appreciated. That period, however, has now passed away. An impulse has been given to common school education, which cannot but render every man definitely sensible of his wants, and consequently eager to supply them. The time then would seem to have arrived, when our institutions of learning are called upon to place themselves in harmony with the advanced and rapidly advancing condition of society.

3. IT IS NECESSARY.—To us, it seems that but little option is left to the colleges in this matter. Any one who will observe the progress which, within the last thirty years, has been made by the productive classes of

society, in power, wealth, and influence, must be convinced that a system of education, practically restricted to a class vastly smaller, and rapidly decreasing in influence, cannot possibly continue. Within a few years, the manufacturing interest has wrung the corn laws from the aristocracy of Great Britain. Let any one recall the relative position of the professions, and of the mercantile and manufacturing interests, in any of our cities, twenty years since, and compare it with their relative position now, and he cannot but be convinced, that a great and a progressive change has taken place. Men who do not design to educate their sons for the professions, are capable of determining upon the kind of instruction which they need. If the colleges will not furnish it, they are able to provide it themselves; and they will provide it. In New York and Massachusetts, incipient measures have been taken for establishing agricultural colleges. The bill before the legislature of New York, provides for instruction in all the branches taught in our colleges, with the exception of languages. It is to be, in fact, an institution for giving all the education which we now give, agricultural science being substituted for Latin and Greek. What is proposed to be done for the farmers, must soon be done either for or by the manufacturers and merchants. In this manner, each productive department will have its own school, in which its own particular branch of knowledge will be taught, besides the other ordinary studies of a liberal education. A large portion of the instruction communicated will thus be the same in all. Mathematics, Mechanics, Chemistry, Physiology, Rhetoric, Moral and Intellectual Philosophy, and Political Economy, will be taught in them all. The Colleges teach precisely the same sciences, with the addition of Latin and Greek, in the place of the knowledge designed in these separate schools, for a particular profession.

If the *prestige* of colleges should be thus destroyed, and it be found that as good an education as they furnish, can be obtained in any of those other schools, the number of their students will be seriously diminished. If, by this dissemination of science among all the other classes of society, the tendency towards the professions should be still farther arrested, the colleges will be deserted by yet larger numbers. They may become very good foundations for the support of instructors, but very few will be found to avail themselves of their instructions.

Is not such a result as this to be deplored? Is it desirable that so many teachers should be employed in teaching precisely the same things? All the branches of general science, taught in any one generous school,

must be taught in them all. The colleges already have existing arrangements for teaching them. They are, to a considerable extent, supplied
with libraries, apparatus, and all the means of instruction. Would it
not seem desirable, that they should so far modify their system, as to
furnish all the instruction needed by the various classes of society, who
desire special professional teaching, and so arrange their courses of
general knowledge, that all, of every class, may, with equal facility,
avail themselves of their advantages? In this manner the colleges will
reap all the benefit arising from the diffusion and progress of knowledge. Pursuing any other course, they would seem to suffer injury
from one of the most hopeful indications of the progress of civilization.

But two subjects remain to be considered by your committee. They
are, the relations which, under such a system, would exist between the
corporation and the officers of instruction; and the subject of academical degrees.

The relation existing at present between the corporation and the
instructors in our colleges, so far as it can be gathered from pretty
constant practice, is substantially the following:

The corporation pledge themselves to the public to furnish all the
instruction which is generally demanded, in order to qualify a student
for the degree of Bachelor of Arts. They appoint professors for life,
who are to give this instruction, and they hold themselves responsible
to furnish the professors with an adequate support; they themselves,
by theory, observing from time to time whether their intentions are
adequately fulfilled. If an officer's salary be insufficent for his support,
be the number of students greater or less, both he and the public may
justly charge the corporation with injustice; and corporations are frequently so charged, though they have already distributed every dollar
of income over which they have any control.

It will at once appear, that if an extended and various system of education, such as has been indicated above, be adopted, the relation of
the parties to each other must be made more simple and definite. The
corporation cannot pretend any longer to hold themselves responsible
for the support of every professor; nor can they pretend to oversee him
in the discharge of his duty. They have really no means of supporting
an instructor, except those derived from the funds committed to their
charge by the public. These they can appropriate on some equitable
principle to each *professorship*. The officer who accepts of a professorship will then be entitled to whatever income is attached to it, and he

will look to his fees for instruction for the remainder of his compensation. Like every other man, the instructor will be brought directly in contact with the public, and his remuneration will be made to depend distinctly upon his industry and skill in his profession.

The corporation would thus be responsible for the support of the officer of instruction, only to the amount of the funds under its control. It would furnish every instructor with a lecture room, the necessary apparatus, and the use of the library, holding every individual separately responsible for the condition of all the public property intrusted to his care. In the universities on the continent of Europe, it is always held, that, in case a professor does not justify the expectations of the public, the government is at liberty, without removing such incumbent, to appoint another in the same department. It deserves to be considered whether such power might be advantageously reserved by the visitors of colleges in this country. It is also found, in other countries, to be of great advantage, to allow any person, of suitable character and qualifications, to teach in a university any branch of science in which he may excel. In this manner every enterprising young man, endowed with a talent for teaching, has the opportunity of making known to the public his qualifications; and teaching is thus placed in the same condition as the other professions. Whether this plan might not be adopted here, will deserve the attention of the corporation. . . .

The objection that would arise to this plan, would probably be its effect upon the classics. It will be said, that we should thus diminish the amount of study bestowed on Latin and Greek. To this the reply is easy. If, by placing Latin and Greek upon their own merits, they are unable to retain their present place in the education of civilized and Christianized man, then let them give place to something better. They have, by right, no preëminence over other studies, and it is absurd to claim it for them. But we go further. In our present system we devote some six or seven years to the compulsory study of the classics. Besides innumerable academies, we have one hundred and twenty colleges, in which, for a large part of the time, classical studies occupy the labors of the student. And what is the fruit? How many of these students read either classical Greek or Latin after they leave college? If, with all this labor, we fail to imbue our young men with a love for the classics, is there any reason to fear that any change will render their position less advantageous? Is there not reason to hope, that by rendering this study less compulsory, and allowing those who have a taste for it to devote themselves more thoroughly to classical reading, we shall raise it from its present depression, and derive from it all the benefit which it is able to confer?

In view of these facts and arguments, the committee have arrived at the following conclusions.

1. This college cannot, under any circumstances, be long sustained without large addition to its funds.

2. In the present condition of collegiate education in New England, it is not probable that addition to its funds would increase the number of its students, unless large provision were also made for gratuitous tuition.

3. Such funds might attract students from other colleges, but would do little either to increase the aggregate number of educated men, or to extend the advantages of education to those classes of the community which do not now enjoy them.

4. There is reason to hope that the same amount of funds which would be necessary to sustain the college under the present system, might, if the system were modified in the manner above suggested, add greatly to the number of students, and, at the same time, confer inestimable advantages on every class of society.

The committee, therefore, recommend to the corporation the adoption of the following resolutions.

Resolved, that the system of instruction in Brown University be modified and extended in the manner indicated in the above Report, as soon as the sum of $125,000 can be added to its present funds.

Resolved that [   ] be authorized to carry the proposed changes into effect, by perfecting the details and completing the necessary arrangements previously, if possible, to the commencement of the next collegiate year.

All which is respectfully submitted.

For the committee,

F. WAYLAND, *Chairman*

Brown University, March 28, 1850

2. Henry P. Tappan on University Education, 1851

Henry P. Tappan (1805–81) was born in Rhinebeck, New York, and received his B.A. from Union College (1825). In 1827 he graduated from Auburn Theological Seminary; he was ordained in the Congregational church in 1828 and four years later became professor of moral and intellectual philosophy at the University of the City of New York (later New York University), where he served until his dismissal as the result of an academic controversy in 1837. His books on philosophy and theology won for him a widening reputation, and in 1852 he was called to the presidency of the University of Michigan. The views expressed in the previous year in his *University Education,* here reprinted in part, were those he tried to realize in Michigan. Much influenced by the Prussian system of education, which he had inspected at first hand, he envisioned a full-fledged university, with advanced studies, at the head of an integrated system of state education. In this book he was a pioneer among American writers in stating the ideal of the state university as a place for advanced study. In practice he made Michigan a leader among the midwestern state universities as Jefferson's University of Virginia had been among those of the South. Despite his outstanding achievements, much sectarian and personal hostility was mobilized against him, and after an unfriendly board of regents came into control he was asked to resign in 1863. Twelve years later the regents acknowledged their regret by passing resolutions hailing his contributions to the university. Tappan spent the last years of his life in Europe.

See Docs. 4 and 5; Charles M. Perry, *Henry Philip Tappan* (Ann Arbor, 1933); I. N. Demmon (ed.), *University of Michigan, Regents Proceedings, 1837–1864* (Ann Arbor, 1915), pp. 1119–66; Wilfred Shaw, *The University of Michigan* (New York, 1920).

We have spoken of the German Universities as model institutions. Their excellence consists in two things: first, they are purely Universities, without any admixture of collegial tuition. Secondly, they are complete as Universities, providing libraries and all other material of learning, and having professors of eminence to lecture on theology, law, and medicine, the philosophical, mathematical, natural, philological, and political Sciences, on history and geography, on the history and principles of Art, in fine, upon every branch of human knowledge. The professors are so numerous that a proper division of labor takes place, and every subject is thoroughly discussed. At the University every student selects the courses he is to attend. He is thrown upon his own responsibility and diligence. He is left free to pursue his studies; but, if he wishes to become a clergyman, a physician, a lawyer, a states-

Henry P. Tappan, *University Education* (New York, 1851), pp. 43–46, 63–101.

man, a professor, or a teacher in any superior school, he must go through the most rigid examinations, both oral and written.

Collegial tuition in the German Universities does not exist, because wholly unnecessary, the student being fully prepared at the Gymnasium before he is permitted to enter the University. Without the Gymnasium, the University would be little worth. The course at the Gymnasium embraces a very thorough study of the Latin and Greek languages, a knowledge of the mathematics below the Differential and Integral Calculus, general history, and one or two modern languages besides the German, and Hebrew if the student design to study theology. The examinations are full and severe, the gradations of merit are accurately marked, and no one below the second grade is permitted to enter the University.

The Gymnasia thus guard the entrance of the Universities. Besides, the University course would not be available to him who had not prepared himself for it. It presumes certain attainments, and passes by the elements of the sciences. It is true, indeed, that a student may neglect his opportunities in the University, but then he throws away all hopes of professional life, and of employment in the State.

The Educational System of Germany, and particularly in Prussia, is certainly a very noble one. We cannot well be extravagant in its praise. Thorough in all its parts, consistent with itself, and vigorously sustained, it furnishes every department of life with educated men, and keeps up at the Universities themselves, in every branch of knowledge, a supply of erudite and elegant scholars and authors, for the benefit and glory of their country, and the good of mankind.

In comparing the University system of Germany with that of England, it is worthy of remark that Germany has also admirable common-school systems for popular education, while England is strikingly deficient in this respect. In the one case a properly-developed University system has reached its natural result of invigorating general education; in the other the priestly privilege of a cloistered learning is still maintained.

The Colleges of America are plainly copied from the Colleges of the English Universities. The course of studies, the President and Tutors, the number of years occupied by the course, are all copied from the English model. We have seen that in the English Institutions, the name of University alone remained, while the collegial or tutorial system absorbed all the educational functions. In America, while Colleges were professedly established, they soon assumed a mixed character. Professors were appointed, but they discharged only the duty of tutors in the higher grades of study; so that the tutors were really assistant professors, or the professors only tutors of the first rank. Our Colleges also have from the beginning conferred degrees in all the faculties, which in England belongs only to the University. By establishing the faculties of Theology, Law and Medicine, some of our colleges have approached still more nearly to the forms and functions of a University. By assuming the title of University and College indifferently, as we are prone to do, we seem to intimate that we have some characteristics belonging to both, and that we deem it in our power to become Universities whenever we please. Sometimes the only advance made to the higher position, is by establishing a medical school; which, however, has little other connection with the college than its dependence upon it for conferring the degree of Doctor of Medicine. . . .

As to the defects in the system of education in our country, we have already given our assent to the Report of Brown University, in respect to the first; we believe that education has become superficial by attempting too much in the short period allotted. The other defects do not strike us so forcibly. A review of the college studies does not show an especial adaptation to the learned professions, unless it be in the space given to Latin and Greek. Indeed, the Report admits that it is not well adapted to the learned professions, and that good classical scholars under the received system are as rare as good mathematicians and civil engineers. Some of our colleges, too, have introduced a scientific course in distinction from a classical, to afford an opportunity to prepare for the other forms of life besides the learned professions. We think, too, that the idea of accomplishing a general discipline of the mind preparatory to any sphere of active duty, has not been absent from our collegiate systems. We confess, however, that this idea has not been well carried out and made effective. We have been aiming to do great things; we have called our colleges universities; we have tried to enlarge our course of studies more and more; we seem to have been struggling to afford every imaginable facility; and yet we have only a superficial and inadequate education.

Must we not seek for our great error somewhere else? We inspire no general desire for high education, and fail to collect students, because we promise and do not perform. Hence we fall into disrepute, and young men of ability contrive to prepare themselves for active life without our aid. In connection with this the commercial spirit of our country, and the many avenues to wealth which are opened before enterprise, create a distaste for study deeply inimical to education. The manufacturer, the merchant, the gold-digger, will not pause in their career to gain intellectual accomplishments. While gaining knowledge, they are losing the opportunities to gain money. The political condition of our country, too, is such, that a high education and a high order of talent do not generally form the sure guarantees of success. The tact of the demagogue triumphs over the accomplishments of the scholar and the man of genius.

Put these causes together, and the phenomena we witness and lament are explained. Our colleges are complacently neglected when they neither afford the satisfaction and distinction of a thorough and lofty education, and yield no advantages in gaining wealth and political eminence.

We have multiplied colleges so as to place them at every one's door; we have multiplied the branches of study so as to give every one enough to do, and to satisfy the ambition of learning, if all are to be required; we have cheapened education so as to place it within the reach of every one; we have retained the short term of four years, so that no great portion of life need be spent in study; and we have made the terms of admission quite easy enough. Now all this would tend to the popularity of these institutions, if the education acquired helped us to gain money and political influence. But as it does not, it is not valued by a commercial people, and a people of political institutions like ours.

And even if our educational systems should be made more thorough, requiring more time, we see not that it would make a strong appeal to the commercial spirit and to political ambition, while men continue to succeed so well without high education. The idea of fitting our colleges to the temper of the multitude does not, therefore, promise great results. They do not answer to the commercial and political spirit of our country; nor to the philosophical or ideal—the architectonic conception of education. To attempt to make them answer to the former would be of doubtful success. But we can make them answer to the latter; and doing this, we shall meet every want of the human mind, and of society; for if we educate men as men, we prepare them for all the responsibilities and duties of men. And educating men on this principle, we should in due time have great examples of the true form; and the charm, and power, and dignity of learning would become apparent to all. And then education would stand out, as in truth it is, not as a mere preparation for the facile doing of the business of the world, but as the highest aim of the human being; as Milton has nobly said, "The end of learning is to repair the ruins of our first parents, by regaining to know God aright, and out of that knowledge to love him, to imitate him, to be like him, as we may the nearest by possessing our souls of true virtue, which being united to the heavenly grace of faith, makes up the highest perfection." In this way we should raise up a powerful counter influence against the excessive commercial spirit, and against the chicanery and selfishness of demagogueism which now prevail. Men thus worthily built up would get into all the relations of society, and throw a new aspect over the arts, commerce, and politics, and a high-minded patriotism and philanthropy would everywhere appear. Then it would be seen how much more mighty and plastic are great ideas and fundamental principles than all the arts, tact, and accomplishments of expediency. Then the host of penny-a-liners, stump orators, discoursers upon socialism, bigots, and partisans would give way before sound writers, true poets, lofty and truthful orators, and profound philosophers, theologians, and statesmen. We should have a pure national literature, and a proud national character.

To bring about this great change, we must do something besides multiplying colleges after the same model, pouring forth a tide of school-books, and making experiments upon a facile system of education full of pretension and fair promises, but containing no philosophical and manly discipline.

The multiplication of colleges after the same model only serves to increase our difficulties. We set about putting up the same kind of buildings; we create the same number of professors, to teach the same things on the same principle; we get together a few books and some philosophical apparatus; and then we have the same annual commencements, with orations and poems, and the conferring of degrees; and we get under the same pressure of debt, and make the same appeals to the public to help us out of it; and then with our cheap education, to induce many to get educated, we experience the same anxiety to gather in as many students as possible; and, since where we cannot get money it is something to get appearance, we show the same readiness to educate for nothing those who will submit to be educated, but who cannot pay. In all this we are improving nothing; but we are taking away all dignity from our system of education, and proving its inadequacy.

It were well to commence about this time some experiment of a different kind—a new experiment, and yet one of no doubtful issue, if we can carry it out to its issue. If we can give it a beginning and a middle, we know what its end must be. The establishment of Universities in our country will reform, and alone can reform our educational system. By the Universities we mean such as we have before described—*Cyclopædias* of education: where, in libraries, cabinets, apparatus, and professors, provision is made for studying every branch of knowledge in full, for carrying forward all scientific investigation; where study may be extended without limit, where the mind may be cultivated according to its wants, and where, in the lofty enthusiasm of growing knowledge and ripening scholarship, the bauble of an academical diploma is forgotten. When we have such institutions, those who would be scholars will have some place to resort to; and those who have already the gifts of scholarship will have some place where to exercise them. With such institutions in full operation, the public will begin to comprehend what scholarship means, and discern the difference between sciolists and men of learning. Then we shall hear no more inane discussions about the expediency of discarding Latin and Greek; for, classical scholars there will then be, who will have an opportunity of showing the value of the immortal languages, and the immortal writings of the most cultivated nations of antiquity. Then we shall have mathematicians prepared for astronomers and engineers. Then we shall have philosophers who can discourse without text-books. Then, too, we shall have no more acute distinctions drawn between scholastic and practical education; for, it will be seen that all true education is practical, and that practice without education is little worth; and then there will be dignity, grace, and a resistless charm about scholarship and the scholar.

The philosophic idea of education being thus developed in the highest form of an educational institution—where alone it can be adequately developed—it will begin to exert its power over all subordinate institutions. There will now be demanded a preparation suitable for undertaking the higher degrees of scholarship, and schools and colleges will receive a new impulse and will be determined to their proper form. We shall not now attempt to learn a little of everything in the lower institutions; but we shall learn that which is requisite to prepare for the higher, and we shall learn that well. The influence of the higher will be to give limitation, order, consistency, and thoroughness to the lower. And there will be diffused through all schools of every grade, and for both sexes, new ideas of intellectual discipline, and the sense of an elevated life and duty. Education now will have an authority to define it, examples to illustrate it, and the voice of a Divine spirit to call it forth.

We might have had Universities ere this, had we not wasted our means and energies in unfruitful schemes and misappropriations. We have wasted large sums in erecting expensive buildings in many different places for small collections of students, which, had they been concentrated, would have given for several uncertain colleges a stable University, with ample provision of books and the whole material of learning, and with endowed professorships.

Some of the States, like the State of New York, have made large appropriations from a literature fund to common schools, where, scattered in feeble streams through a thousand channels, it has produced no other effect than cheapening a little more what was cheap enough already. Massachusetts, with no literature fund, has a common and free school system no less, if not more complete and efficient, than New York. Common schools required no such attenuated patronage. But this fund, on an obvious principle of political economy, might have been concentrated into a power that would have given to the State of New York Colleges or Gymnasia, and Universities on an organized and connected system that would have justified her claim to be the Empire State, in a high and noble sense; and have made her, in her educational development, second to no country in the world.

The proposed changes in Brown University set forth in the Report of the Corporation, and which we understand have since been adopted, indicate that it is not preposterous to hope that some of our colleges may be brought under a higher organization. This Institution has hitherto been only a college, but it has been one of the best in our country in respect to its endowments, its library, and its faculty. It has also been one of the most respectable in point of the number of its students: nevertheless, it finds a change necessary, and it dares to make it.

There are some features of this new organization, which have very much the air of a University. The number of courses of instruction, the freedom of choice allowed to the student, and the abolition of the fixed term of four years, and the graduation of the time allotted to each particular course by the nature of the course itself—all these seem to point to a University. But the Corporation do not, after all, propose to do away the collegial character of their Institution, but only to modify it. Their leading conceptions are, first, the introduction of a better scholarship, by giving to each study more time, or not attempting to do more than can be well done; secondly, to adapt the Institution to the wants of all classes; thirdly, by this wider adaptation to call in a larger number of students.

The experiment alone can determine whether the modifications introduced will realize these conceptions of an improved and more widely-diffused education. We believe that an attempt to modify our collegiate institutions emanating from so respectable a source, cannot but have weight in determining other institutions to consider the necessity of introducing reforms into our educational system. We sincerely desire that the experiment may prove successful. And since the Corporation, in making the present changes, reserve the power of making still further changes, if called for, we shall entertain the hope that, in carrying forward this experiment, they may be led to form the purpose of making Brown University a University proper. As yet we do not discern the legitimate idea of a University.

The very conception of adapting the Institution to the wants of "young men who are devoting themselves to the productive professions," intimates that pupils will be received who have made very little scholastic preparation, and that, therefore, the courses intended for the "productive professions" will be quite elementary. The courses here proposed will undoubtedly be very useful to young men engaged in commerce and manufactures, and who propose to cultivate farms on scientific principles. The increase of students anticipated is likely to be chiefly from this class of youth; and thus, instead of the old college with its Greek and Latin, and Mathematics, shall we not have a large commercial institution, which, instead of gathering around itself classical associations, and impressing us with the worth and dignity of scholarship, shall only give us the hum of preparation for the business of life in the industrial and productive direction? The Latin and Greek scholars—the old-fashioned plodding students seeking after science and philosophy for their own sake, and dreaming of high mental cultivation and profound learning, will be rarely seen, we fear, when candidates for the "productive professions" form the overwhelming majority and create the *esprit de corps*.

We do not feel confident that this new organization will elevate the tone of scholarship. One of the principles laid down reads thus: "The various courses should be so arranged, that in so far as practicable, every student might study what he chose, all that he chose, and nothing but what he chose." This principle is intended to obtain universally, unless the parent or guardian should place his child or ward under the authoritative direction of the Faculty. Now it is possible for a student to choose either too much or too little, and either to renew the old evil of attempting so much as to lead to superficial acquisition, or to fall into the opposite evil of undertaking so little as to leave overmuch leisure on his hands. And we must not forget that these students are of no higher grade than those who usually enter college; youths, whose habits of application are yet to be formed, and their judgment ripened, and not, like the students of the German Universities, young men grown, and formed under the discipline of years spent in the Gymnasia, and who, therefore, may be presumed to have some ground to stand upon when they make choice of the kind and the number of the courses they are to pursue.

Nor do we feel confident that the colleges can be made the best institutions for all those who are devoting themselves to the "productive professions." Some who wish to become particularly scientific, would find such an institution congenial. But of the multitude who contemplate the productive professions, the majority will feel inclined to take a more limited course, and to enter as early as possible upon their apprenticeship. Indeed, we are doubtful of Agricultural and Commercial Colleges, however developed. We believe that the common schools, generally, can be so improved, or schools of a degree higher, branching directly out from them, can be established, where instruction in the principles of Agriculture embracing Chemistry, and in the application of Chemistry and of other sciences to the arts, can be more fitly and successfully given.

It appears to us that this plan of the Corporation of Brown University is defective, inasmuch as it attempts a union in one institution of three different grades of education, which can be more philosophically and successfully conducted in three different kinds of institutions. We have here combined something of the University, a good deal of the College, and a good deal of the Commercial, Manufactural, and Agricultural School, in which the one element may preponderate over the others, but in which a harmonious action of the three, and a suitable development of all, it is hard to conceive of. But, granting that this scheme should be followed by a reasonable measure of success; that, at least, it should sustain itself by the number of its students, still it cannot meet the highest educational want of our country, which, indeed, is the highest educational want of every country. It will not form the University where philosophical education can be carried out to its last results.

We feel no hostility to the experiment of Brown University. The better it turns out, the better pleased we shall be. We shall even be happy to confess our error, if it shall appear that we have erred in any part of our criticism. The Report of the Corporation is an admirable one, and points out in a strong and lively manner the defects of our College system. The friends of the institution are now making a generous effort to place under its control the means of developing the new scheme. We cannot but feel a strong sympathy with this, and whatever may be the defects of the incipient movement, we repeat, that we shall cherish the hope, that eventually the noblest form of a literary institution may come out of it.

Another plan for improving our educational system is presented in the very able Report recently made to the Trustees of the University of Rochester, by the Committee appointed to draw up a Plan of Instruction for that Institution.

The University of Rochester does not profess to be a University in the strict use of the word: in reality it contemplates only a collegial course of instruction. The plan proposed and adopted aims to make this course more effective, by insisting upon an adequate and thorough preparation for admission; by adjusting the studies properly to the term of four years; by adopting two courses—a classical and a scientific—adapted to two different classes of students, the first to graduate as Bachelors of Arts, the second as Bachelors of Sciences; by limiting the voluntary plan to a choice between these two courses; and by demanding a mastery of the studies prescribed, to be decided by rigid examinations, ere candidates are admitted to the degrees for which they are enrolled. The Report expresses its leading principle in one sentence, *"Thorough* is the word which we need to have written upon all our seminaries and modes of teaching—upon the mind of every teacher, and on the daily task of every scholar."

The Report is filled with just and admirable views of education. In proposing an improvement of our collegial course, it undertakes a very important and necessary part of the great work of perfecting our educational system. If the University of Rochester is enabled to carry out its plan on the lofty principle it avows, it will make a real advance. We cannot but entertain cheering hopes of its success from the intelligence and liberal spirit which pervade the Report and from the names which are appended to it.

It is not necessary to our purpose to enter upon a critical examination of the plan itself. We only remark that the features to which we would take exceptions are those which are unavoidable under the present limitations of our educational system. We have only Colleges, and we feel the want of Universities; hence, we are continually struggling to give our Colleges as much of a University character as possible. "It would be a beautiful consummation to it (Modern History) if at an advanced period in the whole course, some higher instruction in History could be given by lectures, opening great philosophical views, tracing its currents in the channels of political organizations, viewing it in its connections with the science of Ethnology, and showing other aspects of this interesting subject."

We perceive here a looking forward to, a yearning after a University element. The whole plan bears marks, and we say unavoidably, of an endeavor to bring into the College as much of the University as the enlightened Committee deem consistent with their aim at a more thorough scholarship. The want exists and must be in some degree met, and until we have Universities in full, perhaps nothing better or more worthy of commendation could be offered. Still the limited term of study must preclude a ripe scholarship; and after the College course is completed with all its advantages, the student who wishes to pursue his studies still further will look in vain for an Institution to receive him. Indeed the Report itself announces the very feature of the proposed plan to which we have called attention. "The time devoted to what is considered a good education with us is entirely too limited to produce any high degree of scholarship. We deceive ourselves if we suppose that by any improvement in our systems we shall raise to a very elevated point the standard of attainments in any particular department of science or literature, unless there be evinced a disposition on the part of our young men to devote to their education a larger space of time than they are now willing to spare. When that period arrives, we shall be led to found great Universities, each one of which shall be the centre and crown of a system of Colleges, exerting a useful control over them and completing the education thus commenced. Until that desirable consummation, all that can be done is, to administer our Colleges wisely, and provide in them, as far as possible, the opportunity of more advanced instruction in some important branches, where it is now too limited to answer the ends in view." The College is thus proposed, under an improved form, to supply the more advanced instruction as far as possible until Universities shall arise.

While these commendable, although limited experiments are making in different quarters, all scholars and all true friends of learning will do well to inquire, whether there really be any good reason why we should not now create in our country at least one great institution of learning that may vie with the best of the old world. Have we not the means in abundance? Shall the little principalities of Germany surpass these wealthy and powerful States? Nor is it a question that such institutions are required to crown and perfect a system of education.

That the want of Universities is felt, is evident from the Report of Brown University, from the Report of the University of Rochester, and from the very evils complained of in the enlargement of the College course beyond the measure of the time allotted to collegial study. This general movement of the Colleges toward a higher position, by adding more studies to their curriculum, by endeavoring to shape themselves to more numerous classes of students, by introducing voluntary courses of study, by attempting lectures on the more advanced branches of study, and by assuming the name of University, is not a mere freak of ambitious folly, but an attempt to meet the demands of the age. The lofty-sounding curriculums of elementary schools for boys and girls, and the attempt to introduce University lectures even there, are indications also of an all-pervading idea which is striving in various ways to become realized. Now, everything appears crude and disjointed, and sometimes even grotesque: the fused elements are running in every direction, until they find the moulds which are to give them repose in proportion and symmetry.

Our Colleges grasp at a University amplitude of studies, at University capacities and functions, and take the name of Universities, and yet Universities they cannot be within the prescribed limits, with the general paucity of learned material and appliances, and while offering themselves as institutions for students in the elementary course. They were elementary schools of a higher grade in their inception, such they have ever continued to be, as such their existence will ever be demanded, and as such they require to be perfected. By retaining their original designation, while endeavoring to graft upon them what belongs properly to a University, we have only embarrassed them in their proper and possible functions, given them an equivocal character, and lessened their usefulness.

In order to perfect our Colleges, we need to bring them back to a more limited range of studies, comprising a thorough elementary discipline in languages and mathematics and other kindred studies, conducted with respect to a University course which is to follow. This University course might, in some of the older and more amply provided Colleges, be developed after the manner of the English Universities as they originally existed. The College, in this case, would not be enlarged to a University after the present fashion, but the University would be constituted as distinct—beginning its courses of lectures just where the College completes its discipline of prescribed lessons and the recitation-rooms.

Between the University and the Colleges there would be no competition, and the relations would be altogether noble and generous: each would be necessary to the other, and tend to sustain the other; for without Colleges there can be no Universities, and in the Universities alone can the Colleges find their ripened results.

Education, in general, is of two kinds, and of two kinds only: an education imposed by tutors and governors; and an education self-imposed. The first relates to that period of our being embracing childhood and youth, when the faculties are yet immature, and knowledge is in its elementary stages. The second relates to that period commencing with early manhood, when the faculties are comparatively ripened, when elementary knowledge has been attained, and actual experience has taken the place of imagination and conjecture.

The first period requires of necessity authoritative direction, and plastic superintendence. The second period is competent, unless the first has been neglected and suffered to run to waste, to form plans, make decisions, exercise choice, and to apply itself, as from itself, to self-culture, the formation of character, and the duties of life.

All men do, in some sort, attain to both kinds of Education; for all men are disciplined in some degree, well or ill, by a controlling power in early life; and all men have some sense of independence and new responsibilities, when they reach the age of manhood. Education, of both kinds, is a law of our being more or less perfectly developed.

The idea of Educational Institutions, embraces the reduction of educational means and influences to method and system.

For the first period, various institutions have sprung up, from the most elementary Schools to Gymnasia or Colleges. For the second period there is only one institution—the University.

According to the present condition of our Educational System, the higher, self-determined, and manly course of study belonging to this period, appears only as an imperfect appendage to the College under the form of certain voluntary studies, and a limited range of lectures on the loftier sciences, conducted under manifest embarrassments arising from the want of a suitable preparation on the part of the student, and the inadequate amount of time covered by the Collegiate course. Hence, where the higher culture is gained, it is gained rather by studies pursued by the individual amid the duties and cares of life after the institutions of learning have been departed from, than by means of the institutions themselves. The culture which men, who are determined to make the most of life, attain to amid its active pursuits, is invaluable, and will be prized no less by those who have studied at the University than by those who have not. But who does not see the value, nay, the necessity of an Institution which opens its doors to us just when we escape from governors and tutors, and provides us with all the means, and affords us the example and fellowship of manly self-discipline? It is here alone that we can properly pursue the study of philosophy, which implies more than mere acquisition, and is the self-conscious growth of thought. It is here that we can become disciplined to independent scientific investigation, or lay broad and deep the foundations of professional and political life. It is here, also, that teachers and professors can be prepared for the scientific and classical departments of our educational institutions, in general.

The University thus stands just where the first period of education closes, and where the other begins. The second period, indeed, never closes. But as education, during the first period, requires for its orderly development institutions of learning; so education during the second, requires for its proper determination and successful prosecution, the formation of habits of independent thought and study, an acquaintance with method, and a general survey of the field of knowledge, such as can be gained only in an institution especially founded and furnished for these high ends. The University receives the *alumnus* of the *Alma Mater,* and ripens him into the man prepared for the offices of the Church and the State, and for the service of Science and Letters.

We do not entertain the doubt expressed in the Report of the Committee of the University of Rochester, as to a disposition on the part of our young men to devote to their education a larger space of time. The time which they now devote, is the time which has long been prescribed, and not the time which they have themselves appointed. On the other hand, the very pressure which the Colleges are under to enlarge their courses of study, shows plainly enough the demand for higher and more general education. We believe there are many young men who enter College smitten with the love of knowledge and with high hopes of a lofty education, and who now leave with disappointment, whose enthusiasm would at once rekindle at the prospect of a University. Nor is it an uncommon event for students now to seek in foreign countries for that which, as yet, they cannot find at home.

Besides, we must calculate upon the effects which would naturally follow the creation of Universities. They would stand before the community as the culmination of our educational system,—as containing everything to meet the highest wants and aspirations of the human mind,—as spreading out the fair fields of knowledge to their utmost extent,—as presenting an invitation to the ripest cultivation of every branch of science and literature,—as opening retreats where the studious may retire in the fullest satisfaction,—as affording the highest possibilities, and stimulating the noblest endeavors. There would now no longer exist any temptation or necessity for the Colleges to make more or less successful, more or less abortive attempts to pass beyond their just measure, and to sacrifice their invaluable offices and benefits in trespassing upon grounds which do not naturally belong to them. They would explode those jejune schemes of education which seek to introduce juvenile minds, in the incipient stages of discipline, to the higher forms of education for which they have acquired no preparation. They would define clearly the distinction between an elementary and preparatory discipline, and that independent and manly and self-determined pursuit of knowledge which belongs to students who have learned the art of study, and who know how to avail themselves of books and lectures of distinguished and finished scholars. Hence they would introduce order, method, and consistency into the whole course of education. Now, in entering upon the very first stages of education, the student would have the whole line of progress clearly marked out before him; he would know the point to which he is tending and where he might, without uncertainty, realize his highest hopes. The spirit of scholarship would thus be thoroughly awakened, the life of a scholar be clearly defined, and, instead of calculating the time of study, his regards would be fixed upon the ends of study—the glorious attainments to be realized.

William of Champeaux did not wait until the spirit of scholarship had permeated masses of men: he commenced his lectures, laid the foundations of a University, and created the spirit of scholarship. In our country and age, we are not called upon to create the spirit of scholarship, it already exists; we have only to inform it with ideas, and to quicken it to a higher life.

We hold, therefore, that Universities are natural and necessary institutions in a great system of public education. To delay their creation is to stop the hand upon the dial-plate which represents the progress of humanity.

We have delayed this great work of founding Universities too long. We cannot well afford to wait for any new sign from heaven before we begin this work. Is there any impertinence in calling upon all scholars and true friends of learning to consider whether we may not now create at least one great institution of learning that may vie with the best of the old world? And if we designed to show the spirit of this undertaking in a few words, we would say, that it is required for the successful development of such an institution, that it should neither cheapen its education at the expense of its intellectual life and aliment, nor be tempted to do so; that it should be adequate to educate the many, and yet not be destroyed if compelled, for a time, to educate the few; that it should be removed alike from the conflicts and jealousies of sects in the Church, and of parties in the State; and that it should be faithfully consecrated to science, literature, and art.

No part of our country presents equal facilities with the city of New York, for carrying out this great undertaking. New York is really the metropolitan city of our country. The centre of commercial activity, the vast reservoir of wealth, it takes the lead in the elegancies and splendor of life, in the arts of luxury and amusement. It is also the great emporium of books and the fine arts. Here resort the professors of music and of the arts of design. Here literary men are taking up their abode. Here literary institutions of various kinds and grades have already come into being. Here are libraries established by associations or by individual munificence, which are enlarging themselves from year to year. Commerce, wealth, and elegance invite, nay, demand the invigorating life, the counterbalancing power and activity of intellectual cultivation. Whatever is requisite for a great Institution of Learning can here be most readily collected; and here are the means in profusion of creating whatever the well-being and glory of our city and of our country may require. By adding to the natural attractions of a metropolitan city the attractions of literature, science, and art, as embodied in a great University, students from every part of the Union would be naturally drawn together. We should thus have a fully appointed national Institution where the bonds of our nationality would be strengthened by the loftiest form of education, the sympathy of scholars, and the noblest productions of literature.

A great Institution would collect together all that is now scattered and isolated among us, be the home of scholars, the nurse of scholarlike endeavors, the regulating and harmonizing centre of thought and investigation. Our whole population would feel the plastic power of intellectual development and progress; society would receive new forms and habitudes from a learned class, and knowledges be widely diffused by public lectures under the direction of an elite corporation.

But what shall be the form of this Institution?

We would take as models, in general, the University of Paris, the Universities of England before they were submerged in the Colleges, and the Universities of Germany.

In the creation of such a University we would at the very beginning collect a choice, varied, and ample library, second to none in the world in books to aid students in attaining ripe scholarship, and in promoting investigation in every department of knowledge—a library distinguished more for valuable and directly available resources of scholarship than for curious and antiquarian collections, estimated rather by the character than the number of its volumes. At the same time we would collect all the necessary apparatus for Physics and Chemistry; we would furnish a noble Observatory; we would found a rich Cabinet of Natural History; and we would open a gallery of the Fine Arts.

Thus with a full store of the material of science, literature, and the arts, would we lay the foundation of a University. We should thus meet aspirations and wants which, in our country, have hitherto been only disappointed, and call into the walks of learning, by commanding attractions, ingenuous minds that in despair have hitherto given themselves to other pursuits.

We would constitute four Faculties, a Faculty of Philosophy and Science, a Faculty of Letters and Arts, a Faculty of Law, and a Faculty of Medicine. Under these should be comprised a sufficient number of professorships to make a proper distribution of the various subjects comprehended under the general titles. These professorships should be endowed to an extent to afford the incumbents a competency independently of tuition fees. The necessity of such endowments must be obvious when we reflect that studious men require undisturbed minds, and that there are branches of knowledge which the interests of the world demand to have taught—such as Philology, Philosophy, the higher Astronomy, Mathematics, and Physics, while at the same time the number of students will be comparatively few.

It may be a question whether fees of tuition should be required of students, or whether the lectures, together with the libraries and cabinets, should be thrown open gratuitously to the public, as is done in the University of Paris. In this case the professorships, of course, would require to be more amply endowed.

The Professors of the different Faculties should be required to give courses of lectures, on the subjects assigned to them, to the Academical Members of the University. They should also be required to give popular courses to the public in general, on subjects selected by themselves.

By the *Academical* Members, we mean those who shall be admitted upon examination, or upon a Bachelor's degree from any College, and who shall enrol themselves as candidates for the University degrees.

These degrees may be of two grades. The lower grade may comprise Master of Arts, Doctor of Philosophy, Doctor of Medicine, and Bachelor of Laws; the higher grade may comprise Doctor of Laws, Doctor of Theology, and other degrees to mark a high and honorable advance in Medicine, and in Philosophy, Science, Letters and Art.

Those of the first grade to be awarded after three or four years' study, and upon examination. Those of the second grade to be awarded as honorary degrees to men distinguished in the walks of life for their attainments and professional eminence, and to individuals who remain for a still longer term of years connected with the University in learned pursuits. It is, of course, understood that the provisions of the University are to be such as to enable students to pursue favorite branches of science, or learning in general, for an indefinite term of years.

One concurrent effect of this organization would be to elevate the character of Academical degrees, by making them the expression of real attainments, and honorable badges of real merit.

In connection with the popular courses of lectures, there should, also, be established courses particularly designed for the benefit of those engaged in commerce and the useful arts. This would give rise to another class of students besides the Academical, who might avail themselves of every advantage of the University possible to them under the degree of preparation they may have made, and under the pressure of daily business avocations. So also, others besides Academical students might attend the lectures in Law and Medicine, or indeed any courses which they might please to select, but without being considered as candidates for University degrees.

The result would be that the libraries, cabinets, laboratories, and lecture rooms of the University would become the resort of students of every grade; it would thus become the great centre of intellectual activity, and a fountain of learning open to the whole populace.

The different public libraries of the city might, also, be connected with it under their distinctive names; and new libraries might be founded by new donors, under new names, in the same connection, like the different libraries of the English Universities.

It will be remarked that we have omitted a Faculty of Theology in the constitution of this University. As each denomination of Christians has its peculiar Theological views and interests, it would be impossible to unite them harmoniously in one Faculty. It is most expedient, therefore, to leave this branch to the Theological Institutions already established by the several denominations. But still a connection of an unobjectionable character might be formed between Theological Institutions, especially those existing in this city, and the University, productive of very rich benefits. The students of the former might be admitted not only to the libraries of the latter, but also to the lectures on history, philosophy, philology, and general literature, when distinguished lecturers on these subjects gave promise of advantages additional to those enjoyed in the Theological Institutions. Indeed an arrangement might be made by which students undergoing prescribed examinations in philosophy, natural theology, philology, and history, and presenting certificates from their Professors of having completed satisfactorily their Theological courses, might be admitted to the degree of Bachelor in Theology. Students of the Free Academy, also, after having completed their courses in that Institution, might be admitted into the University as Academical Students, or otherwise according to the preparation they may have made.

Thus all our Institutions of learning would grow into a harmonious whole.

With respect to its religious and moral character it should embody in its constitution: First, an entire separation from ecclesiastical control and a renunciation of all sectarian partialities. Secondly, but as every thing that relates to human welfare, needs to be taken under the protecting and nurturing wings of Christianity, it should acknowledge Christianity to be the only true religion, the Bible to be of Divine inspiration, and the supreme rule of Faith and Duty, given freely to all men to be read and received with entire freedom of conscience and opinion.

To carry out these principles it should provide for an equal control of all denominations of Christians acknowledging these principles; it should institute a course of lectures on the evidences of Christianity and on Christian morality; and the reading of the Scriptures together with prayer should constitute a daily public service to be conducted by the Professors in the presence of the students.

No religious profession, however, should be required for admission to the University, but it should be open to students of all creeds as well as of all nations.

For the full development of such an institution, ample funds are required; but that private munificence can accomplish it we fully believe. If the attention of our community can be aroused to the necessity, the interest, the glory of such a work, the accomplishment of it cannot be long delayed.

As examples of what private munificence can give, we need only appeal to various institutions of our land, and to the noble effort now making for Brown University. Nay, we need only look at the example of individuals in our own city with respect to the University of the City of New York; an institution which, although, like other similar institutions bearing the name of University, will claim to be only a College, and, therefore, not in its nature calculated to call forth as lively and as general an interest as the creation of a great University. There has been expended in money and liabilities on this institution, we have been informed, not less than four hundred thousand dollars, obtained chiefly by subscriptions.

Now all that will be required to put into full operation a University like the one we propose, will be about the sum expended on the above-named College. We will call the sum four hundred and fifty thousand dollars.

We can realize with this sum the following preparations and endowments:

A University building, for lecture-rooms, &c.	$75,000
A Library building,	50,000
Books—50,000 volumes,*	50,000
Observatory, to be located on Staten Island, with Instruments,	20,000
Apparatus for Experiments in Physics and Chemistry,	4,000
Incipient Cabinet of Natural History,	5,000
Incipient Gallery of Fine Arts,	6,000
Six fully endowed Professorships at $40,000 each, or ten partially endowed, at $24,000 each,	240,000
Total,	$450,000**

The rate of endowment for the professorships would be regulated, within certain limits, by the decision of the question, whether fees of tuition should be required of students, or not.

Such a foundation would ensure its permanent existence, and enable it to commence at once with all the forms of University education. This once accomplished, additions would afterwards be made as required, by a community now thoroughly awake to the interests of a great institution, and constantly experiencing its benefits.

Ten individuals giving 45,000 dollars each, would raise the sum required; or, fifty giving 9,000 dollars each; or, one hundred giving 4,500 dollars each; or, one thousand giving 450 dollars each. Or, we might distribute it as follows:

---

* This is based on the average cost of the 20,000 volumes already collected in the Astor Library.

** If that noble public benefaction—The Astor Library, could become the centre of a University, and if the contemplated Observatory at Brooklyn could be connected with it, then $120,000 of the above estimate would be deducted.

Ten donors at 10,000 dollars each	$100,000
Twenty donors at 5,000 dollars each	100,000
Forty donors at 2,500 dollars each	100,000
Eighty donors at 1,000 dollars each	80,000
Five hundred donors at 140 dollars each	70,000
	$450,000

No one will doubt that our city contains the individuals who could do this with ease, by the above or by other distributions.

The men who should endow such an Institution, would raise to themselves a grander and more imperishable monument than the obelisks and pyramids of Egypt.

That the plan we have thus generally indicated is not chimerical is demonstrated by the fact that similar Institutions exist and flourish in France and Germany. Take the University of Berlin as an example, with its hundred professors and its two thousand students. These Universities are supported by the State. In Germany, several Universities receive from thirty to fifty thousand dollars annually. The University of Berlin must receive still more.

In our country we desire our Universities to be under the control neither of the Government, nor of any religious denomination, for we wish to preserve such Institutions free alike from political and sectarian influence and partialities. The different sects may have their Colleges and Theological Seminaries. But a great University should be the resort simply of scholars, and be scrupulously devoted to those general interests of learning which are common to men of every creed and of every political bias. Hence, it is required that they be established by private munificence, and be placed under a corporation of private individuals, comprising men devoted to science and letters and the commanding interests of education.

Did we live under a monarchical government, Universities might be established by the government, and be connected with a national church; and then by taxation the people would be compelled to sustain them. Let it not be our reproach that monarchies alone can establish Universities: let us prove to the world that we can voluntarily create them, and that the spirit of a free people is mightier to the production of everything that can elevate and adorn humanity than the will of princes.

Universities are not the natural appendages or nurselings of monarchies. We have shown that they had their origin in the spirit of liberal and rational research, and that they were first established by individual enterprise. In Germany, particularly, so rife have been liberal opinions, and so strong the advocacy of constitutional governments in the Universities, that they have at times called out the most vigorous persecution from the State.

They are eminently Institutions for the people, inasmuch as they place within the reach of all who are disposed to high education, all the means for its attainment. They are fountains whence universal knowledge may be diffused, and whose all-pervading influence goes to quicken, and to give order and consistency to every form of education.

That will be a proud day for the city of New York when it shall see such an Institution arise in the midst of its marts of business and its splendid palaces, and giving to its prosperity the crown of intellectual glory.

Why should we leave to another generation a work which we ourselves can accomplish, and which shall carry down our influence to the future under a form so good and beautiful, and so worthy of all that we claim for our enterprise, our far-seeing wisdom, our devotion to our country's welfare, and our confident hopes of its ultimate destiny?

Should we fail in our expectations of finding in the community men with views ready to grasp this design, and a liberality adequate to meet its demands, then why may not a band of assimilated scholars enter upon the work themselves, aided by a few liberal patrons of learning, or wholly unaided if need be, and renewing the scenes of past ages, institute courses of lectures like Roscelin, William of Champeaux, and Abelard?

Their success might at first be small; but, doing their work ably, faithfully, and with indomitable perseverance, they would ultimately prevail, and collect around them ingenuous young men, and awaken an enthusiasm for glorious scholarship, and so commend themselves and their work to the public, that wealth and influence would be enforced into their service by a charm which human nature has always obeyed. Universities meet a real want of humanity—a want which is now deeply felt in our own country; and the existing Universities of the old world, which we now from a distance admire and long for, stand forth as guarantees of our success. We earnestly hope that the struggle of such an experiment, in our day, may not be called for; but, if it is, are there not scholars who dare to make it?

3. F. A. P. Barnard Decries Principles Governing College Communities, 1855

See Part IV, Docs. 24 and 25.

Is there no other remedy? There is one to which, little favor as it may find at present, especially with colleges which have invested large sums in costly buildings, I sincerely believe that the whole country will come at last; it is *to abandon the cloister system entirely,* and with it the attempt to do, what is now certainly done only in pretense, to watch over the conduct and protect the morals of the student. I am aware that this is high ground to take. Deeply satisfied as I have been, from the day I became a freshman in college to the present hour, of the vast evil and the little good inherent in the prevalent system of government in American colleges, I perhaps should not even yet have felt emboldened to speak out so publicly my convictions, in the face of the quiet contentment with which my compeers and the public everywhere apparently regard the existing state of things, had not one of the most eminent of our American educators long since condemned the system as publicly and as decidedly as I have done, and upon the same grounds. But Dr. Wayland, though he exhibits the evils which necessarily attend this system, in a manner irresistibly conclusive, hesitates to pronounce them sufficient to call for or to justify the abandonment of buildings already erected to serve as residences for college students. He confines himself to deprecating the erection of any more. I am disposed to take one step further. I say that Dr. Wayland himself has proved the system to be so pernicious, as to require that the ax should be laid directly at the root of it, no matter what the expense may be. . . .

In looking at this question in its moral aspects, Dr. Wayland takes

Frederick A. P. Barnard, *Letters on College Government* (New York, 1855), pp. 70–71, 76–79, 91–93.

altogether the view which I have already presented. He enforces his opinion by one or two considerations which seem to me to have a peculiar importance. In regard to the dangerous influence of evil example, he observes that the votaries of vice are much more zealous in making proselytes than the devotees of virtue. No remark could be more emphatically or more sadly true. There is apparently a malignant pleasure felt by the vile in marking the gradual steps by which the pure in heart become wicked like themselves; and it is with a sort of fiendish ingenuity that they invent allurements and ply seductive arts, to the end that they may ruin where they profess to befriend. The unsuspicious, unreflecting natures of youth, make them especially prone to yield to those whose greater familiarity with what is called life, but is in fact too often only the road to death, gives them a seeming superiority and lends to their opinions and their example a most mischievous fascination. Some such, we may say with too unfortunate a certainty, will usually be found wherever one or two hundred young men are assembled together as members of the same community. Some such will, indeed, have been almost unavoidably attracted to our colleges, by the peculiar social features which they present; and by the undeniable fact, which I have heretofore illustrated, that the college is a place of freedom rather than of restraint. Is there not here an exposure dangerous to every unsophisticated youth, and liable too often to become absolutely ruinous?

It is further observed by Dr. Wayland, that where a number of persons are collected together, and by the circumstances of their association are disconnected almost wholly from the surrounding world, there will inevitably come to be recognized among them certain peculiar principles of action, there will come to be received certain peculiar convictions of duty, which are not elsewhere recognized, but derive their character from that of the community among whom they originate. . . . In the college code, the highest honor is not bestowed upon that which is good and right; nor the sternest disapprobation awarded to that which is bad and wrong. To be gentlemanly, is better than to be moral; to be generous, is better than to be just. It is much to be doubted whether a protracted residence in a moral atmosphere, characterized by the prevalence of doctrines like these, can exert a healthy influence upon the character; or whether the usages to which it familiarizes the youth are such as to render the man either better or happier.

Dr. Wayland does not forget to glance at the prejudicial effect which the long-continued intercourse of young men, exclusively or nearly so, with each other, cannot fail to exert upon their manners; to which I might add the tendency, so constantly noticed that I suppose it must be esteemed inevitable, of the language of their conversation, under similar circumstances, to degenerate into rudeness, or something even worse. . . .

While thus every argument derived from the fitness of things, and from considerations of health, of morals, and of manners, seems directly to condemn the college cloister system prevalent in this country, hardly, I think, on the other hand, will a single substantial advantage be found to recommend it. That it is cheaper to the student, Dr. Wayland has, in my opinion, satisfactorily disproved. That it is immensely more expensive to the public at large, where colleges are created and sustained by their munificence, he made equally evident. Indeed, where money to the amount of one hundred thousand dollars or more, has, in a single institution, been invested in dormitories alone, and where, as in the University of Alabama, not one single dollar of revenue is derived from this investment, in the way of rent or otherwise, it requires no argument to show that, if the dormitories were unnecessary, all this is a dead loss. In our own particular case, it is worse than a dead loss; for not only do these buildings return no income to the treasury, but they keep up a continued drain upon it, to the extent of several hundred dollars per annum, to preserve them in decent repair, and in tolerably habitable condition. Is there a single plausible reason to be urged in favor of the perpetuation of such a system, but the unfortunate fact that it cannot now be abandoned here without a heavy pecuniary loss?

We find . . . that a large number of the colleges of our country are planted in retired and quiet portions of the interior; and secondly, that instead of being placed in the midst of any community, even that of a small country village, they are situated at some moderate distance from such a spot, sufficient to be measured by a walk of perhaps half an hour. There has evidently been a common design in all this, and it is clearly traceable to a fear of the dangerous temptations which are presumed to lie in wait for youth, wherever human beings are gathered together in society. These temptations are greater in large towns; therefore large towns are, first of all, sedulously avoided. They are not absent even from small towns and villages; therefore small towns and villages are in like manner tabooed. Yet as neither young men nor their instructors can conveniently live cut off from all communication with their fellow beings, the neighborhood of the lesser towns is tolerated; but it is held at such a convenient distance that, if it possesses any allurements to lead young men astray, such yielding youths can find them out without any trouble at all, and enjoy them with that satisfaction of conscious security which arises out of the knowledge that their instructors and guardians are quietly housed a mile and a half off. The fact is, that all this reasoning, from beginning to end, is founded in the most mistaken impressions in the world. The temptations of great cities do not corrupt the youth of great cities, any more than the differing, but no less real, ones of the country, as a general rule, corrupt the youth of the country. The grand melo-drama which is placarded all over Royal street in Mobile, arrests no eager glance from the Mobile lad as he passes along on his way to his schoolboy tasks. Familiarity breeds contempt, indifference, unconsciousness. And so it is with all other presumed fascinations of the same nature. In like manner, young men from abroad, sent to commercial towns to become initiated into the ways of trade, though entirely free to dispose of their evenings as they please, do not more frequently contract bad habits in such places, than students in our most secluded colleges. Facts further demonstrate that there is actually less complaint of irregularity and dissipation in those colleges in cities which have no dormitories, than is often heard in those country institutions where compulsory residence in college buildings is a feature of the system. This is true of Columbia College and the City University, in New York; and also, according to Dr. Wayland, of the Universities of Glasgow and Edinburgh, in Scotland. . . .

4. Henry P. Tappan on the Idea of the True University, 1858

This lecture, delivered on June 22, 1858, at the request of the Christian Library Association, reflects Tappan's increasing concern with sectarian problems and states his ideal of university independence and freedom. See Docs. 2 and 5.

Gentlemen of the Board of Regents, of the Faculty, and of the Christian Library Association:

It will not be deemed superfluous, at the outset of my discourse, to recall to your minds, as well as to inform the public, of the origin of this association.

The original organization of a religious character was that of the Society of Inquiry for missions. This society existed for a number of years and was conducted with various degrees of efficiency and success. The order of exercises required monthly reports on Christian missions which were delivered in public by students appointed for that purpose by the members. A curious feature of this organization was that, although its objects apparently were calculated to interest only religious students, and especially those who were contemplating the gospel ministry, it admitted members with little or no discrimination. Many excellent reports were indeed read; but the diversity of character and views which the association necessarily embraced were adverse to that harmony and energy which are essential to success and which can be secured only by a unity in the governing principle.

During the present collegiate year, by common consent the Society of Inquiry was abolished. After this the Christian Association was organized. This differs from the former organization both in its terms of admission, and in its objects. It is composed of students who are members of Christian churches, or who, at least, profess to be aiming at a religious life as a cardinal interest.

Its objects too, are more comprehensive; and, while not discarding Christian missions, embrace general religious cultivation, and especially in relation to collegiate life. By this association religious students will be led to know each other more intimately, to cherish a more lively

Henry P. Tappan, *The University: Its Constitution and Its Relations, Political and Religious* (Ann Arbor, 1858).

interest in each others welfare, to watch over and sustain each other, and to co-operate in all wise and legitimate methods of promoting religion in the University generally.

But the new movement did not stop here. The deficiency of the University Library, and of the Libraries of the Students' Societies, in religious books, arrested the attention of professors and students, and of certain friends of the University. These libraries, like those of similar institutions, consisted mainly of scientific works, and works of general literature.

It would be difficult, if not impossible, to supply this deficiency from the general funds of the University. A State institution and not designed to be controlled by any particular religious denomination—an attempt, on its part, to supply religious books might stir up denominational prejudices, and lead to a conflict of denominational interests inimical to its peace and prosperity. If the Students' Literary Societies were to attempt it, the religious and secular elements would be liable to constant disagreement respecting the proper proportion of religious and secular books.

A new association, therefore, having this for its leading object seemed to be the only way of meeting the exigency. This association is open to all who choose to enter into it, and is formed upon principles so simple and catholic that there seems to be no just ground of apprehension for its success.

The annual subscription of the members will contribute a steady, although not a very large fund, for purchasing books; the wise and good from different parts of the country will make donations, from time to time, in money and books; authors and publishers will not forget us; and thus, from various sources there will be collected, as we hope, and continue to grow, a library composed of the varied, remarkable, and, to a great extent, rich and magnificent literature which has sprung from religious ideas and the word of God; and for which our English tongue is distinguished, perhaps, beyond all other forms of human speech.

Indeed, gentlemen, our University is like the Virgin Earth when Eden was planted—when the hand of God sowed the soil with seeds which should germinate and multiply into boundless bounty and beauty throughout the coming generations.

We who are called to the work of building up this University, are instruments of a Divine benignity working for the future through the present; and if we do our work truly and uprightly, are sowing seeds of knowledge and of just and fundamental principles in this new and virgin region for all time to come; and surrounding ourselves with such rich and hallowed memories, that men of after ages will rise up and call us blessed. We must look for something far higher than temporary expedients, or to gain a vain and fleeting reputation in our own day. If we build on a false foundation, our work will perish, and our names be dishonored: For we cannot prevent the ultimate and righteous judgement of history. If we build fairly and truly our work shall live and we shall live with it.

Of all mere human institutions there are none so important and mighty in their influence as Universities; because, when rightly constituted, they are made up of the most enlightened, and the choicest spirits of our race; they embrace the means of all human culture, and they act directly upon the fresh and upspringing manhood of a nation. To them must be traced science, literature, and art; the furniture of religious faith; the lights of industry; the moving forces of civilization; and the brotherly unity of humanity.

Do we ask, what are their grand constituents? There is but one reply —scholars and books. Wherever you collect the treasures of knowledge, and the men who know how to use and apply them, there, and there only, you have properly a University. The organization is simple; for the power employed is self-governing—self-directing: like the element of light, give it room, and it makes its unerring way. Hence it will be found in the history of Universities, that they have been the work of individuals rather than of governments. Governments may charter and endow them; but scholars must mould them and build them up. Governments may provide, and should provide that the two great constituents—scholars and books—be made sure and ample; but after that, let them have freedom and scope for the work which scholars only can accomplish. Let there be no jealous and tyrannical interference; let there be no religious or political tests; let there be no barbarous attempt to harness the winged Pegasus to the drag of beggarly elements. Knowledge can flourish only in the air of freedom; beauty can grow only under the sunlight of heaven; truth can walk in majesty and vigor only when unfettered; goodness can be pure and without hypocrisy only amid the sanctities of trust. Let us have the aliment of thought; but then leave us to think.

Freedom—this is the grand characteristic of University Education, as it is the essential attribute of manhood. Childhood and youth, of necessity, must be trained and disciplined under authority: but when the mind has come to know itself, and has gained the art of study, then it must lead on its own development. The educational system has attained its most perfect organization, when the boundary between the pre-disciplinary stage, and the University, is most sharply defined; and the early and authoritative training is conducted in primary reference to the self-training which is to follow. Professors and books aid, guide, and stimulate; but the scholar makes himself. He must be self-made or he is not made at all. Indeed, in the pre-disciplinary stage there is an incipient self-making, for all study and learning, even the most elementary, imply a thoughtful self-application; and every act of thought is an act of freedom.—But the University ever holds this distinction, that here, the student has attained a position from whence he can estimate the ends and aims of thought, and can map out to himself the fields of scholarship.

In the present state of our institutions, the pre-disciplinary stage, and the university stage run together, so that the boundaries overlap each other and confuse the lines of separation. We name our colleges, universities, while our universities are little more than colleges.

It is evident, however, that clearer views on educational organization are spreading over the country; and more positive efforts are made towards the development of universities. The State of Michigan has already gained distinction for efforts of this kind; and gives fair promise of eventually reaching the goal. She has conceived the plan, and laid the foundations of a university. Within a short period great advances have been made. What is now of the greatest moment to us is to avoid mistakes which may impede our prosperity; if not lead to disorganization and ruin. We must endeavor to keep clearly before us the great end, to employ the right means, and to make every movement a step in the right direction. It is disastrous to do only to make it necessary to undo again. It is running too great a hazard to venture upon doubtful experiments. But this is by no means necessary, for there is no subject whose principles are simpler or better defined, or sustained and illustrated by more numerous facts.

How simple the idea of a university! An association of eminent scholars in every department of human knowledge; together with books embodying the results of human investigation and thinking, and all the means of advancing and illustrating knowledge.

How simple the law which is to govern this association!—That each member as a thinker, investigator, and teacher shall be a law unto himself, in his own department.

Is there any authority competent to prescribe to Bacon, Leibnitz, Kant, Cousin, Hamilton, the methods of philosophical thinking, and exposition? To Gallileo [sic], Newton, Herschell, Struve, La Place, Arago, Le Verrier, Airy, how to demonstrate the mechanism of the heavens, and to pursue the stars in their courses? To Dalton, Davy, Faraday, Liebig, how to conduct the analyses of the Laboratory, and to determine the laws of chemistry? To Macauley [sic] and Prescott how to write histories? To Burke and Brougham how to debate in the English parliament; to Webster and Clay in the American Senate? To Milton, Shakespeare, Goethe, Schiller how to write poems? To Titian and Raphael how to cover the canvass with Divine Forms? To Michael Angelo how to build St. Peters? Nay, nay, to go to humbler things. Is not the ship builder entrusted with the building of the ship; the engineer with the construction of the Rail Road? Governments and corporations do not construct public works any more than they make poems, paintings and statues: They only grant charters, and provide the means; and then entrust them to the men who by capacity, knowledge, and experience are qualified to do the work. To have the work well done, the essential thing is to find the men qualified to do it.

The same principle applies to universities. "Every man to his trade." Governments cannot make universities by enactments of law: Nor corporations by the erection of edifices: The church cannot create them under the authority of heaven: The flattering eulogies of orators cannot adorn them with learning: Newspapers cannot puff them into being. Learned men—scholars—these are the only workmen who can build up universities. Provide charters and endowments—the necessary protection and capital: provide books and apparatus—the necessary tools: Then seek out the sufficient scholars, and leave them to the work, as the intellectual engineers who are alone competent to do it.

The history of all art, of all great undertakings proves that this is the only way of success. Nay, it is an exceedingly plain thing which every man of common sense cannot fail to see. And the history of universities proves most decisively that this is the only way by which they have risen to eminence and success. It may be very difficult to find men equal to this, as it is often difficult to find men equal to any great undertaking. But the principle of success lies luminously before us. Says Sir William Hamilton—the very highest authority on the subject: "Universities are establishments founded and privileged by the State for public purposes: They accomplish these purposes through their professors; and the right of choosing professors is a public trust confided to an individual or body of men, solely to the end, that the persons best qualified for its duties, may be most certainly procured for the vacant chair."

This distinguished philosopher and author has shown, in pursuing the history of European Universities, how their eminence and prosperity have ebbed and flowed just as this principle of seeking the ablest professors has been departed from or adhered to. The instances of the Universities of Padua and Pisa show how even sectarian prejudices yielded to the interests of learning. "From the integrity of their patrons, and the lofty standard by which they judged, the call to a Paduan or Pisan chair was deemed the highest of all literary honors. The status of Professors was in Italy elevated to a dignity, which in other countries it has never reached; and not a few of the most illustrious teachers in the Italian Seminaries, were of the proudest nobility of the land. While the Universities of other countries had fallen from Christian and cosmopolite, to sectarian and local schools, it is the peculiar glory of the Italian, that under the enlightened liberality of their patrons, they still continued to assert their Universality: creed and country were in them no bar; the latter not even a reason for preference. Foreigners of every nation are to be found among their professors; and the most learned man of Scotland—Dempster—sought in a Pisan chair, that theatre for his abilities which he could not find at home."

Sir William Hamilton adduces Leyden as a marked illustration of the results of the principle which he advocates, in his very able paper on "Academical Patronage and Superintendence,"—by which he means the appointing power of Universities. The passage is too remarkable to be omitted. "It is mainly to John Van der Does, Lord of Noortwyck, a distinguished soldier and statesman, but still more celebrated as a universal scholar under the learned appellative of Janus Douza, that the school of Leyden owes its existence and reputation. As Governor of that city, he had baffled the league of Requesens; and his ascendency which had moved the citizens to endure the horrors of a blockade, subsequently influenced them to prefer, to a remission of imposts, the boon of a University. In the constitution of the new Seminary it was he who was principally consulted; and his comprehensive erudition which earned for him the titles of the 'Batavian Varro,' and 'common oracle of the University,' but still more his lofty views and unexclusive liberality, enabled him to discharge, for above thirty years, the function of first curator with unbounded influence and unparalleled success.— Gerard Van Hoogeveen, and Cornelius de Coning, were his meritorious colleagues. Douza's principles were those which ought to regulate the practice of all academical patrons; and they were those of his successors. He knew, that at the rate learning was seen prized by the State in the academy, would it be valued by the nation at large. In his eyes a University was not a mere mouth piece of necessary instruction, but at once a pattern of lofty erudition, and a stimulus to its attainment. He knew that professors wrought more even by example and influence than by teaching; that it was theirs to pitch high or low the standard of learning in a country; and that as it proved arduous or easy to come up to them, they awoke either a restless endeavor after an ever loftier attainment, or lulled into a self-satisfied conceit. And this relation between the professorial body and the nation, held also between the professors themselves.

"Imperative in all, it was more particularly incumbent on the first curators of a University, to strive after the very highest qualifications; for it was theirs to determine the character which the school should afterwards maintain; and theirs to give a higher tone to the policy of their successors. With these views Douza proposed to concentrate in Leyden a complement of professors, all illustrious for their learning; and if the *most* transcendent erudition could not be procured for the University with the obligation of teaching, that it should still be secured to it without. For example, *Lipsius,* 'the Prince of Latin literature' had retired. Who was to replace him? *Joseph Scaliger,* the most learned man whom the world has ever seen, was then living a dependent, in the family of Rochepozay.—He, of all men, was, if possible, to be obtained. The celebrated Baudius, and Tuningius, professor of Civil Law, were commissioned to proceed as Envoys to France, with authority to tender the appointment, and to acquiesce in any terms that the illustrious scholar might propose. Nor was this enough. Not only did the curators of the University and the Municipality of Leyden write in the most flattering strain to the 'Prince of the Literary Senate,' urging his acquiescence, but also the States of Holland, and Maurice of Orange. Nay, the States and Stadtholder preferred likewise strong solicitations to the King of France to employ his influence in their behalf with the 'Phoenix of Europe,' which the great Henry cordially did. The negotiations succeeded. Leyden was illustrated; the general standard of learned acquirement, and the criterion of professorial competency, were elevated to a lofty pitch; erudition was honored above riches and power, in the person of her favorite son. After the death of Scaliger his place was to be filled by the only man who may contest with him the supremacy of learning; and *Salmasius,* who though a Protestant had been invited to Padua, but under the obligation of lecturing, preferred the literary leisure of Leyden, with the emoluments and honors which its curators and magistracy lavished on him:—simply, that, as his call declares, 'he might improve by conversation, and stimulate by example, the learned of the place;' or in the words of his funeral orator, 'ut nominis sui honorem academiæ huic impertiret, scriptis eandem illustraret, præsentia condecoraret.' And yet the working professors of Leyden, at that time, formed a constellation of great men which no other University could exhibit.

"Such is a sample of the extraordinary efforts (for such sinecures were out of rule) of the first curators of Leyden, to raise their school to undisputed preeminence, and their country to the most learned in Europe. In this attempt they were worthily seconded by their successors, and favored by the rivalry of the patrons of the other Universities, and Scholæ Illustres of the United Provinces. And what was their success? In the Batavian Netherlands, when Leyden was founded, erudition was at a lower ebb than in most other countries; and a generation had hardly passed away when the Dutch scholars, of every profession, were the most numerous and learned in the world. And this not from artificial encouragement and support, in superfluous foundations, affording at once the premium of education, and the leisure for its undisturbed pursuit, for of these the Provinces had none; not from the high endowment of academic chairs, for the moderate salaries of the professors were returned (it was calculated) more than twelve times to the community, by the resort of foreign students alone; but simply through the admirable organization of all literary patronage, by which merit and merit alone, was always sure of honor, and of an honored, if not lucrative appointment; a condition without which colleges are nuisances, and universities only organized against their end.—Leyden has been surpassed by many other Universities, in the emoluments and in the number of her chairs, but has been equalled by none in the average eminence of her professors. Of these, the obscurer names would be luminaries in many other schools; and from the circle of her twelve professors, and in an existence of two hundred years, she can select a more numerous company of a higher erudition than can be found among the public teachers of any other seminary in the world."

Such is the language of Sir William Hamilton—himself a prodigy of erudition, one of the most eminent philosophers and professors of his times, and the most distinguished writer on education in the English language. What he has said of Leyden is borne out by all the great Universities of the world. Their intellectual vitality, their power as educational institutions, their distinction and prosperity, and the general state of learning in the countries to which they belong have always kept pace with the ability and erudition of the professorial corps they could bring together and maintain. And wherever the grand point of an elite body of professors was once gained, all things else of greatest value followed rapidly.

In the year 1810, when the Kingdom of Prussia was crushed by the weight of the French invasion, the University of Berlin was established under the patronage of the King. The philosopher Fichte, was the principal instrument employed in moulding its form, and breathing into it life and power. The great principle of its creation was that of bringing together the most eminent men from every part of Germany. Leibnitz had indeed already founded the Academy of Sciences, and Berlin was the home of Humboldt; Fichte and the King had congenial coadjutors. But who could have anticipated that the experiment of Leyden was here to be so gloriously renewed! From the siege of Leyden arose a University beside which the old Universities of Spain became insignificant: and from the French invasion arose, at Berlin, a University which in less than a quarter of a century rivalled the Sorbonne and the College of France.

Under the great Napoleon, the grandeur of the Institute sprang from a similar cause with the grandeur of his army. In the first he aimed to collect men of the highest genius and learning: The unexampled tactics, and terrible efficiency of the latter arose from that band of generals and marshals whom his sagacity detected, and his example moulded and inspired. It was by the men that he gathered around him in war and in science, that he well nigh made France the centre of empire, as he made it the centre of civilization.

It is a law of God's universe that great ends require great principles and adequate means and instruments. History will be searched in vain for instances where mean conceptions and pretentious feebleness have led on revolutions, advanced art and science, or laid the stable foundations of national greatness. A Brigham Young may lead his hordes to Utah; but *there* are no seeds of truth and liberty such as the Mayflower bore over the Atlantic wave: *there* is no germ of a future Washington. The Toledo war could give us no heroes of Lexington and Bunker Hill. To do manly things, we must have brave men. To do good things, we must have virtue. Patriotic deeds demand patriots. Commercial prosperity demands both honesty and enterprise. The poet only can write poems.—The artist only can mould the forms of beauty. The hopes of our country can repose only in the true statesman. The cunning politician is but a stock jobber. The hero is our safety in war. The thinker alone reveals principles of improvement. The educated alone can lead on the great cause of education. All great and enduring institutions must spring from minds adequate to conceive them, from hands skillful and powerful to build them. And if there be any institutions which might claim even the aid of divinities, they are those from whence shall gush forth, as from the rock smitten by the wand of the prophet, the streams which are to nourish the intelligence and invigorate the character of a free and mighty people like this, which is swarming from the Atlantic to the Pacific, and from the "frozen North," to the amber and flowery South.

I conceive of the University of Michigan as capable of becoming one of these great and distinguished institutions; a rock to be smitten by the wand of a prophet that the streams of knowledge may gush forth for the people. I see in the plan originally adopted by its founders, in its origin as a gift from the general government to this young and vigorous State, in its very name—THE UNIVERSITY OF THE STATE OF MICHIGAN—and in its entire history, the marks of greatness, of wide spread influence, of national glory. Let the State of Michigan collect here, the means of all knowledge and liberal culture: Let the curators appointed by the people aim at one thing—to bring together, here, all the talent and erudition possible, independently of political or sectarian considerations, and no doubtfulness can overhang the result. Where you collect the treasures of learning and learned men, you cannot fail of a University. This is the way in which Universities have always been made: it is the fixed law of their creation.

When I received a call from the late Board of Regents to take charge of this University, I felt as all men in middle life must feel when called to break up long cherished associations, to forsake the home places of childhood, youth and manhood, to enter new regions however glorious and beautiful they may be. I had been so long accustomed to see the sun rise from the Atlantic wave, and "scatter the east wind upon the earth," that I recoiled from the thought of watching him in his noontide splendor looking down upon these vast lakes as upon "a molten looking glass," or of watching his setting over these unbroken prairies as if wearily travelling to find his rest beyond the rocky mountains; and I had been so long accustomed, on solstitial summer days like this, to track the shadows upon the hills and mountains which embosom the Hudson, on whose enchanted banks I breathed the air of spring as my first taste of life, that it seemed to me I should lose alike my identity and all "local habitation" amid these boundless plains and forests, and in this mighty rushing tide of human life. Believe me, it was a painful decision for me to make to accept that call, although so honorable, and implying so much public trust. But I saw that I was called for no ordinary purpose, to enter upon no common work. A young, vigorous, free, enlightened, and magnanimous people, had laid the foundations of a State University: they were aiming to open for themselves one of the great fountains of civilization, of culture, of refinement, of true national grandeur and prosperity: while leveling the forests, and turning up the furrows of the virgin soil to the sunlight, they would enter upon the race of knowledge, and beautify and refine their new homes with learning and the liberal arts; they would reduce the rude Pan to the graceful measures of the beautiful Apollo and his "sacred nine," and cause the Huron to repeat the wizard murmurs of the Ilissus. It was the charm of this high promise and expectation that drew me here.

As a trust was reposed in me, so I came trustfully. If I had not something to bring; if I were not capable of doing something, why was I called? wherefore should I presume to come? No one should be called to such a work who has not given pledges of competency: no one should undertake it who is entirely dubious of himself. I hold it as a fixed principle, that a true man must know himself; and that he who undertakes a public trust, must have principles settled, methods defined, a course of action conceived of, and a brave heart to govern a ready and not unskillful hand.

I am now just closing the sixth year of my presidency. One lustrum is past; another is just entered upon. Let me be judged of by my works.

You will all bear me witness that I have ever expounded the true and established idea of a University—an association of scholars together with books and all other means of knowledge.

The late Board of Regents have themselves testified that we attained to harmony in our views and cordially co-operated in our endeavors to build up this University.

In the appointment of professors, we aimed to be governed by the principle illustrated in the history of all great and prosperous Universities: we sought for the most competent men. The advancement and prosperity of this institution has added another illustration of the soundness of the principle.

What was inaugurated by former Boards of Curators will, I doubt not, be followed up by the enlightened gentlemen who compose the present Board. Indeed, as the President of the Board of Regents, I feel, that I am not the less speaking their sentiments than my own. The magnitude of the work committed to us cannot well be exaggerated. Why cannot we accomplish in this great North-west, with such abundant sources of Public Wealth and in a state of profound peace, what Douza and his colleagues accomplished for Leyden in the midst of the exhaustion and horrors of war? What Frederick William and Fichte accomplished for Prussia when their country was trodden down by the armed heel of the invader? O! it is not possible for us to calculate how beautiful and rapid may be the developments of a wise, adequate and united action! Nor can we penetrate that future of glory which, by a law of heaven, shall be unfolded from the institutions which we plant to-day—the harvests that will be reaped by the coming generations from the seeds which earnest and holy hands are now sowing in the soil of freedom.

Believe me, that the eyes of the nation are upon us—nay, the eyes of the friends of learning and education, in other nations.—This young University is a son of the morning—the light bearer of the great Sun of Knowledge which is rising upon the Empire of the West.

When I was last in Paris that distinguished philosopher, and friend, and promoter of education, Victor Cousin, after enquiring respecting our State and the condition and promise of our University, turned to Professor Ampère and remarked with an emphatic tone, and beaming eye, "It is a great destiny to plant philosophy in that vast region of the West!" It is a great destiny. The men who engage wisely and faithfully in building up this University will have their names written in a proud and imperishable history.

I have alluded to mistakes to be avoided that our work may not be marred or impeded.

We have avoided one grand and fatal mistake, in not misconceiving the true character of a University, and the means by which alone its development is possible.

There are three others to which in all honesty, fidelity and plainness, I would now call your attention. These three mistakes would be the introduction of political partizanship and aims, local jealousies and competitions, and sectarian prejudices and demands into the management of the University.

I would here remark at the outset, that I am not aware of a single fact in the past management of the University which indicates any influence from these sources in the Board of Regents. However these gentlemen have been elected, by whatever political party, from whatever part of the State, out of the bosom of whatever religious denomination, they have always seemed to me, to forget political, local, and religious connections in this common State interest, and to look steadily at the responsibilities of the great trust reposed in them, by a people alike interested in the cause of education.

There is certainly no more honorable office in the gift of the people, or one more grateful to a noble and proper ambition.

These influences perhaps, are more liable to exist in the body of the people than elsewhere, and to produce their effect by an outside pressure, I would remark, too, that in speaking of them I have reference to what may occur, rather than to anything which has already occurred. I would speak in a strain of premonition as to the future, rather than in a strain of rebuke as to the past.

The University, as strictly as the common schools, belongs to the entire people.

Politics can never be admitted to influence its appointments and measures, for two plain reasons. First, in its nature it has nothing to do with politics. It is an institution constituted not for political movements, but for the advancement of science and literature; and for the education of youth in science and literature, and not in the doctrines and arts of political parties. To divert it from the one object to the other would be to destroy it.

Secondly, it being essential to its success to procure the most able professors, no respect can be had to political sympathies, but purely to scientific and literary qualifications. To make appointments on any other principles, would be to destroy the standard of scholarship, to change it from a literary to a political institution, to introduce conflict and confusion, and to explode it as an ill-begotten experiment.

The tendency of local jealousies is either to destroy a common and hearty interest in its welfare, to prevent a common union in promoting its interest, and to narrow it from a State to a sectional institution, or to institute measures for dividing and distributing its departments and resources.

The first evil is that of reducing it from greatness to insignificance by shutting it up within narrow bounds. The second evil is the destruction of a force, by dispersion, which can exist only by concentration. Waters collected in one deep channel may turn a thousand mills, which if divided in a thousand channels may be insufficient to turn one.

The very idea of a University is that of concentrating books and apparatus, and learned men in one place. All branches of human learning are cognate, and require for their successful prosecution, cordial co-operation and mutual support. Nay, they are logically interdependent, so that to separate them would be to render their development impossible. The relations existing between the branches of knowledge symbolize the relations of the professors and students in these branches. Together they form a learned society, the members of which operate upon each other by the communication of ideas in daily converse, by the force of example, and by the excitement of noble and generous competition. We have seen how highly the University of Leyden rated the effects of this association in the efforts which they made to secure merely the residence of Joseph Scaliger, and after him, of Salmasius, at Leyden, that both professors and students might be guided and stimulated by their conversation and example. No one can visit Berlin, in our day, without perceiving that a certain grace, dignity and inspiring influence exist there from the presence of the illustrious Humboldt—the unrivalled model of a scientific man. Merely to see him, quickens one's intellectual nature; and only a brief conversation with him leaves an ennobling impression never to be forgotten.

I do not wish to speak with severity of those who may differ from me in opinion; nor does it become me to impugn any man's motives. But I certainly have a right to state what I believe to be an indisputable fact, that no true University has ever yet been established by a distribution of its parts in different localities; and that none of those great men who have hitherto created these institutions, and whom the world accounts an unquestionable authority on this subject, have ever attempted it.

If you remove one department from the common locality, you admit the right and possibility of removing other departments. If you find reasons for removing the Medical Department to Detroit, you may find reasons for establishing the Law Department at Lansing. The Upper Peninsula, from its abundant mineral resources, and its geological indications, may claim to be the proper seat of the Department of Geology and Mineralogy: The vast northern forests of the lower Peninsula would offer great facilities for Botany and Zoology: The island of Mackinaw might be deemed a beautiful location for the Observatory: The professor of Greek might be tempted by the Arcadian beauty of the banks of the St. Joseph, at Niles: The professor of Latin might find something to remind him of the Roman energy in the enterprising character of Grand Rapids: The professor of History might be charmed to Monroe by the historical associations which cluster on the banks of the Raisin: The professor of Mathematics might find attractions in his old associations among the lakes of Pontiac: The rural shades of Pinckney have not lost their hold upon the imagination of the professor of Modern Languages: Grand Haven might claim the professor of Chemistry: The sylvan beauty of Kalamazoo might seem fit haunts for Belles Lettres and the fine arts: and Physics and Civil Engineering might be divided between the thriving towns of Marshall and Jackson. An equitable division of books and apparatus might also be made. Then the President in solitary dignity might extend his gardens into the College Campus without rebuke; and unmolested lead about his class in philosophy, and rival the great Stagyrite in practical peripateticism. Room too, he would have in abundance, for the accommodation of the professors in their occasional visits, and for the learned men of other countries, who, attracted by our fame, should come to search out the University of Michigan. Some of us, however, notwithstanding the brilliancy and charms of these novel experiments, may deem it less hazardous to listen to the teachings of experience, and to yield to the authority of well established precedents. Much has already been done by adhering to the principle of concentration. We see much more that can be undertaken, on this principle, with the surest prospects of success. The University in its present location has been found quite accessible to the youth both of our State and of other States. Local jealousies, if they have existed, must soon subside before a generous common sense. Every part of Michigan will recognise the University as its own; and even Ann Arbor itself as the seat of this common possession, will come to be regarded as in some sort belonging to the people of the State. Least of all do I apprehend that Detroit will be ambitious of taking possession of one of the Departments of the University, when I behold on yonder hill a work of her own liberality consigned to this locality. She has enriched and adorned the University with an Observatory; she has given it her name; but she has not lopped it from the parent stem. And her intelligent citizens have doubtless well considered that although a Medical College might be planted there, as such Colleges have been planted in other cities, yet the mere name of the University could give it no real elevation above others of the same class, while cut off from a vital connection with it; and while removed from that circle of learned association which alone supplies to a University school, in any of the professions, a real distinction and a higher character in comparison with those isolated schools which are merely private establishments. Foregoing then all doubtful and impracticable questions, let us consider the location of the University as a point determined, and, with a hearty union, bend our efforts to perfect all its departments, by enlarging the means of instruction, by introducing higher standards of scholarship, and by increasing fidelity and devotion to the noble work we have undertaken. In the fable of the bundle of twigs we are taught how each twig taken separately may be broken by an infant's hand; while all bound firmly together may bid defiance to a giant's strength.

The third evil to be avoided is sectarian prejudices and demands in the management of the University.

In an institution professedly belonging to a particular religious denomination, or belonging to the State where a State religion exists, a Theological Faculty can be established as freely as any other.—Here of course the authorised tenets will be taught. But it would be a great and manifest mistake, even in such an institution, to introduce religious any more than political tests in the appointment of professors. Professors in every department should be men of pure and honorable characters. This is essential indeed, no less, in political appointments, or in men entrusted with commercial responsibilities. But beyond this, in the appointment of professors, reference should be had only to scientific and literary qualifications, and aptitude to teach. It is indispensable to a teacher in any branch of science or literature, that he should be master of the branch which he professes to teach. However amiable his character, however pure his religious or political creed according to the judgement of any sect or party, if he have not the requisite literary or scientific qualifications, he is of no account. It is on this common sense principle that we select a physician, a lawyer, a mechanic, a laborer of any description; and it would be the height of infatuation to reject it in the appointment of professors. Nor, would the institution in question avoid the error by adopting the principle of selecting the best man of one's own sect or party; for it might often happen that the best man of the sect or party would not be the best man for the vacant chair; and some man of extraordinary ability, and whose accession would bring incalculable strength and reputation to the institution would be set aside. There is no safe principle but that of looking directly at the qualifications of the individual, relatively to the chair to be filled.

Hence the most eminent Universities have ever been governed by this principle: and it would be easy to show from the history of Universities, that wherever the opposite principle has been adopted, it has brought barrenness and mediocrity into the professorial corps.

We have seen that even Roman Catholic institutions have adopted this wise principle, and like the Universities of Padua and Pisa, above referred to, have by it, rendered themselves illustrious.

In institutions of our own country belonging to particular sects, their usefulness and prosperity have been in proportion to their liberality. Take Yale College as an example—an institution, with the exception of Harvard, more fully developed than any institution in our country. Yale College belongs to the Congregationalists; it has a Theological Faculty, and a chaplain and preacher of its own order; and yet there is no sectarian exclusiveness in the appointment of professors in departments outside of the theological, and no sectarian pressure in its interior discipline and management. It cannot be said of Yale that it has been devoted to the interests of congregationalism, or that it has tended to extend congregationalism. The country does not think of it as a sectarian institution. It attracts attention and is valued generally for its educational benefits. Let it but change its policy and become intensely sectarian, and its glory would depart. Now it is resorted to by youth of all denominations, from all political parties, and from every section of

the country, North and South, East and West; and it presents the largest number of students of any college or University of the United
States. Indeed Yale College derives no benefit from being attached to a
particular sect, save the privilege of establishing a Theological Faculty.

Every sect has the right of establishing its own institutions: but no
such institution can arise to eminence, or gain large success, by making
the promotion of sectarian interests its great aim. Let any one carefully
examine the institutions of our country, and he will find the above assertion fully sustained. Hence we find the sectarian institutions, so
called, tending more and more to a liberal policy. The genius of our
country demands, that if sectarian in name, they should not be so in
their educational organization and procedures.

One is led by the consideration of these facts to enquire why sectarian colleges or universities exist, at all, where no Theological Faculty
is established? Their origin is very easily accounted for.

In England the Universities proper of Oxford and Cambridge fell
into disuse; and the Colleges, which were private and special endowments, originally designed to furnish board and lodging to Theological
students, and eventually came to have teachers attached to them, supplanted the former as educational institutions. Thus Oxford and Cambridge merged into collections of Colleges under ecclesiastical control.

It was natural therefore, that when a University was established at
Cambridge, Massachusetts, it should begin with a college after the
English form. This precedent was followed as other similar institutions came into being. Besides, all education in our country began under the patronage of religious sects, or of individuals belonging to
these sects. Men who emigrated to this country from religious principles, naturally connected all their institutions both educational and
political, with their peculiar church organization.

But it did not follow, because, this connection was originally demanded, or could not be avoided, on account of the peculiar exigencies
of the times, that it was to continue when these exigencies had passed
away. Hence, in time, the Church and State came to be separated; and
education in the common schools, at least, came to be separated from
the Church also. This movement has proceeded farther and farther;
and we now have not only common schools, but also High Schools and
Academies, Normal Schools, and even many Colleges and Universities,
removed from particular ecclesiastical connections.

Indeed, it is hard to perceive any necessity for such a connection in any instance, save where a sect desires to create a Theological Faculty. If it be said that Colleges and Universities require to be under religious control, and this can be best secured by a particular denominational connection, the argument proves too much. For why is not the same demanded for Common Schools, Union Schools, High Schools, Academies, Normal Schools, and the various private institutions? Nay, the lower schools, and especially the common schools, would seem to demand the very highest conditions for religious influence, since in *these,* pupils are received at the most impressible period of human life, and when the strongest bent is given to character and habits. It is on this very ground that the Roman Catholics have claimed the control of the apportionment of school money falling to their children. They say, we deem it essential to educate our children under those religious influences which our consciences approve of. Now, are we consistent, if we deny the necessity of denominational control in our common schools, and indeed in many other schools below the College and the University, but the moment we reach this highest grade of education, claim it as essential?

If the State is competent to establish, and to provide for the management of Common, Union and Normal Schools without denominational interference, why is it not competent to do the same with respect to Colleges and Universities? And if the religious interests of the former can be secured under State organization, why not of the latter?

Besides, as a matter of fact, we cannot perceive what peculiar religious discipline is exercised in denominational institutions which does not exist elsewhere, unless these institutions should take rigid measures for the inculcation of their peculiar tenets. In this case their pupils could be derived only from their own communions, and they would become exceedingly limited in their sphere of operation. This, we know, they do not generally attempt, but aiming to afford education in science and literature, leave the conscience unfettered, and establish only a moral and religious discipline which shall commend itself to the community generally without distinction of sect. And this is the very discipline which is introduced into State institutions, and into institutions generally which are not denominational.

We come now to consider the University of Michigan under its moral and religious aspects.

First, as to the appointment of professors.

If the principle we have above laid down, that the appointment of professors to chairs of literature and science, to all chairs, at least, out-side of the Theological, is to be made independently alike of political and religious tests, and solely in reference to literary and scientific qualifications, and aptitude to teach, and that too in institutions pro-fessedly attached to particular religious denominations; and if the ex-ample not only of Protestant Leyden, but also of Roman Catholic Padua and Pisa is worthy of all commendation, and its wisdom at-tested by its brilliant success; then, when we come to the "University of Michigan," established as a State institution on a fund provided by the General Government for no other purpose than that of promoting science and literature, and advancing education, and whose great ob-ject is declared to be, in the first ordinance of the State passed in refer-ence to it, and approved March 18, 1837, "to provide the inhabitants of the State with the means of acquiring a thorough knowledge of the various branches of literature, science, and the arts;" then, I say, when we come to this institution, the principle of regulating appointments by qualifications, alone, cannot fail us. Here, if any where, political and religious tests must be utterly abolished, nor even a shadow of them appear.

All sects and parties, every individual in the State would probably agree to this general statement. But a plan has somehow sprung up, and in one or two instances been acted upon, which, on the one hand, by proclaiming the equal rights of all religious denominations in Uni-versity appointments seems to avoid exclusiveness; while on the other hand, in the very attempt to adjust these rights, it involves us in all the evils of denominational tests. For, on this plan, wherever a chair is to be filled, instead of confining ourselves to the considerations of the lit-erary and scientific qualifications of the candidates, and their aptitude to teach, we must raise two additional enquiries; first, to which of the denominations does the appointment about to be made, of right be-long? and secondly, which of the candidates possesses the requisite denominational qualifications? Now, it is plain, that in both these questions, we depart from the true principle before vindicated; and that were this plan once adopted, every appointment afterwards made to the University would be governed by some denominational test. But this would not be the only evil we should have to encounter. There would be the evil of denominational jealousy and competition. How would it be possible to adjust these denominational rights? Which de-nomination shall have the largest number of professors? Shall it be determined by the numbers, the wealth, the political influence, or the educated intelligence of the sect? Or, shall the same number be distributed alike to all the sects? But some professorships may be regarded as more influential than others; and the full professorship would generally be regarded as taking precedence of the assistant. Then how many assistant professorships shall be considered equivalent to one full professorship? Shall it be two or one and a half? How shall we determine the relative importance of the full professorships? Which sect shall have the right to nominate the President? Or shall it be given to all in rotation? And shall he be elected for a limited term of years? Then again, it must be determined how far the power of the sects shall extend: Shall they have the power to make all nominations; or shall the Regents be required to elect the proper number from each sect? Or will each sect be satisfied with one representative, and leave the Regents to elect the remainder according to their pleasure? Or suppose the rights of some sects have hitherto been neglected, as for example, the Roman Catholics, who have not at present a single professor in the University—indeed the same is true with respect to the Dutch Reformed, the Unitarian, Universalist, and it may be other denominations—and that one or all of these should come forward and claim their rights when the chairs are all filled; would this difficulty be removed by creating new chairs, or by vacating some of the chairs already filled in order to make way for what may be demanded as an equitable adjustment?

When once we admit the principle of denominational representation, we can exclude no denomination. When once we allow denominational interference, every denomination has an equal right to interfere. We must hear all: we must attend to all: and we must enter upon the impracticable task of satisfying all. And then this impracticable and unproductive work of endeavoring to harmonize the conflicting claims of numerous sects, ever prone to become more and more inflamed by competition, and rendered more and more unreasonable, will absorb the attention and labors of the Regents, instead of the practicable, legitimate, and noble work of securing for the University eminent professors, and providing them with the means of fulfilling their functions, and carrying out the ends of public instruction.

And when these representatives of the different sects are introduced into the University, acknowledged and known in this capacity, then the question arises, how they are to act out this representative capacity,

and to maintain the interests of the bodies which they represent? Shall
they all remit the peculiarities of their respective sects, and endeavor to
stand upon certain principles in which they all agree? Then there will,
in reality, be no representation of sects, and the ends of the whole arrangement become null and void. Shall each one assert his sectarian
peculiarities? Then will the University be split into conflicting parties,
and the professors be found heading their respective clans, and instead
of an institution "providing the inhabitants of the State with the means
of acquiring a thorough knowledge of the various branches of literature, science, and the arts," we shall have a grand gymnasium where
Catholics and Protestants, the orthodox and the heterodox, engaged in
endless logomachies shall renew Milton's chaos—

> "A universal hubbub wild
> Of stunning sounds and voices all confused."

Better, far better, than to run the hazard of such confusion and ruin,
would it be to consign the University to any one denomination, Catholic, or Protestant, animated by the noble spirit of Padua, Pisa, or Leyden. One alone possessing it, might be generous and enlightened; a
number attempting to share its functions, and divide its spoils, would
only rend it in pieces. But egregiously do those mistake the character
and ends of this institution who imagine that, because, it belongs to no
sect or party in particular, it therefore belongs to all sects and parties
conjointly, and of equal right. It not only does not belong to any sect
or party in particular; it belongs to no sect or party at all. It belongs to
the people of this State simply as the people of the State. The deed of
trust by which it was founded, the ordinance by which its objects are
defined, makes no allusion to Catholic or Protestant, to Presbyterian,
Methodist, Episcopalian, Baptist, Congregationalist, Unitarian, Universalist, or any other religious denomination. It speaks not of political
parties; it refers to no particular localities: It speaks only of the State
of Michigan, or of the people of the State. It is a purely literary and
scientific institution; it is in no sense ecclesiastical. It is designed for a
simple purpose—advancing knowledge and promoting education. Occupying a higher grade, it is as purely a popular and educational institution as the common school itself. It is as absurd to speak of the University as belonging to religious sects conjointly, as it would be to speak
of the asylum, the State prison, the Legislature, or any public body,
institution, or works, as thus belonging. The State is not composed of

religious sects, but of the people. And the institutions of the State do not belong to the sects into which the people may chance to be divided by their religious opinions and practices; but to the people considered as the body politic, irrespective of all such divisions.

The people of the State, and not the religious sects, elect, by districts, ten Judges and ten Regents, who are responsible to their constituents, the people of the State, and not to the religious sects. As well may the religious sects prescribe to the one as to the other. The duties of these Judges and Regents are fixed, not by the religious sects, but by the constitution, and organic laws enacted under it.

Both Judges and Regents fulfill their duty when they faithfully obey the constitution and laws of the State and their manifest intent. No religious body or ecclesiastical organization—no association whatever, whether political, religious or benevolent, has a right to prescribe to Judges or Regents, to interfere with their functions or to call them to account. They stand before the people as simply the body politic.

The Regents, as ordered by the constitution and organic law, appoint the President and Professors of the University, manage its funds and direct its affairs generally. They are the proper, and legal, and only curators. All their doings, and the doings of the President and Professors under them, including the receipts and expenditures of all monies, are, according to law, fully embodied in a report to the Superintendent of Public Instruction, who prints the same, lays it before the legislature, and sends it abroad among the people. In addition to this a Board of Visitors is appointed by the Superintendent, who have full power and opoprtunity to examine into the condition of the University, and who make a report of the same. In these ways the people are made fully acquainted with the affairs of the University, annually, by its responsible and known guardians and visitors.

The President and Professors are entrusted with the instruction and discipline of the Institution according to a system of by-laws enacted by the Regents. They fulfill their duties when they faithfully obey and administer these laws. The are directly accountable only to the Regents, and through them to the people of the State.

No political association, no ecclesiastical body, and no association whatever, secular or religious, have any authority to prescribe to the Faculty, to interfere with their functions, or to call them to account. The State has determined their responsibilities. The right of prescription, interference, or of any control conceded to one religious body would involve a concession of the same to all similar bodies. What is conceded to the Protestants, the Catholics may equally claim. What is conceded to the Methodists or Presbyterians, all other protestant sects may equally claim. Nay, what is conceded to religious sects must be conceded also to those who belong to no sect. We might thus have various codes of morals, various rules of discipline, and conflicting laws of duty: And we certainly should have little independence or discretion.

The institution has laws stringently enforcing faithful study, good order, and good morals. With respect to religious duties, every student is required to attend public worship on the Sabbath in whatever church his parent or guardian shall direct. In addition to this, the Faculty are required to have daily prayers for the students.—The duty of conducting prayers is not imposed particularly upon the President, or upon any member of the Faculty. How and by whom the duty shall be performed is left under the direction of that body.

Now if the Faculty faithfully fulfill these laws in respect to religious services, no one has a right to find fault with them. If more services, or different services are required, the Regents are the proper authority to order them.

In a strictly sectarian College or University, the President and professors, if ordered by the body to whom it belongs, to inculcate their creed, and to abide by their ecclesiastical organization, may indeed, be compelled to move in a contracted sphere, but they will have a clearly defined position, and need never be in doubt as to the religious management of the institution. But if a State University, in belonging to no sect in particular, is consigned to all the sects, to be censured, dictated to, and called to account at their pleasure, it will only serve to exemplify the fable anew, where an attempt to please every body ended in pleasing nobody, and made the actors supremely ridiculous.

The only practical alternative is that of committing an institution of learning to one sect, or to none at all. State institutions, of course are committed to none at all.

From the liberal course which the Colleges and Universities, attached to particular denominations in our country, have generally pursued, led on by the generous and elevated spirit of learning, or influenced by our free political institutions and public opinion, I find on a comparison of the rules of our State University respecting religious services and moral discipline, with those of the leading denomina-

tional institutions, no important difference whatever. All alike inculcate strict morality and honorable conduct: all alike require a daily
attendance upon prayers; all alike require an attendance upon divine
worship on the Sabbath: And those institutions, such as Yale and
Harvard, which have a University preacher of the denomination, excuse those students whose parents or guardians request it, from attendance on the College Chapel, in order that they may attend the services
of churches which have their preference. This is all that the best regulated, the most popular, the most influential and successful institutions
of our country undertake to do, whether they be denominational or
not; and this is just what the University of Michigan undertakes to do.
These services manifestly require no particular denominational superintendence, and no infusion of the particular tenets of any sect. Far
less do they require the mutually jealous and necessarily conflicting
superintendence of many sects. It would be a portentous distinction to
draw between a denominational and a State Institution, that the first
is under the control of one sect; the other under the control of all sects;
that the first is embalmed in the brotherly love, and defended by the
watchful jealousy of one sect; the other divided among the opposing
interests, or thrown as a prize among the rampant competitions of all.

The presence of benign and charitable religion should pervade the
hearts, and hallow the hands of men in all human organizations and
offices; but it does not thence follow that the object of all is directly to
inculcate religious doctrines and duties. It were well that all our legislators, judges, and State officers generally, as well as our men of business, were religious men. Heavenly thoughts and prayerful habits
would be great safe guards of virtue and pledges of integrity everywhere. It would be exceedingly desirable that all teachers from a common school teacher, to a University professor, should be men of piety.
But the prime object of a seminary of learning is not like that of a
church, to inculcate religion or perform its services; but, to afford education. If we are content in our common schools with proper fitness to
teach the required branches, and a good moral character, why demand
denominational qualifications in the higher institutions? And why
force the church into the State University any more than into our halls
of legislation or on the bench of judges?

The Regents of the University have ever regarded themselves as
State officers, and not as the representatives of special religious or political interests. I believe their proceedings will defy scrutiny on this

point. In only one instance within my knowledge has an appointment been made with reference to denominational connections.

Before I left New York to take charge of the University, I was informed by a member of the Board of Regents, that the Board deemed it expedient to fill Professor Whedon's place from his own denomination. When I arrived in Michigan, I was advised with by highly respectable gentlemen in Detroit and Ann Arbor, belonging to that denomination, on the subject. I found that such an expectation existed. The consequence was, through my own instrumentality, Professor Haven was elected. He was a gentleman who I had reason to believe, possessed the requisite professorial qualifications. His denominational connection was to me no objection.—Indeed, neither in his case, nor in that of any other professor elected, was it to me a matter of any personal consideration. The appointment proved satisfactory to all parties; and never, during his residence with us, did I feel that he was a denominational representative; I regarded him as a truly liberal man as well as an efficient officer.

But farther reflection made it perfectly plain to me that the principle of denominational representation could never with safety be adopted. I found from the public prints as well as from various conversations that the idea was getting abroad that appointments were to be made on that principle. A clergyman of another denomination wrote me a letter, bringing before me the claims of the body to which he was attached. It was evident that the experiment ought never to be repeated. Should a precedent be once established, there would be no end to the difficulties and evils in which we would become involved. I believe the Regents were unanimously of the same opinion. On thing is certain, no appointment has since been made with any reference to denominational connection. After Dr. Brunnow reached Ann Arbor, I for the first time asked him whether he were a Catholic or a Protestant, when he informed me that he was a Lutheran protestant. Dr. Haven, who brought Professor Winchell's name before the Board of Regents, affirmed that he was ignorant of his denomination connection. Prof. Frieze was known to be an Episcopalian, but he was elected through the instrumentality of Prof. Boise, himself a Baptist. Dr. Ford and Prof. Wood were elected while we were entirely ignorant of their denominational connections. Messrs. Clarke and Brooks, alumni of the University, were known to be Methodists, but this did not, as I am aware, have the least influence in their appointment as assistant professors. Messrs. Peck and Trowbridge were elected without any knowledge on our part of their religious predilections. Mr. White, although known to be an attendant in the Episcopal Church, was elected on the recommendation of the Congregational president, and, among others, of Congregational clergymen and professors at New Haven, who valued him so highly that they were desirous of having a chair of History endowed for him in Yale College. As for myself, my name was first brought before the Regents, without any knowledge of the fact on my part, by George Bancroft who is not a presbyterian, and until of late has been accounted a Unitarian. Sure I am that I was not elected for my presbyterianism. I have always disclaimed, as I now disclaim, being the representative of my sect, in the University. I should deem myself wholly unfit for my place, were I willing to be considered in that light. As the President of the University of Michigan, I claim to be an officer of the State. I have been called here by no ecclesiastical body; and as President of the University, I am accountable to none. I have been appointed under an express provision of the Constitution. I have been appointed by Regents elected by the people. I am accountable directly to them, and to the people through them.

As to religious duties in the University, there is nothing specially assigned to the President. The execution of the requirement that the students shall attend Divine Worship on the Sabbath, and the maintaining of daily prayers are not committed particularly to the President. The ordinance of the University requires these duties of the Faculty and consequently of the President only as one of the Faculty. The Faculty, however, have by common consent committed the daily prayers to the President. The manner of performing this duty has been left entirely to himself, and I am not aware that he has not fully met the approbation both of the Faculty and the Regents.

The religious duties imposed upon the President and Faculty by the Regents, are all that can be required of them as officers of the Institution.

But the question here arises are there any additional duties which, as private christians they can with propriety exercise towards the students committed to them? There, certainly, are various ways in which religious instruction can be given; by graceful and apt episodes in the class room when the subject naturally suggests them; by employing scientific truths to illustrate natural theology; by the easy familiarity of daily converse opened by the relation of teacher and pupil; by visitations in sickness; by rendering themselves accessible to the students as religious advisers; by habitually manifesting a parental interest in them; by maintaining the attitude of experienced and earnest friendship; by a pure and upright example; and by the exercise of all those tender charities which are as remote from sectarian bigotry, as they are near the vital heart of christianity.

Separate from the institution the spirit of denominational and proselytism; and you can admit the gospel under its purest, most benignant and redeeming aspects. Indeed, in a State institution of learning, where youth who have been nurtured under every variety of religious opinion are congregated, the strict inculcation of the peculiarities of any one sect would be far less successful than a familiar teaching of those fundamental principles of the gospel, which are generally admitted. Hence that very religious influence which alone is admissible in a State University, would be that which, in its very nature, is calculated to do most good. But no specific rules can be laid down on this subject: every thing will depend on the good sense, truthfulness, and tact of the teacher himself. The part of the Regents is, to take the utmost pains to procure professors who are qualified for their office, and then to trust to their uprightness and discretion; always, of course, holding in reserve the power to check imprudence, and to correct evils. Indeed a well selected body of professors will so assimilate as to check and regulate each other.

Since I have been acquainted with the University of Michigan, there has been an entire harmony on religious subjects among both professors and students. Denominationalism and proselytism have not appeared among us, and yet much healthful religious influence has been exerted—as much I believe as in any other institution of learning; and with consequences no less marked and happy. As to myself I may be permitted to say that I have conscientiously endeavored to make the daily religious services as effective as possible. Beyond this, at the Sabbath morning prayers, I have always given brief practical remarks drawn from the passage read. And on Sabbath afternoon, I have generally given a lecture either on natural theology, or the evidences of Christianity, or morals, or on some point of practical Christianity. Attendance on this lecture has always been at the option of the students. This lecture has also been open to the public.

I have never learned that either the professors, the students, or the public have charged me with any appearance of sectarianism or prose-

lytism. If in any religious efforts on the part of the professors or myself beyond what is prescribed by the University ordinance, there have
been any improprieties or excess, we are open to correction and restraint from the Regents—the legal guardians of the University. But
while we hold ourselves amenable to the Regents, we claim exemp-
tion from the authority of all ecclesiastical bodies either as imposing
on us duties, restraining our actions, or censuring our measures. Legally, such bodies have no right to extend their authority over us in
any way: Morally, they have no power to aid us, from the very fact
that what one attempts all have an equal right to attempt; and that
therefore as their advice or prescriptions would not be likely to harmonize, their interference would only serve to confuse and embarrass
us.

One of the most effectual ways of promoting religion among the
students is to afford every encouragement to their voluntary associations for religious purposes, such as the Student's Christian Association,
and the Christian Library Association. The latter is especially to be
commended to Christians of all denominations, and to all persons desirous of aiding the best interests of the Institution.—Give us religious
books: Give us as freely as you please. Give us the noble works of the
old English Divines—of the established church and of the Dissenters.
Give us the excellent works of our American Divines of all Schools.
There the books will stand, open to the choice of the students. Each
one can consult his own taste and peculiarities; and all can profit by the
spirit of Christianity nobly diffused through so many channels. Perhaps an opportunity thus afforded of consulting the choice works of
the great and good men of all parties will lead many a mind to adopt
the grand and Catholic sentiment of Cyprian: "The Church is one,
which by reason of its fecundity is extended into a multitude, in the
same manner as the rays of the sun, however numerous, constitute but
one light; and the branches of a tree, however many, are attached to
one trunk, which is supported by its tenacious root; and where various
rivers flow from the same fountain, though moisture is diffused by the
redundant supply of waters, unity is preserved in their origin."

The University as an institution of the State, open to all the people
of the State, and affording to them the means of the highest education,
is a symbol of the essential union of all religious sects, and of all political parties. We are all Christians, we are all American citizens. Whatever may be our differences, we have a common agreement—a com-

mon interest in the great subject of education.—It is the part of wisdom to preserve the University intact from the questions on which we differ, and to maintain and foster it purely as an educational institution. The Regents and Faculty may have their own opinions on politics, their own attachments for the sects to which they severally belong, their own views on questions of moral reform. These as men, and as American citizens, they claim to entertain in perfect freedom, without any interference, or any rebuke. But they would violate the trust reposed in them, did they allow these to influence their measures in respect to the University.

The great principle in respect to the management of the University is very plain, and commends itself to the common sense of every one; and that is, that it is to be left to the Regents who are appointed by the people for that purpose, and who make an annual report of their doings which every one may read. The irresponsible reports of newspaper writers who write under fictitious names; and who when they do not manufacture, like scavengers, collect gossip, are of little worth, except they be regarded as humorous advertisements of the University. It is to be presumed that the people of Michigan know the difference between fancy sketches drawn at a distance, and facts and statistics given over the signatures of the legal guardians whom they have themselves elected. The University of Michigan has nothing to be ashamed of, and nothing to conceal. There is nothing that it desires more than to be fully known to the people to whom it belongs. If there be any individuals who are not satisfied with the reports of the Regents, let them come and examine for themselves, and take sufficient time to make themselves acquainted with the University in all its departments. Let them come and introduce themselves to the President and Professors, and every facility will be afforded them. Let them not merely walk through the grounds, but let them visit the Library, the gallery of Fine Arts, the Museum, the Laboratory, the Observatory, and attend the lectures of the Professors and the examinations of the students. Every thing here is open to the public eye. *Si monumentum quaeris, circumspice*—Do you ask for the evidences of our doings, look around. Here are laid the stable foundations of a magnificent institution. Nay, here already exists an institution of which any people might be proud. Only let there be a hearty union, enlightened councils, and an honorable appreciation. Let political and sectarian jealousies and competitions never invade us. Let all idle questions of partition and removal be laid forever.—We have greater work to do than to discuss them. Let the people see that the State University, like the State Capitol, must have some fixed location; and that as the last is not the Capitol of Lansing because it is planted there; so neither is this the University of Ann Arbor, because it is planted here. Nay, develope this University to the grand measure which such a name implies, and it will become the attractive centre of so wide a circle, it will shed abroad so far its glorious light, its enkindling influence—that even the title, University of Michigan, will be too limited to characterize it: it will be the University of the great North-west, it will be one of the great central institutions, which like Leyden, and Padua, and Pisa, in their days of glory, and like Paris, Munich, and Berlin in our own times, are the Universities of Nations, the fountains of universal civilization.

5. Andrew D. White's Description of Michigan under Tappan, ca. 1860

Andrew D. White (1832–1918), the descendant of New England ancestors, was born in central New York, educated at Yale (1853), and seasoned by considerable study and travel abroad during the next two years. After taking an M.A. at Yale, he became professor of history at the University of Michigan in 1857, at the time when it was profiting from Tappan's leadership. The example of Tappan, reported in this brief excerpt from White's *Autobiography*, confirmed ideas about education that White had already formed from his critical observations at Yale and his studies in Paris and Berlin. After leaving Michigan, White went on to a distinguished career as a historian, diplomat, and educator, of which the crowning achievement was the founding of Cornell. Among the university builders of the great epoch of educational growth that followed the Civil War, he was equaled only by his friends, Charles William Eliot and Daniel Coit Gilman.

See Docs. 6, 7, 8, and 9; Part VIII, Doc. 8; Carl Becker, *Cornell University: Founders and the Founding* (Ithaca, N.Y., 1943); Walter P. Rogers, *Andrew D. White and the Modern University* (Ithaca, N.Y., 1942).

The more I threw myself into the work of the university the more I came to believe in the ideas on which it was founded, and to see that it was a reality embodying many things of which I had previously only

Andrew D. White, *Autobiography* (New York, 1905), I, 271–72, 275–81.

dreamed. Up to that time the highest institutions of learning in the United States were almost entirely under sectarian control. Even the University of Virginia, which Thomas Jefferson had founded as a center of liberal thought, had fallen under the direction of sectarians, and among the great majority of the Northern colleges an unwritten law seemed to require that a university president should be a clergyman. The instruction in the best of these institutions was, as I have shown elsewhere, narrow, their methods outworn, and the students, as a rule, confined to one simple, single, cast-iron course, in which the great majority of them took no interest. The University of Michigan had made a beginning of something better. The president was Dr. Henry Philip Tappan, formerly a Presbyterian clergyman, a writer of repute on philosophical subjects, a strong thinker, an impressive orator, and a born leader of men, who, during a visit to Europe, had been greatly impressed by the large and liberal system of the German universities, and had devoted himself to urging a similar system in our own country. On the Eastern institutions—save, possibly, Brown—he made no impression. Each of them was as stagnant as a Spanish convent, and as self-satisfied as a Bourbon duchy; but in the West he attracted supporters, and soon his ideas began to show themselves effective in the State university over which he had been called to preside.

The men he summoned about him were, in the main, admirably fitted to aid him. . . .

The features which mainly distinguished the University of Michigan from the leading institutions of the East were that it was utterly unsectarian, that various courses of instruction were established, and that options were allowed between them. On these accounts that university holds a most important place in the history of American higher education; for it stands practically at the beginning of the transition from the old sectarian college to the modern university, and from the simple, single, cast-iron course to the form which we now know, in which various courses are presented, with free choice between them. The number of students was about five hundred, and the faculty corresponded to these in numbers. Now that the university includes over four thousand students, with a faculty in proportion, those seem the days of small things; but to me at that period it was all very grand. It seemed marvelous that there were then very nearly as many students at the University of Michigan as at Yale; and, as a rule, they were students worth teaching—hardy, vigorous, shrewd, broad, with faith in the greatness of the country and enthusiasm regarding the nation's future. It may be granted that there was, in many of them, a lack of elegance, but there was neither languor nor cynicism. One seemed, among them, to breathe a purer, a stronger air. Over the whole institution Dr. Tappan presided, and his influence, both upon faculty and students, was, in the main, excellent. He sympathized heartily with the work of every professor, allowed to each great liberty, yet conducted the whole toward the one great end of developing a university more and more worthy of our country. His main qualities were of the best. Nothing could be better than his discussions of great questions of public policy and of education. One of the noblest orations I have ever heard was an offhand speech of his on receiving for the university museum a cast of the Laocoön from the senior class; yet this speech was made without preparation, and in the midst of engrossing labor. He often showed, not only the higher qualities required in a position like his, but a remarkable shrewdness and tact in dealing with lesser questions. . . .

Every winter Dr. Tappan went before the legislature to plead the cause of the university, and to ask for appropriations. He was always heard with pleasure, since he was an excellent speaker; but certain things militated against him. First of all, he had much to say of the excellent models furnished by the great German universities, and especially by those of Prussia. This gave demagogues in the legislature, anxious to make a reputation in buncombe, a great chance. They orated to the effect that we wanted an American and not a Prussian system. Moreover, some unfortunate legends were developed. Mrs. Tappan, a noble and lovely woman belonging to the Livingston family, had been brought up in New York and New England, and could hardly suppress her natural preference for her old home and friends. A story grew that in an assembly of Michigan ladies she once remarked that the doctor and herself considered themselves as "missionaries to the West." This legend spread far and wide. It was resented, and undoubtedly cost the doctor dear.

The worst difficulty by far which he had to meet was the steady opposition of the small sectarian colleges scattered throughout the State. Each, in its own petty interest, dreaded the growth of any institution better than itself; each stirred the members of the legislature from its locality to oppose all aid to the State university; each, in its religious assemblages, its synods, conferences, and the like, sought to stir preju-

dice against the State institution as "godless." The result was that the
doctor, in spite of his eloquent speeches, became the butt of various
wretched demagogues in the legislature, and he very rarely secured
anything in the way of effective appropriations. The university had been
founded by a grant of public lands from the United States to Michigan; and one of his arguments was based on the fact that an immensely valuable tract, on which considerable part of the city of Toledo
now stands, had been taken away from the university without any suitable remuneration. But even this availed little, and it became quite a
pastime among demagogues at the State Capitol to bait the doctor. On
one of these occasions he was inspired to make a prophecy. Disgusted
at the poor, cheap blackguardism, he shook the dust of the legislature
off his feet, and said: "The day will come when my students will take
your places, and then something will be done." That prophecy was
fulfilled. In a decade the leading men in the legislature began to be
the graduates of the State university; and now these graduates are
largely in control, and they have dealt nobly with their alma mater.
The State has justly become proud of it, and has wisely developed it.

Dr. Tappan's work was great, indeed. He stood not only at the beginning of the institution at Ann Arbor, but really at the beginning of
the other universities of the Western States, from which the country is
gaining so much at present, and is sure to gain vastly more in the future. The day will come when his statue will commemorate his services.

But there was another feature in his administration to which I refer
with extreme reluctance. He had certain "defects of his qualities." Big,
hearty, frank, and generous, he easily became the prey of those who
wrought upon his feelings; and, in an evil hour, he was drawn into a
quarrel not his own, between two scientific professors. This quarrel
became exceedingly virulent; at times it almost paralyzed the university, and finally it convulsed the State. It became the main object of the
doctor's thoughts. The men who had drawn him into it quietly retired
under cover, and left him to fight their battle in the open. He did this
powerfully, but his victories were no less calamitous than his defeats;
for one of the professors, when overcome, fell back upon the church to
which he belonged, and its conference was led to pass resolutions
warning Christian people against the university. The forces of those
hostile to the institution were marshaled to the sound of the sectarian
drum. The quarrel at last became political; and when the doctor un-

wisely entered the political field in hopes of defeating the candidates put forward by his opponents, he was beaten at the polls, and his resignation followed. A small number of us, including Judge Cooley and Professors Frieze, Fasquelle, Boise, and myself, simply maintained an "armed neutrality," standing by the university, and refusing to be drawn into this whirlpool of intrigue and objurgation. Personally, we loved the doctor. Every one of us besought him to give up the quarrel, but in vain. He would not; he could not. It went on till the crash came. He was virtually driven from the State, retired to Europe, and never returned.

6. The "Cornell Idea" Forms in White's Mind, 1860–65

See Doc. 5.

Every feature of the little American college seemed all the more sordid. But gradually I began consoling myself by building air-castles. These took the form of structures suited to a great university:—with distinguished professors in every field, with libraries as rich as the Bodleian, halls as lordly as that of Christ Church or of Trinity, chapels as inspiring as that of King's, towers as dignified as those of Magdalen and Merton, quadrangles as beautiful as those of Jesus and St. John's. In the midst of all other occupations, I was constantly rearing these structures on that queenly site above the finest of the New York lakes, and dreaming of a university worthy of the commonwealth and of the nation. This dream became a sort of obsession. It came upon me during my working hours, in the class-rooms, in rambles along the lake shore, in the evenings, when I paced up and down the walks in front of the college buildings, and saw rising in their place and extending to the pretty knoll behind them, the worthy home of a great university. But this university, though beautiful and dignified, like those at Oxford and Cambridge, was in two important respects unlike them. First, I made provision for other studies besides classics and mathemat-

Andrew D. White, *Autobiography*, I, 288–92.

ics. There should be professors in the great modern literatures—above all, in our own; there should also be a professor of modern history and a lecturer on architecture. And next, my university should be under control of no single religious organization; it should be free from all sectarian or party trammels; in electing its trustees and professors no questions should be asked as to their belief or their attachment to this or that sect or party. So far, at least, I went in those days along the road toward the founding of Cornell.

The academic year of 1849–1850 having been passed at this little college in western New York, I entered Yale. This was nearer my ideal; for its professors were more distinguished, its equipment more adequate, its students more numerous, its general scope more extended. But it was still far below my dreams. Its single course in classics and mathematics, through which all students were forced alike, regardless of their tastes, powers, or aims; its substitution of gerund-grinding for ancient literature; its want of all instruction in modern literature; its substitution of recitals from text-books for instruction in history—all this was far short of my ideal. Moreover, Yale was then far more under denominational control than at present—its president, of necessity, as was then supposed, a Congregational minister; its professors, as a rule, members of the same sect; and its tutors, to whom our instruction during the first two years was almost entirely confined, students in the Congregational Divinity School. . . .

There was also in my dream another special feature, which no one has as yet attempted to realize—a lofty campanile, which I placed sometimes at the intersection of College and Church, and sometimes at the intersection of College and Elm streets—a clock-tower looking proudly down the slope, over the traffic of the town, and bearing a deep-toned peal of bells.

My general ideas on the subject were further developed by Charles Astor Bristed's book, "Five Years in an English University," and by sundry publications regarding student life in Germany. . . .

The next period in the formation of my ideas regarding a university began, after my graduation at Yale, during my first visit to Oxford. Then and at later visits, both to Oxford and Cambridge, I not only reveled in the architectural glories of those great seats of learning, but learned the advantages of college life in common—of the "halls," and the general social life which they promote; of the "commons" and "combination rooms," which give a still closer relation between those most directly concerned in university work; of the quadrangles, which give a sense of scholarly seclusion, even in the midst of crowded cities; and of all the surroundings which give a dignity befitting these vast establishments. Still more marked progress in my ideas was made during my attendance at the Sorbonne and the Collège de France. In those institutions, during the years 1853–1854, I became acquainted with the French university-lecture system, with its clearness, breadth, wealth of illustration, and its hold upon large audiences of students; and I was seized with the desire to transfer something like it to our own country. My castles in the air were now reared more loftily and broadly; for they began to include laboratories, museums, and even galleries of art. . . .

My student life at Berlin, during the year following, further intensified my desire to do something for university education in the United States. There I saw my ideal of a university not only realized, but extended and glorified—with renowned professors, with ample lecture-halls, with everything possible in the way of illustrative materials, with laboratories, museums, and a concourse of youth from all parts of the world.

I have already spoken, in the chapter on my professorship at the University of Michigan, regarding the influence on my ideas of its president, Henry Philip Tappan, and of the whole work in that institution. Though many good things may be justly said for the University of Virginia, the real beginning of a university in the United States, in the modern sense, was made by Dr. Tappan and his colleagues at Ann Arbor. Its only defects seemed to me that it included no technical side, and did not yet admit women. As to the first of these defects, the State had separated the agricultural college from the university, placing it in what, at that period, was a remote swamp near the State Capitol, and had as yet done nothing toward providing for other technical branches. As to the second, though a few of us favored the admission of women, President Tappan opposed it; and probably, in view of the condition of the university and of public opinion at that time, his opposition was wise.

7. *Organizing Cornell, 1865*

See Docs. 5 and 8.

Although my formal election to the university presidency did not take place until 1867, the duties implied by that office had already been discharged by me during two years.

While Mr. Cornell devoted himself to the financial questions arising from the new foundation, he intrusted all other questions to me. Indeed, my duties may be said to have begun when, as chairman of the Committee on Education in the State Senate, I resisted all efforts to divide the land-grant fund between the People's College and the State Agricultural College; to have been continued when I opposed the frittering away of the entire grant among more than twenty small sectarian colleges; and to have taken a more direct form when I drafted the educational clauses of the university charter and advocated it before the legislature and in the press. This advocacy was by no means a light task. The influential men who flocked to Albany, seeking to divide the fund among various sects and localities, used arguments often plausible and sometimes forcible. These I dealt with on various occasions, but especially in a speech before the State Senate in 1865, in which was shown the character of the interested opposition, the farcical equipment of the People's College, the failure of the State Agricultural College, the inadequacy of the sectarian colleges, even though they called themselves universities; and I did all in my power to communicate to my colleagues something of my own enthusiasm for a university suitably endowed, free from sectarian trammels, centrally situated, and organized to meet fully the wants of the State as regarded advanced education, general and technical.

Three points I endeavored especially to impress upon them in this speech. First, that while, as regards primary education, the policy of the State should be diffusion of resources, it should be, as regards university education, concentration of resources. Secondly, that sectarian colleges could not do the work required. Thirdly, that any institution for higher education in the State must form an integral part of the whole system of public instruction; that the university should not be isolated from

---

Andrew D. White, *Autobiography*, I, 330–32, 336–37.

the school system, as were the existing colleges, but that it should have a living connection with the system, should push its roots down into it and through it, drawing life from it and sending life back into it. Mr. Cornell accepted this view at once. Mr. Horace Greeley, who, up to that time, had supported the People's College, was favorably impressed by it, and, more than anything else, it won for us his support. To insure this vital connection of the proposed university with the school system, I provided in the charter for four "State scholarships" in each of the one hundred and twenty-eight Assembly districts. These scholarships were to be awarded to the best scholars in the public schools of each district, after due examination, one each year; each scholarship entitling the holder to free instruction in the university for four years. Thus the university and the schools were bound closely together by the constant and living tie of five hundred and twelve students. As the number of Assembly districts under the new constitution was made, some years later, one hundred and fifty, the number of these competitive free scholarships is now six hundred. They have served their purpose well. Thirty years of this connection have greatly uplifted the whole school system of the State, and made the university a life-giving power in it; while this uplifting of the school system has enabled the university steadily to raise and improve its own standard of instruction. . . .

Just previously to my election to the university presidency I had presented a "plan of organization," which, having been accepted and printed by the trustees, formed the mold for the main features of the new institution; and early among my duties came the selection and nomination of professors. In these days one is able to choose from a large body of young men holding fellowships in the various larger universities of the United States; but then, with the possible exception of two or three at Harvard, there was not a fellowship, so far as I can remember, in the whole country. The choosing of professors was immeasurably more difficult than at present. With reference to this point, a very eminent graduate of Harvard then volunteered to me some advice, which at first sight looked sound, but which I soon found to be inapplicable. He said: "You must secure at any cost the foremost men in the United States in every department. In this way alone can a real university be created." Trying the Socratic method upon him, I asked, in reply, "How are we to get such men? The foremost man in American science is undoubtedly Agassiz, but he has refused all offers of high position at Paris made him by the French Emperor. The main objects of his life are the creation of his great museum at Harvard and his investigations and instruction in connection with it; he has declared that he has 'no time to waste in making money!' What sum or what inducement of any sort can transfer him from Harvard to a new institution on the distant hills of central New York? So, too, with the most eminent men at the other universities. What sum will draw them to us from Harvard, Yale, Columbia, the University of Virginia, and the University of Michigan? An endowment twice as large as ours would be unavailing." Therefore it was that I broached, as a practical measure, in my "plan of organization," the system which I had discussed tentatively with George William Curtis several years before, and to which he referred afterward in his speech at the opening of the university at Ithaca. This was to take into our confidence the leading professors in the more important institutions of learning, and to secure from them, not the ordinary, conventional paper testimonials, but confidential information as to their young men likely to do the best work in various fields, to call these young men to our resident professorships, and then to call the most eminent men we could obtain for non-resident professorships or lectureships. This idea was carried out to the letter. The most eminent men in various universities gave us confidential advice; and thus it was that I was enabled to secure a number of bright, active, energetic young men as our resident professors, mingling with them two or three older men, whose experience and developed judgment seemed necessary in the ordinary conduct of our affairs.

As to the other part of the plan, I secured Agassiz, Lowell, Curtis, Bayard Taylor, Goldwin Smith, Theodore Dwight, George W. Greene, John Stanton Gould, and at a later period Froude, Freeman, and others, as non-resident professors and lecturers. Of the final working of this system I shall speak later.

8. Ezra Cornell Denies That He Founded an "Aristocratic" University, 1865

Ezra Cornell (1807–74) was born at Westchester Landing, New York, and taken upstate as a child by his father, who was a farmer and a maker of pottery. At eighteen, having relatively little formal education, Cornell went to work as a laborer but soon rose to a managerial post in a flour mill. Enterprise in the development of the magnetic telegraph made him a rich man by his middle years and freed him for active participation in politics and philanthropy. As a member of the state senate, he met Andrew D. White, who soon interested him in the project of a university for central New York. As a self-made man, Cornell naturally rejected with indignation the notion that he was erecting an "aristocratic" institution. Indeed, his most famous remark was: "I would found an institution in which any person can find instruction in any study." But a prejudice against alleged aristocracy was one of the several obstacles that had long since stood in the way of the development of great universities.

See Doc. 5 and references; also Philip Dorf, *The Builder: A Biography of Ezra Cornell* (New York, 1952).

The great effort made by the Attorney of Charles Cook to prejudice the minds of the Ass[embly] Com. against the bill chartering the "Cornell University" in his speeches of thursday & friday last—on the assumption of the aristocratic character of the proposed institution, or of myself as its patron, has led me to examine my own position to ascertain if it was obnoxious [?] to the charge of aristocracy. My parents were quakers, and I was brought up in that faith and have only deviated from the direct line by marrying a lady who was not a member of the society, and by falling into the popular form of dress and speech. My grand parents & great grand parents on the side of both father and mother were of the same religious denomination. I am a mechanic and farmer and my wealth is the legitimate fruit of those pursuits, I have never speculated, in any kind of property, stocks or securities. My wealth has arisen from carefully investing my surplus earnings in a business which has grown with the growth of the country [The Telegraph]. I have not even speculated in the stock of telegraph companies. When I could sell stock to make money, I have been content with the belief that I could make more by holding the stock and profiting by the increase in its value from the growing increase in the business. My

Carl Becker, *Cornell University: Founders and the Founding,* pp. 168–70.

father was a mechanic and depended on his trade to support his family —his brothers were all mechanics or farmers, as were my mothers brothers. My father's father was a farmer, my mothers father was a mechanic—My brothers and my sisters husbands, are all either farmers or mechanics—My wife's father & grand father were mechanics, her brothers and her sisters husbands are mechanics, farmers, manufacturers & engineers.

I have no relation of any degree within my knowledge who is or has been a lawyer, physician, Minister of the Gospel, merchant, politician, office holder, gentleman loafer or common idler—None who have been drunkards or recipiants of charity. All have procured an honest and compleat support for their families by *productive labor,* none but myself have acquired anything like a fortune, and mine is placed at the disposal of the industrial classes. I cannot conceive it to be possible that any man can be more thoroughly identified with the industrial, laboring, and productive classes, than I am, and my ruling desire is to dispose of so much of my property as is not required for the reasonable wants of my family, in a manner that shall do the greatest good to the greatest number of the industrial classes of my native state, and at the same time to do the greatest good to the state itself, by elevating the character and standard of knowledge of the industrial and productive classes. I tender the sum of $500,000 to the State to be added to the donation of congress, for the sole object contemplated by congress, for the education of the Agricultural & Mechanical classes. In the Organization of such an institution, I am controlled to a great extent by circumstances. I find the only two institutions in the state which were organized on the basis of educating the industrial classes, failures, from the want of adequate means, and from other causes, which in my judgment render it unwise to attempt to rear the desired edifice on their foundation.

Therefore after a consultation with the best and most influential trustees of both the State Agricultural College at Ovid—and the Peoples College at Havana, they advised the new organization—for the new institution and tendered the name of "Cornell University." The name I demurred to, fearing it would be charged that I have an undue ambition in that particular. I was met with assurances that it was eminently proper that the institution should bear my name, and I made no further objection.

The trustees were thus selected from the trustees of the two old boards, and from persons outside both boards.

The ten persons named, represents, three mechanics,—three farmers —one manufacturer—one merchant—one lawyer, one engineer—and one literary gentleman. The ex-officio trustees represent the State government, the common school interest of the state, the State Agricultural Society, the County of Tompkins through its public librarian—and the Cornell family. Can the industrial classes of the State select a board of trustees more likely to protect and foster its interests than the one here selected? I think not.

As to the manner of my using money, I may be permitted to say that I never in any instance exacted or accepted in any form more than seven percent (this was the usual rate at that time) for money loaned, and the only loans which I have made to individuals have been to persons who were unable to furnish such securities as capitalists or bankers exact, and who required the money to protect their business and property from the grasp of the usurer, or from some misfortune in business—to young men to purchase farms—to widows of soldiers to purchase a small house (or, perhaps, home) and for like objects—I have $100,000 thus invested, on what bankers call doubtful securities, but the loans are such as humanity demanded, and the security such as the parties could give.

Of donations, I will not speak other than to say, since the war commenced, they have been given for the support of soldiers families, supply substitutes for drafted men and kindred objects for the support of the government.

9. Sectarian Attacks upon Cornell, 1868–74

See Docs. 5, 6, 7, and 8.

Beside these financial and other troubles, another class of difficulties beset us, which were, at times, almost as vexatious. These were the continued attacks made by good men in various parts of the State and Nation, who thought they saw in Cornell a stronghold—first, of ideas

---

Andrew D. White, *Autobiography*, I, 422–26.

in religion antagonistic to their own; and secondly, of ideas in education likely to injure their sectarian colleges. From the day when our charter was under consideration at Albany they never relented, and at times they were violent. The reports of my inauguration speech were, in sundry denominational newspapers, utterly distorted; far and wide was spread the story that Mr. Cornell and myself were attempting to establish an institution for the propagation of "atheism" and "infidelity." Certainly nothing could have been further from the purpose of either of us. He had aided, and loved to aid, every form of Christianity; I was myself a member of a Christian church and a trustee of a denominational college. Everything that we could do in the way of reasoning with our assailants was in vain. In talking with students from time to time, I learned that, in many cases, their pastors had earnestly besought them to go to any other institution rather than to Cornell; reports of hostile sermons reached us; bitter diatribes constantly appeared in denominational newspapers, and especially virulent were various addresses given on public occasions in the sectarian colleges which felt themselves injured by the creation of an unsectarian institution on so large a scale. Typical was the attack made by an eminent divine who, having been installed as president over one of the smaller colleges of the State, thought it his duty to denounce me as an "atheist," and to do this especially in the city where I had formerly resided, and in the church which some of my family attended. I took no notice of the charge, and pursued the even tenor of my way; but the press took it up, and it recoiled upon the man who made it.

Perhaps the most comical of these attacks was one made by a clergyman of some repute before the Presbyterian Synod at Auburn in western New York. This gentleman, having attended one or two of the lectures by Agassiz before our scientific students, immediately rushed off to this meeting of his brethren, and insisted that the great naturalist was "preaching atheism and Darwinism" at the university. He seemed about to make a decided impression, when there arose a very dear old friend of mine, the Rev. Dr. Sherman Canfield, pastor of the First Presbyterian Church in Syracuse, who, fortunately, was a scholar abreast of current questions. Dr. Canfield quietly remarked that he was amazed to learn that Agassiz had, in so short a time, become an atheist, and not less astonished to hear that he had been converted to Darwinism; that up to that moment he had considered Agassiz a deeply religious man, and also the foremost—possibly, indeed, the last—

great opponent of the Darwinian hypothesis. He therefore suggested that the resolution denouncing Cornell University brought in by his reverend brother be laid on the table to await further investigation. It was thus disposed of, and, in that region at least, it was never heard of more. Pleasing is it to me to chronicle the fact that, at Dr. Canfield's death, he left to the university a very important part of his library.

From another denominational college came an attack on Goldwin Smith. One of its professors published, in the Protestant Episcopal "Gospel Messenger," an attack upon the university for calling into its faculty a "Westminster Reviewer"; the fact being that Goldwin Smith was at that time a member of the Church of England, and had never written for the "Westminster Review" save in reply to one of its articles. So, too, when there were sculptured on the stone seat which he had ordered carved for the university grounds the words, "Above all nations is humanity," there came an outburst. Sundry pastors, in their anxiety for the souls of the students, could not tell whether this inscription savored more of atheism or of pantheism. Its simple significance—that the claims of humanity are above those of nationality—entirely escaped them. Pulpit cushions were beaten in all parts of the State against us, and solemn warnings were renewed to students by their pastors, to go anywhere for their education rather than to Cornell. Curiously, this fact became not only a gratuitous, but an effective, advertisement: many of the brightest men who came to us in those days confessed to me that these attacks first directed their attention to us.

We also owed some munificent gifts to this same cause. In two cases gentlemen came forward and made large additions to our endowment as their way of showing disbelief in these attacks or contempt for them.

Still the attacks were vexatious even when impotent. Ingenious was the scheme carried out by a zealous young clergyman settled for a short time in Ithaca. Coming one day into my private library, he told me that he was very anxious to borrow some works showing the more recent tendencies of liberal thought. I took him to one of my bookcases, in which, by the side of the works of Bossuet and Fénelon and Thomas Arnold and Robertson of Brighton, he found those of Channing, Parker, Renan, Strauss, and the men who, in the middle years of the last century, were held to represent advanced thought. He looked them over for some time, made some excuse for not borrowing any of them just then, and I heard nothing more from him until there came, in a denominational newspaper, his eloquent denunciation of me for possessing such books. Impressive, too, must have been the utterances of an eminent "revivalist" who, in various Western cities, loudly asserted that Mr. Cornell had died lamenting his inability to base his university on atheism, and that I had fled to Europe declaring that in America an infidel university was, as yet, an impossibility.

For a long time I stood on the defensive, hoping that the provisions made for the growth of religious life among the students might show that we were not so wicked as we were represented; but, as all this seemed only to embitter our adversaries, I finally determined to take the offensive, and having been invited to deliver a lecture in the great hall of the Cooper Institute at New York, took as my subject "The Battle-fields of Science." In this my effort was to show how, in the supposed interest of religion, earnest and excellent men, for many ages and in many countries, had bitterly opposed various advances in science and in education, and that such opposition had resulted in most evil results, not only to science and education, but to religion. This lecture was published in full, next day, in the "New York Tribune"; extracts from it were widely copied; it was asked for by lecture associations in many parts of the country; grew first into two magazine articles, then into a little book which was widely circulated at home, reprinted in England with a preface by Tyndall, and circulated on the Continent in translations, was then expanded into a series of articles in the "Popular Science Monthly," and finally wrought into my book on "The Warfare of Science with Theology." In each of these forms my argument provoked attack; but all this eventually created a reaction in our favor, even in quarters where it was least expected. One evidence of this touched me deeply. I had been invited to repeat the lecture at New Haven, and on arriving there found a large audience of Yale professors and students; but, most surprising of all, in the chair for the evening, no less a personage than my reverend instructor, Dr. Theodore Dwight Woolsey, president of the university. He was of a deeply religious nature; and certainly no man was ever, under all circumstances, more true to his convictions of duty. To be welcomed by him was encouragement indeed. He presented me cordially to the audience, and at the close of my address made a brief speech, in which he thoroughly supported my positions and bade me Godspeed. Few things in my life have so encouraged me.

Attacks, of course, continued for a considerable time, some of them violent; but, to my surprise and satisfaction, when my articles were finally brought together in book form, the opposition seemed to have exhausted itself. There were even indications of approval in some quarters where the articles composing it had previously been attacked; and I received letters thoroughly in sympathy with the work from a number of eminent Christian men, including several doctors of divinity, and among these two bishops, one of the Anglican and one the American Episcopal Church.

The final result was that slander against the university for irreligion was confined almost entirely to very narrow circles, of waning influence; and my hope is that, as its formative ideas have been thus welcomed by various leaders of thought, and have filtered down through the press among the people at large, they have done something to free the path of future laborers in the field of science and education from such attacks as those which Cornell was obliged to suffer.

10. F. H. Hedge on University Reforms, 1866

Frederic Henry Hedge (1805–90) retained a lifelong interest in German literature and academic ideals after he, at thirteen, accompanied George Bancroft (see Part IV, Doc. 5) to Germany. It is illustrated in the diagnosis of the American college system, here partly reproduced, that appeared three years before Charles William Eliot (see Part VII, Doc. 2) began his Harvard presidency. Hedge's scholarly devotion to German life and letters was also exhibited throughout his active Unitarian ministry (1829–56), his role among New England transcendentalists, his professorship of ecclesiastical history in the Harvard Divinity School (1857–76), and his professorship of German literature in Harvard College (1872–84).

On Hedge see Orie W. Long, *Frederic Henry Hedge: A Cosmopolitan Scholar* (Portland, Me., 1940); and George H. Williams, *Rethinking the Unitarian Relationship with Protestantism: An Examination of the Thought of Frederic Henry Hedge* (Boston, 1949).

Individuals have done their part, but slow is the growth of institutions which depend on individual charity for their support. As an illustration of what may be done by public patronage, when States are in earnest with their universities, and as strangely contrasting the

---

Frederic Henry Hedge, "University Reform, An Address to the Alumni of Harvard, at Their Triennial Festival," *Atlantic Monthly*, XVIII (July, 1866), 299–307.

sluggish fortunes of our own *Alma,* look at the State University of Michigan. Here is an institution but twenty-five years old, already numbering thirty-two professors and over twelve hundred students, having public buildings equal in extent to those which two centuries have given to Cambridge, and all the apparatus of a well-constituted, thoroughly furnished university. All this within twenty-five years! The State itself which has generated this wonderful growth had no place in the Union until after Harvard had celebrated her two hundredth birthday. In twenty-five years, in a country five hundred miles from the seaboard,—a country which fifty years ago was known only to the fur trade,—a University has sprung up, to which students flock from all parts of the land, and which offers to thousands, free of expense, the best education this continent affords. Such is the difference between public and private patronage, between individual effort and the action of a State.

A proof of the broad intent and œcumenical consciousness of this infant College appears in the fact that its Medical Department, which alone numbers ten professors and five hundred students, allows the option of one of four languages in the thesis required for the medical degree. It is the only seminary in the country whose liberal scope and cosmopolitan outlook satisfy the idea of a great university. Compared with this, our other colleges are all provincial; and unless the State of Massachusetts shall see fit to adopt us, and to foster our interest with something of the zeal and liberality which the State of Michigan bestows on her academic masterpiece, Harvard cannot hope to compete with this precocious child of the West. . . .

With the multiplication of religious sects, with the progress of secular culture, with the mental emancipation which followed the great convulsions of the eighteenth century, the maintenance of the ecclesiastical type originally impressed on the College ceased to be practicable,— ceased to be desirable. The preparation of young men for the service of the Church is still a recognized part of the general scheme of University education, but is only one in the multiplicity of objects which that scheme embraces, and can never again have the prominence once assigned to it. This secularization, however it might seem to compromise the design of the founders of the College, was inevitable,—a wise and needful concession to the exigencies of the altered time. Nor is there, in a larger view, any real contravention here of the purpose of the founders. The secularization of the College is no violation of its motto, *"Christo et Ecclesiae."* For, as I interpret those sacred ideas, the cause of Christ and the Church is advanced by whatever liberalizes and enriches and enlarges the mind. All study, scientifically pursued, is at bottom a study of theology; for all scientific study is the study of Law; and "of Law nothing less can be acknowledged than that her seat is in the bosom of God."

But something more than secularization of the course of study is required to satisfy the idea of a university. What is a university? Dr. Newman answers this question with the ancient designation of a *Studium Generale,*—a school of universal learning. "Such a university," he says, "is in its essence a place for the communication and circulation of thought by means of personal intercourse over a wide tract of country."[1] Accepting this definition, can we say that Harvard College, as at present constituted, is a University? Must we not rather describe it as a place where boys are made to recite lessons from text-books, and to write compulsory exercises, and are marked according to their proficiency and fidelity in these performances, with a view to a somewhat protracted exhibition of themselves at the close of their college course, which, according to a pleasant academic fiction, is termed their "Commencement"? This description applies only, it is true, to what is called the Undergraduate Department. But that department stands for the College, constitutes the College, in the public estimation. The professional schools which have gathered about it are scarcely regarded as a part of the College. They are incidental appendages, of which, indeed, one has its seat in another city. The College proper is simply a more advanced school for boys, not differing essentially in principle and theory from the public schools in all our towns. In this, as in those, the principle is coercion. Hold your subject fast with one hand, and pour knowledge into him with the other. The professors are taskmasters and police-officers, the President the chief of the College police.

Now, considering the great advance of our higher town schools, which carry their pupils as far as the College carried them fifty years ago, and which might, if necessary, have classes still more advanced of such as are destined for the university, I venture to suggest that the time has come when this whole system of coercion might, with safety and profit, be done away. Abolish, I would say, your whole system of marks, and college rank, and compulsory tasks. I anticipate an objection drawn from the real or supposed danger of abandoning to their

---

[1] *The Office and Work of Universities,* by John Henry Newman,

own devices and optional employment boys of the average age of college students. In answer, I say, advance that average by fixing a limit of admissible age. Advance the qualifications for admission; make them equal to the studies of the Freshman year, and reduce the college career from four years to three; or else make the Freshman year a year of probation, and its closing examination the condition of full matriculation. Only give the young men, when once a sufficient foundation has been laid, and the rudiments acquired, the freedom of a true University,—freedom to select their own studies and their own teachers from such material, and such *personnel,* as the place supplies. It is to be expected that a portion will abuse this liberty, and waste their years. They do it at their peril. At the peril, among other disadvantages, of losing their degree, which should be conditioned on satisfactory proof that the student has not wholly misspent his time.

An indispensable condition of intellectual growth is liberty. That liberty the present system denies. More and more it is straitened by imposed tasks. And this I conceive to be the reason why, with increased requirements, the College turns out a decreasing proportion of first-class men. . . .

The question has been newly agitated in these days, whether knowledge of Greek and Latin is a necessary part of polite education, and whether it should constitute one of the requirements of the academic course. It has seemed to me that those who take the affirmative in this discussion give undue weight to the literary argument, and not enough to the glossological. The literacy argument fails to establish the supreme importance of a knowledge of these languages as a part of polite education. The place which the Greek and Latin authors have come to occupy in the estimation of European scholars is due, not entirely to their intrinsic merits, great as those merits unquestionably are, but in part to traditional prepossessions. When after a millennial occultation the classics, and especially, with the fall of the Palaeologi, the Greek classics burst upon Western Europe, there was no literature with which to compare them. . . . What wonder that the classics were received with boundless enthusiasm! It was through the influence of that enthusiasm that the study of Greek was introduced into schools and universities with the close of the fifteenth century. It was through that influence that Latin, still a living language in the clerical world, was perpetuated, instead of becoming an obsolete ecclesiasticism. The language of Livy and Ovid derived fresh impulse from the reappearing stars of secular Rome.

It is in vain to deny that those literatures have lost something of the relative value they once possessed, and which made it a literary necessity to study Greek and Latin for their sakes. The literary necessity is in a measure superseded by translations, which, though they may fail to communicate the aroma and the verbal felicities of the original, reproduce its form and substance. It is furthermore superseded by the rise of new literatures, and by introduction to those of other and elder lands. The Greeks were masters of literary form, but other nations have surpassed them in some particulars. . . .

But, above all, the literary importance of Greek and Latin for the British and American scholar is greatly qualified by the richness and superiority of the English literature which has come into being since the Graecomania of the time of the Tudors, when court ladies of a morning, by way of amusement, read Plato's Dialogues in the original. If literary edification is the object intended in the study of those languages, that end is more easily and more effectually accomplished by a thorough acquaintance with English literature, than by the very imperfect knowledge which college exercises give of the classics. . . .

Give them Shakespeare's Tempest to read, and with no other pony than their own good will, though they may not penetrate the deeper meaning of that composition, they will gain more ideas, more nourishment from it, than they will from compulsory study of the whole trio of Greek tragedians. . . .

The literary argument for enforced study of Greek and Latin in our day has not much weight. What I call the glossological argument has more. Every well-educated person should have a thorough understanding of his own language, and no one can thoroughly understand the English without some knowledge of languages which touch it so nearly as the Latin and the Greek. Some knowledge of those languages should constitute, I think, a condition of matriculation. But the further prosecution of them should not be obligatory on the student once matriculated, though every encouragement be given and every facility afforded to those whose genius leans in that direction. The College should make ample provision for the study of ancient languages, and also for the study of the mathematics, but should not enforce those studies on minds that have no vocation for such pursuits. . . . There are also exceptional natures that delight in mathematics, minds whose young affections run to angles and logarithms, and with whom the computation of values is itself the chief value in life. The College should accommodate either bias, to the top of its bent, but should not enforce either with compulsory twist. It should not insist on making every alumnus a linguist or a mathematician. If mastery of dead languages is not an indispensable part of polite education, mathematical learning is still less so. Excessive requirements in that department have not even the excuse of intellectual discipline. More important than mathematics to the general scholar is the knowledge of history, in which American scholars are so commonly deficient. More important is the knowledge of modern languages and of English literature. More important the knowledge of Nature and Art. May the science of sciences never want representatives as able as the learned gentlemen who now preside over that department in the mathematical and presidential chairs. Happy will it be for the University if they can inspire a love for the science in the pupils committed to their charge. But where inspiration fails, coercion can never supply its place. If the mathematics shall continue to reign at Harvard, may their empire become a law of liberty.

I have ventured, fellow-graduates, to throw out these hints of University Reform, well aware of the opposition such views must encounter in deep-rooted prejudice and fixed routine; aware also of the rashness of attempting, within the limits of such an occasion, to grapple with such a theme; but strong in my conviction of the pressing need of a more emancipated scheme of instruction and discipline, based on the facts of the present and the real wants of American life. It is time that the oldest college in the land should lay off the *praetexta* of its long minority, and take its place among the universities, properly so called, of modern time.

One thing more I have to say while standing in this presence. The College has a duty beyond its literary and scientific functions,—a duty to the nation,—a patriotic, I do not scruple to say a political duty. . . .

Universities are no longer political bodies, but they may be still political powers,—centres and sources of political influence. Our own College in the time of the Revolution was a manifest power on the side of liberty, the political as well as academic mother of Otis and the Adamses. In 1768, "when the patronage of American manufactures was the test of patriotism," the Senior Class voted unanimously to take their degrees apparelled in the coarse cloths of American manufacture.

In 1776, the Overseers required of the professors a satisfactory account of their political faith. So much was then thought of the influence on young minds of the right or wrong views of political questions entertained by their instructors. The fathers were right. When the life of the nation is concerned,—in the struggle with foreign or domestic foes, —there is a right and a wrong in politics which casuistry may seek to confuse, but which sound moral sentiment cannot mistake, and which those who have schools of learning in charge should be held to respect. Better the College should be disbanded than be a nursery of treason. Better these halls even now should be levelled with the ground, than that any influence should prevail in them unfriendly to American nationality. No amount of intellectual acquirements can atone for defective patriotism. Intellectual supremacy alone will not avert the downfall of states. . . .

Soon after the conquest of American independence, Governor Hancock, in his speech at the inauguration of President Willard, eulogised the College as having "been in some sense the parent and nurse of the late happy Revolution in this Commonwealth." Parent and nurse of American nationality,—such was the praise accorded to Harvard by one of the foremost patriots of the Revolution! Never may she cease to deserve that praise! . . .

We have no professorship at Cambridge founded for the express purpose of making good citizens. In the absence of such, may all the professorships work together for that end. The youth intrusted to their tutelage are soon to take part, if not as legislators, at least as freemen, in the government of our common land. May the dignity and duty and exceeding privilege of an American citizen be impressed upon their minds by all the influences that rule this place! Trust me, Alumni, the country will thank the University more for the loyalty her influences shall foster, than for all the knowledge her schools may impart. Learning is the costly ornament of states, but patriotism is the life of a nation.

11. The Morrill Act, 1862

The first Morrill Act, setting aside land revenues for the support of state colleges teaching "such branches of learning as are related to agriculture and the mechanic arts," marked a great step forward in federal educational policy. It not only created land-grant colleges but gave a powerful impulse to the movement for state universities. The best use of the funds made available under the act came, in fact, where the land-grant funds were added to a pre-existing state university endowment. In New York the land-grant funds were constructively used for the promotion of Cornell. In states where funds were divided among a number of competing colleges, the results were less happy. The land-grant colleges, which did not thrive under the original Morrill Act endowment, were much strengthened by the second Morrill Act of 1890, providing annual federal appropriations for these institutions and stimulating state legislatures to do the same. Further financial support was given to the land-grant institutions by the Nelson Amendment of 1907 and the Bankhead-Jones Act of 1905.

See Doc. 14; Earle D. Ross, *Democracy's College: The Land-Grant Movement in the Formative Stage* (Ames, Iowa, 1942); I. L. Kandel, *Federal Aid for Vocational Education* (New York, 1917); Carl Becker, *Cornell University: Founders and the Founding;* Whitney Shepardson, *Agricultural Education in the United States* (New York, 1929).

Section 4. *And be it further enacted,* That all moneys derived from the sale of the lands aforesaid by the States to which the lands are apportioned, and from the sales of land scrip hereinbefore provided for, shall be invested in stocks of the United States or of the States, or some other safe stocks, yielding not less than five per centum upon the par value of said stocks; and that the moneys so invested shall constitute a perpetual fund, the capital of which shall remain forever undiminished (except so far as may be provided in section five of this act), and the interest of which shall be inviolably appropriated by each State which may take and claim the benefit of this act, to the endowment, support, and maintenance of at least one college where the leading object shall be, without excluding other scientific and classical studies, and including military tactics, to teach such branches of learning as are related to agriculture and the mechanic arts, in such manner as the legislatures of the States may respectively prescribe, in order to promote the liberal and practical education of the industrial classes in the several pursuits and professions in life. . . .

---

12 *United States Statutes at Large,* 503–5.

Section 5. *And be it further enacted* . . .

Third. Any State which may take and claim the benefit of the provisions of this act shall provide, within five years, at least not less than one college, as described in the fourth section of this act, or the grant to such State shall cease; and said State shall be bound to pay the United States the amount received of any lands previously sold and that the title to purchasers under the State shall be valid.

Fourth. An annual report shall be made regarding the progress of each college, recording any improvements and experiments made, with their cost and results, and such other matters, including state industrial and economical statistics, as may be supposed useful, one copy of which shall be transmitted by mail free, by each, to all the other colleges which may be endowed under the provisions of this act, and also one copy to the Secretary of the Interior. . . .

Approved, July 2, 1862.

12. *James Morgan Hart Compares the German University and the American College during the 1860's*

James Morgan Hart (1839–1916) was born at Princeton and educated at the College of New Jersey where he took his B.A. in 1860, the year his alma mater's name was changed to Princeton University. He then studied for four years in Berlin, Geneva, and Göttingen, receiving a law degree from the latter institution in 1864. It was upon his experiences in these postgraduate years that his comparison between the American college and the German university is mainly based, but, after some years as a teacher of law and then of philology, he returned to Europe in 1872 for a briefer stay. On this occasion he studied at Leipzig, Marburg, and Berlin, deepening his knowledge of philology. Upon his return he published this narrative, which became standard reading for American students contemplating graduate study in Germany. For fourteen years he taught modern languages and English literature at the University of Cincinnati. In 1890 he was called back to Cornell, where he had taught from 1868 to 1872, now as professor of rhetoric and English philology. His influence in this field and in the teaching of English in the schools of New York was considerable.

James Morgan Hart, *German Universities: A Narrative of Personal Experience* (New York, 1874), pp. v–vii, 249–64, 267–68, 292–93, 296–97, 303–4, 339–41, 344–46.

There is no more adequate account of Hart generally available than Albert B. Faust's sketch in the *Dictionary of American Biography*. See Part IV, Docs. 3, 4, 5, and 18.

Much has been published in a fugitive form upon the fruitful topic of university life in Germany. One man has taken up the lecture-system, another the dueling, a third the manners and customs of the instructors or of the students. But no one, I believe, has told, in a plain, straightforward narrative, how he himself passed his time at the university, what he studied, and what he accomplished. It seemed to me, therefore, that I might do the cause of education in America some service, by offering my own experience as a sample of German student-life in the average. Had my career in Göttingen been an extraordinary one, full of exciting episodes, I should have hesitated to make it public. But precisely because it was so uneventful, so like the lives of my associates, I have deemed it fit to serve as a model for illustration, not imitation, and as a basis for digression. I have had throughout but one aim: to communicate facts and impressions from which the reader might draw his own inferences. Even those portions of the Personal Narrative which assume the form of argument are intended to remove prejudices, not to state final conclusions.

The General Remarks must abide the verdict as they stand. If they contain aught that is erroneous or distorted, the present is not the place for correction. I can only say that I have striven faithfully to make them both accurate and just. Should the reader be disposed to regard my estimate of the German Universities as extravagant, of the English as too unfavourable, I would refer him to an oration delivered by von Sybel, in 1868, upon "German and Foreign Universities." It forms part of a volume entitled *Vorträge und Aufsätze,* recently published under the auspices of the *Allgemeiner Verein für deutsche Literatur.* The renowned historian, who is certainly the last man to be taxed with blind, unreasoning patriotism, approaches the subject from a different side, yet his views bear such close resemblance, both in form and spirit, to those set forth in the present work, that, to escape the imputation of unfair borrowing, I feel bound to state explicitly that I did not read the oration, in fact was not aware of its existence, until my own manuscript had passed entirely into the hands of the printer. After all, there can be but one opinion as to the merits of the several university systems of England, France and Germany.

It may not be superfluous to add that the present work is not an attack upon the American College. Although holding that the German method of Higher Education is far above our own, I should be very sorry to see that method adopted at once, and in the lump. Before taking decided steps towards the expansion of our colleges into quasi universities, it will be advisable for us to consider thoroughly what a university really is, what it accomplishes, what it does not accomplish, the basis upon which it rests, the relations that it holds to the nation at large. Until we have formed clear and stable conceptions upon all these points, innovation, I fear, will be only tinkering, not reform. If I have succeeded in throwing any light upon the subject, my wish is abundantly realized. . . .

From the foregoing personal narrative the reader will probably be able to obtain a glimpse at the mode of life at a German university, to the extent at least of realizing how an American may live and study there. Yet there are certain features of the German method of higher education that can be adequately elucidated only by eliminating the personal element and discussing them in their more general bearings. I have deemed it proper, therefore, to supplement the personal narrative with the following remarks in the way of criticism.

I revisited Germany in 1872–3. In that time I studied at Leipsic, Marburg, and Berlin, and passed a summer at Vienna. Brought thus in contact with professors, students and men of letters in the great German centers of thought, I had ample opportunity of reviewing and modifying early impressions, and of judging the university system as a whole. I venture to offer these remarks, then, as the result of recent comparative investigation.

The first question that suggests itself is naturally this,

I

WHAT IS A UNIVERSITY?

To the German mind the collective idea of a university implies a *Zweck,* an object of study, and two *Bedingungen,* or conditions. The object is *Wissenschaft;* the conditions are *Lehrfreiheit* and *Lernfreiheit.* By *Wissenschaft* the Germans mean knowledge in the most exalted sense of that term, namely, the ardent, methodical, independent search after truth in any and all of its forms, but wholly irrespective of utilitarian application. *Lehrfreiheit* means that the one who teaches, the professor or *Privatdocent,* is free to teach what he chooses, as he chooses.

Lernfreiheit or the freedom of learning, denotes the emancipation of the student from *Schulzwang,* compulsory drill by recitation.

If the object of an institution is anything else than knowledge as above defined, or if either freedom of teaching or freedom of learning is wanting, that institution, no matter how richly endowed, no matter how numerous its students, no matter how imposing its buildings, is not, in the eye of a German, a *university*. On the other hand, a small, out-of-the-way place like Rostock, with only thirty-four professors and docents, and one hundred and thirty-five students, is nevertheless as truly a university as Leipsic, where the numbers are one hundred and fifty and three thousand respectively, because Rostock aims at theoretical knowledge and meets the requirements of free teaching and free study. The difference is one of size, not of species.

If we examine the list of lectures and hours of universities like Leipsic, Berlin, and Vienna, we shall be overwhelmed, at first sight, with the amount and the variety of literary and scientific labor announced. The field seems boundless. All that human ingenuity can suggest is apparently represented. On examining more closely, however, we shall find that this seemingly boundless field has its limits, which are very closely traced and which are not exceeded. Strange as it may sound to the American, who is accustomed to gauge spiritual greatness by big numbers and extravagant pretensions, a German university, even the greatest, perceives what it can do and what it *can not do.*

It is not a place "where any man can study anything." Its elevated character makes it all the more modest. It contents itself with the theoretical, and leaves to other institutions the practical and the technical. The list of studies and hours for Leipsic in the semester 1872–3 fills thirty octavo pages. In all that list we shall discover scarcely one course of work that can be called in strictness practical. A German university has one and only one object: to train thinkers. It does not aim at producing poets, painters, sculptors, engineers, miners, architects, bankers, manufacturers. For these, the places of instruction are the Art Schools of Dresden, Munich, Düsseldorf, the Commercial Schools at Bremen, Hamburg, Berlin, Frankfort, the Polytechnicums at Hanover, Frankenberg, Stuttgart, etc. Even in the professions themselves, theory and practice are carefully distinguished, and the former alone is considered as falling legitimately within the sphere of university instruction. Taking up the four faculties in order: theology, law, medicine, philosophy, and watching them at work, we shall perceive that the evident tendency of their method is to produce theologians rather than pastors, jurists rather than lawyers, theorizers in medicine rather than practitioners, investigators, scholars, speculative thinkers rather than technologists and school-teachers. Yet every pastor, lawyer, doctor, teacher, botanist, geologist has passed through the university course. What is meant, then, by the assertion that the university gives only theoretical training? Do not the practical men in all the professions receive their professional outfit at the university and can receive it nowhere else? The seeming discrepancy is to be explained only by considering the university as a permanent, self-supporting institution, a world in itself, existing for itself, rather than a mere ladder by which to ascend from a lower to a higher plane. Self-supporting, I mean, of course, in the sense that the university is a detached organism assimilating and growing in accordance with its own laws. In a pecuniary sense, it is wholly or almost wholly dependent upon state subvention. The distinction, subtle as it may appear, is essential in forming a just conception of the character of university work. The university supplies itself with its educational staff exclusively from its own graduate members, who pass their entire lives within its precincts. The professors, assistant-professors, docents whose names one reads in the catalogue of Berlin or Leipsic or Heidelberg are one and all, with scarcely an exception, men who started in life as theoreticians and never made the effort to become practitioners. To them the university was not a mere preparatory school, where they might remain long enough to get their theoretical training, and then turn their backs upon it forever. On the contrary, it was an end, a career in itself. They have always been university men, and never expect to become anything else. In this place I must guard against being misunderstood. The reader would receive a very unfair impression of Göttingen, for instance, if he were to infer, from what has been said, that the Göttingen faculty is made up exclusively of Göttingen graduates. Quite the reverse is the case. Probably two thirds come from elsewhere. As a rule, the young *Privatdocent* receives his first call as professor from a university where he has not been known as a student. There exists in this respect complete parity among the German institutions of learning. The feeling which prompts an American college to prefer its own graduates for professors is something quite unknown in Germany I leave it to the reader's judgement to decide which of the two systems is better: that of liberal selection, or that of "Breeding-in." When I speak of a university as recruiting exclusively from its graduates, I mean neither Berlin nor Leipsic nor Heidelberg in particular, but the twenty universities of the German empire regarded as one body, the members of which are perfectly co-ordinate. Professors and docents, and even students, pass from one to another with a restlessness, we might say, that would be surprising in America, but which is looked upon in Germany as a matter of course. It is the exception, not the rule, when a man passes his entire career as instructor in one place. The key-note of the system is simply this. To those who are connected with the university in any instructional capacity whatever, it is an end and not a means, a life and not a phase of life, a career and not a discipline. The professors are not selected from among the leading lawyers, pastors, doctors, teachers, scientists of the country or province. When a chair already existing becomes vacant, or a new chair is created, and the question of filling it comes up, the Senatus Academicus does not scrutinize the bench or the bar or the gymnasium for an available man. It endeavors to ascertain who is the most promising *Privatdocent*, either in its own midst or at some other seat of learning, the young man who has made his mark by recent publications or discoveries. The newly organized university of Strassburg is a signal instance in point. Within two years after the close of the French war, Strassburg was opened with a full corps of instructors in all the departments. The total number at present is eighty. Yet of these eighty not one, so far as I can ascertain, is what might be called a practitioner. They are all full or half-professors or docents called from other institutions of learning. One who is familiar with the muster-roll of the universities can resolve the Strassburg list into its elements, saying: This man came from Berlin, that one from Vienna, that one from Würzburg, and so on. The reader will probably say: Is not this the case in America also? Are not our college professors all college graduates? To which the answer must be: Not in the same way, not to the same extent. How many of our college professors have been professors, and nothing else? How many have qualified themselves directly for the respective chairs which they occupy, by a life of special study? How many of them formed the resolve while still students, to lead a college life forever, to devote themselves exclusively to instructing others in turn, either at their own Alma Mater or at some other college? I do not have in view such institutions as Yale or Harvard, old, well endowed, fed from the rich soil of New England culture. I mean the typical American college as it exists in the Middle, Southern, and Western States. How many of the professors have been in business, or tried their skill at farming, engineering, journalism? Has or has not the professor of Latin served an apprenticeship as mathematical tutor, or kept a boarding school for young ladies? How few of the hundreds and thousands of men, from New York to San Francisco, calling themselves professors, can say with a comfortable degree of pride: I selected my specialty in youth, I have pursued it without intermission, without deviation ever since, and I have produced such and such tangible evidences of my industry as a specialist.

No, the reader may rest assured that the character and atmosphere of a German university differ radically from the character and atmosphere of the typical American college. It is a difference of kind, not merely of degree. Comparisons, according to the popular adage, are odious. Yet even at the risk of giving offense, I take the liberty of drawing a comparison that may serve, perhaps, to throw some light on this vital point. At all events, the comparison shall be a just one. Marburg, in Hesse, has at present 430 students; Princeton, my Alma Mater, has 420. The numbers, then, are almost identical. Each is located in a small country town. Yet Princeton has, all told, not more than 18 professors and tutors; Marburg has 62. Among them are men renowned throughout the world for their original investigations. The same might be said, indeed, of the Princeton faculty, but only with grave restrictions. No one professor at Princeton has the opportunity of working either himself or his students up to his or their full capacity. The instruction goes by routine, each professor contributing his quota to the supposed general development of all the students in a body. At Marburg there is the fourfold division of faculties; there are students pursuing theology, law, medicine, classic philology, modern philology, the natural sciences, history, orientalia. Each instructor has his select band of disciples, upon whom he acts and who re-act upon him. There is the same quiet, scholarly atmosphere, the same disregard for bread-and-butter study, the same breadth of culture, depth of insight, liberality of opinion and freedom of conduct, that one finds in the most favored circles of Leipsic, Berlin, Heidelberg, or Vienna. During every hour of the two months that I passed at Marburg, I was made to feel that a German university, however humble, is a world in and for itself; that its aim is not to turn out clever, pushing, ambitious graduates, but to engender culture.

This condition is both cause and effect. Many of the students who attend the university do so simply with a view to becoming in time professors. The entire *personnel* of the faculty is thus a close corporation, a spiritual order perpetuating itself after the fashion of the Roman Catholic hierarchy. Inasmuch as every professional man and every schoolteacher of the higher grades has to pass through the university, it follows that the shaping of the intellectual interests of the country is in the hands of a select few, who are highly educated, perfectly homogeneous in character and sympathies, utterly indifferent to the turmoils and ambitions of the outer-world, who regulate their own lives and mould the dispositions of those dependent upon them according to the principles of abstract truth. The quality of university education, then, is determined by its object, and that object is to train not merely skillful practitioners, *but also future professors.* In fact, the needs of the former class are subordinated to the needs of the latter. In this respect, the faculty acts, unconsciously, in accordance with the promptings of the instinct of self-preservation. If thorough scientific culture is an essential element in national life, it must be maintained at every cost. The slightest flaw in the continuity of spiritual descent would be as dangerous as a break in the apostolic succession of the church. Every inducement, therefore, must be held out to young men to qualify themselves in season for succeeding to their present instructors. The lectures and other instruction must be adapted to train and stimulate *Privat-docenten,* for they are the ones who are to seize and wear the mantles of the translated Elijahs. For every professor dead or removed, there must be one or two instantly ready to fill his place.

This is not the *avowed* object of the university course. One might pass many years in Germany without perceiving it stated so bluntly. Yet I am persuaded that it is at bottom the determining factor in the constitution of university life It will explain to us many incidental features for which there is elsewhere no analogy; for instance, the sovereign contempt that all German students evince for everything that savors of "bread-and-butter." The students have caught, in this respect, the tone of their instructors. Even such of them as have no intention of becoming *Privat-docenten* pass three and four years of their life in generous devotion to study pure and simple, without casting a single forward glance to future "business." All thought of practical life is kept in abeyance. The future practitioners and the future theoreticians sit side by side on the same bench, fight on the same *Mensur,* drink at the same *Kneipe,* hear the same lectures, use the same books, have every sentiment in common; hence the perfect *rapport* that exists in Germany between the lawyer and the jurist, the pastor and the theologian, the practicing doctor and the speculative pathologist, the gymnasial teacher of Latin and Greek and the professed philologist. Hence the celerity with which innovating ideas spread in Germany. . . .

To repeat, the university instruction of Germany does not attempt to train successful practical men, unless it be indirectly, by giving its students a profound insight into the principles of the science, and then turning them adrift to deduce the practice as well as they can from the carefully inculcated theory. Its chief task, that to which all its energies are directed, is the development of great thinkers, men who will extend the boundaries of knowledge.

Viewed from this point, then, the two conditions, *Lehrfreiheit* and *Lernfreiheit,* are not only natural and proper, but are absolutely essential. Were the object of higher education merely to train "useful and honorable members of society," to use the conventional phrase of the panegyrists of the American system, the German universities might possibly change their character. In place of professors free to impart the choicest results of their investigations, they might substitute pedagogues with text-books and class-books, noting down the relative merits and demerits of daily recitations. In place of students free to attend or to stay away, free to agree with the professor or to differ, free to read what they choose and to study after their own fashion, they might create a set of undergraduates reciting glibly from set lessons and regarding each circumvention of the teacher as so much clear gain. . . . The professor has but one aim in life: scholarly renown. To effect this, he must have the liberty of selecting his studies and pushing them to their extreme limits. The student has but one desire: to assimilate his instructor's learning, and, if possible, to add to it. He must, therefore, be his own master. He must be free to accept and reject, to judge and prove all things for himself, to train himself step by step for grappling with the great problems of nature and history. Accountable only to himself for his opinions and mode of living, he shakes off spiritual bondage and becomes an independent thinker. He *must* think for himself, for there is no one set over him as spiritual adviser and guide, prescribing the work for each day and each hour, telling him what he is to believe and what to disbelieve, and marking him up or down accordingly.

The universities occupy, then, an impregnable position. Recruiting their tuitional forces (*Lehrkräfte*) from among themselves, they are independent of the outer world. . . .

II

PROFESSORS

The character of the German professor will be best understood by first disposing of the preliminary question: What is he not?

The professor is not a teacher, in the English sense of the term; he is a specialist. He is not responsible for the success of his hearers. He is responsible only for the quality of his instruction. His duty begins and ends with himself.

No man can become a professor in a German university without having given evidence, in one way or another, that he has pursued a certain line of study, and produced results worthy to be called novel and important. In other words, to become a professor, he must first have been a special investigator. Professional chairs are not conferred "on general principles," or because the candidate is "a good teacher," or "well qualified to govern the young." . . .

The chief attraction in the professorial career, however, is the nature of the work itself. No human lot, it is true, is without its trials. The life of a professor is anything but a bed of roses. It means severe intellectual toil from morning till evening, from manhood to declining years. But there is a freedom about it that is inexpressibly fascinating. The professor is his own master. His time is not wasted in cudgeling the wits of refractory or listless reciters. His temper is not ruffled by the freaks or the downright insults of mutinous youths. He lectures upon his chosen subject, comments upon his favorite Greek or Roman or early German or Sanscrit author, expounds some recently discovered mathematical theorem, discusses one or another of the grave problems of history or morals, and is accountable only to his own conscience of what is true and what is false. He lectures only to those who are willing and able to hear. He is sustained by the consciousness that his words are not scattered by the wayside, but that they fall upon soil prepared to receive them, and will bring forth new fruit in turn. His relation with his hearers is that of one gentleman speaking to another. . . .

IV

STUDENTS

. . . The German students exhibit such varieties of character that it would be useless to attempt to reduce them to one category and label them thus and so. They have only one trait in common: individuality of thought and freedom of action. Such a sentiment as "class-feeling" does not exist among them. In America, where the same set of young men recite side by side in the same recitation-rooms for four years, it is perhaps only natural that the feeling of class unity should exist as it does. It is not in itself an evil, although liable to grave perversion. Three fourths of the public disorder in our colleges are due to it in one or another shape. In Germany, it simply does not exist. There are no courses of study, no classes. Even those who are pursuing the same general studies do not take the same lectures in the same order. . . .

The German student is older than the American. The average age of admission of this year's graduating class at Yale was eighteen. This is for America a high average. The German rarely attends the university before his twentieth year. Many students are even older. In the next place, the German is much more thoroughly trained. On this point, I must beg the reader to dismiss all prejudice and look the facts full in the face. That we have a few good schools, is a truism which nobody will deny. But that we have not anything like a school-system, by virtue of which all young men, wherever they may live, can be trained for their higher education, is equally true. I except the eastern part of Massachusetts, where wealth and intelligence are so diffused that almost every district has an excellent preparatory school. But where, I venture to ask, outside of the eastern part of Massachusetts, shall we find the match for a German gymnasium? . . .

The only just way of comparing two systems is to take them at points widely apart. The idler of Germany, I am confident, has forgotten twice as much as the idler of America, the industrious student knows twice as much as the industrious undergraduate, and the future scholar of Germany is a man of whom we in America have no conception. He is a man who could not exist under our system, he would be choked by recitations and grades. What he studies, he studies with the devotion of a poet and the trained skill of a scientist. The idea of competing, of putting forth all his energies in a trial of skill after the fashion of the English university examination, has never occurred to him.

He studies to learn, to master what has been done before him, and to contribute if possible to the growth of knowledge. He reads with a view to permanent results, not to examinations To justify these assertions, it will be necessary to define more precisely what I mean by "knowledge." Life in Germany is not so free as in America. It presents fewer elements of excitement, moves rather in a prescribed routine. It does not exhibit a like frantic haste after fame and wealth. The newspaper press, vegetating rather than flourishing under humdrum circumstances, is deficient in everything that we call enterprise. Any one of our great dailies gives its readers more and better reading than the entire press of Berlin. The Germans do not look upon their newspapers as daily pabulum. The German boy, although well informed, grows up in comparative ignorance of the great social and political movements around him. He knows much less of the world, his mind is not stocked with scraps of news gathered from papers and magazines. The American boy, to use an Americanism, is much more wide-awake. He can tell you what has happened yesterday in China or Africa, what is likely to happen to-morrow in South America. Yet we can scarcely call this knowledge, in the highest sense of the term. It is rather *allotria,* the unsifted, unarranged, undigested materials of knowledge. What the German gynasiast knows at all, he knows well, because he knows it as an item of general training, and in its relations to other things. For instance, although Germany and France are next-door neighbors, the gymnasiast does not watch from day to day, from month to month, the political convulsions at Paris and Versailles. Yet he has probably read with a good deal of care the history of France from its origin, and is in a position to form a correct judgment as to what these convulsions really betoken. If you lay before him the events as they transpire from time to time, he will *understand* them, because he will view them as the present out-cropping of forces which he has traced in their operation for centuries. . . .

VII

COMPARISON WITH AMERICAN COLLEGES

. . . The American public is still indifferent, as a public. It is not aroused to the vital connection between the State and education in all its stages, highest as well as lowest. The explanation of the signal failure of the movement in behalf of Civil Service Reform is to be found in the circumstance that the public is apathetic. The nation at large does not care whether it has better office-holders or not. It secretly approves, rather than disapproves, of the principle of succession in office. After a man has been post-master or revenue-collector for four years, it is only fair—argues the American mind—that he give some one else "a chance." Such is public opinion, and it is idle to quarrel with it. A similar view is taken of education. We do not need highly educated men. So long as our graduates can spell with tolerable accuracy, have a modicum of the classics and mathematics, can write and declaim with fluency, what more do you expect of them? They must become "practical," must learn the theory through the practice, and rough it with the others. Right or wrong, this is the average estimate set upon the value of college education. The public does not perceive the importance of any thing higher and more systematic. Indeed, I am tempted at times to believe that the colleges have exceeded, on some points, the demands of their friends. They give more than is expected of them. There are symptoms of a desire to react from the progress made during the past fifteen years. In making this assertion, I have in view, not so much Yale and Harvard as the colleges in the Middle and Western States. Urged on by a spirit of rivalry which is in itself deserving only of praise, these latter have made their curriculum more extensive and have also enforced its requirements more strictly. In doing this, they have gone a step too far, they have outrun the capacities of the preparatory schools. Up to the outbreak of the Civil War, the American college was an easy-going institution, where one was not forced beyond his natural gait, but had leisure to follow his inclinations, and especially to read. This has been changed. New professorships in the natural sciences have been created, and the chairs have been filled with energetic young men, enthusiastic in their vocation, and—I trust they will pardon the bluntness of expression—rather intolerant towards those who do not keep pace with them. Many of the professors in the older departments are also young men who have studied abroad, are equally enthusiastic, and equally intolerant. The result is that we are called upon to witness a curious phenomenon, one that must act as a disturbing element in every system of education, to wit, a direct conflict of studies. Our undergraduates have at the present day too many studies, and are hurried through difficult and disconnected subjects at too rapid a rate. The new professors in the classics and the new professors in the natural sciences threaten to tear the child asunder between them, and there is no Solomon at hand to decide upon the true

alma mater. Viewed in this light, the assertion now going the rounds
of the press and attributed variously to Mr. Beecher and Mr. Fields,
namely, that our colleges have not succeeded in producing one first-
rate man in any department since 1855, will perhaps receive its explanation. Whatever the college of bygone days may have failed to do, it
certainly gave its pupil a better opportunity than his successor now enjoys, of maturing in conformity to the laws of individual being. . . .

It would not be difficult to show that in point of economy also our
colleges have much to learn from Germany. The reader's most careful
attention is invited to the tabular statement of income and expenditure
for the university of Leipsic, presented elsewhere. Two of our colleges,
Harvard and Yale, have each—if I mistake not—as large an income as
that of Leipsic. If smaller, the difference is certainly inconsiderable.
Yet both Harvard and Yale would be slow in provoking a comparison
between themselves and Leipsic. To what, then, must we look for the
explanation of this disproportion in America between the outlay and
the results effected? In part, but only in a small part, to the relatively
higher figures of professors' salaries in America. Each one of the full
professors at Harvard receives $4,000 a year, I believe. At Yale, the sala-
ries are very nearly as high. No one will have the shabbiness to assert
that the pay is too high. As a class, American professors are insuffi-
ciently recompensed. After years of toil and annoyance, they can be
thankful if they are able to keep themselves and their families out of
debt. Were the salary of every professor doubled, the increase would be
nothing more than justice. It is difficult to understand why professors,
who are men of ability and culture, who devote themselves unselfishly
to the best interests of the nation, should not be paid as liberally as our
best lawyers and physicians, why the guardians of the spiritual interests
of men should fare worse than those who look merely after their bodies and estates. It is not more than six years ago that the president of
Harvard was forced to admit in public that his senior professor received less than the chief cook of the Parker House! Things have been
bettered since then, but they have not been radically cured.

Now for this state of affairs the party chief in responsibility is the
college itself. Not Harvard, nor Yale, nor Princeton, nor Cornell alone,
but the spirit of our college system. We have been misled by rivalry
into copying after England in the feature that is least worthy of imita-

tion. I mean—buildings! Had the money which has been sunk in brick and stone and mortar during the past twenty years been judiciously invested, the salary of every professor in America might be doubled at this moment.

13. The Governing Board of the Sheffield Scientific School Calls for New Principles in Education, 1868

In 1847 Yale College established a new Department of Philosophy and the Arts, whose purpose was to embrace advanced work in the arts and new work in the sciences. The new department had responsibility for graduate instruction in the arts and sciences and for undergraduate instruction primarily in the applied sciences. During the 1850's work in this area was beginning to become systematic. As a part of the movement toward more advanced study, the School of Applied Chemistry, which had existed since 1847, was regrouped in 1854 with the School of Engineering as the Yale Scientific School. The existence of the new school was made secure and its success possible by the donations of the Connecticut merchant and railroad entrepreneur Joseph Earl Sheffield (1793–1882), which, beginning in 1854, eventually reached over a million dollars. In 1861 the school was renamed the Sheffield Scientific School. Daniel Coit Gilman (see Part VII, Docs. 1, 5, and 6), who had helped to draw up the plan of organization of the school, served as its librarian, secretary, and professor of physical and political geography. Seizing upon the implications of the Morrill Act (Doc. 11), he made the Sheffield Scientific School the first institution to use funds allotted under it. At the time this report was prepared, the influence of the new school was growing rapidly, but the tendency it represented was still being resisted by old-fashioned Yale men. The philosophy of this brief statement should be compared with that of the Yale Report of 1828 (Part IV, Doc. 11).

See Part VII, Doc. 3; Russell H. Chittenden, *History of the Sheffield School of Yale University, 1846–1922* (2 vols.; New Haven, 1928); George W. Pierson, *Yale College: An Educational History, 1871–1921* (New Haven, 1952).

Governing Board and Faculty of the Sheffield Scientific School of Yale College, "Statement . . . Presented to the State Board of Visitors, at Their Annual Meeting, March, 1868," in *Third Annual Report of the Sheffield Scientific School of Yale College, 1867–8* (New Haven, 1868), pp. 10–17.

The object of all education is to increase our capacity of happiness and usefulness, to enable us the better to enjoy our own lives and help others to enjoy theirs. In calling forth and training the powers of the individual, it has this double end distinctly in view. . . .

No theory of education can possibly be sound which does not recognize the absolute worth of all human knowledge, or which contemns "facts" of any kind, philological, historical, or scientific. . . .

Formerly only members of the "learned professions," and gentlemen who could afford to train themselves after their pattern, were regarded as needing to be "educated;" and a little of the old feeling remains, though put out of date by the different aspect of affairs in our time. Other occupations used to be mere trades, the preparation for which consisted in the acquisition of a certain amount of mental and manual dexterity, handed down in guilds and the like, and communicated by private instruction. Now, nearly all the arts of life are raised to a vastly higher plane; the causes and modes of action which they involve are understood; underneath each lies a science, whose comprehension is necessary to their highest and most successful pursuit; a science, too, whose establishment has perhaps required as much learning and insight, as much faithful labor in investigation and logical acuteness of deduction, as much accumulation of wisdom, as high gifts of intellect, as any known branch of human knowledge; whose acquisition costs as thorough preparation, as long study, and as distinguished capacity; and which offers as keen satisfaction to the curious intellect, and has as wide and direct a bearing upon human happiness. All is here included that can give dignity to a calling and to the preparation for it. The scientific man, as he is often called—for example, the engineer, the chemist, the naturalist—is by his occupation challenged to not less ability and disinterestedness, and promised not less usefulness, than the lawyer or physician; his due training is as real a part of the higher education, all that fits him for his work is as truly disciplinary, as anything else in the whole scheme of study.

It is not well possible to lay too much stress upon discipline; but it is comparatively easy to misunderstand what is meant by that word. Anything is disciplinary which prepares the mind for the worthy exercise of its powers, which fits it to receive and utilize truth. There is a too current disposition now-a-days to divorce discipline from acquisition of knowledge, to contemn the useful as ignoble. This is a natural reaction against the opposite tendency, to regard no knowledge as worth acquiring of which the utility is not immediate and obvious. Either error is equally detrimental; and either, when nakedly presented, is sure to be rejected by any enlightened mind; but it is not so easy to avoid some admixture of the one or the other. . . . There is discipline in the acquisition of all knowledge, because the mere effect of acquirement helps to acquire farther; and also because all knowledge is in itself valuable, as connected with and leading to other knowledge, as enriching and expanding the mind, giving it the taste to acquire and the power to retain. But its worth for discipline lies vastly more in the latter mode of action on the mind than in the former. Nothing is more really disciplinary, in the highest sense, than the gaining of valuable knowledge, along with the comprehension of its value, and the understanding how to use it. Nothing thus given is mere fact or information, nor is the process of so giving it a cram. This is the material on which the mind must work, in order to test and increase its powers, and without which what it may do is only mock work, which exhausts while it exercises. The idea of spending the season of "education" wholly or mainly in a sort of mental gymnastics, of laying out a scheme of preparation for the active work of life which does not include as an essential part the storing of the mind with a variety of useful information, is as erroneous as anything can be. . . . The ends of education must not be lost sight of in the means; those ends are practical, and must be pursued by means likely to result in their attainment. What is the best discipline for one is not the best for another, even though both may aim at an equal degree of general culture, if their disposition is different, or if they are to follow different walks in life. Each method must be judged by the fruit it yields; that is wasted labor from which in the end no appreciable advantage is derived; the mental effort spent in it might better have been given to something else. . . .

Classical studies put us in communication with the best thought of both ancient and modern times; they give a kind and degree of mental culture which has been attainable by no other means, and which long custom, as well as its intrinsic character, leads the community to estimate at, to say the least, its full worth.

It is true that, as already noticed, the prominence of the classics as a means of education is upon the wane—not by their loss of absolute value, but by the uprise of other means to the same end, possessing a not less urgent and conspicuous importance; partly, also, by the transfusion of their valuable content into other and modern forms, so that their influence is obtainable indirectly. . . . They will demand not less attention in amount than they have hitherto won—although there will be large classes of students whose training may and must be gained without them, by the aid of the abundant fruits of culture which have now been stored up outside of them; and although, on the other hand, he who is versed in them alone can no longer make the same pretension to discipline as formerly. There was a time when to be merely a good Latin and Greek scholar was to be well educated; now, such a one is only a specialist, and may be a narrow-minded pedant, as really deficient in due discipline as if he knew nothing but mathematics, or chemistry, or zoölogy.

The objection is often brought against classical study that those who devote to it so large a proportion of the time given to training never carry it, after all, beyond the stage of preliminary discipline, do not begin to derive fruit and enjoyment from it, and drop it abruptly when the work of life is begun, hardly if at all conscious of benefit obtained. Much more is apt to be made of this objection than it is really worth; for, on the one hand, no one is capable of measuring the good that a study does him in exercising the powers of his mind and increasing its range and capacity; and, on the other hand, the higher benefits of education are not within the reach of every one; a host of minds are only limitedly receptive of general culture; are capable, perhaps, of becoming fair specialists in some line which engages all their energies; nothing more. All education is to this extent experimental and liable to failure. The liability does, however, constitute a powerful and valid argument against limiting education to one unvarying pattern, since many a mind which is repelled and stagnated by one set of studies, may be incited to independent and healthy action by another.

We have entered into so much of detail respecting classical study because the scientific courses are mainly peculiar, and exposed to distrust on the part of many in the community, in virtue of the inferior place which they assign to such study, and because they seem to some to deny hereby its value, and cast reproach upon it. This is not at all our intent: we hold that every scientist is the better for all the classical training he can get, even for vastly more than is given in the ordinary college course. Only we also hold that it does not outweigh in importance everything else, and constitute to every one the *summum bonum* of mental training.

14. A State Senator Argues for a Liberal Curriculum at Iowa State Agricultural College, 1884

Preston M. Sutton of Marshalltown, Iowa, put forward the following case for liberal training in the agricultural college at Ames, which had inherited the Morrill grant. He argued that the narrow course of agricultural subjects in the college was defeating the original intent of the Morrill Act of 1862, and he even received a cautious word of support from Justin Morrill. Sutton was a graduate of Illinois Normal University and taught in Iowa schools and colleges before entering law. See Doc. 11, and E. D. Ross, *History of Iowa State College,* chap. vii.

Mr. President:—This bill provides that there shall be adopted and taught at the Iowa State Agricultural College a broad, liberal and practical course of study, in which the leading branches of learning shall relate to agriculture and the mechanic arts, but which shall also include such other branches of learning as will most liberally and practically educate the agricultural and industrial classes in the several pursuits and professions in life, including military tactics. It proposes to enact this in lieu of section 1621, which it repeals, and which specifies as a course of study Geology, Minerology, Meteorology, Entomology, Zoology, animal and Vegetable Anatomy, Veterinary Surgery and Book-keeping, and permits no other studies except such as are directly connected with agriculture. It will thus be seen that this bill proposes to change the law so as to provide a general and liberal course of study in which agriculture and the mechanics' arts shall have a leading place, and to repeal the exclusive course that is now provided by the statute. . . . It has received the careful consideration of the present faculty of the college, and has the approval, as I believe, of all the more particularly informed friends of the school of whatever faction (if there be different factions,) and comes to the senate with the unanimous approval of the committee on the Agricultural College. . . .

Mr. Morrill says it was the intention to give prominence to the industries, but not to prevent states having a sufficient fund to give the

Senator Preston M. Sutton, "Speech in Behalf of the Bill Relating to a Course of Study for the State Agricultural College," in Earle D. Ross, *A History of the Iowa State College of Agriculture and Mechanic Arts* (Ames, Iowa, 1942) pp. 382–83, 388, 392–98, 400–402.

school the efficiency of a university in the languages and mathematics. The education must be practical, and just as liberal as the funds of the state will permit. Now, I insist that Iowa with a fund of three-quarters of a million of dollars, has no excuse for clinging to a narrow course of study, for this is its richest and should be its best school. Its pupils should be taught agriculture, together with such other studies as will give them a liberal as well as a practical education. Or, in other words, the purpose of the grant as made by congress, and as accepted by the state, should be adhered to with strictest fidelity and without any attempt to avoid it. . . .

Now the Act of Congress was passed July 2, 1862, when this college and farm was little over four years old. It was to create a college for the purpose of benefiting agriculture and the mechanic arts, by educating the agricultural and mechanical classes liberally for all the pursuits and professions in life. . . . The honorable gentlemen who composed that board, had planned a purely Agricultural College devoted wholly to agriculture, which they no doubt had good reason to believe would best benefit agriculture and stand as a lasting monument of what they had done for the greatest of all great industries. The college was their pride, and justly so. They had made it, and they had built their hopes upon it, and they wanted to see it stand just as they had planned it. But they wanted these lands. Now there came a struggle, and I have no doubt it was an honest one, but I must contend it was not a successful one. They desired to be the trustees of this great trust from the government, but wanted to avoid the plain expressed purpose of the trust, which was a liberal and practical education in the several pursuits in life, and misappropriate it to special and technical education in the sole pursuits of agriculture and such mechanic arts as are directly connected with agriculture. The legislature undertook to help the board out of their dilemma by getting up an act which would seem to turn the Agricultural College over to the purpose required by the Act of Congress and yet retain to the old college its original character. Now we will see if they succeeded. They took a part of the act of the legislature of 1858, and thus sought to unite the two so as to appear to embrace the provisions of both. I say that I have no doubt that it was an honest attempt, but I do say it was not a successful one. It was unsuccessful because it was impossible. They took out of the title of the Act of Congress, keeping well clear of the body of it, "colleges for the benefit of agriculture and the mechanic arts," and then took out of the act of the legislature, a "State Agricultural College and model farm, to be connected with the entire agricultural interests of the state," and then put these two together and adopted word for word the course of study prescribed in the act of the legislature, and thought they had solved the question. But in place of providing a college for "the liberal and practical education of the industrial classes in the several pursuits and professions in life," they only provided a college for technical education in the sole pursuits of agriculture. . . . I am not here to say that the Agricultural College has not been a benefit to agriculture and the mechanic arts, but I am here to contend that the purpose of the Act of Congress is different from that adopted by the legislature. Agriculture and the mechanic arts can be benefited in different ways. For instance, by schools of invention, by agricultural stations, by agricultural fairs and in many ways different and diverse. If the Act of Congress were silent as to the character of the benefit required, then we might consider whether some other kind of benefit might not do, but the Act of Congress is not silent. It speaks aloud, and it speaks with no uncertain sound. . . .

The whole plan of the congressional agricultural college was liberal and practical education. The plan of the old state agricultural college was technical and exclusive education. The two plans were entirely different, and when the legislature interposed the plan of the state college and applied this fund to its exclusive use, the legislature misappropriated these funds.

The one plan was for an exclusive and special education in a single pursuit and the other for a liberal education in the several pursuits. One was to teach exclusively agriculture and the other to teach such branches of learning as related to agriculture and the mechanic arts, together with such other studies as would give to the industrial classes a broad and liberal education. I say it was unwise to attempt a compromise between two plans, so absolutely different, and it has proved to have been very unwise. . . .

There has been an irrepressible conflict in this school. The energies of the school have been divided, and much of its strength exhausted in unfriendly and fruitless contention. Were it not too serious it would be almost amusing to witness the struggle that has gone on in this college between the old plan and the new. We would see one set of men reciting the Act of Congress and construing it for broad and liberal education, and then another set reading the act of the legislature and clinging with all the fondness of a father to the old farm. One side would read from the act of congress: "The branches of learning relating to agriculture and the mechanic arts," without "excluding" anything, not even the classics, necessary to promote the liberal and practical education of the industrial classes in the several pursuits and professions of life, and then insist that the funds devoted by the act of congress should be used for the purposes as herein set forth, and would beg that History and Literature might be made regular studies in the school so that the students could be taught the history of agriculture, the history of liberty, the history of their country, the history of all great causes, and the history of the world's great men. The other side would read from the act of the legislature the course of study provided for the old Legislative College of 1858, as follows: Mineralogy, Meteorology, Entomology, Zoology, Geology, etc., and such other studies only as will directly connect the college with the agricultural interest of the State, and that side would insist that History was a dangerous study that led the youths to long for other than agricultural pursuits, and thus would they contend for absolute technical agricultural education. To this day there is not a word of history to be found in any one of the five studies in this college for young men. Young ladies are allowed nine weeks of History, but no young man need apply. It seems to be concluded, I presume, that girls will read something besides Mineralogy, Geology, Entomology, Meteorology and Zoology, anyway. Girls will read, but they seldom read Geology, and so for fear they might read something worse, they give them a few weeks of History.

It has been suggested that History is properly a preparatory study, but it is not. It may be contended that History should be completed before entering college, but it cannot be. The best colleges and universities of the country admit it. There is not a respectable college in the country but makes History one of its leading and most essential studies. . . .

History is not only absolutely essential to learning but history may be said to be learning itself. Learning without history is Hamlet with Hamlet left out. . . . There is nothing that America is so proud of as of her history. Nothing so inspires the American heart to high ambition as the study of American history, and yet we have a college pretending to give a liberal education with her doors locked against history.

Now is this liberal education? I ask you is it even practical education? What is practical education? It certainly is not a bare technical knowledge of physical science. A man may read the rocks and all of the lessons they teach, and study the flowers till he can call them all by name, and be able to analyze all the minerals and measure their component parts, and be able to give the name and character of every specimen of animal or insect life and still not be able practically to apply his learning to the solution of a single problem in life. The German nation is a nation of scientists, who are possessed of most profound learning, but it is technical and in no degree practical or liberal. The learned men of Germany should have been its rulers, and would have been, had their schools been practical and liberal. The German schools have been technical. The German education has ever been of the most technical character. It has made profound scholars in the technical sciences, but it has failed to develop great men in the affairs of life or of state. It spent itself in the solution of abstract questions until Germany retrograded into absolute and iron monarchy. The framers of this great educational law were not in favor of that kind of education. . . .

Our Agricultural College is altogether the best endowed institution of learning in the state, and we should not narrow or dwarf its powers. We should make it what it was intended to be and what it is so well capable of becoming, the most liberal and most practical institution of learning in Iowa. But it may be asked if this college is to be a college in which only the leading branches of learning shall relate to agriculture, and from which the other branches of learning shall not be excluded, how is it to be different from other colleges. Even if this college were no different from other colleges it would be no reason why we should violate the plain letter of the law that endowed it. We should faithfully perform the trust, and not seek to avoid its plain provisions. But it is different from other colleges. It is very different indeed. True it is that the state and country are full of colleges of general instruction, but they are not full of colleges in which the leading branches of learning are related to agriculture; nor colleges that are in any great degree such colleges as this Act of Congress requires. A poor boy who goes unaided through the common colleges of the country, is looked upon as a hero. It is so hard to do, and we have but few who have ever attempted to do it. . . . These common colleges furnish no labor to speak of, and what little they do furnish is of the most servile kind, and few enter them except those whose parents can pay their way. The idea of this new college is to furnish work to every boy. To furnish such work as combined with study will educate the mind and body together, and neither at the expense of the other, wholesome, honest, ennobling work, not scrubbing floors and sweeping stairs alone, but beautiful fields to be plowed and planted, ripened harvests to be gathered in, the finest of cattle to tend and feed, and the noblest of horses to care for and drive, work that the farmer's boy knows how and loves to do, remunerative work, a college where every boy and girl is expected to work, a college where work is made honorable and where work confers a dignity, a college where honest poverty even is welcome, a college where a poor boy can go without a dollar and proudly earn his way, as hundreds have already done, a college where labor can earn not only learning, but the most liberal and practical learning under the sun, that learning which, rightly wedded with labor, made a Franklin possible. . . . But this labor that the new college furnishes is not the only difference. The common college is in the city and in the towns, where baneful influences make hazing possible. The new temple of learning is a country home which has always been the object of deepest love, and the subject of gladdest sentiment. . . . When the sentiments and habits of young men are being formed, how grand the thought to have them ever surrounded by the lasting sublime influences of a country home. When I visited our Agricultural College last fall, and saw its beautiful fields and herds of cattle, its lawns and its woods, and its commodious buildings, and its laboratories and libraries, and contemplated its magnificent endowment fast nearing a million, I thought I could see the possibility of one of the grandest institutions of learning that the world has ever known—a grand temple of learning where learning shall lead labor by the hand, and confer upon him all her manifold blessings. A college that may carry the broadest of learning into every toiler's home, and that may prepare the sons of toil for the broadest possible usefulness to all mankind. The providing of such a college I believe it to be true purpose of the Act of Congress that gave us these lands. I believe by the acceptance of these lands we have pledged the honor of the state to the maintenance of that purpose alone.

Part VII

ORGANIZING THE MODERN
AMERICAN UNIVERSITY

I<small>T WOULD BE</small> difficult, in a brief introduction to this section, to improve on the historical review of the era of university organization
given us by Daniel Coit Gilman (Doc. 1) from the retrospective van-
tage point of 1906 in his *Launching of a University*. In this period of
revolutionary change, however, certain broad outlines should be clearly
marked out. The first was the immense scale on which the enterprise
took place. The great sums now at last made available for Cornell, the
Johns Hopkins, Chicago, Stanford, and supplied as well to enlarge the
state universities and the older private universities were so large as to
dwarf the means available to previous enterprises in higher education.
The second was the growing importance of science, itself one of the
things that attracted the attention of men of great wealth to the importance of the university. When Charles William Eliot wrote in 1869
about what he called "The New Education" (Doc. 3), it was the demand for the applied sciences and the stimulating work of the scientific schools (Part IV, Doc. 13) that he mainly had in mind. A further
consideration is that the universities, enlarged and enriched as they
were, could now support a program of advanced study and offer inducements for serious scholars. The growing specialization of knowledge and the rising determination that knowledge must be not merely
conserved but also advanced in universities finally had their impact

even on the undergraduate college, where the old required curriculum gradually gave way before the elective system (Doc. 2, and Part VIII).

Three educational pioneers particularly left their impact upon the educational scene. One of them, Andrew D. White, Ezra Cornell's adviser and the first president of Cornell University, realized in the 1860's, with the founding of the new university in Ithaca, a dream that had been maturing in his mind since his dissatisfied student days at Yale and his visits to European universities (Doc. 9, and Part VI, Doc. 6). Another was Eliot, the first scientist to become president of Harvard, who took the occasion of his inaugural address (Doc. 2) to publish a ringing manifesto for higher standards, for more science, the elective system, and a relaxation of the narrow paternal college discipline of the old days. It was Eliot who led the way in showing that the new trend in education need not wait upon such newly established universities as Cornell and the Johns Hopkins but that the old private universities that had always been at the top in the quality of their work could also be in the vanguard of important changes. The third leader was Gilman, whom the trustees of the Johns Hopkins were everywhere advised (Doc. 4) to take on as the first president of their new university, founded in Baltimore in 1876. The Hopkins was unique in the sense that its founder was specifically concerned to create a great *graduate* school, completely untrammeled by the old incubus of sectarianism—a school in which Gilman was free (Doc. 5) to do what he could to attract the finest scholars available and create for them an atmosphere thoroughly conducive to their noblest efforts. As G. Stanley Hall put it (Doc. 6), Gilman became "a spiritual father of his faculty, the author of their careers, and for years made the institution the paradise and seminarium of young specialists." Not quite of the same rank among educational promoters as Eliot, White, and Gilman was John W. Burgess of Columbia (Doc. 7), who, however, did as much as anyone to bring his own university into the stream of university development. It was one of Burgess' accomplishments to show how important the new university developments could be for the social and political sciences. He created and became the first head of Columbia's faculty of political science, which he built into a center of social studies that at the turn of the century was as distinguished as any in the United States. In good part because of Burgess' energy and vision, New York at last got the great urban university that had been so long proposed for her (Part IV, Docs. 12–18, and Part V, Doc. 11).

So rapid was the transformation of the American university between the 1860's and the end of the century that teachers and administrators with a strong sense of tradition were almost overwhelmed. Men who were building state universities in the West, like Professor Charles Kendall Adams of Michigan, were constantly bucking the tide of sentiment directed against public, tax-supported institutions (Doc. 8). Among those who hoped to balance innovation with a keen sense for the values of the past was Woodrow Wilson, who, speaking from the perspective of an old institution like Princeton with a long record of influence, could well remind the world that American higher education had a notable past as well as a promising future. In his essay, "Princeton in the Nation's Service" (Doc. 10), published in 1896, six years before he became the university's president, Wilson hearkened back to the contributions of Princeton in the days of Witherspoon (Part II, Doc. 10) and observed that it is "the duty of an institution of learning . . . not merely to implant a sense of duty, but to illuminate duty by every lesson that can be drawn out of the past." Stoutly he defended the unique value of the classics; and, in words that were beginning to be thought heretical in many quarters, he affirmed: "I am much mistaken if the scientific spirit of the age is not doing us a great disservice, working in us a certain great degeneracy. Science has bred in us a spirit of experiment and a contempt for the past. It has made us credulous of quick improvement, hopeful of discovering panaceas, confident of success in every new thing." In these remarks he anticipated cleavages and gaps in the educational as well as the social structure which the next generation would try to remedy (Part XI).

1. Daniel Coit Gilman Reviews the Accomplishments of the University Era, 1869-1902

Gilman (1831–1908) was born in Connecticut and graduated from Yale in 1852. In 1853 he went with Andrew D. White to St. Petersburg, where both men were attachés of the American legation. In 1855 he returned to Yale, where, in the following year, he participated in planning what later became the Sheffield Scien-

D. C. Gilman, *The Launching of a University* (New York, 1906), pp. 3–10, 12; first published with some variations in *Scribner's Magazine*, XXXI (March, 1902), 327–31.

tific School (see Part VI, Doc. 13), showing that he had made extensive observations of European schools of science. He subsequently served the newly organized school for many years as librarian, secretary, and professor of physical and political geography. In 1872 he accepted the presidency of the University of California, where his difficulties with the regents made it impossible for him to bring to fruition his great gifts as an educational administrator. But when the trustees of the Johns Hopkins were seeking a first president, they were everywhere recommended to invite Gilman (see Doc. 4), and he accepted the invitation in 1875. One of his first acts in this capacity was his call for a policy of intellectual freedom (Part X, Doc. 1). From the first he committed the Johns Hopkins to the search for distinguished men and not to ambitious or expensive plans for buildings. His hunt for talent took him to Britain and Germany as well as many quarters of the United States, and he succeeded in organizing the first great graduate school, as well as the historically important Johns Hopkins School of Medicine and the Johns Hopkins Hospital. He continued throughout his life to be active in civic and educational affairs. See Fabian Franklin, *The Life of D. C. Gilman* (New York, 1910); John C. French, *A History of the University Founded by Johns Hopkins* (Baltimore, 1946); and Hugh Hawkins, *Pioneer: A History of the Johns Hopkins University, 1874–1889* (Ithaca, N.Y., 1960).

During the last half century American universities have grown up with surprising rapidity. It is not necessary to fix an exact date for the beginning of this progress. Some would like to say that the foundation of the Lawrence Scientific School in Harvard University, and, almost simultaneously, the foundation of the Sheffield School of Science in New Haven were initial undertakings. These events indicated that the two oldest colleges of New England were ready to introduce instruction of an advanced character, far more special than ever before, in the various branches of natural and physical science. An impulse was given by the passage of the Morrill Act, by which a large amount of scrip, representing public lands, was offered to any State that would maintain a college devoted to agriculture and the mechanic arts, without the exclusion of other scientific and literary studies. The foundation of Cornell University was of the highest significance, for it fortunately came under the guidance of one who was equally devoted to historical and scientific research, one whose plans showed an independence of thought and a power of organisation then without precedent in the field of higher education. The changes introduced in Harvard, under masterful leadership, when the modern era of progress began, had profound influence. The subsequent gifts of Johns Hopkins, of Rockefeller, of Stanford, of Tulane, promoted the establishment of new institutions, in sympathy with the older colleges, yet freer to introduce new subjects and new methods. The State universities of the North-west and of the Pacific coast, as population and wealth increased, became an important factor. These multiform agencies must all be carefully considered when an estimate is made of the progress of the last half-century.

I was a close observer of the changes which were introduced at Yale in the fifties and sixties, the grafting of a new branch—"a wild olive," as it seemed—upon the old stock. Then I had some experience, brief but significant, in California, as the head of the State University, at a time when it was needful to answer the popular cry that it should become chiefly a school of agriculture, and when it was important to show the distinction between a university and a polytechnic institute. Then came a call to the East and a service of more than a quarter of a century in the organisation and development of a new establishment. These are three typical institutions. Yale was a colonial foundation, wedded to precedents, where an effort was made to introduce new studies and new methods. California was a State institution, benefited by the so-called agricultural grant, where it was necessary to emphasise the importance of the liberal arts, in a community where the practical arts were sure to take care of themselves. Baltimore afforded an opportunity to develop a private endowment free from ecclesiastical or political control, where from the beginning the old and the new, the humanities and the sciences, theory and practice, could be generously promoted.

In looking over this period, remarkable changes are manifest. In the first place, science receives an amount of support unknown before. This is a natural consequence of the wonderful discoveries which have been made in respect to the phenomena and laws of nature and the improvements made in scientific instruments and researches. Educational leaders perceived the importance of the work carried on in laboratories and observatories under the impulse of such men as Liebig and Faraday. With this increased attention to science, the old-fashioned curriculum disappeared, of necessity, and many combinations of studies were permitted in the most conservative institutions. Absolute freedom of choice is now allowed in many places. Historical and political science has come to the front, and it is no longer enough to learn from a text-book wearisome lists of names and dates; reference must be made to original sources of information, or, at any rate, many books must be consulted in order to understand the progress of human society. Some knowledge of German and French is required of every-one. English literature receives an amount of attention never given to it in early days. Medicine is no longer taught by lectures only, but the better schools require continued practice in biological laboratories and the subsequent observation of patients in hospitals and dispensaries. The admission of women to the advantages of higher education is also one of the most noteworthy advances of the period we are considering.

The historian who takes up these and allied indications of the progress of American universities will have a difficult and an inspiring theme. It has been a delightful and exhilarating time in which to live and to work, to observe and to try. All the obstacles have not been overcome, some mistakes have been made, much remains for improvement, but on the whole the record of the last forty or fifty years exhibits substantial and satisfactory gains. The efforts of scholars have been sustained by the munificence of donors, and more than one institution now has an endowment larger than that of all the institutions which were in existence in 1850.

In the middle of the century the word "university" was in the air. It was cautiously used in Cambridge and New Haven, where a number of professional schools were living vigorous lives near the parental domicile, then called "the college proper," as if the junior departments were colleges improper. To speak of "our university" savoured of pretence in these old colleges. A story was told at Yale that a dignitary from a distant State introduced himself as chancellor of the university. "How large a faculty have you?" asked Dominie Day. "Not any," was the answer. "Have you any library or buildings?" "Not yet," replied the visitor. "Any endowment?" "None," came the monotonous and saddening negative. "What have you?" persisted the Yale president. The visitor brightened as he said, "We have a very good charter."

Among enlightened and well-read people, the proper significance of a university was of course understood. Students came home from Europe, and especially from Germany, with clear conceptions of its scope. Everett, Bancroft, Ticknor, Hedge, Woolsey, Thacher, Whitney, Child, Gould, Lane, Gildersleeve and others were familiar with the courses of illustrious teachers on the Continent. European scholars were added to the American faculties—Follen, Beck, Lieber, Agassiz, Guyot, and others also distinguished. But the American colleges had been based on the idea of an English college, and upon this central nucleus the limited funds and the unlimited energies of the times were concentrated, not indeed exclusively, but diligently. Any diversion of the concentrated resources of the treasury to "outside" interests, like law, medicine, and theology, was not to be thought of. Even now, one hears occasionally the question, "after all, what *is* the difference between a university and a college?" To certain persons, the university simply means the best place of instruction that the locality can secure. The country is full of praiseworthy foundations which ought to be known as high-schools or academies or possibly as colleges, but which appear to great disadvantage under the more pretentious name they have assumed. Just after the war the enthusiastic sympathy of the North for the enfranchised blacks led to the bestowal of the highest term in educational nomenclature upon the institutes where the freedmen were to be taught. Fortunately, Hampton and Tuskegee escaped this christening, but Fiske, Atlanta, and Howard foundations were thus named. It is nearer the truth to say that the complete university includes four faculties—the liberal arts or philosophy, law, medicine, and theology. Sometimes a university is regarded as the union, under one board of control, of all the highest institutions of a place or region. There is one instance,—the State of New York,—where the name "university" is given to a board which in a general way supervises all the degree-giving institutions in the State.

When the announcement was made to the public, at the end of 1873, that a wealthy merchant of Baltimore had provided by his will for the establishment of a new university, a good deal of latent regret was felt because the country seemed to have already more higher seminaries than it could supply with teachers, students, or funds. Another "college" was expected to join the crowded column, and impoverish its neighbours by its superior attractions. Fortunately, the founder was wise as well as generous. He used the simplest phrases to express his wishes; and he did not define the distinguished name that he bestowed upon his child, nor embarrass its future by needless conditions. Details were left to a sagacious body of trustees whom he charged with the duty of supervision. They travelled east and west, brought to Baltimore experienced advisers, Eliot, Angell, and White, and procured many of the latest books that discussed the problem of education. By and by they chose a president, and accepted his suggestion that they should give emphasis to the word "university" and should endeavour to build up an institution quite different from a "college," thus making an addition to American education, not introducing a rival. Young men who had already gone through that period of mental discipline which commonly leads to the baccalaureate degree were invited to come and pursue those advanced studies for which they might have been prepared, and to accept the inspiration and guidance of professors selected because of acknowledged distinction or of special aptitudes. Among the phrases that were employed to indicate the project were many which then were novel, although they are now the commonplaces of catalogues and speeches.

Opportunities for advanced, not professional, studies were then scanty in this country. In the older colleges certain graduate courses were attended by a small number of followers—but the teachers were for the most part absorbed with undergraduate instruction, and could give but little time to the few who sought their guidance. ...

As the day has now come when there is almost a superfluity of advanced courses, let me tell some of the conditions which brought the Johns Hopkins foundations into close relations with these upward and onward movements.

Before a university can be launched there are six requisites: An idea; capital, to make the idea feasible; a definite plan; an able staff of coadjutors; books and apparatus; students. On each of these points I shall briefly dwell, conscious of one advantage as a writer—conscious, also, of a disadvantage. I have the advantage of knowing more than anyone else of an unwritten chapter of history; the disadvantage of not being able or disposed to tell the half that I remember.

"The idea of the university" was a phrase to which Cardinal Newman had given currency in a remarkable series of letters in which he advocated the establishment of a Catholic foundation in Dublin. At a time when ecclesiastical or denominational colleges were at the front, and were considered by many people the only defensible places for the education of young men, his utterances for academic freedom were emancipating; at a time when early specialisation was advocated, his defence of liberal culture was reassuring. The evidence elicited by the British university commissions was instructive, and the writings of Mark Pattison, Dr. Appelton, Matthew Arnold, and others were full of suggestions. Innumerable essays and pamphlets had appeared in Germany discussing the improvements which were called for in that land of research. The endeavours of the new men at Cambridge and New Haven, and the instructive success of the University of Virginia, were all brought under consideration. Under these favourable circumstances, *Zeitgeist* they may be called, the Johns Hopkins was founded upon the idea of a university as distinct from a college.

The capital was provided by a single individual. No public meeting was ever held to promote subscriptions or to advocate higher education; no speculation in land was proposed; no financial gains were expected; no religious body was involved, not even the Society of orthodox Friends, in which the founder had been trained, and from which he selected several of his confidential advisers. He gave what seemed at the time a princely gift; he supplemented it with an equal gift for a hospital. It was natural that he should also give his name. That was then the fashion. . . .

Given the idea and the funds, the next requisite was a plan. In my first interviews with the trustees, I was strongly impressed by their desire to do the very best that was possible under the circumstances in which they were placed. We quickly reached concurrence. Without dissent, it was agreed that we were to develop, if possible, something more than a local institution, and were at least to aim at national influence; that we should try to supplement, and not supplant, existing colleges, and should endeavour to bring to Baltimore, as teachers and as students, the ablest minds that we could attract. It was understood that we should postpone all questions of building, dormitories, commons, discipline, and degrees; that we should hire or buy in the heart of the city a temporary perch, and remain on it until we could determine what wants should be revealed, and until we could decide upon future buildings. We were to await the choice of a faculty before we matured any schemes of examination, instruction, and graduation. . . .

2. *Charles William Eliot, Inaugural Address as President of Harvard, 1869*

Charles William Eliot (1834–1926) was born in Boston and graduated from Harvard in 1853, after which he became tutor of mathematics and assistant professor of mathematics and chemistry. From 1863 to 1865 he studied abroad, returning to take up a professorship of chemistry at the Massachusetts Institute of Technology. His observations of European education led to the publication of his

C. W. Eliot, *Educational Reform: Essays and Addresses* (New York, 1898), pp. 1–38.

important articles on "The New Education: Its Organization," excerpted in Doc. 3. His command of educational problems was among the factors leading to his choice as Harvard's president in 1869. His administration was one of great quantitative growth and qualitative progress for Harvard, involving among other things a complete reformation of the law school, the medical school, and Harvard College. Besides his general university reforms, Eliot espoused the "elective system" (see Part VIII, Doc. 2). In 1872 Harvard began to award advanced degrees, and in 1890 the graduate school was organized. Eliot was a vigorous and active figure, who published many works on educational and other problems. See Eliot's *Educational Reform* and *A Late Harvest*, with an introduction by M. A. DeWolfe Howe (Boston, 1924), as well as Henry James, *Charles W. Eliot* (2 vols.; Boston, 1930).

The endless controversies whether language, philosophy, mathematics, or science supplies the best mental training, whether general education should be chiefly literary or chiefly scientific, have no practical lesson for us to-day. This University recognizes no real antagonism between literature and science, and consents to no such narrow alternatives as mathematics or classics, science or metaphysics. We would have them all, and at their best. To observe keenly, to reason soundly, and to imagine vividly are operations as essential as that of clear and forcible expression; and to develop one of these faculties, it is not necessary to repress and dwarf the others. A university is not closely concerned with the applications of knowledge, until its general education branches into professional. Poetry and philosophy and science do indeed conspire to promote the material welfare of mankind; but science no more than poetry finds its best warrant in its utility. Truth and right are above utility in all realms of thought and action.

It were a bitter mockery to suggest that any subject whatever should be taught less than it now is in American colleges. The only conceivable aim of a college government in our day is to broaden, deepen, and invigorate American teaching in all branches of learning. It will be generations before the best of American institutions of education will get growth enough to bear pruning. The descendants of the Pilgrim Fathers are still very thankful for the parched corn of learning.

Recent discussions have added pitifully little to the world's stock of wisdom about the staple of education. Who blows to-day such a ringing trumpet-call to the study of language as Luther blew? Hardly a significant word has been added in two centuries to Milton's description of the unprofitable way to study languages. Would any young American learn how to profit by travel, that foolish beginning but excellent sequel to education, he can find no apter advice than Bacon's. The practice of England and America is literally centuries behind the precept of the best thinkers upon education. A striking illustration may be found in the prevailing neglect of the systematic study of the English language. How lamentably true to-day are these words of Locke: "If any one among us have a facility or purity more than ordinary in his mother-tongue, it is owing to chance, or his genius, or anything rather than to his education or any care of his teacher."

The best result of the discussion which has raged so long about the relative educational value of the main branches of learning is the conviction that there is room for them all in a sound scheme, provided that right methods of teaching be employed. It is not because of the limitation of their faculties that boys of eighteen come to college, having mastered nothing but a few score pages of Latin and Greek, and the bare elements of mathematics. Not nature, but an unintelligent system of instruction from the primary school through the college, is responsible for the fact that many college graduates have so inadequate a conception of what is meant by scientific observation, reasoning, and proof. It is possible for the young to get actual experience of all the principal methods of thought. There is a method of thought in language, and a method in mathematics, and another of natural and physical science, and another of faith. With wise direction, even a child would drink at all these springs. The actual problem to be solved is not what to teach, but how to teach. The revolutions accomplished in other fields of labor have a lesson for teachers. New England could not cut her hay with scythes, or the West her wheat with sickles. When millions are to be fed where formerly there were but scores, the single fish-line must be replaced by seines and trawls, the human shoulders by steam-elevators, and the wooden-axled ox-cart on a corduroy road by the smooth-running freight-train. In education, there is a great hungry multitude to be fed. The great well at Orvieto, up whose spiral paths files of donkeys painfully brought the sweet water in kegs, was an admirable construction in its day; but now we tap Fresh Pond in our chambers. The Orvieto well might remind some persons of educational methods not yet extinct. With good methods, we may confidently hope to give young men of twenty to twenty-five an accurate general knowledge of all the main subjects of human interest, besides a minute and thorough knowledge of the one subject which each may select as his principal occupation in life. To think this impossible is to despair of mankind; for unless a general acquaintance with many branches of knowledge, good so far as it goes, be attainable by great numbers of men, there can be no such thing as an intelligent public opinion; and in the modern world the intelligence of public opinion is the one indispensable condition of social progress.

What has been said of needed reformation in methods of teaching the subjects which have already been nominally admitted to the American curriculum applies not only to the university, but to the preparatory schools of every grade down to the primary. The American college is obliged to supplement the American school. Whatever elementary instruction the schools fail to give, the college must supply. The improvement of the schools has of late years permitted the college to advance the grade of its teaching, and adapt the methods of its later years to men instead of boys. This improvement of the college reacts upon the schools to their advantage; and this action and reaction will be continuous. A university is not built in the air, but on social and literary foundations which preceding generations have bequeathed. If the whole structure needs rebuilding, it must be rebuilt from the foundation. Hence, sudden reconstruction is impossible in our high places of education. Such inducements as the College can offer for enriching and enlarging the course of study pursued in preparatory schools, the Faculty has recently decided to give. The requirements in Latin and Greek grammar are to be set at a thorough knowledge of forms and general principles; the lists of classical authors accepted as equivalents for the regular standards are to be enlarged; an acquaintance with physical geography is to be required; the study of elementary mechanics is to be recommended, and prizes are to be offered for reading aloud, and for the critical analysis of passages from English authors. At the same time the University will take to heart the counsel which it gives to others.

In every department of learning the University would search out by trial and reflection the best methods of instruction. The University believes in the thorough study of language. It contends for all languages —Oriental, Greek, Latin, Romance, German, and especially for the mother-tongue; seeing in them all one institution, one history, one means of discipline, one department of learning. In teaching languages, it is for this American generation to invent, or to accept from abroad, better tools than the old; to devise, or to transplant from Europe, prompter and more comprehensive methods than the prevailing; and to command more intelligent labor, in order to gather rapidly and surely the best fruit of that culture and have time for other harvests.

The University recognizes the natural and physical sciences as indispensable branches of education, and has long acted upon this opinion; but it would have science taught in a rational way, objects and instruments in hand—not from books merely, not through the memory chiefly, but by the seeing eye and the informing fingers. Some of the scientific scoffers at gerund grinding and nonsense verses might well look at home; the prevailing methods of teaching science, the world over, are, on the whole, less intelligent than the methods of teaching language. The University would have scientific studies in school and college and professional school develop and discipline those powers of the mind by which science has been created and is daily nourished—the powers of observation, the inductive faculty, the sober imagination, the sincere and proportionate judgment. A student in the elements gets no such training by studying even a good text-book, though he really master it, nor yet by sitting at the feet of the most admirable lecturer.

If there be any subject which seems fixed and settled in its educational aspects, it is the mathematics; yet there is no department of the University which has been, during the last fifteen years, in such a state of vigorous experiment upon methods and appliances of teaching as the mathematical department. It would be well if the primary schools had as much faith in the possibility of improving their way of teaching multiplication.

The important place which history, and mental, moral, and political philosophy, should hold in any broad scheme of education is recognized of all; but none know so well how crude are the prevailing methods of teaching these subjects as those who teach them best. They cannot be taught from books alone, but must be vivified and illustrated by teachers of active, comprehensive, and judicial mind. To learn by rote a list of dates is not to study history. Mr. Emerson says that history is biography. In a deep sense this is true. Certainly, the best way to impart the facts of history to the young is through the quick interest they take in the lives of the men and women who fill great historical scenes or epitomize epochs. From the centers so established, their interest may be spread over great areas. For the young especially, it is better to enter with intense sympathy into the great moments of history, than to stretch a thin attention through its weary centuries.

Philosophical subjects should never be taught with authority. They are not established sciences; they are full of disputed matters, open questions, and bottomless speculations. It is not the function of the teacher to settle philosophical and political controversies for the pupil, or even to recommend to him any one set of opinions as better than another. Exposition, not imposition, of opinions is the professor's part. The student should be made acquainted with all sides of these controversies, with the salient points of each system; he should be shown what is still in force of institutions or philosophies mainly outgrown, and what is new in those now in vogue. The very word "education" is a standing protest against dogmatic teaching. The notion that education consists in the authoritative inculcation of what the teacher deems true may be logical and appropriate in a convent, or a seminary for priests, but it is intolerable in universities and public schools, from primary to professional. The worthy fruit of academic culture is an open mind, trained to careful thinking, instructed in the methods of philosophic investigation, acquainted in a general way with the accumulated thought of past generations, and penetrated with humility. It is thus that the university in our day serves Christ and the church.

The increasing weight, range, and thoroughness of the examination for admission to college may strike some observers with dismay. The increase of real requisitions is hardly perceptible from year to year; but on looking back ten or twenty years, the changes are marked, and all in one direction. The dignity and importance of this examination have been steadily rising, and this rise measures the improvement of the preparatory schools. When the gradual improvement of American schools has lifted them to a level with the German gymnasia, we may expect to see the American college bearing a nearer resemblance to the German faculties of philosophy than it now does. The actual admission examination may best be compared with the first examination of the University of France. This examination, which comes at the end of a French boy's school life, is for the degree of Bachelor of Arts or of Sciences. The degree is given to young men who come fresh from school and have never been under university teachers; a large part of the recipients never enter the university. The young men who come to our examination for admission to college are older than the average of French Bachelors of Arts. The examination tests not only the capacity of the candidates, but also the quality of their school instruction; it is a great event in their lives, though not, as in France, marked by any degree. The examination is conducted by college professors and tutors who have never had any relations whatever with those examined. It would be a great gain if all subsequent college examinations could be as impartially conducted by competent examiners brought from without the college and paid for their services. When the teacher examines his class, there is no effective examination of the teacher. If the examinations for the scientific, theological, medical, and dental degrees were conducted by independent boards of examiners, appointed by professional bodies of dignity and influence, the significance of these degrees would be greatly enhanced. The same might be said of the degree of Bachelor of Laws, were it not that this degree is, at present, earned by attendance alone, and not by attendance and examination. The American practice of allowing the teaching body to examine for degrees has been partly dictated by the scarcity of men outside the faculties who are at once thoroughly acquainted with the subjects of examination, and sufficiently versed in teaching to know what may fairly be expected of both students and instructors. This difficulty could now be overcome. The chief reason, however, for the existence of this practice is that the faculties were the only bodies that could confer degrees intelligently, when degrees were obtained by passing through a prescribed course of study without serious checks, and completing a certain term of residence without disgrace. The change in the manner of earning the University degrees ought, by right, to have brought into being an examining body distinct from the teaching body. So far as the College proper is concerned, the Board of Overseers have, during the past year, taken a step which tends in this direction.

The rigorous examination for admission has one good effect throughout the college course: it prevents a waste of instruction upon incompetent persons. A school with a low standard for admission and a high standard of graduation, like West Point, is obliged to dismiss a large proportion of its students by the way. Hence much individual distress, and a great waste of resources, both public and private. But, on the other hand, it must not be supposed that every student who enters Harvard College necessarily graduates. Strict annual examinations are to be passed. More than a fourth of those who enter the College fail to take their degree.

Only a few years ago, all students who graduated at this College passed through one uniform curriculum. Every man studied the same subjects in the same proportions, without regard to his natural bent or preference. The individual student had no choice of either subjects or teachers. This system is still the prevailing system among American colleges, and finds vigorous defenders. It has the merit of simplicity. So had the school methods of our grandfathers—one primer, one catechism, one rod for all children. On the whole, a single common course of studies, tolerably well selected to meet the average needs, seems to most Americans a very proper and natural thing, even for grown men.

As a people, we do not apply to mental activities the principle of division of labor; and we have but a halting faith in special training for high professional employments. The vulgar conceit that a Yankee can turn his hand to anything we insensibly carry into high places, where it is preposterous and criminal. We are accustomed to seeing men leap from farm or shop to court-room or pulpit, and we half believe that common men can safely use the seven-league boots of genius. What amount of knowledge and experience do we habitually demand of our lawgivers? What special training do we ordinarily think necessary for our diplomatists?—although in great emergencies the nation has known where to turn. Only after years of the bitterest experience did we come to believe the professional training of a soldier to be of value in war. This lack of faith in the prophecy of a natural bent, and in the value of a discipline concentrated upon a single object, amounts to a national danger.

In education, the individual traits of different minds have not been sufficiently attended to. Through all the period of boyhood the school studies should be representative; all the main fields of knowledge should be entered upon. But the young man of nineteen or twenty ought to know what he likes best and is most fit for. If his previous training has been sufficiently wide, he will know by that time whether he is most apt at language or philosophy or natural science or mathematics. If he feels no loves, he will at least have his hates. At that age the teacher may wisely abandon the school-dame's practice of giving a copy of nothing but zeros to the child who alleges that he cannot make that figure. When the revelation of his own peculiar taste and capacity comes to a young man, let him reverently give it welcome, thank God, and take courage. Thereafter he knows his way to happy, enthusiastic work, and, God willing, to usefulness and success. The civilization of a people may be inferred from the variety of its tools. There are thousands of years between the stone hatchet and the machine-shop. As tools multiply, each is more ingeniously adapted to its own exclusive purpose. So with the men that make the State. For the individual, concentration, and the highest development of his own peculiar faculty, is the only prudence. But for the State, it is variety, not uniformity, of intellectual product, which is needful.

These principles are the justification of the system of elective studies which has been gradually developed in this College during the past forty years. At present the Freshman year is the only one in which there is a fixed course prescribed for all. In the other three years, more than half the time allotted to study is filled with subjects chosen by each student from lists which comprise six studies in the Sophomore year, nine in the Junior year, and eleven in the Senior year. The range of elective studies is large, though there are some striking deficiencies. The liberty of choice of subject is wide, but yet has very rigid limits. There is a certain framework which must be filled; and about half the material of the filling is prescribed. The choice offered to the student does not lie between liberal studies and professional or utilitarian studies. All the studies which are open to him are liberal and disciplinary, not narrow or special. Under this system the College does not demand, it is true, one invariable set of studies of every candidate for the first degree in Arts; but its requisitions for this degree are nevertheless high and inflexible, being nothing less than four years devoted to liberal culture.

It has been alleged that the elective system must weaken the bond which unites members of the same class. This is true; but in view of another much more efficient cause of the diminution of class intimacy, the point is not very significant. The increased size of the college classes inevitably works a great change in this respect. One hundred and fifty young men cannot be so intimate with each other as fifty used to be. This increase is progressive. Taken in connection with the rising average age of the students, it would compel the adoption of methods of instruction different from the old, if there were no better motive for such change. The elective system fosters scholarship, because it gives free play to natural preferences and inborn aptitudes, makes possible enthusiasm for a chosen work, relieves the professor and the ardent disciple of the presence of a body of students who are compelled to an unwelcome task, and enlarges instruction by substituting many and various lessons given to small, lively classes, for a few lessons many times repeated to different sections of a numerous class. The College therefore proposes to persevere in its efforts to establish, improve, and extend the elective system. Its administrative difficulties, which seem formidable at first, vanish before a brief experience.

There has been much discussion about the comparative merits of lectures and recitations. Both are useful—lectures, for inspiration, guidance, and the comprehensive methodizing which only one who has a view of the whole field can rightly contrive; recitations, for securing and testifying a thorough mastery on the part of the pupil of the treatise or author in hand, for conversational comment and amplification, for emulation and competition. Recitations alone readily degenerate into dusty repetitions, and lectures alone are too often a useless expenditure of force. The lecturer pumps laboriously into sieves. The water may be wholesome, but it runs through. A mind must work to grow. Just as far, however, as the student can be relied on to master and appreciate his author without the aid of frequent questioning and repetitions, so far is it possible to dispense with recitations. Accordingly, in the later College years there is a decided tendency to diminish the number of recitations, the faithfulness of the student being tested by periodical examinations. This tendency is in a right direction, if prudently controlled.

The discussion about lectures and recitations has brought out some strong opinions about text-books and their use. Impatience with text-books and manuals is very natural in both teachers and taught. These books are indeed, for the most part, very imperfect, and stand in constant need of correction by the well-informed teacher. Stereotyping, in its present undeveloped condition, is in part to blame for their most exasperating defects. To make the metal plates keep pace with the progress of learning is costly. The manifest deficiencies of text-books must not, however, drive us into a too sweeping condemnation of their use. It is a rare teacher who is superior to all manuals in his subject. Scientific manuals are, as a rule, much worse than those upon language, literature, or philosophy; yet the main improvement in medical education in this country during the last twenty years has been the addition of systematic recitations from text-books to the lectures which were formerly the principal means of theoretical instruction. The training of a medical student, inadequate as it is, offers the best example we have of the methods and fruits of an education mainly scientific. The transformation which the average student of a good medical school undergoes in three years is strong testimony to the efficiency of the training he receives.

There are certain common misapprehensions about colleges in general, and this College in particular, to which I wish to devote a few moments' attention. And, first, in spite of the familiar picture of the moral dangers which environ the student, there is no place so safe as a good college during the critical passage from boyhood to manhood. The security of the college commonwealth is largely due to its exuberant activity. Its public opinion, though easily led astray, is still high in the main. Its scholarly tastes and habits, its eager friendships and quick hatreds, its keen debates, its frank discussions of character and of deep political and religious questions, all are safeguards against sloth, vulgarity, and depravity. Its society and, not less, its solitudes are full of teaching. Shams, conceit, and fictitious distinctions get no mercy. There is nothing but ridicule for bombast and sentimentality. Repression of genuine sentiment and emotion is indeed, in this College, carried too far. Reserve is more respectable than any undiscerning communicativeness; but neither Yankee shamefacedness nor English stolidity is admirable. This point especially touches you, young men, who are still undergraduates. When you feel a true admiration for a teacher, a glow of enthusiasm for work, a thrill of pleasure at some excellent saying, give it expression. Do not be ashamed of these emotions. Cherish the natural sentiment of personal devotion to the teacher who calls out your better powers. It is a great delight to serve an intellectual master. We Americans are but too apt to lose this happiness. German and French students get it. If ever in after years you come to smile at the youthful reverence you paid, believe me, it will be with tears in your eyes.

Many excellent persons see great offense in any system of college rank; but why should we expect more of young men than we do of their elders? How many men and women perform their daily tasks from the highest motives alone—for the glory of God and the relief of man's estate? Most people work for bare bread, a few for cake. The college rank-list reinforces higher motives. In the campaign for character, no auxiliaries are to be refused. Next to despising the enemy, it is dangerous to reject allies. To devise a suitable method of estimating the fidelity and attainments of college students is, however, a problem which has long been under discussion, and has not yet received a satisfactory solution. The worst of rank as a stimulus is the self-reference it implies in the aspirants. The less a young man thinks about the cultivation of his mind, about his own mental progress,—about himself, in short,—the better.

The petty discipline of colleges attracts altogether too much attention from both friends and foes. It is to be remembered that the rules concerning decorum, however necessary to maintain the high standard of manners and conduct which characterizes this College, are nevertheless justly described as petty. What is technically called a quiet term cannot be accepted as the acme of university success. This success is not to be measured by the frequency or rarity of college punishments. The criteria of success or failure in a high place of learning are not the boyish escapades of an insignificant minority, nor the exceptional cases of ruinous vice. Each year must be judged by the added opportunities of instruction, by the prevailing enthusiasm in learning, and by the gathered wealth of culture and character. The best way to put boyishness to shame is to foster scholarship and manliness. The manners of a community cannot be improved by main force any more than its morals. The Statutes of the University need some amendment and reduction in the chapters on crimes and misdemeanors. But let us render to our fathers the justice we shall need from our sons. What is too minute or precise for our use was doubtless wise and proper in its day. It was to inculcate a reverent bearing and due consideration for things sacred that the regulations prescribed a black dress on Sunday. Black is not the only decorous wear in these days; but we must not seem, in ceasing from this particular mode of good manners, to think less of the gentle breeding of which only the outward signs, and not the substance, have been changed.

Harvard College has always attracted and still attracts students in all conditions of life. From the city trader or professional man, who may be careless how much his son spends at Cambridge, to the farmer or mechanic, who finds it a hard sacrifice to give his boy his time early enough to enable him to prepare for college, all sorts and conditions of men have wished and still wish to send their sons hither. There are always scores of young men in this University who earn or borrow every dollar they spend here. Every year many young men enter this

College without any resources whatever. If they prove themselves men of capacity and character, they never go away for lack of money. More than twenty thousand dollars a year is now devoted to aiding students of narrow means to compass their education, besides all the remitted fees and the numerous private benefactions. These latter are unfailing. Taken in connection with the proceeds of the funds applicable to the aid of poor students, they enable the Corporation to say that no good student need ever stay away from Cambridge or leave college simply because he is poor. There is one uniform condition, however, on which help is given: the recipient must be of promising ability and the best character. The community does not owe superior education to all children, but only to the élite—to those who, having the capacity, prove by hard work that they have also the necessary perseverance and endurance. The process of preparing to enter college under the difficulties which poverty entails is just such a test of worthiness as is needed. At this moment there is no college in the country more eligible for a poor student than Harvard on the mere ground of economy. The scholarship funds are mainly the fruit of the last fifteen years. The future will take care of itself; for it is to be expected that the men who in this generation have had the benefit of these funds, and who succeed in after life, will pay manyfold to their successors in need the debt which they owe, not to the College, but to benefactors whom they cannot even thank, save in heaven. No wonder that scholarships are founded. What greater privilege than this of giving young men of promise the coveted means of intellectual growth and freedom? The angels of heaven might envy mortals so fine a luxury. The happiness which the winning of a scholarship gives is not the recipient's alone: it flashes back to the home whence he came, and gladdens anxious hearts there. The good which it does is not his alone, but descends, multiplying at every step, through generations. Thanks to the beneficent mysteries of hereditary transmission, no capital earns such interest as personal culture. The poorest and the richest students are equally welcome here, provided that with their poverty or their wealth they bring capacity, ambition, and purity. The poverty of scholars is of inestimable worth in this money-getting nation. It maintains the true standards of virtue and honor. The poor friars, not the bishops, saved the church. The poor scholars and preachers of duty defend the modern community against its own material prosperity. Luxury and learning are ill bedfellows. Nevertheless, this College owes much of its distinctive character to those who, bringing hither from refined homes good breeding, gentle tastes, and a manly delicacy, add to them openness and activity of mind, intellectual interests, and a sense of public duty. It is as high a privilege for a rich man's son as for a poor man's to resort to these academic halls, and so to take his proper place among cultivated and intellectual men. To lose altogether the presence of those who in early life have enjoyed the domestic and social advantages of wealth would be as great a blow to the College as to lose the sons of the poor. The interests of the College and the country are identical in this regard. The country suffers when the rich are ignorant and unrefined. Inherited wealth is an unmitigated curse when divorced from culture. Harvard College is sometimes reproached with being aristocratic. If by aristocracy be meant a stupid and pretentious caste, founded on wealth, and birth, and an affectation of European manners, no charge could be more preposterous: the College is intensely American in affection, and intensely democratic in temper. But there is an aristocracy to which the sons of Harvard have belonged, and, let us hope, will ever aspire to belong—the aristocracy which excels in manly sports, carries off the honors and prizes of the learned professions, and bears itself with distinction in all fields of intellectual labor and combat; the aristocracy which in peace stands firmest for the public honor and renown, and in war rides first into the murderous thickets.

The attitude of the University in the prevailing discussions touching the education and fit employments of women demands brief explanation. America is the natural arena for these debates; for here the female sex has a better past and a better present than elsewhere. Americans, as a rule, hate disabilities of all sorts, whether religious, political, or social. Equality between the sexes, without privilege or oppression on either side, is the happy custom of American homes. While this great discussion is going on, it is the duty of the University to maintain a cautious and expectant policy. The Corporation will not receive women as students into the College proper, nor into any school whose discipline requries residence near the school. The difficulties involved in a common residence of hundreds of young men and women of immature character and marriageable age are very grave. The necessary police regulations are exceedingly burdensome. The Corporation are not influenced to this decision, however, by any crude notions about the innate capacities of women. The world knows next to nothing about the natural mental capacities of the female sex. Only after generations of civil freedom and social equality will it be possible to obtain the data necessary for an adequate discussion of woman's natural tendencies, tastes, and capabilities. Again, the Corporation do not find it necessary to entertain a confident opinion upon the fitness or unfitness of women for professional pursuits. It is not the business of the University to decide this mooted point. In this country the University does not undertake to protect the community against incompetent lawyers, ministers, or doctors. The community must protect itself by refusing to employ such. Practical, not theoretical, considerations determine the policy of the University. Upon a matter concerning which prejudices are deep, and opinion inflammable, and experience scanty, only one course is prudent or justifiable when such great interests are at stake— that of cautious and well-considered experiment. The practical problem is to devise a safe, promising, and instructive experiment. Such an experiment the Corporation have meant to try in opening the newly established University Courses of Instruction to competent women. In these courses the University offers to young women who have been to good schools as many years as they wish of liberal culture in studies which have no direct professional value, to be sure, but which enrich and enlarge both intellect and character. The University hopes thus to contribute to the intellectual emancipation of women. It hopes to prepare some women better than they would otherwise have been prepared for the profession of teaching, the one learned profession to which women have already acquired a clear title. It hopes that the proffer of this higher instruction will have some reflex influence upon schools for girls—to discourage superficiality, and to promote substantial education.

The governing bodies of the University are the Faculties, the Board of Overseers, and the Corporation. The University as a place of study and instruction is, at any moment, what the Faculties make it. The professors, lecturers, and tutors of the University are the living sources of learning and enthusiasm. They personally represent the possibilities of instruction. They are united in several distinct bodies, the academic and professional Faculties, each of which practically determines its own processes and rules. The discussion of methods of instruction is the principal business of these bodies. As a fact, progress comes mainly from the Faculties. This has been conspicuously the case with the Academic and Medical Faculties during the last fifteen or twenty years. The undergraduates used to have a notion that the time of the Academic Faculty was mainly devoted to petty discipline. Nothing could be further from the truth. The Academic Faculty is the most active, vigilant, and devoted body connected with the University. It indeed is constantly obliged to discuss minute details, which might appear trivial to an inexperienced observer. But, in education, technical details tell. Whether German be studied by the Juniors once a week as an extra study, or twice a week as an elective, seems, perhaps, an unimportant matter; but, twenty years hence, it makes all the difference between a generation of Alumni who know German and a generation who do not. The Faculty renews its youth, through the frequent appointments of tutors and assistant professors, better and oftener than any other organization within the University. Two kinds of men make good teachers—young men and men who never grow old. The incessant discussions of the Academic Faculty have borne much fruit: witness the transformation of the University since the beginning of President Walker's administration. And it never tires. New men take up the old debates, and one year's progress is not less than another's. The divisions within the Faculty are never between the old and the young officers. There are always old radicals and young conservatives.

The Medical Faculty affords another illustration of the same principle—that for real university progress we must look principally to the teaching bodies. The Medical School to-day is almost three times as strong as it was fifteen years ago. Its teaching power is greatly increased, and its methods have been much improved. This gain is the work of the Faculty of the School.

If then the Faculties be so important, it is a vital question how the quality of these bodies can be maintained and improved. It is very hard to find competent professors for the University. Very few Americans of eminent ability are attracted to this profession. The pay has been too low, and there has been no gradual rise out of drudgery, such as may reasonably be expected in other learned callings. The law of supply and demand, or the commercial principle that the quality as well as the price of goods is best regulated by the natural contest between producers and consumers, never has worked well in the province of high education. And in spite of the high standing of some of its advocates, it is well-nigh certain that the so-called law never can work well in such a field. The reason is that the demand for instructors of the highest class on the part of parents and trustees is an ignorant demand, and the supply of highly educated teachers is so limited that the consumer has not sufficient opportunities of informing himself concerning the real qualities of the article he seeks. Originally a bad judge, he remains a bad judge, because the supply is not sufficiently abundant and various to instruct him. Moreover, a need is not necessarily a demand. Everybody knows that the supposed law affords a very imperfect protection against short weight, adulteration, and sham, even in the case of those commodities which are most abundant in the market and most familiar to buyers. The most intelligent community is defenseless enough in buying clothes and groceries. When it comes to hiring learning and inspiration and personal weight, the law of supply and demand breaks down altogether. A university cannot be managed like a railroad or a cotton-mill.

There are, however, two practicable improvements in the position of college professors which will be of very good effect. Their regular stipend must and will be increased, and the repetitions which now harass them must be diminished in number. It is a strong point of the elective system that, by reducing the size of classes or divisions, and increasing the variety of subjects, it makes the professors' labors more agreeable.

Experience teaches that the strongest and most devoted professors will contribute something to the patrimony of knowledge; or if they invent little themselves, they will do something toward defending, interpreting, or diffusing the contributions of others. Nevertheless, the prime business of American professors in this generation must be regular and assiduous class teaching. With the exception of the endowments of the Observatory, the University does not hold a single fund primarily intended to secure to men of learning the leisure and means to prosecute original researches.

The organization and functions of the Board of Overseers deserve the serious attention of all men who are interested in the American method of providing the community with high education through the agency of private corporations. Since 1866 the Overseers have been elected by the Alumni. Five men are chosen each year to serve six years. The body has, therefore, a large and very intelligent constituency, and is rapidly renewed. The ingenious method of nominating to the electors twice as many candidates as there are places to be filled in any year is worthy of careful study as a device of possible application in politics. The real function of the Board of Overseers is to stimulate and watch the President and Fellows. Without the Overseers, the President and Fellows would be a board of private trustees, self-perpetuated and self-controlled. Provided as it is with two governing boards, the University enjoys that principal safeguard of all American governments—the natural antagonism between two bodies of different constitution, powers, and privileges. While having with the Corporation a common interest of the deepest kind in the welfare of the University and the advancement of learning, the Overseers should always hold toward the Corporation an attitude of suspicious vigilance. They ought always to be pushing and prying. It would be hard to overstate the importance of the public supervision exercised by the Board of Overseers. Experience proves that our main hope for the permanence and ever-widening usefulness of the University must rest upon this double-headed organization. The English practice of setting up a single body of private trustees to carry on a school or charity according to the personal instructions of some founder or founders has certainly proved a lamentably bad one; and when we count by generations, the institutions thus established have proved shortlived. The same causes which have brought about the decline of English endowed schools would threaten the life of this University were it not for the existence of the Board of Overseers. These schools were generally managed by close corporations, self-elected, self-controlled, without motive for activity, and destitute of external stimulus and aid. Such bodies are too irresponsible for human nature. At the time of life at which men generally come to such places of trust, rest is sweet, and the easiest way is apt to seem the best way; and the responsibility of inaction, though really heavier, seems lighter than the responsibility of action. These corporations were often hampered by founders' wills and statutory provisions which could not be executed, and yet stood in the way of organic improvements. There was no systematic provision for thorough inspections and public reports thereupon. We cannot flatter ourselves that under like circumstances we should always be secure against like dangers. Provoked by crying abuses, some of the best friends of education in England have gone the length of maintaining that all these school endowments ought to be destroyed, and the future creation of such trusts rendered impossible. French law practically prohibits the creation of such trusts by private persons.

Incident to the Overseers' power of inspecting the University and

publicly reporting upon its condition, is the important function of suggesting and urging improvements. The inertia of a massive University
is formidable. A good past is positively dangerous, if it make us content with the present, and so unprepared for the future. The present
constitution of our Board of Overseers has already stimulated the
Alumni of several other New England colleges to demand a similar
control over the property-holding board of trustees which has heretofore been the single source of all authority.

We come now to the heart of the University—the Corporation. This
board holds the funds, makes appointments, fixes salaries, and has, by
right, the initiative in all changes of the organic law of the University.
Such an executive board must be small to be efficient. It must always
contain men of sound judgment in finance; and literature and the
learned professions should be adequately represented in it. The Corporation should also be but slowly renewed; for it is of the utmost
consequence to the University that the Government should have a
steady aim, and a prevailing spirit which is independent of individuals
and transmissible from generation to generation. And what should this
spirit be? First, it should be a catholic spirit. A university must be indigenous; it must be rich; but, above all, it must be free. The winnowing breeze of freedom must blow through all its chambers. It takes a
hurricane to blow wheat away. An atmosphere of intellectual freedom
is the native air of literature and science. This University aspires to
serve the nation by training men to intellectual honesty and independence of mind. The Corporation demands of all its teachers that
they be grave, reverent, and high-minded; but it leaves them, like their
pupils, free. A university is built, not by a sect, but by a nation.
Secondly, the actuating spirit of the Corporation must be a spirit of
fidelity—fidelity to the many and various trusts reposed in them by
the hundreds of persons who, out of their penury or their abundance,
have given money to the President and Fellows of Harvard College in
the beautiful hope of doing some perpetual good upon this earth. The
Corporation has constantly done its utmost to make this hope a living
fact. One hundred and ninety-nine years ago, William Pennoyer gave
the rents of certain estates in the county of Norfolk, England, that
"two fellows and two scholars forever should be educated, brought up,
and maintained" in this College. The income from this bequest has
never failed; and to-day one of the four Pennoyer scholarships is held

by a lineal descendant of William Pennoyer's brother Robert. So a lineal descendant of Governor Danforth takes this year the income of the property which Danforth bequeathed to the College in 1699. The Corporation have been as faithful in the greater things as in the less. They have been greatly blessed in one respect: in the whole life of the Corporation, seven generations of men, nothing has ever been lost by malfeasance of officers or servants. A reputation for scrupulous fidelity to all trusts is the most precious possession of the Corporation. That safe, the College might lose everything else and yet survive; that lost beyond repair, and the days of the College would be numbered. Testators look first to the trustworthiness and permanence of the body which is to dispense their benefactions. The Corporation thankfully receive all gifts which may advance learning; but they believe that the interests of the University may be most effectually promoted by not restricting too narrowly the use to which a gift may be applied. Whenever the giver desires it, the Corporation will agree to keep any fund separately invested under the name of the giver, and to apply the whole proceeds of such investment to any object the giver may designate. By such special investment, however, the insurance which results from the absorption of a specific gift in the general funds is lost. A fund invested by itself may be impaired or lost by a single error of judgment in investing. The chance of such loss is small in any one generation, but appreciable in centuries. Such general designations as salaries, books, dormitories, public buildings, scholarships graduate or undergraduate, scientific collections, and expenses of experimental laboratories, are of permanent significance and effect; while experience proves that too specific and minute directions concerning the application of funds must often fail of fulfilment, simply in consequence of the changing needs and habits of successive generations.

Again, the Corporation should always be filled with the spirit of enterprise. An institution like this College is getting decrepit when it sits down contentedly on its mortgages. On its invested funds the Corporation should be always seeking how safely to make a quarter of a per cent. more. A quarter of one per cent. means a new professorship. It should be always pushing after more professorships, better professors, more land and buildings, and better apparatus. It should be eager, sleepless, and untiring, never wasting a moment in counting laurels won, ever prompt to welcome and apply the liberality of the community, and liking no prospect so well as that of difficulties to be overcome and labors to be done in the cause of learning and public virtue.

You recognize, gentlemen, the picture which I have drawn in thus delineating the true spirit of the Corporation of this College. I have described the noble quintessence of the New England character—that character which has made us a free and enlightened people; that character which, please God, shall yet do a great work in the world for the lifting up of humanity.

Apart from the responsibility which rests upon the Corporation, its actual labors are far heavier than the community imagines. The business of the University has greatly increased in volume and complexity during the past twenty years, and the drafts made upon the time and thought of every member of the Corporation are heavy indeed. The high honors of the function are in these days most generously earned.

The President of the University is primarily an executive officer; but, being a member of both governing boards and of all the faculties, he has also the influence in their debates to which his more or less perfect intimacy with the University and greater or less personal weight may happen to entitle him. An administrative officer who undertakes to do everything himself will do but little, and that little ill. The President's first duty is that of supervision. He should know what each officer's and servant's work is, and how it is done. But the days are past in which the President could be called on to decide everything from the purchase of a door-mat to the appointment of a professor. The principle of divided and subordinate responsibilities, which rules in government bureaus, in manufactories, and all great companies, which makes a modern army a possibility, must be applied in the University. The President should be able to discern the practical essence of complicated and long-drawn discussions. He must often pick out that promising part of theory which ought to be tested by experiment, and must decide how many of things desirable are also attainable, and what one of many projects is ripest for execution. He must watch and look before—watch, to seize opportunities to get money, to secure eminent teachers and scholars, and to influence public opinion toward the advancement of learning; and look before, to anticipate the due effect on the University of the fluctuations of public opinion on educational problems; of the progress of the institutions which feed the University; of the changing condition of the professions which the University supplies; of the rise of new professions; of the gradual alteration of social and religious habits in the community. The University must accommodate itself promptly to significant changes in the character of the people for whom it exists. The institutions of higher education in any nation are always a faithful mirror in which are sharply reflected the national history and character. In this mobile nation the action and reaction between the University and society at large are more sensitive and rapid than in stiffer communities. The President, therefore, must not need to see a house built before he can comprehend the plan of it. He can profit by a wide intercourse with all sorts of men, and by every real discussion on education, legislation, and sociology.

The most important function of the President is that of advising the Corporation concerning appointments, particularly about appointments of young men who have not had time and opportunity to approve themselves to the public. It is in discharging this duty that the President holds the future of the University in his hands. He cannot do it well unless he have insight, unless he be able to recognize, at times beneath some crusts, the real gentleman and the natural teacher. This is the one oppressive responsibility of the President: all other cares are light beside it. To see every day the evil fruit of a bad appointment must be the cruelest of official torments. Fortunately, the good effect of a judicious appointment is also inestimable; and here, as everywhere, good is more penetrating and diffusive than evil.

It is imperative that the statutes which define the President's duties should be recast, and the customs of the College be somewhat modified, in order that lesser duties may not crowd out the greater. But, however important the functions of the President, it must not be forgotten that he is emphatically a constitutional executive. It is his character and his judgment which are of importance, not his opinions. He is the executive officer of deliberative bodies, in which decisions are reached after discussion by a majority vote. Those decisions bind him. He cannot force his own opinions upon anybody. A university is the last place in the world for a dictator. Learning is always republican. It has idols, but not masters.

What can the community do for the University? It can love, honor, and cherish it. Love it and honor it. The University is upheld by this public affection and respect. In the loyalty of her children she finds strength and courage. The Corporation, the Overseers, and the several faculties need to feel that the leaders of public opinion, and especially the sons of the College, are at their back, always ready to give them a generous and intelligent support. Therefore we welcome the Chief Magistrate of the Commonwealth, the Senators, Judges, and other dignitaries of the State, who by their presence at this ancient ceremonial bear witness to the pride which Massachusetts feels in her eldest university. Therefore we rejoice in the presence of this throng of the Alumni testifying their devotion to the College which through all changes, is still their home. Cherish it. This University, though rich among American colleges, is very poor in comparison with the great universities of Europe. The wants of the American community have far outgrown the capacity of the University to supply them. We must try to satisfy the cravings of the select few as well as the needs of the average many. We cannot afford to neglect the Fine Arts. We need groves and meadows as well as barracks; and soon there will be no chance to get them in this expanding city. But, above all, we need professorships, books, and apparatus, that teaching and scholarship may abound.

And what will the University do for the community? First, it will make a rich return of learning, poetry, and piety. Secondly, it will foster the sense of public duty—that great virtue which makes republics possible. The founding of Harvard College was an heroic act of public spirit. For more than a century the breath of life was kept in it by the public spirit of the Province and of its private benefactors. In the last fifty years the public spirit of the friends of the College has quadrupled its endowments. And how have the young men nurtured here in successive generations repaid the founders for their pious care? Have they honored freedom and loved their country? For answer we appeal to the records of the national service; to the lists of the Senate, the cabinet, and the diplomatic service, and to the rolls of the army and navy. Honored men, here present, illustrate before the world the public quality of the graduates of this College. Theirs is no mercenary service. Other fields of labor attract them more and would reward them better; but they are filled with the noble ambition to deserve well of the republic. There have been doubts, in times yet recent, whether culture were not selfish; whether men of refined tastes and manners could really love Liberty, and be ready to endure hardness for her sake; whether, in short, gentlemen would in this century prove as loyal to noble ideas as in other times they had been to kings. In yonder old playground, fit spot whereon to commemorate the manliness which there was nurtured, shall soon rise a noble monument which for generations will give convincing answer to such shallow doubts; for over its gates will be written: "In memory of the sons of Harvard who died for their country." The future of the University will not be unworthy of its past.

3. *Eliot on the Scientific Schools, 1869*

See Doc. 2.

"What can I do with my boy? I can afford, and am glad, to give him the best training to be had. I should be proud to have him turn out a preacher or a learned man; but I don't think he has the making of that in him. I want to give him a practical education; one that will prepare him, better than I was prepared, to follow my business or any other active calling. The classical schools and the colleges do not offer what I want. Where can I put him?" Here is a real need and a very serious problem. The difficulty presses more heavily upon the thoughtful American than upon the European. He is absolutely free to choose a way of life for himself and his children; no government leading-strings or social prescriptions guide or limit him in his choice. But freedom is responsibility. Secondly, being thus free, and being also in face of prodigious material resources of a vast and new territory, he is more fully awake than the European can be to the gravity and urgency of the problem. Thirdly, he has fewer means than any other, except the English parent, of solving the problem to his son's advantage. . . .

No thoughtful American in active life reaches manhood without painfully realizing the deficiencies and shortcomings of his own early training. He knows how ignorance balks and competition overwhelms, but he knows also the greatness of the material prizes to be won. He is anxious to have his boys better equipped for the American man's life than he himself was. It is useless to commend to him the good old ways, the established methods. He has a decided opinion that there are

C. W. Eliot, "The New Education," *Atlantic Monthly,* XXIII (February and March, 1869), 202–20, 365–66.

or ought to be better ways. He will not believe that the same methods which trained some boys well for the life of fifty or one hundred years ago are applicable to his son; for the reason, that the kind of man which he wants his son to make did not exist in all the world fifty years ago. So without any clear idea of what a practical education is, but still with some tolerably distinct notion of what it is not, he asks, "How can I give my boy a practical education?"

Thanks to the experience gained during the last twenty years in this country, it is easier to answer this question than it used to be. Certain experiments have been tried whose collective results are instructive. There have been found many American parents willing to try new experiments even in the irrevocable matter of their children's education, so impressed were they with the insufficiency of the established system. It requires courage to quit the beaten paths in which the great majority of well-educated men have walked and still walk. . . .

Without a wide-spreading organization, no system of education can have large success. The organization of the American colleges and their connections is extensive and inflexible. Endowed institutions offer teaching at less than its cost. A large number of professors trained in the existing methods hold firm possession, and transmit the traditions they inherited. Then there are the recognized text-books, mostly of exquisite perverseness, but backed by the reputation of their authors and the capital of their publishers. Lastly, the colleges have regular inlets and outlets. They are steadily fed by schools whose masters are inspired by the colleges, and they as regularly feed all the real and all the so-called learned professions.

The new education must also be successfully organized, if it would live. A system of education which attracts no great number of boys, which unites its disciples in no strong bonds of common associations and good-fellowship, and which, after years of trial, is not highly organized with well-graded schools, numerous teachers, good text-books, and a large and increasing body of attached alumni, has no strong hold upon the community in which it exists. Let us see what has been done towards this organization.

We wish to review the recent experience of this country in the attempt to organize a system of education based chiefly upon the pure and applied sciences, the living European languages, and mathematics, instead of upon Greek, Latin, and mathematics, as in the established college system. The history of education is full of still-born theories;

the literature of the subject is largely made up of theorizing; whoever reads it much will turn with infinite relief to the lessons of experience. But it should be observed that it is experience in mass, the experience of institutions, the experience of a generation, and not individual experience, which is of value. To have been a schoolmaster or college professor thirty years only too often makes a man an unsafe witness in matters of education: there are flanges on his mental wheels which will only fit one gauge. On the other hand, it must be acknowledged that conservatism is never more respectable than in education, for nowhere are the risks of change greater. . . .

We must begin our survey with the institutions of highest grade, because from the parent's point of view the higher school necessarily determines in large measure the nature of the lower school, just as the shape, weight, and bearings of a superstructure determine the form and quality of its foundations. The foundation-plan is the last to leave a careful architect's office. In choosing a preparatory school, the careful parent will consider to what it leads; above all, he will make sure that the school is not an *impasse*. The higher and lower institutions are, indeed, mutually dependent; if the admission examinations of the colleges and polytechnic schools seem, on the one hand, to sharply define the studies of the preparatory schools; on the other hand, it is quite as true that the colleges and advanced schools are practically controlled in their requisitions by the actual state of the preparatory schools. They can only ask for what is to be had. They must accept such preparation as the schools can give.

Institutions which exist only on paper, or which have been so lately organized that their term of actual work is only counted by months, will not be alluded to. The agricultural colleges begotten by Congress are all in this category. A large school can hardly get under way in less than four or five years. Three kinds of institutions or organizations for giving the new education are to be distinguished: the scientific "schools" connected with colleges; the scientific "courses" organized within colleges; and the independent "schools" especially devoted to non-classical education. These three organizations will be considered in succession.

The greater part of the "scientific schools" of the United States are connected with colleges. Such are the Sheffield Scientific School of Yale College, the Lawrence Scientific School at Harvard College, the Chandler Scientific School of Dartmouth College, and the School of Mines of Columbia College. Two considerations seemed to justify this connection: first, the natural desire to utilize the libraries, collections, and cabinets of apparatus already belonging to the colleges; and, secondly, the expectation of engaging the professors of the colleges in the work of the new schools. It was thought that an unnecessary duplication of buildings, equipments, and salaries might thus be avoided. These advantages have been in part realized, but only in part. The scientific schools have needed separate buildings, and to a large extent separate apparatus and separate professorships; but the college libraries have been a gain to them, and some courses of lectures, delivered to undergraduates of the colleges, have been open to the students of the scientific schools, though not always much resorted to by them. Except at Dartmouth, the aid of the college professors has been more apparent than real, because, being greatly overtasked with college work, these professors have had little time or energy to spare for the scientific schools.

A decided disadvantage is to be offset against any advantages which the scientific schools may have gained from their association with established colleges. A new system of education, crude, ill-organized, and in good degree experimental, has been brought into direct comparison and daily contact with a well-tried system in full possession of the field. The foundling has suffered by comparison with the children of the house. Even where there have been no jealousies about money or influence, and no jarrings about theological tendencies or religious temper, the faculty and students of the scientific school have necessarily felt themselves in an inferior position to the college proper as regards property, numbers, and the confidence of the community. They have been in a defensive attitude. It is the story of the ugly duckling.

An impression prevailed at the outset, that a scientific school was to be a professional school in the same sense as a law or medical school, and that graduates of the colleges would continue their studies in the scientific schools precisely as they do in the schools of law, medicine, and theology. The men who projected the Harvard and Yale schools were evidently under this impression. Experience has shown that the scientific schools proper are not recruited in this manner to any considerable extent. . . .

Whatever, therefore, may have been the anticipations of their founders, it is evident that, as a matter of fact, the scientific schools, as they have been actually conducted, have not attracted college graduates in any considerable number. They have not been professional schools in the same sense as the schools of law, medicine, and theology; nor, speaking generally, have they been schools of higher grade than the colleges, in respect to the average quality of their students. The methods of instruction at some of them have been such as are suitable for advanced students; but the methods have been in advance of the students.

In plan, these scientific schools are not all alike. They agree in requiring no knowledge of Latin and Greek for admission, and in excluding the dead languages from their schemes of instruction, but in many essential respects they differ widely. Thus, the minimum age of admission is eighteen at the Cambridge School, seventeen at the Columbia School, sixteen at the Sheffield School; and fourteen at the Chandler School. The requisites for admission are very various, and the schemes of study and methods of instruction are not the same at any two of these four schools. Each school must be examined by itself.

The history of the development of the Department of Philosophy and the Arts in Yale College is so full of instruction as to justify us in dwelling upon it at some length; it is at once an epitome of the past history of scientific instruction in this country, and a prophecy of its future. The department was established in 1847, at a time when a thrill of aspiration and enthusiasm seems to have run through all the New England colleges. As at Harvard in 1846 and at Columbia in 1864, it was a laboratory of applied chemistry which was really the principal feature of the new scheme; but at Yale, advanced instruction in philology, philosophy, and pure science, suitable for graduates, was also offered. In the five years from 1847 to 1852 the average annual number of students was only about sixteen. In 1852 a department of engineering was added to the department of chemistry; and a degree of Bachelor of Philosophy was offered to students who remained two years in *either* department, and passed satisfactory examinations in three branches of study within the same department. The two departments of chemistry and engineering were entirely distinct. A student might take the degree in either department without knowing anything of the studies pursued in the other. As there was no examination for admission, and only a narrow, one-sided, two years' course of study in either department, it is not surprising that the degree of Bachelor of Philosophy soon came to be slightly considered; it really stood for very little culture. In the eight years from 1852 to 1860 the average annual number of students was about forty-seven. A slight change for the better occurred in 1858, when candidates for a degree were required to pass an examination in French or German.

Thus far the Yale Scientific School had borne a strong resemblance to what the Lawrence Scientific School at Cambridge then was, and has always remained; but in 1860 the teachers in the Yale Department of Philosophy and the Arts, dissatisfied with the fruits of their labors, took a great step in advance.

They first systematized the post-graduate instruction in philosophy, philology, and science by offering the degree of Doctor of Philosophy to Bachelors of Arts, Science, or Philosophy, who after two additional years of study should give good evidence of high attainment in two distinct branches of learning. Candidates for this degree, not already Bachelors, were required to pass an admission examination equivalent to that required for the bachelor's degree, the three bachelor degrees taking equal rank. This Doctor's degree has been given thirteen times since 1861. The existence of this programme of instruction at Yale, unpretentious but genuine, and perseveringly offered to a few real students, taken in connection with the facts, that one hundred and sixty-nine persons possessed of degrees have studied something additional to the ordinary college course in this Yale Department of Philosophy and the Arts since its foundation; that one hundred and sixty-four persons possessed of degrees have been members of the Lawrence Scientific School within the same period; that the Columbia School of Mines has received a few persons possessed of degrees; and that young Americans go every year to Europe, in search of better educational facilities than they suppose their own country to afford them,—proves that there is a small but steady demand in the older American communities for instruction higher than that of the ordinary college course, and yet different from that of the law, medical, and theological schools. This legitimate success at Yale, on a really high level, if also on a modest scale, points the way to improvements which ought soon to be made at all the more important American "universities," which will then better deserve their ambitious title.

At the same time, the Yale instructors in the Department of Philosophy and the Arts reorganized completely the Scientific School by constituting, first, a three years' "general course" of studies, embracing mathematics, physical science, modern languages, literature, history, political economy, and commercial law; secondly, a special course in chemistry, which included French, German, English, botany, physical geography, physics, history of the inductive sciences, geology, and logic, besides the chemistry; and, thirdly, a special course in engineering, which included French and German, and lectures upon astronomy, chemistry, physics, mineralogy, and geology, besides the studies which bear most directly upon engineering. These two special courses at first covered but two years; but in 1862 the first year of the general course was required of all candidates for a degree in the chemical department, besides the two years' special course; and in 1864 a three years' course of study was definitely adopted as the plan of the whole school. Other special departments have since been added to the original ones of chemistry and engineering, but the fundamental plan of the school is essentially unchanged since 1864. A year's course of general studies precedes a two years' course in some one of seven different departments. These departments are chemistry and mineralogy, natural history and geology, engineering, mechanics, agriculture, mining, and a selected course in science and literature. The studies of these seven departments are in large measure common; but there is nevertheless a very decided divergence into different ways at the beginning of the second year of the school, according to the student's bent or to his choice of a profession. Since 1864 every candidate for the degree of Bachelor of Philosophy has been required to pass successfully through a three years' course of carefully selected studies,—a generous course, embracing mathematics, English, French, and German, moral, mental, and political philosophy, and history, besides a large variety of scientific subjects. This scheme is of course analogous to that of the common American college, with a large elective element in the last two years. The classics are omitted, the course is only three years long instead of four, and the studies of the last two years have a distinctly practical or professional turn; but there is the same regular course of studies leading to a degree, the same movement by classes, and a range of subjects as extensive as in the common college course. It should be said that, in 1864, the Congressional grant to promote the giving of instruction in agriculture and the mechanic arts, so wisely given to Yale College by the Connecticut Legislature, began to influence for good the development of the Scientific School.

Another marked change in the policy of this school deserves attention. Up to 1860 there was no real examination for admission. Anybody, no matter how ignorant, could join the chemical department;

and, in the engineering department, some acquaintance with algebra, geometry, and plane trigonometry was all that was required. No previous knowledge of chemistry was expected of students entering the laboratory. The Yale school did not differ from the Cambridge school in this respect. In fact, the Lawrence Scientific School had no other requisites for admission than those mentioned until this year (1868). In 1860 the Yale Scientific School established an examination for admission to any department of the school. This examination comprised arithmetic, algebra, geometry, plane trigonometry, the elements of natural philosophy and chemistry, English grammar, and geography. The same preparation in Latin as for the college proper was also recommended to the candidate for admission to the Scientific School. This admission examination has been but slightly modified since 1860. The history of the United States has been substituted for chemistry, and Latin is about to be insisted upon as a qualification for admission.

The changes in the Yale school since 1860 have all had one aim, namely, to raise the grade of the school by getting in a better class of students, and then teaching them more and better. The methods of a professional school have been abandoned as unsuitable, and those of a college have been taken up; but the apparent declension is a real elevation. For the loose-jointed, one-sided scheme has been substituted one which is both methodical and comprehensive. It is interesting to see that the improvement has been appreciated. The average annual number of students in the period from 1847 to 1852 was sixteen; in the period from 1852 to 1860 it was forty-seven, but the average attendance was largest in the earlier years of this period; since 1860 the annual number of students has steadily risen from thirty-eight, the number of that year, to one hundred and twenty-two in 1867–68. Nineteen teachers now take an active part in the work of instruction. Every legitimate effort is made to carry as many students as possible through the regular course, and bring them up to the standard fixed by the examination for the degree. Effort in this direction is needed; for numbers of students resort to the school for brief periods, to their own injury and that of the school. Since the foundation of the school, only one hundred and twenty-eight degrees of Bachelor of Philosophy have been given.

The Lawrence Scientific School at Cambridge is, and always has been, what the Yale school also was at first,—a group of independent professorships, each with its own treasury and its own methods of instruction. The several departments are so distinct that the student in one department has no necessary connection with any other. . . .

There is no common discipline, and no general course of co-ordinated studies which all candidates for any degree must pass through. A young man who has studied nothing but chemistry, or nothing but engineering, and who is densely ignorant of everything else, may obtain the sole degree given by the school,—that of Bachelor of Science. There appears never to have been any examination for admission, except that some knowledge of algebra, geometry, and trigonometry has been required, before a student could join the department of engineering. It has been the practice to receive students into the chemical laboratory without requiring any previous knowledge of chemistry, or indeed of anything else. Nominally, students have not been admitted until they were eighteen years of age, but practically this rule has proved quite elastic. The degree of Bachelor of Science can be obtained in any one department by residing at least one year in Cambridge, and passing the examination of that single department. This examination has usually been passed after a residence of from eighteen to thirty months. This system, or, rather, lack of system, might do for really advanced students in science, for men in years and acquired habits of study,—in fact, the school has been of great service to a score or two of such men,—but it is singularly ill adapted to the wants of the average American boy of eighteen. The range of study is inconceivably narrow; and it is quite possible for a young man to become a Bachelor of Science without a sound knowledge of any language, not even his own, and without any knowledge at all of philosophy, history, political science, or of any natural or physical science, except the single one to which he has devoted two or three years at the most. . . .

Up to 1864 the average annual number of students in the Chandler Scientific School was less than forty. Since that year it has materially increased, reaching sixty-three in 1867–68. Dartmouth College has lately received two gifts which will materially add to its resources, and enable it to elevate the character of its scientific instruction. Sylvanus Thayer, Brigadier-General of Engineers, U.S.A., has given the college fifty thousand dollars as a foundation for a school of architecture and engineering; and the New Hampshire Legislature has wisely transferred to the college the Congressional grant in aid of technical instruction in agriculture and the mechanic arts.

The Chandler Scientific School has labored under the serious disadvantage of having too intimate a connection with the college proper. It has borne another name, and offered instruction of a lower character than that of Dartmouth College. It cannot be said to have had a distinct faculty. Some of the teachers in the college have given a part of their time to the subordinate course. It has been distinctly in a position of inferiority.

The Columbia School of Mines was founded in 1864, with a somewhat narrower scope than the schools thus far described. Its object was to give instruction in those branches of science which relate to mining and metallurgy; and, perhaps unintentionally, it held out to persons engaged in mining and metallurgical enterprises the hope that graduates of the school would be competent forthwith to conduct works, whether new or old. . . .

A technical school lays the best foundation for later work; if well organized, with a broad scheme of study, it can convert the boy of fair abilities and intentions into an observant, judicious man, well informed in the sciences which bear upon his profession; so trained, the graduate will rapidly master the principles and details of any actual works, and he will rise rapidly through the grades of employment; moreover, he will be worth more to his employers from the start than an untrained man. Nevertheless, after the school, a longer or shorter term of apprenticeship upon real works of engineering, mining, building, or manufacturing will be found essential for the best graduates of the best technical schools. When people are content with the services of the last graduates of the medical school as family physicians, when the youngest bachelors of laws are forthwith retained with heavy fees for important cases, it will be time enough to expect that young men who have just completed their school training for the difficult professions of the engineer, manufacturer, miner, or chemist, will be competent at once to take charge of mines, manufacturing establishments, or large works of engineering. No matter how good the polytechnic, scientific, technological, or mining schools may be, it is a delusive expectation that their graduates will be able to enter at once the highest grades of employment, and assume the direction of practical affairs upon a large scale immediately upon leaving the schools. Common sense brings any one who considers the magnitude of the investments necessary in mining and metallurgical works to this conclusion. Young men of twenty to twenty-four are seldom equal to great money responsibilities. . . .

We come now to the examination of the scientific or English

"courses" organized within colleges. These courses run parallel with the classical course of instruction which it has been the primary object of the American colleges to provide. They are cast in the same mould as the classical course; but the metal is of a different composition. The experiment of conducting parallel classical and scientific courses in one and the same institution is by no means a new one. It is merely being tried afresh on a large scale and under new conditions in this country, after having failed in Europe. In Brown University, Union College, and the University of Michigan, for example, there have existed for several years two or more parallel courses,—one the common semi-classical course; the other, or others, constructed on the same framework as the classical course by simply replacing Latin and Greek, or Greek alone, by living European languages, and at the same time expanding a little the mathematical and scientific instruction. A student may choose either course, but not two; at the end of one course he will probably be a Bachelor of Arts; at the end of the other, a Bachelor of Science or Philosophy. . . .

The simultaneous carrying on of what should be such different courses of instruction within the same walls, in the same community of students, and by one and the same corps of instructors, is, we believe, very disadvantageous to both systems of training. Such a combination has been thoroughly tried in the Lycées of France, and has completely failed and been abandoned. In Germany it has seemed expedient to separate the two courses, even during the school-boy period; and for the higher instruction of both systems entirely separate institutions have been found necessary. The fact is, that the whole tone and spirit of a good college ought to be different in kind from that of a good polytechnic, or scientific school. In the college, the desire for the broadest culture, for the best formation and information of the mind, the enthusiastic study of subjects for the love of them without any ulterior objects, the love of learning and research for their own sake, should be the dominant ideas. In the polytechnic school should be found a mental training inferior to none in breadth and vigor, a thirst for knowledge, a genuine enthusiasm in scientific research, and a true love of nature; but underneath all these things is a tempter or leading motive unlike that of a college. The student in a polytechnic school has a practical end constantly in view; he is training his faculties with the express object of making himself a better manufacturer, engineer, or teacher; he is studying the processes of nature, in order afterwards to turn them to human uses and his own profit; if he is eager to penetrate the mysteries of electricity, it is largely because he wants to understand telegraphs; if he learns French and German, it is chiefly because he would not have the best technical literature of his generation sealed for him; if he imbues his mind with the profound and exquisite conceptions of the calculus, it is in order the better to comprehend mechanics. This practical end should never be lost sight of by student or teacher in a polytechnic school, and it should very seldom be thought of or alluded to in a college. Just as far as the spirit proper to a polytechnic school pervades a college, just so far that college falls below its true idea. The practical spirit and the literary or scholastic spirit are both good, but they are incompatible. If commingled, they are both spoiled.

It is not to be imagined that the mental training afforded by a good polytechnic school is necessarily inferior in any respect to that of a good college, whether in breadth, vigor, or wholesomeness. Certain it is that an average graduate of the Zurich Polytechnicum or the Paris École Centrale has a much better title to be called "learned"[1] than most graduates of American colleges and professional schools. He has

[1] The term "learned profession" is getting to have a sarcastic flavor. Only a very small proportion of lawyers, doctors, and ministers, the country over, are Bachelors of Arts. The degrees of LL.B. and M.D. stand, on the average, for decidedly less culture than the degree of A.B., and it is found quite possible to prepare young men of scanty education to be successful pulpit exhorters in a year or eighteen months. A really learned minister is almost as rare as a logical sermon.

On the catalogue of the University of Michigan for 1867–68, there stand the names of three hundred and eighty-seven law students, not one of whom appears to have possessed at that stage of his education any degree whatever. There are four teachers. To enter the school, a young man must be eighteen years of age, and he must present a certificate of good moral character. Nothing else is required. To obtain a degree he must follow certain courses of lectures through two terms of six months each. Nothing else is required. It is possible that the degrees really possessed by law students have been omitted; but degrees are printed against the names of their possessors in other departments of the University on the same catalogue. Among one hundred and forty-six persons who received the degree of LL.B., in that year, seventeen had other degrees,—a very small proportion.

On the same catalogue there are enrolled four hundred and eleven medical students, of whom nineteen already possess a Bachelor's degree.. There are eleven teachers. The school is established in the small town of Ann Arbor, quite remote from large hospitals. Poor humanity shudders at the spectacle of so large a crop of such doctors.

Such professional schools may, indeed, be the best which the hastily organized, fast-growing American communities will support; but the word "learned" can only be conventionally applied to professions for which the preliminary training exacted is so short and so loose.

studied more, harder, and to better effect, though in a different spirit. But the two kinds of education cannot be carried on together, in the same schedules, by the same teachers. The classical course will hurt the scientific, and the scientific the classical. Neither will be at its best. The experience of the world and common sense are against such experiments as those of Brown, Union, and Michigan. Nevertheless, they may be good temporary expedients during a transition period, or in crude communities where hasty culture is as natural as fast eating. They do good service in lack of better things.

The incompatibility of the practical spirit and the literary spirit, which has here been dwelt upon, may appear to some to limit unduly the number of subjects proper to be taught in colleges. The tendency to the practical side of every subject which befits a good polytechnic school would be improper in a college; but the same subjects may to a very great extent be taught in both. One and the same subject may be studied in two very unlike frames of mind. We have only desired to urge the incompatibility of one temper with another temper, both being good in their separate places.

Another unjust inference might be drawn from what has been said of the impossibility of carrying on two long courses of instruction of different aims and essence within the same schedules of hours and terms and the same walls. It might be inferred that the applied sciences are necessarily unfit to be taught or studied in a university, taking that word in its best sense. It cannot be said too loudly or too often, that no subject of human inquiry can be out of place in the programme of a real university. It is only necessary that every subject should be taught at the university on a higher plane than elsewhere. Even scholars are apt to be intolerant of this subject or that in university schemes; one can see no sense in archaeology; another condemns natural history as being without practical applications, useless for training, and frightfully absorbent of money; a third finds pure science wholesome meat, but applied science utilitarian chaff. It is impossible to be too catholic in this matter. But the American university has not yet grown out of the soil, and we are rather meeting a theoretical than a practical objection. The incidental remark may be permitted, that a university, in any worthy sense of the term, must grow from seed. It cannot be transplanted from England or Germany in full leaf and bearing. It cannot be run up, like a cotton-mill, in six months, to meet a quick demand. Neither can it be created by an energetic use of the inspired editorial, the advertising circular, and the frequent telegram. Numbers do not constitute it, and no money can make it before its time. There is more of the university about the eight or ten Yale graduates who are studying in the Yale Department of Philosophy and the Arts, than in as many hundred raw youths who do not know more than a fair grammar school may teach. When the American university appears, it will not be a copy of foreign institutions, or a hot-bed plant, but the slow and natural outgrowth of American social and political habits, and an expression of the average aims and ambitions of the better educated classes. The American college is an institution without a parallel; the American university will be equally original.

Besides the scientific schools connected with colleges, and the scientific or English courses within colleges, there exist in the United States several independent schools in which mathematics, the exact sciences and their applications, the modern languages, and philosophy form the staple of instruction. Such are the Rensselaer Polytechnic Institute at Troy, and the School of the Massachusetts Institute of Technology at Boston. These two schools have a certain general resemblance; they are independent establishments; they have the same minimum age of admission, namely, sixteen years, although practically the average age of the students who enter these institutions is decidedly above this minimum; they do not require any Latin or Greek for admission, and do not admit these languages to their courses of study; finally, in each the course of study lasts four years. In the comprehensiveness of their courses of instruction, in the number of teachers employed, and in their general scale of operations, these schools differ materially. . . .

The most ample course of instruction which has been thus far offered in this country to students who demand a liberal and practical education as well as a training specially adapted to make them ultimately good engineers, manufacturers, architects, chemists, merchants, teachers of science, or directors of mines and industrial works, is that organized by the Massachusetts Institute of Technology at Boston. The course extends through four years. The studies of the first and second years, and certain general studies in the third and fourth years, are required of all regular students. At the beginning of the third year each student selects one of six courses, which he follows during his third and fourth years at the school. These six courses are:—

1. Mechanical Engineering.
2. Civil Engineering.

3. Chemistry.
4. Geology and Mining.
5. Building and Architecture.
6. General Science and Literature. . . .

It is very obvious that the student who should be led by competent men, provided with the necessary tools, through such a four years' course of study as this, would have received a training which would be neither loose, superficial, nor one-sided. Between this course and the ordinary semi-classical college course there is no question of information by one and formation by the other; of cramming utilitarian facts by one system, and developing mental powers by the other. Both courses form, train, and educate the mind; and one no more than the other, only the disciplines are different. Either course, well organized, can make out of a capable boy a reasoning man, with his faculties well in hand. One man swings dumb-bells, and walks; another rows, and rides on horseback; both train their muscles. One eats beef, another mutton; but both are nourished.

People who think vaguely about the difference between a good college and a good polytechnic school are apt to say that the aim of the college course is to make a rounded man, with all his faculties impartially developed, while it is the express object of a technical course to make a one-sided man,—a mere engineer, chemist, or achitect. Two truths are suppressed in this form of statement. First, faculties are not given by God impartially,—to each round soul a little of each power, as if the soul were a pill, which must contain its due proportion of many various ingredients. To reason about the average human mind as if it were a globe, to be expanded symmetrically from a centre outward, is to be betrayed by a metaphor. A cutting-tool, a drill, or auger would be a juster symbol of the mind. The natural bent and peculiar quality of every boy's mind should be sacredly regarded in his education; the division of mental labor, which is essential in civilized communities in order that knowledge may grow and society improve, demands this regard to the peculiar constitution of each mind, as much as does the happiness of the individual most nearly concerned. Secondly, to make a good engineer, chemist, or architect, the only sure way is to make first, or at least simultaneously, an observant, reflecting, and sensible man, whose mind is not only well stored, but well trained also to see, compare, reason, and decide. The vigorous training of the mental powers is therefore the primary object of every well-organized technical school. At the same time a well-arranged course of study, like that of the New Haven school, the Troy school, or the Institute of Technology, will include a vast deal of information and many practical exercises appropriate to the professions which the students have in view....

These partial or special students are of two sorts in most of the technical schools. First, men of age and acquirements, who come to add to their previous attainments a special training in some professional subject, some one application of science to the arts; to meet the wants of such men has been and is one of the most useful functions of the technical schools. Secondly, young men of imperfect preliminary training, whose parents think, or who themselves think, that they can best become chemists by studying nothing but chemistry, or engineers by only attending to the mathematics and their applications, or architects by ignoring all knowledge but that of architectural design. This notion is certainly a very crude one; but it deceives many uninstructed parents and inexperienced young men.... The scientific schools, in their earlier days, sent many such illiberally educated men into the scientific professions, and it will still take them years to recover from the bad effects of this serious mistake. Some of the most vigorous of these very men have since realized the defects of their early training, and are now the warmest friends of the improved methods of scientific education....

The scientific schools have been recruited in large part, of course, from that excellent and numerous class of young men who have more taste and capacity for science than for language and literature, and who have followed their natural bent in making choice of a school and a profession; but they have also been the refuge of shirks and stragglers from the better organized and stricter colleges. This evil is a temporary one, incident to what has been the experimental condition of education through science. It will correct itself, when the new system of education is as well organized as the old, and when the community understands the legitimate inlets and outlets of the new schools,—how to get into them, and what they lead to.

To avoid misapprehension, let it be distinctly stated that the scientific schools have already done a very timely and necessary work in this country by training, although hastily and imperfectly, a certain number of specialists, such as assayers, analysts, railroad engineers, and teachers of science, to very useful functions. And again, let it be acknowledged with thankfulness, that genius, or even an unusual vigor of mind and will, often overcomes in after life that worst of obstacles, insuperable for common men,—an inadequate or mistaken training in youth.

At present it is the wise effort of the faculties of all the leading polytechnic or scientific schools to carry as many of their pupils as possible through the "regular" course of study; in other words, they recommend their pupils to lay, during three or four years between seventeen and twenty-two, a broad and strong foundation for the strictly professional studies, of which a part are pursued in the school, and a part during the apprenticeship which should follow their school life. . . .

Three difficulties beset the establishment of such new schools in this country. The first danger is the tendency to reckless preliminary expenditure upon buildings and mechanical fittings. Many American schools and colleges have been wrecked on this rock. The American trustee has a deplorable propensity to put what should be quick capital into more or less unsuitable bricks and mortar. This danger escaped, the second difficulty is the scarcity of teachers having the necessary training and the equally necessary enthusiasm. There must be brought together a harmonious body of teachers, young, if possible, both in years and spirit, but at any rate in spirit, allowed the leisure necessary for men to keep themselves on a level with the rapid progress of the arts and sciences, and paid enough to have a mind at ease. High reputation is not necessary; but conscientiousness in the discharge of routine duties, fair talents well improved, and a genuine enthusiasm are essential. If to these qualifications there can be added personal devotion to the head of the institution, the happiest conditions are united. The American scientific schools and colleges and the European universities have trained a few Americans to such functions; but they are still scarce, because the active industries of the country absorb the greater number of energetic young men possessed of the requisite training. The supreme difficulty remains. Men competent to administer a large school of science are rare in all communities; they are not only rare in this country, but are here peculiarly liable to be drawn into other pursuits. A steady, careful, and kindly administration is required, not thrusting itself into notice, but quietly felt alike by teachers, students, and servants. The building up in any new place of a great school for the new education must be in the main the work of a single man, or, in rare cases, of two or three men animated by the same spirit. To find this man should always be the first step; it will certainly be the hardest in the whole undertaking.

The American colleges have taken, and still take, their presidents from the clerical profession almost exclusively. This course has been perfectly natural for the colleges, because almost all of them have been founded expressly to propagate and perpetuate the Gospel as the founders understood it, or, in other words, to breed ministers and laymen of some particular religious communion. It is gradually becoming apparent that even the colleges are suffering from this too exclusively clerical administration. Fortunately for the country, education is getting to be a profession by itself. For the discharge of the highest functions in this profession, the training of a divinity student, years of weekly preaching, and much practice in the discharge of pastoral duties, are no longer supposed to be the best, or at least the only preparation. Several other classes of men are now as cultivated as the clergy. As a class, ministers are as fit to be suddenly transferred to the bench at forty-five or fifty years of age, as they are to be put at the head of large educational establishments. The legal profession would be somewhat astonished at such an intrusion. Yet in their capacity of trustees, lawyers and men of business are constantly putting clergymen into the highest posts of the profession of education, which is thus robbed of its few prizes, and subjected to such indignity as soldiers feel when untried civilians are put over their heads. But, however it may be with the colleges, to transplant a successful clergyman in the prime of life from the charge of a parish to the charge of a polytechnic school would be felt to be absurd. The difficulty of finding a good head is not to be surmounted in any such ready fashion. . . .

4. The Johns Hopkins Trustees Are Advised To Select Gilman, 1874

The incident here described occurred on September 30, 1874.
See Doc. 1, and Hawkins, *Pioneer,* p. 15.

This reminds me of a circumstance connected with his transfer from Berkeley and San Francisco to Baltimore. Our University at Ithaca had been established for a few years when there appeared one day at my office a deputation of trustees from the newly founded Johns Hopkins University. Of course I made it my duty to show them what we had done at Cornell thus far, taking them especially through the library, lecture rooms, laboratories, and, above all, the schools of civil and mechanical engineering. As we came out of Sibley College and were standing on the stone platform from which a few months before Daniel had made his admirable address at the opening of that building, the chairman of the Johns Hopkins trustees, Judge Brown, in the presence of his colleagues, who were standing about us, asked me, with some solemnity, whether I knew of any person whom I could recommend for the presidency of their proposed university at Baltimore. To this question I at once replied that there was one man whom I could recommend thoroughly, President Gilman of the University of California. At this the whole company burst into a laugh which greatly disconcerted me; but Judge Brown most kindly came to the rescue. He informed me that on the same errand which brought them to Ithaca they had first visited Cambridge and after looking through Harvard, had asked of President Eliot the same question which they had just asked me and had received the same answer which I had given;—that they had then visited Yale and, having been shown through its main buildings by President Porter, had received the same answer from him. Never was an answer more conscientiously given and never was expectation more completely fulfilled. The success of Dr. Gilman as President of Johns Hopkins I have always regarded as the most remarkable of its kind achieved during my time.

Andrew D. White to Mrs. Gilman, May 3, 1909, in Fabian Franklin, *The Life of Daniel Coit Gilman* (New York, 1910), pp. 324–25.

5. *Gilman Recalls the Early Days of the Johns Hopkins, 1876*

The founder made no effort to unfold a plan. He simply used one word,—UNIVERSITY,—and he left it to his successors to declare its meaning in the light of the past, in the hope of the future. There is no indication that he was interested in one branch of knowledge more than in another. He had no educational "fad." There is no evidence that he had read the writings of Cardinal Newman or of Mark Pattison, and none that the great parliamentary reports had come under his eye. He was a large-minded man, who knew that the success of the foundation would depend upon the wisdom of those to whom its development was entrusted; and the Trustees were large-minded men who knew that their efforts must be guided by the learning, the experience, and the devotion of the Faculty. There was a natural desire, in this locality, that the principal positions should be filled by men with whom the community was acquainted, but the Trustees were not governed by an aspiration so provincial. They sought the best men that could be found, without regard to the places where they were born, or the colleges where they had been educated. So, on Washington's birthday, in 1876, after words of benediction from the President of Harvard University, our early counsellor and constant friend, the plans of this University were publicly announced in the President's inaugural speech. . . .

Let me now proceed to indicate the conditions which existed in this country when our work was projected. You will see that extraordinary advances have been made. The munificent endowments of Mr. John D. Rockefeller and of Mr. and Mrs. Leland Stanford, the splendid generosity of the State legislatures in Michigan, Wisconsin, Minnesota, California, and other Western States, the enlarged resources of Harvard, Yale, Columbia, Princeton, Pennsylvania and other well established universities, and now the unique and unsurpassed generosity of Mr. Carnegie, have entirely changed the aspects of liberal education and of scientific investigation.

As religion, the relation of finite man to the Infinite, is the most im-

---

Johns Hopkins University Celebration of the Twenty-fifth Anniversary of the Founding . . . (Baltimore, 1902), pp. 15–16, 19–27.

portant of all human concerns, I begin by a brief reference to the attitude of universities toward Faith and Knowledge. The earliest universities of Europe were either founded by the Church or by the State. Whatever their origin, they were under the control, to a large extent, of ecclesiastical authorities. These traditions came to our country, and the original colleges were founded by learned and godly men, most of them, if not all, ministers of the gospel. Later, came the State universities and later still, the private foundations like that in which we are concerned. Gradually, among the Protestants, laymen have come to hold the chief positions of authority formerly held by the clergy. The official control, however, is less interesting at this moment than the attitude of universities toward the advancement of knowledge. To-day, happily, apprehensions are not felt, to any great extent, respecting the advancement of science. It is more and more clearly seen that the interpretation of the laws by which the universe is governed, extending from the invisible rays of the celestial world to the most minute manifestations of organic life, reveal one plan, one purpose, one supreme sovereignty—far transcending the highest conceptions to which the human mind can attain respecting his sovereign and infinite Power. Sectarian supremacy and theological differences have dwindled therefore to insignificance, in institutions where the supreme desire is to understand the world in which we are placed, and to develop the ablest intellects of each generation, subservient to the primeval injunction "replenish the earth and subdue it; and have dominion over the fish of the sea, and over the fowl of the air, and over every living thing that moveth upon the earth." Notwithstanding these words, the new biology, that is the study of living creatures, encountered peculiar prejudices and opposition. It was the old story over again. Geology, early in the century, had been violently attacked; astronomy, in previous centuries, met its bitter opponents; higher criticism is now dreaded. Yet quickly and patiently the investigator has prosecuted and will continue his search for the truth,—heedless of consequences, assured by the Master's words,—"the Truth shall make you free."

Still the work goes on. Science is recognized as the handmaid of religion. Evolution is regarded by many theologians as confirming the strictest doctrines of predestination. The propositions which were so objectionable thirty years ago are now received with as little alarm as the propositions of Euclid. There are mathematicians who do not regard the Euclidean geometry as the best mode of presenting certain mathematical truths, and there are also naturalists who will not accept the doctrines of Darwin, without limitation or modification, but nobody thinks of fighting over the utterances of either of these philosophers. In fact, I think it one of the most encouraging signs of our times that devout men, devoted to scientific study, see no conflict between their religious faith and their scientific knowledge. Is it not true that as the realm of Knowledge extends the reign of Faith, though restricted, remains? Is it not true that Science to-day is as far from demonstrating certain great propositions, which in the depths of our souls we all believe, as it was in the days of the Greek philosophers? This university, at the outset, assumed the position of a fearless and determined investigator of nature. It carried on its work with quiet, reverent, and unobtrusive recognition of the immanence of divine power,— of the Majesty, Dominion, and Might, known to men by many names, revered by us in the words that we learned from our mothers' lips, Almighty God, the Father Everlasting.

Another danger, thirty years ago, was that of conflict between the advocates of classical and scientific study. For many centuries Greek and Latin were supreme in the faculty of liberal arts, enforced and strengthened by metaphysics and mathematics. During the last half century, physical and natural sciences have claimed an equal rank. The promotion has not been yielded without a struggle, but it is pleasant to remember that in this place, no conflict has arisen. Among us, one degree, that of Bachelor of Arts, is given alike to the students of the Humanities and the students of Nature, and the degree of Doctor of Philosophy may be won by advanced work in the most remote languages of the past or in the most recent developments of biology and physics. Two illustrious teachers were the oldest members of the original faculty;—one of them universally recognized as among the foremost geometricians of the world,—the other, renowned for his acquaintance with the masters of thought in many tongues, and especially for his appreciation of the writers of ancient Greece, upon whose example all modern literature is based.

Our fathers spoke of "Church and State," and we but repeat their ideas when we say that universities are the promoters of pure religion and wise government. This university has not been identified with political partisanship,—though, its members, like all patriots, have held and expressed their opinions upon current questions, local and national. Never have the political views of any teacher helped or hindered his preferment; nor have I any idea what would be the result of the party classification of our staff. This, however, may be claimed. The study of politics, in the sense of Freeman, "History is past politics, and politics present history," has been diligently promoted. The principles of Roman law, international arbitration, jurisprudence, economics and institutional history have here been set forth and inculcated,—so that in every part of the land, we can point to our graduates as the wise interpreters of political history, the strong promoters of democratic institutions, the firm believers in the merit system of appointments, and in local self-government.

A phrase which has lately been in vogue is original research. Like all other new terms, it is often misapplied, often misunderstood. It may be the highest occupation of the human mind. It may be the most insignificant. A few words may therefore be requisite to explain our acceptance of this word. When this university began, it was a common complaint, still uttered in many places, that the ablest teachers were absorbed in routine and were forced to spend their strength in the discipline of tyros, so that they had no time for carrying forward their studies or for adding to human knowledge. Here the position was taken at the outset that the chief professors should have ample time to carry on the higher work for which they had shown themselves qualified, and also that younger men, as they gave evidence of uncommon qualities, should likewise be encouraged to devote themselves to study. Even those who were candidates for degrees were taught what was meant by profitable investigation. They were shown how to discover the limits of the known; how to extend, even by minute accretions, the realm of knowledge; how to coöperate with other men in the prosecution of inquiry; and how to record in exact language, and on the printed page, the results attained. Investigation has thus been among us the duty of every leading professor, and he has been the guide and inspirer of fellows and pupils, whose work may not bear his name, but whose results are truly products of the inspiration and guidance which he has freely bestowed.

The complaint was often heard, in the early seventies, that no provision was made in this country for post-graduate work except in the three professional schools. Accordingly, a system of fellowships, of scholarships, and of other provisions for advanced study was established here, so well adapted to the wants of the country at that time that its provisions have been widely copied in other places. It now seems as if there was danger of rivalry in the solicitation of students, which is certainly unworthy, and there is danger also that too many men will receive stipendiary encouragement to prepare themselves for positions they can never attain. In the early days of the French Academy when a seat in that body was a very great prize, a certain young man was told to wait until he was older, and the remark was added that in order to secure good speed from horses, a basket of oats should always be tied to the front of the carriage pole as a constant incitement. It would indeed be a misfortune if a system of fellowships should be open to this objection. Nevertheless, whoever scans our register of Fellows will discover that many of the ablest men in the country, of the younger generation, have here received encouragement and aid.

When this university began, the opportunities for scientific publication in this country were very meagre. The American Journal of Science was the chief repository for short and current papers. The memoirs of a few learned societies came out at slow intervals and could not be freely opened to investigators. This university, in the face of obvious objection, determined to establish certain journals which might be the means of communication between the scholars of this country and those abroad. Three journals were soon commenced: The American Journal of Mathematics; the American Journal of Philology; the American Chemical Journal. Remember that these were "American" journals, in fact as well as in name, open to all the scholars of the country. Other periodicals came afterwards, devoted to History and Politics, to Biology, to Modern Languages, to Experimental Medicine and to Anatomy. Moderate appropriations were made to foreign journals of great importance which lacked support, the English Journal of Physiology and the German Journal of Assyriology. Nor were the appropriations of the Trustees restricted to periodical literature. Generous encouragement was given to the publication of important treatises, like the researches of Dr. Brooks upon Salpa; to the physiological papers of Dr. Martin; to the studies in logic of Mr. Peirce and his followers; to Professor Rowland's magnificent photographs of the solar spectrum; to the printing of a facsimile of the earliest Christian document after the times of the Apostles; and recently, with the coöperation of the University of Tübingen, to the exact reproduction by Dr. Bloomfield of a unique manuscript which has an important bearing upon comparative philology.

I am not without apprehensions that our example to the country has been infelicitous, not less than thirty institutions being known to me, which are now engaged in the work of publication. The consequence is that it is almost impossible for scholars to find out and make use of many important memoirs, which are thus hidden away. One of the problems for the next generation to solve is the proper mode of encouraging the publication of scientific treatises.

6. G. Stanley Hall Describes Gilman's Policies at the Hopkins in the 1880's

G. Stanley Hall (1844–1924) was born in Massachusetts and graduated from Williams College (1867). From college he went to Union Theological Seminary, but growing skepticism caused him to abandon the thought of the ministry, and he decided to go to Germany, where he remained for two years, studying philosophy and theology and enjoying his psychological liberation from the cramped outlook of rural New England. From 1872 to 1876 he taught literature and philosophy at Antioch College. He turned thence to Harvard, where he taught English for two years and took his Ph.D. (1878), after which he returned for another two years to Germany, where he studied physics, physiology, and experimental psychology with such men as Helmholtz, Ludwig, and Wundt. In 1882 he was given a special lectureship and a psychological laboratory at Gilman's new university, and in the following year he became professor of psychology and pedagogics. A leader in experimental psychology, he also founded the *American Journal of Psychology* (1887) and founded the American Psychological Association (1891), of which he became the first president. He achieved wide fame for his writings on children and on education, and in 1888 was called by the millionaire Jonas Gilman Clark (1815–1900) to head the new Clark University at Worcester, Massachusetts. Clark's eccentric policies, and uncertain support, combined with William Rainey Harper's seduction of a large part of its excellent faculty (Part IX, Doc. 5), prevented the new institution from realizing Hall's well-laid plans for its development, but Hall remained in his position until 1919, combining administration with extensive contributions to psychology and education.

See Part IX, Docs. 5 and 7; E. L. Thorndike, *Biographical Memoir of G. Stanley Hall* (New York, 1928); Lorine Pruette, *G. Stanley Hall, A Biography of a Mind* (New York, 1926).

G. Stanley Hall, *Life and Confessions of a Psychologist* (New York, 1923), pp. 246–53. Reprinted with the permission of Appleton-Century-Crofts, Inc.

True history in the field of higher education was perhaps never so hard to write as in this country, pervaded as it is with insidious biases for competing institutions, and the day of impartiality and competency of judgment will dawn late; but just in proportion as love of the highest learning and research prevails, Dr. Gilman's qualities will become the ideals of leaders in our American system.

Gilman was essentially an *inside* president. His interest in the work of the individual members of his faculty did not end when they were engaged, but began. He loved to know something of their every new investigation, however remote from his own specialty, and every scientific or scholarly success felt the stimulus of his sympathy. His unerring judgment of men was triumphantly justified in the achievements of those he appointed; and although in selecting young men he had to walk by faith, he nowhere showed more sagacity than in applying individual stimuli and checks, so that in this sense and to this extent he was a spiritual father of many of his faculty, the author of their careers, and for years made the institution the paradise and seminarium of young specialists. This made stagnation impossible, and the growth of professors there in their work was, I believe, without precedent....

Dr. Gilman was not preëminently an outside president or an outside organizer. He was never known as an apostle of uniformity. It could never be said of him that there were dollars and students in all or even in anything he said, in the sense that these considerations determined either what was said or left unsaid. He had, I believe, no place on any committee of ten, twelve, or fifteen, and had no share in the unhappy business by which in some parts of the country secondary education has been dominated by or subordinated to college interests or requirements. He believed in individuality and held that institutions were made for men, and not men for institutions. He knew no selfishness or interinstitutional rivalry; nor did he take part in the tendency to absorb or incorporate other foundations into a great educational trust. His faith and services were for the university invisible, not made with hands, which consists in the productive scientific work of gifted minds wherever they are, sympathetic by nature and made still more so by the coördination of studies, as one of the most characteristic features of our age....

The new policies which mark Gilman as the most creative mind in the field of the higher education that this country has yet produced may be summarized as follows. First of all, he realized that as civilization advanced, all critical decisions and new steps must be made by experts who could command all the available knowledge in their field and perhaps add something new to the sum of the world's knowledge. To have made a contribution to this, however small, marks the real attainment of majority in our world. Scholarship is a prime condition but erudition is not enough; each must have had the unique experience of having contributed some tiny brick, however small, to the Temple of Science, the construction of which is the sublimest achievement of man. In everything else there may be docility but at some point each must be an authority and have passed beyond apprenticeship, and be able to light his own way with independent knowledge. Then alone is he a real citizen in the culture world of to-day. Thus intellectual creativeness must be made the real standard and test of any system of higher education of to-day. Anything and everything must be subordinated to this, and Gilman must have had great satisfaction in realizing that in this kind of productivity the Hopkins University, at least for a decade or two, was the leader and pioneer in this land. He was never dismayed to be told that this ideal was "made in Germany." It found the warmest response in every able and original mind in all academic America, as is abundantly witnessed by the fact that the Hopkins fashions have been so generally cultivated in later years by all our higher institutions. And although this tradition has been sedulously maintained and so far as possible is ever advancing at Baltimore, the leadership of this institution is now relatively less pronounced only because its ideals have been so infectious in so many other centers.

Another item in the Gilman policy was to avoid excessive or premature specialization. It was to this end that so many popular courses were established and so many eminent men were brought to the Johns Hopkins for brief periods; that the interdepartmental scientific club was established, where specialists tried to interest those in other lines in their own work; and that the *Bulletin* and *Circular,* in which each was urged to present in brief and popular form the results of his own investigations, were maintained. This work, although welcomed by broader minds, always encountered some opposition and more inertia. Students were prone to focus on their major subject and neglect the larger opportunities thus provided. Some of the professors found it irksome to summarize their technical studies in a way intelligible to cultured minds in other fields. A few thought it rather beneath their academic dignity to explain in courses open to the public what they were doing. But these methods of mutual acquaintance were always diligently fostered by Gilman....

He never entered the mad race for dollars and students, which was the ultimate aim of nearly everything that college presidents said and did. His appeal always was to quality rather than to size and numbers, and his very temperament made him keenly sympathetic with the non-belligerency and cult of peace which characterized the Quakers, so that he shrank constitutionally from all antagonisms. Just why he never introduced physical geography, a subject of great significance and academic possibilities already so well developed in Germany, and which he himself had represented in his early days at Yale, no one ever knew unless it was that he felt that any manifestation of partiality for his own chair might be construed as selfishness.

Again, I never quite understood why he opposed my earnest wish to give a course on the history of universities and learned societies, which seemed to me an essential part of the work of pedagogy, but preferred that I should limit my activities here to primary and secondary education. Perhaps he distrusted my competence, and if so he was probably wiser than I, although I always felt that it would require a remarkable degree of self-abnegation in any college or university president to develop such a course in which his own policies might perhaps be shown to be imperfect in the larger light of history. Or perhaps he felt that if such a course were given it really ought to be by the president himself, although I had no reason whatever to suspect Gilman of wanting to preëmpt this field....

[At the close of the next paragraph in the original, Hall added a footnote, which is here printed as the conclusion of this extract.]

Gilman established, if he did not introduce, the custom of printing in the Register the academic record of each professor and graduate student, and also calling attention in his annual reports and otherwise to the special achievements in research in each department, one year stressing some and in other years other of the branches, and always publishing the names and number of student attendants upon each course. This was another fine psychological spur to wholesome emulation so characteristic of the first president of the Hopkins. He also arranged the order of the courses in a somewhat Comtean, hierarchic way, for example, mathematics, physics, chemistry, biology, language, literature, history, sociology, with psychology last, and always favored early publication of every result of investigation, so that besides the journals established in various departments there were often long series of monographs. He was always sympathetic and glad to listen to anything we would tell him about our work and always seemed to be doing his best to understand it, no matter how technical it was, so that we all felt, along with a sense that he always had the final decision with regard to all our appointments and promotions, that he had a personal as well as official satisfaction in anything we did.

7. John W. Burgess' Program for the American University, 1884

John W. Burgess (1844–1931), a Tennesseean and a graduate of Amherst College, spent three profitable years at Berlin, Leipzig, and Göttingen before returning to become professor of history, political science, and political economy at his alma mater. His greatest achievements were at Columbia, which he joined in 1876. As creator and first dean of its faculty and school of political science, he was one of the men most influential in transforming the college into Columbia University.

See also Burgess, *Reminiscences of an American Scholar* (New York, 1934), and R. G. Hoxie and others, *A History of the Faculty of Political Science, Columbia University* (New York, 1955).

At a juncture when the mind of the educated public is so earnestly occupied with the problem of the higher education, it cannot be premature or out of place to attempt to give something more of point and precision to this general tendency of thought, by analyzing the question into its component parts and giving a separate statement of its natural elements. The American University, then: When shall it be? Where shall it be? What shall it be? Already have we thus three questions in regard to it, and when we come to examine each of the three we find that each is more than a simple interrogation and requires a further analysis.

First, then, When shall it be?

As concisely as we can put it the reply will consist of three conditions; viz.: It shall be when there exists in the nation the surplus of

---

J. W. Burgess, *The American University: When Shall It Be? Where Shall It Be? What Shall It Be?* (Boston, 1884).

wealth to support it, the body of scholars to form its Faculties and the body of students qualified by previous training and acquirements to profit by University work.

Do these conditions now exist in the United States? Without doubt the first does, in many parts of this great and wealthy land. The home of the greatest Universities of the world, Germany, is poor in comparison with the United States. We certainly cannot plead poverty as a reason for deferring the establishment of the University. This is so manifest that I will spend no more words upon this part of the inquiry.

Have we now, in the second place, the body of scholars qualified to form its Faculties? It would seem to be, at the first glance, unquestionable that from the three hundred and more College Faculties now existing in the United States a sufficient number of true scholars might be drawn to constitute the Faculties of a half-dozen real Universities; but to the critical student of pedagogy this reply will not be entirely satisfactory. He will object that the American College Professor is not, as a rule, a University Professor, nor capable of becoming so by the mere change of position from the College to the University chair; that he is generally a person who has himself never seen the inside of a real University, and knows nothing of its matter or methods of investigation and instruction, save what he may, perchance, have gleaned from some superficial article or book professing to describe the same; that he is the peculiar product of the American College, a hybrid somewhat between the drill-master of the Gymnasium[1] and the University Professor,—too much of the former to be the latter, and just enough of the latter to spoil him for the former, he is really neither, and belongs nowhere in a really scientific gradation of an educational system. It cannot be gainsaid that there is some truth in this rather harsh sounding criticism, but it is not wholly true. During the last twenty-five years a large number of our most promising scholars have qualified themselves for professorial chairs in the best Universities of Europe, especially of Germany, and we have the testimony of the German Professors for it that their industry and success suffer in no respect by comparison with the work of the German students themselves; and it would not be impossible to name American scholars, who, though having never enjoyed such advantages, would yet adorn the University

---

[1] I shall use this term to designate the curriculum of elementary and disciplinary studies requisite for entrance upon University work.

chair anywhere. Notwithstanding the pessimistic remarks of some of our English cousins,—one of them in particular, who has lately been our guest,—I think the better judgment of educated foreigners about us is that we do now possess the material necessary for the creation of University Faculties. The problem reduces itself to the matter of judicious selection, which can be best solved at the outset, in my opinion, by the choice of a President who is himself deeply learned in the science of Education, a broad scholar and an accurate judge of men, and then confiding to him the selection of the Professors. After the Faculties are once successfully constituted they themselves are the best judges as to who should be their coadjutors and successors. I will return to the consideration of this point, however, further on.

In the third place, have we now the body of students prepared to appreciate the work of the University, and eager to enter upon it? This is in itself a most comprehensive question,—one not easy to answer, or even to reduce to intelligible statement. It is, in short, the whole question of our secondary education[2] and its relation to superior education. The first response which suggests itself to the mind of the inquirer upon this point is that the eight to ten thousand graduates per annum of the American Colleges furnish the body of students prepared and ready to enter upon University work; but the critical student of American pedagogy will object here again that the average graduate of the average American College is neither fitted to become nor desirous of becoming, a student in the University; that he is a smatterer in the elements of knowledge, and possesses thereto just enough of advanced learning to make him ignorant of his own defects, and impatient of the minute and exact processes of a true University method, as well as unable to appreciate and apply them. It is to be deplored that there is a very great deal of truth in this criticism. I would venture to affirm that very few graduates of American Colleges have been able to pursue successfully a course in a German University and attain to a degree, without learning their Greek, or Latin, or modern languages, or their elements of natural science, or even their mathematics (though this less frequently), over again. The American College graduate is not the equal of the "Abiturient" of the German Gymnasium in an exact comprehension and facile use of the elements of all knowledge, though

---

[2] By secondary education, I intend all that comes between primary education and the University. The gymnastic curriculum.

he may have more of what is sometimes called "general information." There was a time in our educational history when the Fitting School and the College, taken together, furnished a student with a pretty fair gymnastic preparation for the University, or at least for some courses of the University. At that time a diligent student could, at the end of the College period, read Greek and Latin with a good deal of facility, and by his mathematical training had become something of a logician; but now the overloading of the College course with University studies, causing the breaking up of the same into a variety of special courses before the student has become generally prepared to select or to profit by the selection, and the introduction of University methods into the College by over-ambitious Professors have put an end to that condition of things in the most of our better Colleges. Before the student learns really to read any language he is now dragged into the most minute philological study, which so limits the amount read that the formation of the vocabulary is stopped; before he learns the elements of the different natural sciences he is invited to enter the laboratory of some particular one and encouraged to seek to become a discoverer ere he knows the first principles of what has already been discovered; while a considerable number make good use of the opportunity to escape in large degree the great disciplinary influence of the pure mathematics, and come thus with immature reasoning powers to the work of the University.

I confess that I am unable to divine what is to be ultimately the position of Colleges which cannot become Universities and which will not be Gymnasia. I cannot see what reason they will have to exist. It will be largely a waste of capital to maintain them, and largely a waste of time to attend them. It is so now. It seems to me that when the American public comes to a clear consciousness of its educational needs it will demand a pretty thorough reformation of our system of secondary education, and that this will be, in outline, the direction which it will take; viz.: the addition of two or three years to the courses of the Academies and High Schools, making in these a continuous curriculum of seven to nine years, during which the pupil shall be taught a thorough knowledge of the English language and a good reading knowledge of at least the Greek, Latin, German and French, the pure mathematics to the Calculus, the elements of the natural sciences, and the elements of universal history and general literature; then the establishment of such institutions in every town of any considerable population, and the advance of the successful graduates of these direct to the University. Such institutions will be, as compared with our present Colleges, inexpensive, and within the reach of every considerable community. They will fit the students better and in larger numbers for the University then the Academy and College now taken together do, and they will enable the student to reach the University by his twentieth or twenty-first year, whereas now the double, and, to a great degree, doubled curricula of Academy and College detain him from the University until the completion of his twenty-second or twenty-third year, on the average.

There is, however, still another difficulty in relying upon College graduates to make up a body of University students, and that is they have no desire, as a rule, to become real University students. It is disheartening to a true lover of learning to hear the talk in which the graduates of Colleges generally indulge concerning the uselessness of any study for them which does not connect itself *directly* with the practice of some profession. They will enter the Law department, or the Medical department, or the Theological department of a University, but they will limit their studies to what they call the practical side of their profession; *i.e.,* they will eschew carefully the cognate and auxiliary studies in what the Germans call the Faculty of Philosophy,— studies which lift their professions out of the condition of a mere technique into the position of a true science. They are therefore not University students, in the true sense, but undergraduates of technical schools. It would not be just, however, to let these observations go without some qualification. They are true, indeed, for the mass of our College graduates, but there are many honorable exceptions which should be remarked. Many of our College graduates have had the wisdom and the energy to make their College course a real gymnastic training in all the elements, and not yield to the temptation to enter special fields, and many of them have manifested the true scholastic zeal and spirit. The fact that our Colleges furnish annually several hundreds of students to the Universities of Germany, the majority of whom study under the Faculty of Philosophy, and many of whom make with marked success their Doctor's degree, is ample evidence upon these points. Upon the whole, I think it would be correct to assume that our College graduates do now furnish us with a body of students prepared to do fair University work. All beginnings are surrounded with difficulties, and we must not be too fastidious as to the order of the start or we shall never go. We should, however, keep always in view these great failings in our system of secondary education and seek most earnestly to remedy them, for the ultimate success of the University will depend most largely upon this being rightly effected.

In the light of this brief analysis and discussion, it seems to me we may claim, without risk of being called vain or visionary, that the conditions necessary to the development of a true university do *now* exist in our country.

II. Where shall the American University be?

Briefly we answer, it must be at or near a centre of wealth and culture.

The University anywhere is in great advantage when placed at or near such a centre, because of the aids and auxiliaries which it furnishes to University work,—its galleries and museums of art and science, its libraries, its hospitals, and its varied life. Berlin, Vienna, Munich, Leipzig and Paris are the natural seats of the great Universities of Europe. But in the United States there is another and if anything a more imperative reason why the University should be so located; viz., its sole reliance upon private support. A State which confides to its Government the direction and support of its higher education may use the State treasury to establish a University anywhere; but in a State which does not vest its governmental organs with any such powers and where, therefore, private donation is the sole source of University support the University must, as a rule, be located near by where the individuals reside who have the wealth to bestow upon it and the disposition to bestow it. Some individuals will indeed be found who are willing to bestow aid upon far off enterprises, but the greatness of the amount necessary to found and maintain a University can hardly be secured without the incentive of local pride.

Have we now any such centres in the United States? We can affirm unhesitatingly that we have already at least one which fulfils all of these requirements; where the surplus wealth exists and the disposition to give it to the support of the higher education, and where the many auxiliaries of University culture above referred to also exist through the same munificent generosity of cultured men. It will hardly be necessary that I should name this community, but it may be profitable to call to mind the origin of that cultured public spirit which distinguishes it so markedly. There can be no doubt that it took its beginning from the character of the men who originally founded that community. Winthrop and his companions were neither seedy noblemen, seeking to retrieve broken fortunes by founding feudal estates or trading-posts in a new land nor destitute men from the middle class, compelled to emigrate in order to win a livelihood. They were men of fair means, of good blood and of high culture,—many of them graduates of Cambridge, and by profession ministers of the Gospel; men who knew that the highest good is the culture of the community, and not the enrichment of the individual. They came to found what they termed a commonwealth, and they viewed the weal of the community as consisting first of all in piety, morality and intelligence. One of their earliest acts was to set aside a large portion of the common property to the purpose of the higher education, in order, as they expressed it, that piety and good learning should not perish from the earth. The descendants of these men in every generation have been true to the principles of their forefathers, and they have established a community possessing the wealth and the spirit to bestow it for the culture of its own citizens and of all who will go and partake thereof. Whether we have more than one such community remains yet to be seen. We have other cities in which riches abound to a higher degree even than in Boston, but the reign of excessive individualism and the elaboration of private luxury have thus far largely negatived the conditions for the development of a cultured community and a cultured public spirit. Where the rich man considers that he must have his palace in the city, his villa in the country and his cottage by the sea, his steam-yacht, his coach and four and his private car in order to be comfortable, little will remain from the largest income for the higher education of the community or the nation. Let us not, however, be too desponding. If it still remains to be seen whether we have more than one such community, it also remains to be seen that we have not. We are not yet so far advanced in the formation of our public habits to say what we now are, that we shall be always and no more. A few devoted and cultivated spirits can do much in training a community to a proper application of its surplus wealth, and there are not a few such spirits abroad now in many of our great cities, the success or failure of whose efforts will, at no very distant day, give the practical answer to the question as to whether or not we are to have more than one University.

III. What shall the American University be?

This is the triple question of organization, curricula, and method.

First, What should be the form of organization, *i.e.,* what would be the form most consonant with the genius of American Institutions?

I think we may safely assume at the outset that the University will not now thrive here as an institution of the State. The rapidly shifting policies in legislation and the rapidly rotating personnel of administration render the government, either of the Nation or Commonwealth, utterly unfit to direct the development of the higher education. Moreover, there is nothing which would offer to the universal demagogism of American politics so capital a point of attack as the appropriations necessary to the support of the University. No party would be able, in all probability, to hold the reins of power here for a second term which should dare to expend the public moneys, in any sufficient amount, upon what, in the eyes of the great majority of voters, is a useless luxury.

The American University must therefore be a private institution, supported by private donations, and directed by an association of private persons. It would be a waste of time and exertion to enter upon a discussion of the advantages and disadvantages of this condition. It cannot be otherwise so long as the politic which has reigned here for a good half-century continues, and there is little prospect discoverable at this moment that it will ever cease. As first principle and point of departure we would say, then, that the central point in the organization of the American University must be the Corporation,—a body vested with the powers of acquiring, holding, and using property, of establishing Faculties, and granting University degrees. This body may originate in one of three ways: either through voluntary association, or through nomination by a donor or donors, or through appointment by the Government. Of course, if through either of the first two methods, the members must be accepted and *formally* appointed by the Government which confers the corporate powers. So far the matter is clear and simple, and unavoidably dictated by the genius of American institutions. When we come, however, to consider the questions as to how the Corporation shall be perpetuated, and what shall be its permanent relation to the Government on the one side and the Faculties on the other, then we touch upon points capable of a variety of solutions, no one of which is so rigorously required by the conditions of American life as to exclude the rest. We have here, then, debatable ground, upon which private judgment, if supported by sound reasoning and experience, may be of some weight in suggesting the principles for these relations best adapted to produce successful results. First, then, as to the method of perpetuating the Corporate body. It may be done in one of three ways, or in some combination thereof; viz.: the Government may appoint to the vacancies, or the Corporation may cooptate, or the graduates of the University may elect. It seems to me that the first method is with us to be unqualifiedly condemned. The higher education cannot, in my opinion, be too far emancipated from governmental interference in a political system where nothing is done except with a partisan purpose. With us the alternative lies between cooptation or election by the graduates or some combination of the two methods. The advantage of the first is conservativeness. Its danger is fogyism. The advantages of the second are to be found in its progressiveness, and in its tendency to attach the graduates more closely to the institution. Its dangers are radicalness, and tendency to create factions and breed a spirit of bitter partisanship. While the third, which, at first sight, might seem to combine the excellencies and avoid the defects of the other two, is really the most objectionable of the three. It furnishes the best conditions for the bitterest feuds in the Corporation between the members elected by the graduates and those chosen by the Corporation. To my mind the self-perpetuating Corporation is the most practicable form. It will be the more experienced and harmonious; a disappointed minority therein will not be invoking the interference of any outside body in its behalf, as it certainly would do if the graduates stood behind the Corporation as its creator and superior; and most important of all, it will give a readier ear to the advice of the Faculties, and confer upon them a wider and wider autonomy. Practically the Corporation will fill its vacancies from the graduates and, in time, the body will be almost entirely composed of graduates; and if the interest of the graduates in the institution can only be kept alive by according to them the right to elect the Trustees, then it seems to me that such interest is hardly worth so great a sacrifice of advantage in administration that we should essay its preservation. I know it is possible that a board of ultra-conservative Trustees may select for vacancies only ultra-conservative men, and thus perpetuate a spirit of illiberality in itself and in the Faculties which it appoints; still, I prefer this possibility to the probability that the tricks of politics will dominate the elections and the elected body be rendered useless by factiousness. When we come fully to understand that, in the true University, the Corporation must be a controlling body rather than an initiating body, then we shall appreciate the proposition that it should be as compact and simple as possible in its constitution and procedure.

Secondly. I have already said enough to indicate the view which I entertain concerning the relation which should exist between the Corporation and the Government. It should, of course, be held by the Courts to the fulfilment of its trusts, but any supervision by Legislature or Executive should be most decidedly repelled. It is far rather to be supposed that a company of respectable gentlemen, who have public spirit enough to give their time, thoughts and energies and often their money to the creation and maintenance of an institution of superior learning, will honestly and efficiently manage its affairs of their own motion and accord, than that the meddling of such Commissioners therein as would most likely be here intrusted with inspecting powers could be of any service whatsoever. The partisanship which, as the rule, dominates all appointments here renders any governmental agent unfit to tamper with such delicate relations; for partisanship seeks to manipulate every thing for personal or party advantage and does nothing, intentionally, for such abstractions as civilization and culture.

Thirdly. The relation of the Corporation to the Faculties. It would be most awkward and disadvantageous if the Government should undertake to fix these relations in the charter; for, in the first place, the Government would not know how to make the adjustment, and, in the second place, it must, in the developing period of the University, be a constantly shifting line. The Corporation should be made the starting-point and the ultimate authority for everything further, and the Faculties should have only such functions and powers as are conferred upon them by the Corporation. In the earlier periods of the life of the institution, the Corporation must necessarily exercise more of its powers in detail itself. After it has succeeded in establishing Faculties who shall have proved their capacity and fidelity, then it will be both safe and expedient and necessary to the success of the University that the Corporation should accord the Faculties a much wider discretion and autonomy. When that time arrives, the nature of the case would suggest that the Corporation should hold the property and administer the finances, the Faculties should control the system of discipline and education, while both should participate in the further selection of the officers of instruction. This is the solution to which the

German Universities have come. It is a solution, however, which contains nothing exclusively German about it, except that the Government, represented by its Minister of Education, stands in the place of the Corporation; and that is hardly exclusively German,—it is Continental European. The Germans have come to this solution of the question of these relations first, simply because they are further along in the development of the true University than any other nationality.

Finally, we come to the subject of the organization of the Faculties. In the German system the rule is the distinction of the University corps into four Faculties, viz., Theology, Jurisprudence, Medicine, and Philosophy, placing thus all non-professional branches under the latter head. Neither is there anything exclusively German about this. It is the natural division of University pursuits, and is as applicable in New York as in Berlin. The question has often been mooted in Germany as to division of the Philosophical Faculty into two or three bodies, as for instance into a Faculty of Moral Science and one of Natural Science, but the best thought there condemns this *in toto,* upon the ground that the Natural Sciences would tend, by the separation, more and more to the methods and purposes of the Polytechnicum. The Philosophical Faculty is the life and glory of the University. It is the foundation for everything further. Without it Theology becomes a dreary dogmatism, Law a withering letter, and Medicine a dangerous empiricism. It is possible to have a Theological School which is no *University Faculty* of Theology at all. In fact, most of the Theological Schools in the United States are not; and for the simple reason that there is no Philosophical Faculty connected with them to furnish the broad basis of Psychology, Logic, History, Literature, and Philology, upon which all development and progress in Theology must rest. The mere acquirement of creeds and ritual is not University Theology. It is only the technique of Theology. Likewise we may have a Law School which is not a University Faculty of Jurisprudence. Few, if any, of our Law Schools have risen to the dignity of such a place. Cases and rules of practice make up the substance of the instruction which the pupils want and which the Professors usually give. But this, again, regards Law only as a bread and butter industry. This is again technique, but not Jurisprudence. The Philosophical Faculty, again, must place the broad basis of History, Logic, Ethics, and Philosophy under the rules and judgments of Courts before the Law School is entitled to be called a Faculty of Jurisprudence. The same is true in regard to the

School of Medicine. It will stagnate and degenerate into a machine for grinding out half-fitted practitioners unless the Chemistry, Botany, Anatomy, Physiology, Logic and Psychology of the Philosophical curriculum give it the life and energy for an ever-continuing development.

The German system, then, unites these four Faculties, usually by representation, into a single body,—the Senate of the University,—and vests in this body the general supervision and administration of the University. In this manner, also, the full and well-proportioned growth of all branches is secured. This organization is as necessary to the success of the American University as to the German. The want of it is one of the causes of the curious malformations that are to be observed in those American institutions which are striving to become Universities upon a plan suggested by some bias-minded President, some officious Professor, some zealous Trustee, or some crotchety donor.

Thus far the German system will serve us as the example in regard to the organization of the Faculties, which we will do best to accept and imitate. We come now, however, to a question in the solution of which the German experience does not render us any aid, viz., that of the University Presidency. The German University has a Rector, chosen annually from among the Professors by the Assembly of the ordinary[3] Professors of the entire University, and a Dean for each Faculty, likewise chosen by the Professors in that Faculty for the term of a single year. These officers preside over these bodies and are responsible for the execution of their acts, but a permanent Presidency is no actual part of the German system. On the other hand, for the American University this office is, it seems to me, indispensable, at least until the University is fully and completely developed. That necessity springs out of the fact that the American University must be a private institution, resting upon voluntary contribution for its support. To meet this condition successfully in our American society the University must have a permanent representative before the public,—a man who shall not only be a great scholar and a sound pedagogue, but who shall be possessed of social position, dignity of manner and business tact, of energy, enthusiasm and the power to inspire. In other words, a man who can direct the surplus of great incomes into the University treasury and give wisest counsel to the Trustees in its expenditure. Moreover, in the earlier periods of the foundation and growth of the Uni-

---

[3] This is the word which the Germans use to designate a full Professor.

versity, a President, great in scholarship and in the knowledge of educational systems, keen in discrimination and sound in his judgment and estimation of men, is the best means which a Board of Trustees can employ for the original constitution of the Faculties; and though we grant that, this once successfully accomplished, his powers should largely pass over upon them in respect to discipline and educational policy, yet the functions first mentioned never should and never can. The successful accomplishment of these requires an experience, a reputation, and an influence which permanency alone can lend.

Secondly. The University Curricula.

It is not easy to draw the line between the Gymnasium and the University in regard to the subjects of their curricula. I think we may get at it better through a series of adjustments than by a direct survey. First, then, the entire realm of the Unknown belongs to the University. The primest function of the University is the discovery of *new* truth, the *increase* of knowledge in every direction. The fitting out of Academies and even Colleges with extensive laboratories, cabinets, museums, and libraries is a great waste of substance. These things all belong to the University, to be used, not as curiosities to entertain, but as means to new discoveries. Secondly, all professional science belongs to the University,—Theology, Jurisprudence, Medicine. This is the universal practice, and is so patent and necessary that I need not expend time in attempting to give reasons. So far there is no difficulty. It is, thirdly, then only when we come to draw the line between the Gymnasium and the non-professional curriculum of the University, the Faculty of Philosophy, that we are driven to take closer observation, since, apparently, many of the studies pursued in the latter are but a continuation of the same subjects taught in the former. Shall, then, the University begin in this curriculum where the Gymnasium leaves off, or the Gymnasium leave off where the University begins, no matter where, or is there a natural line of division between them? It seems to me that the latter is or should be the case, and that the difference of *purpose* between the Gymnasium and the University should dominate in the solution of this question as well as in that of University method. The University curriculum of Philosophy is a collection of *non-professional specializations,* and the student should enter upon it only after he has become prepared, through the variety, quantity, and quality of his discipline and knowledge, to specialize in *any* and *every* direction. He should be able to read those ancient and modern languages which contain the chief literature upon the subjects of all knowledge; he should have the drill and the ground-work of the pure mathematics, and of the elements of the natural sciences generally; he should have stored and classified in his memory the names, dates, and principal events of history; and he should be brought under the discipline of logical thought and composition. He must have all of the disciplines and knowledges in an extent and to a degree that he shall be able to pursue with intelligence and success any branch of Philology, or Literature, or History, or Philosophy, or Moral or Political Science, or enter with profit upon the work of the laboratories, observatories, and cabinets of the Natural Sciences. On the other hand, Philology, Literature, Philosophy, Moral, Historical and Political Science, and the studies of the Laboratories, Observatories, and Cabinets, belong to the University, and should be kept jealously apart from the Gymnasium. If they are not, they will never be successfully pursued. Without the completion of the gymnastic curriculum they cannot be appreciated, and if they be injected into it this must be at the cost of displacing something of far more importance to the gymnast. They will prove a quicksand instead of a rock. This, then, is the general line between the curriculum of the Gymnasium and that of the Philosophical Faculty of the University. It cannot be pretended that the adjustment is minute and exhaustive, but a careful and an intelligent application of the general principles of distinction here advanced would, I think, arrive ultimately thereto. It should be added, however, that although the University should instruct as well as discover and conserve, yet its means and its energies should not be expended upon the mere *pratique* of its subjects. In Theology, for instance, it should not be held to teach forms and rubrics, better learned at the reading-desk of some church; nor in Medicine the methods of practice, better seen in the wards of the hospital; nor in Jurisprudence the technique of procedure and deministration, better acquired in the office of an attorney or as clerk in a governmental bureau; and not in the Natural Sciences is its work their application to the exploitation of the wealth of the universe,—that is the object of the Polytechnicum; and all of these things are the industrial side of knowledge and instruction, which should take care of itself, or else be taken care of by those immediately interested therein, and has no claim upon the community at large for sacrifice and support.

Thirdly and lastly, the methods of University instruction.

The German system presents, we may say, three fundamental principles upon this subject; viz.: the combination of studies at the election of the student, the giving of the instruction by original lecture, and the exercise of the student in the Seminarium. There is, however, nothing exclusively German in these principles. The reasons for them are as general as humanity, and have the same force here as there. First, the combination of studies by the student for himself proceeds upon the ground that the student is the best judge of his own bent and genius. If his gymnastic training has not brought him to this point, then he is not fit to be a University student at all. He either has no genius for anything, or has not been disciplined sufficiently to bring it out. In either case the University is not the place for him, and consideration for such persons must never lead to the abandonment of this only real method for the cultivation of a true intellectual peculiarity; for without such a development there can be no advance in the discovery of new truth or in a fuller comprehension of old truth. Secondly, the giving of instruction by original lecture stands upon the ground that the University Professor must be a worker among original material. He must present to his students *his own* view and arrangement, derived from *his own* investigation of the sources. If he does not do this, but contents himself with simply repeating the views of others, it is probably because he is not capable of anything else, in which case he is no University Professor at all, but at best only a drill-master for the Gymnasium. And, thirdly the Seminarium of picked students for special work in the study or laboratory of the Professor rests upon the obvious reason that those students who have a special genius for any subject should have the opportunity for special exercise in its development under the special direction of more experienced genius in the same line.

Manifestly these grounds and reasons are of universal force, and likewise the principles of method which rest upon them. We can do no better, therefore, than follow, in the main, the German example in these respects again and should not be repelled from it by the indiscriminate charge of slavish imitation.

If, now, these reflections in regard to the American University be correct, I think we must conclude that we have not yet attained to anything like a full realization of it and that there is no doubt many a hard pull ahead before we arrive thereto; but it is something to know where the difficulties lie and how some of them have been elsewhere overcome, and it is much to feel that we have already gone too far to turn back in discouragement and be forced to the contemplation of ultimate failure.

8. Charles Kendall Adams Argues the Merits of the State University, 1875

When Charles Kendall Adams (1835–1902) wrote this review, he had been Andrew D. White's successor in the professorship of history at the University of Michigan for twelve years. Adams, a Vermonter, graduated from Michigan as White's star pupil and the influence of White (see Doc. 9, and Part VI, Docs. 5–7) was seen in Adams' introduction of the seminary method of instruction for advanced students at Michigan, and in his presidencies of Cornell (1885–92) and Wisconsin (1892–1900). As an administrator Adams was particularly adept in appointing eminent professors and in conducting ambitious and imaginative campaigns of university expansion. So great was his affection for the University of Wisconsin that he left his entire property to it as a fellowship fund for graduate work in English, Greek, and history.

See Charles F. Smith, *Charles Kendall Adams: A Life Sketch* (Madison, 1924), and Merle Curti and Vernon Carstensen, *The University of Wisconsin, 1848–1925* (Madison, 1949), Vol. I, chap. xx.

Every one knows that at the present day public opinion inclines to the establishment of a sharply defined line between our upper and our lower schools. The belief is almost universal that our common schools ought to be supported by general taxation. The welfare of the State manifestly demands that the children of the poor, as well as those of the rich, receive an elementary education. This interest could not be subserved, if the poor were to be left to their own unaided efforts. The State, therefore, says to the rich: You shall contribute of your abundance for the education of your poor neighbors' children. It matters not that you educate your own children at a private school and at your own private expense; it matters not even if you have no children whatever of your own to educate. You are a part of the State. You receive the benefits of that enlightened condition of society which comes from the general prevalence of schools; and, consequently, you must bear such a part of the burden of their support as your property is a part of the whole property of the State. But while this argument seems to be

C. K. Adams, [Review of] *"American State Universities, Their Origin and Progress, a History of Congressional University Land Grants, a Particular Account of the Rise and Development of the University of Michigan, and Hints toward the Future of the American University System.* By Andrew Ten Brook. Cincinnati . . . 1875," *North American Review,* CXXI (October, 1875), 365–408.

generally satisfactory when applied to the support of the common schools, it is often objected to when applied to the support of schools of a higher grade. The fact is obvious that throughout the country the opinion prevails to a great extent that our colleges and universities, and even our academies, ought to be supported largely, if not indeed exclusively, not at the expense of the public, but by means of private munificence. Not long since a case occurred in one of the most enlightened of our States where a gentleman of high standing raised the question concerning the right of the school board to expend any portion of the school money for the support of a high school. Before the court it was argued on ethical as well as on constitutional grounds that the public moneys could not properly be expended in support of instruction in any other than what are commonly known as elementary branches. Happily this position was not sustained by the court; but it must be confessed that the arguments advanced were quite in harmony with the views on the question which, at present, are more or less generally enlightened.

Now it is our firm conviction that the distinction which we have noted is without substantial foundation. It seems to us that the arguments advanced in support of it are essentially fallacious; and, furthermore, that it is entirely at variance with the early views and habits of our own country.

It would scarcely seem necessary to plead the cause of higher education in a republic. In general and abstract terms everybody admits the necessity of it. It is too obvious to admit of question that there can be no intelligent guidance of the intricate affairs of state, without something of that discriminating knowledge which comes from a thorough training of the higher faculties. Of course it is impossible for all men to have large personal experience, and therefore it is best that, so far as possible, they should acquire large knowledge of the personal experience of others. Therefore the more of higher education you can have in a state the better. All this is commonplace, and will be universally assented to. But it is languidly admitted, rather than earnestly felt. It is, probably, after all, not too much to say that the masses of the people, as represented in the average legislature, half believe that higher education is a luxury to be privately enjoyed, rather than a necessity to be publicly supported. The consequence is that in most of our States, while the people guard strenuously all encroachments upon the system of common schools, they are quite willing to leave the care of their higher institutions of learning in the hands of those over whom they have no control. This willingness, encouraged by the arguments to which we have already alluded, has resulted in the general adoption of a policy of non-interference.

But is it true that higher education is in any sense less necessary to the welfare of a state than the education afforded by the common schools? Is it not, after all, quite as essential that the men who are to make and administer our laws should be thoroughly trained, as that those who choose the lawmakers should know how to read and write? Nay, is there any ethical or logical reason why, if you provide a certain grade of education for the voter, you may not also provide a certain grade for the lawmaker? Is there any justification of the one, that is not a possible justification of the other? If these questions are answered as we apprehend they must be, the problem reduces itself to a very simple query: Is there any method by which higher education can be more certainly and more satisfactorily secured than by committing it to the charge of the state?

Those who answer this question in the affirmative, so far as we have observed, found their objections to the policy of state support either on the belief that it is unjust to the tax-payer, or that it is unsafe for the student. It is sometimes urged that, as, in the nature of things, higher education can only be acquired by the few, it ought not to be secured at the expense of the many. But to this it is a complete answer to say that such an education is a public benefit, and that unless it can be shown that this benefit can be better secured in some other manner, it ought to be provided for just as other public benefits are provided for. It is no argument against the establishment of hospitals and asylums by the state, to say that they are chiefly beneficial to the few only. No member of Congress presumes to argue against appropriations for lighthouses and harbor improvements, on the ground that such improvements are chiefly advantageous to merchants and navigators; and, therefore, that merchants and navigators or their friends ought to construct them. The truth is, that a very large part of what are known as public improvements are directly beneficial to no more than a very small portion of the community, while the advantage derived from them by members of the public at large is only of that general and indefinite nature which comes from the improved condition of the state as a whole. It requires but a moment's reflection to perceive that no state could thrive, that no true civilization could exist even, if the principle were to be admitted that no man is to be taxed save for that which to him personally is to be of direct and tangible advantage. To admit the principle, and act upon it, would be to strike away the very possibility of social improvement. The argument, therefore, that our legislatures have no *right* to tax the people for the purposes of higher education, is utterly fallacious. The position can only be sustained when it is admitted that such education is of no advantage whatever to the state at large.

The other objection to which we alluded, is that in universities supported by the state, students are unsafe. This objection is not, perhaps, very loudly urged, but it is, without doubt, to a very considerable extent, secretly entertained. Occasionally it crops out in unseemly ways. We happened to know of a zealous editor who, not long since in a moment of thoughtlessness, allowed his spirit to escape his control, and to make an antic display of itself. In announcing the admission of a large class to one of our Eastern universities, which he did not think sufficiently religious, he headed his article, *"Two hundred raw recruits for Satan!"* It would, of course, be unjust to declare this editorial Boanerges as strictly representative of any large class of persons; and yet we fancy the number is not altogether inconsiderable who would differ from him chiefly in method of expression. It has to be admitted that there are vast numbers of good men and women who entertain the notion that those colleges which are in some way or other under the supposed control of the Church are the only safe resorts of our young men in search of an education.

Now, we wish to state explicitly that, in our opinion, this notion is not only without foundation, but that it exerts a pernicious influence on the cause of higher education in the country.

In the first place, the notion is founded on exaggerated views of the difference between the state and the denominational universities. It is often represented, and, indeed, believed, that institutions of the one class are distinctively religious, while those of the other class are distinctively irreligious. Such representations are really the most efficient means by which a numerical majority of the colleges in our country are kept alive. But these representations are almost as far as possible from the truth. There is, indeed, a manifest difference between the dominant spirit of a great state university and that of an obscure denominational college. But the very moment you bring to the college a large faculty and a large number of students, the difference vanishes.

We have no disposition to make invidious comparisons. But we have repeatedly heard men of earnest religious faith and life, who have had professional experience in both classes of institutions, declare that the difference in this respect is imaginary rather than real. Nay, further, we have never heard the contrary asserted by any one who has had good opportunity of judging. We have come to believe, therefore, that the comparisons so frequently made are either outright cant, or are the product of entire ignorance on the subject.

The real distinction, then, is between the small colleges and the large ones. Here, no doubt, there is a marked difference. In the smaller institutions the student is under the more direct supervision of the faculty. The professors know far more intimately the characteristics of individual pupils. The peculiar wants of each are recognized, and are treated in their appropriate manner. It is also true that the individual peculiarities of the professors themselves leave a more positive impression on the mind of the student. If the instructor is ardently religious, as in a college of this class he is likely to be, a restraining, and perhaps even a religious influence may be exerted. These, in general terms, are the advantages held out by the small college. For certain purposes they are, doubtless, not to be despised, but they are entirely different in kind from the advantages presented at a great university. They are the characteristics which direct rather than develop the mind. They stand guard over it, doubtless often keeping it out of danger, but they do not inspire it for its highest efforts. They keep it from utter failure, but they do not move it to the highest success. If the best education consisted simply of making perfect recitations and keeping out of mischief, the smallest college would be incomparably the best college. But the best education is far more than that. Perhaps it is correct to say it is an inspiration rather than an acquisition. It comes not simply from industry and steady habits, but far more largely from that kindling and glowing zeal which is best begotten by familiar contact with large libraries and museums, and enthusiastic specialists. It shows itself not so much in the amount which its possessor has made himself master of, as in the spirit with which he takes what he knows, and goes out with it to grapple with his life work. This is the reason, it may be said in passing, why valedictorians and senior-wranglers so often disappoint the hopes of their friends. For the moment a student begins to covet a given position, he is tempted, for obvious reasons, to limit his efforts to the work which will favorably affect his standing. His success depends upon the regularly perfect performance of the task assigned. He keeps himself, therefore, within very narrow limits. So long as this spirit dominates, it tends to narrowness rather than breadth. Its possessor is working for a price, whereas all genuine scholarship is, and must be, its own sufficient reward. The difference is quite enough to account for innumerable failures as well as innumerable successes in life. It needs scarcely to be said that the highest successes are to be awaited when to the exact scholarship of the one is joined the enthusiastic spirit of the other; and it is this combination of excellences which the large university is best adapted to secure. While the small college affords guidance and protection, the large one offers guidance, inspiration, and opportunity. What the respective merits of the city and of the country are to the man of business, those of the large institution and those of the small one are to the student. As the young merchant will be less exposed to financial perils in a village grocery than in the whirl of a commercial metropolis, so will the student be less exposed to danger in the quiet retreat of a rural college than in the more exciting atmosphere of a metropolitan university. But in both of these avocations it is the stir, the enthusiasm, the unceasing activity, and, above all, the constant intercourse with men of the same pursuits and the same ambitions, that develop the greatest energies and secure the highest successes.

The advantages of a concentration of energies for higher education have long been felt in every nation of Europe. England, Ireland, and Scotland, with a population not much less than our own, have scarcely half a score of institutions empowered to grant degrees. In France there is, strictly speaking, but a single one. In Germany, where the system of education has been brought to the highest perfection, the number is only twenty-one, or one for about two millions of inhabitants. In our own country the latest announcement is that we have three hundred and twenty-two colleges and universities, each entitled, so far as municipal law can bestow it, to rank itself as one of our highest institutions of learning. A single one of our States has the enormous number of thirty-three colleges and nine universities, with an average gross income of somewhat less than nine thousand dollars each: forty-two faculties, forty-two libraries, forty-two museums, forty-two complete sets of apparatus, to say nothing of laboratories and observatories to be provided for and administered out of an income which scarcely exceeds, if indeed it does exceed, the insufficient income of Harvard College!

Now, it is to be noted that this fatal isolation of educational appliances is the direct result of our methods of supporting our colleges and universities. In our opinion the system of private endowments could never have resulted otherwise. Local interests and ambitions are ever active, and have ever exerted a powerful influence. Men will give money for a college in their town, when they would give nothing for a college at a distance. Then, too, the attitude of the different religious sects has tended powerfully in the same direction. Every denomination knows that, if it is to push its way in the civilization of the present century, it must have an educated clergy. It must also guard its members, especially its members in process of education, against the influence of opposing creeds. To accomplish this result it must have schools. As our system practically excludes parochial schools, it is limited to the college and to the theological seminary. These, therefore, it must have in as great abundance as possible. Whenever a rich sectarian dies, therefore, he is exhorted to leave his money to one of the sectarian schools already founded; or, if he is unwilling to do that, to found a school in his own name. The exhortation is often made effectual by the fact that the cost of an efficient college is ridiculously under-estimated.

Not long since occurred an example that will serve as an illustration. An effort was made to endow a denominational school in the heart of one of our largest States. A great meeting was held for the purpose. Within less than a hundred miles were several colleges already in operation, besides a university with an endowment of more than two millions of dollars. And yet one of the most zealous members was reported as using substantially these words: "We must endow a great Christian university. Yes, we must have the greatest and best university in the country, *even if it takes an endowment of five hundred thousand dollars!*" Here was pious simplicity indeed; and yet the speech was not altogether exceptional either in piety or simplicity. It was the identical spirit which has dotted the country all over with mendicant colleges and universities, whose chief work in the general cause of higher education has been to keep down the standards of scholarship, and to stand in the way of something better.

Now, in our opinion the public has not sufficiently understood and appreciated the leading cause of this condition of affairs. We have no doubt that the immense number of our colleges is very generally deplored. But we are not sure that the public is ready to admit either the extent of the evil, or the fact that the evil is the legitimate and necessary product of our system. That it is such a product, we believe it is easy to show. We believe that as soon as it was determined that the colleges and universities were not to be supported in the same manner as the lower schools are supported, it was fixed as a necessary consequence, that, while the lower schools would flourish, the colleges and universities would multiply beyond all demand, and a vast majority of them would languish beyond all recovery. We believe that under the change of policy to which we have referred, the importance of higher education has declined in public estimation; that while a comparison of the state of the learned professions at the present time with the same of fifty years ago will reveal a degeneracy, a careful study of statistics, like those prepared by President Barnard in 1870, will also show that the number of students seeking a college education has relatively declined. We believe, furthermore, that nothing but a return to the early policy of our country will reinstate the general cause of higher education in the position of relative importance which it formerly occupied. . . .

It is evident that the number of undergraduate students in the country, for the thirty or forty years previous to 1870, was not only diminishing, but that the diminution during the last ten years of the period was very remarkable. What the tendency since 1870 has been, we have at hand no means of determining.

Now, whatever may have been the specific causes that have contributed to this diminution,—and they are doubtless several in number, —it is evident we are forced to the general conclusion that the colleges of to-day, as a whole, present less attractions to young men than did the colleges in the early part of the century. It may have been partly because courses of study have not conformed to the public demand. It may have been in a measure owing to the intense mercenary spirit which for the last forty years has had possession of the country. But in our opinion it is far more largely due to the insignificance of the modern college in the popular imagination. Ambitious young men who aspire to professional and political honors bend their chief energies to the means of helping themselves on. Forty-two colleges in a single State are sure to be insignificant, and are sure to be thought insignificant. The popular imagination attaches to them very little importance; and, as a matter of fact, the graduate finds that his degree has given him little or no advantage over his fellow. The ambitious young man, therefore, is quite likely to eschew the college and betake himself at once to the more attractive experiences of the office and the political stump.

This is no fanciful picture, but one that may be shown to be absolutely true to the facts. The popular impression, at least among literary men, is that college graduates are considerably less numerous and less conspicuous in the professions and in political life than were men of a similar education fifty or a hundred years ago. The popular impression is doubtless correct. In regard to the professions it is, perhaps, difficult to speak with great confidence or precision; but in regard to the prominence of college-bred men in political life, the position admits of absolute demonstration. A study of the dictionaries will show beyond all question that the number of graduates elected to the last Congresses is considerably less than was the number elected in the early days of the Republic. We had supposed this to be the case; but after a somewhat wearisome turning over of Drake and Lanman, we have found the difference to be even greater than we had suspected. Of the signers of the Declaration of Independence, for example, thirty out of fifty-six were college-bred; of the Senate of the First Congress, fifteen out of twenty-six; while of the Forty-first Congress, the latest of which we could procure exact information, the proportion from the same States was only seven out of twenty-six. If the investigation were to be extended to the House of Representatives and to the other States, the comparison would probably be still less favorable. Be that as it may, it is too evident that for some reason or other the graduate of to-day is not so likely to be the man chosen by the people as was the graduate in the early days of the Republic. It thus becomes just as obvious that college graduates, as a class, are less conspicuous than they were formerly, as we just saw it to be that they are relatively less numerous.

It needs only to be said, in concluding this part of our subject, that the responsibility of this serious, if not even alarming, tendency rests alone with our present educational system. It cannot be said to rest with the colleges, for it would be unjust to demand of them the impossible. They accomplish all, be it said without qualification, that colleges under these limitations are able to accomplish. As a rule they are administered by men who, for ability, for earnestness, and for devotion would at least compare favorably with any other class of men to be found in the country. But they are bound hand and foot by the poverty of the means they have to do with. Probably no American educator has visited the alcoves and the museums of a European university without turning away heartsick at the thought of the meagre appliances to which he must return.

For this meagreness there is of course no remedy, except by removing its cause. There is no reason to hope for any radical change for the better until, by some means or other, the number of colleges ranking themselves with the highest is reduced. To this end we believe that every consideration of true policy requires that the interest of the people should be concentrated upon a limited number of the larger and stronger colleges and universities. We believe that these should be raised into such conspicuous pre-eminence that the smaller and weaker ones will cease to be regarded as on the same level or to be entitled to rank in the same class. We believe that no other way can higher education be raised to the rank which it now holds in Europe, or even to the rank which it formerly held in our own country. If in the older States it is impracticable to enlist the legislatures in the work of raising the few at the expense of the many, the hope of a favorable change must rest upon the basis of private benevolence. But in the newer States where State universities have been established, no such limitations are imposed. There would seem to be no obstacle in the way of a large policy of legislative liberality similar to that which characterized the early history of New England. With the vast wealth of the West to support it, such a policy could not fail to build up a series of universities that would be a real credit to the land.

9. Andrew D. White Reviews His Achievements at Cornell, 1893

This letter, despite its boasting tone, serves as an excellent résumé of White's educational work. It was written to the two Cornell professors in response to remarks made by White's successor, Jacob Gould Schurman, at Schurman's inauguration. Schurman referred to White as being "among those who had most to do with securing the original charter of Cornell University." This slighting reference, a gross understatement of White's contribution, impelled the indignant ex-president to write these words from Finland, where his service as minister to Russia had taken him. On White, see Part VI, Docs. 5, 6, and 7.

Andrew D. White to George L. Burr and Ernest W. Huffcut, Helsingfors, Finland, September 8, 1893, White Papers, Cornell University Library, as printed in Carl Becker, *Cornell University: Founders and the Founding* (Ithaca, N.Y., 1943), pp. 173–80. Reprinted with the permission of Cornell University Press.

Permit me to write you in regard to a matter of much delicacy and in which I must put myself somewhat unreservedly into your hands, trusting to your kindness and discretion as to the result. At the inauguration of President Schurman he referred to me, no doubt with the most kindly feeling, stating in effect that "among those who had most to do with securing the original charter of Cornell University" was myself, but that I "had now returned to my first love."

I trust that you will not think me unduly egotistical when I say that this seems to me an inadequate statement.

It is simply unhistorical and absolutely misleading to those who shall hereafter look for the history of the University in documents issued under the highest sanction.

Both of you have to some extent acquainted yourselves with the University history, and I think that you will both allow that the statement above is either too little or too much.

This strikes me with all the more force in view of the approaching anniversary. I shall be content if at that time not one of the orators sees fit to mention my name; I should prefer infinitely to have it go unmentioned rather than that any statement should be made like that above referred to.

If my name is not mentioned at all no one will be misled, & perhaps some person hereafter looking into the matter will bring out something near the truth.

The main facts are simply these.

The first suggestion ever made having in view the keeping of the Land Grant Fund together for a *single* university came from me.

The one man who prevented in 1864 the division of the Land Grant Fund amounting then, according to the estimate of the Comptroller, to about $600,000, between the twenty & more colleges, which sought to divide it, was myself, as chairman of the Senate "Committee on Literature."

The one man who prevented its division at a later date [this can only mean at a later date in this the same year, 1864—C. B.] between the "People's College" at Havana, and the State Agricultural College at Ovid, was myself as chairman of the same committee.

During an entire winter in that capacity I opposed Mr. Cornell & the State Agricultural Society on this point. . . .

When, during the summer following . . . Mr. Cornell made his proposal to divide the fund, he to give three hundred thousand dollars

($300,000) to the State Agricultural College at Ovid, so that this added to half the Land Grant Fund ... would make up a sum equal to the entire estimated proceeds of the Land Grant, and when this was applauded to the echo by the authorities of the State Agricultural Society at Rochester [this was in fact a meeting of the trustees of the Agricultural College—C. B.], I, in their presence, still refused to accede to this division, but told Mr. Cornell that I would bring in a Bill to give the *entire* Land Grant Fund to a new institution provided he would make this same offer to it.

It was to me that during the following Session of the Legislature Mr. Cornell stated that he had five hundred thousand dollars ($500,-000) more than he or his family needed, asking what I would suggest as to the disposal of it.

It was I who answered as follows; "as regards institutions of a charitable sort we can always rely on the kindly instincts of the people at large; as to primary education, we can rely upon the State; as to advanced education, but few & chosen men understand it & see the value of it, & for this we must rely on individual munificence."

I then told him in a general way what sort of an institution for advanced instruction was needed;—one which should be unsectarian, fully equipped for the highest instruction in the sciences & the arts, and in history & in modern literature as well as for the branches hitherto carried on in the Colleges of the State, an institution in which various courses should be maintained, carried on in the same buildings & estimated of equal dignity, & in which women might receive an education equal to that given to men.

I showed him that here was a chance which might never happen again.

I had many conversations with him on this subject & at last he made his proposal to give half a million of dollars ($500,000) to a university to be established at Ithaca on the lines suggested by me.

It was I who suggested the name of *Cornell University;* he at first opposed it, but I conquered his scruples by showing him that this was simply in accordance with a time-honored custom in our own & other countries, citing the names Harvard, Yale, Brown, Williams & others.

I then made a rough draft of a charter, to which Mr. Cornell contributed parts relating to the Land Grant, and this was put into shape by Charles Folger, at that time Chairman of the Judiciary Committee of the Senate, afterwards Chief-Justice of the State and Secretary of the Treasury of the United States.

It was I who suggested both in the interest of the State & to secure the hearty co-operation of Judge Folger that the Willard Asylum—which had just been authorized—should be established on the Agricultural College property at Ovid, within Judge Folger's district, & this was done.

It was I, who, during the winter addressed small meetings of members of both houses in Mr. Cornell's rooms, explaining the plan to them, showing its necessity & various advantages.

It was I who, when a crisis came, in the Senate, & we found the lobby of the New York Central Railroad opposed to us, in order to secure the votes of the Anti-Cornell men in the Assembly, held the New York Central bill from passing the Senate & prevailed on a majority of the Senate not to take it up until justice was done us.

It was I who, at Mr. Cornell's request, nominated one half of the original Charter Trustees, he naming the other half.

It was I who, in the bitter struggle for our Charter against all the Colleges of the State, saw personally all the leading Editors of New York & enlisted them on our side by a full & fair presentation of the whole subject, inducing them to support us thoroughly, as they did in their papers. [An examination of the leading papers indicates that Manton Marble of the WORLD was the only editor who had anything much (favorable or unfavorable) to say about the matter—C. B.]

I do not underrate Mr. Cornell's work—I set it far above my own.

That he, a man who had never had the advantage of a University or Collegiate education, should have been willing to make so munificent a gift & in so broad a spirit was the greatest thing of all; that I have always acknowledged, & in his scheme for the "location" of the lands he showed foresight equal to his devotion to the interests of his fellow-men. . . .

Nor do I depreciate in the slightest degree the admirable service rendered by Mr. Lord in the Assembly, nor do I underrate the suggestions made from time to time by Judge—then Mr. Finch.

But the facts are as above stated.

I may add another point; Mr. Cornell was then one of the oldest—if not the oldest—members of the Senate, austere, not communicative to his associates generally, in fact, so reserved in his intercourse with his fellow-senators that they hardly knew him personally, I was the youngest member of the Senate & in my enthusiasm made the interest of the proposed university a personal matter, laboring individually with the other members & obtaining thus the co-operation which could not otherwise have been secured.

The idea of founding a University worthy of the State of New York was an old dream of mine cherished even while I was at Geneva (now Hobart) College, strengthened at Yale, developed more & more during my student days abroad; whether I live to return or not you will find marked passages in my European diary showing this.

Among my old letters, too, will be found a correspondence with Gerrit Smith, in which I offered him one half of all that I possessed on condition that he should carry out a plan, which he at one time favored, of establishing a University in the State of New York.

It was this hope of contributing to the establishment of a university freed from the old shackles which led me to accept the Professorship at the University of Michigan, since I saw there an opportunity to make a beginning of such an institution as I had dreamed of.

It may be said that I published too little after the organization of the university on the general subject.

As to this, I had stated my views in my speech in the Senate on the University bill, had developed them in the "Plan of Organization" & in my Inaugural Address, had defended them in sundry newspaper articles, & afterwards presented them in my Address to the State Agricultural Society, & in various magazine articles, lectures, etc.; but after we had opened the University came my conviction that mere writing & talking about Universities was not what was wanted,—that to establish an institution of a general university character & on the lines I had suggested to Mr. Cornell was what was wanted; that if this succeeded there was no need of elaborate treatises on the subject & that if it did not succeed such treatises would not accomplish the end which I had in view.

This is what led me to be silent under President Porter's attack; I could have answered him fully, but I left it to time to answer him & time has done it—Yale following our example in things which he declared preposterous—adopting them even during his presidency.

I think I may claim in this matter to have been free from any unworthy personal ambition; I had not the remotest expectation of being elected to any place in the institution, my election to its Presidency was a surprise to me and I accepted it only because the election was unanimously made by the Trustees & so earnestly pressed upon me by Mr. Cornell, but I accepted making a distinct statement that I should be regarded simply as *locum tenens,* holding the place until some man more fit for it could be secured.

Such a man, indeed, I had endeavored to secure—President Martin Anderson of Rochester, & was only dissuaded when Mr. William Kelly, President of the State Agricultural Society informed Mr. Cornell & myself that, if we insisted on choosing Dr. Anderson, his duty would be to retire from his Cornell Trusteeship & devote himself to the interests of Rochester as against Cornell.

Whatever ambition I had, & in this I was strengthened by the counsels of my dear wife, was in the direction of accepting a Professorship which had been tendered me at Yale.

As to the period following the struggle for the Charter; it was I who visited the foremost technical institutions of England, Germany, France, & Italy, with reference to the best organization of similar departments at Cornell, & this was without any cost to the University— either for salary or expenses.

It was I who laid the foundations of the Library & the collections of various sorts by purchases in Europe & elsewhere, securing special donations from Mr. Cornell, Mr. Kelly, and others, & adding to them myself.

It was I who suggested at the very outset the plan of non-resident Professors, which I had thought out long before & to which I had called George William Curtis' attention years previous at Ann Arbor —as you will see by referring to his speech at the opening of the University in 1868. [There is in Mr. Curtis' speech no reference to the idea of non-resident professors—C. B.]

It was I who enlisted Agassiz, Lowell, Curtis, Goldwin Smith, Bayard Taylor, James Law, Froude, Freeman & others, who came & gave a most valuable impulse to the new movement.

It was I who suggested and carried through the Legislature the Amendment to our Charter providing for the election of Alumni Trustees, &, so far as I know, this was the first admission of Alumni to such privileges in the United States.

As to the admission of women my simple claim is that as I had advocated it some years before at the University of Michigan, so I urged it in my Inaugural Address, & pressed it later upon the Trustees, drawing up the Report to the Board in favor of it.

It was I who suggested the establishment of fully equipped mechanical laboratories & workshops in connection with the Department of Mechanical Engineering, purchasing the first power-lathe for that purpose with my own funds, since I hardly dared approach the Trustees at that time with a proposal to make such purchase of which they could hardly then see the advantage.

It was immediately following a suggestion of mine in an Annual Report that Mr. Sibley broached to me first of all his wish to erect a College Building for us & and it was in accordance with my suggestion, made at various times from Berlin as well as from Ithaca, that he made various additions to the Sibley Building & Equipment.

It was immediately after a conversation with me on the subject of the University, & especially the University Library, that Miss McGraw—afterwards Mrs. Fiske—avowed to her father her wish to do something for the institution, &, receiving his permission, gave us the chimes as a beginning of gifts.

It was immediately after an Address of mine that John McGraw came to me and said, "I will stand by you", & in response to my suggestion gave us the building, which bears his name, & other things.

It was upon a suggestion of mine & for the purpose of anchoring Classical studies at the University that Mr. Cornell purchased The Anthon Library.

It was I who, as Professor Anthony will testify, suggested the establishment at Cornell of the first Department of Electrical Engineering ever erected in the United States, indeed, ever created anywhere, as far as I know, asking him to prepare a plan of instruction & to come before our Executive Committee with it, &, when Judge Boardman & others opposed it & seemed likely to defeat it, I pledged myself that it should not make any demands upon the University Treasury during its first year & that I would myself meet all the cost of it beyond the appropriations already made for that year.

What I had done for the development of historical studies at the University of Michigan & in the country at large Professor Herbert Adams & President Adams have told you—what I did at Cornell to found a proper department you know.

As to the department of Political Science for practical training so far as I know I was the first to suggest it in any country;—in my Johns Hopkins address and in my Report as Commissioner to the Paris Exposition on Political Education in Europe—& was prompt to carry it into effect at Cornell—as far as our means allowed.

From me came the first successful plan for an Unsectarian University or College Chapel in the United States, & the establishment of a Christian but non sectarian pulpit. Mr. Dean Sage's proposal was for a Chaplaincy, with a suggestion that it be held by a resident Clergyman of some one denomination. This I declined to urge upon the Trustees, but presented my plan which he accepted and which other institutions have since imitated.

It was I who, by the aid of Mr. Schuyler against great opposition—which defeated the plan during several meetings, led the Trustees to establish the Scholarships and Fellowships out of the monies which had been advanced by various Trustees at an earlier day to pay the University debt.

And I may add one more fact, for your eyes alone;—I do it with reluctance, but I propose making a clean breast of the matter;—No other man, so far as I know, has given so large a proportion of his fortune to the University as I have, & I have given not showy things, but have scattered my gifts among many of the lesser things, which, while scarcely noted, have given a University tone & character to the institution.

There is also another thing of which I may justly remind you; in view of the great increase in the number of professors & of their high character, it should, I think, not be forgotten that in the early days it was with the utmost difficulty that men of ability & standing could be induced to cast in their lot with Cornell; it was an untried experiment, laughed at by conservative University men throughout the country, the surroundings on the hill at Ithaca were not at first attractive, much had to be done with very small means, &, as I look back, I feel surprised that I was able to secure & hold such admirable men as I induced to come into the College faculty & to remain in it.

And one thing more. The curse of American Colleges & universities of the newer type had long been dissensions in Boards of Trustees & Faculties. The history of Union, Hamilton, Michigan, Wisconsin, & a multitude of others, showed promising institutions absolutely paralyzed by such dissensions. With all the difficulties at Cornell in the early days there were plenty of inducements to dislike & dissension. I have never ceased to congratulate myself that these were kept under & that I never had a quarrel with any person connected with the institution, & that my influence from the first was exercised effectively in favor of peace. . . .

The one thing in my life to which I look back with pride [with greatest pride, he must surely have meant—C. B.] is my connection with the foundation of the institution.

You know, to some extent, the opposition which confronted me but you can hardly know how bitter & trying it was at times.

[There are three more pages of the letter, answering the statement that he had "now returned to his first love," and suggesting that perhaps some more adequate recognition of his part in the founding might be made in the coming anniversary celebration. The letter then closes as follows—C. B.]

Pardon me for writing you so long a letter.

It was mainly written at Upsala when there came to me a vivid idea of the value of work done in founding & maintaining a University; there is no statement in it which cannot be confirmed either by living witnesses or by documents.

I ask you to consider it, to preserve it, but for the present to keep it to yourselves.

I remain to both of you,

Most sincerely your friend,

ANDREW D. WHITE

I prefer to have this remain in custody of Prof Burr at the White Library. A.D.W.

10. Woodrow Wilson on "Princeton in the Nation's Service," 1896

Woodrow Wilson (1856–1924) had had a long academic career before he became governor of New Jersey and then President. Born in Virginia, he graduated from Princeton in 1879, studied law at the University of Virginia, and entered law practice in Atlanta, Georgia. But the law disappointed him, and he entered the flourishing graduate school at the Johns Hopkins in 1883. Two years later he published his doctoral thesis, and his best book, *Congressional Government*. He taught history at Bryn Mawr and then Wesleyan, and in 1890 became professor

Forum, XXII (December, 1896), 450–66.

of jurisprudence and political economy at Princeton. At the time this essay was published, he was rapidly coming to the fore as one of his university's most prominent spokesmen; and in 1902, when President Francis L. Patton resigned, he was named his successor, the first layman to become president of Princeton. His accomplishments at Princeton brought him into the public eye and led to his political career.

On Wilson at Princeton see Arthur S. Link, *Wilson: The Road to the White House* (Princeton, 1947), chaps. ii, iii. The best account of Wilson's earlier academic connections and his ideas during his years as a graduate student and teacher is William Diamond, *The Economic Thought of Woodrow Wilson* (Baltimore, 1943).

It has never been natural, it has seldom been possible, in this country for learning to seek a place apart and hold aloof from affairs. It is only when society is old, long settled to its ways, confident in habit, and without self-questionings upon any vital point of conduct, that study can effect seclusion and despise the passing interests of the day. America has never yet had a season of leisured quiet in which students could seek a life apart without sharp rigors of conscience, or college instructors easily forget that they were training citizens as well as drilling pupils; and Princeton is not likely to forget that sharp schooling of her youth, when she first learned the lesson of public service. She shall not easily get John Witherspoon out of her constitution. . . .

Dr. Witherspoon could have pupils at will. He was so much else besides schoolmaster and preceptor, was so great a figure in the people's eye, went about so like an accepted leader, generously lending a great character to a great cause, that he could bid men act and know that they would heed him. . . .

And the Revolution, when it came, seemed but an object lesson in his scheme of life. It was not simply fighting that was done at Princeton. The little town became for a season the centre of politics, too; and once and again the Legislature of the State sat in the college hall, and its revolutionary Council of Safety. Soldiers and public men whose names the war was making known to every man frequented the quiet little place, and racy talk ran high in the jolly tavern where hung the sign of Hudibras. Finally the Federal Congress itself sought the place and filled the college hall with a new scene, sitting a whole season there to do its business,—its president a trustee of the college. A commencement day came which saw both Washington and Witherspoon on the platform together,—the two men, it was said, who could not be

matched for striking presence in all the country,—and the young salu-
tatorian turned to the country's leader to say what it was in the hearts
of all to utter. The sum of the town's excitement was made up when,
upon that notable last day of October, in the year 1783, news of peace
came to that secluded hall, to add a crowning touch of gladness to the
gay and brilliant company met to receive with formal welcome the
Minister Plenipotentiary but just come from the Netherlands, Washington moving amongst them the hero whom the news enthroned.

It was no single stamp that the college gave its pupils. James Madison, Philip Freneau, Aaron Burr, and Harry Lee had come from it almost at a single birth, between 1771 and 1773—James Madison, the
philosophical statesman, subtly compounded of learning and practical
sagacity; Philip Freneau, the careless poet and reckless pamphleteer of
a party; Aaron Burr, with genius enough to have made him immortal
and unschooled passion enough to have made him infamous; "Light-
horse Harry" Lee, a Rupert in battle, a boy in counsel, high-strung,
audacious, wilful, lovable, a figure for romance. These men were types
of the spirit of which the college was full; the spirit of free individual
development which found its perfect expression in the president himself. . . .

Whatever we may say of these matters, however, one thing is certain:
Princeton sent upon the public stage an extraordinary number of men
of notable quality in those days; became herself for a time in some visible sort the academic centre of the Revolution, fitted, among the rest,
the man in whom the country was one day to recognize the chief author of the Federal Constitution. Princetonians are never tired of telling how many public men graduated from Princeton in Witherspoon's
time,—twenty Senators, twenty-three Representatives, thirteen Governors, three Judges of the Supreme Court of the Union; one Vice-
President, and a President; all within a space of twenty years, and
from a college which seldom had more than a hundred students. Nine
Princeton men sat in the Constitutional Convention of 1787; and,
though but six of them were Witherspoon's pupils, there was no other
college that had there so many as six, and the redoubtable Doctor
might have claimed all nine as his in spirit and capacity. Madison
guided the convention through the critical stages of its anxious work,
with a tact, a gentle quietness, an art of leading without insisting, ruling without commanding,—an authority, not of tone or emphasis, but
of apt suggestion,—such as Dr. Witherspoon could never have exer-

cised. Princeton men fathered both the Virginia plan, which was adopted, and the New Jersey plan, which was rejected; and Princeton men advocated the compromises without which no plan could have won acceptance. The strenuous Scotsman's earnest desire and prayer to God to see a government set over the nation that should last was realized as even he might not have been bold enough to hope. No man had ever better right to rejoice in his pupils.

It would be absurd to pretend that we can distinguish Princeton's touch and method in the Revolution or her distinctive handiwork in the Constitution of the Union. We can show nothing more of historical fact than that her own president took a great place of leadership in that time of change, and became one of the first figures of the age; that the college which he led and to which he gave his spirit contributed more than her share of public men to the making of the nation, outranked her elder rivals in the roll-call of the Constitutional Convention, and seemed for a little a seminary of statesmen rather than a quiet seat of academic learning. What takes our admiration and engages our fancy in looking back to that time is the generous union then established in the college between the life of philosophy and the life of the state.

It moves her sons very deeply to find Princeton to have been from the first what they know her to have been in their own day,—a school of duty. The revolutionary days are gone, and you shall not find upon her rolls another group of names given to public life that can equal her muster in the days of the Revolution and the formation of the Government. But her rolls read since the old days, if you know but a little of the quiet life of scattered neighborhoods, like a roster of trustees, a list of the silent men who carry the honorable burdens of business and of social obligation,—of such names as keep credit and confidence in heart. They suggest a soil full of the old seed, and ready, should the air of the time move shrewdly upon it as in the old days, to spring once more into the old harvest. The various, boisterous strength of the young men of affairs who went out with Witherspoon's touch upon them, is obviously not of the average breed of any place, but the special fruitage of an exceptional time. Later generations inevitably reverted to the elder type of Paterson and Ellsworth, the type of sound learning and stout character, without bold impulse added or any uneasy hope to change the world. It has been Princeton's work, in all ordinary seasons, not to change but to strengthen society, to give, not yeast, but bread for the raising. . . .

No one who looks into the life of the Institution shall find it easy to say what gave it its spirit and kept it in its character the generations through; but some things lie obvious to the view in Princeton's case. She had always been a school of religion, and no one of her sons, who has really lived her life, has escaped that steadying touch which has made her a school of duty. Religion, conceive it but liberally enough, is the true salt wherewith to keep both duty and learning sweet against the taint of time and change; and it is a noble thing to have conceived it thus liberally, as Princeton's founders did.

Churches among us, as all the world knows, are free and voluntary societies separated to be nurseries of belief, not suffered to become instruments of rule; and those who serve them can be free citizens, as well as faithful churchmen. The men who founded Princeton were pastors, not ecclesiastics. Their ideal was the service of congregations and communities, not the service of a church. Duty with them was a practical thing, concerned with righteousness in this world, as well as with salvation in the next. There is nothing that gives such pith to public service as religion. A God of truth is no mean prompter to the enlightened service of mankind; and character formed as if in His eye has always a fibre and sanction such as you shall not obtain for the ordinary man from the mild promptings of philosophy.

This, I cannot doubt, is the reason why Princeton has formed practical men, whom the world could trust to do its daily work like men of honor. . . .

The world has long thought that it detected in the academic life some lack of sympathy with itself, some disdain of the homely tasks which make the gross globe inhabitable,—not a little proud aloofness and lofty superiority, as if education always softened the hands and alienated the heart. It must be admitted that books are a great relief from the haggling of the market, libraries a very welcome refuge from the strife of commerce. We feel no anxiety about ages that are past; old books draw us pleasantly off from responsibility, remind us nowhere of what there is to do. We can easily hold the service of mankind at arm's length while we read and make scholars of ourselves. But we shall be very uneasy, the while, if the right mandates of religion are let in upon us, and made part of our thought. The quiet scholar has his proper breeding, and truth must be searched out and held aloft for men to see for its own sake, by such as will not leave off their sacred task until death takes them away. But not many pupils of a college are to be investigators; they are to be citizens and the world's servants in every field of practical endeavor, and in their instruction the college must use learning as a vehicle of spirit, interpreting literature as the voice of humanity,—must enlighten, guide, and hearten its sons, that it may make men of them. If it give them no vision of the true God, it has given them no certain motive to practise the wise lessons they have learned. . . .

There is nothing so conservative of life as growth; when that stops, decay sets in and the end comes on apace. Progress is life, for the body politic as for the body natural. To stand still is to court death.

Here, then, if you will but look, you have the law of conservatism disclosed: it is a law of progress. But not all change is progress, not all growth is the manifestation of life. Let one part of the body be in haste to outgrow the rest and you have malignant disease, the threat of death. The growth that is a manifestation of life is equable, draws its springs gently out of the old fountains of strength, builds upon old tissue, covets the old airs that have blown upon it time out of mind in the past. Colleges ought surely to be the best nurseries of such life, the best schools of the progress which conserves. Unschooled men have only their habits to remind them of the past, only their desires and their instinctive judgments of what is right to guide them into the future: the college should serve the State as its organ of recollection, its seat of vital memory. It should give the country men who know the probabilities of failure and success, who can separate the tendencies which are permanent from the tendencies which are of the moment merely, who can distinguish promises from threats, knowing the life men have lived, the hopes they have tested, and the principles they have proved. . . .

It is plain that it is the duty of an institution of learning set in the midst of a free population and amidst signs of social change, not merely to implant a sense of duty, but to illuminate duty by every lesson that can be drawn out of the past. It is not a dogmatic process. I know of no book in which the lessons of the past are set down. I do not know of any man whom the world could trust to write such a book. But it somehow comes about that the man who has travelled in the realms of thought brings lessons home with him which make him grave and wise beyond his fellows, and thoughtful with the thought-fulness of a true man of the world.

He is not a true man of the world who knows only the present fashions of it. In good breeding there is always the fine savor of gener-ations of gentlemen, a tradition of courtesy, the perfect knowledge of long practice. The world of affairs is so old no man can know it who knows only that little last segment of it which we call the present. We have a special name for the man who observes only the present fashions of the world, and it is a less honorable name than that which we use to designate the grave and thoughtful gentlemen who keep so steadily to the practices that have made the world wise and at ease these hun-dreds of years. We cannot pretend to have formed the world, and we are not destined to reform it. We cannot even mend it and set it for-ward by the reasonable measure of a single generation's work if we forget the old processes or lose our mastery over them. We should have scant capital to trade on were we to throw away the wisdom we have inherited and seek our fortunes with the slender stock we have our-selves accumulated. This, it seems to me, is the real, the prevalent argument for holding every man we can to the intimate study of the ancient classics. Latin and Greek, no doubt, have a grammatical and syntactical habit which challenges the mind that would master it to a severer exercise of analytical power than the easy-going synthesis of any modern tongue demands; but substitutes in kind may be found for that drill. What you cannot find a substitute for is the classics as liter-ature; and there can be no first-hand contact with that literature if you will not master the grammar and the syntax which convey its subtle power. Your enlightenment depends on the company you keep. You do not know the world until you know the men who have possessed it and tried its ways before ever you were given your brief run upon it. And there is no sanity comparable with that which is schooled in the thoughts that will keep. It is such a schooling that we get from the world's literature. The books have disappeared which were not gen-uine,—which spoke things which, if they were worth saying at all, were not worth hearing more than once, as well as the books which spoke permanent things clumsily and without the gift of interpreta-tion. The kind air which blows from age to age has disposed of them like vagrant leaves. There was sap in them for a little, but now they are gone, we do not know where. All literature that has lasted has this claim upon us: that it is not dead; but we cannot be quite so sure of any as we are of the ancient literature that still lives, because none has lived so long. It holds a sort of primacy in the aristocracy of natural selection. . . .

It has always seemed to me an odd thing, and a thing against nature that the literary man, the man whose citizenship and freedom are of the world of thought, should ever have been deemed an unsafe man in affairs; and yet I suppose there is not always injustice in the judgment. It is a perilously pleasant and beguiling comradeship, the company of authors. Not many men when once they are deep in it will leave its engaging thought of things gone by to find their practical duties in the present. But you are not making an undergraduate a man of letters when you keep him four short years at odd, or even at stated, hours in the company of authors. You shall have done much if you make him feel free among them.

This argument for enlightenment holds scarcely less good, of course, in behalf of the study of modern literature, and especially the literature of your own race and country. You should not belittle culture by esteeming it a thing of ornament, an accomplishment rather than a power. A cultured mind is a mind quit of its awkwardness, eased of all impediment and illusion, made quick and athletic in the acceptable exercise of power. It is a mind at once informed and just,—a mind habituated to choose its course with knowledge, and filled with full assurance, like one who knows the world and can live in it without either unreasonable hope or unwarranted fear. It cannot complain, it cannot trifle, it cannot despair. Leave pessimism to the uncultured, who do not know the reasonableness of failure. Show that your mind has lived in the world ere now; has taken counsel with the elder dead who still live, as well as with the ephemeral living who cannot pass their graves. Help men, but do not delude them.

I believe, of course, that there is another way of preparing young men to be wise. I need hardly say that I believe in full, explicit instruction in history and in politics, in the experiences of peoples and the fortunes of governments, in the whole story of what men have attempted and what they have accomplished through all the changes both of form and purpose in their organization of their common life. Many minds will receive and heed this systematic instruction which have no ears for the voice that is in the printed page of literature. But, just as it is one thing to sit here in republican America and hear a credible professor tell of the soil of allegiance in which the British monarchy grows, and quite another to live where Victoria is queen and hear common men bless her with full confession of loyalty, so it is one thing to hear of systems of government in histories and treatises and quite another to feel them in the pulses of the poets and prose writers who have lived under them.

It used to be taken for granted—did it not?—that colleges would be found always on the conservative side in politics (except on the question of free trade); but in this latter day a great deal has taken place which goes far toward discrediting the presumption. The college in our day lies very near indeed to the affairs of the world. It is a place of the latest experiments; its laboratories are brisk with the spirit of discovery; its lecture rooms resound with the discussion of new theories of life and novel programmes of reform. There is no radical like your learned radical, bred in the schools; and thoughts of revolution have in our time been harbored in universities as naturally as they were once nourished among the Encyclopedists. It is the scientific spirit of the age which has wrought the change. I stand with my hat off at the very mention of the great men who have made our age an age of knowledge. No man more heartily admires, more gladly welcomes, more approvingly reckons the gain and the enlightenment that have come to the world through the extraordinary advances in physical science which this great age has witnessed. He would be a barbarian and a lover of darkness who should grudge that great study any part of its triumph. But I am a student of society and should deem myself unworthy of the comradeship of great men of science should I not speak the plain truth with regard to what I see happening under my own eyes. I have no laboratory but the world of books and men in which I live; but I am much mistaken if the scientific spirit of the age is not doing us a great disservice, working in us a certain great degeneracy. Science has bred in us a spirit of experiment and a contempt for the past. It has made us credulous of quick improvement, hopeful of discovering panaceas, confident of success in every new thing.

I wish to be as explicit as carefully chosen words will enable me to be upon a matter so critical, so radical as this. I have no indictment against what science has done: I have only a warning to utter against the atmosphere which has stolen from laboratories into lecture rooms and into the general air of the world at large. Science—our science—is new. It is a child of the nineteenth century. It has transformed the world and owes little debt of obligation to any past age. It has driven mystery out of the Universe; it has made malleable stuff of the hard world, and laid it out in its elements upon the table of every class-room. Its own masters have known its limitations: they have stopped short at the confines of the physical universe; they have declined to reckon with spirit or with the stuffs of the mind, have eschewed sense and confined themselves to sensation. But their work has been so stupendous that all other men of all other studies have been set staring at their methods, imitating their ways of thought, ogling their results. We look in our study of the classics nowadays more at the phenomena of language than at the movement of spirit; we suppose the world which is invisible to be unreal; we doubt the efficacy of feeling and exaggerate the efficacy of knowledge; we speak of society as an organism and believe that we can contrive for it a new environment which will change the very nature of its constituent parts; worst of all, we believe in the present and in the future more than in the past, and deem the newest theory of society the likeliest. This is the disservice scientific study has done us: it has given us agnosticism in the realm of philosophy, scientific anarchism in the field of politics. It has made the legislator confident that he can create, and the philosopher sure that God cannot. Past experience is discredited and the laws of matter are supposed to apply to spirit and the make-up of society.

Let me say once more, this is not the fault of the scientist; he has done his work with an intelligence and success which cannot be too much admired. It is the work of the noxious, intoxicating gas which has somehow got into the lungs of the rest of us from out the crevices of his workshop—a gas, it would seem, which forms only in the outer air, and where men do not know the right use of their lungs. I should tremble to see social reform led by men who had breathed it; I should fear nothing better than utter destruction from a revolution conceived and led in the scientific spirit. Science has not changed the laws of social growth or betterment. Science has not changed the nature of society, has not made history a whit easier to understand, human nature a whit easier to reform. It has won for us a great liberty in the physical world, a liberty from superstitious fear and from disease, a freedom to use nature as a familiar servant; but it has not freed us from ourselves. It has not purged us of passion or disposed us to virtue. It has not made us less covetous or less ambitious or less self-indulgent. On the contrary, it may be suspected of having enhanced our passions, by making wealth so quick to come, so fickle to stay. It has wrought such instant, incredible improvement in all the physical setting of our life, that we have grown the more impatient of the unreformed condition of the part it has not touched or bettered, and we want to get at our spirits and reconstruct them in like radical fashion by like processes of experiment. We have broken with the past and have come into a new world.

Can any one wonder, then, that I ask for the old drill, the old memory of times gone by, the old schooling in precedent and tradition, the old keeping of faith with the past, as a preparation for leadership in days of social change? We have not given science too big a place in our education; but we have made a perilous mistake in giving it too great a preponderance in method in every other branch of study. We must make the humanities human again; must recall what manner of men we are; must turn back once more to the region of practicable ideals.

Of course, when all is said, it is not learning but the spirit of service that will give a college place in the public annals of the nation. It is indispensable, it seems to me, if it is to do its right service, that the air of affairs should be admitted to all its class-rooms. I do not mean the air of party politics, but the air of the world's transactions, the consciousness of the solidarity of the race, the sense of the duty of man toward man, of the presence of men in every problem, of the significance of truth for guidance as well as for knowledge, of the potency of ideas, of the promise and the hope that shine in the face of all knowledge. There is laid upon us the compulsion of the national life. We dare not keep aloof and closet ourselves while a nation comes to its maturity. The days of glad expansion are gone, our life grows tense and difficult; our resource for the future lies in careful thought, providence, and a wise economy; and the school must be of the nation.

I have had sight of the perfect place of learning in my thought: a free place, and a various, where no man could be and not know with how great a destiny knowledge had come into the world—itself a little world; but not perplexed, living with a singleness of aim not known without; the home of sagacious men, hard-headed and with a will to know, debaters of the world's questions every day and used to the rough ways of democracy; and yet a place removed—calm Science seated there, recluse, ascetic, like a nun, not knowing that the world passes, not caring, if the truth but come in answer to her prayer; and Literature, walking within her open doors, in quiet chambers, with men of olden time, storied walls about her, and calm voices infinitely sweet; here "magic casements, opening on the foam of perilous seas, in fairy lands forlorn," to which you may withdraw and use your youth for pleasure; there windows open straight upon the street, where many stand and talk, intent upon the world of men and business. A place where ideals are kept in heart in an air they can breathe; but no fool's paradise. A place where to hear the truth about the past and hold debate about the affairs of the present, with knowledge and without passion; like the world in having all men's life at heart, a place for men and all that concerns them; but unlike the world in its self-possession, its thorough way of talk, its care to know more than the moment brings a light; slow to take excitement, its air pure and wholesome with a breath of faith; every eye within it bright in the clear day and quick to look toward heaven for the confirmation of its hope. Who shall show us the way to this place?

Part VIII

THE DEVELOPMENT OF THE
ELECTIVE SYSTEM

THE ABANDONMENT of the old required classical curriculum and its replacement by a more complex curriculum in which the undergraduate was able to exercise a large amount of choice in the selection of studies was the most important single consequence for the undergraduate college in the development of the modern university. If the wide range of modern studies in languages, science, and social studies was to be made available in any considerable measure to the college student, it was no longer possible for his four-year course to cover all available subjects. Inevitably there must be choice; and to a large degree it was proposed that the decision as to what courses the individual was to "take" would depend in greater or lesser part upon him and not upon the curriculum-planners. This change was not made without a good deal of resistance, especially in the long-established colleges of the East and in small colleges without the resources to develop a varied curriculum. President Noah Porter of Yale, the citadel of the old system (Part IV, Doc. 11), proposed (Doc. 1) to yield as little as possible to the new, in which he saw tendencies destructive to the tradition of liberal education. But to such a persuasive exponent of the new dispensation in education as President Charles William Eliot of Harvard (Doc. 2), the elective system was simply a part of that expanding freedom of spirit that the new university represented. It left the student free in large measure to determine his course of study; it offered him an inducement to single out areas of special interest in which he would go on to do work of genuine distinction; and by leaving him free to make choices and initiate study it would encourage him, without the imposition of external discipline, to form his own habits of work and guide his own conduct.

Perhaps the most comprehensive and incisive answer to the views of Eliot and other proponents of the elective system was made by President James McCosh of Princeton (Doc. 3), an immensely capable exponent of old-school views. He was not, he insisted, an old fogy; he welcomed educational progress, but he hoped that progress would not involve abandoning everything that had been good in the old ways. Prophetically, McCosh insisted that students would have a tendency to "choose the branches [of study] which will cost them the least study, and put themselves under the popular professors who give them the highest grades with the least labor." Whatever freedom the student was to have, McCosh thought, it must be exercised within the framework of a strong, required system of studies. Attendance on lectures and recitations should remain obligatory. Once these things were required, the student might have the choice of a few specialties that represent his particular talents and interests. But the college should never leave him outside the framework of a closely textured system of moral and religious as well as intellectual discipline.

The elective system became the object of a great deal of discussion in the entire community. Lay discussion (Doc. 4), though not altogether unsympathetic to the ideals and techniques of the old-time college, saw that the future rested for the most part with the exponents of the elective system. By the end of the century most of the conservative colleges had bent a long way before the strong winds of the elective system. But it was also beginning to be clear that the open curriculum had its problems as well as its merits. Harvard, the leader of the movement for election, now herself began to re-examine it (Docs. 5 and 6). This re-examination did not by any means lead once again to a desire to retrace the steps educational planning had made during the preceding thirty years, but it did show certain weaknesses, not least of which was that the students' curricular selection was often far from balanced; the large lecture course had brought its own problems as well. In Harvard's self-criticism one may discern the first faint rumblings of the effort to reconstitute in some part a systematic curriculum that was to be uppermost in the minds of college educators after 1920 (see Part XI).

1. Noah Porter Rejects the Elective System, 1871

Noah Porter (1811–92) was born in Connecticut and graduated from Yale in 1831. After some years in teaching and the study of divinity he was ordained in 1836. In 1846 he was called to Yale to be Clark Professor of Moral Philosophy and Metaphysics, a position from which he attained a wide influence. In 1871 he became president of the college. A conservative in almost all things, he opposed not only the elective system but the intellectual positivism of the post-Darwinian era. See George W. Pierson, *Yale College . . . 1871–1921* (New Haven, 1952), chap. iii; Walter James, "The Philosophy of Noah Porter" (Ph.D. diss., Columbia University, 1951); and Part X, Doc. 4.

To relieve the college system of the difficulties adverted to, the plan of *elective studies* has been proposed—not of elective courses or schools, of which we have spoken and which the college provides,—but the choice of studies from time to time, to be directed by the real or fancied aptitudes or preferences of the pupil, and the possible relation of these studies to his future profession or career. We grant for this plan a temporary satisfaction to the more earnest students and the more ardent enthusiasm which attends the continued prosecution of a favorite study. But we cannot overlook the very serious evils to which it is exposed. The majority of undergraduate students have neither the maturity nor the data which qualify them to judge of the relative value of studies or their bearing on their future employments. The few who have a definite career, or pronounced tastes, may be misled by their feelings to judge in the direction which is most injurious because for the present it is more pleasing. The plan involves the certain evil of breaking into the common life of the class and the college as well as of unprofitable expenditure and insuperable complexity.

A still more serious objection to a wide range of elective studies in the college is found in its tendency to limit the cycle of the studies

Noah Porter, "Inaugural Address," in *Addresses at the Inauguration of Professor Noah Porter, D.D., LL.D., as President of Yale* (New York, 1871), pp. 44–46.

acknowledged to be liberal, and to contract the period of university education. We urge in this connection that the higher education of this country *ought in its forecast of the future, to contemplate a longer rather than a shorter period of time for its completion*.... The more urgent is this noisy tumult of life without, and the stronger its pressure against the doors of the college, the greater need is there that certain studies which have little relation to this life should be attended to, and the less occasion that those should be anticipated which will absorb all the energies of life. We prefer the theory of liberal culture which assumes that an increasing rather than a diminishing number of our choicest youth of leisure will continue their literary and scientific studies, and thus be able to dignify and adorn their life by habits of systematic research and of earnest literary activity—that some who are devoted to business will acquire the strength to withstand the absorbing cares and the insatiable greed of money getting; that here and there a professional man may be saved from the narrowness which the exclusive claims of his calling must engender if science, and literature, and history are not actively attended to. What this country demands is a larger number of educated men who are elevated and refined by a culture which is truly liberal; men whose convictions are founded in manifold reading and comprehensive thought; men with the insight which comes only from a larger converse with history, a profound meditation on the problems of life and speculation, and a catholic taste in literature. The more such men mingle in the concerns of life, the more do they soften our controversies and dignify our discussions, refine upon our vulgarities and introduce amenities into our social life. They are needed in our politics and literature, at the bar and in the pulpit, in our newspapers and journals. We have plenty of cheap glitter, of tawdry bedizenment and showy accomplishments; plenty of sensational declamation, coarse argument, and facile rhetoric; much moral earnestness which needs tolerance and knowledge, and religious fervor which runs into dogmatism and rant. We need a higher and more consummate culture, in some of the men at least whom we educate for the work of life, and for this reason the arrangements for university education should contemplate a prolonged period of study....

2. Charles William Eliot Expounds the Elective System as "Liberty in Education," 1885

See Part VI, Docs. 2 and 3.

How to transform a college with one uniform curriculum into a university without any prescribed course of study at all is a problem which more and more claims the attention of all thoughtful friends of American learning and education. To-night I hope to convince you that a university of liberal arts and sciences must give its students three things:

I. Freedom in choice of studies.

II. Opportunity to win academic distinction in single subjects or special lines of study.

III. A discipline which distinctly imposes on each individual the responsibility of forming his own habits and guiding his own conduct.

These three subjects I shall take up in succession, the first of them taking the greater part of the time allotted me.

I. Of freedom in choice of studies.

Let me first present what I may call a mechanical argument on this subject. A college with a prescribed curriculum must provide, say, sixteen hours a week of instruction for each class, or sixty-four hours a week in all for the four classes, without allowing for repetitions of lectures or lessons. Six or eight teachers can easily give all the instruction needed in such a college, if no repetitions are necessary. If the classes are so large that they need to be divided into two or more sections, more teachers must be employed. If a few extra or optional studies, outside of the curriculum, are provided, a further addition to the number of teachers must be made. Twenty teachers would, however, be a liberal allowance for any college of this type; and accordingly there are hundreds of American colleges at this moment with less than twenty teachers all told. Under the prescribed system it would be impossible for such a college to find work for more teachers, if it

Charles William Eliot, *Educational Reform: Essays and Addresses* (New York, 1898), pp. 125–48.

had them. Now there are eighty teachers employed this year in Harvard College, exclusive of laboratory assistants; and these eighty teachers give about four hundred and twenty-five hours of public instruction a week without any repetitions, not counting the very important instruction which many of them give in laboratories. It is impossible for any undergraduate in his four years to take more than a tenth part of the instruction given by the College; and since four fifths of this instruction is of a higher grade than any which can be given in a college with a prescribed curriculum, a diligent student would need about forty years to cover the present field; and during those years the field would enlarge quite beyond his powers of occupation. Since the student cannot take the whole of the instruction offered, it seems to be necessary to allow him to take a part. A college must either limit closely its teaching, or provide some mode of selecting studies for the individual student. The limitation of teaching is an intolerable alternative for any institution which aspires to become a university; for a university must try to teach every subject, above the grade of its admission requirements, for which there is any demand; and to teach it thoroughly enough to carry the advanced student to the confines of present knowledge, and make him capable of original research. These are the only limits which a university can properly set to its instruction—except indeed those rigorous limits which poverty imposes. The other alternative is selection or election of studies.

The elective system at Harvard has been sixty years in developing, and during fourteen of these years—from 1846 to 1860—the presidents and the majority of the faculty were not in favor of it; but they could find no way of escape from the dilemma which I have set before you. They could not deliberately reduce the amount of instruction offered, and election of studies in some degree was the inevitable alternative.

The practical question then is, At what age, and at what stage of his educational progress, can an American boy be offered free choice of studies? or, in other words, At what age can an American boy best go to a free university? Before answering this question I will ask your attention to four preliminary observations.

1. The European boy goes to free universities at various ages from seventeen to twenty; and the American boy is decidedly more mature and more capable of taking care of himself than the European boy of like age.

2. The change from school to university ought to be made as soon

as it would be better for the youth to associate with older students under a discipline suited to their age, than with younger pupils under a discipline suited to theirs—as soon, in short, as it would be better for the youth to be the youngest student in a university than the oldest boy in a school. The school might still do much for the youth; the university may as yet be somewhat too free for him: there must be a balancing of advantages against disadvantages; but the wise decision is to withdraw him betimes from a discipline which he is outgrowing, and put him under a discipline which he is to grow up to. When we think of putting a boy into college, our imaginations are apt to dwell upon the occasional and exceptional evil influences to which his new freedom will expose him, more than upon those habitual and prevailing influences of college companionship which will nourish his manliness and develop his virtue; just as we are apt to think of heredity chiefly as a means of transmitting vices and diseases, whereas it is normally the means of transmitting and accumulating infinitely various virtues and serviceable capacities.

3. A young man is much affected by the expectations which his elders entertain of him. If they expect him to behave like a child, his lingering childishness will oftener rule his actions; if they expect him to behave like a man, his incipient manhood will oftener assert itself. The pretended parental or sham monastic régime of the common American college seems to me to bring out the childishness rather than the manliness of the average student; as is evidenced by the pranks he plays, the secret societies in which he rejoices, and the barbarous or silly customs which he accepts and transmits. The conservative argument is: a college must deal with the student as he is; he will be what he has been, namely, a thoughtless, aimless, lazy, and possibly vicious boy; therefore a policy which gives him liberty is impracticable. The progressive argument is: adapt college policy to the best students, and not to the worst; improve the policy, and in time the evil fruits of a mistaken policy will disappear. I would only urge at this point that a far-seeing educational policy must be based upon potentialities as well as actualities, upon things which may be reasonably hoped for, planned, and aimed at, as well as upon things which are.

4. The condition of secondary education is an important factor in our problem. It is desirable that the young men who are to enjoy university freedom should have already received at school a substantial training, in which the four great subdivisions of elementary knowl-

edge—languages, history, mathematics, and natural science—were all adequately represented; but it must be admitted that this desirable training is now given in very few schools, and that in many parts of the country there are not secondary schools enough of even tolerable quality. For this condition of secondary education the colleges are in part responsible; for they have produced few good teachers, except for the ancient languages; and they have required for admission to college hardly anything but the elements of Greek, Latin, and mathematics. But how should this condition of things affect the policy of an institution which sees its way to obtain a reasonable number of tolerably prepared students? Shall we stop trying to create a university because the condition of secondary education in the country at large is unsatisfactory? The difficulty with that policy of inaction is that the reform and development of secondary education depend upon the right organization and conduct of universities. It is the old problem: Which was first created, an egg or a hen? In considering the relation of college life to school life, many people are confused by a misleading metaphor —that of building. They say to themselves: on weak foundations no strong superstructure can be built; schools lay the foundations on which the university must build; therefore, if preparatory schools fail to do good work, no proper university work can subsequently be done. The analogy seems perfect, but has this fatal defect: education is a vital process, not a mechanical one. Let us, therefore, use an illustration drawn from a vital function, that of nutrition. A child has had poor milk as an infant, and is not well developed; therefore, when its teeth are cut, and it is ready for bread, meat, and oatmeal, you are to hold back this substantial diet, and give it the sweetened milk and water, and Mellin's Food, which would have suited it when a baby. The mental food of a boy has not been as nourishing and abundant as it should have been at school; therefore when he goes to college or university his diet must be that which he should have had at school, but missed. Education involves growth or development from within in every part; and metaphors drawn from the process of laying one stone upon another are not useful in educational discussions. Harvard College now finds itself able to get nearly three hundred tolerably prepared students every year from one hundred or more schools and private tutors scattered over the country; and she is only just beginning to reap the fruit of the changes in her own policy and discipline which the past eighteen years have wrought. Schools follow universities, and will be what universities make them.

With these preliminary suggestions I proceed to answer the question, At what age can an American boy best go to a university where choice of studies is free? and to defend my answer. I believe the normal age under reasonably favorable conditions to be eighteen. In the first place, I hold that the temperament, physical constitution, mental aptitudes, and moral quality of a boy are all well determined by the time he is eighteen years old. The potential man is already revealed. His capacities and incapacities will be perfectly visible to his teacher, or to any observant and intimate friend, provided that his studies at school have been fairly representative. If his historical studies have been limited to primers of Greek, Roman, and American history, his taste and capacity for historical study will not be known either to his teacher or to himself; if he has had no opportunity to study natural science, his powers in that direction will be quite unproved; but if the school course has been reasonably comprehensive, there need be no doubt as to the most profitable direction of his subsequent studies. The boy's future will depend greatly upon the influences, happy or unhappy, to which he is subjected; but given all favorable influences, his possibilities are essentially determined. The most fortunate intellectual influences will be within his reach, if he has liberty to choose the mental food which he can best assimilate. Secondly, at eighteen the American boy has passed the age when a compulsory external discipline is useful. Motives and inducements may be set vividly before him; he may be told that he must do so and so in order to win something which he desires or values; prizes and rewards near or remote may be held out to him; but he cannot be driven to any useful exercise of his mind. *Thirdly,* a well-instructed youth of eighteen can select for himself—not for any other boy, or for the fictitious universal boy. but for himself alone— a better course of study than any college faculty, or any wise man who does not know him and his ancestors and his previous life, can possibly select for him. In choosing his course he will naturally seek aid from teachers and friends who have intimate knowledge of him, and he will act under the dominion of that intense conservatism which fortunately actuates civilized man in the whole matter of education, and under various other safeguards which nature and not arbitrary regulation provides. When a young man whom I never saw before asks me what studies he had better take in college, I am quite helpless, until he tells me what he likes and what he dislikes to study, what kinds of exertion are pleasurable to him, what sports he cares for, what reading interests him, what his parents and grandparents were in the world, and what he means to be. In short, I can only show him how to think out the problem for himself with such lights as he has and nobody else can have. The proposition that a boy of eighteen can choose his own studies, with the natural helps, more satisfactorily than anybody else can choose them for him, seems at first sight absurd; but I believe it to be founded upon the nature of things, and it is also for me a clear result of observation. I will state first the argument from the nature of things, and then describe my own observations.

Every youth of eighteen is an infinitely complex organization, the duplicate of which neither does nor ever will exist. His inherited traits are different from those of every other human being; his environment has been different from that of every other child; his passions, emotions, hopes, and desires were never before associated in any other creature just as they are in him; and his will-force is aroused, stimulated, exerted, and exhausted in ways wholly his own. The infinite variety of form and feature, which we know human bodies to be capable of, presents but a faint image of the vastly deeper diversities of the minds and characters which are lodged in these unlike shells. To discern and take due account of these diversities no human insight or wisdom is sufficient, unless the spontaneous inclinations, natural preferences, and easiest habitual activities of each individual are given play. It is for the happiness of the individual and the benefit of society alike that these mental diversities should be cultivated, not suppressed. The individual enjoys most that intellectual labor for which he is most fit; and society is best served when every man's peculiar skill, faculty, or aptitude is developed and utilized to the highest possible degree. The presumption is, therefore, against uniformity in education, and in favor of diversity at the earliest possible moment. What determines that moment? To my thinking, the limit of compulsory uniform instruction should be determined by the elementary quality and recognized universal utility of the subjects of such instruction. For instance, it is unquestionable that every child needs to know how to read, write, and, to a moderate extent, cipher. Therefore primary schools may have a uniform programme. One might naturally suppose that careful study of the mother-tongue and its literature would be considered a uniform need for all youth; but as a matter of fact there is no agreement to this effect. The English language and literature have hardly yet won a place for themselves in American schools. Only the elements of two foreign languages and the elements of algebra and geometry can be said to be generally recognized as indispensable to the proper training of all young people who are privileged to study beyond their seventeenth year. There is no consent as to the uniform desirableness of the elements of natural science, and there is much difference of opinion about the selection of the two foreign languages, the majority of educated people supposing two dead languages to be preferable, a minority thinking that living languages are permissible. The limit of that elementary knowledge, of which by common consent all persons who are to be highly educated stand in need, is therefore a narrow one, easily to be reached and passed, under respectable instruction, by any youth of fair ability before he is eighteen years old. There, at least, ceases justifiable uniformity in education. There, at least, election of studies should begin; and the safest guides to a wise choice will be the taste, inclination, and special capacity of each individual. When it comes to the choice of a profession, everybody knows that the only wisdom is to follow inclination. In my view, the only wisdom in determining those liberal studies which may be most profitably pursued after eighteen is to follow inclination. Hence it is only the individual youth who can select that course of study which will most profit him, because it will most interest him. The very fact of choice goes far to secure the coöperation of his will.

I have already intimated that there exist certain natural guides and safeguards for every youth who is called upon in a free university to choose his own studies. Let us see what these natural aids are. In the first place, he cannot help taking up a subject which he has already studied about where he left it off, and every new subject at the beginning and not at the middle. Secondly, many subjects taught at a university involve other subjects, which must therefore be studied first. Thus, no one can get far in physics without being familiar with trigonometry and analytic geometry; chemical analysis presupposes acquaintance with general chemistry, and paleontology acquaintance with botany and zoölogy; no one can study German philosophy to advantage unless he can read German, and no student can profitably discuss practical economic problems until he has mastered the elementary principles of political economy. Every advanced course, whether in language, philosophy, history, mathematics, or science, presupposes acquaintance with some elementary course or courses. Thirdly, there is a prevailing tendency on the part of every competent student to carry far any congenial subject once entered upon. To repress this most fortunate tendency is to make real scholarship impossible. So effective are these natural safeguards against fickleness and inconsecutiveness in the choice of studies, that artificial regulation is superfluous.

I give, in the next place, some results of my own observation upon the working of an elective system; and that you may have my credentials before you I will describe briefly my opportunities of observation. I had experience as an undergraduate of a college course almost wholly required; for I happened upon nearly the lowest stage to which the elective system in Harvard College ever fell, after its initiation in 1825. During the nine years from 1854 to 1863 I became intimately acquainted with the working of this mainly prescribed curriculum from the point of view of a tutor and assistant professor who had a liking for administrative details. After a separation from the University of six years, two of which were spent in Europe as a student and four at the Massachusetts Institute of Technology as a professor, I went back as president in 1869, to find a tolerably broad elective system already under way. The wishes of the governing boards and external circumstances all favoring it, the system was rapidly developed. Required studies were gradually abolished or pushed back; so that first the Senior year was made completely elective, then the Junior, then the Sophomore, and finally in June last the Freshman year was made chiefly elective. No required studies now remain except the writing of English, the elements of either French or German (one of these two languages being required for admission), and a few lectures on chemistry and physics. None of the former exclusive staples, Greek, Latin, mathematics, logic, and metaphysics, are required, and no particular combinations or selections of courses are recommended by the faculty. I have therefore had ample opportunity to observe at Harvard the working of almost complete prescription, of almost complete freedom, and of all intermediate methods. In Europe I studied the free university method; and at the Institute of Technology I saw the system—excellent for technical schools—of several well-defined courses branching from a common stock of uniformly prescribed studies.

The briefest form in which I can express the general result of my observation is this: I have never known a student of any capacity to select for himself a set of studies covering four years which did not apparently possess more theoretical and practical merit for his case than the required curriculum of my college days. Every prescribed curriculum is necessarily elementary from beginning to end, and very heterogeneous. Such is the press of subjects that no one subject can possibly be carried beyond its elements; no teacher, however learned and enthusiastic, can have any advanced pupils; and no scholar, however competent and eager, can make serious attainments in any single subject. Under an elective system the great majority of students use their liberty to pursue some subject or subjects with a reasonable degree of thoroughness. This concentration upon single lines develops advanced teaching, and results in a general raising of the level of instruction. Students who have decided taste for any particular subject wisely devote a large part of their time to that subject and its congeners. Those who have already decided upon their profession wisely choose subjects which are related to, or underlie, their future professional studies; thus, the future physician will advantageously give a large share of his college course to French, German, chemistry, physics, and biology; while the future lawyer will study logic, ethics, history, political economy, and the use of English in argumentative writing and speaking. Among the thousands of individual college courses determined by the choice of the student in four successive years, which the records of Harvard College now preserve, it is rare to find one which does not exhibit an intelligible sequence of studies. It should be understood in this connection that all the studies which are allowed to count toward the A.B. at Harvard are liberal or pure, no technical or professional studies being admissible.

Having said thus much about the way in which an American student will use freedom in the choice of studies, I desire to point out that a young American must enjoy the privileges of university life between eighteen and twenty-two, if at all. From two thirds to three fourths of college graduates go into professions or employments which require of them elaborate special preparation. The medical student needs four years of professional training, the law student at least three, the good teacher and the skilful architect quite as much. Those who enter the service of business corporations, or go into business for themselves, have the business to learn—a process which ordinarily takes several years. If a young man takes his A.B. at twenty-two, he can hardly hope to begin the practice of his profession before he is twenty-six. That is quite late enough. It is clearly impossible, therefore, that the American university should be constructed on top of the old-fashioned American college. The average Freshman at Harvard is eighteen and two thirds years old when he enters, and at the majority of colleges he is older still. For the next three or four years he must have freedom to choose among liberal studies, if he is ever to enjoy that inestimable privilege.

Two common objections to an elective system shall next have our attention. The first is often put in the form of a query. Election of studies may be all very well for conscientious or ambitious students, or for those who have a strong taste for certain studies; but what becomes, under such a system, of the careless, indifferent, lazy boys who have no bent or intellectual ambition of any sort? I answer with a similar query: What became of such boys under the uniform compulsory system? Did they get any profit to speak of under that régime? Not within my observation. It really does not make much difference what these unawakened minds dawdle with. There is, however, much more chance that such young men will get aroused from their lethargy under an elective system than under a required. When they follow such faint promptings of desire as they feel, they at least escape the sense of grievance and repugnance which an arbitrary assignment to certain teachers and certain studies often creates. An elective system does not mean liberty to do nothing. The most indifferent student must pass a certain number of examinations every year. He selects perhaps those subjects in which he thinks he can pass the best examinations with the smallest amount of labor; but in those very subjects the instruction will be on a higher plane than it can ever reach under a compulsory system, and he will get more benefit from them than he would from other subjects upon which he put the same amount of labor but attained less success. It is an important principle in education, from primary school to university, that the greater the visible attainment for a given amount of labor the better; and this rule applies quite as forcibly to a weak student as to a strong one. Feeble or inert students are considerably influenced in choosing their studies by the supposed quality of the teachers whom they will meet. As a rule they select the very teachers who are likely to have the most influence with them, being guided by traditions received from older students of their sort. It is the unanimous opinion of the teachers at Cambridge that more and better work is got from this class of students under the elective system than was under the required.

Having said thus much about the effects of free choice of studies upon the unpromising student, I must add that the policy of an institution of education, of whatever grade, ought never to be determined by the needs of the least capable students; and that a university should aim at meeting the wants of the best students at any rate, and the wants of inferior students only so far as it can meet them without impairing the privileges of the best. A uniform curriculum, by enacting superficiality and prohibiting thoroughness, distinctly sacrifices the best scholars to the average. Free choice of studies gives the young genius the fullest scope without impairing the chances of the drone and the dullard.

The second objection with which I wish to deal is this: free choice implies that there are no studies which are recognized as of supreme merit, so that every young man unquestionably ought to pursue them. Can this be? Is it possible that the accumulated wisdom of the race cannot prescribe with certainty the studies which will best develop the human mind in general between the ages of eighteen and twenty-two? At first it certainly seems strange that we have to answer no; but when we reflect how very brief the acquaintance of the race has been with the great majority of the subjects which are now taught in a university the negative answer seems less surprising. Out of the two hundred courses of instruction which stand on the list of Harvard University this year it would be difficult to select twenty which could have been given at the beginning of this century with the illustrations, materials, and methods now considered essential to the educational quality of the of the courses. One realizes more easily this absence of accumulated experience on considering that all the natural sciences, with comparative philology, political economy, and history, are practically new subjects, that all mathematics is new except the elements of arithmetic, algebra, and geometry, that the recent additions to ethics and metaphysics are of vast extent, and that the literatures of the eighteenth and nineteenth centuries have great importance in several European languages. The materials and methods of university education always have been, and always will be, changing from generation to generation. We think, perhaps with truth, that the nineteenth century has been a period of unprecedented growth and progress; but every century has probably witnessed an unprecedented advance in civilization, simply because the process is cumulative, if no catastrophes arrest it. It is one of the most important functions of universities to store up the accumulated knowledge of the race, and so to use these stores that each successive generation of youth shall start with all the advantages which their predecessors have won. Therefore a university, while not neglecting the ancient treasures of learning, has to keep a watchful eye upon the new fields of discovery, and has to invite its students to walk in new-made as well as in long-trodden paths. Concerning the direct educational influence of all these new subjects the race cannot be said to have much accumulated wisdom.

One presumption of considerable scope may, however, be said to be established by experience. In every new field of knowledge the mental powers of the adventurers and discoverers found full play and fruitful exercise. Some rare human mind or minds must have laboriously developed each new subject of study. It may fairly be presumed that the youth will find some strenuous exercise of his faculties in following the masters into any field which it taxed their utmost powers to explore and describe. To study the conquests of great minds in any field of knowledge must be good training for young minds of kindred tastes and powers. That all branches of sound knowledge are of equal dignity and equal educational value for mature students is the only hopeful and tenable view in our day. Long ago it became quite impossible for one mind to compass more than an insignificant fraction of the great sum of acquired knowledge.

Before I leave the subject of election of studies, let me point out that there is not a university of competent resources upon the continent of Europe in which complete freedom of studies has not long prevailed; and that Oxford and Cambridge have recently provided an almost complete liberty for their students. In our own country respectable colleges now offer a considerable proportion of elective studies, and as a rule the greater their resources in teachers, collections, and money, the more liberal their application of the elective principle. Many colleges, however, still seem to have but a halting faith in the efficacy of the principle, and our educated public has but just begun to appreciate its importance. So fast as American institutions acquire the resources and powers of European universities, they will adopt the methods proper to universities wherever situate. At present our best colleges fall very far short of European standards in respect to number of teachers, and consequently in respect to amplitude of teaching.

As yet we have no university in America—only aspirants to that eminence. All the more important is it that we should understand the conditions under which a university can be developed—the most indispensable of which is freedom in choice of studies.

II. A university must give its students opportunity to win distinction in special subjects or lines of study. The uniform curriculum led to a uniform degree, the first scholar and the last receiving the same diploma. A university cannot be developed on that plan. It must provide academic honors at graduation for distinguished attainments in single subjects. These honors encourage students to push far on single lines; whence arises a demand for advanced instruction in all departments in which honors can be won, and this demand, taken in connection with the competition which naturally springs up between different departments, stimulates the teachers, who in turn stimulate their pupils. The elaborate directions given by each department to candidates for honors are so many definite pieces of advice to students who wish to specialize their work. It is an incidental advantage of the system that the organization of departments of instruction is promoted by it. The teachers of Latin, of history, or of philosophy, find it necessary to arrange their courses in orderly sequence, to compare their methods and their results, and to enrich and diversify as much as possible the instruction which they collectively offer. Many European universities, but especially the English, offer honors, or prizes, or both of these inducements, for distinguished merit in specialities; and the highly valued degree of Ph.D. in Germany is a degree given for large attainments in one or two branches of knowledge, with mention of the specialty. The Harvard faculty announced their system of honors in 1866–67, and they certainly never passed a more effective piece of legislation. In 1879 they devised a lesser distinction at graduation called honorable mention, which has also worked very well. To get honors in any department ordinarily requires a solid year and a half's work; to get honorable mention requires about half that time. The important function of all such devices is to promote specialization of work and therefore to develop advanced instruction. It is unnecessary to point out how absolutely opposed to such a policy the uniform prescription of a considerable body of elementary studies must be.

III. A university must permit its students, in the main, to govern themselves. It must have a large body of students, else many of its numerous courses of highly specialized instruction will find no hearers, and the students themselves will not feel that very wholesome influence which comes from observation of and contact with large numbers of young men from different nations, States, schools, families, sects, parties, and conditions of life. In these days a university is best placed in or near the seat of a considerable population; so that its officers and students can always enjoy the various refined pleasures, and feel alike the incitements and the restraints, of a highly cultivated society. The universities of Rome, Paris, Vienna, Berlin, Leipsic, Christiania, Madrid, and Edinburgh forcibly illustrate both of these advantages. These conditions make it practically impossible for a university to deal with its students on any principle of seclusion, either in a village or behind walls and bars. Fifteen hundred able-bodied young men living in buildings whose doors stand open night and day, or in scattered lodging-houses, cannot be mechanically protected from temptation at the university any more than at the homes from which they came. Their protection must be within them. They must find it in memory of home, in pure companionship, in hard work, in intellectual ambition, religious sentiment, and moral purpose. A sense of personal freedom and responsibility reinforces these protecting influences, while the existence of a supervising authority claiming large powers which it has no effective means of exercising weakens them. The *in loco parentis* theory is an ancient fiction which ought no longer to deceive anybody. No American college, wherever situated, possesses any method of discipline which avails for the suppression or exclusion of vice. The vicious student can find all means of indulgence in the smallest village, and the worst vices are the stillest. It is a distinct advantage of the genuine university method that it does not pretend to maintain any parental or monastic discipline over its students, but frankly tells them that they must govern themselves. The moral purpose of a university's policy should be to train young men to self-control and self-reliance through liberty. It is not the business of a university to train men for those functions in which implicit obedience is of the first importance. On the contrary, it should train men for those occupations in which self-government, independence, and originating power are preëminently needed. Let no one imagine that a young man is in peculiar moral danger at an active and interesting university. Far from it. Such a university is the safest place in the world for young men who have anything in them—far safer than counting-room, shop, factory, farm, barrack, forecastle, or ranch. The student lives in a bracing atmosphere; books engage him; good companionships invite him; good occupations defend him; helpful friends surround him; pure ideals are held up before him; ambition spurs him; honor beckons him.

3. James McCosh Attacks the New Departure and President Eliot, 1885

James McCosh (1811–94) was born in Scotland and educated at the universities of Glasgow and Edinburgh. An important figure in the religious life of Scotland, he soon became one of the leading defenders of supernaturalism against the influence of men like John Stuart Mill, and in 1852 he was appointed to the chair of logic and metaphysics in Queen's College, Belfast. From this post the productive McCosh became one of the most influential thinkers in the Anglo-American world, and in 1868 he was invited to assume the presidency of Princeton, and with it, in effect, the intellectual leadership of American Presbyterianism. Assuming this role at a time when older verities were being questioned, McCosh defended conservatism with commendable flexibility. As an educator he was immensely successful in rehabilitating Princeton, which had reached a low state at the time of his accession. Although he opposed what he considered to be the extremes of the elective system, he did allow elective studies at Princeton and encouraged the development of graduate work and the study of science. See William M. Sloane (ed.), *The Life of James McCosh* (New York, 1896); John Brubacher and Willis Rudy, *Higher Education in Transition* (New York, 1958), chap. vi; and T. J. Wertenbaker, *Princeton: 1746–1896* (Princeton, 1946), pp. 294–307.

I have been drawn into this three-cornered debate[1] by no merit or demerit of mine. I was told by the Nineteenth Century Club that the President of Harvard was to advocate what was called his "new departure," and I was invited to criticize it. I have noticed with considerable anxiety that departure as going on for years past without parents or the public noticing it. I am glad that things have come to a crisis. Fathers and mothers and the friends of education will now know what is proposed, what is in fact going on, and will have to decide forthwith whether they are to fall in with and encourage it, or are to oppose it.

I asked first what the question was. President Eliot has shaped it as follows: "IN A UNIVERSITY THE STUDENT MUST CHOOSE HIS STUDIES AND GOVERN HIMSELF." I saw at once that the question thus announced was large and loose, vague and ambiguous, plausible to the ear, but with

---

James McCosh, *The New Departure in College Education, Being a Reply to President Eliot's Defense of It in New York* (New York, 1885).

[1] The Nineteenth Century Club meant to make the debate three-cornered, but somehow one of the sides of the triangle fell out, and instead of a triangle we have two sides facing each other.

no definite meaning. But it commits its author to a positive position and gives me room to defend a great and good cause. The form is showy but I can expose it; I can prick the bubble so that all may know how little matter is inside.

On the one hand I am sorry that the defence of solid and high education should have devolved on me rather than on some more gifted advocate. But on the other hand I feel it to be a privilege that I am invited to oppose proposals which are fitted, without the people as yet seeing it, to throw back in America (as Bacon expresses it) "The Advancement of Learning."

I will not allow any one (without protest) to charge me with being antiquated, or old-fashioned, or behind the age—I may be an old man but I cherish a youthful spirit. For sixteen years I was a professor in the youngest and one of the most advanced universities in Great Britain, and I have now been sixteen years in an American college, and in both I have labored to elevate the scholarship. I act on the principle that every new branch of what has shown itself to be true learning is to be introduced into a college. My friends in America have encouraged me by generously giving me millions of money to carry out this idea. I am as much in favor of progress as President Eliot, but I go on in a different, I believe a better way. I adopt the new, I retain what is good in the old. I am disappointed, I am grieved when I find another course pursued which allows, which encourages, which tempts young men in their caprice to choose easy subjects, and which are not fitted to enlarge or refine the mind, to produce scholars, or to send forth the great body of the students as educated gentlemen.

Freedom is the catch-word of this new departure. It is a precious and an attractive word. But, O Liberty! what crimes and cruelties have been perpetrated in thy name! It is a bid for popularity. An entering Freshman will be apt to cheer when he hears it—the prospect is so pleasant. The leader in this departure will have many followers. The student infers from the language that he can study what he pleases. I can tell you what he will possibly or probably choose. Those who are in the secrets of colleges know how skilful certain students are in choosing their subjects. They can choose the branches which will cost them least study, and put themselves under the popular professors who give them the highest grades with the least labor. I once told a student in an advanced stage of his course, "If you had shown as much skill in pursuing your studies as in choosing the easiest subjects you would have been the first man in your class." I am for freedom quite as much as Dr. Eliot is, but it is for freedom regulated by law. I am for liberty but not licentiousness, which always ends in servitude.

I am to follow the President of Harvard in the three roads which he has taken; placing positions of mine face to face with his:

    I. FREEDOM IN CHOOSING STUDIES

    II. FREEDOM IN CHOOSING SPECIALTIES

    III. FREEDOM IN GOVERNMENT

I

Freedom in Choosing Studies.—I am for freedom, but it must be within carefully defined limits. First, a young man should be free to enter a university or not to enter it. He is to be free to choose his department in that university, say Law or Medicine, or the Academic terminating in the Bachelor or Master's Degree. But, having made his choice, is he to have all possible freedom ever after? At this point the most liberal advocate of liberty will be obliged to tell the student, "We are now required to lay some restraints upon you," and the youth finds his liberty is at an end. He has to take certain studies and give a certain amount of time to them, say, according to the Harvard model, to select four topics. He goes in for Medicine: he may make his quartette Physical Geography, which tells what climate is; and Art, which teaches us to paint the human frame; and Music, which improves the voice; and Lectures on the Drama, which show us how to assume noble attitudes. These seem more agreeable to him than Anatomy and Physiology, than Surgery and Materia Medica, which present corpses and unpleasant odors. I tell you that, though this youth should get a diploma written on parchment, I would not, however ill, call him in to prescribe to me, as I might not be quite sure whether his medicines would kill or cure me. Or the intention of the youth is Engineering in order to make or drive a steam engine, and he does not take Mathematics, or Mechanics, or Graphics, or Geodesy; but as unlimited choice is given him, he prefers drawing and field work—when the weather is fine, and two departments of gymnastics—now so well taught in our colleges—namely, boxing and wrestling. I tell you I am not to travel by the railway he has constructed. But he has a higher aim: he is to take a course in the Liberal Arts and expects a Master's Degree; but Greek and Mathematics and Physics and Mental Philosophy are all old and waxing older, and he takes French to enable him to travel in Europe, and Lectures on Goethe to make him a German scholar, and a Pictorial History of the age of Louis XIV., and of the Theatre in ancient and modern times. This is a good year's work, and he can take a like course in each of the four years; and if he be in Yale or Princeton College, he will in Spring and Fall substitute Base Ball and Foot Ball, and exhibit feats more wonderful than were ever performed in the two classical countries, Greece and Rome, at their famous Olympian Games and Bull Fights.

I have presented this designedly rude picture to show that there must be some limits put to the freedom of choice in studies. The able leader of the new departure, with the responsibilities of a great College upon him, and the frank and honest gentleman, who has such a dread of a Fetish—the creature of his own imagination—will be ready to admit that in every department of a University there should be a well considered and a well devised curriculum of study. It is one of the highest and most important functions of the governing bodies to construct such a scheme. It should have in it two essential powers or properties.

First, there should be branches required of all students who pursue the full course and seek a degree. This is done in such departments as Engineering and Medicine and should be done in Arts. The obligatory branches should be wisely selected. They should all be fitted to enlarge or refine the mind. They should be fundamental, as forming the basis on which other knowledge is built. They should be disciplinary, as training the mind for further pursuits. Most of them should have stood the test of time and reared scholars in ages past. There will be found to be a wonderful agreement among educated men of high tastes as to what these should be.

There should be included in them the eight studies on which examinations are held in order to entrance [*sic*] into Harvard College. These are 1, English; 2, Greek; 3, Latin; 4, German; 5, French; 6, History; 7, Mathematics; 8, Physical Science. This is the scheme of preparatory studies just issued by Harvard. It seems to me to require too much from our schools. It will prevent many teachers who have hitherto sent students to college from doing so any more. Teachers in smaller towns and country districts will have to look to this. If the scheme is carried out fewer young men will come up to our colleges from such places. They will find that they cannot get French and German and physical apparatus in the schools available to them. Some of the branches had better be reserved for college, where they will be taught more effectively. But passing this by as not just to our present point, I put all these cardinal studies in the branches which should be required in a college.

In the farther courses of a college other obligatory studies should be added, such as Biology, including Botany and Zoology, Geology, Political Economy or better Social Science, and at least three branches of Mental Science, Psychology, Logic, and Ethics. All these by a wise arrangement could be taught in the three or four years at school and the four years of college. They should be judiciously spread over the years of school and college training; a certain number of them in each successive year for every student. They should advance with the age and progress of the student. They should follow one after another in logical order from the more elementary to the higher, which presuppose the lower. Thus Mathematics should come before Physics, and Biology before Geology, and Psychology before Logic and Ethics.

Education is essentially the training of the mind—as the word *educare* denotes—the drawing forth of the faculties which God has given us. This it should especially be in a University, in a *Studium Generale,* as it used to be called. The powers of mind are numerous and varied, the senses, the memory, the fancy, judgment, reasoning, conscience, the feelings, the will; the mathematical, the metaphysical, the mechanical, the poetical, the prosaic (quite as useful as any); and all these should be cultivated, the studies necessary to do so should be provided, and the student required so far to attend to them, that the young man by exercise may know what powers he has and the mental frame be fully developed. To accomplish this end the degrees of Bachelor of Arts and of Master of Arts were instituted. These titles have acquired a meaning. For centuries past tens of thousands of eager youths have been yearly seeking for them and the attainments implied in them. True, the standard adopted in some colleges has been low—some who have got the diploma could not read the Latin in which it is written; still it has a certain prestige and a considerable attractive power. It indicates, as to the great body of those who possess it, that they have some acquaintance with elevated themes, that in short they have some culture. I do not wish to have this stimulus withdrawn. I have been laboring for the last thirty-two years to elevate the requirements for the degree.

But let it retain its meaning and carry out its meaning thoroughly. Let it be an evidence that the possessor of it has some knowledge of literature, science, and philosophy.

I have no objection that other degrees be instituted, such as Bachelor of Literature, Bachelor of Science, but only on one condition, that examinations be deep, that they be rigid, that they imply a knowledge of the principles as well as of the details of the branches taught, that they cultivate the mind and elevate the tastes as well as fit men for professions. But let us retain in the meanwhile the old Bachelor and Master Degrees, only putting a new life into them. They should not be given to one who knows merely English and German, or one who knows merely chemistry and physics, still less to one who knows merely music and painting. Eminence in these has no right to assume, or in fact steal, the old title. Let each kind of degree have its own meaning and people will value it accordingly. But let A.B. and A.M. abide to attract youths to high general scholarship.

Under this Academic Degree I would allow a certain amount of choice of studies, such as could not be tolerated in professional departments, as Law or Medicine. But there are branches which no candidate for the degree should be allowed to avoid. There should be English, which I agree with President Eliot in regarding as about the most essential of all branches, it being taught in a scientific manner. There should be Modern Languages, but there should also be Classics. A taste and a style are produced by the study of the Greek and Latin with their literatures, which are expressively called *Classic*. It may be difficult to define, but we all feel the charm of it. If we lose this there is nothing in what is called our Modern Education to make up for the loss. President Eliot has a high opinion of German Universities, but the eminent men in their greatest University, that of Berlin, have testified that a far higher training is given in the Classical Gymnasia than in the scientific Real Schule.[2]

There should be physical science, but there should also be mental and moral science required of all. In knowing other things our young men should be taught to know themselves. When our students are instructed only in matter they are apt to conclude that there is nothing

---

[2] Professor Hoffman, as Rector of Berlin University, says that it is the opinion of the University that "all efforts to find a substitute for the classical languages, whether in mathematics, in the modern languages or in the natural sciences, have been hitherto unsuccessful." In Princeton College Dr. Young and the scientific professors unanimously are, if possible, more strongly in favor of Latin and Greek than even the classical professors.

but matter. Our colleges should save our promising youths, the hope of the coming age and ages, from materialism with its degrading consequences. We must show them that man has a soul with lofty powers of reason and conscience and free will, which make him immortal and enable him so far to penetrate the secrets of nature, and by which he can rise to the knowledge of God.

We in Princeton believe in a Trinity of studies: in Language and Literature, in Science, and in Philosophy. Every educated man should know so much of each of these. Without this, man's varied faculties are not trained, his nature is not fully developed and may become malformed.

A college should give what is best to its students, and it should not tempt them to what is lower when the higher can be had. Harvard boasts that it gives two hundred choices to its students, younger and older.[3] I confess that I have had some difficulty in understanding her catalogue. I would rather study the whole Cosmos. It has a great many perplexities, which I can compare only to the cycles, epicycles, eccentricities of the old astronomy, so much more complex than that of Newton. An examination of students upon it would be a better test of a clear head than some of their subjects, such as "French Plays and Novels." As I understand it, one seeking a degree, may, in his free will choose the following course:

In Sophomore Year—
1. French Literature of the Seventeenth Century.
2. Mediaeval and Modern European History.
3. Elementary Course in Fine Art, with collateral instruction in Water-coloring.
4. Counterpoint (in music).

---

[3] In Princeton we have nearly all the branches taught in Harvard, but we do not subdivide and scatter them as they do; we put them under compacted heads. In his address to the Johns Hopkins University, Dr. Eliot refers to the supposed deficiency in teaching history in Princeton. In reply I have to state that we have a small examination on the subject for entrance; that in the Sophomore year we use one of Freeman's textbooks to give an elementary view of universal history; that in the Junior and Senior the Professor of the Philosophy of History gives a historical and critical survey of the science and methods of history. More particularly each Professor is expected to give a history of his own branch, and so we have histories of Politics, of Philosophy, of Greece, of Rome, of the literature of Germany and of France, etc. I do not agree with Mr. J. S. Mill that history cannot be taught in a college (it would take forty years and more to go over all history); but I think the numerous narrative histories of epochs is just a let-off to easy-going students from the studies which require thought.

In Junior Year—
  1. French Literature of the Eighteenth Century.
  2. Early Mediaeval History.
  3. Botany.
  4. History of Music.
In Senior Year—
  1. French Literature of the Nineteenth Century.
  2. Elementary Spanish.
  3. Greek Art.
  4. Free Thematic Music.[4]

There are twenty such dilettanti courses which may be taken in Harvard. I cannot allow that this is an advance in scholarship. If this be the modern education, I hold that the old is better. I would rather send a young man, in whom I was interested, to one of the old-fashioned colleges of the country, where he would be constrained to study Latin, Greek, Mathematics, Rhetoric, Physics, Logic, Ethics, and Political Economy, and I am persuaded that his mind would thereby be better trained and he himself prepared to do higher and more important work in life. From the close of Freshman year on it is perfectly practicable for a student to pass through Harvard and receive the degree of Bachelor of Arts, without taking any course in Latin, Greek, Mathematics, Chemistry, Physics, Astronomy, Geology, Logic, Psychology, Ethics, Political Economy, German, or even English! (If, as President Eliot insists, a knowledge of our mother-tongue is the true basis of culture, what is to be said of this?)

Secondly. It should be an essential feature of the course for a degree, that the attendance of the student on lectures and recitations should be obligatory. This is a very important matter. The student may have freedom in his choice, but having made his election he should be bound to attend on the instruction imparted. He should not be allowed to attend the one day and stay away the next. A professor should not be subjected to the disadvantage of only a portion of his students, say a half or a third, being present at any one lecture, and of the students who attend not being the same continuously. Parents living far away from the college-seat should have some security that their sons professing to be at college are not all the winter skating on the ice, or shooting canvasback-ducks on Chesapeake Bay.

---

[4] In the debate we were told that this is a deep study; then the Degree of Master of Music (M.M.) should be given to it but not M.A.

But it is said that if a student can stand an examination, it is no matter where he gets his knowledge. There is an enormous fallacy lurking here. I admit that a youth may make himself a scholar without being at a college or submitting to its examinations. But if he goes to college let him take all its advantages. One of these is to be placed under a continuous course of instruction in weekly, almost daily, intercourse with his professors, keeping him at his work and encouraging him in it. It is thus that the academic taste, thus that the student spirit with its hard work is created and fostered.

I have had thorough means of becoming acquainted with those systems in which there is no required attendance; and I testify that they do not tend to train high scholars. Everything depending on a final examination, the student is sure to be tempted to what is called *cramming*. A student once told me what this led to in his own experience. In five of the branches taught to his class, he spread his daily studies over the year; but in one he trusted to cramming. I said to him, "Tell me honestly what is the issue." He answered, "In the five branches I remember everything and could stand another examination to-day, but in the one—it happened to be botany—it is only four weeks since I was examined on it, but my mind is a blank on the whole subject."

I know that in Germany they produce scholars without requiring a rigid attendance, and I rather think that in a few American colleges, they are aping this German method, thinking to produce equally diligent students. They forget that the Germans have one powerful safeguard which we have not in America. For all offices in Church and State there is an examination by high scholars following the college course. A young man cannot get an office as clergyman, as teacher, as postmaster, till he is passed by that terrible examining bureau, and if he is turned by them his prospects in life are blasted.[5] Let the State of Massachusetts pass a law like the Prussian, and Harvard may then relax attendance, and the State will do what the colleges have neglected to do.[6]

---

[5] The Germans have, besides, their admirable gymnasien, where all is prescribed, and which give instruction equivalent to that of the Freshman and Sophomore years in American colleges.

[6] President Eliot would not have students enter college till they are eighteen years of age. If this be carried out it is evident that we shall have fewer young men taking a college education. A large number cannot afford to continue till twenty-five before they earn money; not entering college till eighteen, continuing three or four years and spend-

Specialties in Study.—Men have special talents, and so they should have special studies provided for them. They are to have special vocations in life, and college youth should so far be prepared for them. Every student should have Obligatory studies, but he should also be allowed Elective studies. The branches of knowledge are now so numerous and literature is so wide and varied, that no one can master it all; should he try to do so, he would only be "a jack of all trades and a master of none."

The student should have two kinds of electives provided for him. He may be allowed to take subjects which could not be required of all, such, for example, as Sanscrit, Anglo-Saxon, the Semitic Tongues, and in science, Histology and Physical Geography. No college should make these obligatory, and yet considerable numbers of students would prize them much and get great benefit from them, to fit them for their farther study and life-work. Or, the student, after taking certain elementary branches, should have higher forms of the same provided for him, and be encouraged to take them. Of all the rudimentary branches or cardinal studies, there should be a course or courses required of all in order to make them educated gentlemen, but there should be advanced courses—Electives, to produce high scholars in all branches, literary, linguistic, scientific, philosophic. All students should know several of the highest languages, ancient and modern, but there should be advanced linguistic studies, and especially a science of Comparative Language. I defy you to make all master Quaternions, or Quantics, or Functions, but these should be in the college for a select few. All should be taught the fundamental laws of the human mind, but there should also be a number entering into the depths and climbing the heights, of the Greek, the Scotch, and the German philosophies.

I hold that in a college with the variety there should be a unity. The circle of the sciences should have a wide circumference but also a fixed

---

ing another three years in learning a profession. In many cases many young men might be ready to enter college at sixteen, graduate at twenty, and then learn their professions. This would suit the great body of students. But one in ten, or one in five who have acquired a taste for more should be encouraged to remain in college, to take post-graduate courses and devote themselves to special studies. We encourage this in Princeton by seven or eight endowed Fellowships, and have always 30, 40, or 50 post-graduate students. In this way we hope to rear scholars.

centre. In every year there should be certain primary and radical studies required of every student, with all the while a diversity in his electives. This I take the liberty of saying is the difference between Harvard and Princeton. In Harvard there are now in no year any studies
obligatory on all except a part of Freshman year studies—everything
is scattered like the star dust out of which worlds are formed. Greek is
not obligatory; Mathematics are not obligatory; Logic and Ethics are
not obligatory. In Princeton a number of disciplinary branches are required, and so many are required in each year to give us a central sun
with rotating planets. In Nature, as Herbert Spencer has shown, there
is differentiation which scatters, but there is also concentration which
holds things together. There should be the same in higher education.
In a college there may be, there should be specialists, but not mere
specialists, who are sure to be narrow, partial, malformed, one-sided,
and are apt to become conceited, prejudiced, and intolerant. The other
day a gymnast showed me his upper arm with the muscle large and
hard as a mill-stone. It is a picture of the mental monstrosities produced by certain kinds of education. The tanner insists that "there is
nothing like leather," and the *literateur,* that there is nothing like language; while the mathematician assures you that there is nothing to be
believed except what can be demonstrated; leading Goethe to say, "As
if, forsooth, things only exist when they can be mathematically demonstrated. It would be foolish in a man not to believe in his mistress'
love because she could not prove it to him mathematically; she can
mathematically prove her dowry but not her love."

Dr. Eliot tells us he has found great difficulties in combining the
Prescribed and the Elective Courses. In my thirty-two years' college
teaching I have met with no such difficulty. On the contrary I have
found them working in harmony. Thus I have found the Prescribed
study in Greek helping me in the Elective History of Philosophy.[7]

It is now shown that all science is correlated, and every one thing
depends on every other. Humboldt had his "Cosmos," and Mr. Grove
his "Correlation of the Forces," and the Duke of Argyll has his "Unity
of Nature." Nature is a system like the solar, with a sun in the centre
and planets and satellites all around, held together by a gravitating

---

[7] At the New York meeting I distributed the *Plan of Study in Princeton College,*
showing how we carry into practical operation the principles laid down in this paper and
combine the general with the special.

power which keeps each in its proper place, and all shining on each other. You cannot study any one part comprehensively without so far knowing the others. In like manner, all the parts of a good college curriculum should be connected in an organic whole. Make a man a mere specialist and the chance is he will not reach the highest eminence as a specialist. The youth most likely to make discoveries is one who has studied collateral subjects; the well gushes out at a certain point because the rains have descended on a large surface and entered the earth, and must find an outlet.

I may here point out the evils little noticed arising from a boy having too many choices; they say two hundred in Harvard. I believe that comparatively few young men know what their powers are when they enter college. Many do not yet know what their undeveloped faculties are; quite as many imagine that they have talents which they do not possess. Fatal mistakes may arise from a youth of sixteen or eighteen commiting himself to a narrow-gauge line of study, and he finds when it is too late that he should have taken a broader road.

A young man, we may suppose, when he enters college leaves out Greek, attracted by a popular teacher of French. When he has done so he finds, as he comes to Junior year, that a voice, as it were, from God, calls him to preach the gospel of salvation. Then he comes to see his mistake, for if he has to be an expounder of Scripture, he must know the language of the New Testament, and to attain this he must go back two or three years to school, and, unwilling to do this, he gives up studying for the ministry. The Churches of Christ will do well to look to this new departure, for they may find that they have fewer candidates for the office of the ministry. The colleges may have to look to this, for the churches furnish to them the most constant supply of students. For myself, I fear that the issue will be an unfortunate division of colleges into Christian and infidel.

A like result may follow from other unfortunate choices, as we say, from young men "mistaking their trade." One who might have turned out a splendid teacher devotes himself to metaphysics and neglects classics and mathematics. Another who might have become a statesman has avoided logic and political economy, being allured by music and plays. The boy has turned away from mathematics to find that in his future study and professional work he absolutely needs them.

III

Self Government.—I hold that in a college, as in a country, there should be government; there should be care over the students, with inducements to good conduct, and temptations removed, and restraints on vice. There should be moral teaching; I believe also religious teaching—the rights of conscience being always carefully preserved. But one part of this instruction should be to inculcate independence, independence in thinking, independence in action and self-control. The student should be taught to think for himself, to act for himself. If he does not acquire this spirit, no external authority will be able to guide and restrain him. I abhor the plan of secretly watching students, of peeping through windows at night, and listening through key-holes. Under the *spy* system, the students will always beat their tutors. The tricky fellows will escape, while only the simple will be caught.

But is there, therefore, to be no moral teaching, no restraint on conduct? Are students to be allured away from their homes, hundreds and thousands of miles away, from California, Oregon, and Florida, to our Eastern colleges, and there do as they please—to spend their evenings according to their inclinations, to keep no Sabbaths, and all the while get no advice, no warning from the college authorities? They see a student going into a liquor store, a dancing saloon, a low theatre, a gambling-house. Are they to do nothing? Are they precluded from doing anything? A student is seen drunk. What are you to do with him? "The law is not made for the righteous man, but for the lawless and disobedient." Have you no law to reach him? You have no right to discipline him. It is an interference with his freedom. He is a man, and not a boy, and he should resent it. He is able to guide himself. His widowed mother lives a thousand miles away, and cannot reach him. He continues in this course. Are you to allow him to remain in the institution to ruin himself and corrupt others? You answer, we will send him away. But you cannot do so (so I hope) without evidence, and this implies that horrid thing, discipline. But you dismiss him. I have been obliged to dismiss students on rare occasions. It is a terrible ordeal to me. I have sometimes felt more than the student himself. And when the father comes to me, the father trying to suppress the bursting feeling, and the mother in agony which cannot be restrained, I am crushed, I am prostrated. But my creed is, prevention is better than punishment. Surely, if we have the right to dismiss and expel (I never expelled a student), we have the liberty to instruct, to advise, to remonstrate, nay, to discipline. I have some painful scenes to pass through in the government of a college, but I have had more pleasant ones. I have to testify that three-fourths, I believe nine-tenths, of the cases of discipline I have administered have ended in the reformation of the offender. I have been gratified by many fathers and mothers thanking me for saving their sons from ruin. Scores of graduates, when they meet me, have said, "I thank you for that sharp rebuke you gave me; you gave it heartily, and I was irritated at the time, but now I thank you as heartily, for I was arrested thereby when rushing into folly."

It is time that fathers and mothers should know what it is proposed to do with their sons at college. The college authorities are in no way to interfere with them. They are to teach them Music and Art, and French Plays and Novels, but there is no course in the Scriptures—in their poetry, their morality, their spirituality. The President of Harvard recommends that all colleges should be in great cities. Students are to be placed in the midst of saloons, and gambling-houses, and temples of Venus, but meanwhile no officer of the college is to preach to them, to deal with them. Suppose that under temptation the son falls. I can conceive a father saying to the head of the institution, "I sent my son to you believing that man is made in the image of God, you taught him that he is an upper brute, and he has certainly become so; I sent him to you pure, and last night he was carried to my door drunk. Curse ye this college; 'curse ye bitterly,' for you took no pains to allure him to good, to admonish, to pray for him." I was once addressed by a mother in very nearly these words. I was able to show that her son had come to us a polluted boy from an ungodly school, and that we had dealt with him kindly, warned him solemnly, disciplined him, given notice of his conduct to his mother, and prayed for him. Had I not been able to say this conscientiously I believe I would that day have given in my resignation of the office I hold, and retired to a wilderness to take charge of myself, feeling that I was not competent to take care of others.

It is a serious matter what we are to do to provide religious studies in our colleges. Professor Huxley knows that there is little or nothing in our ordinary school books to mould and form the character of children, and so, as member of the London School Board, he votes for the reading of the Scriptures in the schools, not that he believes them, but because they are fitted to sway the mind,—which I remark they are able to do, because they are divine. Everybody knows that science alone is not fit to form or guard morality; and Herbert Spencer is very anxious about this transition period, when the old has passed away (so he thinks) and the new morality is not yet published. Emerson stood up manfully for the retention of prayers in Harvard University. Are we now in our colleges to give up preaching? to give up Bible instruction? to give up prayers? But I am on the borders of the religious question, on which I now formally propose that *This club should have another meeting, in which President Eliot will defend the new departure in the religion of colleges, and I engage with God's help to meet him.*[8]

In closing, I have to confess that I regard this new departure with deep anxiety. The scholarship of America is not yet equal to that of Germany or Great Britain. Some of us are anxious to raise it up to the standard of Europe. We are discouraged by this plan of Harvard to allow and encourage its students to take branches in which there is so little to promote high intellectual culture. We know what a galaxy of great men appeared in Harvard an age ago, under the old training. I know that it is keenly discussed, within the college itself, whether there is anything in the present and coming modes of dissipated instruction to rear men of the like intellectual calibres. Has there been of late any great poem, any great scientific discovery, any great history, any great philosophic work, by the young men of Cambridge? I observe that the literary journals, for which our young writers prepare articles, have now fixed their seat in New York rather than Boston.

The wise leaders of the new departure do not propose to fight against religion. They do not fight with it, but they are quite willing to let it die out, to die in dignity. They have put severe learning on a sliding scale, not it may be in order to a sudden fall, but insensibly to go down to the level of those boys who do not wish to think deeply or study hard. I am glad things have come to a crisis. Let parents know it, let the churches know it, let all America know it, let scholars in Europe know it, let the world know it—for what is done in Harvard has influence over the world. But some timid people will say, "Tell it not in the lands whence our pious fathers came that the college whose motto is *Pro Christo et Ecclesia* teaches no religion to its pupils. Tell it not in Berlin or Oxford that the once most illustrious university in America no longer requires its graduates to know the most perfect language, the grandest literature, the most elevated thinking of all antiquity.

---

[8] I am waiting to hear whether this challenge is accepted.

Tell it not in Paris, tell it not in Cambridge in England, tell it not in Dublin, that Cambridge in America does not make mathematics obligatory on its students. Let not Edinburgh and Scotland and the Puritans in England know that a student may pass through the once Puritan College of America without having taken a single class of philosophy or a lesson in religion. But whatever others may do, *I say, I say,* let Europe know in all its universities—I wish my voice could reach them all—that in a distinguished college in America a graduate need no longer take what the ages have esteemed the highest department of learning; and I believe that such an expression of feeling will be called forth, that if we cannot avert the evil in Harvard we may arrest it in the other colleges of the country.

4. The New Curriculum: Some Views from the Nation, 1882

The incursions of the elective system upon the old curriculum were calculated to excite the interest not only of professional educators but of all laymen with an interest in higher education. These remarks serve as a sample of educational discussion among laymen who read the *Nation,* then the country's foremost weekly, edited by E. L. Godkin (1831–1902). William Goodell Frost (1854–1938), writer of the letter included as the second selection here, was then a recent graduate of Oberlin College and later went to a lengthy presidency (1892–1920) of Berea (Kentucky) College.

EDITORIAL

YALE AND HARVARD

Yale College has apparently taken up the practice begun by Harvard of issuing an annual report, in which the president not only gives an account of the actual condition of the college, but briefly discusses various university problems. The appearance of the two reports simultaneously will hereafter furnish those who are interested in the higher education with materials for a very instructive comparison of what may be called the two rival methods in university administration. The

"Yale and Harvard," *The Nation,* XXXIV (January 19, 1882), 50–51; "The American College *vs.* the European University," *ibid.,* February 16, 1882, pp. 142–44.

prominent part which Harvard has taken in introducing the elective system and the system (among the higher classes at least) of voluntary recitation, makes her in a certain sense the representative of those who think that the true function of a university is simply to provide the means of learning for those who wish to learn, and that no part of the energy or ability of its instructors should be expended either in stimulating the stupid or inert, or in bringing to punitive justice those who neglect their opportunities.

Yale, on the other hand, has hitherto represented, and, if we may judge by President Porter's report, still represents, those who consider a university a place for general training, moral as well as intellectual, in which the professor should stand literally *in loco parentis,* and not only provide the student with the means of instruction, but see that he gets it whether he likes it or not. The former is the European idea, and it is to the European type that Harvard is gradually approximating. The latter may be called the American idea, and in preaching it President Porter seeks to uphold what may be called the distinctively American college. There is nothing on the Continent exactly like the Yale view of the "college boy," and nothing in England except in the public schools. The relation of the professors to the students which President Porter upholds in the report before us, resembles nothing so much as the relation of the assistant master toward the boys at Eton, or Rugby, or Harrow. There could not be a better description of the role of the English assistant master, who teaches classics and mathematics in school hours, and afterward superintends the cricket and boating, than President Porter gives when he says that "the true and radical remedy" for the tendency in public schools and colleges to disregard "the plainest axioms of manners and morals," and to violate "the accepted axioms of courtesy and truth," is, first, to "hold the student to his duties in no mask or disguise," and then to introduce as "great variety into the student's life as practicable—making reasonable provision for attractive amusements and athletic activities."

Harvard, on the other hand, seems to aim more and more at leaving the student to take as much or as little of the advantages in the direction of learning which the place offers him as he pleases, and at withdrawing more and more from any charge of his morals and manners which is not necessary to the maintenance of public decency and good order. The elective system, in which the student picks out, within certain very wide limits, the course of study he will pursue, and the system of voluntary recitation, in which the student of the upper classes—also within certain very wide limits—uses attendance on recitations as an aid to his studies or not as he pleases, are leading features in a regime which takes for granted that a young man who goes to college begins life, and becomes his own master, to the same degree and in the same sense as a young man who gets a clerkship in the city, and leaves his parents in order to earn his bread. That this regime is found to give satisfaction we conclude from President Eliot's assertion that—

"Whoever reads the history of the development of the elective system, as it is recorded in the successive annual reports of the dean of the college faculty since 1870, will arrive at the well-grounded conviction that every extension of the system has been a gain to the individual student, to the college, and to every interest of education and learning; and will also see reason to believe that the time is not far distant when the few subjects still prescribed for all students will in their turn become elective."

We have called President Porter's idea of the duties of a university toward the undergraduates the American idea; but it is becoming every day more and more doubtful whether it will remain so, and for several reasons. One is that no large college seems to be able to play successfully the part either of the schoolmaster or parent. Yale has long plumed herself on being emphatically what religious parents would consider a "safe" college, or a college in which exemplary care was taken of the student's morals. Nevertheless, President Porter almost confesses that parents have begun to lose confidence in her from this point of view, and that those who wish to have their sons well looked after are beginning to prefer the smaller colleges; and apropos of this he reads his own staff a long lecture on the need of stricter discipline and closer attention to faith and morals. If Yale cannot succeed in the role of a guardian, no large college can. In fact, we venture to assert that, allowing for numbers and opportunity, the standard of conduct, or what may be called the tone, is—if there be any difference—higher among students in the colleges which allow them largest liberty than in the colleges which take most pains to exert a direct influence on character either by exhortation or fines and penalties. In managing all large bodies of young men by means of restraint, if the restraint be mild and easily evaded, it constitutes in itself, owing to one of the best-known peculiarities of human nature, a strong incentive to excess or disobedience. To be effective, therefore, it has to be overwhelmingly powerful and fortified by the sternest sanctions, such as those of military discipline. But no college can use any such discipline, and, therefore, every college which attempts to treat youths of eighteen as children through its rules fails lamentably in securing their enforcement. That a very large body of parents prefer colleges which promise large control of conduct is quite true. But if they are now finding out, as President Porter hints, that the large colleges at least cannot keep this promise, they are simply coming to a kind of knowledge which has long been within the reach of those who know anything of college life. There is no American college which, in order to provide adequate supervision of morals and manners on the parental theory, would not need double its present force of officers, and a very different kind of officers from those who now fill its chairs. The present professors would make poor policemen, or drill-sergeants, even if their time were not fully occupied with their duties as instructors.

Taking all this in connection with the dismal complaints of poverty which both universities make, we cannot help inclining to the belief that the American college of the future will belong rather to the European or Harvard type than to the present American or Yale one. No efficient seat of learning can, with any endowment which any American college now possesses or hopes to possess, undertake anything approaching to parental care of the students. They will all soon cease to promise anything of the kind....

THE AMERICAN COLLEGE *vs.* THE EUROPEAN UNIVERSITY

To the Editor of the Nation:

The one positive (and commendable) feature of the university is its wide range of electives: beyond this all is negative—no required studies or compulsory attendance, no rules, no responsibility for the moral or even the intellectual improvement of the student. The advantages of this *laissez-faire* system as applied to college students are not to be overlooked. It is a great relief to the instructor to feel that it is none of his business whether his pupils improve or abuse their opportunities. It stimulates both teacher—or rather professor, for in the university scheme the professor does not condescend to *teach*—it stimulates both professor and pupil to specially fine work in special departments. It has given Germany perhaps the leading position in the intellectual world.

We must remember, however, that German universities correspond rather to our professional schools than to our colleges, and are intended for older students, and designed to give eminence in a single branch rather than general culture. Just here has been their success, and also their failure. It seems to us improbable that any such system can be imported bodily and made to supplant the American college. The latter is a growth indigenous to our soil. Starting with the moral earnestness of the Puritans, it has grown up with other American institutions. It admits of indefinite improvement, but its fundamental ideas, resting upon real human wants, cannot be set aside.

The idea of a curriculum or fixed circle of required studies may be old-fashioned, but so is the multiplication-table. That the required studies may be supplemented by electives all will admit, but to make all studies elective must defeat the very object of a liberal education. Here lies the fallacy of the elective system. It dazzles us with the rich variety of electives, and somehow produces the impression that a student can take them *all* in the four years. Its advocates eagerly point out this and that and the other branch which the student may elect, but they studiously conceal the fundamental and essential branches which the student may omit. A student may graduate from Harvard without studying political economy, English literature, mental or moral philosophy. Natural history is wholly elective. Hitherto logic and outlines of history have been required, but we can all see with President Eliot that there is "reason to believe that the time is not far distant when the few subjects still prescribed for all students will in their turn become elective." The idea that a certain amount of information and a certain familiarity with the lines of thought in each of the leading departments of human knowledge is essential to an education, is wholly ignored. What will Harvard's degree mean? Not that the graduate has been trained in the methods of classical, scientific, and metaphysical thought, and introduced to history, political science, and all the more important branches of study. It will mean simply that he has pursued for four years the studies most agreeable to his yet unformed taste—those which are easiest to him, or which look toward his profession.

There is an immense pressure in our age, and in every age, for superficial education—something to give reputation and polish at the least expense of time and effort. We have scientific, normal, and business schools, each having a legitimate sphere, but each professing to give its patrons all the advantages of a full college course. For these short courses a sort of fiat-parchment is given: "This is an educated man— by order of the president and trustees." Now, the elective system is pandering to this very thing. The colleges in which it prevails virtually say to the student: "You cannot afford, you do not need, to spend four years in general culture. You may omit all that is hardest for you, and spend four years in those branches in which you are already most proficient, and which will shorten your professional studies, and we will give you the same degree."

The idea, also, that the college and its instructors must stand in a sense *in loco parentis* has a justification in the nature of things. The parental relation need not be confounded with that of the policeman or drill-sergeant. Parents who put their sons at an early age into a store or shop desire to know something more of the employer or foreman than that they are successful and efficient in their business. Such men stand *in loco parentis* to the young men under their influence, and ought to have some paternal qualities and some sense of responsibility. How much more the college professor, whose influence is tenfold greater. He is the only friend of mature years the student has. . . .

The university methods have their place in post-graduate courses. We shall all be glad to send our young men to Cambridge or Baltimore after they have completed a thorough curriculum under teachers who really teach, and who feel some responsibility for their welfare; but the American college will not soon be supplanted by the European university. Both are needed. The university is on a par with professional schools, the college is a second home; the university instructs, the college educates.

WILLIAM GOODELL FROST

Oberlin, O., Jan. 23, 1882

EDITOR'S REPLY

The student is often not competent to choose his course, or, if competent, has not the moral strength to choose rightly, or comes from an uneducated family which can give him no advice and exercise no influence over him in this matter. We presume it is safe to say that fully one-half the undergraduates of American colleges are the sons of fathers who are unable to help them in deciding what branches of study will make a college education most valuable to them, either for the purposes of intellectual training or of professional success. But it does not follow from this that, as our correspondent seems to think, there is no alternative except the "curriculum, or fixed circle of required studies"; nor do we think anybody of authority has ever seriously objected to this because it was "old-fashioned." What is needed is something between the "fixed circle" and absolute freedom. In other words, the college should assist the student in selecting, with due regard to his needs and his capacity. The best system would be one in which each student should make up his course under the special supervision or with the special assistance of a professor. But this is probably hardly practicable. If not, the best way out of the difficulty would seem to be the division of the studies into groups or courses, and the restriction of the election to these groups. They might be so made up as to meet the needs of every type of mind sufficiently common to be worth recognition, and would prevent the indulgence of pure laziness, or the total neglect of subjects with which every liberally-educated man should be acquainted.

As regards the "loco-parentis" college for which our correspondent pleads, there is only one thing to be said, and that is, that, however desirable it may be, it does not exist. There are no such colleges as he describes, and no professors who supply the student with "wholesome family restraint." Moreover, it is almost certain that in the present conditions of American life they cannot be created. We cannot find the professors competent to be parents to the undergraduates, or find the undergraduates ready to accept professors as parents. One of the most singular delusions of our time is the notion prevalent among American fathers and mothers that they can secure this restraint in small colleges and in colleges where the faculty is religious. Small country colleges doubtless offer fewer temptations and attract students bred in simpler homes than the large ones, but they are also compelled to put up with an inferior quality of instructors and inferior instruction. As regards the large ones, we shall simply say that a boy is notoriously just as "safe"—and we believe safer—in those which are trying hardest to be universities as in those which are trying hardest to stay colleges, and that the influence of the professor diminishes in the direct ratio of his eagerness to exert parental authority....

5. How the Elective System Actually Worked at Harvard in 1900

The following facts (with many others) were obtained from a detailed examination of the programs of study of 448 members of the Class of 1901. This examination was made by the Pedagogical Seminary (Education 20a) under the guidance of Professor Hanus in the winter of 1900–1901, and in particular by a committee of four, whose partial reports were discussed by the Seminary, and who made a final report upon the subject at the close of the academic year.

During the winter of 1901–1902 this report was revised, enlarged, and entirely rewritten by the writer of this article, who had general charge of the work of the committee. The purpose from the start has been to secure the facts, and then to present them without bias. It is hoped that the entire data, embodied in about 35 tables accompanied by explanatory text may, at no distant date, be published. No similar detailed study of the actual working of the Elective System has been made since Pres. Eliot, in his Report of 1886, presented the programs of 350 members of the classes of 1884 and 1885. Dean Briggs in his report for 1899–1900 gives "certain statistics of the use to which the Elective System was put by the various college classes between and including the classes of 1886 and 1900." The work of the Seminary, it will be seen, carried on, but with more detail, the studies already made of the Elective System at Harvard.

Some objections to the Elective System at Harvard imply that the choice of studies thereunder is practically unrestricted. It should, however, be understood that the choice of the Freshmen is practically limited to certain specified elementary courses, comprising only about 20 per cent of all the courses offered to undergraduates, and that a Freshman cannot take more than two courses in any one subject. Besides, English, and either French or German, must be taken by almost all Freshmen. Freshmen and Special Students must secure the approval of their choices by specially appointed advisers. Elementary courses must, of course, be taken prior to more advanced courses in the same subject, and a large number of the courses offered may be taken

Charles S. Moore, "The Elective System at Harvard," *Harvard Graduates Magazine,* XI (June, 1903), 530–34.

only in case the applicants satisfy the instructors in those courses of their fitness to take them. Furthermore, the whole body of courses offered is divided into about 14 examination groups, and no two courses in the same group may be taken at the same time. No more than six courses may be taken at a time, the requirement being five courses for a Freshman, and four for upper classmen with an extra half course in English Composition for those whose work in Freshman English was not satisfactory.

Let us now see what general lines of choice are followed at Harvard, the facts being obtained from an examination of the programs of study of 448 members of the Class of 1901. Of 33 subjects offered for choice, the first 14 that were chosen (the order being based upon the number of students making the choice and also substantially, upon the number of courses taken in each subject) were as follows:—

English (facile princeps), History, Economics, German, French, Philosophy, Fine Arts, Chemistry, Latin, Geology, Government, Greek, Mathematics, and Physics.

Arranged according to the average number of courses taken by each student, the first 14 are English, History, Music, Economics, Engineering, Chemistry, Philosophy, German, French, Architecture, Greek, Fine Arts, Latin, and Spanish. Mathematics drops to the 19th place, Geology and Government to the 22d, Physics to the 26th. While relatively few students chose Music, Engineering, and Architecture, each of those students took a large number of courses, and while relatively many took Geology, Government, and Physics, each one took but little in each subject. . . .

Examining the 448 programs for evidence of evasion of hard work, we find 20 that show from six to eight choices (out of a total of about 20 choices) among courses having the reputation to a greater or less degree of being "snap" courses. Several of these are the programs of men of high rank who graduated with a *magna cum*. Fewer than one eighth of the choices of the entire class were made from such courses, and but a few programs (only five indisputably) show a preponderance of "snap" and elementary, *i.e.* introductory, courses.

It is to be recognized that the term "snap" is a very inexact term, and also that a number of lecture courses of an introductory character are essential both for later work, and also for general culture. It would be unfortunate should the Elective System, through its marked tendency to increase the standard of work, change the character of such courses.

Let us consider next the extent to which the Elective System has led to specialization. We are met at once by the necessity of defining specialization. Dean Briggs, in his Report for 1899–1900, presents a table "of those who began to specialize not later than the Sophomore year, that is, of those who after the Freshman year took at least half of their work in one department." It seems useful, however, for our purposes, to recognize the fact that there may be specialization for but one year or for but two years, and to construct a definition to include this element of time. The following is offered as the basis upon which the programs in question have been classified with regard to specialization. A student is regarded as specializing who has taken 2 full courses or more in one department (*i.e.* Greek, Latin, Mathematics) in one year, or $3\frac{1}{2}$ full courses or more in one department in two years, or 5 full courses or more in one department in three years, or 6 full courses or more in one department in four years, with not less than $1\frac{1}{2}$ courses in any one year.

The definition will be more complete if groups of kindred departments be included, as, the Classics, History, Government, and Modern Languages. So we will say in addition to the above definition that a student is regarded as specializing who has taken

3 full courses or more in one *group* in one year,

5 full courses or more in one *group* in two years,

7 full courses or more in one *group* in three years,

$8\frac{1}{2}$ full courses or more in one *group* in four years, with not less than two courses in any one year.

The tables show that of the four-year men 6 per cent have specialized throughout the four years; 12 per cent more for three years; and 19 per cent failed to specialize even for one year.

It is interesting to note that of the men who completed the four years' work in three years, but 4 per cent specialized throughout the three years, while on the other hand but 12 per cent failed to specialize even for one year. Three fourths of the men who, coming from other colleges, were admitted to the senior class, specialized during their one year.

Nearly one half of the men who specialized during three and four years, did so in English, one sixth in Modern Languages (except English), and less than one eighth in the Classics, and also in History and Government.

If we seek out the programs that show such specialization every year, or for some part of the time that the work was confined to a narrow field, we find that there are 29 which appear open to the charge of showing undue specialization. This is 7.8 per cent of the 372 who did the full work for a diploma at Harvard. Of these 29, 14 specialized in History and Political Science, and nine of the 14 are now studying Law. Ten specialized in History and Modern Languages, of whom two are studying Law, and two are teaching Modern Languages. Three specialized in the Classics, two now being candidates for the doctor's degree, and one studying for the Ministry. Of the remaining two, one specialized in Engineering and is now studying Engineering, and one in Psychology, and is now studying Medicine. Nine of the 29 were three-year men.

If we examine the data to see to what extent there was a lack of proper concentration of energy, we find 17 students (or 4½ per cent of the 372 who did full work at Harvard) whose programs show a small amount of work in any one subject or group together with a wide range of subjects or groups. The work of these 17 is so scattered that thoroughness seems impossible; yet three of them received the A.B. *magna cum laude,* one of them being a Phi Beta Kappa man, and one received the A.B. *cum laude.*

There is another point of view which should be taken in studying the actual working of the Elective System. A program should be well-balanced, that is, should include some work in each of, say, three groups of subjects, Languages, Social Studies, and Science. It seems a reasonable requirement that each of these groups should be represented by at least 15 per cent of the total work of the student. This would leave 55 per cent for distribution according to interest, aptitude, or future needs. It might be stated in this way, that the presence of this minimum of 15 per cent would save a program from condemnation as ill-balanced. Turning now to the actual programs of the three hundred and seventy-two who completed their work at Harvard, we find that there was no one who failed to take some work in the Linguistic group, but two who failed to take some work in the Sociological group, and sixteen who failed to take some work in the Scientific group, while three failed to take the minimum of 15 per cent in the Linguistic group, twenty-one in the sociological, and one hundred and ninety in the Scientific.

Taking into consideration individual subjects, we find that of the 372 who completed at Harvard all the requirements for the degree of A.B. 254 (68%) took no Physics; 250 (67%) took no Mathematics; 247

(66%) took no Greek; 215 (58%) took no Chemistry; 178 (48%) took no Latin; 147 (39%) took no Fine Arts; 140 (37%) took no Philosophy; 137 (36%) took neither Greek nor Latin; 87 (23%) took neither Latin nor Mathematics; 29 (8%) took no science of any kind; 8 (2%) took neither Physics nor Chemistry; 60 (16%) took neither Botany, Zoölogy, Mineralogy, nor Hygiene.

These facts are interesting, and are given without comment as evidence of the actual working of the Elective System as at present administered at Harvard. The writer has at his command similar sets of statistics from Wellesley, Dartmouth, and Radcliffe, which may be made public at a later date.

6. Harvard's Appraisal of Her Elective System in 1904

On the 27th of May, 1902, the Faculty of Arts and Sciences voted: "That a committee be appointed to inquire and report what further measures may be advantageously taken to improve the quality of the work done in satisfaction of the requirements for the degree of Bachelor of Arts."...

Early in the deliberations of the Committee, it became clear that neither the Faculty nor any member of the Faculty possessed accurate and detailed knowledge of the methods and the efficiency of instruction in all the different courses, and that the Committee, if it would speak intelligently, must get such knowledge. The Committee undertook, therefore, to obtain information both from the instructors and from the students; and with this object it sent two circular letters of inquiry,—copies of which are appended to this report,—one to the head of every course conducted in the academic year 1901–02, the other to students in each course, the number of students varying with the size of the course.... From the instructors 245 replies were received; from the students 1757. The grades of the students who replied were as follows: A, 540; B, 560; C, 375; D, 210; E, 72.

"Report of the Committee on Improving Instruction in Harvard College," *Harvard Graduates Magazine*, XII (June, 1904), 611–14, 616–19.

The large proportion of A and B men is due in part to the fact that the better scholars answered the inquiries more freely, but in part also to the small number of men not in high standing who complete the work in the most advanced courses....

The instructors, as a rule, replied with fulness and care; the students with frankness, good feeling, and intelligence. The Committee believes that the replies, taken together, afford, with due allowance for occasional prejudice and eccentricity, the best documentary evidence now existing in regard to the teaching in Harvard College; and that they bear witness to the high quality of the students and to the strength of the teaching force. Now and then, naturally enough, the same course and the same instructor that inspired some students repelled others; but there was an unexpected and gratifying amount of evidence that students who got low marks—even those who failed—could respect instruction from which, according to the official records, they had seemed to profit little. There was also enough adverse criticism to leave no doubt of the students' sincerity.

The replies of the students showed a general satisfaction with their choice of elective studies in all departments. The exceptions are sometimes personal, and sometimes spring from a misconception of the ground covered by a course. Of the 1757 answers to the question, "Did your experience justify your choice?" only 197, or one in nine, were negative; and only 99 declared that the choice of the course in question was but partly justified. On the average, therefore, the students who replied were satisfied with five out of six of their elective courses. Such figures show that the choice of studies is intelligent, and that the courses are well conducted. It is not surprising that the good scholars were satisfied with their choice in a larger proportion of cases than the poor ones. Among the A men, only one elective course in 12 did not justify, or only partly justified, the choice; among the B men, one in 7; among the C men, one in 5; among the D men, one in $3\frac{1}{2}$; among the E men, about one in 2.

A student who was not satisfied with his choice commonly gave his reasons; and even those who felt that their choice was thoroughly justified were not slow to make suggestions for the improvement of their courses. The students made, however, no adverse criticism of a general character beyond the extremely common complaint that they feel the need of being kept up to their work more regularly....

There can be no doubt that our instructors as a body deceive themselves as to the amount of work which their courses require. Their answers, though often vague, suggest a general impression that the amount of time for a single course, outside of the recitation or lecture room, ought to be about six hours a week. It is impossible to tell exactly from the answers of the students the amount of time that they give on the average to a course, because it is frequently impossible to tell whether they include time spent in the laboratory or on a thesis; but, apart from laboratory courses and courses requiring theses, the students' estimates give the following results:

[Figures with a dash between them indicate the number of hours of work a week done outside of the lecture room; figures underneath indicate the number of courses in which that work was done, two half courses counting as a whole course. Thus, in one course less than one hour of work per week was done outside of the lecture room; in each of six courses as much as one hour, and less than two.]

0–1	1–2	2–3	3–4	4–5	5–6	6–7	7–8
1	6	20½	30½	35	19½	10	3

From this array one can see that the average work done in a course is a little over four hours a week. This result, however, is misleading; first, because the figures include the estimates of some members of the Graduate School; and, secondly, because in the table small courses with few students have the same weight as large courses with many students. The important point, therefore, in relation to the courses which require little work is not the number of such courses but the Number of students taking them, a number shown in the following table.

0–1	1–2	2–3	3–4	4–5	5–6	6–7	7–8
21	876	2498	2117	2056	355	82	29

[The upper numbers indicate the number of hours of work per week; the lower ones the number of students who did that amount of work.]

From this array it will be seen that the average amount of work done by an undergraduate in a course is less than 3½ hours a week outside of the lecture room. It should be added that more than half of the answers from which these results are derived came from men who attained the grade of *A* or *B*.

Such an amount of work the Committee regards as far too small. . . .

The Committee would suggest that a statement be made by the Faculty for the benefit of instructors of the number of hours a week which they should expect of men in their courses, and that a serious effort be made to maintain that standard in every course. In the large lecture courses, however, it is not always easy to raise the present standard. Increasing the prescribed reading, for example, does not necessarily increase the hours of work. On the contrary, it may lead to neglect of the reading altogether, or to reliance on bought summaries. What should be demanded is more intelligence in reading, and more effort in applying what is read. Such intelligence and such effort may be tested by "quizzes" and the like. Students themselves express the opinion that the instructor or assistants should by means of frequent "quizzes" or conferences keep them up to their work, and enable them to read with greater understanding. "Quizzes" and conferences belong with elementary work. Theses can hardly be demanded in large elementary courses; they should begin, as the students themselves suggest, where "quizzes" cease. In 1901–02 theses were required in 32 of the courses open to students in the College. . . .

Among the methods adopted with a view to raising the standard of work in these courses, two are in common use to-day. One of these, which may be called the conference method, employs a number of assistants who meet the students individually, talk over their reading with them in order to ascertain that it has been done, and assist them by explanation, advice, and suggestion. As the number of men assigned to each assistant is large, he can give little time to each, and that only at long intervals, usually seeing each of his men for 10 or 15 minutes at a time about once a month. The other method, which may be called the section method, confines the lectures to two of the three hours in the course, and divides the class into sections, each of which meets an assistant for examination, "quiz," and discussion, in the third hour. Under this system, each assistant has charge of about 120 men, who are divided into three or four sections. The former method is probably better for the more capable students who are willing to work, but does not stimulate the indolent. . . .

The students found fault to some extent with the injustice of marking done in the same course by a number of different assistants, an injustice which it is probably impossible to obviate altogether. Much more important is the fault they found with some of the assistants themselves, and the complaint that the value of a course depends in large measure on the chance of getting a good assistant....

The replies received by the Committee leave no reasonable doubt that there is a place, and an important place, for large lecture courses in Harvard College, and that they are not destined to pass away with the further development of the elective system.

In 1882–83 there were only 5 courses with more than 100 members, and none with more than 200; in 1892–93 there were 18 with between 100 and 200 members, and 10 with more than 200; in 1901–02 there were 25 with between 100 and 200 members, and 14 with more than 200. Moreover, the very large courses containing two fifths or more of a whole class have increased from three in 1882–83 to eight and a half in 1901–02; and in 1901–02 there were two elective courses each of which contained more than four fifths as many students as could be found in the whole Freshman class. The larger courses grow, the more evident it becomes that the object of the lectures in them is not so much to impart concrete information as to stimulate thought and interest in the subject; and since the stimulus depends in part on the attitude in which the audience stands towards the lecturer, it is important that these courses should be conducted by the men who have already achieved a reputation. Indeed, the replies of the students make it clear that to be effective the lecture courses must be conducted by the best lecturers in the University....

The Committee believes that the lectures in the large courses should treat general principles rather than details which may be readily obtained from books, and that in these and all other courses much which instructors now dictate or put upon the board should be printed or mimeographed. Furthermore, it believes that, though large lecture courses which maintain the proper standard of work are both valuable and necessary, it is a misfortune when they are required as preliminary to all further study of the subjects that they treat. Such a requirement in some Departments amounts to little less than the reëstablishment of prescribed courses.

An interesting problem was brought to the attention of the Committee by the students' answers to the question why they had chosen this or that elective course. Among both students and members of the Faculty there appears to be a growing tendency to regard certain subjects as designed peculiarly for general culture, and certain others as designed for the scholastic training of specialists. That a student's opinion of the motives which induced him to elect a certain course is often far from correct is shown by the fact that the motive of general fashion was recognized by only two persons. . . . It is noticeable that the students regard English and other modern languages, philosophy, history, geology, and some other studies, as culture subjects in a higher sense than mathematics, the classics, and most of the sciences. The Committee believes that such a distinction is unfortunate, and that, so far as possible, every Department ought to provide courses for students who are not to be specialists in it, and that such courses should require as much systematic work as other courses in the Department. . . .

In connection with this subject, the Committee would point out the importance of encouraging a greater number of men to take honors at graduation, and of making honors something more than a purely scholastic distinction for young specialists; for the Committee believes that students in pursuit of general culture should be encouraged in a thorough and somewhat advanced study of subjects to which they do not intend to devote their lives. The fact that ambitious students find little incentive to take honors is one of the glaring failures of our system. . . .

The Committee proposes no formal vote, but summarizes its conclusions as follows:

1. The relation between the instructors and the students is good, and the students are in general satisfied with their elective studies.

2. The average amount of study, however, is discreditably small.

3. The difficulty of raising the standard is seriously increased by students taking six courses each.

4. The requirements of time and study in the various courses should be as nearly equivalent as possible. Certainly there should not be such discrepancies as exist at present.

5. Large lecture courses have come to stay.

6. Yet in the large lecture courses a special effort should be made to increase the amount and the thoroughness of the work.

7. For this purpose the number of assistants should be increased.

8. Every effort should be made to secure such a number and such an apportionment of lecture rooms as shall enable the instructor to use his lecture room before and after the hour of his lecture.

9. It is a mistake to prescribe introductory lecture courses as a preliminary to all further study of the subjects that they treat.

10. Every subject in the College should be taught on the principle that a thorough knowledge of it is a valuable part of a liberal education.

11. Every serious man with health and ability should be encouraged to take honors in some subject.

L. B. R. Briggs	B. S. Hurlbut
W. E. Byerly	J. B. Woodworth
A. L. Lowell	R. Cobb
M. H. Morgan	O. M. W. Sprague

C. H. Grandgent

Part IX

UNIVERSITY FACULTIES AND
UNIVERSITY CONTROL

I n the old-time college little thought was given to securing professors of great distinction, to the means by which their scholarly work could be forwarded, or to how they could be made reasonably happy and harmonious. Indeed, the small, overworked, harassed faculties of the sectarian colleges had often been ill-tempered and feud-ridden, and one of the first achievements of the university era was to create a state of mind in which faculties could live in peace and avoid the squabbles that all too often destroyed the small colleges (Doc. 1). The new organizers of universities, like White and Gilman, were given free hands by their trustees not merely in recruiting faculties but also in arranging their work so that they could be kept content (Doc. 2). Ancient sectarian limitations on recruitment were brushed aside. The announced policy of the organizers of the Johns Hopkins (Doc. 3) was not to be "governed by denominational or geographic considerations in the appointment of any teacher; but . . . to select the best person whose services they can secure in the position to be filled, irrespective of the place where he was born, or the college in which he was trained, or the religious body with which he has been enrolled." To the contemporary reader this may seem obvious policy; in 1876 it was still revolutionary outside a handful of eminent institutions.

749

Trustees soon found that the more eminent the faculty they could gather, the more it was likely to claim an active role in the management of academic affairs, and the freer it would insist on being. In the old college the trustees had inquired closely into student discipline, faculty conduct, curriculum, and other academic affairs. In the modern university, they tended to be pushed further and further away from the foreground of university business—teaching and research—and confined to the vital but restricted tasks of financial management. Even the role of the president, always of the greatest importance, was more susceptible to suspension or delegation, as Andrew D. White found (Doc. 4) on his fairly frequent and prolonged absences from the business of the president's office at Cornell. Faculties found themselves competent in administration as well as scholarship, an almost unknown characteristic of academic men that was utilized by William Rainey Harper in building effective departmental chairmanships and sustaining a high level of faculty morale during his first decade as president at Chicago (Doc. 8).

As had so often been the case with other groups and social classes in history, the rising dignity and position of the professor caused him to be more exigent, not less, in his demands for the control of his own affairs. In the never-ending search for more adequate academic performance, professors became increasingly critical of the management of universities by lay trustees who knew nothing about teaching or scholarship. A literature of protest grew up (Docs. 6, 7, and 9) in which professors, looking at the self-governing bodies of academic men abroad, began to ask if the powers of trustees should not be further reduced; and some began to ask why there should be any academic government by laymen at all. In the most momentous, though hardly the soberest, document produced during this movement of protest, Thorstein Veblen's satire, *The Higher Learning in America: A Memorandum on the Conduct of Universities by Business Men* (Doc. 11), the constant tension between the life of practice, of money-making, and the life of scholarship and intellect was explored. The feeling so widespread among academic men in the best universities, that they needed still more control over their own affairs, had much to do with the background of some academic freedom controversies (Part X, Docs. 10 and 12) as well as with the formation of the American Association of University Professors (Part X, Doc. 8). President Lowell of Harvard, among other administrators, found it necessary to restate (Doc. 12) what he considered to be the legitimate functions of lay trustees. Reminding his audience of the public functions of education, he stated that without the oversight of laymen, teaching "will become in time narrow, rigid or out of harmony. . . . Experts should not be members of a non-professional body that supervises experts." Regardless of the sentiment of professors, lay trustees had law and tradition on their side, as well as the more powerful elements in the community.

1. Andrew D. White on Faculty Status in the 1870's and 1880's

See Part VI, Docs. 5, 6, 9, and Part VII, Doc. 8.

The faculty, which was at first comparatively small, was elected by the trustees upon my nomination. In deciding on candidates, I put no trust in mere paper testimonials, no matter from what source; but always saw the candidates themselves, talked with them, and then secured confidential communications regarding them from those who knew them best. The results were good, and to this hour I cherish toward the faculty, as toward the trustees, a feeling of the deepest gratitude. Throughout all the hard work of that period they supported me heartily and devotedly; without their devotion and aid, my whole administration would have been an utter failure. . . .

From one evil which has greatly injured many American university faculties, especially in the middle and western States, we were virtually free. This evil was the prevalence of feuds between professors. Throughout a large part of the nineteenth century they were a great affliction. Twice the State University of Michigan was nearly wrecked by them; for several years they nearly paralyzed two or three of the New York colleges; and in one of these a squabble between sundry professors and the widow of a former president was almost fatal. Another of the larger colleges in the same State lost a very eminent president from the same cause; and still another, which had done excellent work, was dragged down and for years kept down by a feud between its two fore-

A. D. White, *Autobiography* (New York, 1905), I, 428–30.

most professors. In my day, at Yale, whenever there was a sudden in-flux of students, and it was asked whence they came, the answer always was, "Another Western college has burst up"; and the "burst up" had resulted, almost without exception, from faculty quarrels.

In another chapter I have referred to one of these explosions which, having blown out of a Western university the president, the entire board of trustees, and all the assistant professors and instructors, con-vulsed the State for years. I have known gifted members of faculties, term after term, substitute for their legitimate work impassioned ap-peals to their religious denominations, through synods or conferences, and to the public at large through the press,—their quarrels at last en-tangling other professors and large numbers of students.

In my "Plan of Organization" I called attention to this evil, and laid down the principle that "the presence of no professor, however gifted, is so valuable as peace and harmony." The trustees acquiesced in this view, and from the first it was understood that, at any cost, quarrels must be prevented. The result was that we never had any which were serious, nor had we any in the board of trustees. One of the most satis-factory of all my reflections is that I never had any ill relations with any member of either body; that there was never one of them whom I did not look upon as a friend. My simple rule for the government of my own conduct was that I had *no time* for squabbling; that life was not long enough for quarrels; and this became, I think, the feeling among all of us who were engaged in the founding and building of the university.

2. Daniel Coit Gilman on the Spirit of the First Johns Hopkins Faculty and Trustees, 1876

See Part VII, Docs. 1, 4, 5, 6, and Part X, Doc. 1.

Those of us who initiated, in 1876, the methods of instruction and government in the new foundation at Baltimore were young men. Syl-vester alone had more than three score years to his credit. Gildersleeve

Daniel Coit Gilman, *The Launching of a University* (New York, 1906), pp. 47–50.

and I, now patriarchs, were forty-five years old. Morris was a little older. Remsen, Rowland, and Martin were not thirty years of age. The original Associates, many of whom became leaders in their several departments of study, Adams, Brooks, Cross, Elliott, Hastings, Morse, Scott, were still younger. All were full of youthful enthusiasm and energy. There were none to say, "This is not our way"; none to fasten on our ankles the fetters of academic usage. Duty, youth, hope, ambition, and the love of work were on our side. Laboratories were to be constructed, instruments and books to be bought, colleagues and assistants to be chosen, regulations to be formulated, conditions of admission, promotion and graduation to be determined, plans of study to be matured.

As I have intimated, we brought to the council room many prejudices and preferences derived from our previous training and from our personal idiosyncrasies. Two of the staff had been professors in the University of Virginia, two had been Fellows in the great English universities, two had received degrees in German universities and others had studied abroad, two had been connected with New England colleges, two had been teachers in scientific schools, and one had been at the head of a State university. Our discussions were free and familiar, as of friends around a council board. It was rarely, if ever, necessary to "make a motion" or to put a question to the vote. By processes well known to Friends, "the sense of the meeting" was taken and recorded.

It was our dominant purpose to hold on to the principles and adhere to the methods which experience had established in this and in other countries, and at the same time to keep free from the slavery of traditions and conditions which are often more embarrassing and retarding than positive laws. We often reminded one another that the rule of to-day was liable to become the custom of to-morrow, the immemorial usage of next month, the iron-clad law of the future, and we tried to preserve spontaneity of action, not only for ourselves but for our successors. "Evolution" was then beginning to be the note of the times, and our best advisers urged upon us "Development." "Be slow," they said, "plant good seeds and see what they yield." So we did not undertake to establish a German university, nor an English university, but an American university, based upon and applied to the existing institutions of this country. Not only did we have no model to be followed; we did not even draw up a scheme or programme for the government of ourselves, our associates and successors. For a long time our proceedings were "tentative," and this term was used so often that it became a by-word for merriment. Such considerations carried with them this corollary. Every head of a department was allowed the utmost freedom in its development, subject only to such control as was necessary for harmonious co-operation. He could select his own assistants, choose his own books and apparatus, devise his own plans of study,— always provided that he worked in concord with his fellows. To secure this concord and the support of the Trustees, it was necessary that close relations should be kept up with the President, and that wishes and wants, purposes and plans, should be freely talked over with him. As the University grew, it was not so easy to maintain this usage, but it was maintained and is still a most serviceable feature in the administration.

The Trustees wisely refrained from interference with the faculty, to whom the government and instruction of the students was entrusted. The Trustees made the appointments, it is true, but they were always guided by the counsel of the President and professors. They awarded the degrees, the scholarships and the fellowships, but only on the nomination and recommendation of the academic staff. The professors, on the other hand, had no part in the financial management. They were not consulted in respect to investments: they did not fix the salaries nor the appropriations for the library and apparatus. In the construction of buildings their wishes were paramount, their advice indispensable; but the building contracts were in the hands, exclusively, of the Trustees.

An enormous number of applications for professorships were received, and filed; but I do not think they had much weight with the Trustees, who, according to their promise, kept themselves aloof from all dangerous entanglements, and were determined to make their selections with sole regard to the welfare of the University. They preferred to consult, confidentially, those on whose judgment they relied, rather than to be governed by the written endorsements and recommendations which came by every mail, often supported by strong personal influence. . . .

3. Gilman Recounts the Founding Principles at the Johns Hopkins, 1876

See Doc. 2.

It is the desire of the authorities, I said at that time [Jan. 1, 1876] (speaking in the name of the Trustees), that the institution now taking shape should forever be free from the influences of ecclesiasticism or partisanship, as those terms are used in narrow and controversial senses; that all departments of learning,—mathematical, scientific, literary, historical, philosophical,—should be promoted, as far as the funds at command will permit, the new departments of research receiving full attention, while the traditional are not slighted; that the instructions should be as thorough, as advanced and as special as the intellectual condition of the country will permit; that the glory of the University should rest upon the character of the teachers and scholars here brought together, and not upon their number, nor upon the buildings constructed for their use; that its sphere of influence should be national, while at the same time all the local institutions of education and science should be quickened by its power; and finally that among the professional departments, special attention should be first given to the sciences bearing upon medicine, surgery, and hygiene, for which some provision has been made by the munificent gift of our founder to establish the Johns Hopkins Hospital.

The selection of professors and teachers upon whom will devolve the instruction of youth, the chief work of the University, is peculiarly difficult because there are here no traditions for guidance, no usages in respect to the distribution of subjects, and none in respect to the kind of instruction to be given; and also because the plans of the Trustees must depend very much upon the character of the teachers whom they bring together.

A very large number of candidates have been suggested to the Trustees; but among them all there are but a few who have attained distinction as investigators or as teachers. Most of those whose names have been thus presented are young men, usually of much promise,

Daniel Coit Gilman, *The Launching of a University*, pp. 41–43.

who have not yet had an opportunity to show their intellectual power in any department of higher instruction; and yet among this very class a discerning choice will doubtless discover those who are soon to be the men of scientific and literary renown. The Trustees promise to open freely the doors of promotion to those young men who seem to be capable of the highest work,—appointing them at first for restricted and definite periods. Moreover they hope for a while to gain much of the influence and co-operation of older and more distinguished men by inviting one and another to come here from time to time with courses of lectures. But the idea is not lost sight of that the power of the University will depend upon the character of its resident staff of permanent professors. It is their researches in the library and the laboratory; their utterances in the classroom and in private; their example as students and investigators, and as champions of the truth; their publications, through the journals and the scientific treatises, which will make the University of Baltimore an attraction to the best students, and serviceable to the intellectual growth of the land.

In selecting a staff of teachers, the Trustees have determined to consider especially the devotion of the candidate to some particular line of study and the certainty of his eminence in that specialty; the power to pursue independent and original investigation, and to inspire the young with enthusiasm for study and research; the willingness to co-operate in building up a new institution; and the freedom from tendencies toward ecclesiastical or sectional controversies. The Trustees will not be governed by denominational or geographical considerations in the appointment of any teacher; but will endeavour to select the best person whose services they can secure in the position to be filled, irrespective of the place where he was born, or the college in which he was trained, or the religious body with which he has been enrolled.

4. White on the Distribution of Administrative Powers in the 1880's

See Doc. 1.

But my greater opportunities—those which kept me from becoming a mere administrative machine—were afforded by various vacations, longer or shorter. During the summer vacation, mainly passed at Saratoga and the sea-side, there was time for consecutive studies with reference to my work, my regular lectures, and occasional addresses. But this was not all. At three different times I was summoned from university work to public duties. The first of these occasions was when I was appointed by President Grant one of the commissioners to Santo Domingo. This appointment came when I was thoroughly worn out with university work, and it gave me a change of great value physically and intellectually. During four months I was in a world of thought as different from anything that I had before known as that wonderful island in the Caribbean Sea is different in its climate from the hills of central New York swept by the winds of December. And I had to deal with men very different from the trustees, faculty, and students of Cornell. This episode certainly broadened my view as a professor, and strengthened me for administrative duties.

The third of these long vacations was in 1879–80–81, when President Hayes appointed me minister plenipotentiary in Berlin. My stay at that post, and especially my acquaintance with leaders in German thought and with professors at many of the Continental universities, did much for me in many ways.

It may be thought strange that I could thus absent myself from the university, but these absences really enabled me to maintain my connection with the institution. My constitution, though elastic, was not robust; an uninterrupted strain would have broken me, while variety of occupation strengthened me. Throughout my whole life I have found the best of all medicines to be travel and change of scene. Another example of this was during my stay of a year abroad as commissioner at the Paris Exposition. During that stay I prepared several ad-

A. D. White, *Autobiography*, I, 434–36.

ditions to my course of general lectures, and during my official stay in Berlin added largely to my course on German history. But the change of work saved me: though minor excursions were frequently given up to work with book and pen, I returned refreshed and all the more ready for administrative duties.

As to the effect of such absences upon the university, I may say that it accorded with the theory which I held tenaciously regarding the administration of the university at that formative period. I had observed in various American colleges that a fundamental and most injurious error was made in relieving trustees and faculty from responsibility, and concentrating all in the president. The result, in many of these institutions, had been a sort of atrophy,—the trustees and faculty being, whenever an emergency arose, badly informed as to the affairs of their institutions, and really incapable of managing them. This state of things was the most serious drawback to President Tappan's administration at the University of Michigan, and was the real cause of the catastrophe which finally led to his break with the regents of that university, and his departure to Europe, never to return. Worse still was the downfall of Union College, Schenectady, from the position which it had held before the death of President Nott. Under Drs. Nott and Tappan the tendency in the institutions above named was to make the trustees in all administrative matters mere ciphers, and to make the faculty more and more incapable of administering discipline or conducting current university business. That system concentrated all knowledge of university affairs and all power of every sort in the hands of the president, and relieved trustees and faculty from everything except nominal responsibility. From the very beginning I determined to prevent this state of things at Cornell. Great powers were indeed given me by the trustees, and I used them; but in the whole course of my administration I constantly sought to keep ample legislative powers in the board of trustees and in the faculty. I felt that the university, to be successful, should not depend on the life and conduct of any one man; that every one of those called to govern and to manage it, whether president or professor, should feel that he had powers and responsibilities in its daily administration. Therefore it was that I inserted in the fundamental laws of the university a provision that the confirmation by the trustees of all nominations of professors should be by ballot; so that it might never be in the power of the president or any other trustee unduly to influence selections for such positions. I also exerted myself to provide that in calling new professors they should be nominated by the president, not of his own will, but with the advice of the faculty and should be confirmed by the trustees. I also provided that the elections of students to fellowships and scholarships and the administration of discipline should be decided by the faculty, and by ballot. The especial importance of this latter point will not escape those conversant with university management. I insisted that the faculty should not be merely a committee to register the decrees of the president, but that it should have full legislative powers to discuss and to decide university affairs. Nor did I allow it to become a body merely advisory; I not only insisted that it should have full legislative powers, but that it should be steadily trained in the use of them. On my nomination the trustees elected from the faculty three gentlemen who had shown themselves especially fitted for administrative work to the positions of vice-president, registrar, and secretary; and thenceforth the institution was no longer dependent on any one man. . . .

5. G. Stanley Hall Describes William R. Harper's Raid upon the Clark Faculty, 1892

See Part VII, Doc. 6. On Harper see Doc. 8.

Very soon after this, President Harper of the University of Chicago appeared upon the scene. He had made many proposals to eminent men to join his staff but they had been turned down because of a critical attitude toward a "Standard-Oil institution," a very grave obstacle at that time to that very able and sagacious organizer but which has long since been forgotten in the splendid work the institution has accomplished. Dr. Harper, learning of the dissatisfaction here, had at Professor Whitman's house met and engaged one morning the majority of our staff, his intentions and even his presence being unknown to me. Those to whom we paid $4,000, he gave $7,000; to those we paid $2,000, he offered $4,000, etc., taking even instructors, docents, and fel-

G. Stanley Hall, *Life and Confessions of a Psychologist* (New York, 1923), pp. 295-97. Reprinted with the permission of Appleton-Century-Crofts, Inc.

lows. This proved really to be the nucleus and, I think, the turning point in the early critical stage of the development of the Chicago institution.

When this was done he called on me, inviting me also to join the hegira at a salary larger than I was receiving—which of course I refused—and then told me what he had done. I replied that it was an act of wreckage for us comparable to anything that the worst trust had ever attempted against its competitors but he asked, "What could I do?" recounting the above difficulties he had had in gathering a staff. I finally told him that if he would revise his list, releasing a few of our men and taking one or two others whom he had omitted, I would bear the calamity silently and with what grace I could, although I felt his act comparable to that of a housekeeper who would steal in at the back door to engage servants at a higher price. To this he demurred, and I finally threatened, unless he would make such few revisions of his list as I suggested, to make a formal appeal to the public and to Mr. Rockefeller himself to see if this trust magnate (who was at that time about at the height of his unpopularity and censure and who was said to have driven many smaller competing firms out of existence by slow strangling methods of competition) would justify such an assassination of an institution as had that day been attempted here (for Harper had made advances to nearly all of our staff, even those who remained loyal, and was evidently ready to make a clean sweep). He finally assented, even taking at least one man here who covered the exact field of another he had previously engaged and canceling his engagements with one or two of the younger men I particularly wanted, although to my surprise and regret he felt himself justified in informing those whose status was changed by this revision that it was at my direction.

I had spent much time, travel, and effort in gathering this very distinguished group of men, and I told him that his action was like that of the eagle who robbed the fishhawk of his prey. The accession of these men to the few whom President Harper had at that time enlisted, I have often been told, as indeed was evident, marked an epoch in his endeavors. Their action in enlisting with the new institution by the lake gave the public assurance that it would not be Chatauquaean but would have a solid scientific nucleus, and, moreover, their influence at Chicago would of course be important for advanced work and research, as indeed it so abundantly proved. Three of these men were made heads of the large and admirable buildings and departments devoted respectively to chemistry, physics, and biology. Thus Clark had served as a nursery, for most of our faculty were simply transplanted to a richer financial soil.

6. An Academic Scientist's Plea for More Efficient University Control, 1902

John James Stevenson (1841–1924) was born in New York City and graduated (1863) from the University of the City of New York, which later became New York University. After some years of teaching in an academy, he also became editor of the *American Educational Monthly*. Over a period of a dozen years he taught chemistry and geology and participated in a number of major geological surveys. In 1881 he became professor of geology at New York University. He was first secretary of the Geological Society of America and represented the United States at the International Geological Congress in 1903.

The pessimism with which some recent writers regard the university outlook in our country is, unfortunately, not wholly unreasonable. Yet the conditions, far though they be from the ideal, are not such as to make one despondent. The rapid development of our country has brought difficulties to colleges and universities as it did to business enterprises. The business world recognized the difficulties and overcame them at the cost of complete change in methods. Let the business common sense, which has made the United States preeminent in commerce, be applied to university matters and it will give us equal preeminence in education. It is necessary to recognize the conditions frankly, to cast aside injurious makeshifts and to adjust the methods to the new surroundings and the new demands. For the surroundings and the demands are new. Within the last thirty years, the relations between the teaching and the corporate boards have undergone a serious transformation; the relations of college professors to the community, as well as to their students, have been revolutionized; the manner and the matter of the professor's work in many departments bear no resemblance to those of thirty years ago. The extent and nature of these changes are

---

J. J. Stevenson, "University Control," *The Popular Science Monthly*, LXI (September, 1902), 396–406.

known in but slight degree to those in the corporate boards of colleges and universities; the community is wholly ignorant of them. Let us understand them.

At the close of the Civil War, American colleges were comparatively small. Their trustees, for the most part, were alumni or professional men familiar with college work, as it then existed, and personally acquainted with the professors with whom they were in sympathy and for whose benefit they held their place. But, within a generation, the small colleges have become large, many of them have expanded into true universities with numerous departments, hundreds of instructors and thousands of students; while the financial interests, expanding more rapidly than the institutions, have attained a magnitude in some cases as great as that of New York's finances fifty years ago. No trustee in a large college to-day can know much of college work as such, can be acquainted with the faculties, can do much more than bear his share of the business responsibility. Vast sums of money needed for expansion, even for continued existence, are sought from men, who, having accumulated wealth, desire to leave the world better than they found it. Such men, in many cases, hesitate to entrust the disposition of their gifts wholly to others and each year finds them in increasing numbers upon corporate boards of colleges and universities—sometimes because they have contributed, sometimes because it is hoped that they will contribute.

These patrons, if not college graduates, labor under a disadvantage in that they are unacquainted with the nature of the work for which colleges have been founded; even if they be college graduates they are at an almost equal disadvantage, as absorption in business or professional pursuits has prevented them from keeping track of the changes which have come about since their graduation. As a rule, their new responsibility does not tend to create or to renew acquaintance with college work; the trustees' duties usually begin and end with labors on committees, so that naturally enough the business affairs with which they have to do become for them the all-important work of the institution. And this conception is strengthened by thoughtless assertions of men who ought to know better. Only recently this community was informed that the millionaires make the universities. With such flattery ringing in their ears, one is not surprised that some trustees forget the object for which the university exists and think of professors, when they think of them at all, as merely employees of the corporation, whose personality and opinions are as unimportant as those of a bank clerk.

Unacquainted with the faculty, unfamiliar with the extent and even character of the work done by individual professors, the trustees depend for knowledge of the educational affairs upon reports by the college or university president, for in rare instances only have faculties, as such, representatives in the board. Unfortunately, very few of our college presidents have taken a preliminary course to qualify them for the position. Indeed, it must be confessed that ability to superintend educational work has not been regarded in all cases as the essential prerequisite; in some cases that appears to have been thought less important than a supposed ability to collect money. But at the best no one man is able now to understand all the phases of university or even college work, as many college presidents already recognize; but were he able and willing, he has little opportunity to make his trustees comprehend them. Discussion of purely business matters occupies so much attention during board meetings that discussion of other matters must be deferred and the president's report is printed that it may be read at leisure. The best of presidents becomes weakened by the overwhelming importance of the financial side and comes to look upon increasing numbers as the sure proof of success. He soon finds himself between the upper millstone of the trustees and the nether millstone of the faculty, the former insisting upon numbers, the latter upon a high standard, so that in an honest effort to perform his duty, he is in danger of receiving censure from both.

The change in relations of the educational and corporate boards is due to a drifting apart of the two boards, leading to the loss of that sympathy, which was the bond, and to a reversal of the relative importance of the boards. Formerly trustees existed to care for the faculties; now many trustees evidently feel that the faculties are appendages to the board of trustees.

But while the conditions in respect to the relations between educational and corporate boards have undergone a change, on the whole, decidedly for the worse, the conditions in respect to the professor's relations to the community and to his work have undergone a change no less radical, not indeed for the worse, but at a cost to himself so serious as to impair his usefulness and to threaten that of the institutions themselves. Here lies, in the opinion of many thoughtful men, the secret of deterioration observable in the output.

The common belief is that the college professor's teaching work is purely incidental, an easy method of obtaining a good living, that he may pursue his studies without anxiety respecting worldly matters. Whatever may have been the case in some prehistoric period, it is certain that in our day there is no calling in which the pecuniary compensation is so low, while the intellectual requirement is so high as in that of college professor. The average salary of college men in New York city is much less than the average salary of clergymen. The expansion, one may almost say the very existence, of American colleges is due to the consecrated devotion of those who give the instruction. Of the immense gifts made to American colleges, comparatively little goes toward increasing salaries of professors already at work; almost the whole goes to meet the insatiable demand for expansion.

Nor is the college instructor a man of 'abundant literary leisure,' as many still suppose. College professors of a generation and a half ago were, for the most part, recluses—made so by the nature of the studies then included in the college curriculum. The hours of teaching were short, and beyond those the institution demanded little. There was abundant leisure and it was used well in study. But now, in many departments the hours are long, often covering in one way or another the whole day, while other requirements are severe. The college demands that the professors be encyclopedic in knowledge of the subjects covered by their chairs, no matter how broad these may be, that they contribute frequently to the journals, that they be prominent in social, scientific, political or religious affairs. How much of the literary leisure remains in some departments one may imagine—and the increasing requirements, all involving pecuniary expenditure, have come with decreasing salaries. For the most part, professors are no longer doctrinaires; the character of their work compels close contact with the world. Museums of applied chemistry, physics, biology and geology are notable features in all the larger universities and are not unknown in the smaller institutions. Social science and psychology no longer deal in merely *à priori* discussions; they deal with facts for which search is made everywhere.

But far more important is the change in the professor's relation to his work. And here reference may be made parenthetically to a matter of some importance. The college curriculum of forty years ago was, to say the least, elementary. A reasonably good graduate was fit to be tutor in any branch and a professional man, who had kept up his literary tastes was not thought to be presumptuous when he applied for any one of the chairs. The college president was usually professor of mental and moral science, because a clergyman of rather more than average ability was, of course, fitted for that chair. But in this day, special, prolonged preparation is required for any chair, be it philosophy, history or chemistry. The progress which this condition indicates has led to an unforeseen difficulty which is becoming a subject of anxiety. For a long period the college curriculum, framed on narrow lines, remained practically unchanged and the secondary schools, with small equipment, prepared pupils in a leisurely way. As a rule the preparation was good and the boys entered college practically on a level. Within twenty years our colleges have not only increased the entrance requirements for some parts of the old course, but they have introduced new courses, even new departments, each with special entrance requirements, often very high. In great part, the secondary schools, with their limited resources, have been unable to increase their staff so as to keep pace with increasing demands from the colleges, and the students from different schools, though nominally alike in sum of preparatory work, are no longer approximately on the same plane. The college instructor, who has to do with the earlier years, finds himself burdened not merely with the work legitimately belonging to him, but also with much of the preliminary training. This combination of preparatory drill and advanced work is perplexing.

It is very true that the burden of changed conditions in respect to college work is not felt equally in all departments. Professors in charge of some of the older chairs have an increased burden, in that the method of teaching differs, yet, taken as a whole, matters, in so far as undergraduate work is concerned, remain with them pretty much as they were thirty years ago. But the teaching of concrete subjects is so completely changed both in matter and manner that one must dwell somewhat in detail upon the conditions; the more so because they have come about so rapidly that even professors in other departments are unaware of their extent.

Science, for a long time, was an insignificant feature of the college curriculum; its treatment was more elementary than that of history. The professor had an immense field to cover—the whole of nature aside from man's achievements in a few directions—but, while he taught many subjects after a fashion, he studied only one. The stock of knowledge was very small and anything new to one observer was likely to be new to all others. Investigation was a simple matter; ingenuity, industry and keen discrimination made up most of the necessary equipment; so that there were few earnest teachers who failed to contribute frequently to the common stock. But, by their earnestness, these men worked their destruction as investigators; for while each had his chosen field of study, he still covered the whole area as teacher. Many of the discoveries made by these men were startling and were discussed in a more or less inaccurate way by the newspapers. Students sought explanation from the professor who was supposed to know everything. The botanist was puzzled by questions respecting chemical physics or psychology; the physicist was worried by questions respecting alleged discoveries in biology or geology. Practical application of newly discovered principles followed quickly to add to the teacher's trials. There was no longer time for special investigations and all one's energies had to be devoted to a vain effort to keep pace with investigations in the several directions.

The danger of this condition was recognized early in some of the older and wealthier institutions, so that in them, as in some of the newly organized and well-endowed universities, the fact was accepted that the several sciences were soon to be independent professions, and the departments of chemistry, physics, biology, psychology, geology, paleontology and mineralogy became practically schools, each with its own staff of professors and assistants.

But in too many of our colleges the danger was not recognized at an early period and in too many it is still unrecognized. Only a few of our institutions have more than four chairs in natural science, many have only two, and far too many are still in the sub-high school stage of only one. Yet the catalogues of such institutions offer a long series of courses, graduate as well as undergraduate, in several departments. A rather prominent college trustee not long ago informed the writer that a professorship of psychology or physics or geology is hardly equal in extent to one of Latin or pure mathematics. Yet any one of the chairs first named covers a group of subjects as unrelated as those embraced by the old-time chair of 'mental and moral science, history and belles lettres.' It is broader in scope than that other chair of 'ancient and modern languages' which existed in many colleges thirty-three years ago. A professor who teaches three branches of chemistry, physics or geology in three successive hours deals with three wholly different matters, three distinctly unrelated lines of investigation, requiring independent methods of preparation and each demanding as much knowledge as does the whole work of a professor holding a chair of languages. But, aside from this class-room labor, the teacher of science in the average institution must prepare demonstrative lectures, must keep apparatus in proper condition, must procure and care for museum material, must spend time with classes in field demonstration, while, in addition, he has the never-ending grind required to keep him in touch with the growth of knowledge respecting subjects embraced in his department. These are burdens from which professors in the older courses are happily free.

It is true that the science teacher in most of our colleges has only himself to blame for the severity of his burden. Determination to give to his students what he believes due to them has led him to make exertions which were not required but which, once begun, came to be regarded as part of his duties. Had he not manufactured apparatus and begged money with which to procure more, he would have had little for which to care; had he not expended ingenuity in preparing elaborate experiments with limited advantages, he would have had no occasion for greater expenditure; had he not expended his money and his vacations in procuring museum material and his energy in pestering acquaintances for generous donations of such material, he would have little labor in connection with a museum; had he not insisted upon the introduction of laboratory teaching no one else would have insisted upon it. But having a clear conception of duty, he has sacrificed himself deliberately. The great expansion of the scientific departments of American colleges is due to the exertions of the teachers of science; and they in many instances have received neither gratitude nor any other acknowledgment.

And yet not without reward, for the influence of the science teacher has gone out far beyond the college limits. The great discoveries, up to within a few years, were made by college professors, and these, applied by inventors, have changed the face of the civilized globe, while those to whom the world is indebted for its comforts are unknown even by name. Their work has spread intelligence and revolutionized educational methods. . . .

Especial emphasis has been laid upon the burden of the scientific side, because the writer is more familiar with its changes during the last thirty-five years; but the condition is serious enough for incumbents of many chairs not scientific. Men in most of the American colleges and universities are badly handicapped by routine work; not that too many hours are spent in actual teaching, but as a rule the teaching covers too many things, while too much is expected or required outside of purely college duties. The condition is unfortunate for the world, which no longer reaps the fruit of college men's work as investigators; but it is many times more unfortunate for the student. To be a thorough educator, the college instructor must possess the instinct and the experience of an investigator, otherwise he cannot train men to think. The present method of utilizing professors tends to convert them into superficial purveyors of second-hand knowledge; it must lead to decay in our educational system which has owed its virility to professors who were independent thinkers because they were thorough investigators.

The condition is serious, so serious as to inspire hope for the future. Many suggestions have been presented, most of them good but almost all of them premature. Changes more radical than any yet proposed must be made before those suggestions can be considered.

American colleges have still to contend with two fundamental difficulties—poverty and an ancient method of control.

A college professor can hardly administer the remedy for poverty, but he may suggest what is on the surface. There are too many colleges which ought to be merely academies, too many which should be high schools, too many so-called universities which ought to be modest colleges, and there are enough of true universities to supply the country's need for a long time. Unquestionably, coalition in some cases and consolidation in others would go far toward relieving the stress; but consideration of even this matter is premature, for a radical change in the method of control must be brought about before either coalition or consolidation become possible.

Originally, in most of our institutions, the college was the only school under control of the degree-granting corporation and the professional schools which grew up around it had but a nominal connection, managing their own affairs, both educational and financial. But the college is no longer the all-important portion of our universities; professional, technical and scientific schools, some of them in part replacing the college, predominate and all are actually, as well as nominally, under one corporate control. The college itself is not the school of thirty-five years ago; the whole system of training has been changed, and there is offered not a narrow but a broad education. Yet one finds in control of the vast institution the same president as in the olden time, with powers like those of an academy principal and often with the same sense of personal ownership; the same board of trustees, with authority and privileges as in the days when the college was the whole and itself little better than an academy. In other words, we are controlling the great university with its thousands of students in many schools, with its many groups offering hundreds of courses, after the fashion which prevailed when there was but one group of courses, arranged expressly with reference to the needs of those looking forward to the clerical profession. The method is not adapted to the conditions; as well try to manage the New York Central of to-day by the railroad methods of forty years ago.

The time has come for a complete reorganization of the system; the educational work and the business management must be under separate boards, and the boundaries of the provinces should be definite.

The faculties, each for itself, should control appointments of professors and instructors; should determine all matters concerning curricula; should decide questions as to expansion or contraction of work; should have the final word respecting internal arrangement of buildings—in short should be the supreme authority in all matters directly affecting the educational work. Matters affecting the work of the university as a whole should be referred to a council composed of representatives from all of the faculties whose determination should be final. In very many institutions most of these powers are still vested in the board of trustees, which means simply that in these matters the whole control is in the hands of one or two members; since no board of trustees can possibly be competent to decide respecting qualifications of candidates for professorships or upon changes in curricula, decisions respecting these matters are most likely to be rendered in deference to the opinion of some trustee or officer who is supposed by the rest to know something about them. In other words, the individual trustees have transferred their powers while nominally retaining them.

The presiding officer of the council, the educational head of the university, should be one who has studied the educational problem from all sides; not necessarily a great scholar in any one department, but a broad scholar, possessing tact and executive force. Such men are not rare, though one may be pardoned for regretting that so many have chosen other professions in preference to that of college president. The faculties should select this officer.

The trustees should have charge of the financial interests of the institution. In some of our universities, those interests exceed those of some western states; even in less pretentious institutions they are very large. They are sufficient every where to require not merely close attention but an amount of business skill and shrewd foresight beyond that demanded by ordinary business of equal extent. The trustees cannot be the architects or the builders; but their work, if confined to its proper province, would be so important that unless it were well performed, that of architects and builders would be imperfect. They should plan liberal things for the work, but should not leave the execution, as now, chiefly to one man. Under such conditions the bond between the boards would be close, for in frequent conferences each would become familiar with the general conditions and needs of the other, so that they would work, not merely in harmony, but also with the view to mutual helpfulness.

The writer has been informed that this plan is impracticable; that it has in itself the seeds of destruction; the faculties would be self-perpetuating bodies; conservatism would be crystallized; it is hard enough now to get rid of incompetent or antiquated professors, it would be impossible then; available funds would be applied to salaries and not to development; jealousies would paralyze the work; *et cetera* to the end of a list which does credit to its author's power of imagination.

An answer in part would be *Tu quoque,* for certainly trustees are usually self-perpetuating bodies and it is equally certain that crystallization of conservatism in trustee boards has not been the least of the difficulties with which energetic faculties have had to contend. It is quite possible that salaries might be increased, or that an effort would be made to increase them so that a college instructor could live in modest comfort upon his salary. But there is no need of trustee supervision to prevent selfish grasping of funds. Chairs have been divided, new courses established, new methods introduced, the grade of instruction elevated—all upon the initiative of the faculties, and this in face of the fact that such expansion means decreasing salaries.

With educational matters under control of the faculties more attention would be paid to the qualifications of candidates for appointments than to the qualifications of their supporters; there would be fewer instructors of the type which some regard as burdensome; a college professorship would not be a haven of rest in which a failure might be anchored by his friends; expansion at the expense of efficiency would cease; there would be an end to extreme specialization in narrow groups but a wiser specialization in studies of a different type. No doubt mistakes, and many of them, would be made, as college professors are like other men; but the faculties are less likely to err in their management than are those who know very little about educational affairs. . . .

As business principles would prevail in the management, funds for endowments could be obtained with less difficulty because there would be less dread of waste through bad investment. Patrons would be more ready to found departments, equipped with men, materials and buildings, seeing in them more enduring monuments than mere memorials of stone.

The writer has been a college professor for thirty-three years. Familiar with the changes for good and ill to which this article refers, he has felt compelled to write without reserve and it may be with some emphasis, that the conditions may be brought sharply before those who really control the future of American colleges and universities. He appeals to that business common sense which characterizes the great majority of college trustees. American colleges and universities have outgrown their swaddling clothes; no amount of patching can make them fit; the new garments must be of different cut and of different material.

7. G. Stanley Hall on Academic Unrest before World War I

See Doc. 5.

In this country academic unrest has been largely directed against organization and administration. In old days the college president, though he usually taught, was supreme and autocratic, and as leading institutions grew and he ceased to teach, the concentration of power in his hands became altogether excessive. The foundation of new institu-

G. Stanley Hall, *Life and Confessions of a Psychologist*, pp. 345–47. Reprinted with the permission of Appleton-Century-Crofts, Inc.

tions, the Hopkins, and a little later Stanford and Chicago, greatly augmented his power under our system. He had to determine the departments, select professors, fix their status, build, organize, represent the institution to the board and public and perhaps the legislature, plunge into the mad, wasteful competition for students and money, and lay supply pipes to every institution that could feed his. Never was the presidential function so suddenly enlarged nor its power so great and uncontrolled as a decade ago. Even the University of Virginia and other southern universities, which had only a president of the faculty elected by its members, fell into line, and a reaction toward democratization, which in its extreme form seemed sometimes almost to adopt the slogan, *"Delindus [sic] est prex,"* was inevitable. In the Cattell movement abundant incidents of arrogance and arbitrary, if not usurped, power were collected, and it was even insisted that although charters or conditions of bequest, to say nothing of American tradition, would have to be revised, the president should be only chairman of the faculty, elected perhaps annually by them, and in the literature of this movement we find occasionally the radical plea that some or all of the powers of the board should be turned over to the faculty, who should at least be given control of the annual budget.

More lately the movement of protest here was against the autocracy of the dean, whom the president had created in his own image and who sometimes exercised a power that he would never dare to do, and who in large institutions constructed a mechanism of rules, methods, procedures, and standards that have almost come to monopolize the deliberations of the Association of American Universities, which fortunately cannot prescribe or legislate for its individual members. University deans have often created rules which they themselves can suspend for individuals, and this has greatly augmented their power. It is they largely who have broken up knowledge into standardized units of hours, weeks, terms, credits, blocking every short cut for superior minds and making a bureaucracy which represses personal initiative and legitimate ambition. Just before the war perhaps we heard most remonstrance against head professors, and statements that the assistant professors and younger instructors in their departments were entirely at their mercy, that they were burdened with the drudgery of drills, examinations, markings (all at small pay) while their chiefs took the credit, so that the best years of the best young men, who are the most precious asset of any institution, or even of civilization, were being wasted. Indeed, we have vivid pictures of the hardships which often crush out the ambitions of young aspirants for professorial honors and tend to make them, if they ever do "arrive," parts of a machine with no ideals of what sacred academic freedom really means. Happily the best sentiment of the best professors now organized interinstitutionally to safeguard their own interests and those of their institutions represents a most wholesome and needed movement which is sure to prevail.

Thus at the outbreak of the war, with all these and many more problems pressing for solution, with the wholesome influence of de-nominalization and stimulus to higher standards and comparative views emanating from the Carnegie Foundation, and with the very slow and hard but real progress we were making in developing the true university spirit in this practical and material age and land, it seemed as though we were slowly but surely entering upon a new era.

8. William Rainey Harper's Decennial Report, 1902

When William Rainey Harper (1856–1906) accepted the presidency of the University of Chicago in 1892, he already had turned down several college presidencies offered to him because of his national reputation as a biblical scholar, Hebraist, editor, and lecturer. A brilliant academic career that saw him a graduate of Muskingum College (Ohio) at fourteen and a holder of the Ph.D. from Yale at eighteen and that included teaching posts at Denison University (1876–79), the Baptist Union Theological Seminary in Chicago (1879–86), and Yale (1886–91) prepared him for an even greater presidency in a university established through the tremendous support of John D. Rockefeller. He administered its affairs until his death, and it became a monument to his energy, tolerance, and vision. Among his many novel accomplishments were a university extension, the quarter system incorporating a summer school, a university press, and faculty control of athletics. Throughout it all Harper found time for full time teaching as chairman of his department as well as the Sunday school superintendency (1897–1905) of his own Baptist church.

On Harper see T. W. Goodspeed, *William Rainey Harper* (Chicago, 1928), the brief biography by Paul Shorey in the *Dictionary of American Biography,* and Doc. 5.

William Rainey Harper, "The President's Report: Administration," *University of Chicago Decennial Publications,* 1st Ser., I (Chicago, 1903), xii–xxiv, cxliii.

On nearly every important question the action of the Trustees has been unanimous. I can recall only half a dozen matters, some of them of very minor importance, which have passed the Board with votes recorded in the negative. This seems an almost incredible statement when it is recalled that over ten thousand distinct recommendations, covering every imaginable subject both of educational and business character, have been presented to the Board for its consideration. That this unanimity has not grown out of indifference is seen from the further fact that many matters have been debated through a period of one, two, or even three years before a conclusion has been reached.

No man can calculate the actual value of the time given the University by the Trustees in Board meetings, committee meetings, and conferences; but, in addition to all this, the Trustees have themselves contributed about $1,000,000 to the University treasury, thus giving indubitable evidence of their personal interest in the great enterprise intrusted to their charge. In some instances these gifts have been made with considerable cost to the donor, but in every case with a splendid enthusiasm.

In the first years, and in connection with the financial panic of 1893, there were times of serious concern. It was not altogether certain that the new institution could meet the heavy demands made upon it in view of the generous scale on which it had been started. In these times of crisis the strength and courage of the Trustees individually and collectively appeared at its best. One may never forget some of these meetings in times when only the greatest skill and wisdom prevented disaster. . . .

During the larger portion of this period the work of the Trustees has been placed in the hands of committees. The Committee on Instruction and Equipment has considered and made recommendations on all appointments, all matters of educational policy, all purchases of equipment and apparatus, including books and collections. The work of this committee has been exceedingly arduous. All nominations for positions on the staff have received careful study, and all questions of promotion and salary have here been taken up. During the period under review the committee has supervised the expenditure of about $5,000,000. The Committee on Buildings and Grounds has had the most important and responsible task of determining the character of buildings, selecting architects, and passing final judgment on plans and specifications. The success or failure of this work will be determined by the estimate placed upon the results accomplished as they appear in the twenty-nine buildings, costing $4,000,000, which now stand upon the University Quadrangles. . . .

An Expenditure Committee, consisting of the President of the University, the Secretary of the Board of Trustees and the Auditor, together with the President of the Board of Trustees—who, however, has been unable ordinarily to be present at the meetings of the committee —has supervised the expenditure of the various appropriations in accordance with general rules established by the Trustees. No officer of the University has been accorded the privilege of expending even the smallest sum of money unless that expenditure has beforehand been authorized under an appropriation made by the Trustees. The establishment of the Budget from year to year and the rigid adherence to its provisions have made it possible to reduce the work of the University to a thoroughly business basis, and it may fairly be claimed that the affairs of no business corporation are conducted more strictly on business lines than are those of the University. . . .

The history of these years shows conclusively that the attitude of the Trustees toward the Faculties of the University has been broad and liberal. It is understood that all questions involving financial expenditure fall within the province of the Trustees and are to be considered by them; that all appointments to office in the University are made directly by the Trustees upon recommendation of the President; and that on questions of fundamental policy, involving the establishing of new Faculties and the change of statutes as established by the Trustees, final action is reserved for the Trustees themselves. But it is a firmly established policy of the Trustees that the responsibility for the settlement of educational questions rests with the Faculties, and although in some instances the request of a Faculty has not been granted for lack of the funds required, in no instance has the action of a Faculty on educational questions been disapproved. It is clearly recognized that the Trustees are responsible for the financial administration of the University, but that to the Faculties belongs in the fullest extent the care of educational administration. During the years covered by this Report there has been no case of an appeal to the Trustees by a minority in any Faculty or governing Board against the action of a majority or against the action of the President.

The history of the growth of the University is in itself the best testimony of the largeness of view taken by the Board of Trustees. With a body of Trustees less intelligent or less able, such progress would have been impossible. It is fair to say that in the breadth of view which has characterized the work of the trustees there is to be seen an expression of the spirit of the city of Chicago—a spirit to which the University is indebted for many of the important elements that have entered into its constitution. . . .

Not least among the virtues of the Trustees has been the measure of sympathy and support which has uniformly been accorded by them to the President of the University. . . . There has been no moment in the ten years when I have not felt that each Trustee was a warm personal friend to whom I might go for that intangible help which a cold officialism does not furnish, but which exists only in connection with personal friendship. . . .

I desire to present the following suggestion . . . :

Since the period of first organization has now passed, and the work of the University is better comprehended; and since also the details of the work are growing with great rapidity and will continue so to grow, it should be considered whether the present plan of organization in committees will prove in the future to be the most effective. This plan undoubtedly possesses many advantages, chief of which is the fact that the work and responsibility are thus divided, and the various members of the Board are enabled to become more thoroughly acquainted with certain divisions of the University than they could possibly become with all its divisions. But it is a question whether by this organization sufficient unity is secured; whether, as in the case of the ruling bodies of large cities, it would not be better to throw the responsibility of all the details upon a smaller number of men who might be able or willing to give a larger share of their time to the work; and whether, as in the case of business concerns, larger responsibility may not be placed upon the administrative officers. Such a smaller body would constitute an Executive Committee, to which might be given large powers in the intervals between Board meetings. It is perhaps true that in the case of no institution in the country are details presented to the Board of Trustees to such an extent as in the case of the University of Chicago. This policy has surely justified itself in the past, but with the growth of the University it may be doubted whether such men as are desired to serve as Trustees will have the time, aside from their other duties, to consider the work of the University in so great detail. . . .

This distribution [of instructors] shows for the ten years that practically little attention has been given to work, on the one hand, in subjects connected with Aesthetics, and, on the other hand, in subjects connected with Technology. It appears that the strength of the institution has been devoted, outside of the Divinity School, to the regular subjects in Arts, Literature, and Science. It may be claimed that in the distribution between the Humanities and Science the latter has been fairly dealt with. When account is taken of the several laboratories erected, the considerable amount of equipment purchased, and the strong staff appointed in the various departments of Science, it will be recognized that a large share of the facilities of the University has been turned in this direction. Criticism has been made more than once to the effect that it would have been better to have inaugurated work in the Technological Departments from the beginning—in other words, that the practical side deserved a larger consideration than it received. It is certainly true that the demand for the more practical departments of Engineering has been very great, and that if these departments had been organized at the beginning they would today be perhaps the strongest departments in the University. My answer to the suggestion, however, is twofold: First, it seemed upon the whole wise to devote the entire energy of the institution in scientific lines to departments of pure science, with the purpose of establishing these upon a strong foundation. This work being finished, there would be ample opportunity for the other work, and the other work would be all the stronger when it came, because of the earlier and more stable foundation of pure science. Second, it was also thought wise not to lay too much emphasis on the practical side of education at the outset. No one could fail to see that sooner or later in an environment like that of Chicago the practical side would be sufficiently cared for. The greater danger was that pure science might be left without provision. In any case, the plan adopted was the one which at the time seemed to be the correct one; and events, so far as I can interpret them, do not appear to have contradicted this opinion.

Some interest was excited in the first years of the organization of the University in view of the larger salaries paid to Heads of Departments. The position taken by the Trustees in this matter has never been challenged, nor does any one today regret the action. In my opinion this action was one of utmost importance. I do not mean to suggest that men of prominence in the field of letters and science are mercenary, but this action was taken as an expression of the serious interest of the Trustees in the work which they had proposed for themselves. Two policies were open for the organization of the staff of instruction. The first, strongly urged by many educators, was that of selecting a few younger instructors and allowing the work to grow more gradually under the domination of a single spirit. The other policy, which was regarded as impracticable by many, was the one adopted, namely, to bring together the largest possible number of men who had already shown their strength in their several departments, each one of whom, representing a different training and a different set of ideas, would contribute much to the ultimate constitution of the University. Considerable risk attended the adoption of the second policy, for it was an open question whether with so large a number of eminent men, each maintaining his own ideas, there could be secured even in a long time that unity of spirit without which an institution could not prosper. During the first year there were times when to some it seemed doubtful if the experiment of bringing together so large a number of strong men would prove successful; but during the middle of the second year certain events occurred which led up to the birth, as it were, of the spirit of unity which had not been hoped for. . . .

The organization in Departments with recognized Heads was effected more rigidly than in any other institution. This organization secured to each Department a separateness and an independence which exhibited both advantages and disadvantages. It was advantageous in that it located responsibility, drew sharp lines, and made more evident points of strength and weakness. It was disadvantageous in that for a time it prevented a much-needed correlation of work between closely related Departments, and laid perhaps too great emphasis upon the difference in rank of officers. Both of these difficulties, however, soon took care of themselves. After a period of three or four years, the process of synthesizing began, and of their own accord Departments, without losing their independence, began to come together for conference on all questions of common interest. Out of this voluntary association there grew up at first Conferences, and very recently by legislative enactment the Group Faculties. . . . The other difficulty was also largely removed. It soon became apparent that those Departments in which all the members of the staff came together in democratic fashion and worked out the plans of the Department were best organized for securing good results. Despotism on the part of a Head of Department was short-lived, and while some Heads of Departments reserved larger authority than others, the general relationship of the members of the staff in almost every Department was adjusted to the characteristics of those concerned. The organizing spirit in not a few Departments became that of some other officer than the Head, who perhaps gave himself more exclusively to the work of research instead of to that of administration. Upon the whole, therefore, the plan has probably developed as few difficulties as any other plan which might have been followed. It has the supreme advantage of being exceedingly flexible, and the administration of the different Departments is today almost as varied as the number of the different Departments. This is as it should be. The machinery is a secondary matter, and should be as far as possible that which the men most closely interested themselves prefer. . . .

It is generally believed that the lines of departmental organization may not be strictly drawn. From a more scientific point of view, it is quite certain that the study of special problems will carry the student into two or more of the different Departments as they are now constituted. In general little difficulty has arisen from the divisions. There have been times when the line between Political Economy and the Social Science was not satisfactory; as also that between Geology and Zoölogy. The relationship of Paleontology on the one hand to the geological work, and on the other to that of Zoölogy, has been disputed, but the departmental organization as originally adopted, with the slight modifications which have been made, seems upon the whole the one best adapted to the interests of all concerned.

A spirit of co-operation has grown up which has shown itself in many ways, and from the more developed growth of which much good may be expected. The staff has been singularly free from cliques. A caucus is something practically unknown. Debate is always free and outspoken. The division of the Faculties varies with almost every question which comes forward. Men who oppose each other vigorously on one subject work together most harmoniously when another subject comes forward for consideration. At two or three times within the ten years there has been more or less excitement. This has demonstrated the sincerity of men in the expression of their convictions, and, as stated above, men who on one of these cases were vigorous opponents, on another clasped hands as allies. Upon the whole, it is perhaps strange that such periods when feeling has become, perhaps, too intense, have not been more frequent. In no community in the world has there been shown a greater readiness to permit the rule of the majority.

It seems evident that a closer bond of union will exist between the

Professional Faculties and the staff of the Faculties of Arts, Literature, and Science than is ordinarily found in institutions of learning. No sharp line has yet been drawn between the members of the Professional Faculties and those of the other Faculties. It is my most earnest hope that the tendency which has already shown itself in this matter may continue, and that as other Professional Faculties shall be organized they shall not be isolated from the University at large or from any portion of it, but rather that they shall take their full share in the discussion and disposition of all questions which concern the University life and policy. The future of professional work in this country is largely dependent, in my opinion, upon the closeness of its relationship to the University. . . .

I . . . repeat . . . here a statement made at a recent Convocation. . . .

". . . I may be permitted to present a statement adopted unanimously by the members of the Congregation of the University on June 30, 1899:

"*Resolved,* 1. That the principle of complete freedom of speech on all subjects has from the beginning been regarded as fundamental in the University of Chicago, as has been shown both by the attitude of the President and the Board of Trustees and by the actual practice of the President and the professors.

"2. That this principle can neither now nor at any future time be called in question.

"3. That it is desirable to have it clearly understood that the University, as such, does not appear as a disputant on either side upon any public question; and that the utterances which any professor may make in public are to be regarded as representing his opinions only.

"To this statement of the Congregation I wish to add, first, that whatever may or may not have happened in other universities, in the University of Chicago neither the Trustees, nor the President, nor anyone in official position has at any time called an instructor to account for any public utterances which he may have made. Still further, in no single case has a donor to the University called the attention of the Trustees to the teaching of any officer of the University as being distasteful or objectionable. Still further, it is my opinion that no donor of money to a university, whether that donor be an individual or the state, has any right, before God or man, to interfere with the teaching of officers appointed to give instruction in a university. . . . Neither an individual, nor the state, nor the church has the right to interfere with the search for truth, or with its promulgation when found. Individuals, or the state, or the church may found schools for propagating certain special kinds of instruction, but such schools are not universities, and may not be so denominated. A donor has the privilege of ceasing to make his gifts to an institution if, in his opinion, for any reason the work of the institution is not satisfactory; but *as donor* he has no right to interfere with the administration or the instruction of the university. The trustees in an institution in which such interference has taken place may not maintain their self-respect and remain trustees. They owe it to themselves and to the cause of liberty of thought to resign their places rather than to yield a principle the significance of which rises above all else in comparison. In order to be specific, and in order not to be misunderstood, I wish to say again that no donor of funds to the University—and I include in the number of donors the founder of the University, Mr. Rockefeller—has ever by a single word or act indicated his dissatisfaction with the instruction given to students in the University, or with the public expression of opinion made by an officer of the University. I vouch for the truth of this statement, and I trust that it may have the largest possible publicity.

"Concerning the second subject, the use and abuse of the right of free expression by officers of the University staff: As I have said, an instructor in the University has an absolute right to express his opinion. If such an instructor is on an appointment for two or three or four years, and if during these years he exercises this right in such a way as to do himself and the institution serious injury, it is of course the privilege of the University to allow his appointment to lapse at the end of the term for which it was originally made. If an officer on permanent appointment abuses his privilege as a professor, the University must suffer and it is proper that it should suffer. This is only the direct and inevitable consequence of the lack of foresight and wisdom involved in the original appointment. The injury thus accruing to the University is, moreover, far less serious than would follow if, for an expression of opinion differing from that of the majority of the Faculty, or from that of the Board of Trustees, or from that of the President of the University, a permanent officer were asked to present his resignation. The greatest single element necessary for the cultivation of the academic spirit is the feeling of security from interference. It is only those who have this feeling that are able to do work which in the highest sense will be beneficial to humanity. Freedom of expression must be given the members of a university faculty, even though it be abused; for, as has been said, the abuse of it is not so great an evil as the restriction of such liberty. But it may be asked: In what way may the professor abuse his privilege of freedom of expression? Or, to put the question more largely: In what way does a professor bring reproach and injury to himself and to his institution? I answer: A professor is guilty of an abuse of his privilege who promulgates as truth ideas or opinions which have not been tested scientifically by his colleagues in the same department of research or investigation. A professor has no right to proclaim to the public a truth discovered which is yet unsettled and uncertain. A professor abuses his privilege who takes advantage of a class-room exercise to propagate the partisan views of one or another of the political parties. The university is no place for partisanship. From the teacher's desk should emanate the discussion of principles, the judicial statement of arguments from various points of view, and not the one-sided representations of a partisan character. A professor abuses his privilege who in any way seeks to influence his pupils or the public by sensational methods. A professor abuses his privilege of expression of opinion when, although a student and perhaps an authority in one department or group of departments, he undertakes to speak authoritatively on subjects which have no relationship to the department in which he was appointed to give instruction. A professor abuses his privilege in many cases when, although shut off in large measure from the world, and engaged within a narrow field of investigation, he undertakes to instruct his colleagues or the public concerning matters in the world at large in connection with which he has had little or no experience. A professor abuses his privilege of freedom of expression when he fails to exercise that quality ordinarily called common sense, which, it must be confessed, in some cases the professor lacks. A professor ought not to make such an exhibition of his weakness, or to make an exhibition of his weakness so many times, that the attention of the public at large is called to the fact. In this respect he has no larger liberty than other men.

"But may a professor do all of these things and yet remain an officer in the University? Yes. The professor in most cases is only an ordinary man. Perfection is not to be expected of him. Like men in other professions, professors have their weaknesses. But will a professor under any circumstances be asked to withdraw from the University? Yes. His resignation will be demanded, and will be accepted, when, in the opinion of those in authority, he has been guilty of immorality, or when for any reason he has proved himself to be incompetent to perform the service called for. The public should be on its guard in two particulars: The utterance of a professor, however wise or foolish, is not the utterance of the University. No individual, no group of individuals, can speak for the University. A statement, by whomsoever made, is the statement of an individual.

"And further, in passing judgment, care should be taken that the facts are known. It is a habit of modern journalists, and especially of the average student reporter for the newspapers, so to supply facts, so to dress up the real facts, so to magnify and exaggerate, so to belittle and ridicule universities and university men, that serious injury is wrought, where perhaps no such injury was intended. It is the fashion to do this sort of thing, and it is done regardless of the consequences. Real regard for the interests of higher education would lead to the adoption of a different policy; but as matters stand, the professor is often charged with acts and utterances implying an imbecility which is not characteristic of him and to him there are frequently ascribed startling and revolutionary sentiments and statements of which he is wholly innocent. I may sum up the point in three sentences: (1) college and university professors do make mistakes, and sometimes serious ones; but (2) these are to be attributed to the professor and not to the university; and (3) in a large majority of instances the mistake, as published to the world, is misrepresented, exaggerated, or, at least, presented in such a form as to do the professor, the university, and the cause of truth itself, gross injustice." . . .

On the basis of the ten years of history one may reasonably make certain predictions without incurring the charge of boldness. The most difficult part of the work of organization has been finished. Some traditions have actually been established, and upon these as a foundation others will soon grow up. The essential characteristics of the institution have been determined. The institution promises to become a university, and not simply a large college. Its professional work will be on a level with the so-called graduate work, and will indeed itself be graduate work of the highest order. The Senior Colleges will serve as a clearing-house for the Graduate and Professional Schools; that is, as a period during which the student will work according to his own choice and with his best spirit.

With the Divinity School thoroughly established, the Law School in substantial shape, and the Medical School practically arranged for, there remain only (1) the School of Technology and (2) the Schools of Music and Art. It is hoped that the second ten years will bring these remaining schools, and with them the great Library, with its surrounding buildings for the Departments of the Humanities, a great University Chapel, and the remaining Laboratories of which the institution today stands in such need.

The first ten years have seen the foundations laid and the superstructure erected in the rough. The second ten years will witness the development of the aesthetic side of life and thought.

WILLIAM R. HARPER
President

9. J. McKeen Cattell on Reforming University Control, 1913

J. McKeen Cattell was born in Pennsylvania in 1860, educated at Lafayette College (1880), and spent his first two postgraduate years studying at Göttingen, Leipzig, Paris, and Geneva. After a year at Johns Hopkins as a fellow, he returned to Leipzig for further study in psychology, taking his Ph.D. in 1886. For some time thereafter he taught at the University of Pennsylvania and Bryn Mawr, and in 1891 he went to Columbia as professor of psychology. A distinguished authority in experimental psychology, he edited two major psychological journals and also for a time the *Popular Science Monthly*. In 1895 he was elected president of the American Psychological Association. Problems of academic government always interested Cattell, and his interest was doubtless heightened by his inability to get along with President Nicholas Murray Butler of Columbia. The work from which this excerpt was taken was an outgrowth of his concern with academic reform. His difficulties at Columbia had their climax in a celebrated wartime academic freedom case (see Part X, Docs. 10, 11, and 12).

Hofstadter and Metzger, *The Development of Academic Freedom in the United States* (New York, 1955), pp. 471–73, 499–502.

THE CORPORATION AND THE PRESIDENT

In a review of the different factors concerned with the administration of a university the corporation in ultimate control is the natural starting-point. It was becoming that the fellows of Yale College, a collegiate school primarily for the education of the clergy, should be

J. McKeen Cattell, *University Control* (New York, 1913), pp. 26–62.

representative clergymen of the state. In general the trustees of the primitive American college were competent to administer its simple economy. But even then there were difficulties. Before the American Institute of Instruction meeting in Worcester, Mass., in 1837, the Rev. Jasper Adams, president of Charleston College, gave a lecture on "The relations subsisting between the board of trustees and the faculty of the university," stating that as far as he knew this had never been the subject of special investigation. He argues that the trustees should manage the funds of their institution, while the faculty should regulate the courses of instruction and the internal administration. Professors should be appointed by the trustees on the advice of and in accordance with the wishes of the faculty. It appears that in those days there was trouble through the trustees interfering with what the faculties regarded as their rights, notably at Hamilton College, concerning which the president wrote a pamphlet entitled "A Narrative of the Embarrassments and Decline of Hamilton College," which he attributed to meddling by the trustees with the business of the faculty. At that time President Adams and President Davis seem to have regarded themselves as professors rather than as trustees.

The legal powers of trustees and regents are similar everywhere, but their actual part in the conduct of the institution varies greatly. It is likely to be larger when the board is small and when the members reside nearby. In his Harris lectures on "University Administration" President Eliot says: "The best number of members for a university's principal board is seven," and with pleasing naïveté he adds a little later: "It is a curious fact that the university with the most fortunate organization in the country is the oldest university, the principal governing board, the President and Fellows of Harvard College, consisting of seven men." When the board of trustees is large and meets but rarely, there is usually an executive committee which with the president is in substantial control. The members of this committee are likely to be the friends and adherents of the president—in practise the president is likely to select the trustees and the members of their executive committee—and the faculties and professors are supposed to communicate with the trustees only through the president. Under our existing system, there should be an elected committee of the faculties which would meet with the executive committee of the trustees. It would in addition be advisable to permit the professors and other officers to elect for limited terms representatives—not necessarily from among themselves—on the board of trustees in the manner now becoming usual for alumni representation. It is undesirable for the individual professor to tease the trustees with his needs or grievances; but there should surely be some way by which trustees and professors can consider together the problems confronting the university. A joint committee of trustees and professors such as has just now been constituted to administer the Crocker Cancer Research Fund of Columbia University is an excellent plan.

If trustees are trustees and not directors, it does not greatly matter in practise how many of them there are or how they are chosen, so long as they are men of integrity and honor, representative of the common sense of the community. Even if the trusteeship is an acknowledgment of gifts made or hoped for, no great harm is done. But a self-perpetuating board with absolute powers, even though for a generation the powers may not be abused or even used, is intolerable in a democratic community. The president and directors of industrial corporations are elected by the shareholders and are increasingly supervised by the state. In the state universities the regents are elected by the people or appointed by their representatives, and the people may be regarded as the ultimate corporation. In the case of the private universities, it would apparently be wise to have a large corporation consisting of the professors and other officers of the university, the alumni who maintain their interest in the institution and members of the community who ally themselves with it. This corporation—or perhaps better the three groups of which it is composed—should elect the trustees. Thus there might be a board of nine trustees, one being elected annually for a three-year period by each of the three divisions of the corporation.

Several of my correspondents hold that members of the community permitted to join the corporation of a university should be carefully selected. I should myself like to see the widest possible participation. If 10,000 or 50,000 people would join such a corporation, so much the better. They would pay dues, perhaps five or ten dollars a year, and would enjoy certain privileges such as attendance at lectures and concerts, the use of libraries, museums, rooms for meetings and the like. If many people are concerned with their university, it is well for them and for it. Some of them will become seriously interested, ready to aid with their counsel, their influence and their money. In New York City several institutions—the Metropolitan Museum of Art, the American Museum of Natural History, the Zoological Park, the Botanical Garden—are partly supported by the city, partly by boards of trustees and partly by members. The buildings are owned and the curators are paid by the city; the collections are owned and the research work is paid for by the trustees; the members have certain privileges in return for dues. In spite of obvious difficulties, the plan has worked well.

A large corporation holding the university in trust for all the people is clearly a step in the direction of public ownership. It is the ultimate fate of every corporation to be controlled by the state, and our private universities will surely become part of the system of public education. This should develop gradually rather than through such measures as have been required to obtain control of church property in other nations. When the people own their universities they will probably see the wisdom of delegating to those concerned—namely, the officers of the university, its alumni and members of the community taking an interest in higher education and having knowledge of it—the right to elect the trustees. True democracy does not consist of government by the uninformed, but of government by those most competent, selected by and responsible to the people. In one of the leading state universities one third of the trustees are elected by the alumni; a second third might to advantage be elected by the teachers, the remaining third being elected by the people or their representatives.

When trustees in the state universities are elected by the people or their representatives and in the private universities are elected by the corporation consisting of officers of the university, alumni and members of the community, the question as to their powers and duties is perplexing. Much can be said in favor of giving them no more power than is vested in a trust company designated as trustee of an estate, and arguments can be urged in favor of a small paid board of experts having the ultimate decision on all questions. I seem to have been almost the only educational person in the country who approved of the principle of Mayor Gaynor's plan for a small paid board of education for New York City, and I should regard its present adoption as risky. This, however, is the correct method of democracy—experts selected by the people and paid for their work. The professors and other officers of the university should be such. Whether in addition to them it is desirable or necessary to have a board to coordinate and control their work, to regulate their duties and fix their salaries, is a question which can only be settled by experience. Certainly the commission form of government is preferable to an individual autocrat.

In the academic jungle the president is my black beast. I may seem to be in the condition of the animal suffering from the complication of diseases described in a recent issue of a New England paper: "Patrolman Lindstrum went to East Elm Street recently and shot an alleged mad dog. The dog also was declared to have hydrophobia and rabies." As a matter of fact neither barking nor biting is warranted. An eminent philosopher of Harvard University in a lecture to a class at Radcliffe is alleged to have depicted in eloquent terms the darkness of the life of him who has lost his religious faith and then to have added that the only compensation is a sense of humor. Whereat, first one and then another of the students began to weep until all the eighty girls were in tears. It is more becoming for university professors to appreciate the semi-humorous absurdity of the situation than to fall to weeping together. I once incited one of my children to call her doll Mr. President, on the esoteric ground that he would lie in any position in which he was placed. Of course, the president is by nature as truthful, honorable and kind as the rest of us, and is likely to have more ability or enterprise, or both. But he really finds himself in an impossible situation. His despotism is only tempered by resignation; and in the meanwhile he must act as though he were a statue of himself erected by public subscription. In Tennyson's words:

Who should be king save him who makes us free.

The argument for giving a free hand to the president is that this is the way to get things done. It should, however, be remembered that it is quite as important—and this holds especially in the university—not to do the wrong thing as it is to do the right thing. The time of the president is largely occupied with trying to correct or to explain the mistakes he has made, and the time of the professor is too much taken up with trying to dissuade the president from doing unwise things or in making the best of them after they have been done. Administrative details should be attended to promptly and correctly; this is the proper business of secretaries and clerks. Then we need leaders, most of all in a democracy. But in a democracy leaders are the men we follow, not the men who drive us. In the university each should lead in accordance with his ability and his character.

The trouble in the case of the university president is that he is not a leader, but a boss. He is selected by and is responsible to a body practically outside the university, which in the private corporations is responsible to nobody. In our political organization, the mayor, governor or president has great power, too great in my opinion, if only because it demoralizes the legislature; but they are responsible to the people who elect them. I object even more to the irresponsibility of the university president than to his excessive powers. The demoralization that the president works in the university is not limited to his own office; it has given us the department-store system, the existing exhibit of sub-bosses—deans, heads of departments, presidential committees, professors appointed by, with salaries determined by, and on occasion dismissed by, the president, all subject to him and dependent on his favor.

It is not my wish to depreciate unfairly the services of the American university president. Like the promoter in business and the boss in politics, he has doubtless been a factor natural and perhaps desirable in a given stage of evolution, when the growth of the complexity of society and the need of new adjustments have outrun the adaptability of the individual. It is probable that the president has increased appropriations and gifts; it is possible that he has promoted rather than hindered the development of the university and the extension of its work. The president, however, has not usually been the cause of gifts, professors and students, but only the means of diverting them from one institution to another, and on occasion of doing so in ways unworthy of the institution which he then misrepresents. The president has not infrequently sacrificed education to the fancied advantage of his own institution. Thus college entrance requirements have imposed studies on the high school which drive from it the majority of boys. The opposition of certain presidents of proprietary universities to a national university is not less pernicious if it results from honest prejudice. The prestige of the president is due to the growth of the university, not conversely. He is like the icon carried with the Russian army and credited with its victories. President Eliot claimed that he had never asked for a gift for Harvard. During the lean years he was regarded as a poor money-getter; when the fat years came with the increasing wealth of the alumni and of the country, this opinion was reversed, but he had not changed. President Eliot is a truly great man, but his remarks on all sorts of subjects, usually wise but occasionally otherwise, were reported everywhere, not for their wisdom, but on account of his position.

While I regard it as desirable to do what little I can to make ridiculous an institution which has become a nuisance, and while I should find my state of dependence on a president for my opportunity to serve the university intolerable if I concealed my views, I certainly do not wish to be understood as lacking in appreciation of the fine characters and high motives of most of the men who have served as professors and later become presidents. They do not considerably, if at all, surpass in character or ability the average standard of the professorship, but they exploit before the world how high this standard is. The practise of many presidents is a sacrifice of their real convictions to the imagined exigencies of the situation. Most of them would agree that autocracy in the university is undesirable. Thus President Eliot writes: "The president of a university should never exercise an autocratic or one-man power. He should be often an inventing and animating force, and often a leader; but not a ruler or autocrat. His success will be due more to powers of exposition and persuasion combined with persistent industry, than to any force of will or habit of command. Indeed, one-man power is always objectionable in a university, whether lodged in president, secretary of the trustees, dean or head of department."

Dr. Seelye, then president of Smith College, at the inauguration of Dr. Rhees as president of Rochester University, said: "Autocracy, however, is a hazardous expedient, and is likely to prove ultimately as pernicious in a college as it is in a state. It induces too great reliance upon the distinctive characteristics of a despot, and too little upon those of a gentleman. One-man power is apt to enfeeble or to alienate those who are subject to it. . . . Successful autocrats are few, and however long their term of service, it is short compared with the life of an institution. If they leave as an inheritance a spirit which has suppressed free inquiry, and which has made it difficult to secure and retain teachers of strong personality, the loss will probably be greater than any apparent gain which may have come through the rapid achievements of a Napoleonic policy."

Under existing conditions—at least in our proprietary universities—it appears that the place which the president now fills, or wobbles about in, might be divided into three parts. There might be a chancellor, as in the English universities, a man of influence and of prominence, representing the corporation and the relations of the institution to the community, concerned with increasing the endowment and prestige of the university. Then there might be a rector, as in the German universities, elected annually or for some other limited period by and from the faculties, presiding at academic functions and the like. In the third place, there would be a secretary or curator, an educational expert in charge of administrative details. In a real democracy and with a people appreciative of the needs and service of the university, the former two officials would become superfluous.

It must be admitted that the situation is difficult. The alumni are no longer predominantly scholars or even professional men. They have more concern for football than for the work of the professor; any university club could get on better without its library than without its bar. But the alumni of a university should be not less intelligent and wise than the electorate of the nation. In both cases the ultimate control must be democratic, unless perchance we are following false gods. Experts and intellectuals are not, as a rule, to be trusted to act for the common good in preference to their personal interests. The professors of an endowed university can not be given the ultimate control. A monastery or a proprietary medical school must ultimately be reformed from without. We need the referendum and the recall because we can not trust those placed in authority, and we fear these measures because we do not trust the people. An aristocracy is deaf; a democracy is blind. But it is our business to do the best we can under the existing conditions of human nature. Advancing democracy has burned its bridges behind it. No one believes that a city should be owned by a small self-perpetuating board of trustees who would appoint a dictator to run it, to decide what people could live there, what work they must do and what incomes they should have. Why should a university be conducted in that way?

THE POSITION OF THE PROFESSOR

The Bible is often misquoted to the effect that "money is the root of all evil." The love of money and the lack of money are indeed factors in most of the difficulties of society. Next after the getting of men, the getting of money for the university is its most troublesome problem, and next after the proper treatment of men, the use of money is the most important question. He who holds the purse strings holds the reins of power. That the president should decide which professor shall be discharged and which have his salary advanced, which department or line of work shall be favored or crippled, is the most sinister side of our present system of university administration, more pernicious in the private universities, where dismissals and salaries are kept secret, than in the state universities, where salaries are published and teachers are, or should be, dismissed, as in the better public-school systems, only after definite charges.

To transfer the control of appointments and finances from the president to the professors would strike many as passing from purgatory to a worse place. A university executive said to me the other day that if the professors were in control the first thing that they would do would be to raise their own salaries. Well, perhaps worse things have been done. It may be admitted that this is what a president usually does for himself and to an extent beyond the dreams of the most avaricious professor. But there are at least two points of difference. First, the president may increase his salary by withholding a small sum from each professor, whereas the professors could only increase their salaries by obtaining the money for the purpose. Second, it is undesirable for a president to receive three or four times the salary of the greatest scholar or teacher on the faculty, as is the case at California, Columbia and other institutions. It is subversive of decent social and educational ideals for the president of Harvard University to be permitted to build on the grounds of the university a house for himself costing $100,000, and for the trustees of Columbia University to build for their president a house which with its grounds may cost twice that amount. But it would be in the interest of the university and of society if the salaries of professors were increased. Abuses are possible, but at present whatever makes the academic career more attractive to men of genius is in the interest of all the people.

The undeniable difficulties in the way of adjusting salaries and the conflicting needs of schools and departments, whether the decision rests primarily with the president, the trustees or a committee of the faculties, may be minimized by permanence of tenure and fixed salaries, and by giving the departments financial autonomy. President Van Hise, of the University of Wisconsin, and President Butler, of Columbia University, have recently pronounced in favor of the competitive system in the university.[1] The former says: "There is no possible excuse

---

[1] Similarly the late E. Benjamin Andrews, then president of the University of Nebraska, concluded an article on "University Administration" (*Ed. Rev.*, March, 1906) with the words:

"It is not thought that a professor who has grown inefficient has a right to his place simply because he has wrought long for the institution, even if his service has been satisfactory. . . . In some cases application of the competitive system appears cruel, and it may now and then be so in fact; but none who compare institutions where this procedure prevails with those using greater apparent clemency can doubt which is the

for retaining in the staff of a university an inefficient man." The latter says: "A teacher who can not give to the institution which maintains him common loyalty and the kind of service which loyalty implies ought not to be retained through fear of clamor or criticism," and further in respect to equality of salaries: "In my judgment such a policy would fill the university with mediocrities and render it impossible to make that special provision for distinction and for genius which the trustees ought always to be able to make."

There are advantages in a system of severe competition for large prizes under honorable conditions, as well as in permanent tenure of office with small salaries and a free life; but confusion and harm result from running with the hare and hunting with the hounds. If there is to be competition in order to retain university chairs, then the university must be prepared to forego able men or to compete with other professions in the rewards it gives. It must offer prizes commensurate with those of engineering, medicine and law, namely, salaries as large as from ten to a hundred thousand dollars a year. It is further true that under these circumstances a man must be judged by his peers. A university which dismisses professors when the president thinks that they are inefficient or lacking in loyalty to him is parasitic on the great academic traditions of the past and of other nations. A single university which acts in this way will in the end obtain a faculty consisting of a few adventurers, a few sycophants and a crowd of mediocrities. If all universities adopt such a policy, while retaining their present meager salaries and systems of autocratic control, then able men will not em-

---

juster practise on the whole and in the long run." Several of the most distinguished university presidents have, however, defended permanence of tenure. Thus the late President Harper said in one of his quarterly statements (1901): "If an officer on permanent appointment abuses his privilege as a professor, the university must suffer and it is proper that it should suffer. This is only the direct and inevitable consequence of the lack of foresight and wisdom involved in the original appointment. The injury thus accruing to the university is moreover far less serious than would follow if, for an expression of opinion differing from a majority of the faculty or from that of the board of trustees or from that of the president of the university, a permanent officer might be asked to present his resignation. The greatest single element necessary for the cultivation of the academic spirit is the feeling of security from interference. It is only those who have this feeling that are able to do work which in the highest sense will be beneficial to humanity." President Eliot in his book on "University Administration" writes: "The statute which defines the tenures of office throughout the university is of fundamental importance; for it is practically the expression of a contract between the university and its teachers and administrators. This contract ought to provide for life-tenures after adequate periods of probation."

bark on such ill-starred ships. They will carry forward scientific work in connection with industry and will attract as apprentices those competent to learn the ways of research.

Permanent tenure of office for the professor is not a unique state of privilege. A president's wife has permanent tenure of office; he can not dismiss her because he regards her as inefficient or because he prefers another woman. Analogous social conditions make it undesirable that he should have power to dismiss a professor for similar reasons. In the army and navy, in the highest courts, to a certain extent in the civil service of every country, there is permanence of office. Indeed it is nowhere completely disregarded; service is always a valid claim for continued employment. A wife may be divorced by the courts, an army officer may be court-martialed, a judge may be impeached; but such actions are taken only after definite charges and opportunity for defence. Permanent tenure of office is intended to improve the service, not to demoralize it. It is attached to honorable offices, where public spirit and self-sacrifice are demanded, and the wages do not measure the performance. In Germany, France and Great Britain the permanence of tenure has given dignity and honor to the university chair, attracting to it the ablest men and setting them free to do their work.

Incitement to the best work of which a man is capable is not excluded from the university if the professorship itself is made a high reward, the essentials of which are permanence, freedom and honor. Men who have proved their ability for research need opportunity rather than extraneous stimulus. Still it is true that while the lack of prizes does not considerably dampen the spirit of research, it makes the academic career less attractive to those who should be drawn to it. Most of the graduate students in our universities are men of mediocre ability, drifting along with the aid of fellowships and underpaid assistantships to an inglorious Ph.D. and a profession with meager rewards. Several of my correspondents write that if large income, power and honor were not attached to the presidency, there would be no prize to attract men to university work. From my point of view it is altogether demoralizing that the reward held before the investigator and teacher should be the position of an executive, politician and promoter, which takes him away from the higher work for which he is fit. It is a curious exposure of the situation when the president of our largest university [Nicholas Murray Butler] can write: "Almost without exception the men who to-day occupy the most conspicuous positions in the United States have worked their way up, by their own ability, from very humble beginnings. The heads of the great universities were every one of them not long ago humble and poorly compensated teachers." It would be well if some universities would maintain professorships so highly rewarded and regarded that the possibility of a call would exercise a beneficial influence throughout the country, and if each university would establish from one to ten professorships having a salary and a prestige equal at least to that of the presidency. Vacancies in these professorships should be filled by cooptation or election by the faculties or by a faculty committee; but even under the present system of presidential nominations, it would be better to have a few important appointments made publicly than a number of small increases in salary made secretly as the result of presidential favor.

It is awkward to urge a reform, such as an increase in the salaries of professors or the advance of a few salaries to that of the presidency, when this would become superfluous or undesirable, if society as a whole could be reorganized on a just economic basis. Elsewhere[2] I have discussed the question as follows:

"The best reward for scholarly work is adequate recognition of the work as preparation for a career in life. At Columbia University a man takes his doctor's degree at the average age of 27 years. He is fortunate if he receives immediately an instructorship at $1,000 a year; the increments of salary are $100 a year for ten years, so that at the age of 37 he receives a salary of $2,000. In a commercial community the imagination is not stirred by such figures. The university is a parasite on the scholarly impulse instead of a stimulus to it.

"The first need of our universities and colleges is great men for teachers. In order that the best men may be drawn to the academic career, it must be attractive and honorable. The professorship was inherited by us as a high office which is now being lowered. Professors and scholars are not sufficiently free or sufficiently well paid, so there is a lack of men who deserve to be highly rewarded, and we are in danger of sliding down the lines of a vicious spiral, until we reach the stage where the professor and his scholarship are not respected because they are not respectable.

"I should myself prefer to see the salaries, earnings and conveyings

---

[2] "The Case of Harvard College," an address before the Harvard Teachers' Association, *The Popular Science Monthly*, June, 1910.

of others cut down rather than to have the salaries of professors greatly increased. When a criminal lawyer—to use the more inclusive term for corporation lawyer—receives a single fee of $800,000, our civilization is obviously complicated. Every professor who is as able as this lawyer and who does work more important for society can not be paid a million dollars a year. But neither is it necessary to pay him so little that he can not do his work or educate his children. I recently excused myself somewhat awkwardly for not greeting promptly the wife of a colleague by saying that men could not be expected to recognize women because they changed their frocks. She replied: 'The wives of professors don't.' It is better to have wit than frocks; but in the long run they are likely to be found together.

"The first step of a really great university president would be to refuse to accept a larger salary than is paid to the professors. The second step would be to make himself responsible to the faculty instead of holding each professor responsible to him. The bureaucratic or department-store system of university control is the disease which is now serious and may become fatal. This subjection of the individual to the machinery of administration and to the rack wage is but an invasion of the university by methods in business and in politics from which the whole country suffers. We may hope that it is only a temporary incident in the growth of material complexity beyond the powers of moral and intellectual control, and that man may soon regain his seat in the saddle."

I myself accept the social ideal: From each according to his ability, to each according to his needs; and I believe that, thanks to the applications of science, the resources of society are sufficient to provide adequately for all. But the first step to take in our present competitive system is to make rewards commensurate with effective ability and a compromise between services and needs. I have pointed out that, apart from exceptional cases, the range of individual differences in many traits is about as two to one. Thus in accuracy of perception and movement, in quickness of recognition and reaction, in rate of learning and retentiveness of memory, in time and variety of the association of ideas, in validity of judgments, I have found in laboratory experiments a range of difference of this magnitude. The able student can prepare a lesson or earn the doctor's degree in about half the time required by the poorer student. For the same kind of work and under similar conditions the value of the services of an individual varies within somewhat the same limits. A good laboring man or a good clerk is worth as much as two who are mediocre. The value of genius to the world is of course inestimable. A great man of science may contribute more than even the most successful promoter—a Rockefeller, a Carnegie or a Morgan—gets. But such contributions are made possible by the organization of society as a whole, and should in large measure be distributed among its members, preferably in the direction of making further contributions possible. Scientific men should receive adequate rewards, and the surplus wealth which directly or indirectly they have produced—it must be counted by the hundreds of thousands of millions of dollars—should, in so far as this can be done to advantage, be spent on further scientific research.

The available wealth in the United States and Great Britain suffices to provide a home and the tools of production for each family and the productivity of labor to provide an annual income of about $1,000 for each producer. If waste in production and expenditure were reduced, even to the extent that now obtains among teachers and scientific men as a group, there would probably be available $1,500 for each adult, including women engaged in the care of the home, or $3,000 for each family. If this were distributed on a range of two to one in accordance with ability, the more deserving teachers and scientific men with their wives would earn salaries of $4,000, in addition to owning their homes. An addition of from $250 to $1,000 should be allowed for each child requiring support and education, to be deducted in part from the incomes of those having no children, and allowance should be made for the varying cost of living in the city or the country and the like.

If the maximum income of a university professor or scientific man with a family should be from $5,000 to $10,000, no one should receive more, except to cover greater risks. There is no occupation requiring rarer ability or more prolonged preliminary training, and there is none whose services to society are greater. If there are to be money prizes—incomes of $20,000 or $100,000 or more—then they should be open to professors and investigators. Scientific ability is as rare as executive or legal ability, and is far more valuable to society. The lawyer who receives a fee of $800,000 for enabling a group of promoters to get ten times as much by evading the intent of the law, does not add to the wealth of society. The scientific man who increases the yield of the cereal crop by one per cent. adds $10,000,000 a year to the wealth of the country and five times as much to the wealth of the world. The scientific man who discovered and those who have developed the Bessemer process of making steel have, according to the estimate of Abram S. Hewitt, added $2,000,000,000 yearly to the world's wealth. There is no reason except the imperfect adjustments of society why the lawyer should receive large rewards and the scientific man a scant salary. Those who render services to an individual or group are likely to be paid in accordance with the value of their services to the individual or group; in our competitive system those who render services to society as a whole are not paid at all, or only partially and indirectly. Of our thousand leading men of science, 738 are employed in universities and colleges, 106 in the government service, 59 in research foundations. It is the duty of these institutions to provide adequately and liberally for their support and for their work.

The rewards of the academic and scientific career deserve detailed discussion because they are of fundamental importance to the university and to society. Professors and investigators should have adequate incomes, as large as is desirable for any social class, but above all they should have opportunity to lead a life free from distracting or dishonorable compromises. It should be emphasized that nothing here written is intended to promote a privileged class of university professors. Valparaiso University and Mr. Edison's Menlo Park Laboratory are useful, as well as Harvard University and the Rockefeller Institute for Medical Research. My concern is only that the university should be of the greatest possible service to the people and to the world. It may be that the great bulk of routine teaching and routine research can be done most economically under the factory system, with a manager to employ and discharge the instructional force and bosses to keep each gang up to a square day's work. But then the highest productive scholarship and creative research must find refuge elsewhere than in such a university.[3]

---

[3] As President Maclaurin, of the Massachusetts Institute of Technology, has put it (*Science,* Jan. 20, 1911):

The superintendent of buildings and grounds, or other competent authority, calls upon Mr. Newton.

Supt. Your theory of gravitation is hanging fire unduly. The director insists on a finished report, filed in his office by 9 A.M. Monday next; summarized on one page; typewritten, and the main points underlined. Also a careful estimate of the cost of the research per student-hour.

Newton. But there is one difficulty that has been puzzling me for fourteen years, and I am not quite . . .

Supt. (with snap and vigor). Guess you had better overcome that difficulty by Monday morning or quit.

It is truly distressing that our universities should be so conventional and unimaginative, each trying to follow the lead of those bigger than itself, all lacking in fineness and distinction. The Johns Hopkins, Clark, Stanford and Chicago were founded one after the other with promise of higher things, and each has relapsed into the common mediocrity. Harvard and Yale maintain the traditions of scholarship; the Johns Hopkins and Chicago have not abandoned the ideals of research; Columbia looms up with the vastness and crudeness of the metropolis; the state universities exhibit the promise and the immaturity of our democracy. But each and all unite the scholasticism of the twelfth century with the commercial rawness of the twentieth century. Can there not be one university where the professor will have a study instead of an office, where the ideal set before the young instructor is something else than answering letters promptly and neatly on the typewriter, where men are weighed rather than counted, where efficiency and machinery are subordinated to the personality of great men? Could there not be a university or school, dominating some field of scholarship and research with its half-dozen professors and group of instructors and students drawn together by them? Might not means be devised by which the professor would be paid for the value of his teaching, service and research, and then be set free to do his work how and when and where he can do it best? It is not inconceivable that there should be a national or state university, with some features of the royal academies, rewarding with fellowships men of unusual promise and with professorships men of unusual performance, endowing the individual instead of the institution.

THE DUTIES OF THE PROFESSOR

If it is not possible at present to have free professors and independent schools, we can at least strive for greater freedom of the individual and larger autonomy of the department within the university. As the position and salary of the professor should not depend on the favor of a president, so the department or school should be allowed substantial autonomy. There is nothing more disheartening to the members of a department or school than to have its activities prescribed or limited, its annual appropriation apportioned, by a centralized system. A great danger confronting the modern university is its own bulk. In the evolution of organic life a limit is placed on the size which an animal can attain. Its surface increases more slowly than its mass, and there must be differentiation and division of labor in order that the animal may grow and react properly to the environment. Even then a limit is fixed; it is doubtful whether apart from the nervous system a structure more complicated than that of the mammal will be reached, or that animals much larger than man will survive. Only a polyp or similar creature can conduct a pure democracy; the organization of higher animals must be more complicated. The growth in size of the American university has been large and rapid. Faculty or town-meeting methods have become difficult or impossible; the institution drifts into autocratic and bureaucratic control. A representative or delegated system of government is necessary for the university as a whole, but its divisions can maintain a family and democratic system.

President Eliot says[4] that a long tenure of office will be an advantage to the president and to the university he serves, but that the chairmen of departments should be chosen for short periods and should generally be junior or assistant professors to give them opportunity and because "dangers from the domination of masterful personages will be reduced to a minimum under this system." It is not evident why it is less desirable to limit "the domination of masterful personages" in the office of the president or of the dean than in the department. But it is true that a departmental autocracy may be even worse than one on a larger scale, and for the reason that it is conducted in the dark. A president may say that a teacher "ought not to be retained through fear of clamor or criticism," but fortunately public opinion does prevent the more serious abuses to which the system is liable. In certain departments of certain universities instructors and junior professors are placed in a situation to which no decent domestic servant would submit. Clearly that is no breeding ground for genius and great personalities.

It can not be denied that the organization of the departments of a university is one of the difficult problems that confront us. The German plan, according to which the individual rather than the department is the unit, is in many ways preferable. But the American university conducts what is practically a secondary school in the first two years of the college, and it conducts professional schools which are not of university grade. The high schools and small colleges should take over the first two years of the college, establish schools of agriculture and

[4] "University Administration."

of the mechanic arts, and conduct courses preparatory to medicine, law, engineering and teaching. In a large state, the state university would have one hundred thousand students, if it received all the young men and women between the ages of sixteen and twenty who should continue educational work. Such education should be provided locally and in connection with productive industry, as in the admirable plan adopted by the school of engineering of the University of Cincinnati, by which students work alternate weeks in the university and in the shop. Under President Eliot, Harvard placed both its college and its professional schools on a university basis; under President Lowell, it has moved backward in the direction of making the college a school of information and culture and of requiring the professional school to begin with the elements. To such an extent is the university the plaything of its president!

For administrative and financial purposes it seems necessary to organize the university into schools, divisions or departments, although for educational purposes as much flexibility as possible should be maintained. The scope and size of such a division should depend on convenience and local conditions, rather than on logical distinctions among the subjects taught. A small college or a small medical school can be conducted to advantage under one faculty. In a large university there is no need to have a separate department for each of the oriental languages because they differ from one another more than do the European languages, though it may be desirable to have separate departments for German and French. When a medical school, or even the work in a special science, such as chemistry, becomes large, it may be advisable to organize it into partly autonomous divisions. There is no gain in economy and usually a loss in cooperation and effectiveness when the entering class of a college or professional school exceeds fifty or a hundred, and when its faculty exceeds twenty or thereabouts. Colleges should remain small; if a university must have a great crowd of college students, they should be divided among separate colleges, as in the English universities. These colleges should not, however, consist of freshmen, as President Lowell plans, or of students belonging to a certain social class, as is likely to happen under the fraternity and club system, but of men having common intellectual interests. Even small colleges for general education should aim to excel and to do research work in some special direction. In the large university the residential colleges and departments should coincide, so that younger men will join a group of older students and instructors having similar interests and ends in life. As I have elsewhere remarked:

The ideal is the zoological hall of the old Harvard, where apprentices of a great man and a great teacher lived together. This is told of again in the charming autobiography of Shaler. A boy from the aristocratic southern classes, with ample means and good abilities but no fixed interests, fell into this group. There he discovered his life-work and pursued it with boundless enthusiasm. Nor did the fact that he devoted himself exclusively to professional work in natural history in college prevent him from writing Elizabethan plays in his old age. The number of men of distinction given to the world from this small Agassiz group is truly remarkable.

A group of some 10 to 20 instructors, having registered primarily under them from 50 to 200 students, is a good size for a school, division or department. Each can be well acquainted with the others and take a personal and intelligent interest in all the work of the department. At the same time the number is sufficient to permit the representation of diverse kinds of work and points of view, and to make possible the election of officers and a democratic control. The chairman or head and an executive committee should of course be elected, not named by a semi-absentee president. In a group of this character questions are not usually brought to a vote. In reaching decisions each member is likely to be weighed as well as counted. In my experience the junior members of a faculty or department take too little rather than too much share in its discussions and its control. If they obtained constitutional rights they might become more aggressive; if they should, so much the better. One of the serious difficulties of the present system is that the younger men do not share in the conduct of the university and do not feel themselves to be part of its life. Those who do not have their ideas before they are thirty are not likely to have them. The paraphernalia and camp baggage of modern civilization have become so heavy that they threaten to block its further advance. If men must devote thirty years to mere acquisition, and be kept even longer in official subjection, there is not much chance that they will do anything else thereafter. What youth can do should be joined with what age can know.

Voting rights in a department might be in proportion to the salary the officers receive; but such statutory regulations are scarcely needed. The real control is vested in the aggregate common sense of those concerned. The group may well be flexible in character. When courses of instruction and educational problems are under discussion, assistants and even graduate students may be admitted to advantage. When the question is the promotion of an instructor, the group would naturally be limited to those of higher office. The chairmanship of the department might rotate among its members or the same head might be reelected continuously, according to convenience. It by no means follows that the professor most eminent in research should be the executive head; on the contrary, it should usually be a man of competent administrative ability whose time is of less value. Every reasonable man believes in economy in administration and letting the men do things who can do them. Even the most important decisions can be left to the head of the department or its executive committee, so long as they represent and are responsible to the whole department.

The school or department should have complete control of its own educational work. So long as there is ample room for differences of opinion as to the value of different subjects and methods, it is well that there be variation and survival of the fit. Entrance requirements and degrees are among the chief obstacles to education. An instructor in Columbia University said recently to a student who had just received the highest grade assigned in the course: "Why did you take the course, if you don't want a degree?" If there must be degrees, it may be necessary to standardize them; but this should be done only to the extent of prescribing the amount of work to be done in the direction called for by the degree, this being determined by the time spent, weighted in accordance with the ability of the students. . . .

Financial as well as educational autonomy should be given to the school or department. Its total income should be held as a trust fund, to be decreased only after full and public investigation. The laboratories, rooms, apparatus, equipment, library, etc., should be held in trust for the department, to be taken away against its will only for clear reasons and on the recommendation of a competent faculty committee. Under these conditions the members of a department will plan on a safe basis for the future, and will seek to increase its funds and facilities. I know of a case in which a professor obtained a gift of $100,000, made expressly "to increase the facilities of the department," and the income was assigned by the president and trustees to pay the salary of that professor against his earnest protest. I also know of a case in which a department which had built up one of the strongest laboratories in the country had those of its rooms especially devoted to research taken away and given to a weak department, to induce a certain professor to accept a call from elsewhere to the headship of the weak department. These are of course extreme cases and might seem incredible, if it were not that interference with the vested rights of departments is of frequent occurrence.

The Harvard plan of visiting committees which may take an active interest in the educational work and financial support of departments is commendable. Under the existing trustee system it might be well if one trustee would concern himself especially with one or two departments, attending their meetings and doing what he could to advance their interests. There can to advantage be within the university departments related to its educational work, but under independent control. Thus the most useful and vigorous division of Columbia University, with the possible exception of the faculty of political science, is the Teachers College, which is under its own trustees with a dean and faculty responsible to them. As a department of education under the trustees of Columbia College it would probably have had no more leadership than the departments at Harvard or Yale. The educational alliance between Columbia University and the Union Theological Seminary is far better than a school of theology under the trustees of the university. There is no valid objection to two schools of law or two schools of chemistry, independently controlled, but enjoying the advantages of educational affiliation with a university. Endowed research institutions and municipal, state or governmental bureaus can to advantage be placed near a university, contributing to and gaining from its educational work.

Appointments and the apportionment of funds are said to be questions insoluble under democratic control. But in spite of the difficulties the case is not so bad as autocratic one-man power. If there are fixed salaries with automatic increases, only three or four decisions must be made. Shall this man be appointed instructor? Shall he be appointed junior professor after five or ten years of service as instructor? Shall he be appointed full professor after five or ten years of service as junior professor? Who shall be appointed to super-professorships, if such exist? As a matter of fact under the existing system instructors and junior professors are nearly always nominated by the department or its head. They alone have the necessary information in regard to the men and the situation. The nomination of a full professor can be entrusted better to the department concerned than to a president. But such an appointment, being for life and of immense consequence, can not be too carefully guarded. It should be passed on by a board or committee composed, say, of two members of the department, two members of allied departments and two distinguished representatives of the subject outside the university concerned. Such control would prevent undesirable inbreeding or the further deterioration of a weak department. Nominations should be made publicly—the English plan of definite candidates with printed records has much to commend it—and the power of veto should perhaps be given to the faculties as well as to the trustees.

The apportionment of the existing income of a department varies but little from year to year, and can safely be left to the department. Questions arise only when an increase which the department can not itself obtain is wanted, and there are general funds available, but not sufficient to supply all the needs of the university. Under the existing system each head of department grabs for everything in sight, and the president plays the part of an inscrutable and sometimes unscrupulous providence in the semi-secret distribution of his favors. No scheme could be more demoralizing. The correct plan is for each department to draw up its budget, with requests for increases and the reasons clearly indicated, the proposed budgets being printed and open to all concerned. Under these conditions unreasonable claims would not often be made by the departments. Plans for new departments and new lines of work could also be submitted by any responsible group. An elected committee of professors, with the assistance of an expert curator or controller, would then pass on the various budgets and proposals and adjust them to the available income, the reductions made by the committee being of course published. The budget for the university would then go to the trustees. It may be objected that under this plan existing work would be strengthened rather than new ground broken. But might not this be better than the existing presidential mania for expansion? It seems in fact probable that if many professors and junior instructors were concerned, there would be more new ideas than when the initiative is left to a single man, and further that wise plans would be more likely to be adopted and inexpedient schemes to be rejected.

When schools and departments have autonomy, there is no need for much super-legislation and super-administration in the university. The machinery should be as simple as may be. Departments may be united into a school or college and elect a dean and a faculty or an executive committee to coordinate the work. A department can elect members to represent it in allied departments and on the faculties of the schools and colleges with whose work it is concerned. There should be an elected council or senate to represent the entire university and an executive committee which can confer with the executive committee of the trustees. There may at times to advantage be faculty meetings or plebiscites of large groups or of all the officers of the university. Questions concerning the entire university can be discussed to advantage by the fly-leaf method of the English universities, and a vote can be taken without a general assembly at a polling booth or by mail.

There are advantages and disadvantages in large faculty meetings. When all important matters are decided by administrative officers or executive committees and only trivial questions are discussed before the faculty, usually by certain polyphasiac members, its meetings are likely to fall into disrepute. Men are efficient in direct proportion to their responsibility. Further, a body of men is effective inversely as its size and directly as the time it works together. A body of fifty men, such as the faculty to which I primarily belong, meeting for an hour three times a year, without power or responsibility, is clearly dedicated to futility. But if any one supposes that university presidents would do better under these conditions, he should call to mind the conduct of the trustees of the Carnegie Foundation. It seems to be the case that in order to make large faculties real legislative bodies, it would be necessary to devote more time to their meetings than is expedient, and perhaps more common sense than is available. All parliaments, congresses and legislatures do their work through cabinets and committees; but these are responsible to the whole body. Some such plan is necessary in the university. Still the cynical attitude toward faculty meetings common in academic circles appears to be one of the sinister symptoms resulting from the existing methods of autocratic control. It is typical of existing conditions that the most recent university school to be established—the School of Journalism of Columbia University—does not have a faculty, but an "administrative board." I belong to a club at the meetings of which each member must speak once and only once, not exceeding his share of the time, and the discussion is followed by a dinner. If faculty meetings could be made into educational and social clubs they would perform a useful function. The meetings of the faculty of arts and sciences at Harvard may give rise to complaints, but they have been of real service to the university.

Truth, openness, publicity, are the safeguards of free institutions. It is better to wash your dirty linen in public than to continue to wear it. The affairs of a university should be conducted in the full light of day. The proceedings of the trustees, the discussions and conclusions of faculties and of committees, the activities of the president, the work of professors, salaries and the provisions of the budget, the appointment of officers and the rare cases in which it is necessary to dismiss a professor, should be open to all. Light is an excellent disinfectant; what is of more consequence, it is essential to healthy life and growth. "And God said, let there be light: and there was light. And God saw the light, that it was good."

Several of my correspondents argue that if the control of a university were vested in its teachers they would be distracted from their proper work of teaching and research. In a recent article[5] on "The University President in the American Commonwealth," President Eliot writes: "Most American professors of good quality would regard the imposition of duties concerning the selection of professors and other teachers, the election of the president, and the annual arrangement of the budget of the institution as a serious reduction in the attractiveness of the scholar's life and the professorial career." Do President Eliot and the lesser presidents and the few professors who share their views believe that university professors and other citizens of a city should not concern themselves with municipal government or vote for a president of the nation? Are we of the world's greatest democracy and in the twentieth century to revert to the theory that the common people should do the daily work imposed on them, and trust to the king and his lords to care for them?

In the preface to the first edition (1906) of the "Biographical Directory of American Men of Science," I wrote: "There scarcely exists among scientific men the recognition of common interest and the spirit of cooperation which would help to give science the place it should have in the community. It is fully as important for the nation as for men of science that scientific work should be adequately recognized

---

[5] *The Educational Review*, November, 1911.

and supported. We are consequently in the fortunate position of knowing that whatever we do to promote our own interests is at the same time a service to the community and to the world." Trade-unions and organizations of professional men, in spite of occasional abuses, have been of benefit not only to those immediately concerned, but to society as a whole.[6] President Eliot did not obtain commendation for calling the "scab" a hero. But if it is expedient to better the conditions under which work of any kind is done, this is of the utmost importance for education and research. If we can unite to improve the conditions of the academic career, so that it will attract the best men and permit them to do their best work, we make a contribution to the welfare of society which is permanent and universal. It may be that the time has now come when it is desirable and possible to form an association of professors of American universities, based on associations in the different universities, the objects of which would be to promote the interests of the universities and to advance higher education and research, with special reference to problems of administration and to the status of the professors and other officers of the university.

The space at my disposal is exhausted and many problems directly and indirectly concerned with the control of a university remain untouched. I am well aware that this essay is written in the spirit of the advocate and the reformer, rather than from the point of view of the judge and the responsible administrator. Against most of the suggestions which have been made valid objections may be urged. The only principle that I am prepared to defend whole-heartedly is that the university should be a democracy of scholars serving the larger democracy of which it is part. A government of laws is better than a government by men; but better than either is freedom controlled by public opinion and common sense, by precedent and good-will.

---

[6] This is illustrated just now by the conflict between the British Medical Association and the British government. It may seem to be of greater advantage to physicians than to the people that the government has been forced to increase the fees which it proposed to provide; but in the end the rewards and the control which physicians have obtained through their organization will be of advantage to the nation.

10. Carl Becker on the Atmosphere of Cornell after 1917

Carl Becker (1873–1945) was born in Iowa in 1873, received his B.Litt. from the University of Wisconsin in 1896, and returned to his alma mater for his Ph.D. in 1907. Between 1899 and 1917 he taught successively at Pennsylvania State College, Dartmouth, and the universities of Kansas and Minnesota. In the latter year he went to Cornell, where he continued a memorable career as the author of works on eighteenth-century politics and thought in Europe and America. In 1931 he was elected president of the American Historical Association. The following excerpt from his remarkable book on the founding of Cornell portrays the atmosphere of that institution in the years after his arrival.

Charlotte W. Smith, *Carl Becker: On History and the Climate of Opinion* (Ithaca, N.Y., 1956); Cushing Strout, *The Pragmatic Revolt in American History: Carl Becker and Charles Beard* (New Haven, 1958); Burleigh Taylor Wilkins, *Carl Becker: A Biographical Study in American Intellectual History* (Cambridge, Mass., 1961).

In the process of acquiring a reputation Cornell acquired something better than a reputation, or rather it acquired something which is the better part of its reputation. It acquired a character. Corporations are not necessarily soulless; and of all corporations universities are the most likely to have, if not souls, at least personalities. Perhaps the reason is that universities are, after all, largely shaped by presidents and professors, and presidents and professors, especially if they are good ones, are fairly certain to be men of distinctive, not to say eccentric, minds and temperaments. A professor, as the German saying has it, is a man who thinks otherwise. Now an able and otherwise-thinking president, surrounded by able and otherwise-thinking professors, each resolutely thinking otherwise in his own manner, each astounded to find that the others, excellent fellows as he knows them in the main to be, so often refuse in matters of the highest import to be informed by knowledge or guided by reason—this is indeed always an arresting spectacle and may sometimes seem to be a futile performance. Yet it is not futile unless great universities are futile. For the essential quality of a great university derives from the corporate activities of such a community of otherwise-thinking men. By virtue of a divergence as well as

Carl Becker, *Cornell University: Founders and the Founding* (Ithaca, N.Y., 1943), pp. 193–96, 198–203. Reprinted with the permission of Cornell University Press.

of a community of interests, by the sharp impress of their minds and temperaments and eccentricities upon each other and upon their pupils, there is created a continuing tradition of ideas and attitudes and habitual responses that has a life of its own. It is this continuing tradition that gives to a university its corporate character or personality, that intangible but living and dynamic influence which is the richest and most durable gift any university can confer upon those who come to it for instruction and guidance.

Cornell has a character, a corporate personality, in this sense, an intellectual tradition by which it can be identified. The word which best symbolizes this tradition is freedom. There is freedom in all universities, of course—a great deal in some, much less in others; but it is less the amount than the distinctive quality and flavor of the freedom that flourishes at Cornell that is worth noting. The quality and flavor of this freedom is easier to appreciate than to define. Academic is not the word that properly denotes it. It includes academic freedom, of course, but it is something more, and at the same time something less, than that—something less formal, something less self-regarding, something more worldly, something, I will venture to say, a bit more impudent. It is, in short, too little schoolmasterish to be defined by a formula or identified with a professional code. And I think the reason is that Cornell was not founded by schoolmasters or designed strictly according to existing educational models. The founders, being both in their different ways rebels against convention, wished to establish not merely another university but a somewhat novel kind of university. Mr. Cornell desired to found an institution in which any person could study any subject. Mr. White wished to found a center of learning where mature scholars and men of the world, emancipated from the clerical tradition and inspired by the scientific idea, could pursue their studies uninhibited by the cluttered routine or the petty preoccupations of the conventional cloistered academic life. In Mr. White's view the character and quality of the university would depend upon the men selected for its faculty: devoted to the general aim of learning and teaching, they could be depended upon to devise their own ways and means of achieving that aim. The emphasis was, therefore, always on men rather than on methods; and during Mr. White's administration and that of his immediate successors there was assembled at Cornell, from the academic and the non-academic world, a group of extraordinary men—erudite or not as the case might be, but at all events as highly individualized, as colorful, as disconcertingly original and amiably eccentric a

group of men as was ever got together for the launching of a new educational venture. It is in the main to the first president and this early
group of otherwise-thinking men that Cornell is indebted for its tradition of freedom.

Many of those distinguished scholars and colorful personalities were
before my time. Many of those whom I was privileged to know are
now gone. A few only are still with us—worthy bearers of the tradition, indefatigable in the pursuit of knowledge, in the service of Cornell, in the promotion of the public good, young men still, barely
eighty or a little more. Present or absent, the influence of this original
group persists, and is attested by stories of their sayings and exploits
that still circulate, a body of ancient but still living folklore. It is a pity
that some one has not collected and set down these stories; properly
arranged they would constitute a significant mythology, a Cornell epic
which, whether literally true or only characteristic, would convey far
better than official records in deans' offices the real significance of this
institution. Some of these stories I have heard, and for their illustrative
value will venture to recall a few of them. Like Herodotus, I give them
as they were related to me without vouching for their truth, and like
Herodotus, I hope no god or hero will take offense at what I say.

There is the story of the famous professor of history, passionate de-
fender of majority rule, who, foreseeing that he would be outvoted in
the faculty on the question of the location of Risley Hall, declared with
emotion that he felt so strongly on the subject that he thought he
ought to have two votes. The story of another professor of history who,
in reply to a colleague who moved as the sense of the faculty that during war time professors should exercise great discretion in discussing
public questions, declared that for his part he could not understand
how any one could have the Prussian arrogance to suppose that every
one could be made to think alike, or the Pomeranian stupidity to suppose that it would be a good thing if they could. The story of the eccentric and lovable professor of English who suggested that it would
be a good thing, during the winter months when the wind sweeps
across the hill, if the university would tether a shorn lamb on the slope
south of the library building; who gave all of his students a grade of
eighty-five, on the theory that they deserved at least that for patiently
listening to him while he amused himself reading his favorite authors
aloud, and for so amiably submitting to the ironical and sarcastic comments—too highly wrought and sophistically phrased in latinized English to be easily understood by them—with which he berated their

indifference to good literature. There is the story of the professor who
reluctantly agreed to serve as dean of a school on condition that he be
relieved of the irksome task at a certain date; who, as the date approached with no successor appointed, repeatedly reminded the president that he would retire on the date fixed; and who, on that date,
although no successor had meantime been appointed, cleared out his
desk and departed; so that, on the day following, students and heads
of departments found the door locked and no dean to affix the necessary signature to the necessary papers. A school without a dean—
strange interlude indeed, rarely occurring in more decorous institutions, I should think; but one of those things that could happen in
Cornell. And there is the story of the professor of entomology, abruptly
leaving a faculty meeting. It seems that the discussion of a serious matter was being sidetracked by the rambling, irrelevant, and would-be
facetious remarks of a dean who was somewhat of a wag, when the
professor of entomology, not being a wag and being quite fed up, suddenly reached for his hat and as he moved to the door delivered himself thus: "Mr. President, I beg to be excused; I refuse to waste my
valuable time any longer listening to this damned nonsense." And
even more characteristic of the Cornell tradition is a story told of the
first president, Andrew D. White. It is related that the lecture committee had brought to Cornell an eminent authority to give, in a certain lecture series, an impartial presentation of the Free-Silver question. Afterwards Mr. White, who had strong convictions on the subject,
approached the chairman of the committee and asked permission to
give a lecture in that series in reply to the eminent authority. But the
chairman refused, saying in substance: "Mr. President, the committee
obtained the best man it could find to discuss this question. It is of the
opinion that the discussion was a fair and impartial presentation of the
arguments on both sides. The committee would welcome an address by
you on any other subject, or on this subject on some other occasion, but
not on this subject in this series in reply to the lecture just given." It is
related that Mr. White did not give a lecture on that subject in that
series; it is also related that Mr. White became a better friend and
more ardent admirer of the chairman of the committee than he had
been. It seems that Mr. White really liked to have on his faculty men
of that degree of independence and resolution. . . .

And so in the summer of 1917 I came to Cornell, prepared to do as I
pleased, wondering what the catch was, supposing that Professor

Hull's amiable attitude must be either an eccentric form of ironic understatement or else a super-subtle species of bargaining technique. Anyway I proposed to try it out. I began to do as I pleased, expecting some one would stop me. No one did. I went on an on and still no one paid any attention. Personally I was cordially received, but officially no one made any plans to entertain me, to give me the right steer, to tell me what I would perhaps find it wise to do or to refrain from doing. Professor Hull's attitude did seem after all to represent, in some idealized fashion, the attitude of Cornell University. There was about the place a refreshing sense of liberation from the prescribed and the insistent, an atmosphere of casual urbanity, a sense of leisurely activity going on, with time enough to admire the view, and another day coming. . . . At least I saw no indication that deans or heads of departments were exerting pressure or pushing any one around. Certainly no head of the history department was incommoding me, for the simple reason, if for no other, that there didn't seem to be any history department, much less a head. There were seven professors of history, and when we met we called ourselves the "History Group," but no one of us had any more authority than any other. On these occasions Professor Hull presided, for no reason I could discover except that we met in his office because it was the largest and most convenient. Whatever the History Group was it was not a department. If there was any department of history, then there were six; in which case I was the sole member, and presumably the head, of the department of Modern European History. The only evidence of this was that twice a year I received a communication from the president: one requesting me to prepare the budget, which consisted chiefly in setting down the amount of my own salary, an item which the president presumably already knew more about than I did; the other a request for a list of the courses given and the number of students, male and female, enrolled during the year. I always supposed, therefore, that there were six departments of history, each manned by one professor, except the department of American history, which ran to the extraordinary number of two. I always supposed so, that is, until one day Professor Hull said he wasn't sure there were, officially speaking, any departments of history at all; the only thing he was sure of was that there were seven professors of history. The inner truth of the matter I never discovered. But the seven professors were certainly members of the Faculty of Arts, the Graduate Faculty, and the University Faculty since they were often present at the meetings of these faculties. They were also, I think, members of the Faculty of Political Science, a body that seemed to have no corporeal existence since it never met, but that nevertheless seemed to be something—a rumor perhaps, a disembodied tradition or vestigial remainder never seen, but lurking about somewhere in the more obscure recesses of Goldwin Smith Hall. I never had the courage to ask Professor Hull about the university—about its corporate administrative existence, I mean—for fear he might say that he wasn't sure it had any: it was on the cards that the university might turn out to be nothing more than forty or fifty professors.

At all events, the administration (I assumed on general principles that there was one somewhere) wasn't much in evidence and exerted little pressure. There was a president (distinguished scholar and eminent public figure) who presided at faculty meetings and the meeting of the Board of Trustees, and always delivered the Commencement address. But the president, so far as I could judge, was an umpire rather than a captain, and a Gallup poll would have disclosed the fact that some members of the community regarded him as an agreeable but purely decorative feature, his chief function being, as one of my colleagues said, "to obviate the difficulties created by his office." I never shared this view. I have a notion that the president obviated many difficulties, especially for the faculty, that were in no sense created by his office. There were also deans, but not many or much looked up to for any authority they had or were disposed to exercise. Even so, the general opinion seemed to be that the appointment of professors to the office was a useless waste of talent. "Why is it," asked Professor Nichols, "that as soon as a man has demonstrated that he has an unusual knowledge of books, some one immediately insists on making him a bookkeeper?" In those days the dean of the College, at all events, was scarcely more than a bookkeeper—a secretary elected by the faculty to keep its records and administer the rules enacted by it.

The rules were not many or much displayed or very oppressive—the less so since in so many cases they were conflicting, so that one could choose the one which seemed most suitable. The rules seemed often in the nature of miscellaneous conveniences lying about for a professor to use if he needed something of the sort. An efficient administrator, if there had been one, would no doubt have found much that was ill-defined and haphazard in the rules. Even to a haphazard professor, like myself, it often seemed so, for if I inquired what the authority for this or that rule was, the answer would perhaps be that it wasn't a rule but only a custom; and upon further investigation the custom, as like as not, would turn out to be two other customs, varying according to the time and the professor. Even in the broad distribution of powers the efficient administrator might have found much to discontent his orderly soul. I was told that according to the Cornell statutes the university is subject to the control of the Board of Trustees, but that according to the laws of the state it is subject to the Board of Regents. It may or may not be so. I never pressed the matter. I was advised not to, on the theory that at Cornell it always creates trouble when any one looks up the statutes. The general attitude, round and round about, seemed to be that the university would go on very well indeed so long as no one paid too much attention to the formal authority with which any one was invested. And, in fact, in no other university that I am acquainted with does formal authority count for so little in deciding what shall or shall not be done.

In this easy-going, loose-jointed institution the chances seemed very good indeed for me to do as I pleased. Still there was an obvious limit. The blest principle of doing as one pleased presumably did not reach to the point of permitting me to do nothing. Presumably, the general expectation would be that I would at least be pleased to do something, and the condition of doing something was that I alone had to decide what that something should be. This was for me something of a novelty. Hitherto many of the main points—the courses to be given, the minimum hours of instruction, the administrative duties to be assumed —had mostly been decided for me. I had only to do as I was told. This might be sometimes annoying, but it was never difficult. Mine not to question why, mine not to ask whether what I was doing was worth while or the right thing to do. It was bound to be the right thing to do since some one else, some one in authority, so decided. But now, owing to the great freedom at Cornell, I was in authority and had to decide what was right and worth while for me to do. This was not so easy, and I sometimes tried to shift the responsibility to Professor Burr, by asking him whether what I proposed to do was the right thing to do. But Professor Burr wasn't having any. He would spin me a long history, the upshot of which was that what I proposed to do had sometimes been done and sometimes not, so that whatever I did I was sure to have plenty of precedents on my side. And if I tried to shift the responsibility to Professor Hull I had no better luck. He too would spin me a history, not longer than that of Professor Burr, but only taking longer to relate, and the conclusion which he reached was always the same: the conclusion always was, "and so, my dear boy, you can do as you please."

In these devious ways I discovered that I could do as I pleased all right. But in the process of discovering this I also discovered something else. I discovered what the catch was. The catch was that, since I was free to do as I pleased, I was responsible for what it was that I pleased to do. The catch was that, with all my great freedom, I was in some mysterious way still very much bound. Not bound by orders imposed upon me from above or outside, but bound by some inner sense of responsibility, by some elemental sense of decency or fair play or mere selfish impulse to justify myself; bound to all that comprised Cornell University, to the faculty that had so politely invited me to join it without imposing any obligations, to the amiable deans who never raised their voices or employed the imperative mood, to the distinguished president and the Board of Trustees in the offing who every year guaranteed my salary without knowing precisely what, if anything, I might be doing to earn it—to all these I was bound to justify myself by doing, upon request and in every contingency, the best I was capable of doing. And thus I found myself working, although without interference and under no outside compulsion, with more concentration, with greater satisfaction, and, I dare say, with better effect, than I could otherwise have done. I relate my own experience, well aware that it cannot be in all respects typical, since it is characteristic of Cornell to permit a wide diversity in departmental organization and procedure. Yet this very diversity derives from the Cornell tradition which allows a maximum of freedom and relies so confidently upon the sense of personal responsibility for making a good use of it.

I should like to preserve intact the loose-jointed administrative system and the casual freedoms of the old days. But I am aware that it is difficult to do so in the present-day world in which the complex and impersonal forces of a technological society tend to diminish the importance of the individual and to standardize his conduct and thinking, a society in which life often seems impoverished by the overhead charges required to maintain it. Universities cannot remain wholly unaffected by this dominant trend in society. As they become larger and more complicated a more reticulated organization is called for, rules multiply and become more uniform, and the members of the instructing staff, turned out as a standardized article in mass production by our graduate schools, are more subdued to a common model. Somewhat less than formerly, it seems, is the professor a man who thinks otherwise. More than formerly the professor and the promoter are in costume and deportment if not of imagination all compact; and every year it becomes more difficult, in the market place or on the campus, to distinguish the one from the other at ninety yards by the naked eye. On the whole we all deplore this trend towards standardization, but in the particular instance the reasons for it are often too compelling to be denied. Nevertheless, let us yield to this trend only as a necessity and not as something good in itself. Let us hold, in so far as may be, to the old ways, to the tradition in which Cornell was founded and by which it has lived.

But after all, one may ask, and it is a pertinent question, why is so much freedom desirable? Do we not pay too high a price for it in loss of what is called efficiency? Why should any university pay its professors a good salary, and then guarantee them so much freedom to follow their own devices? Surely not because professors deserve, more than other men, to have their way of life made easy. Not for any such trivial reason. Universities are social institutions, and should perform a social service. There is indeed no reason for the existence of Cornell, or of any university, or for maintaining the freedom of learning and teaching which they insist upon, except in so far as they serve to maintain and promote the humane and rational values which are essential to the preservation of democratic society, and of civilization as we understand it. Democratic society, like any other society, rests upon certain assumptions as to what is supremely worth while. It assumes the worth and dignity and creative capacity of the human personality as an end in itself. It assumes that it is better to be governed by persuasion than by compulsion, and that good will and humane dealing are better than a selfish and a contentious spirit. It assumes that man is a rational creature, and that to know what is true is a primary value upon which in the long run all other values depend. It assumes that knowledge and the power it confers should be employed for promoting the welfare of the many rather than for safeguarding the interests of the few.

11. Thorstein Veblen Satirizes the Conduct of Universities by Businessmen, 1918

Thorstein Veblen (1857–1929) was born in Wisconsin, the child of immigrant Norwegian parents, and received his B.A. from Carleton College in 1880 and his Ph.D. from Yale in 1884. After some years of discouragement and withdrawal, he returned to academic study at Cornell and finally received a teaching post at the University of Chicago in 1892. His first book, *The Theory of the Leisure Class* (1899), brought him immediate fame. It was followed by a number of sardonic volumes, of which his *The Higher Learning in America* (1918), from which this selection is taken, was among the most bitter. Veblen himself had had an uneven academic career, made more troubled by his own mordant and uncompromising personality. He was probably the most unsparing critic of American capitalist civilization. Among the outstanding works in an ample literature is Joseph Dorfman's full-length biography, *Thorstein Veblen and His America* (New York, 1934). For a brief interpretive study see David Riesman, *Thorstein Veblen* (New York, 1953).

For a generation past, while the American universities have been coming into line as seminaries of the higher learning, there has gone on a wide-reaching substitution of laymen in the place of clergymen on the governing boards. This progressive secularization is sufficiently notorious, even though there are some among the older establishments the terms of whose charters require a large proportion of clergymen on their boards. This secularization is entirely consonant with the prevailing drift of sentiment in the community at large, as is shown by the uniform and uncritical approval with which it is regarded. The substitution is a substitution of businessmen and politicians; which amounts to saying that it is a substitution of businessmen. So that the discretionary control in matters of university policy now rests finally in the hands of businessmen.

The reason which men prefer to allege for this state of things is the sensible need of experienced men of affairs to take care of the fiscal concerns of these university corporations; for the typical modern university is a corporation possessed of large property and disposing of large aggregate expenditures, so that it will necessarily have many and

Thorstein Veblen, *The Higher Learning in America: A Memorandum on the Conduct of Universities by Business Men* (New York, 1918), pp. 63–71, 100–105, 161–67, 220–25. Reprinted with the permission of Viking Press, Inc.

often delicate pecuniary interests to be looked after. It is at the same time held to be expedient in case of emergency to have several wealthy men identified with the governing board, and such men of wealth are also commonly businessmen. It is apparently believed, though on just what ground this sanguine belief rests does not appear, that in case of emergency the wealthy members of the boards may be counted on to spend their substance in behalf of the university. In point of fact, at any rate, poor men and men without large experience in business affairs are felt to have no place in these bodies. If by any chance such men, without the due pecuniary qualifications, should come to make up a majority, or even an appreciable minority of such a governing board, the situation would be viewed with some apprehension by all persons interested in the case and cognizant of the facts. The only exception might be cases where, by tradition, the board habitually includes a considerable proportion of clergymen:

> "Such great regard is always lent
> By men to ancient precedent."

The reasons alleged are no doubt convincing to those who are ready to be so convinced, but they are after all more plausible at first sight than on reflection. In point of fact these businesslike governing boards commonly exercise little if any current surveillance of the corporate affairs of the university, beyond a directive oversight of the distribution of expenditures among the several academic purposes for which the corporate income is to be used; that is to say, they control the budget of expenditures; which comes to saying that they exercise a pecuniary discretion in the case mainly in the way of deciding what the body of academic men that constitutes the university may or may not do with the means in hand; that is to say, their pecuniary surveillance comes in the main to an interference with the academic work, the merits of which these men of affairs on the governing board are in no special degree qualified to judge. Beyond this, as touches the actual running administration of the corporation's investments, income and expenditures,—all that is taken care of by permanent officials who have, as they necessarily must, sole and responsible charge of those matters. Even the auditing of the corporation's accounts is commonly vested in such officers of the corporation, who have none but a formal, if any, direct connection with the governing board. The governing board, or more commonly a committee of the board, on the other hand, will then formally review the balance sheets and bundles of vouchers duly submitted by the corporation's fiscal officers and their clerical force,—with such effect of complaisant oversight as will best be appreciated by any person who has had the fortune to look into the accounts of a large corporation.

So far as regards its pecuniary affairs and their due administration, the typical modern university is in a position, without loss or detriment, to dispense with the services of any board of trustees, regents, curators, or what not. Except for the insuperable difficulty of getting a hearing for such an extraordinary proposal, it should be no difficult matter to show that these governing boards of businessmen commonly are quite useless to the university for any businesslike purpose. Indeed, except for a stubborn prejudice to the contrary, the fact should readily be seen that the boards are of no material use in any connection; their sole effectual function being to interfere with the academic management in matters that are not of the nature of business, and that lie outside their competence and outside the range of their habitual interest.

The governing boards—trustees, regents, curators, fellows, whatever their style and title—are an aimless survival from the days of clerical rule, when they were presumably of some effect in enforcing conformity to orthodox opinions and observances, among the academic staff. At that time, when means for maintenance of the denominational colleges commonly had to be procured by an appeal to impecunious congregations, it fell to these bodies of churchmen to do service as sturdy beggars for funds with which to meet current expenses. So that as long as the boards were made up chiefly of clergymen they served a pecuniary purpose; whereas, since their complexion has been changed by the substitution of businessmen in the place of ecclesiastics, they have ceased to exercise any function other than a bootless meddling with academic matters which they do not understand. The sole ground of their retention appears to be an unreflecting deferential concession to the usages of corporate organization and control, such as have been found advantageous for the pursuit of private gain by businessmen banded together in the exploitation of joint-stock companies with limited liability.

The fact remains, the modern civilized community is reluctant to trust its serious interest to others than men of pecuniary substance, who have proved their fitness for the direction of academic affairs by acquiring, or by otherwise being possessed of, considerable wealth. It is not simply that experienced business men are, on mature reflection, judged to be the safest and most competent trustees of the university's fiscal interests. The preference appears to be almost wholly impulsive, and a matter of habitual bias. It is due for the greater part to the high esteem currently accorded to men of wealth at large, and especially to wealthy men who have succeeded in business, quite apart from any special capacity shown by such success for the guardianship of any institution of learning. Business success is by common consent, and quite uncritically, taken to be conclusive evidence of wisdom even in matters that have no relation to business affairs. So that it stands as a matter of course that businessmen must be preferred for the guardianship and control of that intellectual enterprise for the pursuit of which the university is established, as well as to take care of the pecuniary welfare of the university corporation. And, full of the same naïve faith that business success "answereth all things," these businessmen into whose hands this trust falls are content to accept the responsibility and confident to exercise full discretion in these matters with which they have no special familiarity. Such is the outcome, to the present date, of the recent and current secularization of the governing boards. The final discretion in the affairs of the seats of learning is entrusted to men who have proved their capacity for work that has nothing in common with the higher learning.

As bearing on the case of the American universities, it should be called to mind that the businessmen of this country, as a class, are of a notably conservative habit of mind. In a degree scarcely equalled in any community that can lay claim to a modicum of intelligence and enterprise, the spirit of American business is a spirit of quietism, caution, compromise, collusion, and chicane. It is not that the spirit of enterprise or of unrest is wanting in this community, but only that, by selective effect of the conditioning circumstances, persons affected with that spirit are excluded from the management of business, and so do not come into the class of successful businessmen from which the governing boards are drawn. American inventors are bold and resourceful, perhaps beyond the common run of their class elsewhere, but it has become a commonplace that American inventors habitually die poor; and one does not find them represented on the boards in question. American engineers and technologists are as good and efficient as their kind in other countries; but they do not as a class accumulate wealth enough to entitle them to sit on the directive board of any self-respecting university, nor can they claim even a moderate rank as "safe and sane" men of business. American explorers, prospectors and pioneers can not be said to fall short of the common measure in hardihood, insight, temerity or tenacity; but wealth does not accumulate in their hands, and it is a common saying, of them as of the inventors, that they are not fit to conduct their own (pecuniary) affairs; and the reminder is scarcely needed that neither they nor their qualities are drawn into the counsels of these governing boards. The wealth and the serviceable results that come of the endeavours of these enterprising and temerarious Americans habitually inure to the benefit of such of their compatriots as are endowed with a "safe and sane" spirit of "watchful waiting,"—of caution, collusion and chicane. There is a homely but well-accepted American colloquialism which says that "The silent hog eats the swill." . . .

While it is the work of science and scholarship, roughly what is known in American usage as graduate work, that gives the university its rank as a seat of learning and keeps it in countenance as such with laymen and scholars, it is the undergraduate school, or college, that still continues to be the larger fact, and that still engages the greater and more immediate attention in university management. This is due in part to received American usage, in part to its more readily serving the ends of competitive ambition; and it is a fact in the current academic situation which must be counted in as a chronic discrepancy, not to be got clear of or to be appreciably mitigated so long as business principles continue to rule.

What counts toward the advancement of learning and the scholarly character of the university is the graduate work, but what gives statistically formidable results in the way of numerous enrolment, many degrees conferred, public exhibitions, courses of instruction—in short what rolls up a large showing of turnover and output—is the perfunctory work of the undergraduate department, as well as the array of vocational schools latterly subjoined as auxiliaries to this end. Hence the needs and possibilities of the undergraduate and vocational schools are primarily, perhaps rather solely, had in view in the bureaucratic organization of the courses of instruction, in the selection of the personnel, in the divisions of the school year, as well as in the various accessory attractions offered, such as the athletic equipment, facilities for fraternity and other club life, debates, exhibitions and festivities, and the customary routine of devotional amenities under official sanction.

The undergraduate or collegiate schools, that now bulk so large in point of numbers as well as in the attention devoted to their welfare in academic management, have undergone certain notable changes in other respects than size, since the period of that shifting from clerical control to a business administration that marks the beginning of the current régime. Concomitant with their growth in numbers they have taken over an increasing volume of other functions than such as bear directly on matters of learning. At the same time the increase in numbers has brought a change in the scholastic complexion of this enlarged student body, of such a nature that a very appreciable proportion of these students no longer seek residence at the universities with a view to the pursuit of knowledge, even ostensibly. By force of conventional propriety a "college course"—the due term of residence at some reputable university, with the collegiate degree certifying honourable discharge—has become a requisite of gentility. So considerable is the resulting genteel contingent among the students, and so desirable is their enrolment and the countenance of their presence, in the apprehension of the university directorate, that the academic organization is in great part, and of strategic necessity, adapted primarily to their needs.

This contingent, and the general body of students in so far as this contingent from the leisure class has leavened the lump, are not so seriously interested in their studies that they can in any degree be counted on to seek knowledge on their own initiative. At the same time they have other interests that must be taken care of by the school, on pain of losing their custom and their good will, to the detriment of the university's standing in genteel circles and to the serious decline in enrolment which their withdrawal would occasion. Hence college sports come in for an ever increasing attention and take an increasingly prominent and voluminous place in the university's life; as do also other politely blameless ways and means of dissipation, such as fraternities, clubs, exhibitions, and the extensive range of extra-scholastic traffic known as "student activities."

At the same time the usual and average age of the college students has been slowly falling farther back into the period of adolescence; and the irregularities and uncertain temper of that uneasy period consequently are calling for more detailed surveillance and a more circumspect administration of college discipline. With a body of students whose everyday interest, as may be said without exaggeration, lies in the main elsewhere than in the pursuit of knowledge, and with an imperative tradition still standing over that requires the college to be (ostensibly at least) an establishment for the instruction of the youth, it becomes necessary to organize this instruction on a coercive plan, and hence to itemize the scholastic tasks of the inmates with great nicety of subdivision and with a meticulous regard to an exact equivalence as between the various courses and items of instruction to which they are to be subjected. Likewise as regards the limits of permissible irregularities of conduct and excursions into the field of sports and social amenities.

To meet the necessities of this difficult control, and to meet them always without jeopardizing the interests of the school as a competitive concern, a close-cut mechanical standardization, uniformity, surveillance and acountancy are indispensable. As regards the schedule of instruction, *bona fide* students will require but little exacting surveillance in their work, and little in the way of an apparatus of control. But the collegiate school has to deal with a large body of students, many of whom have little abiding interest in their academic work, beyond the academic credits necessary to be accumulated for honourable discharge, —indeed their scholastic interest may fairly be said to centre in unearned credits.

For this reason, and also because of the difficulty of controlling a large volume of perfunctory labour, such as is involved in undergraduate instruction, the instruction offered must be reduced to standard units of time, grade and volume. Each unit of work required, or rather of credit allowed, in this mechanically drawn scheme of tasks must be the equivalent of all the other units; otherwise a comprehensive system of scholastic accountancy will not be practicable, and injustice and irritation will result both among the pupils and the schoolmasters. For the greater facility and accuracy in conducting this scholastic accountancy, as well as with a view to the greater impressiveness of the published schedule of courses offered, these mechanical units of academic bullion are increased in number and decreased in weight and volume; until the parcelment and mechanical balance of units reaches a point not easily credible to any outsider who might naïvely consider the requirements of scholarship to be an imperative factor in academic administration. There is a well-considered preference for semi-annual or quarterly periods of instruction, with a corresponding time limit on the courses offered; and the parcelment of credits is carried somewhat beyond the point which this segmentation of the school year would indicate. So also there prevails a system of grading the credits allowed for the performance of these units of task-work, by percentages (often carried out to decimals) or by some equivalent scheme of notation; and in the more solicitously perfected schemes of control of this task-work, the percentages so turned in will then be further digested and weighed by expert accountants, who revise and correct these returns by the help of statistically ascertained index numbers that express the mean average margin of error to be allowed for each individual student or instructor.

In point of formal protestation, the standards set up in this scholastic accountancy are high and rigorous; in application, the exactions of the credit system must not be enforced in so inflexible a spirit as to estrange that much-desired contingent of genteel students whose need of an honourable discharge is greater than their love of knowledge. Neither must its demands on the student's time and energy be allowed seriously to interfere with those sports and "student activities" that make up the chief attraction of college life for a large proportion of the university's young men, and that are, in the apprehension of many, so essential a part in the training of the modern gentleman.

Such a system of accountancy acts to break the continuity and consistency of the work of instruction and to divert the interest of the students from the work in hand to the making of a passable record in terms of the academic "miner's inch." Typically, this miner's inch is measured in terms of standard text per time unit, and the immediate objective of teacher and student so becomes the compassing of a given volume of prescribed text, in print or lecture form,—leading up to the broad principle: *"Nichts als was im Buche steht."* Which puts a premium on mediocrity and perfunctory work, and brings academic life to revolve about the office of the Keeper of the Tape and Sealing Wax. Evidently this organization of departments, schedules of instruction, and scheme of scholastic accountancy, is a matter that calls for insight and sobriety on the part of the executive; and in point of fact there is much deliberation and solicitude spent on this behalf. . . .

To return to the academic personnel and their implication in these recurrent spectacles and amenities of university life. As was remarked above, apart from outside resources the livelihood that comes to a university man is, commonly, somewhat meagre. The tenure is uncertain and the salaries, at an average, are not large. Indeed, they are notably low in comparison with the high conventional standard of living which

is by custom incumbent on university men. University men are conventionally required to live on a scale of expenditure comparable with
that in vogue among well-to-do businessmen, while their university
incomes compare more nearly with the lower grades of clerks and
salesmen. The rate of pay varies quite materially, as is well known.
For the higher grades of the staff, whose scale of pay is likely to be
publicly divulged, it is, perhaps, adequate to the average demands
made on university incomes by polite usage; but the large majority of
university men belong on the lower levels of grade and pay; and on
these lower levels the pay is, perhaps, lower than any outsider appre-
ciates.

With men circumstanced as the common run of university men are,
the temptation to parsimony is ever present, while on the other hand,
as has already been noted, the prestige of the university—and of the
academic head—demands of all its members a conspicuously expensive
manner of living. Both of these needs may, of course, be met in some
poor measure by saving in the obscurer items of domestic expense, such
as food, clothing, heating, lighting, floor-space, books, and the like;
and making all available funds count toward the collective end of
reputable publicity, by throwing the stress on such expenditures as
come under the public eye, as dress and equipage, bric-a-brac, amusements, public entertainments, etc. It may seem that it should also be
possible to cut down the proportion of obscure expenditures for creature comforts by limiting the number of births in the family, or by
foregoing marriage. But, by and large, there is reason to believe that
this expedient has been exhausted. As men have latterly been at pains
to show, the current average of children in academic households is not
high; whereas the percentage of celibates is. There appears, indeed, to
be little room for additional economy on this head, or in the matter of
household thrift, beyond what is embodied in the family budgets already in force in academic circles.

So also, the tenure of office is somewhat precarious; more so than the
documents would seem to indicate. This applies with greater force to
the lower grades than to the higher. Latterly, under the rule of business principles, since the prestige value of a conspicuous consumption
has come to a greater currency in academic policy, a member of the
staff may render his tenure more secure, and may perhaps assure his
due preferment, by a sedulous attention to the academic social amenities, and to the more conspicuous items of his expense account; and he

will then do well in the same connection also to turn his best attention in the day's work to administrative duties and schoolmasterly discipline, rather than to the increase of knowledge. Whereas he may make his chance of preferment less assured, and may even jeopardize his tenure, by a conspicuously parsimonious manner of life, or by too pronounced an addiction to scientific or scholarly pursuits, to the neglect of those polite exhibitions of decorum that conduce to the maintenance of the university's prestige in the eyes of the (pecuniarily) cultured laity.

A variety of other untoward circumstances, of a similarly extra-scholastic bearing, may affect the fortunes of academic men to a like effect; as, e.g., unearned newspaper notoriety that may be turned to account in ridicule; unconventional religious, or irreligious convictions —so far as they become known; an undesirable political affiliation; an impecunious marriage, or such domestic infelicities as might become subject of remark. None of these untoward circumstances need touch the serviceability of the incumbent for any of the avowed, or avowable, purposes of the seminary of learning; and where action has to be taken by the directorate on provocation of such circumstances it is commonly done with the (unofficial) admission that such action is taken not on the substantial merits of the case but on compulsion of appearances and the exigencies of advertising. That some such effect should be had follows from the nature of things, so far as business principles rule.

In the degree, then, in which these and the like motives of expediency are decisive, there results a husbanding of time, energy and means in the less conspicuous expenditures and duties, in order to a freer application to more conspicuous uses, and a meticulous cultivation of the bourgeois virtues. The workday duties of instruction, and more particularly of inquiry, are, in the nature of the case, less conspicuously in evidence than the duties of the drawing-room, the ceremonial procession, the formal dinner, or the grandstand on some red-letter day of intercollegiate athletics.[1] For the purposes of a reputable notoriety the

---

[1] So, e.g., the well-known president of a well and favorably known university was at pains a few years ago to distinguish one of his faculty as being his "ideal of a university man"; the grounds of this invidious distinction being a lifelike imitation of a country gentleman and a fair degree of attention to committee work in connection with the academic administration; the incumbent had no distinguishing marks either as a teacher or as a scholar, and neither science nor letters will be found in his debt. It is perhaps needless to add that for reasons of invidious distinction, no names can be mentioned in this connection. It should be added, in illumination of the instance cited, that in the same

everyday work of the classroom and laboratory is also not so effective as lectures to popular audiences outside; especially, perhaps, addresses before an audience of devout and well-to-do women. Indeed, all this is well approved by experience. In many and devious ways, therefore, a university man may be able to serve the collective enterprise of his university to better effect than by an exclusive attention to the scholastic work on which alone he is ostensibly engaged.

Among the consequences that follow is a constant temptation for the members of the staff to take on work outside of that for which the salary is nominally paid. Such work takes the public eye; but a further incentive to go into this outside and non-academic work, as well as to take on supernumerary work within the academic schedule, lies in the fact that such outside or supernumerary work is specially paid, and so may help to eke out a sensibly scant livelihood. So far as touches the more scantily paid grades of university men, and so far as no alien considerations come in to trouble the working-out of business principles, the outcome may be schematized somewhat as follows. These men have, at the outset, gone into the university presumably from an inclination to scholarly or scientific pursuits; it is not probable that they have been led into this calling by the pecuniary inducements, which are slight as compared with the ruling rates of pay in the open market for other work that demands an equally arduous preparation and an equally close application. They have then been apportioned rather more work as instructors than they can take care of in the most efficient manner, at a rate of pay which is sensibly scant for the standard of (conspicuous) living conventionally imposed on them. They are, by authority, expected to expend time and means in such polite observances, spectacles and quasi-learned exhibitions as are presumed to enhance the prestige of the university. They are so induced to divert their time and energy to spreading abroad the university's good repute by creditable exhibitions of a quasi-scholarly character, which have no substantial bearing on a university man's legitimate interests; as well as in seeking supplementary work outside of their mandatory schedule, from which to derive an adequate livelihood and to fill up the comple-

---

university, by consistent selection and discipline of the personnel, it had come about that, in the apprehension of the staff as well as of the executive, the accepted test of efficiency was the work done on the administrative committees rather than that of the class rooms or laboratories.

ment of politely wasteful expenditures expected of them. The academic instruction necessarily suffers by this diversion of forces to extra-scholastic objects; and the work of inquiry, which may have primarily engaged their interest and which is indispensable to their continued efficiency as teachers, is, in the common run of cases, crowded to one side and presently drops out of mind. Like other workmen, under pressure of competition the members of the academic staff will endeavour to keep up their necessary income by cheapening their product and increasing their marketable output. And by consequence of this pressure of bread-winning and genteel expenditure, these university men are so barred out from the serious pursuit of those scientific and scholarly inquiries which alone can, academically speaking, justify their retention on the university faculty, and for the sake of which, in great part at least, they have chosen this vocation. No infirmity more commonly besets university men than this going to seed in routine work and extra-scholastic duties. They have entered on the academic career to find time, place, facilities and congenial environment for the pursuit of knowledge, and under pressure they presently settle down to a round of perfunctory labour by means of which to simulate the life of gentlemen. . . .

Business principles take effect in academic affairs most simply, obviously and avowably in the way of a business-like administration of the scholastic routine; where they lead immediately to a bureaucratic organization and a system of scholastic accountancy. In one form or another, some such administrative machinery is a necessity in any large school that is to be managed on a centralized plan; as the American schools commonly are, and as, more particularly, they aim to be. This necessity is all the more urgent in a school that takes over the discipline of a large body of pupils that have not reached years of discretion, as is also commonly the case with those American schools that claim rank as universities; and the necessity is all the more evident to men whose ideal of efficiency is the centralized control exercised through a system of accountancy in the modern large business concerns. The larger American schools are primarily undergraduate establishments,—with negligible exceptions; and under these current American conditions, of excessive numbers, such a centralized and bureaucratic administration appears to be indispensable for the adequate control of immature and reluctant students; at the same time, such an organization conduces to an excessive size. The immediate and visible effect of such a large and centralized administrative machinery is, on the whole, detrimental to scholarship, even in the undergraduate work; though it need not be so in all respects and unequivocally, so far as regards that routine training that is embodied in the undergraduate curriculum. But it is at least a necessary evil in any school that is of so considerable a size as to preclude substantially all close or cordial personal relations between the teachers and each of these immature pupils under their charge, as, again, is commonly the case with these American undergraduate establishments. Such a system of authoritative control, standardization, gradation, accountancy, classification, credits and penalties, will necessarily be drawn on stricter lines the more the school takes on the character of a house of correction or a penal settlement; in which the irresponsible inmates are to be held to a round of distasteful tasks and restrained from (conventionally) excessive irregularities of conduct. At the same time this recourse to such coercive control and standardization of tasks has unavoidably given the schools something of the character of a penal settlement.

As intimated above, the ideal of efficiency by force of which a large-scale centralized organization commends itself in these premises is that pattern of shrewd management whereby a large business concern makes money. The underlying business-like presumption accordingly appears to be that learning is a merchantable commodity, to be produced on a piece-rate plan, rated, bought and sold by standard units, measured, counted and reduced to staple equivalence by impersonal, mechanical tests. In all its bearings the work is hereby reduced to a mechanistic, statistical consistency, with numerical standards and units; which conduces to perfunctory and mediocre work throughout, and acts to deter both students and teachers from a free pursuit of knowledge, as contrasted with the pursuit of academic credits. So far as this mechanistic system goes freely into effect it leads to a substitution of salesmanlike proficiency—a balancing of bargains in staple credits—in the place of scientific capacity and addiction to study.

The salesmanlike abilities and the men of affairs that so are drawn into the academic personnel are, presumably, somewhat under grade in their kind; since the pecuniary inducement offered by the schools is rather low as compared with the remuneration for office work of a similar character in the common run of business occupations, and since businesslike employés of this kind may fairly be presumed to go unreservedly to the highest bidder. Yet these more unscholarly members of the staff will necessarily be assigned the more responsible and discretionary positions in the academic organization; since under such a scheme of standardization, accountancy and control, the school becomes primarily a bureaucratic organization, and the first and unremitting duties of the staff are those of official management and accountancy. The further qualifications requisite in the members of the academic staff will be such as make for vendibility,—volubility, tactful effrontery, conspicuous conformity to the popular taste in all matters of opinion, usage and conventions.

The need of such a businesslike organization asserts itself in somewhat the same degree in which the academic policy is guided by considerations of magnitude and statistical renown; and this in turn is somewhat closely correlated with the extent of discretionary power exercised by the captain of erudition placed in control. At the same time, by provocation of the facilities which it offers for making an impressive demonstration, such bureaucratic organization will lead the university management to bend its energies with somewhat more singleness to the parade of magnitude and statistical gains. It also, and in the same connection, provokes to a persistent and detailed surveillance and direction of the work and manner of life of the academic staff, and so it acts to shut off initiative of any kind in the work done.

Intimately bound up with this bureaucratic officialism and accountancy, and working consistently to a similar outcome, is the predilection for "practical efficiency"—that is to say, for pecuniary success—prevalent in the American community. This predilection is a matter of settled habit, due, no doubt, to the fact that preoccupation with business interests characterizes this community in an exceptional degree, and that pecuniary habits of thought consequently rule popular thinking in a peculiarly uncritical and prescriptive fashion. This pecuniary animus falls in with and reinforces the movement for academic accountancy, and combines with it to further a so-called "practical" bias in all the work of the schools.

It appears, then, that the intrusion of business principles in the universities goes to weaken and retard the pursuit of learning, and therefore to defeat the ends for which a university is maintained. This result follows, primarily, from the substitution of impersonal, mechanical relations, standards and tests, in the place of personal conference, guidance and association between teachers and students; as also from the imposition of a mechanically standardized routine upon the members of the staff, whereby any disinterested preoccupation with scholarly or scientific inquiry is thrown into the background and falls into abeyance. Few if any who are competent to speak in these premises will question that such has been the outcome. To offset against this work of mutilation and retardation there are certain gains in expedition, and in the volume of traffic that can be carried by any given equipment and corps of employés. Particularly will there be a gain in the statistical showing, both as regards the volume of instruction offered, and probably also as regards the enrolment; since accountancy creates statistics and its absence does not.

12. A. Lawrence Lowell Justifies the Control of Universities by Laymen, 1920

Lowell (1856–1943), a member of the celebrated Lowell clan, was born in Boston in December, 1856, and educated at Harvard, where he took his A.B. in 1877 and his law degree in 1880. For seventeen years he practised law in Boston, but in 1897 he turned to academic life, becoming a lecturer at Harvard. He was professor of government from 1900 to 1909, and in the latter year he accepted a call to the presidency, in which he served for a quarter of a century. He was a brilliant and original contributor to the study of politics, notable for his works on comparative government, political parties, and public opinion.

See Part X, Doc. 9; Henry A. Yeomans, *Abbot Lawrence Lowell* (Cambridge, 1948); Samuel Eliot Morison (ed.), *The Development of Harvard University, 1869–1929* (Cambridge, 1930), and the same author's *Three Centuries of Harvard* (Cambridge, 1936).

The question of the organization of universities and colleges, of the relation between the faculties and the governing boards, has of late years provoked much discussion, and it may not be out of place to consider the problem from the point of view of our own history and traditions. The form of corporate organization with which we are most familiar is the industrial. Concerns of this kind are created by capitalists who take all the risks of the business, conduct it through a board of

A. Lawrence Lowell, "The Relation between Faculties and Governing Boards," in *At War with Academic Traditions in America* (Cambridge, 1934), pp. 281–91. Reprinted with the permission of Harvard University Press.

directors whom they select, and employ the various grades of persons who serve it. The rights and duties of all persons employed are fixed by a contract with the corporation, that is with the owners of the property, and extend only so far as they are contractual. The main reason for the present form of industrial organization is that capital originates the enterprise and takes the risk. For that reason the board of directors is elected by the owners of the capital. Other kinds of industrial organization can be imagined, and have existed. A body of workers may get together, secure the use of capital at a fixed rate of interest, and conduct the business themselves. But whatever other forms of corporate organization might exist, it is natural that we should take our ideas from the one to which we are most accustomed, and apply them to institutions of all kinds. Yet to do so in the case of universities and colleges, where the conditions are very different, creates confusion and does harm. In this case, there are no owners who take the risk of the business. The institutions are not founded for profit, but for the purpose of preserving, transmitting, and increasing knowledge. The trustees, or whatever the members of the governing board may be called, although vested with the legal title to the property, are not the representatives of private owners, for there are none. They are custodians, holding the property in trust to promote the objects of the institution.

In the Middle Ages, when the universities first appeared, their property was held and the enterprise conducted practically by the academic body. This is the condition today of the colleges in Oxford and Cambridge, where the property of a college is vested in, and all its affairs are conducted by, the Fellows. In most places this state of things has not continued. In continental Europe the property has become vested, as a rule, in the State, which has also the ultimate power of control. In the American endowed universities it has become vested in a board, or boards, distinct, for the most part, from the teaching staff.

The transformation at Harvard is interesting. The College was founded in 1636 by a vote of the General Court appropriating money for that object. In 1642 an act was passed for the government of the College, placing the control in the hands of a Board of Overseers, composed of the Governor, the Deputy Governor, the Magistrates, and the Ministers of the six adjoining towns. This was followed in 1650 by another act creating a corporation, after the pattern of an English college, composed of the President, Treasurer, and five Fellows, but acting under the supervision of the Overseers. In the early days a part of the five Fellows were resident teachers, or, as they were then called, Tutors. They could not all have belonged to that class, because it was three-quarters of a century before there were as many as five teachers beside the President. As a rule the Tutors seem to have been young men who served a short time while awaiting a call to a parish. Perhaps it was for this reason that more mature men from outside were elected to the Corporation. Certain it is that by the time the charter was twenty-five years old, if not before, we find among the Fellows ministers of the neighboring towns.

Towards the close of the seventeenth century several attempts were made to revise the charter and introduce outside members, but for various reasons they all failed of adoption, and in 1707 the original charter was declared to be in force and has remained so ever since. The number of settled ministers among its members continued, however, to increase, until in 1721 there had been for some time only one Fellow in the Corporation who was a teacher at the College. In that year two of the Tutors presented to the Overseers a memorial claiming places in the Corporation, apparently on the ground that they were resident fellows giving instruction in the College and as such were the Fellows intended by the Charter of 1650. The Overseers sustained their claim; so did the House of Representatives, and the controversy dragged on for several years until it was finally brought to nought by the opposition of the Governor, backed eventually by his Council. The question was interwoven with an acute religious quarrel and a desire to remove the ministers in the Corporation whose ecclesiastical views were unpopular. Although the Corporation was not overborne, and the obnoxious Fellows were not removed, it yielded so far as to elect Tutors to the next vacancies that occurred, so that by 1725 three of them were members of the body.

There continued to be two or three Tutors or Professors in the Corporation until 1779, when a notable change began. Save during the confused period at the close of the seventeenth century, when new charters were put into operation only to be defeated by refusal of the royal approval, the non-resident Fellows, that is those who were not teachers at the College, were always ministers of the neighboring towns. But the convulsion of the Revolution, the growth of the University, and the financial difficulties caused by the war "indicated to the Corporation," in the words of Quincy, "the wisdom of selecting men of experience in business, and practically acquainted with public affairs." The first man of the new type was James Bowdoin, elected in 1779; and after that time almost every choice was of this kind, the occasional clergymen elected being chosen not because incumbents of the neighboring parishes but for their personal value as counsellors. The only teachers in the University thereafter elected Fellows were Professor Eliphalet Pearson, who served from 1800 to 1806, and Professor Ephraim W. Gurney, who served from 1884 to 1886.[1]

The change, however, did not take place without subsequent protest. In 1824 a memorial signed by eleven members of the instructing staff, claiming that according to the intent of the charter the Fellows ought to be resident, paid teachers, was presented first to the Corporation and then to the Overseers. While it was under consideration, a war of pamphlets was waged between John Lowell in opposition to the memorial and Edward Everett, then a Professor, in support of it. Each of them dealt keenly with as much of the early history of the College as he could find in contemporary records; and the impression left on the reader today is that the framers of the charter had in mind in a vague way the organization of an English college, but that the word "Fellow" was at that time used loosely, and that no distinct limitation was intended to be placed upon the selection. On January 25, 1825, the Overseers voted unanimously: (1) "That it does not appear to this board that the resident instructors of Harvard University have any exclusive right to be chosen members of the Corporation"; (2) "That it does not appear to this board that the members of the Corporation forfeit their offices by not residing in the College"; and (3) "That, in the opinion of this board, it is not expedient to express any opinion on the subject of future elections." The Overseers seem, however, to have thought that the instructing staff should be represented among the Fellows, for they refused to confirm the election to the next vacancy of Judge Jackson, one of their own number, until the Corporation stated its desire and purpose to elect a resident instructor a Fellow as soon as a proper occasion should offer. Within ten years Joseph Story and James Walker were appointed professors while Fellows, and retained their places on the Corporation; so that in a certain way the

---

[1] Joseph Story and James Walker were appointed professors while Fellows and retained their places upon the Corporation. Alexander Agassiz, who was a Fellow 1878–84, 1886–90, although during all that time Curator of the Museum of Comparative Zoölogy, was not a member of the instructing staff of the University.

instructing staff was represented there; but the proper occasion for electing a resident instructor did not come until 1884, and the professor so chosen continued a Fellow for only two years. In short, the question of giving to the instructing staff a representation upon the Corporation was virtually settled in 1825, has never been seriously revived, and there appears to be no desire to revive it today.

The transition which has taken place at Harvard is an example of the differentiation of functions that comes with the growth in size and complexity of an institution. More recent universities and colleges in America have not gone through this evolution, but have started with a body quite distinct from the instructing staff, and containing none of its members except the President; yet a body in which the title to the property and the complete ultimate control are legally vested. This legal situation has no doubt led to the present unfortunate tendency to regard the boards of trustees of institutions of learning as analogous to the boards of directors of business corporations, their legal position being the same. In spite, however, of a difference in legal organization, the best and most fruitful conception of a university or college is the ancient one of a society or guild of scholars associated together for preserving, imparting, increasing, and enjoying knowledge.

If a university or college is a society or guild of scholars why does it need any separate body of trustees at all? Why more than learned societies, which are obviously groups of scholars, and have no such boards recruited outside their own membership? One reason is to be found in the large endowments of our institutions of learning that require for investment a wide knowledge and experience of business affairs. In fact, as already pointed out, the vast complexity of a modern university has compelled specialization of functions, and one aspect thereof is the separation of the scholarly and business organs. Another reason is that higher education has assumed more and more of a public character; its importance has been more fully recognized by the community at large; it must therefore keep in touch with public needs, make the public appreciate its aims and the means essential to attain them; and for this purpose it must possess the influence and obtain the guidance of men conversant with the currents of the outer world.

There is a further reason more fundamental if less generally understood. Teaching in all its grades is a public service, and the administration of every public service must comprise both expert and lay elements. Without the former it will be ineffectual; without the latter it will become in time narrow, rigid, or out of harmony with its public object. Each has its own distinctive function, and only confusion and friction result if one of them strives to perform the function of the other. From this flows the cardinal principle, popularly little known but of well-nigh universal application, that experts should not be members of a non-professional body that supervises experts. One often hears that men with a practical knowledge of teaching should be elected to school boards, but unless they are persons of singular discretion they are likely to assume that their judgment on technical matters is better than that of the teachers, with effects that are sometimes disastrous. Laymen should not attempt to direct experts about the method of attaining results, but only indicate the results to be attained. Many years ago the Board of Overseers, after a careful examination, came to the conclusion that the writing of English by Harvard undergraduates was sadly defective. In this they were acting wholly within their proper province, and the result was a very notable improvement in the teaching of English composition. But if they had attempted to direct how the subject should be taught they would have been hopelessly beyond their province. They would not have known, as the instructing staff did, how it should be done, and they would have exasperated and disheartened the teachers.

But another question may well be asked. Granted that there should be both expert and non-professional elements in the management of a university or college, why in a society or guild of scholars should the non-professional organ be the final authority? For this there are three reasons. In the first place, so far as the object is public—and where teaching is conducted on a large scale the object cannot fail to concern the public deeply—that object must in the final analysis be determined by public, that is by non-professional, judgment. In an endowed university the governing board does not, indeed, represent the public in the sense that it is elected by popular vote, but it is not on that account any less truly a trustee for the public.

In the second place, the non-professional board is responsible for the financial administration, and the body that holds the purse must inevitably have the final control.

Thirdly, the non-professional board is the only body, or the most satisfactory body, to act as arbiter between the different groups of experts. Everyone knows that in an American university or college there is a ceaseless struggle for the means of development between different departments, and someone must decide upon the relative merits of their claims. In a university with good traditions the professors would be more ready to rely on the fairness and wisdom of a well constituted board of trustees than on one composed of some of their own number each affected almost unavoidably by a bias in favor of his particular subject.

Let it be observed, however, that although the governing board is the ultimate authority it is not in the position of an industrial employer. It is a trustee not to earn dividends for stockholders, but for the purposes of the guild. Its sole object is to help the society of scholars to accomplish the object for which they are brought together. They are the essential part of the society; and making their work effective for the intellectual and moral training of youth and for investigation is the sole reason for the existence of trustees, of buildings, of endowments, and of all the elaborate machinery of a modern university. If this conception be fully borne in mind most of the sources of dissension between professors and governing boards will disappear. At Harvard it has, I believe, been borne in mind as a deep-seated traditional conviction.

The differences between the ordinary industrial employment and the conduct of a society or guild of scholars in a university are wide. In the industrial system of employment the employee is paid according to the value of his services; he can be discharged when no longer wanted; and his duties are prescribed as minutely as may be desired by the employer. In a university there is permanence of tenure; substantial equality of pay within each academic grade; and although the duties in general are well understood, there is great freedom in the method of performing them. It is not difficult to see why each of these conditions prevails, and is in fact dependent upon the others. Permanence of tenure lies at the base of the difference between a society of scholars in a university and the employees in an industrial concern. In the latter, under prevailing conditions, men are employed in order to promote its earning power. In a university the concern exists to promote the work of the scholars and of the students whom they teach. Therefore in the industrial concern an unprofitable employee is discharged; but in the university the usefulness of the scholar depends largely upon his sense of security, upon the fact that he can work for an object that may be remote and whose value may not be easily demonstrated. In a university, barring positive misconduct, permanence of tenure is es-

sential for members who have passed the probationary period. The
equality of pay goes with the permanence of tenure. In an industrial
establishment the higher class of officials, those who correspond most
nearly to the grade of professors, can be paid what they may be worth
to the concern, and discharged if they are not worth their salaries. How
valuable they are can be fairly estimated, and their compensation can
be varied accordingly. But professors, whose tenure is permanent, cannot be discharged if they do not prove so valuable as they were expected
to be. Moreover it is impossible to determine the value of scholars in
the same way as that of commercial officials. An attempt to do so would
create injustice and endless discontent; and it would offer a temptation
to secure high pay, from their own or another institution, by a display
wholly inconsistent with the scholarly attitude of mind. The only
satisfactory system is that of paying salaries on something very close
to a fixed scale, and letting every professor do as good work as he can.
In an industrial concern the prospect of a high salary may be needed
to induce the greatest effort; but indolence among professors is seldom
found. They may, indeed, prefer a line of work less important than
some other; a man may desire to do research who is better fitted for
teaching, or he may prefer to teach advanced students when there is a
greater need of the strongest men in more elementary instruction; but
failure to work hard is rare.

The governing boards of universities having, then, the ultimate legal
control in their hands, and yet not being in the position of industrial
employers, it is pertinent to inquire what their relation to the professors
should be. If we bear in mind the conception of a society or guild of
scholars, that relation usually becomes in practice clear. The scholars,
both individually and gathered into faculties, are to provide the expert
knowledge; the governing board the financial management, the general coördination, the arbitral determinations, and the preservation of
the general direction of public policy. In the words of a former member
of the Harvard Corporation, their business is to "serve tables." The
relation is not one of employer and employed, of superior and inferior,
of master and servant, but one of mutual coöperation for the promotion
of the scholars' work. Unless the professors have confidence in the
singleness of purpose and in the wisdom of the governing boards, and
unless these in their turn recognize that they exist to promote the work
of the society of scholars the relations will not have the harmony that
they should. The relation is one that involves constant seeking of

opinion, and in the main the university must be conducted, not by authority, but by persuasion. There is no natural antagonism of interests between trustees and professors. To suggest it is to suggest failure in their proper relation to one another; to suppose it is to provoke failure; to assume it is to ensure failure.

The question has often been raised whether nominations for appointments should be made by the faculties or their committees, or by the president. It would seem that the less formal the provisions the better. Any president of a university or college who makes a nomination to the governing board without consulting formally or informally the leading professors in the subject and without making sure that most of them approve of it, is taking a grave responsibility that can be justified only by a condition that requires surgery. The objection to a formal nomination by a faculty, or a committee thereof, is that it places the members in an uncomfortable position in regard to their younger colleagues, and that it creates a tendency for the promotion of useful rather than excellent men. A wise president will not make nominations without being sure of the support of the instructing staff, but he may properly, and indeed ought to, decline to make nominations unless convinced that the nominee is of the calibre that ought to be appointed.

Attempts have been made to define, and express in written rules, the relation between the faculties and the governing boards; but the best element in that relation is an intangible, an undefinable, influence. If a husband and wife should attempt to define by regulations their respective rights and duties in the household, that marriage could safely be pronounced a failure. The essence of the relation is mutual confidence and mutual regard; and the respective functions of the faculties and the governing boards—those things that each had better undertake, those it had better leave to the other, and those which require mutual concession—are best learned from experience and best embodied in tradition. Tradition has great advantages over regulations. It is a more delicate instrument; it accommodates itself to things that are not susceptible of sharp definition; it is more flexible in its application, making exceptions and allowances which it would be difficult to foresee or prescribe. It is also more stable. Regulations can be amended; tradition cannot, for it is not made, but grows, and can be altered only by a gradual change in general opinion, not by a majority vote. In short, it cannot be amended, but only outgrown.

Part X

ACADEMIC FREEDOM IN THE
UNIVERSITY

T HE OLD-TIME COLLEGE, with its subservience to sects and its stress
on the transmission of the Western cultural heritage rather than on
the search for new knowledge, had never had a code or canon to protect the intellectual freedom of professors in their teaching or publication or religious profession (see Part V). But those who were committed to the development of genuine universities understood, as
Gilman put it in an early communication to the organizers of the
Johns Hopkins (Doc. 1), that a university is not worthy of the name
if it is "devoted to any other purpose than the discovery and promulgation of the truth." As Gilman and other great university promoters
clearly understood, first-rate scholars would not be chosen if qualities
other than scholarly or scientific competence were given weight in the
search for personnel; they would not join a university if some good
measure of scholastic and intellectual freedom were not among its
inducements; and they would not remain or perform at their best if
the institution did not make good on its promises.

But both within and without the universities some of the old con-
straints still existed and made themselves felt. The emergence of the
modern university coincided with the rise of nineteenth-century science; and the most powerful and liberating of all the scientific discoveries were those of Darwin. Academic scientists were quick to em-

brace Darwinism, to which almost all had been converted by the middle 1870's, and many of them came into conflict with the forces of sectarianism. One of these was Alexander Winchell, professor of geology and zoölogy at Vanderbilt University. Vanderbilt, having received a large donation from Commodore Vanderbilt in 1873, was in the process of refashioning itself from Central University, a school for the training of ministers, into a modern university; but the hand of ecclesiasticism, represented by the permanent president of the trustees, the Methodist bishop, Holland N. McTyeire, still rested heavily upon it. In 1878 Winchell wrote a tract on the pre-Adamite origin of man. Although the geologist was a conservative evolutionist, his work was a shock to the faithful, and after a short and bitter controversy with McTyeire (Docs. 2 and 3), he was dismissed from Vanderbilt. It was characteristic of the state of university development, however, that Vanderbilt, not Winchell, was the loser by the incident; for the scientist was immediately called to the chair of geology and paleontology at the University of Michigan.

The existence of academic freedom controversies during the university era was not in every respect a token of bad conditions; on the contrary, it often bespoke the aggressiveness and militancy of the professors in their new-found dedication to the advancement of knowledge and their growing confidence in the ultimate rightness of their case. An excellent illustration was the experience of the doughty William Graham Sumner, one of the most effective and popular teachers in the history of Yale. In the early 1870's Sumner took to using Herbert Spencer's book, *The Study of Sociology,* as a textbook for undergraduates in his classes in sociology. President Noah Porter, who was by no means a doctrinaire opponent of evolution and who was quite receptive to evolutionary teaching at Yale, felt nonetheless that a book like Spencer's, with its militant secularism, was unsuitable to undergraduates (Doc. 4). Sumner stood his ground and circulated among the officers of the Corporation a vigorous letter (Doc. 5) in which he appealed to the intrinsic usefulness of the work in question as the overriding consideration on which to decide whether or not it should be used. In the end Sumner decided that the publicity the dispute aroused had spoiled the usefulness of Spencer's work and withdrew it; but he had demonstrated that power of the professor to appeal to the increasingly solid sanctions of scientific value to justify classroom procedure. In spite of later controversies, over his tariff views and his opposition to the Spanish-American War, he continued to say in the classroom and write in his works exactly what he thought about current issues.

The rights of property, socialism, labor, currency, and other economic questions were also sources of intense academic controversy. Such questions became particularly acute during the agitated nineties, when the severe depression that began in 1893 caused many Americans to question the old economic verities for the first time. Among the outstanding victims was the young economist, Richard T. Ely, who was accused by a member of the board of regents of the University of Wisconsin of believing in "strikes and boycotts, justifying and encouraging the one while practicing the other." In the midst of the hysteria of 1894, the year of great Populist electoral successes and of Coxey's march on Washington, Ely's post was seriously endangered. But the academic profession, including his own host of affectionate students, rallied to his support (Doc. 6); and the regents, after trying Ely, issued a statement on academic freedom (Doc. 7) that Ely himself called "the strongest defense of freedom of instruction which was ever issued authoritatively from an American University." The regents, echoing Gilman's earlier words (Doc. 1), concluded that "we would be unworthy of the position we hold if we did not believe in progress in all departments of knowledge." They called in memorable language for "that continual and fearless sifting and winnowing by which alone the truth can be found." Ely, in being exonerated and retained, won a victory that all too many of his contemporaries might have envied. The general dissatisfaction aroused among academic men between 1890 and the First World War (see Part IX, Docs. 6, 7, 8, and 10), was created in part by continuing violations of academic freedom. It led, in 1915, to the formation of a protective professional organization, the American Association of University Professors, whose statement of academic freedom (Doc. 8) remained for a long time the classic attempt to codify the principles governing the rights of teachers. Such assertions were not without a high measure of assent among enlightened administrators, as was shown by the measured statements of President A. Lawrence Lowell of Harvard on the situation of academic freedom in wartime (Doc. 9).

Unfortunately Lowell's position was far from representative of university authorities during the First World War. President Nicholas Murray Butler of Columbia quite explicitly declared, shortly after

America's entry into the war, that participation in the war suspended all the normal commitments of the university to freedom for its members. "What had been tolerated before becomes intolerable now," he said. "What had been wrongheadedness was now sedition. What had been folly was now treason." This, he said, could be taken as "the University's last and only warning to any among us, if such there be, who are not with whole heart and mind and strength committed to fight with us to make the world safe for democracy." Such men indeed there were—among them the well-known Columbia psychologist, Professor J. McKeen Cattell, who had long been a rebel against American academic conditions (Part IX, Doc. 8) and a thorn in Butler's side. Cattell petitioned three congressmen to oppose the use of American conscripts on European battlefields; and when the congressmen complained to Butler about Cattell's action, he was dismissed by the trustees; they also dismissed Henry Wadsworth Longfellow Dana, a professor of literature who had encouraged students to agitate against the conscription bill while it was pending before Congress.

These dismissals were the last straw for another discontented Columbia professor, one of the most distinguished in its history—Charles A. Beard. In a letter to Butler (Doc. 10), in which he charged that the university was "under the control of a small and active group of trustees who have no standing in the world of education, who are reactionary and visionless in politics, narrow and medieval in religion," Beard presented his immediate resignation. In this letter he urged that the people "speedily enact the legislation which will strip the Boards of Trustees of their absolute power over the intellectual life of the institutions under their management." Beard was already widely (and on the whole rather falsely) reputed to be a radical because of his book on the Constitution and other writings, and his resignation drew venomous comment from ultra-conservatives, exemplified here by a savage *New York Times* editorial (Doc. 11) which declared that the professor, in resigning from Columbia, "has just rendered the greatest service it was in his power to give." The uproar aroused by his resignation impelled Beard to give a full rehearsal of his discontents with Columbia (Doc. 12), one of the most revealing documents of this whole era of agitation over university control.

1. Daniel Coit Gilman's Declaration on Intellectual Freedom, 1875

The institution we are about to organize would not be worthy the name of a University, if it were to be devoted to any other purpose than the discovery and promulgation of the truth; and it would be ignoble in the extreme if the resources which have been given by the Founder without restrictions should be limited to the maintenance of ecclesiastical differences or perverted to the promotion of political strife.

As the spirit of the University should be that of intellectual freedom in the pursuit of truth and of the broadest charity toward those from whom we differ in opinion it is certain that sectarian and partisan preferences should have no control in the selection of teachers, and should not be apparent in their official work.

Permit me to add that in a life devoted chiefly to the advancement of education I have found some of the best cooperators among those from whom I differed on ecclesiastical & political questions; and that I shall find it easy to work in Maryland with all the enlightened advocates and promoters of science and culture. To those who will labor for "The Johns Hopkins University,["] my grateful and cordial appreciation will go forth. We should hope that the Faculty soon to be chosen will be so catholic in spirit; so learned as to what has been discovered and so keen to explore new fields of research; so skillful as teachers; so co-operative as builders; and so comprehensive in the specialties to which they are devoted,—that pupils will flock to their instruction, first from Maryland and the states near to it,—but soon also from the remotest parts of the land. In seeking this result the Board may rely on my most zealous co-operation.

Gilman to Reverdy Johnson, January 30, 1875, in the Johns Hopkins University Trustees' Minutes, February 11, 1875, as quoted in Hugh Hawkins, *Pioneer: A History of the Johns Hopkins University, 1874–1889* (Ithaca, N.Y., 1960), pp. 22–23.

2. *Alexander Winchell's Encounter with Bishop McTyeire, 1878*

Alexander Winchell (1824–91) was born in Dutchess County, New York, and took his B.A. at Wesleyan (Connecticut) in 1847. After several years of teaching, writing, and lecturing on natural history he took the chair of geology, zoölogy, and botany at the University of Michigan in 1873. It was Michigan that again rescued him from his embarrassments at Vanderbilt by re-inviting him in 1879. Winchell later organized and became president of the Geological Society of America. This account comes from a letter to the Nashville newspaper, in which Winchell stated his case. See Richard Hofstadter and Walter P. Metzger, *The Development of Academic Freedom* (New York, 1955), pp. 330–32; Edwin Mims, *History of Vanderbilt University* (Nashville, 1946).

Forty-five minutes before the hour appointed for my late lecture at the University on "Man in the Light of Geology," I met Bishop Mc-Tyeire casually, and he embraced the opportunity to introduce a business which caused me extraordinary surprise. He said, in effect:

"We are having considerable annoyance from the criticisms which are passed by our people on some of your positions in matters of opinion, and it is likely to increase."

"What positions?" I asked.

"The positions taken in your pamphlet on Adamites and Pre-Adamites. Our people do not believe those things; they object to evolution."

"But," said I, "evolution is not professed in that pamphlet; there is not a single position in it which is not generally accepted, save the opinion that perhaps the black races are older than the white and brown."

"Well, our people are of the opinion that such views are contrary to the 'plan of redemption.'"

"The redemption of man," I replied, "could as well operate retroactively from Christ to races older than Adam, as from Christ to Abraham or Adam."

"I am not offering any objections myself," replied the Bishop, "but our people are complaining and the University will suffer, and I thought, perhaps, you might relieve us of our embarrassments. The

Nashville (Tenn.) *Daily American*, June 16, 1878.

Board," he continued, "will be in session in a few minutes, and they will meet again, after your lecture."

"I am unable to understand you. I think you exaggerate the complaints. Besides, the complaints are groundless."

"Well," said the Bishop, "the St. Louis *Advocate* has been hostiling the subject, and you know what the attitude of our *Advocate* has been."

The latter mention aroused equal surprise and indignation; for only a few days previously the Bishop, in a lengthy and confidential interview, which of course I am not at liberty to report, had made statements—revelations—to me, such that I did not expect to see Dr. Summers' perversions and insinuations turned to my disadvantage at the hand of a high official occupying an inside position. I reminded the Bishop of what he had said in the conversation with a view to inducing me to remain till commencement and deliver a lecture. "And you, yourself," I added, "proposed that I should lecture on Evolution."

"That is true," he replied, "for I wanted you to have an opportunity to put yourself right."

He did not explain whether he wished me to recant, or assemble [*sic*] or avow and defend my belief.

Referring again to the two discontented newspapers, he said, "These are feathers—straws."

"A great University ought to know how to withstand feathers and straws," said I.

"But they are likely to become stones," added the Bishop.

"These complaints are puerile," I continued. "They are themselves misconceptions of the facts, and they are prompted by bigotry. There has been no attempt to disprove the positions of my pamphlet. Besides that, I have not been heard; I have had no opportunity to explain or defend."

On repeating his request that I would relieve the Board of an embarrassment, I declared that I did not understand his meaning, and he then explained that he thought I might considerately "decline a reappointment."

"Are professors subject to annual appointment?" I asked.

"Well, yes; special professors are," he replied.

"No," said I, with indignation and scorn, "I will not, on such grounds, decline a reappointment. If the Board have the manliness to dismiss for cause, and declare the cause, I prefer they should do it. No power on earth could persuade me to decline. But the action which you foreshadow will be unjust and oppressive, as well as discrediting to the University. It will recoil upon its authors."

"We do not propose to treat you as the Inquisition treated Galileo," said the Bishop.

"But what you propose is the same thing," I rejoined. "It is ecclesiastical proscription for an opinion which *must be settled by scientific evidence.*"

3. Andrew D. White's Comment on the Winchell Case, 1878

This is part of a letter from White to Daniel Coit Gilman, written in Paris, July 24, 1878.
See Doc. 2.

By the way, I have been rather interested of late in the Winchell imbroglio at Nashville. What an idea of a University those trustees must have! What was tragical in Galileo's case is farcical in this. It appears that Bishop McTyeire took great pains to show to Winchell that there was no similarity between the two cases. Neither of them was aware that the Bishop used precisely the same argument to Winchell—indeed, virtually, *verbatim*—which Cardinal Bellarmin used to Galileo. Bellarmin told Galileo that his ideas "vitiated the plan of salvation"; McTyeire told Winchell that his ideas "were contrary to the plan of redemption." You see how great minds run in the same channel. What a theory of a University it is, to be sure; and yet that is what our opponents all over the country seem to be struggling for. Very hard to see that the world progresses any, if, instead of being in the hands of a Roman Catholic Cardinal, we are to fall into the hands of a Methodist Bishop. The real advance is the fact that they have no longer any power to oppose us with physical torture. In view of the spirit shown, and the articles written, against Winchell for his very moderate tendency to evolution doctrines, it would seem that the absence of torture is not due to any lack of will in the matter. I have written to Winchell for the entire facts, congratulating him on his conduct, which was very

---

Fabian Franklin, *The Life of Daniel Coit Gilman* (New York, 1910), pp. 344–45.

manly, and have a letter written to McTyeire making a similar request. I have not yet decided to send this. I want the facts for my new book.

Winchell is really superior to his reputation among scientific men. I have long known this. You must be aware of a tendency among the later generation of scientists to underrate everything except minute experiments or observation, or what they call "original research." I am not at all satisfied that they are entirely right. Indeed, I am convinced that they are in many respects wrong. There is a very striking remark in one of the last chapters of Buckle's first volume on this point, where he speaks of the piling-up of the results of experiment and observation in this age; and of the painful lack of deeply thoughtful men to group these results, and bring order out of chaos. Winchell seems to me, to some extent, one of these men. He has been fettered by his attempt to "reconcile Religion and Revelation"; but some of his work, I think, is valuable. Why not give him a chance to say his say in one of your lecture rooms? It would have an admirable effect in many ways. If we could afford it, I would not hesitate a moment. . . .

4. Noah Porter Objects to William Graham Sumner's Use of Herbert Spencer in Undergraduate Courses, 1879

William Graham Sumner (1840–1910) was born in Paterson, New Jersey, graduated from Yale in 1863, and further educated in Geneva, Göttingen, and Oxford. After a period in which he served as a rector and editor in the Protestant Episcopal church, he returned to Yale in 1872 to take the newly created chair of political and social science, in which he became possibly the most famous of Yale's teachers. His voluminous writings made him an important influence in political economy, sociology, and the writing of American history.

See Doc. 5 and, in addition to Starr, A. G. Keller, *Reminiscences (Mainly Personal) of William Graham Sumner* (New Haven, 1933). On Porter see Part VIII, Doc. 1.

My Dear Prof. Sumner:

The use of Spencer's 'Study of Sociology' as a textbook has made a great deal of talk and is likely to make still more. When the subject

---

Noah Porter to William Graham Sumner, New Haven, December 6, 1879, as printed in Harris E. Starr, *William Graham Sumner* (New York, 1925), pp. 346–47.

has been brought to my notice I have been able to reply that I have used his First Principles and his Psychology in my graduate classes with very great advantage. I cannot, however, think that this is or ought to be satisfactory, for the reason that the capacity of an undergraduate student when introduced to the elements of a science, to discriminate between the valid and the invalid is much below that of a graduate. A much more cogent reason is that the book itself is written very largely in a pamphleteering style, which is very unlike most of Spencer's more solid treatises. The freedom and unfairness with which it attacks every Theistic Philosophy of society and of history, and the cool and yet sarcastic effrontery with which he assumes that material elements and laws are the only forces and laws which any scientific man can recognize, seem to me to condemn the book as a textbook for a miscellaneous class in an undergraduate course. I ought to have examined the book sooner, but I feel assured that the use of the book will bring intellectual and moral harm to the students, however you may strive to neutralize or counteract its influence, and that the use of it will inevitably and reasonably work serious havoc to the reputation of the college. Having these opinions, I can do nothing else than express them, and as I am presumed to authorize the use of every textbook, I must formally object to the use of this.

Faithfully yours,
N. PORTER

5. Sumner's Review of His Controversy with Porter, 1881

See Doc. 4, and Hofstadter and Metzger, *The Development of Academic Freedom,* pp. 335–38.

DEAR SIR:

On the 27th of December, 1880, Pres. Porter wrote me a letter enclosing a copy of a paper read by him to the Corporation in June, 1880, about the disagreement between him and me arising from the use by

William Graham Sumner, "A private and personal communication to the members of the Corporation and to the permanent officers of Yale College" (New Haven, June, 1881), as quoted in Harris E. Starr, *William Graham Sumner* (New York, 1925), pp. 357–66.

me of Spencer's 'Study of Sociology' as a textbook. Up to the moment
of receiving this communication I had had no knowledge or suspicion
that Pres. Porter had carried that matter before the Corporation on an
ex-parte statement, although the President stated that he had previously
informed some other persons not members of the Corporation. I have,
although suffering much annoyance from misrepresentation and public abuse, entered into no explanations either in public or private, not
even in private conversation, until within a month, believing that public excitement and scandal could do no good. I have hoped that some
change in my own position, or in circumstances, would cause the point
in issue to solve itself. There are, however, very important interests at
stake, as I will show in this paper, and I cannot allow the annual meeting of the Corporation to pass, and another academic year to open,
without placing this matter before the college world as it stands in fact,
and extricating myself from a false position. It will be seen that Pres.
Porter's statement of the issue does not agree at all with my understanding of it.

The facts out of which the trouble arose are as follows: I am professor of political and social science. Four or five years ago my studies led
me to the conviction that sociology was about to do for the social sciences what scientific method has done for natural and physical science,
viz.: rescue them from arbitrary dogmatism and confusion. It seemed
to me that it belonged to me to give my students the advantage of the
new standpoint and method just as fast as I could win command of it
myself, just as every competent professor aims to set before his students
all the speculations, anticipations, efforts, extensions, reconstructions,
etc., etc., which mark the growth of the sciences. Sociology is so new
that only three or four persons in the world have written upon it as an
independent science. It is so difficult that very few indeed prosecute it,
or even know what it is. My studies have led me to independent convictions on certain points of detail in sociology, but I could not lecture
upon it. If I should pretend to do so I could only cram a half dozen
books and reproduce the material. It is a case for using a textbook.
When I looked about for one, Spencer's 'Study of Sociology' was the
only one which could come into account. I considered it very faulty as
a textbook, and I doubted if I could use it, but after considering the
matter for more than a year I made up my mind that the right and
interest of the students to learn something of sociology outweighed
any faults or deficiencies in the book, and that, for want of something

better, I could probably use this book as a means of giving the students the instruction to which they were entitled. In this judgment I did not take into account the religious character or tone of the book, which is not, so far as I can see, open to any fair objection. Mr. Spencer's religious opinions seem to me of very little importance in this connection, and, when I was looking for a book on sociology, the question whether it was a good or available book in a scientific point of view occupied my attention exclusively. Neither did I take into account the horror of Spencer's name, which, as I have since learned, is entertained by some people. If I had known of it, however, I should not have thought that it was a proper consideration to weigh much in the question which presented itself to me. I used the book for two years with the result of interesting and instructing the students, awakening their powers of observation and analysis as to social phenomena, and suggesting to them most valuable trains of thought as to practical questions in society. I have the amplest testimony that this was the most valuable and successful course ever given by me, and one of the most valuable given in the university. I have heard no word of complaint from the classes which used that book of any harm of any kind arising from the use of it, and to inquiries made by me and by others the invariable answer has been that no harm was done.

To all this Pres. Porter opposes in contradiction of the experience of two years his *a priori* judgment that Spencer's book cannot be used without corrupting the students.

Pres. Porter asserts that the Corporation did not intend, when I was appointed in 1872, that I should teach sociology in some sense which, he says, he will not undertake to define. I was not aware the Corporation had any intention in the matter except that I should bend all my efforts to study and teach political and social science according to the advance of sound learning in regard to those matters. I supposed that I was just as free as any other professor, no more and no less, and I did not know that I was limited by any intention. As sociology has taken shape as an independent science since I was appointed, the Corporation cannot have had any intention about it. It is not, therefore, of any importance that a definition of the kind of sociology from which I am debarred should be given, essential as such a definition would be if there were any such limitation as is asserted.

Pres. Porter affirms that sociology is inchoate and tentative. So is psychology; so are many new developments of physics, biology, and other sciences. To object to what is inchoate and tentative is to set up a closed canon of human learning.

He and I therefore came to an issue on which I was on the defensive. His position was that the students might better get no sociology than run the risk of getting agnosticism in getting sociology, and he even seems to maintain that they might better get no sociology than get it from a book by Spencer. I resisted this and maintained that they should have sociology anyhow, from the best means available, and I would not submit to a restraint the motive of which was consideration for metaphysical and theological interests. This is the only issue to which I have been a party. Pres. Porter has never prohibited the use of the book. He has never distinctly claimed authority to prohibit it. He said that, *if* he had any authority, he wanted to be understood as using all the authority he had against it. This left me to act on my own responsibility without coming into direct collision with him. I did so act and I have stood and now stand responsible for using the book.

It will be seen from this statement—

1. That I have had no controversy about the merits of Herbert Spencer's philosophy. Pres. Porter devoted a large part of his paper to stating his objections to that philosophy. This was quite irrelevant to any matter in which I am concerned, but I think it carried a suggestion that I had been teaching an infidel and pernicious philosophy, which is not true in fact. I have taught sociology as a science, from second causes only, and have not meddled with anything outside of my department. In my controversy with Pres. Porter I did not defend agnosticism; I resisted obscurantism.

2. I have had no controversy about the use of a book by Spencer, as an independent and substantive question. I should be very glad if I could obtain my ends by the use of a book to which no one could make either reasonable or unreasonable objection, but I have refused to sacrifice my ends to a silly horror of Spencer's name, or a prejudice against his works. Pres. Porter has used Spencer's books, as he stated in his paper. I had no reason to suppose that Spencer's writings were ruled out. Pres. Porter devoted by far the largest part of his paper to an elaborate argument to prove: 1. That he is glad to have the young men study Spencer's philosophical writings with him, because he is able by using those writings to overthrow Spencer's philosophy; 2. That Spencer's non-philosophical works could not be used by another gentleman (me) without inculcating Spencer's philosophy. In this view of

the matter the use of Spencer's books is a privilege of the President and his use of them does not, then, constitute a precedent for anybody else; but I confess that this view of the matter never suggested itself to me. I may add, in regard to the "maturity" of the students to whom I taught sociology, that they were the same students, at just the same point in their course (second term of senior year), as those to whom Pres. Porter taught Spencer's philosophy.

3. I have had no controversy about the merits of this particular treatise: 'The Study of Sociology.' Pres. Porter has offered me such a controversy both in public and private. I have declined to enter upon it. I have my well-settled opinion about the merits and faults of that book for my purposes, and I could give them if I saw proper occasion. I think I am also in a position to estimate the correctness and fairness of Pres. Porter's strictures on the book, but what could be gained by an argument about that question? Where should it be carried on? Who wants to hear it? I thought that it belonged to me to consider and decide the practical question on my responsibility. I did it and I take the responsibility. Will the Corporation say that Spencer's Study of Sociology is such a book that I ought to be disciplined for using it, or is it such a book that public opinion would sustain them in so deciding? It certainly is not. Cases unfortunately happen very often in life where one has to do without the unanimous approval which it would be pleasant to possess. I suppose this is one of those cases.

4. I have had no controversy on the question whether the President has a veto on textbooks. I do not admit that he has it, and I do not know of any college officer who admits it, but I have not raised that question. It is plain that if a professor is indiscreet, silly, negligent, incompetent, immoral, or otherwise unfit for his position, he ought to be disciplined, and it is plain that the President is the proper agent for bringing him to discipline. It requires no law to prove this. To use an improper textbook would simply be a case under this general principle. But it is plain also that the President can himself impose no sanctions whatever. He is only a reporting officer for that purpose. It is also plain that the Corporation cannot impose sanctions on the report of the President. They could not sustain him in a position of pure prerogative and sustain his authority at the expense of the rights of a professor. Hence if the law is asserted to mean more than that which understands itself, law or no law, it is ridiculous. If the law means only what every one fully admits, then we come back again to what I have al-

ready stated. I used the book and I take the responsibility. If called on to answer to the President's charges I will not object to his jurisdiction within the only form which it can take.

Pres. Porter, in the paper read to the Corporation, represented me as having yielded the point, and he gave assurances that the book would not be used again. Candor compels me to say that he was in error in this matter. I have never yielded the point or authorized any assurances that I would not use the book again, if I should still find myself so situated that I could not teach sociology without it. In January, 1881, the quesion came up again, no book yet having been published which I could use in the place of Spencer's book. But a new factor now came into account. There was reason to fear that, if I used the book, the students and the newspapers would be on the *qui vive* to see what would happen, and also that the students would watch and weigh every word said by me about the book, and report the same to the newspapers, more or less incorrectly, according to the evil modern custom. The consequences of using Spencer's book which I could foresee were, therefore, unedifying and mischievous, and I could not take the responsibility of bringing on these consequences. I suspended the use of the book. The consequence of the outside excitement and uproar which was stirred up in the Spring of 1880 (I know not by whom, but certainly against my most earnest efforts) has therefore been that the class of 1881 has had no opportunity to study sociology. I appended to my annual report the following protest: 'I now, therefore, append to this, my annual report, a formal and official protest against the interference with me in my rights and duty as an instructor which has led to this result, by which the students are deprived of a part of the benefits to which they are entitled in their course of study here, out of regard to metaphysical and theological interests which ought not to come into account in this connection.' So the matter now stands. I have made no concession. I suspended the use of the book out of regard to major considerations, but the matter is not settled at all. I consider that it involves rights and interests which no honest teacher ever ought to concede.

Certain misunderstandings have, unfortunately, been included in this matter. In his letter of December 27, Pres. Porter said: 'The communication was framed designedly so as to preclude the asking of any questions, the necessity of any discussion or passing any resolutions. A written resolution affirming or confirming the oldest form of the law was prepared by Pres. Woolsey, but, at my request, was not presented.'

I saw nothing ambiguous in this statement, and I proceeded to make my arrangements according to my understanding of it. On the first of May it became evident that the plans I had in mind would not be matured at present, and, in view of what it might be necessary to do, I called on Pres. Woolsey, to find out accurately the scope of his resolution. He said he did not recollect having prepared any resolution. In answer to an inquiry from me, Pres. Porter wrote: 'The written resolution which Pres. Woolsey proposed to offer, or not, as I should prefer, related to the power of the President in respect to textbooks and did not concern either your conduct or my own.' I then wrote again to Pres. Porter as follows: 'I understood from yours of Dec. 27, 1880, that you read to the Corporation, at their June meeting, 1880, a paper containing, with other things, an *ex-parte* statement of facts about the use of Spencer's Study of Sociology as a textbook, and about conversations between you and me in that regard. I understood that, thereupon, Pres. W. proposed to offer a resolution which he had written, affirming the "old rule" (which I supposed to be, as you now state, an alleged rule that the President has a veto on the use of all textbooks in the Academical Dept.). I understood that this was intended as a solution of the subject which your paper brought before the Corporation, and that it would have been a vote of censure on me, but that you protected me from it by asking Dr. W. to withhold it. I inferred that you had done this by the assurance which you gave that the book would not be used again. . . . I politely and respectfully beg you to point out wherin I am in error in the understanding of your letter which I have above recited.' To this he answered: 'Allow me to correct what seems a misunderstanding on your part. The resolution prepared by Pres. Woolsey I am sure was not intended "as a vote of censure on you," but solely as a more explicit affirmation of the power of the President which had been questioned by some members of the Faculty, and which Pres. Woolsey supposed I might desire should be phrased in more positive terms.' To this I replied: 'I do not see the appositeness of any such resolution (as that which Pres. Woolsey prepared) aside from the sociology question, although there may have been other occasion for it (and I do not know of any member of the Faculty who admits the rule as claimed by you), but I do not see the point of informing me of Dr. W's. resolution, especially in this connection, if it had nothing to do with the subject matter of the paper of which you were sending me a copy. I do not argue, I only justify my inference.' Here the correspondence ended. It had, at any rate, corrected the impression derived by me from Pres. Porter's letter of Dec. 27 that the Corporation had reached a decision about the sociology matter which they had been prevented from recording in a formal vote framed by Pres. Woolsey, only by the interposition of Pres. Porter. My position, therefore, was by no means such as I had supposed from January to May. The case was not closed and the way was open for such further steps as I thought proper. I have seen nothing more proper than the present communication.

I have always considered that the Corporation did me great honor when they elected me, a young and untried man, to this important chair. I have tried to justify their confidence. I threw myself into the work of my department and of the college with all my might. I had no other interest or ambition. I have refused (until within six months) to entertain any proposition to go away or to go into other work. It is impossible, however, for me to submit to interference in my work. So long as I am interfered with, my relations to the college are constrained, unsatisfactory, and precarious. I have already lost ground in my work which I had won by great exertion, and I have been forced to suspend further plans on account of the interference to which I have been subjected. While my personal relations to the college are in this uncertain condition I cannot coöperate with my colleagues in planning about the institution as I have been accustomed to do. I seek no action and I deprecate none. I simply seek to place myself on the same plane in regard to this matter on which Pres. Porter placed himself a year ago, and to correct any false impressions which may exist as to my position in the minds of members of the Corporation who heard his paper. I also think that my colleagues ought to know about this matter, for I have been in a false position in respect to them for a year, and as I do not know how or why to select some for my confidence I include all.

Yours respectfully,

W. G. SUMNER

6. David Kinley Recalls the Attack on Richard T. Ely, 1894

During his professorship of political economy and directorate of the school of economics, politics, and history at the University of Wisconsin, Richard T. Ely (1854–1943) probably trained more American economists than any other teacher of his day. Born in upstate New York, Ely graduated from Columbia in 1876, received his doctorate at Heidelberg in 1879, and took the chair of political economy at the Johns Hopkins University in 1881. Upon moving to Wisconsin in 1892, he became a leading figure in the move to identify the social sciences with the problems of American life (see Doc. 8).

Ely was accompanied to Wisconsin by a former student at the Hopkins, David Kinley (1861–1944), a Yale graduate of 1884. Kinley left Wisconsin in 1893 for the University of Illinois where he was a prominent figure throughout his academic lifetime.

See Doc. 7.

Aside from my University duties there were several events in the next few years in which I felt I must take an active interest. The first of these was an attack on my teacher and friend, Dr. Ely. It is a weakness to which we all yield at times, in matters that interest us, to base our opinions on preconceived notions or prejudices rather than on accurate information. Of such a nature were charges brought against Ely. I happened to be spending my vacation in Madison in the summer of 1894 when the State Superintendent of Education in Wisconsin published a letter in the New York *Nation* charging Dr. Ely with aiding and abetting a printers' strike in Madison, in conjunction with a "walking labor delegate," and also with teaching socialism. I did not hear of the attack until I reached Madison and was surprised to find that not a voice had been raised in public in his defense, although criticism of the attack was general in private conversation. I knew personally that the first charge was untrue and that the second was largely a matter of definition and personal opinion. I had heard most of Ely's lectures through three years and I could not regard him as a socialist. So without consulting him, as he was then lecturing at a Chautauqua, I took up his defense.

A Yale classmate of mine, Amos Wilder, later U.S. Consul General

David Kinley, *Autobiography* (Urbana, Ill., 1949), pp. 30–31. Reprinted with the permission of University of Illinois Press.

at Shanghai, had just bought the Madison *State Journal*. Amos permitted me to write a note for the *Journal,* in which I treated the charges lightly and suggested that they had slight basis. That stirred interest, and Ely's friends began to come into the open. Among others, Mrs. Charles Kendall Adams, wife of the president of the University, wrote and thanked me. I called on the superintendent, Ely's accuser, and suggested that he withdraw his charges; but he refused, and I began to plan a defense. At Ely's request I employed Hon. Burr Jones, one of Madison's ablest lawyers, to prepare for the hearing which was soon to be held by a committee of the Board of Regents. I then wrote a letter to the walking delegate, whose name and address I did not know, asking him to describe the man he had interviewed. I took the letter to the local printers' union and asked them to supply name and address and forward the letter. They did so and he answered. Of course the letter was not legal evidence, and on motion of the plaintiff's attorney was not admitted at the first meeting of the trial committee. But the plaintiff failed to appear at the second meeting and the letter was introduced. It proved clearly that Ely was not the person to whom the delegate had spoken. The trial broke down, and not only was Dr. Ely fully exonerated but the regents adopted a resolution in favor of freedom of discussion in teaching. In his autobiography Dr. Ely kindly refers to my action in this episode, but I was only discharging a debt of gratitude and affection, and defending our profession.

7. The Wisconsin Regents Speak for Academic Freedom, 1894

See also Doc. 6; Richard T. Ely, *Ground under Our Feet* (New York, 1938), pp. 223–32; and Hofstadter and Metzger, *The Development of Academic Freedom,* pp. 425–36, including the citations therein.

As Regents of the University with over a hundred instructors supported by nearly two millions of people who hold a vast diversity of views regarding the great questions which at present agitate the hu-

"Report of the Investigating Committee," in Papers of the Board of Regents, September 18, 1894, University of Wisconsin, as quoted in Merle Curti and Vernon Carstensen, *The University of Wisconsin, 1848–1925* (Madison, 1949), I, 525.

man mind, we could not for a moment think of recommending the dismissal or even the criticism of a teacher even if some of his opinion should, in some quarters, be regarded as visionary. Such a course would be equivalent to saying that no professor should teach anything which is not accepted by everybody as true. This would cut our curriculum down to very small proportions. We cannot for a moment believe that knowledge has reached its final goal, or that the present condition of society is perfect. We must, therefore, welcome from our teachers such discussions as shall suggest the means and prepare the way by which knowledge may be extended, present evils . . . removed, and others prevented.

We feel that we would be unworthy [of] the position we hold if we did not believe in progress in all departments of knowledge. In all lines of academic investigation it is of the utmost importance that the investigator should be absolutely free to follow the indications of truth wherever they may lead.

Whatever may be the limitations which trammel inquiry elsewhere we believe the great state University of Wisconsin should ever encourage that continual and fearless sifting and winnowing by which alone the truth can be found.

8. The A.A.U.P.'s "General Declaration of Principles," 1915

The exact authorship of this report is not a matter of record, but Professor E. R. A. Seligman, the Columbia economist, was chairman of the committee that prepared it and seems to have had a major role in its drafting. Seligman (1861–1939), the offspring of an important New York banking family, graduated from Columbia in 1879, studied for several years in Germany and France, and then returned to Columbia where he became a professor in 1888. He became a distinguished authority on public finance and an important adviser to local, state, and national political leaders. With Richard T. Ely (see Docs. 6–7) he participated in the organization of the American Economic Association in 1885, and thirty years later was one of

---

American Association of University Professors, *Report of the Committee on Academic Freedom and Tenure* (n.p., December, 1915), pp. 6–29.

the most prominent organizers of the American Association of University Professors, of which he became president in 1921. On Seligman see the sketch by Joseph Dorfman in *Dictionary of American Biography*, Supplement Two. Walter P. Metzger analyzes the philosophy of this statement in Hofstadter and Metzger, *The Development of Academic Freedom*, pp. 407–12. See also the important subsequent statements on academic freedom and tenure by the A.A.U.P. in 1925 and 1940, reprinted in "Academic Freedom and Tenure," *A.A.U.P. Bulletin*, XLIII (Spring, 1957), 113–18.

I. GENERAL DECLARATION OF PRINCIPLES

The term "academic freedom" has traditionally had two applications —to the freedom of the teacher and to that of the student, *Lehrfreiheit* and *Lernfreiheit*. It need scarcely be pointed out that the freedom which is the subject of this report is that of the teacher. Academic freedom in this sense comprises three elements: freedom of inquiry and research; freedom of teaching within the university or college; and freedom of extra-mural utterance and action. The first of these is almost everywhere so safeguarded that the dangers of its infringement are slight. It may therefore be disregarded in this report. The second and third phases of academic freedom are closely related, and are often not distinguished. The third, however, has an importance of its own, since of late it has perhaps more frequently been the occasion of difficulties and controversies than has the question of freedom of intra-academic teaching. All five of the cases which have recently been investigated by committees of this Association have involved, at least as one factor, the right of university teachers to express their opinions freely outside the university or to engage in political activities in their capacity as citizens. The general principles which have to do with freedom of teaching in both these senses seem to the committee to be in great part, though not wholly, the same. In this report, therefore, we shall consider the matter primarily with reference to freedom of teaching within the university, and shall assume that what is said thereon is also applicable to the freedom of speech of university teachers outside their institutions, subject to certain qualifications and supplementary considerations which will be pointed out in the course of the report.

An adequate discussion of academic freedom must necessarily consider three matters: (1) the scope and basis of the power exercised by those bodies having ultimate legal authority in academic affairs; (2) the nature of the academic calling; (3) the function of the academic institution or university.

1. Basis of academic authority

American institutions of learning are usually controlled by boards of trustees as the ultimate repositories of power. Upon them finally it devolves to determine the measure of academic freedom which is to be realized in the several institutions. It therefore becomes necessary to inquire into the nature of the trust reposed in these boards, and to ascertain to whom the trustees are to be considered accountable.

The simplest case is that of a proprietary school or college designed for the propagation of specific doctrines prescribed by those who have furnished its endowment. It is evident that in such cases the trustees are bound by the deed of gift, and, whatever be their own views, are obligated to carry out the terms of the trust. If a church or religious denomination establishes a college to be governed by a board of trustees, with the express understanding that the college will be used as an instrument of propaganda in the interests of the religious faith professed by the church or denomination creating it, the trustees have a right to demand that everything be subordinated to that end. If, again, as has happened in this country, a wealthy manufacturer establishes a special school in a University in order to teach, among other things, the advantages of a protective tariff, or if, as is also the case, an institution has been endowed for the purpose of propagating the doctrines of socialism, the situation is analogous. All of these are essentially proprietary institutions, in the moral sense. They do not, at least as regards one particular subject, accept the principles of freedom of inquiry, of opinion, and of teaching; and their purpose is not to advance knowledge by the unrestricted research and unfettered discussion of impartial investigators, but rather to subsidize the promotion of the opinions held by the persons, usually not of the scholar's calling, who provide the funds for their maintenance. Concerning the desirability of the existence of such institutions, the committee does not desire to express any opinion. But it is manifestly important that they should not be permitted to sail under false colors. Genuine boldness and thoroughness of inquiry, and freedom of speech, are scarcely reconcilable with the prescribed inculcation of a particular opinion upon a controverted question.

Such institutions are rare, however, and are becoming ever more rare. We still have, indeed, colleges under denominational auspices; but very few of them impose upon their trustees responsibility for the

spread of specific doctrines. They are more and more coming to occupy, with respect to the freedom enjoyed by the members of their
teaching bodies, the position of untrammeled institutions of learning,
and are differentiated only by the natural influence of their respective
historic antecedents and traditions.

Leaving aside, then, the small number of institutions of the proprietary type, what is the nature of the trust reposed in the governing
boards of the ordinary institutions of learning? Can colleges and universities that are not strictly bound by their founders to a propagandist
duty ever be included in the class of institutions that we have just
described as being in a moral sense proprietary? The answer is clear.
If the former class of institutions constitute a private or proprietary
trust, the latter constitute a public trust. The trustees are trustees for
the public. In the case of our state universities this is self-evident. In
the case of most of our privately endowed institutions, the situation is
really not different. They cannot be permitted to assume the proprietary attitude and privilege, if they are appealing to the general public
for support. Trustees of such universities or colleges have no moral
right to bind the reason or the conscience of any professor. All claim
to such right is waived by the appeal to the general public for contributions and for moral support in the maintenance, not of a propaganda, but of a non-partisan institution of learning. It follows that
any university which lays restrictions upon the intellectual freedom of
its professors proclaims itself a proprietary institution, and should be
so described whenever it makes a general appeal for funds; and the
public should be advised that the institution has no claim whatever to
general support or regard.

This elementary distinction between a private and a public trust is
not yet so universally accepted as it should be in our American institutions. While in many universities and colleges the situation has
come to be entirely satisfactory, there are others in which the relation
of trustees to professors is apparently still conceived to be analogous to
that of a private employer to his employees; in which, therefore, trustees are not regarded as debarred by any moral restrictions, beyond
their own sense of expediency, from imposing their personal opinions
upon the teaching of the institution, or even from employing the
power of dismissal to gratify their private antipathies or resentments.
An eminent university president thus described the situation not many
years since:

"In the institutions of higher education the board of trustees is the body on whose discretion, good feeling, and experience the securing of academic freedom now depends. There are boards which leave nothing to be desired in these respects; but there are also numerous bodies that have everything to learn with regard to academic freedom. These barbarous boards exercise an arbitrary power of dismissal. They exclude from the teachings of the university unpopular or dangerous subjects. In some states they even treat professors' positions as common political spoils; and all too frequently, both in state and endowed institutions, they fail to treat the members of the teaching staff with that high consideration to which their functions entitle them."*

It is, then, a prerequisite to a realization of the proper measure of academic freedom in American institutions of learning, that all boards of trustees should understand—as many already do—the full implications of the distinction between private proprietorship and a public trust.

2. *The nature of the academic calling*

The above-mentioned conception of a university as an ordinary business venture, and of academic teaching as a purely private employment, manifests also a radical failure to apprehend the nature of the social function discharged by the professional scholar. While we should be reluctant to believe that any large number of educated persons suffer from such a misapprehension, it seems desirable at this time to restate clearly the chief reasons, lying in the nature of the university teaching profession, why it is to the public interest that the professorial office should be one both of dignity and of independence.

If education is the corner stone of the structure of society and if progress in scientific knowledge is essential to civilization, few things can be more important than to enhance the dignity of the scholar's profession, with a view to attracting into its ranks men of the highest ability, of sound learning, and of strong and independent character. This is the more essential because the pecuniary emoluments of the profession are not, and doubtless never will be, equal to those open to the more successful members of other professions. It is not, in our opinion, desirable that men should be drawn into this profession by

---

* From "Academic Freedom," an address delivered before the New York Chapter of the Phi Beta Kappa Society at Cornell University, May 29, 1907, by Charles William Eliot, LL.D., President of Harvard University.

the magnitude of the economic rewards which it offers; but it is for this reason the more needful that men of high gifts and character should be drawn into it by the assurance of an honorable and secure position, and of freedom to perform honestly and according to their own consciences the distinctive and important function which the nature of the profession lays upon them.

That function is to deal at first hand, after prolonged and specialized technical training, with the sources of knowledge; and to impart the results of their own and of their fellow-specialists' investigations and reflection, both to students and to the general public, without fear or favor. The proper discharge of this function requires (among other things) that the university teacher shall be exempt from any pecuniary motive or inducement to hold, or to express, any conclusion which is not the genuine and uncolored product of his own study or that of fellow-specialists. Indeed, the proper fulfilment of the work of the professorate requires that our universities shall be so free that no fair-minded person shall find any excuse for even a suspicion that the utterances of university teachers are shaped or restricted by the judgment, not of professional scholars, but of inexpert and possibly not wholly disinterested persons outside of their ranks. The lay public is under no compulsion to accept or to act upon the opinions of the scientific experts whom, through the universities, it employs. But it is highly needful, in the interest of society at large, that what purport to be the conclusions of men trained for, and dedicated to, the quest for truth, shall in fact be the conclusions of such men, and not echoes of the opinions of the lay public, or of the individuals who endow or manage universities. To the degree that professional scholars, in the formation and promulgation of their opinions, are, or by the character of their tenure appear to be, subject to any motive other than their own scientific conscience and a desire for the respect of their fellow-experts, to that degree the university teaching profession is corrupted; its proper influence upon public opinion is diminished and vitiated; and society at large fails to get from its scholars, in an unadulterated form, the peculiar and necessary service which it is the office of the professional scholar to furnish.

These considerations make still more clear the nature of the relationship between university trustees and members of university faculties. The latter are the appointees, but not in any proper sense the employees, of the former. For, once appointed, the scholar has professional functions to perform in which the appointing authorities have neither competency nor moral right to intervene. The responsibility of the university teacher is primarily to the public itself, and to the judgment of his own profession; and while, with respect to certain external conditions of his vocation, he accepts a responsibility to the authorities of the institution in which he serves, in the essentials of his professional activity his duty is to the wider public to which the institution itself is morally amenable. So far as the university teacher's independence of thought and utterance is concerned—though not in other regards—the relationship of professor to trustees may be compared to that between judges of the Federal courts and the Executive who appoints them. University teachers should be understood to be, with respect to the conclusions reached and expressed by them, no more subject to the control of the trustees, than are judges subject to the control of the President, with respect to their decisions; while of course, for the same reason, trustees are no more to be held responsible for, or to be presumed to agree with, the opinions or utterances of professors, than the President can be assumed to approve of all the legal reasonings of the courts. A university is a great and indispensable organ of the higher life of a civilized community, in the work of which the trustees hold an essential and highly honorable place, but in which the faculties hold an independent place, with quite equal responsibilities—and in relation to purely scientific and educational questions, the primary responsibility. Misconception or obscurity in this matter has undoubtedly been a source of occasional difficulty in the past, and even in several instances during the current year, however much, in the main, a long tradition of kindly and courteous intercourse between trustees and members of university faculties has kept the question in the background.

3. The function of the academic institution

The importance of academic freedom is most clearly perceived in the light of the purposes for which universities exist. These are three in number:

A. To promote inquiry and advance the sum of human knowledge.

B. To provide general instruction to the students.

C. To develop experts for various branches of the public service.

Let us consider each of these. In the earlier stages of a nation's intellectual development, the chief concern of educational institutions is to train the growing generation and to diffuse the already accepted knowledge. It is only slowly that there comes to be provided in the highest institutions of learning the opportunity for the gradual wresting from nature of her intimate secrets. The modern university is becoming more and more the home of scientific research. There are three fields of human inquiry in which the race is only at the beginning: natural science, social science, and philosophy and religion, dealing with the relations of man to outer nature, to his fellow men, and to the ultimate realities and values. In natural science all that we have learned but serves to make us realize more deeply how much more remains to be discovered. In social science in its largest sense, which is concerned with the relations of men in society and with the conditions of social order and well-being, we have learned only an adumbration of the laws which govern these vastly complex phenomena. Finally, in the spiritual life, and in the interpretation of the general meaning and ends of human existence and its relation to the universe, we are still far from a comprehension of the final truths, and from a universal agreement among all sincere and earnest men. In all of these domains of knowledge, the first condition of progress is complete and unlimited freedom to pursue inquiry and publish its results. Such freedom is the breath in the nostrils of all scientific activity.

The second function—which for a long time was the only function—of the American college or university is to provide instruction for students. It is scarcely open to question that freedom of utterance is as important to the teacher as it is to the investigator. No man can be a successful teacher unless he enjoys the respect of his students, and their confidence in his intellectual integrity. It is clear, however, that this confidence will be impaired if there is suspicion on the part of the student that the teacher is not expressing himself fully or frankly, or that college and university teachers in general are a repressed and intimidated class who dare not speak with that candor and courage which youth always demands in those whom it is to esteem. The average student is a discerning observer, who soon takes the measure of his instructor. It is not only the character of the instruction but also the character of the instructor that counts; and if the student has reason to believe that the instructor is not true to himself, the virtue of the instruction as an educative force is incalculably diminished. There must be in the mind of the teacher no mental reservation. He must give the student the best of what he has and what he is.

The third function of the modern university is to develop experts for the use of the community. If there is one thing that distinguishes the more recent developments of democracy, it is the recognition by legislators of the inherent complexities of economic, social, and political life, and the difficulty of solving problems of technical adjustment without technical knowledge. The recognition of this fact has led to a continually greater demand for the aid of experts in these subjects, to advise both legislators and administrators. The training of such experts has, accordingly, in recent years, become an important part of the work of the universities; and in almost every one of our higher institutions of learning the professors of the economic, social, and political sciences have been drafted to an increasing extent into more or less unofficial participation in the public service. It is obvious that here again the scholar must be absolutely free not only to pursue his investigations but to declare the results of his researches, no matter where they may lead him or to what extent they may come into conflict with accepted opinion. To be of use to the legislator or the administrator, he must enjoy their complete confidence in the disinterestedness of his conclusions.

It is clear, then, that the university cannot perform its threefold function without accepting and enforcing to the fullest extent the principle of academic freedom. The responsibility of the university as a whole is to the community at large, and any restriction upon the freedom of the instructor is bound to react injuriously upon the efficiency and the *morale* of the institution, and therefore ultimately upon the interests of the community.

The attempted infringements of academic freedom at present are probably not only of less frequency than, but of a different character from, those to be found in former times. In the early period of university development in America the chief menace to academic freedom was ecclesiastical, and the disciplines chiefly affected were philosophy and the natural sciences. In more recent times the danger zone has been shifted to the political and social sciences—though we still have sporadic examples of the former class of cases in some of our smaller institutions. But it is precisely in these provinces of knowledge in which academic freedom is now most likely to be threatened, that the need for it is at the same time most evident. No person of intelligence believes that all of our political problems have been solved, or that the final stage of social evolution has been reached. Grave issues in the adjustment of men's social and economic relations are certain to call for settlement in the years that are to come; and for the right settlement of them mankind will need all the wisdom, all the good will, all the soberness of mind, and all the knowledge drawn from experience, that it can command. Towards this settlement the university has potentially its own very great contribution to make; for if the adjustment reached is to be a wise one, it must take due account of economic science, and be guided by that breadth of historic vision which it should be one of the functions of a university to cultivate. But if the universities are to render any such service towards the right solution of the social problems of the future, it is the first essential that the scholars who carry on the work of universities shall not be in a position of dependence upon the favor of any social class or group, that the disinterestedness and impartiality of their inquiries and their conclusions shall be, so far as is humanly possible, beyond the reach of suspicion.

The special dangers to freedom of teaching in the domain of the social sciences are evidently two. The one which is the more likely to affect the privately endowed colleges and universities is the danger of restrictions upon the expression of opinions which point towards extensive social innovations, or call in question the moral legitimacy or social expediency of economic conditions or commercial practices in which large vested interests are involved. In the political, social, and economic field almost every question, no matter how large and general it at first appears, is more or less affected with private or class interests; and, as the governing body of a university is naturally made up of men who through their standing and ability are personally interested in great private enterprises, the points of possible conflict are numberless. When to this is added the consideration that benefactors, as well as most of the parents who send their children to privately endowed institutions, themselves belong to the more prosperous and therefore usually to the more conservative classes, it is apparent that, so long as effectual safeguards for academic freedom are not established, there is a real danger that pressure from vested interests may, sometimes deliberately and sometimes unconsciously, sometimes openly and sometimes subtly and in obscure ways, be brought to bear upon academic authorities.

On the other hand, in our state universities the danger may be the reverse. Where the university is dependent for funds upon legislative favor, it has sometimes happened that the conduct of the institution has been affected by political considerations; and where there is a definite governmental policy or a strong public feeling on economic, social, or political questions, the menace to academic freedom may consist in the repression of opinions that in the particular political situation are deemed ultra-conservative rather than ultra-radical. The essential point, however, is not so much that the opinion is of one or another shade, as that it differs from the views entertained by the authorities. The question resolves itself into one of departure from accepted standards; whether the departure is in the one direction or the other is immaterial.

This brings us to the most serious difficulty of this problem; namely, the dangers connected with the existence in a democracy of an overwhelming and concentrated public opinion. The tendency of modern democracy is for men to think alike, to feel alike, and to speak alike. Any departure from the conventional standards is apt to be regarded with suspicion. Public opinion is at once the chief safeguard of a democracy, and the chief menace to the real liberty of the individual. It almost seems as if the danger of despotism cannot be wholly averted under any form of government. In a political autocracy there is no effective public opinion, and all are subject to the tyranny of the ruler; in a democracy there is political freedom, but there is likely to be a tyranny of public opinion.

An inviolable refuge from such tyranny should be found in the university. It should be an intellectual experiment station, where new ideas may germinate and where their fruit, though still distasteful to the community as a whole, may be allowed to ripen until finally, perchance, it may become a part of the accepted intellectual food of the nation or of the world. Not less is it a distinctive duty of the university to be the conservator of all genuine elements of value in the past thought and life of mankind which are not in the fashion of the moment. Though it need not be the "home of beaten causes," the university is, indeed, likely always to exercise a certain form of conservative influence. For by its nature it is committed to the principle that knowledge should precede action, to the caution (by no means synonymous with intellectual timidity) which is an essential part of the scientific method, to a sense of the complexity of social problems, to the practice of taking long views into the future, and to a reasonable regard for the teachings of experience. One of its most characteristic functions in a democratic society is to help make public opinion more self-critical and more circumspect, to check the more hasty and unconsidered impulses of popular feeling, to train the democracy to the habit of look-ing before and after. It is precisely this function of the university which is most injured by any restriction upon academic freedom; and it is precisely those who most value this aspect of the university's work who should most earnestly protest against any such restriction. For the public may respect, and be influenced by, the counsels of prudence and of moderation which are given by men of science, if it believes those counsels to be the disinterested expression of the scientific temper and of unbiased inquiry. It is little likely to respect or heed them if it has reason to believe that they are the expression of the interests, or the timidities, of the limited portion of the community which is in a posi-tion to endow institutions of learning, or is most likely to be repre-sented upon their boards of trustees. And a plausible reason for this belief is given the public so long as our universities are not organized in such a way as to make impossible any exercise of pressure upon pro-fessorial opinions and utterances by governing boards of laymen.

Since there are no rights without corresponding duties, the consid-erations heretofore set down with respect to the freedom of the aca-demic teacher entail certain correlative obligations. The claim to free-dom of teaching is made in the interest of the integrity and of the progress of scientific inquiry; it is, therefore, only those who carry on their work in the temper of the scientific inquirer who may justly as-sert this claim. The liberty of the scholar within the university to set forth his conclusions, be they what they may, is conditioned by their being conclusions gained by a scholar's method and held in a scholar's spirit; that is to say, they must be the fruits of competent and patient and sincere inquiry, and they should be set forth with dignity, cour-tesy, and temperateness of language. The university teacher, in giving instruction upon controversial matters, while he is under no obligation to hide his own opinion under a mountain of equivocal verbiage, should, if he is fit for his position, be a person of a fair and judicial mind; he should, in dealing with such subjects, set forth justly, with-out suppression or innuendo, the divergent opinions of other investiga-tors; he should cause his students to become familiar with the best published expressions of the great historic types of doctrine upon the questions at issue; and he should above all, remember that his business is not to provide his students with ready-made conclusions, but to train them to think for themselves, and to provide them access to those mate-rials which they need if they are to think intelligently.

It is, however, for reasons which have already been made evident, inadmissible that the power of determining when departures from the requirements of the scientific spirit and method have occurred, should be vested in bodies not composed of members of the academic profession. Such bodies necessarily lack full competency to judge of those requirements; their intervention can never be exempt from suspicion that it is dictated by other motives than zeal for the integrity of science; and it is, in any case, unsuitable to the dignity of a great profession that the initial responsibility for the maintenance of its professional standards should not be in the hands of its own members. It follows that university teachers must be prepared to assume this responsibility for themselves. They have hitherto seldom had the opportunity, or perhaps the disposition, to do so. The obligation will doubtless, therefore, seem to many an unwelcome and burdensome one; and for its proper discharge members of the profession will perhaps need to acquire, in a greater measure than they at present possess it, the capacity for impersonal judgment in such cases, and for judicial severity when the occasion requires it. But the responsibility cannot, in this committee's opinion, be rightfully evaded. If this profession should prove itself unwilling to purge its ranks of the incompetent and the unworthy, or to prevent the freedom which it claims in the name of science from being used as a shelter for inefficiency, for superficiality, or for uncritical and intemperate partisanship, it is certain that the task will be performed by others—by others who lack certain essential qualifications for performing it, and whose action is sure to breed suspicions and recurrent controversies deeply injurious to the internal order and the public standing of universities. Your committee has, therefore, in the appended "Practical Proposals" attempted to suggest means by which judicial action by representatives of the profession, with respect to the matters here referred to, may be secured.

There is one case in which the academic teacher is under an obligation to observe certain special restraints—namely, the instruction of immature students. In many of our American colleges, and especially in the first two years of the course, the student's character is not yet fully formed, his mind is still relatively immature. In these circumstances it may reasonably be expected that the instructor will present scientific truth with discretion, that he will introduce the student to new conceptions gradually, with some consideration for the student's preconceptions and traditions, and with due regard to character-building. The teacher ought also to be especially on his guard against taking unfair advantage of the student's immaturity by indoctrinating him with the teacher's own opinions before the student has had an opportunity fairly to examine other opinions upon the matters in question, and before he has sufficient knowledge and ripeness of judgment to be entitled to form any definitive opinion of his own. It is not the least service which a college or university may render to those under its instruction, to habituate them to looking not only patiently but methodically on both sides, before adopting any conclusion upon controverted issues. By these suggestions, however, it need scarcely be said that the committee does not intend to imply that it is not the duty of an academic instructor to give to any students old enough to be in college a genuine intellectual awakening and to arouse in them a keen desire to reach personally verified conclusions upon all questions of general concernment to mankind, or of special significance for their own time. There is much truth in some remarks recently made in this connection by a college president:

"Certain professors have been refused reëlection lately, apparently because they set their students to thinking in ways objectionable to the trustees. It would be well if more teachers were dismissed because they fail to stimulate thinking of any kind. We can afford to forgive a college professor what we regard as the occasional error of his doctrine, especially as we may be wrong, provided he is a contagious center of intellectual enthusiasm. It is better for students to think about heresies than not to think at all; better for them to climb new trails, and stumble over error if need be, than to ride forever in upholstered ease in the overcrowded highway. It is a primary duty of a teacher to make a student take an honest account of his stock of ideas, throw out the dead matter, place revised price marks on what is left, and try to fill his empty shelves with new goods."*

It is, however, possible and necessary that such intellectual awakening be brought about with patience, considerateness and pedagogical wisdom.

There is one further consideration with regard to the classroom utterances of college and university teachers to which the committee thinks it important to call the attention of members of the profession, and of administrative authorities. Such utterances ought always to be

---

* President William T. Foster in *The Nation,* November 11, 1915.

considered privileged communications. Discussions in the class room ought not to be supposed to be utterances for the public at large. They are often designed to provoke opposition or arouse debate. It has, unfortunately, sometimes happened in this country that sensational newspapers have quoted and garbled such remarks. As a matter of common law, it is clear that the utterances of an academic instructor are privileged, and may not be published, in whole or part, without his authorization. But our practice, unfortunately, still differs from that of foreign countries, and no effective check has in this country been put upon such unauthorized and often misleading publication. It is much to be desired that test cases should be made of any infractions of the rule.*

In their extra-mural utterances, it is obvious that academic teachers are under a peculiar obligation to avoid hasty or unverified or exaggerated statements, and to refrain from intemperate or sensational modes of expression. But, subject to these restraints, it is not, in this committee's opinion, desirable that scholars should be debarred from giving expression to their judgments upon controversial questions, or that their freedom of speech, outside the university, should be limited to questions falling within their own specialties. It is clearly not proper that they should be prohibited from lending their active support to organized movements which they believe to be in the public interest. And, speaking broadly, it may be said in the words of a non-academic body already once quoted in a publication of this Association, that "it is neither possible nor desirable to deprive a college professor of the political rights vouchsafed to every citizen."†

It is, however, a question deserving of consideration by members of this Association, and by university officials, how far academic teachers, at least those dealing with political, economic and social subjects, should be prominent in the management of our great party organizations, or should be candidates for state or national offices of a distinctly political character. It is manifestly desirable that such teachers have

* The leading case is Abernethy vs. Hutchinson, 3 L. J., Ch. 209. In this case where damages were awarded the court held as follows: "That persons who are admitted as pupils or otherwise to hear these lectures, although they are orally delivered and the parties might go to the extent, if they were able to do so, of putting down the whole by means of shorthand, yet they can do that only for the purpose of their own information and could not publish, for profit, that which they had not obtained the right of selling."

† Report of the Wisconsin State Board of Public Affairs, December 1914.

minds untrammeled by party loyalties, unexcited by party enthusiasms, and unbiased by personal political ambitions; and that universities should remain uninvolved in party antagonisms. On the other hand, it is equally manifest that the material available for the service of the State would be restricted in a highly undesirable way, if it were understood that no member of the academic profession should ever be called upon to assume the responsibilities of public office. This question may, in the committee's opinion, suitably be made a topic for special discussion at some future meeting of this Association, in order that a practical policy, which shall do justice to the two partially conflicting considerations that bear upon the matter, may be agreed upon.

It is, it will be seen, in no sense the contention of this committee that academic freedom implies that individual teachers should be exempt from all restraints as to the matter or manner of their utterances, either within or without the university. Such restraints as are necessary should in the main, your committee holds, be self-imposed, or enforced by the public opinion of the profession. But there may, undoubtedly, arise occasional cases in which the aberrations of individuals may require to be checked by definite disciplinary action. What this report chiefly maintains is that such action can not with safety be taken by bodies not composed of members of the academic profession. Lay governing boards are competent to judge concerning charges of habitual neglect of assigned duties, on the part of individual teachers, and concerning charges of grave moral delinquency. But in matters of opinion, and of the utterance of opinion, such boards cannot intervene without destroying, to the extent of their intervention, the essential nature of a university—without converting it from a place dedicated to openness of mind, in which the conclusions expressed are the tested conclusions of trained scholars, into a place barred against the access of new light, and precommitted to the opinions or prejudices of men who have not been set apart or expressly trained for the scholar's duties. It is, in short, not the absolute freedom of utterance of the individual scholar, but the absolute freedom of thought, of inquiry, of discussion and of teaching, of the academic profession, that is asserted by this declaration of principles. It is conceivable that our profession may prove unworthy of its high calling, and unfit to exercise the responsibilities that belong to it. But it will scarcely be said as yet to have given evidence of such unfitness. And the existence of this Association, as it seems to your committee, must be construed as a pledge, not only that the profession will earnestly guard those liberties without which it can not rightly render its distinctive and indispensable service to society, but also that it will with equal earnestness seek to maintain such standards of professional character, and of scientific integrity and competency, as shall make it a fit instrument for that service.

II. PRACTICAL PROPOSALS

As the foregoing declaration implies, the ends to be accomplished are chiefly three:

First: To safeguard freedom of inquiry and of teaching against both covert and overt attacks, by providing suitable judicial bodies, composed of members of the academic profession, which may be called into action before university teachers are dismissed or disciplined, and may determine in what cases the question of academic freedom is actually involved.

Second: By the same means, to protect college executives and governing boards against unjust charges of infringement of academic freedom, or of arbitrary and dictatorial conduct—charges which, when they gain wide currency and belief, are highly detrimental to the good repute and the influence of universities.

Third: To render the profession more attractive to men of high ability and strong personality by insuring the dignity, the independence, and the reasonable security of tenure, of the professorial office.

The measures which it is believed to be necessary for our universities to adopt to realize these ends—measures which have already been adopted in part by some institutions—are four:

A. *Action by Faculty Committees on Reappointments.* Official action relating to reappointments and refusals of reappointment should be taken only with the advice and consent of some board or committee representative of the faculty. Your committee does not desire to make at this time any suggestion as to the manner of selection of such boards.

B. *Definition of Tenure of Office.* In every institution there should be an unequivocal understanding as to the term of each appointment; and the tenure of professorships and associate professorships, and of all positions above the grade of instructor after ten years of service, should be permanent (subject to the provisions hereinafter given for removal upon charges). In those state universities which are legally incapable of making contracts for more than a limited period, the governing boards should announce their policy with respect to the presumption of reappointment in the several classes of position, and such announcements, though not legally enforceable, should be regarded as morally binding. No university teacher of any rank should, except in cases of grave moral delinquency, receive notice of dismissal or of refusal of reappointment, later than three months before the close of any academic year, and in the case of teachers above the grade of instructor, one year's notice should be given.

C. *Formulation of Grounds for Dismissal.* In every institution the grounds which will be regarded as justifying the dismissal of members of the faculty should be formulated with reasonable definiteness; and in the case of institutions which impose upon their faculties doctrinal standards of a sectarian or partisan character, these standards should be clearly defined and the body or individual having authority to interpret them, in case of controversy, should be designated. Your committee does not think it best at this time to attempt to enumerate the legitimate grounds for dismissal, believing it to be preferable that individual institutions should take the initiative in this.

D. *Judicial Hearings Before Dismissal.* Every university or college teacher should be entitled, before dismissal* or demotion, to have the charges against him stated in writing in specific terms and to have a fair trial on those charges before a special or permanent judicial committee chosen by the faculty senate or council, or by the faculty at large. At such trial the teacher accused should have full opportunity to present evidence, and, if the charge is one of professional incompetency, a formal report upon his work should be first made in writing by the teachers of his own department and of cognate departments in the university, and, if the teacher concerned so desire, by a committee of his fellow specialists from other institutions, appointed by some competent authority.

The above declaration of principles and practical proposals are respectfully submitted by your committee to the approval of the Association, with the suggestion that, if approved, they be recommended to the

---

* This does not refer to refusals of reappointment at the expiration of the terms of office of teachers below the rank of associate professor. All such questions of reappointment should, as above provided. be acted upon by a faculty committee.

consideration of the faculties, administrative officers, and governing boards of the American universities and colleges.

EDWIN R. A. SELIGMAN, *Chairman*
Columbia University
CHARLES E. BENNETT,
Cornell University
JAMES Q. DEALEY,
Brown University
RICHARD T. ELY,
University of Wisconsin
HENRY W. FARNAM,
Yale University
FRANK A. FETTER,
Princeton University
FRANKLIN H. GIDDINGS,
Columbia University

CHARLES A. KOFOID,
University of California
ARTHUR O. LOVEJOY,
Johns Hopkins University
FREDERICK W. PADELFORD,
University of Washington
ROSCOE POUND,
Harvard University
HOWARD C. WARREN,
Princeton University
ULYSSES G. WEATHERLY,
University of Indiana

At the annual meeting of the American Association of University Professors held in Washington, D.C., on January 1, 1916, it was moved and carried that the report of the Committee on Academic Freedom and Academic Tenure be accepted and approved.

JOHN DEWEY,
President
A. O. LOVEJOY,
Secretary

9. *A. Lawrence Lowell on Academic Freedom in Wartime, 1917*

On Lowell see Part IX, Doc. 11.

The war has brought to the front in academic life many questions which are new, or present themselves to many people in a new light. One of these is liberty of speech on the part of the professor; and it seems a not unfitting time to analyze the principles involved, and seek to discover their limitations. In so doing I shall deal only with higher education, that is with universities and colleges.

A. L. Lowell, "Academic Freedom," in *At War with Academic Traditions in America* (Cambridge, Mass., 1934), pp. 267–72. Reprinted with the permission of Harvard University Press.

Experience has proved, and probably no one would now deny, that knowledge can advance, or at least can advance most rapidly, only by means of an unfettered search for truth on the part of those who devote their lives to seeking it in their respective fields, and by complete freedom in imparting to their pupils the truth that they have found. This has become an axiom in higher education, in spite of the fact that a searcher may discover error instead of truth, and be misled, and mislead others, thereby. We believe that if light enough is let in, the real relations of things will soon be seen, and that they can be seen in no other way. Such a principle, however, does not solve the actual problems, because the difficulty lies in the application; and for that purpose one must consider the question in various aspects. One must distinguish between the matters that fall within and those that lie outside of the professor's field of study; then there is a difference in the professor's position in his class-room and beyond it. These two cross divisions raise four distinct problems that may profitably be discussed in succession.

The teaching by the professor in his class-room on the subjects within the scope of his chair ought to be absolutely free. He must teach the truth as he has found it and sees it. This is the primary condition of academic freedom, and any violation of it endangers intellectual progress. In order to make it secure it is essential that the teaching in the class-room should be confidential. This does not mean that it is secret, but that what is said there should not be published. If the remarks of the instructor were repeated by the pupils in the public press, he would be subjected to constant criticism by people, not familiar with the subject, who misunderstood his teaching; and, what is more important, he would certainly be misquoted, because his remarks would be reported by the student without their context or the qualifications that give them their accuracy. Moreover, if the rule that remarks in the class-room shall not be reported for publication elsewhere is to be maintained, the professor himself must not report them. Lectures open to the public stand on a different footing; but lectures in a private class-room must not be given by the instructor to the newspapers. That principle is, I believe, observed in all reputable institutions.

This brings us to the next subdivision of the inquiry, the freedom of the professor within his field of study, but outside of his class-room. It has been pointed out that he ought not to publish his class-room lectures as such in the daily press. That does not mean a denial of the right to publish them in a book, or their substance in a learned periodical. On the contrary, the object of institutions of learning is not only the acquisition but also the diffusion of knowledge. Every professor must, therefore, be wholly unrestrained in publishing the results of his study in the field of his professorship. It is needless to add that for the dignity of his profession, for the maintenance of its privileges, as well as for his own reputation among his fellows, whatever he writes or says on his own subject should be uttered as a scholar, in a scholarly tone and form. This is a matter of decorum, not of discipline; to be remedied by a suggestion, not by a penalty.

In troublous times much more serious difficulty, and much more confusion of thought, arise from the other half of our subject, the right of a professor to express his views without restraint on matters lying outside the sphere of his professorship. This is not a question of academic freedom in its true sense, but of the personal liberty of the citizen. It has nothing to do with liberty of research and instruction in the subject for which the professor occupies the chair that makes him a member of the university. The fact that a man fills a chair of astronomy, for example, confers on him no special knowledge of, and no peculiar right to speak upon, the protective tariff. His right to speak about a subject on which he is not an authority is simply the right of any other man, and the question is simply whether the university or college by employing him as a professor acquires a right to restrict his freedom as a citizen. It seems to me that this question can be answered only by again considering his position in his class-room and outside of it.

The university or college is under certain obligations to its students. It compels them to attend courses of instruction, and on their side they have a right not to be compelled to listen to remarks offensive or injurious to them on subjects of which the instructor is not a master,—a right which the teacher is bound to respect. A professor of Greek, for example, is not at liberty to harangue his pupils on the futility and harmfulness of vaccination; a professor of economics, on Bacon's authorship of Shakespeare; or a professor of bacteriology, on the tenets of the Catholic Church. Everyone will admit this when stated in such extreme forms; and the reason is that the professor speaks to his class as a professor, not as a citizen. He speaks from his chair and must speak from that alone. The difficulty lies in drawing the line between that which does and does not fall properly within the professor's subject; and where the line ought to be drawn the professor can hardly claim an arbitrary power to judge, since the question affects the rights both of himself and his students. But serious friction rarely arises, I believe, from this cause, and a word of caution would ordinarily be enough.

The gravest questions, and the strongest feelings, arise from action by a professor beyond his chosen field and outside of his class-room. Here he speaks only as a citizen. By appointment to a professorship he acquires no rights that he did not possess before; but there is a real difference of opinion today on the question whether he loses any rights that he would otherwise enjoy. The argument in favor of a restraining power on the part of the governing boards of universities and colleges is based upon the fact that by extreme, or injudicious, remarks that shock public sentiment a professor can do great harm to the institution with which he is connected. That is true, and sometimes a professor thoughtlessly does an injury that is without justification. If he publishes an article on the futility and harmfulness of vaccination, and signs it as a professor in a certain university, he leads the public to believe that his views are those of an authority on the subject, approved by the institution and taught to its students. If he is really a professor of Greek, he is misleading the public and misrepresenting his university, which he would not do if he gave his title in full.

In spite, however, of the risk of injury to the institution, the objections to restraint upon what professors may say as citizens seem to me far greater than the harm done by leaving them free. In the first place, to impose upon the teacher in a university restrictions to which the members of other professions, lawyers, physicians, engineers, and so forth are not subjected would produce a sense of irritation and humiliation. In accepting a chair under such conditions a man would surrender a part of his liberty; what he might say would be submitted to the censorship of a board of trustees, and he would cease to be a free citizen. The lawyer, physician, or engineer may express his views as he likes on the subject of the protective tariff; shall the professor of astronomy not be free to do the same? Such a policy would tend seriously to discourage some of the best men from taking up the scholar's life. It is not a question of academic freedom, but of personal liberty from constraint, yet it touches the dignity of the academic career.

That is an objection to restraint on freedom of speech from the standpoint of the teacher. There is another, not less weighty, from that of the institution itself. If a university or college censors what its professors may say, if it restrains them from uttering something that it does not approve, it thereby assumes responsibility for that which it permits them to say. This is logical and inevitable, but it is a responsibility which an institution of learning would be very unwise in assuming. It is sometimes suggested that the principles are different in time of war; that the governing boards are then justified in restraining unpatriotic expressions injurious to the country. But the same problem is presented in war time as in time of peace. If the university is right in restraining its professors, it has a duty to do so, and it is responsible for whatever it permits. There is no middle ground. Either the university assumes full responsibility for permitting its professors to express certain opinions in public, or it assumes no responsibility whatever, and leaves them to be dealt with like other citizens by the public authorities according to the laws of the land.

All this refers, of course, to opinions on public matters sincerely uttered. If a professor speaks in a way that reveals moral obliquity, he may be treated as he would on any other evidence of moral defect; for character in the teacher is essential to the welfare of the students.

Every human attempt to attain a good object involves some compromise, some sacrifice of lesser ends for the larger ones. Hence every profession has its own code of ethics designed to promote its major objects, and entailing restrictions whose importance is often not clear to outsiders. But for the teachers in American universities and colleges the code of professional ethics does not appear to have been thoroughly developed or to be fully understood either by teachers or trustees. That result requires time, and for this reason few difficulties arise in institutions that have had a long and gradual growth.

Surely abuse of speech, abuse of authority and arbitrary restraint and friction would be reduced if men kept in mind the distinction between the privilege of academic freedom and the common right of personal liberty as a citizen, between what may properly be said in the class-room and what in public. But it must not be forgotten that all liberty and every privilege imply responsibilities. Professors should speak in public soberly and seriously, not for notoriety or self advertisement, under a deep sense of responsibility for the good name of the institution and the dignity of their profession. They should take care that they are understood to speak personally, not officially. When they so speak, and governing boards respect their freedom to express their sincere opinions as other citizens may do, there will be little danger that liberty of speech will be either misused or curtailed.

10. Charles A. Beard Notifies Nicholas Murray Butler of His Resignation from Columbia, 1917

Charles A. Beard (1874–1948) was born in Indiana, graduated from DePauw in 1898, and studied for some years in England. In 1907 he joined the faculty of political science at Columbia University, where he rapidly became one of the most impressive teachers and scholars. His study *An Economic Interpretation of the Constitution of the United States* (1913) made him one of the most controversial thinkers of his time. After his resignation from Columbia, he retired from teaching as a career to his Connecticut farm. From 1901 to his death, Beard published 49 volumes on history and political science, as well as innumerable articles, speeches, pamphlets, and book reviews, all of which made him an imposing influence. See Howard K. Beale (ed.), *Charles A. Beard* (Lexington, Ky., 1954), a series of articles by various hands; on the Beard, Cattell, and Dana cases at Columbia, see esp. pp. 242–45, and Hofstadter and Metzger, *The Development of Academic Freedom*, pp. 495–502.

Having observed closely the inner life at Columbia for many years, I have been driven to the conclusion that the University is really under the control of a small and active group of trustees who have no standing in the world of education, who are reactionary and visionless in politics, narrow and medieval in religion. Their conduct, to use the language of the resolution adopted last spring by one of the most important Faculties "betrays a profound misconception of the true function of a university in the advancement of learning." How widespread and deep is this conviction among the professors only one intimately acquainted with them can know.

If these were ordinary times one might more readily ignore the unhappy position in which the dominant group in the Board of Trustees has placed teachers, but these are not ordinary times. We are in the midst of a great war, and we stand on the threshold of an era which will call for all the emancipated thinking that America can command. As you are aware, I have from the beginning believed that a victory for the German Imperial Government would plunge all of us into the black night of military barbarism. I was among the first to urge a declaration of war by the United States, and I believe that we should now press forward with all our might to a just conclusion. But thousands

Beard to Butler, October 8, 1917, Minutes of the Trustees of Columbia University, XXXVIII (1917–18), 89–90; *Columbia Alumni News,* IX (October 12, 1917), 59.

of my countrymen do not share this view. Their opinions cannot be changed by curses or bludgeons. Arguments addressed to their reason and understanding are our best hope.

Such arguments, however, must come from men whose disinterestedness is above all suspicion, whose independence is beyond all doubt, and whose devotion to the whole country, as distinguished from any single class or group, is above all question. I am convinced that while I remain in the pay of the Trustees of Columbia University I cannot do effectively my humble part in sustaining public opinion in support of the just war on the German Empire or take a position of independence in the days of reconstruction that are to follow. For this reason I herewith tender my resignation as Professor of Politics to take effect on the morning of Tuesday, Oct. 9, 1917.

I can not find words to convey to you what it means to sever close ties of so many years' standing. Above all do I regret to part from my colleagues. As I think of their scholarship and their worldwide reputation and compare with them the few obscure and wilful trustees who now dominate the University and terrorize young instructors, I can not repress my astonishment that America, of all countries, has made the status of the professor lower than that of the manual laborer, who, through his union, has at least some voice in the terms and conditions of his employment. Holding his position literally by the day, the professor is liable to dismissal without a hearing, without the judgment of his colleagues, who are his real peers. I am sure that when the people understand the true state of affairs in our universities they will speedily enact the legislation which will strip the boards of trustees of their absolute power over the intellectual life of the institutions under their management.

In severing relations with my employers I do not leave the great republic of Columbia students, alumni, and professors. With them I have ties that cannot break while I live. And to you, sir, I am deeply indebted for your courtesy and thoughtful consideration that I have always received at your hands.

11. The New York Times Comments on Beard's Resignation, 1917

See Doc. 10.

COLUMBIA'S DELIVERANCE

No man of feeling would deny to Professor BEARD the luxury and the pleasure of berating the Trustees of Columbia University, to which, in resigning from the teaching staff, he has just rendered the greatest service it was in his power to give. It will do these Columbia Trustees no harm to be described as "reactionary and visionless in politics." They certainly have no vision of the benefits to come from the overthrow of our institutions and the re-organization of society by the apostles of radicalism. Doubtless they are "narrow and mediaeval in religion," since having never enjoyed the advantages of a German university training, they have not embraced that blank materialism which so many American professors have imbibed from that source. But these Trustees know, as every man of sound sense and unclouded vision knows, that Columbia University is better for Professor BEARD's resignation.

Some years ago Professor BEARD published a book, in which he sought to show that the founders of this Republic and the authors of its Constitution were a ring of land speculators who bestowed upon the country a body of organic law drawn up chiefly in the interest of their own pockets. It was pointed out to him at the time, with due kindness but frankly, that his book was bad, that it was a book no professor should have written since it was grossy unscientific. It was not based upon candid and competent examination of facts, but it was written to establish a preconceived theory of his own, which he supported by statements unrelated to fact and quite unconvincing in their nature. It was a book that did Columbia much harm, just as the two professors who were recently dropped for seditious utterances did the university much harm. It was the fruit of that school of thought and teaching, again borrowed from Germany, which denies to man in his

New York Times, October 10, 1917, p. 10.

larger actions the capacity of noble striving and self-sacrifice for ideals, that seeks always as the prompting motive either the animal desire to get more to eat or the hope of filling his pockets. If this sort of teaching were allowed to go on unchecked by public sentiment and the strong hands of university Trustees, we should presently find educated American youth applying the doctrine of economic determinism to everything from the Lord's Prayer to the binomial theorem.

It is not so to be. Trustees may be visionless in politics and mediaeval in religion, but they have the hard, common sense to know, as was said in another notable recent case of interference with academic freedom, that infallible wisdom does not perch upon the back of every chair occupied by a professor bearing the degree of Doctor of Philosophy, and they know that if colleges and universities are not to become breeding grounds of radicalism and socialism, it must be recognized that academic freedom has two sides, that freedom to teach is correlative to the freedom to dispense with poisonous teaching. The Trustees of Columbia University have been very tolerant, very patient, and the university has suffered through the acts, the utterances, and the teachings of some of its professors who mistook the chairs they occupied for pulpits from which doctrines might freely be preached that are dangerous to the community and to the nation. A university is not solely responsible to the young gentlemen fresh from Berlin, Bonn, or Heidelberg whom it may engage as members of its corps of professors. The Trustees of Columbia and of all American universities know that they have a responsibility to the communities and to the country that give those seats of learning existence, to the numerous body of their alumni who are jealous of the standing and repute of their Alma Mater, that they are responsible to sane public opinion, which will hold them accountable for errors of indulgence to the teachers of false doctrines sheltering themselves behind the shibboleth of academic freedom.

12. Charles Beard Explains the Reasons for His Resignation, 1917

It has been insinuated by certain authorities of Columbia University that I resigned in a fit of unjustified petulance, and I, therefore, beg to submit the following statement:

1. My first real experience with the inner administration of the university came with the retirement of Professor John W. Burgess. For some time before his withdrawal, his work in American constitutional law had been carried by Professor X and it was the desire of the members of the faculty that the latter should be appointed Ruggles Professor to succeed Mr. Burgess. But Mr. X had published a book in which he justified criticism of the Supreme Court as a means of bringing our constitutional law into harmony with our changing social and economic life. He was therefore excluded from the Ruggles professorship. It was given to Mr. W. D. Guthrie, a successful corporation lawyer, and a partner of one of the trustees of the University. It was understood that Mr. Guthrie should give one lecture a week for one semester each year, in return for the high honor. Mr. Butler is constantly saying that all matters relating to appointment, fitness, and tenure are left to the appropriate faculties, or words to this effect. As a matter of plain fact the Faculty of Political Science as such was not consulted in advance in the selection of the Ruggles professor. The whole affair was settled by backstairs negotiation, and it was understood by all of us who had any part in the business that no person with progressive or liberal views would be acceptable. Mr. Guthrie was duly appointed. Of his contributions to learning I shall not speak, but I can say that he did not attend faculty meetings, help in conducting doctors' examinations, or assume the burdens imposed upon other professors. This was the way in which the first important vacancy in the Faculty of Political Science was filled after my connection with the institution.

2. My second experience with the administration of the University came in 1916. On April 21st of that year I delivered an address before the National Conference of Community Centers in which I advocated the use of the schools as the centers for the discussion of public ques-

New Republic, XIII (December 29, 1917), 249–51.

tions. A few weeks before, a speaker at one of the school forums was alleged to have said, "To Hell with the Flag," and for that reason a number of persons had urged the closing of school centers altogether. Indeed, some of the speakers at the above-mentioned conference advocated a sort of censorship for all school forums. In my address I merely took the reasonable and moderate view that the intemperance of one man should not drive us into closing the schools to others. The reports in the newspapers, with one exception, were fairly accurate. But one sensational sheet accused me of approving the sentiment, "To Hell with the Flag." Dr. Butler, who had had large experience with frenzied journalism quite rightly took the view that I had been the victim of the headline writer and advised me to do my best to correct the wrong impression and then forget it. I immediately wrote to all of the papers and sought to remove the misunderstanding that had arisen.

Nevertheless I was summoned before the committee on education of the board of trustees. I complied because I wanted to clear up any wrong impressions which the members entertained concerning the nature of my address before the Community Center conference.

As soon as the committee of the trustees opened the inquiry I speedily disposed of the "flag incident," by showing that I had said nothing that could be construed as endorsing in any way the objectionable language in question. No one doubted my word. Indeed I had available abundant testimony from reliable men and women who had heard the address. The record was thus soon set straight.

The inquiry as to the flag incident being at an end I prepared to leave the room when I was utterly astonished to have Mr. Bangs and Mr. Coudert launch into an inquisition into my views and teachings. For half an hour I was "grilled" by these gentlemen. Dr. Butler and certain colleagues from the Faculty of Political Science (who were present at the inquisition) made no attempt to stop the proceedings. Mr. Coudert, who had once privately commended my book on the Constitution as "admirably well done," and opening up "a most fertile field," denounced my teachings in vigorous language, in which he was strongly seconded by Mr. Bangs. I realize now that I should have refused to remain in the room, but I was taken unaware and stunned by the procedure. When the inquisitors satisfied themselves, the chairman of the committee ordered me to warn all other men in my department against teachings "likely to inculcate disrespect for American institutions.["] I repeated my order to my colleagues who received it with a shout of derision, one of them asking me whether Tammany Hall and the pork barrel were not American institutions!

I reported to my colleagues in the Faculty of Political Science that I had been subjected by the committee of the trustees to a "general doctrinal inquisition," and urged them, at an informal meeting, to establish a rule that a professor should be examined in matters of opinion only by his peers, namely men of standing in his profession. Several caucuses of the Faculty were held and it was generally agreed that the proceedings of the trustees were highly reprehensible. Action doubtless should have been taken by the Faculty at the time if we had not been told by Dean Woodbridge that "the trustees have learned their lesson and that such an inquisition would never happen again." We were also informed that some of the trustees were "after" President Butler for his pacifist writings and affiliations and that if the Faculty took a firm stand in matters of doctrinal inquisition an open conflict might ensue. In a long conversation President Butler urged me to drop the whole "miserable business" and go on about my work.

For the sake of "peace" I consented. I should not forget, however, the cases of Professor Kendrick and Dr. Fraser who had been haled before the committee of the trustees on the trivial charge that they had criticized Plattsburg and military discipline at a student meeting some time early in 1916. Their cases I regarded as peculiarly open to objection because they were not even accused of saying anything that was indecent or vulgar or unpatriotic. Nevertheless, I dropped the whole matter on the assurance that such an inquisition would not happen again and that the trustees "had learned their lesson."

3. Though I did not agree with some of my exuberant colleagues that a "great battle for academic freedom had been won" I was ready to abide by their decision. Then, to our utter astonishment, the trustees at their March meeting in 1917 gave to the press a set of resolutions instructing a committee "to inquire and ascertain" whether certain doctrines were being taught in the University. President Butler, in whose name we had been assured that no such inquisition would ever happen again, avoided the issue by taking a vacation and leaving the Faculties to deal with the situation.

The action of the Faculty of Political Science was prompt. An informal meeting was held at which a resolution in the following tenor was unanimously adopted:

"Whereas the resolution of the trustees by its very terms implies a general doctrinal inquisition, insults the members of the Faculty by questioning their loyalty to their country, violates every principle of academic freedom, and betrays a profound misconception of the true function of the university in the advancement of learning, *Be it resolved* that we will not individually or collectively lend any countenance to such an inquiry."

The trustees were forced to abandon their plan for a general inquisition. Indeed, when they learned of the spirit of the Faculty of Political Science and other faculties, they hastily disclaimed any intention of making a "doctrinal inquiry"—as their resolution of March, 1917, clearly implied.

It was agreed that such matters should be handled in cooperation with a committee of nine representing the faculties.

4. Notwithstanding this promise of cooperation on the part of the trustees and the committee of nine representing the teaching force, the trustees ignored the recommendations of that committee in the cases of Professors Dana and Cattell and dismissed these gentlemen summarily in the autumn of 1917, after wrongfully charging them with treason and sedition. Professor John Dewey resigned from the committee of nine and the body which was to safeguard the interests of the professors collapsed in ignominy.

5. Some time before Professors Cattell and Dana were expelled, another professor was summarily thrown out of the University without warning or trial. No reasons for his expulsion were advanced and a polite inquiry addressed by his colleagues to President Butler asking for information remained unanswered.

6. Dr. Leon Fraser was an instructor in Politics in Columbia College. With this office he combined that of assistant to Dean Keppel and Dr. Butler in the Association for International Conciliation. Dr. Fraser was assigned the task of organizing forces in colleges throughout the country in pacifism and international conciliation. In other words, he was paid by these gentlemen to engage in pacifist propaganda. In a moment of youthful enthusiasm, early in 1916, Dr. Fraser made some critical remark about the military camp at Plattsburg. For this he was haled before a committee of the trustees. A year later, namely, in the spring of 1917, my department was warned not to re-nominate Dr. Fraser for re-appointment because he was not acceptable to Mr. Bangs, one of the trustees. In spite of our orders we did re-nominate Dr. Fraser, but before action could be taken by the trus-

tees, he, along with other instructors was dropped, on the assumption that the war would reduce materially the number of students in the College. But not content with dropping him, Mr. Butler informed the College authorities that in case the attendance in the College in the autumn warranted the appointment of additional instructors, under no circumstances should Dr. Fraser be re-nominated. In truth, therefore, if not in theory, Dr. Fraser was expelled from the College without notice or hearing. In view of the fact that Mr. Fraser had been inspired by Mr. Butler and Mr. Keppel to engage in pacifist propaganda and had been paid by them for doing it, it seemed to me that they should at least have demanded and insisted upon having a full and fair hearing of the charges against their youthful adherent, especially as those charges grew out of his "pacifist teachings."

7. We are informed by Dr. Butler that nominations for appointment and promotions come from the Faculties. Such may be the theory, but it is the practice for the trustees and president to warn the committee in charge of appointments and promotions against recommending "unacceptable" persons. For example, when the committee on instruction of the Faculty of Political Science, of which I was a member, was considering promotions last spring, it was informed at the outset by "the committee of one on rumor from the president's office" that "certain of the trustees" would not approve the promotion of Professor Y because he had used "disrespectful language" in speaking of the Supreme Court. Professor Y was not recommended for promotion and the trustees could proudly say that they had not rejected a faculty recommendation!

Mr. Butler cannot conceive of a scholar's entertaining progressive ideas. Once, in asking me to recommend an instructor to a neighboring college, he distinctly pointed out that a man of "Bull Moose" proclivities would not be acceptable.

8. Early in October, 1917, I was positively and clearly informed by two responsible officers of the University that another doctrinal inquisition was definitely scheduled for an early date. It was the evident purpose of a small group of the trustees (unhindered, if not aided, by Mr. Butler) to take advantage of the state of war to drive out or humiliate or terrorize every man who held progressive, liberal, or unconventional views on political matters in no way connected with the war. The institution was to be reduced below the level of a department store or factory and I therefore tendered my resignation.

I make no claims in behalf of academic freedom, though I think they are worthy of consideration: I have merely held that teachers should not be expelled without a full and fair hearing by their peers, surrounded by all of the safeguards of judicial process. Professors in Columbia University have been subjected to humiliating doctrinal inquisitions by the trustees, they have been expelled without notice or hearing, and their appointment and promotion depend upon securing, in advance, the favor of certain trustees. Without that favor scholarship and learning avail nothing.

These facts I submit to the candid and impartial reader. I believe that they constitute a full and unanswerable indictment of the prevailing method at Columbia University under the administration of Dr. Nicholas Murray Butler.

Part XI

HIGHER EDUCATION FOR THE

TWENTIETH-CENTURY WORLD

THE EDUCATIONAL PROGRESS of the late nineteenth century had stemmed from the development of science and professionalism, the development of advanced studies, and the recognition in the educational system of the innumerable fronts upon which knowledge was growing. But the emergence of the modern university shattered the unified if somewhat outmoded pattern of the old-time college without replacing it with a firm new pattern of its own. As a consequence, twentieth-century American higher education has assumed a place of leadership among the educational systems of the world, as well as a position of great national responsibility, at a time when it has lacked a clear sense of its own goals and a unifying and ordering philosophy.

With the development of the many-sided large university, the traditional ideal of liberal collegiate education (Doc. 1) was hard pressed. The universities, with their specialization and professionalism, tended to overshadow their own colleges; and since they supplied the teaching staffs for the independent colleges, even these were subjected to the criteria of university education, with its stress on specialized scholarship, advanced degrees, and professional training. The pressure of industrial and commercial society, putting a premium upon science and specialized skills, threatened at times to overwhelm the tradition of a liberal education. The transition from a university system originally designed for small numbers to a system of mass higher education threatened to submerge the college and the university with uneducable numbers. From the high schools there also came a great deal of pressure for vocationalism and for trivializing the curriculum (Doc. 4).

At no time, then, were the problems of education more complex and more confusing. How was one to adjust the competing claims of quantity and quality, of democracy and excellence, of the professional or vocational and the liberal? How would one reconcile the practical and the theoretical, the development of means and the formulation of ends, the criteria of the graduate school and the ideals of the liberal arts college? How many subjects can be effectively taught in an age of specialized knowledge? Is there any longer a common body of knowledge to which it is desirable to expose all college men and women? What kind of a liberal arts curriculum is meaningful in an age of specialization? How much common organization and how much individual choice should such a curriculum provide? Such questions provided an exceptionally wide range for differences of opinion, and there were educators to be found on the side of almost every solution.

In 1930 Abraham Flexner, whose great survey of the American medical schools twenty years earlier had resulted in the complete reformation of American medical education, attempted a similar critique of the American university with less decisive results (Doc. 3). Flexner found in the American university a beehive of triviality and vocationalism and drew up a major indictment. In the universities he found a fundamental confusion of purpose: they were partly secondary schools for boys and girls, partly graduate and professional schools for advanced students, and partly "service stations" for the general public. Somewhat similar was the verdict of Robert M. Hutchins a few years later (Doc. 5), who found that serious criteria of intellectuality were not being met by the American university. "The most striking fact about the higher learning in America," he said, "is the confusion that besets it." It was infused with the love of money, a misapplied notion of democracy, and an erroneous notion of progress.

Defenders of the university system were not lacking. They pointed out that devising a unitary philosophy for modern education might simply impose a single doctrine upon a pluralistic institution and cramp its capacity for further progress. Still others felt that the assessments of men like Flexner and Hutchins did not do justice to the actual achievement of American higher education, which had undeniably taken a leading place among the educational systems of the world.

Hutchins, said Harry D. Gideonse (Doc. 6), had failed to recognize the forces that created the American university. Moreover, "to write volumes in support of the thesis that there should be a unifying philosophy, without specific indication of the type of unity or of philosophy, is to miss the essential problem underlying the modern dilemma." John Dewey (Doc. 7) found in Hutchins' ideal of philosophical unity and authority something "akin to the distrust of freedom and the constant appeal to *some* fixed authority that is now overrunning the world." In Hutchins' proposals for reform Dewey found a "withdrawal from everything that smacks of modernity and contemporaneousness" and suggested that in such a withdrawal we would not find the road "to the kind of intellectuality that will remedy the evils he so vividly depicts."

One of the elements in the ideal of a liberal education, as it had been offered under the custodianship of the old-time colleges, was that educated men should have the same kind of education. If they did not all read precisely the same classical works, they had at least read in a common body of classical literature that would help to make of them a community of the educated. The development of the elective system had destroyed this unity at the college level, and the heterogeneous mass high school of the twentieth century had aggravated the situation by creating even more diverse backgrounds for college entrants. Insofar as the collegiate education of the twentieth century was to remain a liberal education, to what extent, then, could it be made a general education? And if there was to be a general education, designed to guide the student to life in the troubled world of the twentieth century, in what kinds of materials should this general education consist?

The pioneer in attempts to answer these questions had been Columbia. There in 1917 the faculty, moved by a feeling that the war crisis required a new look at the modern world, had started a "war aims" course. At the end of the war, the success of this course suggested the need of a general required course on "peace aims"—or, more accurately, on the problems and values of Western civilization. This new offering, which found its way into the catalogue for the first time in 1919, evolved into Columbia's famous Contemporary Civilization program, which was widely imitated throughout the country (Doc. 2). This model for the ideal of general education was later supplemented by a required course in humanities, and over the years the general education offering was extended to two years. In 1918 roughly one-third of the college course at Columbia was prescribed; by 1938 it had become about one-half. This balance was now typical of many undergraduate programs. By 1947 programs of general education were a problem of such common concern to American colleges that it was seen fit to found a periodical dedicated to its problems—the *Journal of General Education*. The most thorough recent investigation into the problems was made at Harvard in 1945 at the behest of President James Bryant Conant (Docs. 8 and 9).

Finally, an attempt to confront the problem of numbers and the need to maximize opportunity through education was made in 1946–47, when President Truman, impressed by the waves of G.I.'s returning to college, created a presidential commission to assess the needs and goals of American higher education. *The Report of the President's Commission on Higher Education* (Doc. 10) was a startlingly egalitarian document, and its estimate of the great numbers who should receive a higher education in the near future suggested that our educational system had moved into a wholly new dimension. The report aroused much controversy. Many felt that the new numbers sought by the Commission were not needed by the American economy; others (Doc. 11) that the Commission proposed to sacrifice qualitative standards in planning to accommodate the multitude of college applicants it envisaged.

1. Alexander Meiklejohn Defines the Liberal College, 1912

Alexander Meiklejohn was born in Rochedale, England, in 1872. He received his A.B. at Brown in 1893 and his Ph.D. in philosophy at Cornell in 1897. From 1897 to 1912 he taught philosophy at Brown, during the last seven years as professor of logic and metaphysics. In 1912 he became president of Amherst, a post he held for

Alexander Meiklejohn, "What the Liberal College Is," *The Liberal College* (Boston, 1920), pp. 30–42, 44–45, 47–50. Reprinted with the permission of Amherst College.

a dozen years. From 1926 to 1938 he was once again a professor of philosophy at the University of Wisconsin, where he was also noted for his sponsorship of experimental education.

See Walker H. Hill (ed.), *Learning and Living: Proceedings of an Anniversary Celebration in Honor of Alexander Meiklejohn* (Chicago, 1942), and Lucien Price, *Prophets Unawares* (New York, 1924).

What do our teachers believe to be the aim of college instruction? Wherever their opinions and convictions find expression there is one contention which is always in the foreground, namely, that to be liberal a college must be essentially intellectual. It is a place, the teachers tell us, in which a boy, forgetting all things else, may set forth on the enterprise of learning. It is a time when a young man may come to awareness of the thinking of his people, may perceive what knowledge is and has been and is to be. Whatever light-hearted undergraduates may say, whatever the opinions of solicitous parents, of ambitious friends, of employers in search of workmen, of leaders in church or state or business,—whatever may be the beliefs and desires and demands of outsiders,—the teacher within the college, knowing his mission as no one else can know it, proclaims that mission to be the leading of his pupil into the life intellectual. The college is primarily not a place of the body, nor of the feelings, nor even of the will; it is, first of all, a place of the mind. . . .

In a word, the liberal college does not pretend to give all the kinds of teaching which a young man of college age may profitably receive; it does not even claim to give all the kinds of intellectual training which are worth giving. It is committed to intellectual training of the liberal type, whatever that may mean, and to that mission it must be faithful. One may safely say, then, on behalf of our college teachers, that their instruction is intended to be radically different from that given in the technical school or even in the professional school. Both these institutions are practical in a sense in which the college, as an intellectual institution, is not. . . .

In the conflict with the forces within the college our teachers find themselves fighting essentially the same battle as against the foes without. In a hundred different ways the friends of the college, students, graduates, trustees and even colleagues, seem to them so to misunderstand its mission as to minimize or to falsify its intellectual ideals. The college is a good place for making friends; it gives excellent experience in getting on with men; it has exceptional advantages as an athletic club; it is a relatively safe place for a boy when he first leaves home; on the whole it may improve a student's manners; it gives acquaintance with lofty ideas of character, preaches the doctrine of social service, exalts the virtues and duties of citizenship. All these conceptions seem to the teacher to hide or to obscure the fact that the college is fundamentally a place of the mind, a time for thinking, an opportunity for knowing. And perhaps in proportion to their own loftiness of purpose and motive they are the more dangerous as tending all the more powerfully to replace or to nullify the underlying principle upon which they all depend. . . .

How then shall we justify the faith of the teacher? What reason can we give for our exaltation of intellectual training and activity? To this question two answers are possible. First, knowledge and thinking are good in themselves. Secondly, they help us in the attainment of other values in life which without them would be impossible. Both these answers may be given and are given by college teachers. Within them must be found whatever can be said by way of explanation and justification of the work of the liberal college. . . .

In a word, men know with regard to thinking, as with regard to every other content of human experience, that it cannot be valued merely in terms of itself. It must be measured in terms of its relation to other contents and to human experience as a whole. Thinking is good in itself,—but what does it cost of other things, what does it bring of other values? Place it amid all the varied contents of our individual and social experience, measure it in terms of what it implies, fix it by means of its relations, and then you will know its worth not simply in itself but in that deeper sense which comes when human desires are rationalized and human lives are known in their entirety, as well as they can be known by those who are engaged in living them.

In this consideration we find the second answer of the teacher to the demand for justification of the work of the college. Knowledge is good, he tells us, not only in itself, but in its enrichment and enhancement of the other values of our experience. In the deepest and fullest sense of the words, knowledge pays. This statement rests upon the classification of human actions into two groups, those of the instinctive type and those of the intellectual type. By far the greater part of our human acts are carried on without any clear idea of what we are going to do or how we are going to do it. For the most part our responses to our situations are the immediate responses of feeling, of perception, of custom, of tradition. But slowly and painfully, as the mind has developed, action after action has been translated from the feeling to the ideational type; in wider and wider fields men have become aware of their own modes of action, more and more they have come to understanding, to knowledge of themselves and of their needs. And the principle underlying all our educational procedure is that on the whole, actions become more successful as they pass from the sphere of feeling to that of understanding. Our educational belief is that in the long run if men know what they are going to do and how they are going to do it, and what is the nature of the situation with which they are dealing, their response to that situation will be better adjusted and more beneficial than are the responses of the feeling type in like situations.

It is all too obvious that there are limits to the validity of this principle. If men are to investigate, to consider, to decide, then action must be delayed and we must pay the penalty of waiting. If men are to endeavor to understand and know their situations, then we must be prepared to see them make mistakes in their thinking, lose their certainty of touch, wander off into pitfalls and illusions and fallacies of thought, and in consequence secure for the time results far lower in value than those of the instinctive response which they seek to replace. The delays and mistakes and uncertainties of our thinking are a heavy price to pay, but it is the conviction of the teacher that the price is as nothing when compared with the goods which it buys. . . .

Within the limits of this general educational principle the place of the liberal college may easily be fixed. . . . But the college is called liberal . . . because the instruction is dominated by no special interest, is limited to no single human task, but is intended to take human activity as a whole, to understand human endeavors not in their isolation but in their relations to one another and to the total experience which we call the life of our people. . . . To give boys an intellectual grasp on human experience—this, it seems to me, is the teacher's conception of the chief function of the liberal college.

May I call attention to the fact that this second answer of the teacher defines the aim of the college as avowedly and frankly practical? Knowledge is to be sought chiefly for the sake of its contribution to the other activities of human living. But on the other hand, it is as definitely declared that in method the college is fully and unreservedly intellectual. If we can see that these two demands are not in conflict but that they stand together in the harmonious relation of means and ends, of instrument and achievement, of method and result, we may escape many a needless conflict and keep our educational policy in singleness of aim and action. To do this we must show that the college is intellectual, not as opposed to practical interests and purposes, but as opposed to unpractical and unwise methods of work. The issue is not between practical and intellectual aims but between the immediate and the remote aim, between the hasty and the measured procedure, between the demand for results at once and the willingness to wait for the best results. The intellectual road to success is longer and more roundabout than any other, but they who are strong and willing for the climbing are brought to higher levels of achievement than they could possibly have attained had they gone straight forward in the pathway of quick returns. If this were not true the liberal college would have no proper place in our life at all. In so far as it is true the college has a right to claim the best of our young men to give them its preparation for the living they are to do. . . .

It often appears as if our teachers and scholars were deliberately in league to mystify and befog the popular mind regarding this practical value of intellectual work. They seem not to wish too much said about the results and benefits. Their desire is to keep aloft the intellectual banner, to proclaim the intellectual gospel, to demand of student and public alike adherence to the faith. And in general when they are questioned as to results they give little satisfaction except to those who are already pledged to unwavering confidence in their *ipse dixits*. And largely as a result of this attitude the American people seem to me to have little understanding of the intellectual work of the college. Our citizens and patrons can see the value of games and physical exercises; they readily perceive the importance of the social give and take of a college democracy; they can appreciate the value of studies which prepare a young man for his profession and so anticipate or replace the professional school; they can even believe that if a boy is kept at some sort of thinking for four years his mind may become more acute, more systematic, more accurate, and hence more useful than it was before. But as for the content of a college course, as for the value of knowledge, what a boy gains by knowing Greek or economics, philosophy or literature, history or biology, except as they are regarded as having professional usefulness, I think our friends are in the dark and are likely to remain so until we turn on the light. When our teachers say, as they sometimes do say, that the effect of knowledge upon the character and life of the student must always be for the college an accident, a circumstance which has no essential connection with its real aim or function, then it seems to me that our educational policy is wholly out of joint. If there be no essential connection between instruction and life, then there is no reason for giving instruction except in so far as it is pleasant in itself, and we have no educational policy at all. As against this hesitancy, this absence of a conviction, we men of the college should declare in clear and unmistakable terms our creed—the creed that knowledge is justified by its results. . . .

There is a second wandering from the faith which is so common among investigators that it may fairly be called the "fallacy of the scholar." It is the belief that all knowledge is so good that all parts of knowledge are equally good. Ask many of our scholars and teachers what subjects a boy should study in order that he may gain insight for human living, and they will say, "It makes no difference in what department of knowledge he studies; let him go into Sanskrit or bacteriology, into mathematics or history; if only he goes where men are actually dealing with intellectual problems, and if only he learns how to deal with problems himself, the aim of education is achieved, he has entered into intellectual activity." This point of view, running through all the varieties of the elective system, seems to me hopelessly at variance with any sound educational doctrine. It represents the scholar of the day at his worst both as a thinker and as a teacher. In so far as it dominates a group of college teachers it seems to me to render them unfit to determine and to administer a college curriculum. It is an announcement that they have no guiding principles in their educational practice, no principles of selection in their arrangement of studies, no genuine grasp on the relationship between knowledge and life. . . .

I am not urging that the principle of election of college studies should be entirely discontinued. But I should like to inquire by what right and within what limits it is justified. The most familiar argument in its favor is that if a student is allowed to choose along the lines of his own intellectual or professional interest he will have enthusiasm, the eagerness which comes with the following of one's own bent. Now just so far as this result is achieved, just so far as the quality of scholarship is improved, the procedure is good and we may follow it if we do not thereby lose other results more valuable than our gain. But if the special interest comes into conflict with more fundamental ones, if what the student prefers is opposed to what he ought to prefer, then we of the college cannot leave the choice with him. . . .

This lack of a dominating educational policy is in turn an expression of an intellectual attitude, a point of view, which marks the scholars of our time. In a word, it seems to me that our willingness to allow students to wander about in the college curriculum is one of the most characteristic expressions of a certain intellectual agnosticism, a kind of intellectual bankruptcy, into which, in spite of all our wealth of information, the spirit of the time has fallen. . . .

It has become an axiom with us that the genuine student labors within his own field. And if the student ventures forth to examine the relations of his field to the surrounding country he very easily becomes a populariser, a litterateur, a speculator, and worst of all, unscientific. Now I do not object to a man's minding his own intellectual business if he chooses to do so, but when a man minds his own business because he does not know any other business, because he has no knowledge whatever of the relationships which justify his business and make it worth while, then I think one may say that though such a man minds his own affairs he does not know them, he does not understand them. Such a man, from the point of view of the demands of a liberal education, differs in no essential respect from the tradesman who does not understand his trade or the professional man who merely practices his profession. Just as truly as they, he is shut up within a special interest; just as truly as they he is making no intellectual attempt to understand his experience in its unity. And the pity of it is that more and more the chairs in our colleges are occupied by men who have only this special interest, this specialized information, and it is through them that we attempt to give our boys a liberal education, which the teachers themselves have not achieved. . . .

These five elements, . . . a young man must take from a college of liberal training, the contributions of philosophy, of humanistic science, of natural science, of history and of literature. So far as knowledge is concerned, these at least he should have, welded together in some kind of interpretation of his own experience and of the world in which he lives. . . .

To be perfectly frank about the whole matter, I believe that in large measure our pupils are indifferent to their studies simply because they do not see that these are important.

But if we really have a vital course of study to present this difficulty can in large measure be overcome. It is possible to make a freshman realize the need of translating his experience from the forms of feeling to those of ideas. He can and he ought to be shown that now, his days of mere tutelage being over, it is time for him to face the problems of his people, to begin to think about those problems for himself, to learn what other men have learned and thought before him, in a word, to get himself ready to take his place among those who are responsible for the guidance of our common life by ideas and principles and purposes. If this could be done, I think we should get from the reality-loving American boy something like an intellectual enthusiasm, something of the spirit that comes when he plays a game that seems to him really worth playing. But I do not believe that this result can be achieved without a radical reversal of the arrangement of the college curriculum. I should like to see every freshman at once plunged into the problems of philosophy, into the difficulties and perplexities about our institutions, into the scientific accounts of the world especially as they bear on human life, into the portrayals of human experience which are given by the masters of literature. . . . Let him once feel the problems of the present, and his historical studies will become significant; let him know what other men have discovered and thought about his problems, and he will be ready to deal with them himself. But in any case, the whole college course will be unified and dominated by a single interest, a single purpose,—that of so understanding human life as to be ready and equipped for the practice of it. And this would mean for the college, not another seeking of the way of quick returns, but rather an escape from aimless wanderings in the mere by-paths of knowledge, a resolute climbing on the high road to a unified grasp upon human experience.

I have taken so much of your time . . . that an apology seems due for the things I have omitted to mention. . . . I have put these aside deliberately, for the sake of a cause which is greater than any of them—a cause which lies at the very heart of the liberal college. It is the cause of making clear to the American people the mission of the teacher, of convincing them of the value of knowledge: not the specialized knowledge which contributes to immediate practical aims, but the unified understanding which is Insight.

2. *The Columbia College Faculty Devises a Course in Contemporary Civilization, 1919*

The circumstances by which the Faculty of Columbia College was led to adopt this course are explained in the Introduction. At its January, 1919, meeting it resolved to discontinue required courses in history and philosophy and to substitute a course in contemporary civilization required of all freshmen and meeting five times a week. The first of the two selections below is the opening announcement of this course in the college catalogue of 1919–1920; the second is the rationale as presented in the syllabus provided for students.

For the origin of the course, its context in the Columbia curriculum, and the story of its frequent subsequent revision, see Justus Buchler, "Reconstruction in the Liberal Arts," in Dwight C. Miner (ed.), *A History of Columbia College on Morningside* (New York, 1954), pp. 48–135; see also Docs. 8, 9, and Hoyt Trowbridge, "Forty Years of General Education," *Journal of General Education*, XI (July, 1958), 161–69.

The aim of the course is to inform the student of the more outstanding and influential factors in his physical and social environment. The chief features of the intellectual, economic, and political life of to-day are treated and considered in their dependence on and difference from the past. The great events of the last century in the history of the countries now more closely linked in international relations are reviewed, and the insistent problems, internal and international, which they are now facing are given detailed consideration. By thus giving the student, early in his college course, objective material on which to base his own judgments, it is thought he will be aided in an intelligent participation in the civilization of his own day.

The study of contemporary civilization is included in the curriculum of the Freshman year because the Faculty of Columbia College believes that as early as possible young men should be acquainted with the facts and problems which are the common property and common responsibility of their generation.

We are living in a world in which there are great and perplexing

---

"Contemporary Civilization A1—A2—Introduction. . . . Required of Freshmen," *Columbia College Announcement, 1919–1920* (New York, 1919), p. 34; "The Plan and Purpose of the Course," *Introduction to Contemporary Civilization: A Syllabus, Part I* (New York, 1919), p. 1.

issues on which keen differences of opinion have arisen; and it is important now, not less than during the war, that men should understand the forces which are at work in the society of their own day.

In this course, therefore, the intention is to present the features of civilization, past and present, which are of significance for those who expect to take part in the solution of the problems which now confront us. Many interesting questions are omitted because they are not relevant to the discussion and many features of life which seem too simple to need statement are stressed because of their social importance.

The chief divisions of the course are intended to group related facts and to culminate in a discussion of the insistent problems of the present, supplemented by the presentation of various solutions which have been proposed. . . .

3. Abraham Flexner Criticizes the American University, 1930

Abraham Flexner (1866–1959) was born in Louisville, Kentucky, received his A.B. at the Johns Hopkins during its great days, and, after a year of high-school teaching in his native city, went on to graduate study at Harvard and the University of Berlin. In 1908 he joined the staff of the Carnegie Foundation for the Advancement of Teaching, on which he rose to become secretary, a role he filled between 1917 and 1925, and finally director of the division of studies. From 1930 to 1939 he was also director of the Institute for Advanced Study at Princeton, a research institute of his own conception. Probably his greatest contribution to American education was his famous survey, *Medical Education in the United States and Canada* (1910), in which, taking the excellent medical school at the Hopkins as a model, he examined the condition of other medical schools with an extremely critical eye. His scathing report instituted an era of reform in medical education, in the course of which many of the weaker schools were eliminated and the better ones greatly strengthened. The assessment of the universities here excerpted was perhaps an attempt to repeat his earlier success, but the university situation was far more complicated than that of the medical schools and the resistance to his judgments much stronger (see Doc. 6).

See Abraham Flexner, *I Remember* (New York, 1940), and *Abraham Flexner: An Autobiography* (New York, 1960).

Abraham Flexner, *Universities: American, English, German* (New York, 1930), pp. 41–42, 45, 63–64, 66–68, 74–77, 80–82, 99–103, 130–34, 151–55, 188–89, 217–18. Reprinted with the permission of Marie C. Eichelser and Mrs. Paul Lewinson.

I shall have much to say in criticism of American universities. For that very reason, I begin on an appreciative note. Scholars we have always had—usually stranded in the old-fashioned college, the ministry, or the law. But a university in the sense in which I use the term—an institution consciously devoted to the pursuit of knowledge, the solution of problems, the critical appreciation of achievement, and the training of men at a really high level—a university in this sense we did not possess until the Johns Hopkins University modestly opened its portals in 1876. That is slightly more than fifty years ago. A half century ago, therefore, the opportunities for advanced or critical training in America were very scarce and very limited. The change, since that day, has been amazing, immensely to the credit of a people that within a few generation has had to subdue a continent, create a social and political order, maintain its unity, and invent educational, philanthropic, sanitary, and other agencies capable of functioning at all. Higher opportunities have within this brief period become abundant— less abundant, I think, than external appearances frequently indicate, yet abundant in almost every direction—in the older disciplines, in the newer, in the professions and in state-supported as well as in endowed institutions. Sums of which no one could then have dreamed have been assembled; buildings, apparatus, books have been provided. The country cannot, of course, dispense with Europe; but in the realm of higher education America has become in certain fields a country with which Europe cannot any longer dispense, either. I shall go into details as I proceed. But this categorical statement I make now at the outset, in order that the reader may know that, however severely I reprobate many of the doings of our universities, I do full justice to their solid achievements. Perhaps candid criticism may help them to regain the main road. . . .

The term "university" is very loosely used in America; I shall not pause to characterize the absurdities covered by the name. I propose, rather, to concentrate attention on the most highly developed and prominent of American institutions, to ask what they do, how they are constituted, how they fare from the standpoint of the ideal which I have set up. As for the others—and they run into the hundreds—it is impossible in this volume to take them into account; fine minds and souls will be found here and there in them; many of them, more especially in the South and West—though the East is not free—are hotbeds of reaction in politics, industry, and religion, ambitious in pretension, meagre in performance, doubtful contributors, when they are not actual obstacles, to the culture of the nation.

The great American universities which I shall discuss are composed of three parts: they are secondary schools and colleges for boys and girls; graduate and professional schools for advanced students; "service" stations for the general public. The three parts are not distinct: the college is confused with the "service" station and overlaps the graduate school; the graduate school is partly a college, partly a vocational school, and partly an institution of university grade. . . .

It is gratifying to be able to record the fact that there are American colleges which have not succumbed to nonsense. Harvard—I am now speaking of the college work alone in all the institutions which I am about to name—Yale, Princeton, Swarthmore, Vanderbilt, Amherst, Williams, Barnard, Bryn Mawr, Smith, and Wellesley, to select a small number at random—give no credit towards admission or graduation for any of the absurd courses which I have above mentioned; they all offer a varied and solid cultural curriculum to undergraduate students who may care to be educated. No premature or trivial vocational studies confuse the pursuit of a liberal education. Even these institutions are, to be sure, not free from weaknesses—avoidable and unavoidable. They are compelled to accept as college students graduates of the high schools and preparatory schools which are largely ineffective as training institutions; that they cannot help. In the main the student body lacks intellectual background or outlook; that again they cannot help. Their students are in the mass devoid of cultural interests and develop little, for the most part, during their four years at college; it is difficult to say what they can or should do about that, though increasing disquiet is at least a good sign. Where class instruction is pursued, the classes are usually too large; the young instructor's time is too largely consumed in correcting and grading papers, most of which are badly written. With certain important exceptions which I shall mention later,* the colleges count points and units and credits—an abominable system, destructive of disinterested and protracted intellectual effort; any one of them could abolish it root and branch without notice. . . .

---

* I have lately asked one of the most promising of our younger Greek scholars, how many of his Greek students are "worth while." "Of graduate students," he answered, "none; of undergraduates, less than 10%."

I have just said that a few American colleges are endeavouring to break away from the absurd computation of degrees by arithmetical means and to encourage both concentration and scholarship. On paper, the number of institutions that have thus instituted "honours" work is impressively large; but the number so situated, financially or otherwise, as to be able to do it well, is relatively small. Without intending the list to be complete, special attention may be called to Swarthmore, Harvard, certain departments of Columbia, Barnard, Bryn Mawr, Smith, and the Experimental College at Wisconsin, as institutions in which by one method or another the more earnest or better endowed students are enabled to escape the deadly lockstep of the classroom, the deadly grip of the unit system, and to focus their energies on a limited field in close contact with the more competent instructors. Swarthmore, a small college, admitting annually about one hundred and seventy-five students, having made the most careful selection possible from over a thousand applicants, devotes, because it cannot be helped, as much as two years to patching, disciplining, and sorting out the student body before it can give during the last two years independence and concentrated opportunity to a small segregated group, known as candidates for honours; at the end of the last two years, external examiners pass upon their merits. Harvard has in many subjects appointed tutors, who direct the reading of the abler students and by means of a "comprehensive examination" force the student to read more widely than the 'courses' above criticized. I do not imply that salvation lies only on this road. Just as one may make out a case for the tutor, so one may also make out a case for the lecture by means of which William James addressed a large group, some members of which certainly persisted in the study of philosophy—as, without such stimulus, they probably would not have done. There is no single, no royal road to knowledge, education, or culture; there is no single best way to teach at any stage. Over and above the colleges I have named, there are other institutions, some of them modest and inconspicuous where able students may obtain an education that runs beyond, sometimes far beyond, the secondary stage. But in the mass, it is still true that American college students are, at the close of four years, intellectually considered, an unselected and untrained body of attractive boys and girls, who have for the most part not yet received even a strenuous secondary school training.* Surely the Dean of Columbia College knows American college youth. "I am convinced," he has recently said, "that the youth of college age at the present time are as immature morally and as crude socially as they are undeveloped intellectually." In part this is true because, the high school having coddled them, the college continues the coddling process. Every jerk and shock must be eliminated; the students must be "oriented"; they must be "advised" as to what to "take"; they must be vocationally guided. How is it possible to educate persons who will never be permitted to burn their fingers, who must be dexterously and expensively housed, first as freshmen, then as upper classmen, so as to make the right sort of social connections and to establish the right sort of social relationships, who are protected against risk as they should be protected against plague, and who, even though "they work their way through," have no conception of the effort required to develop intellectual sinew? . . .

Following the success of the Baltimore experiment, graduate schools were developed out of or intertwined with the colleges at Harvard, Yale, Columbia, Princeton, and elsewhere; the University of Chicago founded in the early nineties, established strong departments for graduate work. Since that date the quality of graduate opportunity and study has at its best indubitably improved, not deteriorated; its extent has indubitably increased, not decreased. Mathematics, physics, English, history, economics, even mediaeval and classical studies have attained heights that fifty years ago could not possibly have been dreamed of; witness the names of Charles Peirce, Willard Gibbs, Michelson, Moore, Breasted, Manly, Millikan, Richards, Gildersleeve, Turner, Shapley, Rostovtzeff, Capps, R. L. Jones, and scores of others. In some fields, we have been at once sound and original—among them, economics, sanitation, biology, and experimental medicine, in connection with which, to select a few names at random, Taussig, Wesley Mitchell, Welch, Abel, Mall, Morgan, Van Slyke, and Loeb spring to mind. A distinguished English Chaucerian has recently said that not London or Oxford but Chicago is the most productive centre of Chaucerian study today; and the great Scottish scholar, Sir William Craigie, who with Professor Onions brought the Oxford Dictionary to completion, is now compiling a Scottish Dictionary, not at Aberdeen or Edinburgh, but at the University of Chicago. To be sure, these men

---

* "I think that our French student works harder than the American student," remarked M. Henri Bergson on the occasion of a recent visit to American universities.

were mainly trained abroad; but with avidity America welcomed them and created for them congenial centres of teaching and research. Amazing progress has been made in providing scientists with laboratories and scholars with books. The great scientific laboratories of Harvard, Yale, Columbia, Chicago, Pasadena, Michigan, California, Wisconsin, and other state universities are not surpassed in respect to adequacy by the laboratories of any other country. They might be criticized as being too complete, too commodious, too well equipped rather than the reverse; good men have not infrequently been swamped by the expansion and complexities of their facilities and by the burdens of teaching, supervision, and administration connected therewith. . . ."*

A special paragraph should be devoted to libraries. The true university, Carlyle maintained, was a collection of books. But the larger the collection, the more necessary that it be properly housed, properly arranged, and readily accessible. Half a century ago, roughly speaking, America was practically without libraries. It is less than sixty years since Daniel C. Gilman, destined soon to be President of Johns Hopkins University, resigned the librarianship of Yale University, because he could not obtain an assistant and had himself to light the fire in the stove every morning. No staff of experts, no central heating—a stove fire, in a combustible building, so recently as that! Today, universities, municipalities, secondary and elementary schools emulate one another in providing admirable collections of books and journals, made available to readers and borrowers quickly, freely, and comfortably. A library technique has been developed that is genuinely helpful; library construction has steadily improved. And university libraries have been so woven into the texture of university life and activity that, as far as physical arrangements go, work at every legitimate level is relieved of drudgery, inconvenience, and delay. Sound educational ideals have thus been embodied in steel and stone. The advanced worker needs access to catalogue and shelves; he has it. He wants a quiet nook in which he can work secure from interruption; he has it. The professor who meets his students in a common lecture room, equipped with chairs, a rostrum, and a blackboard, might as well lecture in a public hall; he needs, especially for his advanced students, a seminar room, adjoining the stacks devoted to his subject. Thus books are at hand; a

---

* "Es kommt nicht auf den Käfig an
  Ob ein Vogel singen kann."

workshop for him and his students in a congenial atmosphere is created. The American university has achieved this result better than any other university anywhere. It is not too much to say that no university should embark upon library construction without studying the successive and continually improving American contributions to the solution of the problem of the university library. . . .

But there is, alas, another side that one may not ignore. To begin with, the American graduate school suffers from the curious cultural meagreness of American life. One studies Greek, philosophy, or medicine under great masters; but there is something lacking, something subtle and elusive, but vitally real and substantial. An able student at the American Academy in Rome once told me that he "found it necessary to go abroad for a year every few years, else he would suffocate." It could not be otherwise; time may provide the remedy; but we may perhaps expedite the process by acknowledging the situation and by opposing certain dominant currents of American life. Cultivated persons have emigrated to America. But their children are soon bleached —reduced to the standard American pattern. The melting pot has its advantages; but it has cost us dearly.

In addition to this general defect, the graduate school suffers gravely from the inferior training of the high school and the college. So kindly and sympathetic a critic as Professor [T. F.] Tout feels himself bound to note that "American schools seem, according to American testimony, less thorough and the results of their work less permanent, than is the case with the better sorts of British schools. The absence or rarity of compulsions, both at school and college, leads to a neglect of languages, and one of the weak points of the American historical student is that he is even often less familiar with the tongues in which his sources are written than his English counterpart. In making this statement please do not think that I hold any illusions as to the adequacy of the linguistic equipment of many English aspirants to historical fame! But I am bound to confess that foreign languages, and especially Latin, are for many Americans a worse stumbling-block than even the lack of that broad basis of general historical knowledge that the honour school of almost any British university affords. Perhaps one grows more conservative as one gets older, but America certainly made me see that there was more to be said for honour schools and compulsory language subjects than in my hot youth I had ever dreamed was the case. It also taught me that the thesis, though a good servant, is a bad master, and that the cult of the repeated thesis is sometimes a mistake. If America had something like an English honour course for her M.A., and reserved her thesis for the Ph.D., the advantages of both systems might be retained and the disadvantages minimized. In adopting, rather too whole-heartedly, the German thesis system, the American reformers of a generation or two ago forgot that the German youth, when he went to the university, had had in his *Gymnasium* a good old-fashioned, well-rounded education, and had passed an examination that might well be compared to the British or American pass degree." . . .

The members of the first teachers colleges in the United States were themselves scholars; but scholars and scientists are now scarce, very scarce, in these faculties. In their place, one finds hordes of professors and instructors possessing meagre intellectual background whose interests centre in technique and administration viewed in a narrow *ad hoc* fashion. The staff of Teachers College, Columbia University, requires 26 pages for mere enumeration: the roster contains 303 instructors;* the catalogue lists over 10,000 "students" of one kind or another. A few instructors offer courses in educational philosophy, in foreign or comparative education; problems of elementary and secondary education are not slighted. But why do not these substantial and interesting fields suffice? Why should not an educated person, broadly and deeply versed in educational philosophy and experience, help himself from that point on? Why should his attention be diverted during these pregnant years to the trivialities and applications with which common sense can deal adequately when the time comes? Most of 200 pages, filled with mere cataloguing, are devoted to trivial, obvious, and inconsequential subjects, which could safely be left to the common sense or intelligence of any fairly well educated person. Atomistic training—the provision of endless special courses, instead of a small number of opportunities that are at once broad and deep—is hostile to the development of intellectual grasp. A Negro preacher in a popular play declares: "The Lord expects us to figure out a few things for ourselves;" but Teachers College is organized on the opposite principle. Thus in this huge institution thousands are trained *"ad hoc,"* instead of being educated and encouraged to use their wits and

---

* Not including scores of teachers in the Extension Department, Summer School, etc.

their senses. Among the hundreds of courses thus offered, I cite as fair examples "manuscript writing," "teaching of educational sociology," "administrative procedures in curriculum construction," "research in the history of school instruction in history," "music for teachers of literature and history," "methods used in counseling individuals," "research in college administration," "psychology of higher education," "teaching English to foreigners," "teaching the individual," "extracurricular activities, including school clubs, excursions, athletic insignia, class parties and dances, extra-curricular finances, and a record card for pupil activity"! . . .

And that the unconscious effort to frighten away intelligence is usually quite successful is demonstrated by the theses which crown the student with the A.M. or Ph.D. degree. At random I select from the Chicago and Columbia lists: "The City School District," "The Experience Variables: A Study of the Variable Factors in Experience contributing to the Formation of Personality," "Measuring Efficiency in Supervision and Teaching," "City School Attendance Service," "Pupil Participation in High School Control," "Administrative Problems of the High School Cafeteria," "Personnel Studies of Scientists in the United States," "Suggestion in Education," "Social Background and Activities of Teachers College Students,"* "Qualities related to Success in Teaching," "The Technique of estimating School Equipment Costs," "Public School Plumbing Equipment," "An Analysis of Janitor Service in Elementary Schools,"** "The Equipment of the School Theatre," "Concerning our Girls and What They Tell Us," "Evidences of the Need of Education for Efficient Purchasing," "Motor Achievements of Children of Five, Six, and Seven Years of Age," "A Scale of

---

* In this production, the author of which is a dean of women at a teachers college, account is taken of whether in the homes from which the students came is a lawn mower, a desk set, a rag carpet, a built-in bookcase, potted plants, company dishes. Among the leisure activities investigated are "shopping," "heart-to-heart talks," "just sit alone," "think and dream," "going to picnics," "idle conversation (talking about just anything)," "having *dates* with men," "telling jokes," "teasing somebody," "doing almost anything so you are with the gang," "reading."

** I pause for a moment to contemplate the thesis on "An Analysis of Janitor Service in Elementary Schools." Why elementary? There are reasons: first, obviously, the title suggests other theses—and new subjects are in demand, as students multiply—the duties of a junior high school janitor, of a high school janitor, of a college janitor, etc. "Are these really different subjects?" I once asked a professor of school administration.

"Oh, yes," he replied, "the lavatory problem, for example, is with small boys quite different from the same problem at the high school level!"

Measuring Antero-Posterior Posture of Ninth Grade Boys," "A Study of School Postures and Desk Dimensions," "The Technique of Activity and Trait Analysis Applied to Y.M.C.A. Executive Secretaries as a Basis for Curricular Materials," and "Statistical Methods for Utilizing Personal Judgments to Evaluate Activities for Teacher Training Curricula." Harvard is in danger of following the same course: it has recently bestowed the Ph.D. degree for theses on "Vocational Activities and Social Understanding in the Curriculum for Stenographer-Clerks," "Guidance in Colleges for Women," "The Intelligence of Orphan Children in Texas." (Why orphans? Why Texas?) On the other hand, a minority of the theses deal with serious and worthy subjects. That I have not mistaken the drift of intelligence and scholarship away from schools of education is admitted by the head of an important faculty of education, who permits me to quote, from an unpublished memorandum, the following:

"There is in the United States no University School of Education in which a faculty of marked power and distinction is devoting its full time to a highly selected body of graduate students under a program of ample scope systematically directed toward professional leadership."

Why do certain American universities feel themselves under pressure to develop their "service" functions, even to call themselves "public service" institutions? There are many reasons. State universities have to make themselves "useful"—or they think they do—in order to justify themselves to the man in the street or on the farm, since income depends on appropriations of the state legislature; thus large numbers —some resident, others non-resident—get the kind of information or training, which they need or think they need, and from which they feel themselves competent to profit—though, as I have urged and shall continue to urge, this sort of thing does not deserve to be called college or university education at all; endowed institutions think they must be useful in order that alumni, local communities, and the general public may be encouraged to contribute gifts, and in order that they may not be reproached for being aristocratic or "high-brow" or careless of the needs of the general public. And when I say, "useful," I mean directly, immediately useful, for Americans like to see "results." I believe that the intelligence and generosity of the American public— including alumni—are thus underestimated and undermined. But whether this is true or not, universities have a duty to perform and a function to discharge.* On this point, an able and experienced university president has recently written me: "I am inclined to think most Americans do value education as a business asset, but not as the entrance into the joy of intellectual experience or acquaintance with the best that has been said and done in the past. They value it not as an experience, but as a tool. Possibly Americans value everything in that way—value church and religion and marriage and travel and war and peace, never for the sake of themselves, but always for the sake of something just around the corner. The sense of tomorrow has amazing power in our American life. Never was there a people so careless of the past and even so careless of the present, except as a stepping-stone into a tomorrow which shall bring wealth and dynamic and material progress. All this has its good side and its very bad side as well."**

We can, fortunately, illustrate the correct attitude of the university professor towards practice. Pasteur was a professor of chemistry. In the course of his professional career, the prosperity and well-being of France were threatened by silk-worm disease, by difficulties in the making of wines, in the brewing of beer, by chicken cholera, hydrophobia, etc. Pasteur permitted himself to be diverted from his work in order to solve these problems, one after another; having done so, he published his results and returned to his laboratory. His approach was intellectual, no matter whether the subject was poultry, brewing, or chemistry. He did not become consultant to silk-worm growers, wine makers, brewers, or poultry men; he did not give courses in silk-worm growing, wine making, or chicken raising. The problem solved, his interest and activity ceased. He had indeed served, but he had served like a scientist, and there his service ended. This is not the usual way in which the American university does service. To be sure, there are scientists, economists, and others, who are thus interested in pressing practical problems, and who, having reached a scientific result, communicate it to the world and pass on to other problems. These are, as

---

* The new president of a state university, who, to quote his own language, "innocently" began to study the curriculum, discovered that "courses had been divided and subdivided until they had reached a point of attenuation that did not justify recognition on the part of a university. In the professional schools and departments we found emaciation rampant, for the departments had taken in courses that belong to trade and technical schools." (Quotation slightly abridged.)

** Letter (Jan. 16, 1928) from the late President W. H. P. Faunce of Brown University (quoted by permission).

I take it, genuine university workers. I am not therefore making a plea for scholasticism or gerund grinding—only a plea for the use of judgment, dignity, a sense of value, and a sense of humour.

The absurdities into which the ambition to be of "service" has led certain universities will be regarded as incredible outside, at times inside, the United States—yes, at times, I suspect, within the universities which are themselves guilty. Let me begin by admitting that under the conditions of modern life there are thoroughly competent people who are strongly moved to study; and the younger men connected with universities can learn something of the world in which they live and something of the art of teaching by expending a moderate amount of time and strength in conducting classes for mature, competent, and serious persons in subjects worthy of a place within the framework of a university. The conditions which I have incidentally inserted are, however, important: the subjects must be substantial, the students must be competent and serious, the instructors of high quality and thoroughly protected against exploitation. In so far as I know university extension in America, no university that engages in "service" work observes these or any other ascertainable limits. There are of course serious students, who work year after year, whose persistence is more significant than regular college attendance might be; but there are thousands of drifters, floating in and out, and getting nothing. Columbia University in 1928–29 enrolled about 12,000 extension students, over 10,000 of whom were "resident," the rest non-resident. Substantial courses are indeed offered—courses in Shakespeare, economics, modern languages, philosophy, etc. This is, if kept within bounds and upon a high basis, legitimate, though an entirely separate and independent institute of adult education might do even this as well or better. But what is one to say of the ideals of Columbia University when it befuddles the public and lowers its own dignity by offering extension courses to misguided people in "juvenile story writing," "critical writing," "magazine articles," "persuasive speaking," "advertising layouts," "practical advertising writing," "retail advertising and sales promotion," "advertising research," "individual problems in fiction writing," "writing the one-act play," "book selection," "story telling," and "direct-by-mail selling and advertising?" If there is a country in the world, in which the advertiser is destroying individuality and compelling almost everybody, regardless of needs, wants, and solvency, to buy the same things, it is the United States; and Columbia University, which should be a bulwark against uniformity and the home of intellectual and cultural integrity, independence, and idiosyncrasy, plays the purely commercial game of the merchant whose sole concern is profit or of the shop assistant who thinks that an academic certificate in a business subject may bring him an increased salary. The director of this strange and unworthy conglomeration of sense and nonsense is simultaneously professor of Latin epigraphy, director of university extension, director of the school of business, and president of the reactionary medical school in Brooklyn, of which I have spoken above. Of the value and importance which the University attributes to Latin epigraphy, a layman may venture a guess on the basis of the professor's executive responsibility for 20,000 extension and home study students in every imaginable field, not to mention his sallies into the fields of medical education and business education. . . .

It is idle to labour the point further; but one may comment on a flagrant and apparently unnoticed contradiction. The current literature of college education emphasizes the importance of contact between instructor and student and attributes no small part of the failure of the college to mass-education on the campus. The dictum of Mark Hopkins is frequently recalled: the ideal college consists of a log of wood with an instructor at one end and a student at the other. The preceptorial system introduced at Princeton by President Wilson, the honours work at Harvard and Swarthmore, the tutorial system at Harvard—all are efforts to establish close, informal contacts between members of the student body and the instructing staff. If the difficulties thus attacked are real—and no one disputes the fact—in what terms is one to characterize the advertising of Chicago, Columbia, and other institutions which spread before thousands the alluring prospect of obtaining just as good an education—an education of "university grade" (Columbia) —by mail? The problem of America is not "Main Street"; there are Main Streets in all countries. The hopelessness of America lies in the inability and unwillingness of those occupying seats of intelligence to distinguish between genuine culture and superficial veneer, in the lowering of institutions which should exemplify intellectual distinctions to the level of the venders of patent medicines. So, too, there are Babbitts in all countries, not only in the United States; but "Babbittry" in the presidency of great universities is an exclusively—as it is a widespread—American phenomenon. No nation responds to exacting leadership more readily than the United States: witness the response to the Johns Hopkins at its founding, to the advanced work of the California Institute of Technology, to the reorganization of Swarthmore; but the lessons of history, even of recent history, are for the most part lost upon the eminent university heads of our own time. To be sure, universities might be too remote, too cloistral, too academic. But American universities have yet to learn that participation is wholesome only when subordinated to educational function, only when it takes place at a high, disinterested, intellectual level. . . .*

Let us turn for a moment to schools of domestic science. One wonders what "science" means to the university authorities who conduct or condone faculties of domestic science. The departments bloom like the cedars of Lebanon at Columbia, Chicago, and the state universities. Despite the difficulty experienced by universities and their medical faculties in obtaining professors of bio-chemistry, the departments of domestic science or household arts at Columbia and Chicago boast staffs that undertake to deal with nutritional problems and to offer advanced degrees (A.M., Ph.D.) indifferently to persons who write theses on underwear and on topics in the field of physiological chemistry. A course on catering is found side by side with research in food and nutrition. It is of course absurd to suppose that either competent teachers or competent students can be found in departments of this kind, at a time when there is a strong and unsatisfied demand for both in academic and medical departments of superior dignity and importance. None the less Chicago has in the Department of Home Economics and Household Administration given Ph.D. degrees for theses on the "Basal Metabolism and Urinary Creatinine, Creatine and Uric Acid of School Children," the "Coefficient of Digestibility and Specific Dynamic Action of a Simple Mixed Diet in Contrasting Types of Individuals," "Variations in Demand for Clothing at Different Income Levels—A Study in the Behaviour of the Consumer," and M.A. degrees for theses on "Photographic Studies on Boiled Icing," "Trends in Hosiery Advertising," "An Analysis of Paring Knives in Terms of Time and Material Wastes in Paring Potatoes," "A Study of Controlled Conditions in Cooking Hams," "Buying Women's Garments by Mail,"

---

* Of the great American universities that I have mentioned, one, Princeton, still largely a college though in some departments important graduate groups are developing, does no "service" work whatsoever of the type which I have described; another, Yale, mostly a college, does little and "has no ambitions in that direction." (Letter from the President.)

"Style Cycles in Women's Undergarments," and finally "A Time and Motion Comparison on Four Methods of Dishwashing." In form and aspect nothing could be more impressive. The last-mentioned thesis, for example, bears the title page:

THE UNIVERSITY OF CHICAGO

A TIME AND MOTION COMPARISON OF FOUR METHODS

OF DISHWASHING

A DISSERTATION

SUBMITTED TO THE GRADUATE FACULTY IN

CANDIDACY FOR THE DEGREE OF MASTER OF ARTS

Nor does the resemblance to scientific research cease with the title page. The dissertation includes: Introduction, Review of Literature, Purpose, Limitations, Method of Procedure, Results and Comparisons, Conclusions, and Recommendations, Conclusions (once more!), Bibliography. Time was kept and motions counted for "the removal of dishes from table to tea cart" and similar operations. In the washing of dishes, motions are counted and tabulated for "approach stove, grasp teakettle, remove lid at stove," "travel to sink, turn hot water faucet on," "turn hot water faucet partially off," "travel to stove, replace lid, turn fuel on," "approach sink," etc., over a total of a hundred typewritten pages of tables and explanatory comment, such as "stooping and lifting are fatiguing." In the effort to find subjects for dissertations the ingenuity of teachers is taxed to the uttermost and every nook and corner of home and school ransacked for the merest scrap of a suggestion. . . .

We are now in position to understand a mystery. There were in 1927–28 over 900,000 students enrolled in 1,076 colleges, universities, and professional schools reporting to the Bureau of Education at Washington; there must be well-nigh a million today. In the same year, 83,065 baccalaureate degrees were granted. As the population of the country is approximately 120,000,000, one person out of every 125 is today receiving a so-called higher education, and as this process, at approximately this rate, has been going on for some years, the number of "educated" persons in the United States must be enormous; the general level of intelligence and education should be high and should rapidly become higher. Such is not the case. Why not?

Quite clearly, because most of the 900,000 persons enumerated are not being educated at all; they are prematurely being trained in business, journalism, physical training, domestic science, or are registered in extension and other courses. Even if registered as college or graduate students, there is no certainty that they have been properly prepared or that they are pursuing a course that deserves to be called a liberal education. The fact that so enormous a number are interested in getting some sort of education is, from a social point of view, a novelty in the world's history and may ultimately have significance which today no one can foretell; but one cannot be really hopeful on this score, until universities and other educational institutions definitely discriminate between students on the basis of an intellectual standard. As ordinarily given, the figures are deceptive. . . .

Progress might be greatly assisted by the outright creation of a school or institute of higher learning, a university in the post-graduate sense of the word. It should be a free society of scholars—free, because mature persons, animated by intellectual purposes, must be left to pursue their own ends in their own way. Administration should be slight and inexpensive.* Scholars and scientists should participate in its government; the president should come down from his pedestal. The term "organization" should be banned. The institution should be open to persons, competent and cultivated, who do not need and would abhor spoonfeeding—be they college graduates or not. It should furnish simple surroundings—books, laboratories, and above all, tranquillity—absence of distraction either by worldly concerns or by parental responsibility for an immature student body. Provision should be made for the amenities of life in the institution and in the private life of the staff. It need not be complete or symmetrical: if a chair could not be admirably filled, it should be left vacant. There exists in America no university in this sense—no institution, no seat of learning devoted to higher teaching and research. Everywhere the pressure of undergraduate and vocational activities hampers the serious objects for which uni-

---

* A Harvard professor writes me as follows: "I think it is tremendously important at the present time to oppose the tendencies of administrative usurpation of certain academic functions which can only be properly performed by scholars. It has often seemed to me that we might profitably go back, at least in part, to the system which has long and successfully functioned in Germany—namely, to have the purely house-keeping and financial work of educational institutions carried out by business men and clerks, with deans and rectors appointed from the older men of the faculty for periods of one or two years, relieving them for the time from their purely teaching duties and having them concern themselves during their administrations with the guidance of educational policy in consultation with a committee of their colleagues."

versities exist. Thus science and scholarship suffer; money is wasted; even undergraduate training is less efficient than it might be, if left to itself.

What could be expected, if a modern American university were thus established? The ablest scholars and scientists would be attracted to its faculty; the most earnest students would be attracted to its laboratories and seminars. It would be small, as Gilman's Johns Hopkins was small; but its propulsive power would be momentous out of all proportion to its size. It would, like a lens, focus rays that now scatter. The Rockefeller Institute for Medical Research is limited in scope; its hospital contains less than fifty beds. But its uncompromising standards of activity and publication have given it influence in America and Europe throughout the entire field of medical education and research. A university or a school of higher learning at a level I have indicated would do as much for other disciplines and might thus in time assist the general reorganization of secondary and higher education.

4. A Scientist Analyzes a New Mode of Attack on the Colleges, 1931

Glenn R. Wakeham, the author of these sharp comments on pressures operating on the colleges from the high schools, was at the time associate professor of chemistry at the University of Colorado. An Iowan, born in 1884, he had taken his Ph.D. at Colorado and had much experience with foreign schools, having taught in Germany and England.

Symptoms of a curious change in the attitude of high-school educationists towards the colleges reveal a new attack of some ingenuity upon our college system—provisionally upon the first two years of the standard college course.

Twenty years ago the high schools were busy declaring their independence of college domination. They were diluting the classical high-school courses to the extent of from twenty-five to fifty per cent. with

G. Wakeham, "A New Mode of Attack on the College," *School and Society*, XXXIV (July 25, 1931), 127–29. Reprinted with the permission of The Society for the Advancement of Education, Inc.

industrial, economic, artistic and other branches belonging to the new "culture." They were experimenting with various forms of student government among their pupils. They were organizing high-school students into classes and cliques for social, athletic, and other "cultural" purposes. They cut out of the standard five-class-per-week program two or three of these weekly exercises and introduced "supervised study-hours" so that the students, freed from the necessity of home-work, would be able to attend games and dances and crash the gates of moving-picture theaters. It was believed—or at least suggested—that the improved technique of the new education would enable the high-school student to learn, in the reduced time, as much English, mathematics, science, etc., as he had heretofore acquired—or at least as much as he would ever need.

The results have not quite come up to expectations. High-school students, it must be admitted, accepted the new order of things with pronounced enthusiasm. They govern themselves with a fine, artistic abandon of traditional prejudices. They have developed high proficiency as movie, radio, and baseball fans. They have learned to dance, play football and hockey, drink, and, on occasion, commit adultery. Their "culture," in the Freudian sense, has notably increased.

These unexpected results have pained both parents and educationists, although the latter, manifesting an automatic defense mechanism, try to make light of it. Parents have begun to note that the industrial subjects taught in high school are of even less actual, monetary value to the high-school graduate than the much maligned Latin and Greek of the classical curriculum. Notwithstanding high sounding courses in civics, economics and sociology, high-school graduates romp joyously into the modern vortex of political and social pollution without showing any sign that the philosophical and moral presentations of the high-school curriculum have made the slightest dent in their adolescent obtuseness.

What the educationists did not anticipate was the effect of their curricular dispositions upon student attitudes. From their cutting down of the time formerly devoted to English, arithmetic, and language the students naturally assumed that these things were no longer a vitally important part of education. The new branches introduced were obviously the real essentials. Consequently students came to consider the drudgery of learning to spell, "figger," and parse as something to be avoided as far as possible, something to "get by" with minimum effort, so that they would have more time to devote to the new "cultural activities."

But what pains the educationists most is the stubbornness of the colleges against lining up with the new order of things. Endowed universities are using methods of constantly increasing rigor in selecting their freshmen. State schools, unable to reject unsuitable high-school graduates at the outset, flunk them out as soon as possible, with results to the individual rejectees more disastrous than original elimination would have been. Parents resent this, and educationists resent parental criticisms of the high schools.

It was not to be expected that the educationists would meet this situation by any reform of secondary curricula or instruction. Such an attempt, in the face of the intellectually demoralized youth of the nation, would be a labor of Hercules. Rather, they have launched a flank attack upon the college system itself—an attack against which the new junior colleges, in particular, will have little effective means of defense.

It is almost amusing to note how, of late, they have piped down on their erstwhile resonant declarations of educational independence. They are playing up again the old moan of college domination. They have enlisted the services of such eminent educational administrators as President Glenn Frank to point out the lamentably rigid interdependence of the various stages of our educational system upon each other. They have applied to education Lincoln's dictum that the "nation can not continue half slave and half free"—without stating whether the high school is slave and the college free, or the high school itself half slave and half free. More recently they have organized a formidable "Committee on the Relation of School and College" which, while heavily weighted with high-school men, includes a few outstanding college educators. They ask for an extension of "progressive" high-school experimentation into the first two years of college work, knowing full well that if they can get by with this, the whole college system, including the graduate school, will soon be at their mercy.

It is to be hoped that the colleges will do a little research of their own before turning the high-school experimenters loose in their freshman and sophomore departments. They have at their disposal, in the form of high-school graduates, abundant material upon which to base judgments of the educational effectiveness of recently developed educationist techniques. If they find that the new education has brought forth fruits at all commensurate with its vast claims, it will be time to consider possible applications of the new techniques to college teaching.

It can be taken for granted, at the outset, that all the "adjustments" and "cooperation" will be on the part of the colleges. The high-school system, impregnably secure behind its political defenses, will never concede a single point to help the colleges realize their own ideals. It will be a matter of give and take—give on the part of the colleges and take on the part of the high schools. Let the colleges therefore, beware of giving up anything they do not want to lose, for they will certainly never get it back again.

5. Robert M. Hutchins Assesses the State of the Higher Learning, 1936

Robert M. Hutchins was born into an academic family in 1899 in Brooklyn and educated at Oberlin and Yale, receiving his B.A. from the latter in 1921. After a brief experience as a master in a preparatory school, he went to Yale as a student of Law in 1923. Two years later, upon receiving his LL.B. degree, he joined the faculty of Yale Law School as a lecturer, where he rose rapidly to become professor and, finally, in 1928–29 its dean. In 1929, at the age of thirty, he assumed the presidency of the University of Chicago, where he served under that title until 1945 and for six years afterward as chancellor. His reign at Chicago was notable for a vigorous, experimental, and controversial administration, and its stout defense of academic freedom. Hutchins, during this period, became famous as one of the outstanding proponents of intellectualism in education. In 1951 he became associate director of the newly formed Ford Foundation, and in 1954 the president of the Fund for the Republic, an independent foundation established to aid the defense of civil liberties and civil rights. When this organization established the Center for the Study of Democratic Institutions, he became chairman of the consultants of the new organization.

See also Docs. 6, 7, 10, 11, and *Current Biography, 1954.*

The most striking fact about the higher learning in America is the confusion that besets it. This confusion begins in the high school and continues to the loftiest levels of the university. The high school cannot make up its mind whether it is preparing students for life or for college.

Robert Maynard Hutchins, *The Higher Learning in America* (New Haven, 1936), pp. 1–7, 10–14, 29–38, 70–73, 85–87, 117–18. Reprinted with the permission of Yale University Press.

Its student population is miscellaneous and variegated. The course of study is substantially uniform for all groups, whether they are prospective scientists, lawyers, clerks, or laboring men, and is apparently adjusted to the needs of only the smallest of these groups, that destined for the higher learning.

The junior college is in most places an extension of the high-school curriculum, which is there applied to an essentially similar though somewhat smaller student body. Here also the question whether the students are completing their education or are preparing to go on to the university has not been settled, and the aims of the institution are not clear.

The college of liberal arts is partly high school, partly university, partly general, partly special. Frequently it looks like a teacher-training institution. Frequently it looks like nothing at all. The degree it offers seems to certify that the student has passed an uneventful period without violating any local, state, or federal law, and that he has a fair, if temporary, recollection of what his teachers have said to him. As I shall show later, little pretense is made that many of the things said to him are of much importance.

The university is distinguished from the college by two things: professional schools and the Ph.D. degree. At present we do not know why the university should have professional schools or what they should be like. We do not even know what the professions are. Professional education consists either of going through motions that we have inherited or of making gestures of varying degrees of wildness that we hope may be more effectual. The Ph.D. degree, because it has become a necessary part of the insignia of the college or university teacher, has lost any other meaning. But universities also do research and hope to train research men. The same degree is awarded in recognition of research. The students who are going to be teachers are put through a procedure which was designed to produce investigators. The classes, the courses, the content, and the aims of graduate work are as confused as those of the high school.

For the sake of abbreviation I have of course exaggerated the plight of the higher learning. It has, in fact, many admirable qualities, not the least of which is its friendly reception of anybody who would like to avail himself of it. But we who are devoting our lives to it should learn something from the experience of recent years. Up to the onset of the present depression it was fashionable to call for more and more education. Anything that went by the name of education was a good thing just because it went by that name. I believe that the magic of the name is gone and that we must now present a defensible program if we wish to preserve whatever we have that is of value. Our people, as the last few years have shown, will strike out blindly under economic pressure; they will destroy the best and preserve the worst unless we make the distinction between the two somewhat clearer to them.

If then the problem is to clarify the higher learning, let us examine the causes of its confusion. The first of them is very vulgar; it is the love of money. It is sad but true that when an institution determines to do something in order to get money it must lose its soul, and frequently does not get the money. Money comes to education in three ways—from students, from donors, and from legislatures. To frame a policy in order to appeal to any one of the three is fatal, and, as I have suggested, often futile as well. How much of the current confusion in universities would have been eliminated if boards of trustees had declined gifts which merely reflected the passing whims of wealthy men? Few restricted gifts have ever been made to a university that paid the expense of receiving them. If men are supported, they are not housed or given the books and equipment they need. If buildings are given, they are not maintained. If they are maintained, they are not manned. From the financial standpoint alone the university may be worse off after the gift than it was before. And from the educational or scientific standpoint it is likely to be unbalanced and confused. Dependence on the casual interests of donors means that nobody can tell from one year to another what a university's policy is. It will become next year whatever somebody is willing to pay to make it. I do not mean, of course, that universities do not need money and that they should not try to get it. I mean only that they should have an educational policy and then try to finance it, instead of letting financial accidents determine their educational policy.

Even more important is the influence on educational policy of student fees. It is probably fair to say that American universities above the junior year ought to do anything and everything that would reduce their income from students. This is true because most of the things that degrade them are done to maintain or increase this income. To maintain or increase it the passing whims of the public receive the same attention as those of millionaires. If the public becomes interested in the metropolitan newspaper, schools of journalism instantly arise. If it is awed by the development of big business, business schools full of the same reverence appear. If an administration enlarges the activities of the federal government and hence the staff thereof, training for the public service becomes the first duty of the universities. Today public administration, housing, forestry, and aëronautics are the absorbing subjects of university interest, just as international relations after the war was the topic to which we were to devote ourselves. At any moment crime, divorce, child labor, socialized medicine, or the corruption of lawyers may through some sensational incident become the most pressing problem of the higher learning. During the synthetic excitement of last year about communism, socialism, and other forms of redness, it suddenly became the duty of the colleges and universities to give courses in the eradication of these great evils and in the substitution for them of something called Americanism.

Undoubtedly the love of money and that sensitivity to public demands that it creates has a good deal to do with the service-station conception of a university. According to this conception a university must make itself felt in the community; it must be constantly, currently felt. A state university must help the farmers look after their cows. An endowed university must help adults get better jobs by giving them courses in the afternoon and evening. Yet it is apparent that the kind of professors that are interested in these objects may not be the kind that are interested either in developing education or in advancing knowledge. Since a university will not be able to have two kinds of professors and at the same time remain clear as to what it is about, it must follow that extension work can only confuse the institution. . . .

The love of money means that a university must attract students. To do this it must be attractive. This is interpreted to mean that it must go to unusual lengths to house, feed, and amuse the young. Nobody knows what these things have to do with the higher learning. Everybody supposes that students think they are important. The emphasis on athletics and social life that infects all colleges and universities has done more than most things to confuse these institutions and to debase the higher learning in America.

It is supposed that students want education to be amusing; it is supposed that parents want it to be safe. Hence the vast attention given by universities at enormous expense to protect the physical and moral welfare of their charges. Parents must feel that their children are in good hands. It makes no difference whether those hands are already full. The faculty must be diverted from its proper tasks to perform the uncongenial job of improving the conduct and the health of those entrusted to it.

The love of money leads to large numbers, and large numbers have produced the American system of educational measurement. Under this system the intellectual progress of the young is determined by the time they have been in attendance, the number of hours they have sat in classes, and the proportion of what they have been told that they can repeat on examinations given by the teachers who told it to them. Such criteria as these determine progress from one educational unit to another, and are the basis for entrance to and graduation from professional schools. Since it is clear that these criteria are really measures of faithfulness, docility, and memory, we cannot suppose that they are regarded as true indications of intellectual power. They are adopted because some arbitrary automatic methods are required to permit dealing with large masses of students, and these methods are the easiest. Any others would compel us to think about our course of study and to work out ways of testing achievement in it. But large numbers leave us no time to think.

The love of money makes its appearance in universities in the most unexpected places. One would look for it in presidents and trustees. One would think that the last place one could hear it mentioned would be in faculty meeting. On the contrary, a good many professors instantly react to any proposal for the improvement of education by displaying a concern for the university's income that is notably absent when they are pressing for increases in their own research budgets. Two answers are usually made when any such suggestion is advanced: it is said that the students cannot do the work and that the university by frightening away students will reduce its income. What these answers usually mean is that the professors who make them do not want to change the habits of their lives. Since this cannot be made a matter of public knowledge, some philanthropic reason must be put forward instead.

Actually students will respond to a program designed to give them a better education. It usually happens that after the horrid predictions of professors in these cases more and better students desire to enroll, and specifically because of the innovation that was expected to scare them off. This has happened in my own experience with honors courses, general courses, general examinations, and the abolition of course credits and of the requirement of attendance at classes.

Even more important than the love of money as a cause of our confusion is our confused notion of democracy. This affects the length, the content, and the control of education. According to this notion a student may stay in public education as long as he likes, may study what he likes, and may claim any degree whose alphabetical arrangement appeals to him. According to this notion education should be immediately responsive to public opinion; its subject matter and methods may be regulated in great detail by the community, by its representatives, or even by its more irresponsible members. . . .

To the love of money and a misconception of democracy I would add as a major cause of our disorder an erroneous notion of progress. I shall deal with the various aspects of this notion more at large in the three remaining chapters. I may mention them now by way of index. Our notion of progress is that everything is getting better and must be getting better from age to age. Our information is increasing. Our scientific knowledge is expanding. Our technological equipment in its range and excellence is far superior to what our fathers or even our older brothers knew.

Although the depression has shaken our faith a little, we still remain true to the doctrine of progress and still believe in its universal application. Politics, religion, and even education are all making progress, too. In intellectual fields, therefore, we have no hesitancy in breaking completely with the past; the ancients did not know the things we know; they had never seen steam engines, or aëroplanes, or radios, and seem to have had little appreciation of the possibilities of the factory system. Since these are among the central facts in our lives, how can the ancients have anything to say to us?[1]

Descartes, Hume, and Rousseau, for example, did not find it in the least absurd that they should begin to think as though nobody had ever thought before. They did not even regard it as egotistical. It was merely natural; mankind had progressed to the point where it was necessary to cast out old errors and begin to develop a really intelligent program.

The tremendous strides of science and technology seemed to be the

---

[1] Cf. the recent remark of Sir R. W. Livingstone: "The Greeks could not broadcast the Æschylean trilogy, but they could write it."

result of the accumulation of data. The more information, the more discoveries, the more inventions, the more progress. The way to promote progress was therefore to get more information. The sciences one by one broke off from philosophy and then from one another, and that process is still going on. At last the whole structure of the university collapsed and the final victory of empiricism was won when the social sciences, law, and even philosophy and theology themselves became empirical and experimental and progressive.

In some way or other the theory of evolution got involved in these developments; it gave aid and comfort to empiricism and was particularly happy in its effect upon education. Evolution proves, you see, that there is steady improvement from age to age. But it shows, too, that everybody's business is to get adjusted to his environment. Obviously the way to get adjusted to the environment is to know a lot about it. And so empiricism, having taken the place of thought as the basis of research, took its place, too, as the basis of education. It led by easy stages to vocationalism; because the facts you learn about your prospective environment (particularly if you love money) ought to be as immediate and useful as possible.

We begin, then, with a notion of progress and end with an anti-intellectualism which denies, in effect, that man is a rational animal. He is an animal and perhaps somewhat more intelligent than most. As such, a man can be trained as the more intelligent animals can be. But the idea that his education should consist of the cultivation of his intellect is, of course, ridiculous. What it must consist of is surveys, more or less detailed, of the modern industrial, technological, financial, political, and social situation so that he can fit into it with a minimum of discomfort to himself and to his fellow men. Thus the modern temper produces that strangest of modern phenomena, an anti-intellectual university.

Since an anti-intellectual university is a contradiction in terms, it is no wonder that the theories justifying it are very odd. There is, for instance, the great-man theory of education. Under this theory you pay no attention to what you teach, or indeed to what you investigate. You get great men for your faculty. Their mere presence on the campus inspires, stimulates, and exalts. It matters not how inarticulate their teaching or how recondite their researches; they are, as the saying goes, an education in themselves. This is a variant of the nauseating anecdote about Mark Hopkins on one end of the log and the student on the other.

Under any conditions that are likely to exist in this country the log is too long and there are too many people sitting on both ends of it to make the anecdote apposite. Of course we should try to get great men into education, and each president should try to get as many of them as he can for his own faculty. But he can never hope to get very many, even if he knows one when he sees one. If a president succeeds in finding a few great men, he cannot hope to make them useful in an organization that ties them hand and foot and in a course of study that is going off in all directions at the same time and particularly in those opposite to the ones in which the great men are going. The fact is that the great-man theory is an excuse, an alibi, a vacuous reply to the charge that we have no intelligent program for the higher learning. It amounts to saying that we do not need one; we could give you one if we wanted to. But if you will only accept the great-man theory you will spare us the trouble of thinking.

Another theory we have developed is the character-building theory. It may be that we don't teach our students anything, but what of it? That isn't our purpose. Our purpose is to turn out well-tubbed young Americans who know how to behave in the American environment.[2] Association with one another, with gentlemanly professors, in beautiful buildings will, along with regular exercise, make our students the kind of citizens our country needs.[3] Since character is the result of choice it is difficult to see how you can develop it unless you train the mind to make intelligent choices. Collegiate life suggests that the choices of undergraduates are determined by other considerations than thought. Undoubtedly, fine associations, fine buildings, green grass, good food, and exercise are excellent things for anybody. You will note that they are exactly what is advertised by every resort hotel. The only

---

[2] See the remarks attributed to Father R. I. Gannon, President of Fordham University, *New York Herald Tribune*, June 26, 1936, p. 21: "From now on we must realize that the task of the university is to graduate men of *contacts*, men whose social life has been developed quite as earnestly as their funds of information, men who bear a definite and easily recognizable university stamp."

[3] For a variation on this theme see an article in the *Yale Alumni Weekly*, May 1, 1936, p. 7, in which the writer suggests that the curriculum is of little importance and that students really educate themselves best by informal association with one another and with professors. If this is true, there is no reason for worrying about what to teach.

reason why they are also advertised by every college and university is that we have no coherent educational program to announce.

The character-building theory turned inside out is the doctrine that every young person ought to learn to work hard; and that it is immaterial what he works at as long as he has to work. Under the theory in this form the subject matter of legal study, for example, might just as well be botany or ornithology or any subject that is of such scope and difficulty as to require a substantial amount of hard labor. The prospective lawyer would have learned to work; anything else he must learn in practice anyway.

We shall all admit, I suppose, that learning how to work is perhaps the prime requisite for a useful life. It does seem unfortunate, however, that the higher learning can contribute nothing which clerking, coal-heaving, or choir practice cannot do as well or better. It is possible that apprenticing the young in some trade from the age of fourteen on might get the result here sought after with less expense and trouble. The hard-working doctrine would seem to be a defense-mechanism set up to justify our failure to develop anything worth working on.

The great-man theory and the character-building theory amount to a denial that there is or should be content to education. Those among us who assert that there is a content to education are almost unanimous in holding that the object of the higher learning is utility, and utility in a very restricted sense. They write articles showing that the educated get better jobs and make more money. Or they advocate changes in education that will, they think, make it more effective in preparing students to get better jobs and make more money. Here we are brought back to the love of money as a cause of our confusion. As the institution's love of money makes it sensitive to every wave of popular opinion, and as the popular opinion is that insofar as education has any object it is economic, both the needs of the universities and the sentiments of the public conspire to degrade the universities into vocational schools. To these then a distorted notion of democracy leads us to admit any and all students; for should not all our youth have equal economic opportunities?

This is the position of the higher learning in America. The universities are dependent on the people. The people love money and think that education is a way of getting it. They think too that democracy means that every child should be permitted to acquire the educational insignia that will be helpful in making money. They do not believe in the cultivation of the intellect for its own sake. And the distressing part of this is that the state of the nation determines the state of education.

But how can we hope to improve the state of the nation? Only through education. A strange circularity thus afflicts us.[4] The state of the nation depends on the state of education; but the state of education depends on the state of the nation. How can we break this vicious circle and make at last the contribution to the national life that since the earliest times has been expected of us? We can do so only if some institutions can be strong enough and clear enough to stand firm and show our people what the higher learning is. As education it is the single-minded pursuit of the intellectual virtues. As scholarship it is the single-minded devotion to the advancement of knowledge. Only if the colleges and universities can devote themselves to these objects can we look hopefully to the future of the higher learning in America. . . .

There is a conflict between one aim of the university, the pursuit of truth for its own sake, and another which it professes too, the preparation of men and women for their life work. This is not a conflict between education and research. It is a conflict between two kinds of education. Both kinds are found in all parts of a university. As I shall show in a moment, professional training is given in almost every department, and the pursuit of truth for its own sake may occasionally be met with even in a professional school.

I need not tell you which of these two aims of the modern university has lately been more popular. A mere recital of the new schools, avowedly professional in purpose, that have appeared in the past thirty-five years will convince you that we have seen a dramatic shift in the composition of our universities. Since the beginning of the century the following units designed to fit students for specific occupations have appeared and have become respectable: schools of journalism, business, librarianship, social service, education, dentistry, nursing, forestry, diplomacy, pharmacy, veterinary surgery, and public administration. There are many others that have appeared, but have not yet become

---

[4] On the difficulty of educating contrary to the prevailing views of society, see Plato, *Republic,* Book VI. And contrast Book IV: " 'And moreover,' said I, 'the state, if it once starts well, proceeds as it were in a cycle of growth. I mean that a sound nurture and education if kept up creates good natures in the state, and sound natures in turn receiving an education of this sort develop into better men than their predecessors. . . .' "

respectable. I have confined myself to what might be called the standard subjects.

These new schools, of course, consume a very large portion of the attention of students, faculty, and administrators. New developments in older professional disciplines are having the same effect. The growth of university medicine since 1910 has been phenomenal. The total assets contributing to medical education and research at the University of Chicago are more than forty million dollars, and medicine now consumes 25 per cent of the University's annual budget. Full-time faculties in law and engineering lead, of course, to greater expense than we were formerly put to; for part-time professors ordinarily carried away little or nothing as direct salary. In engineering the equipment becomes more elaborate as technology advances, and no end to the process is in sight. The modest requirements of a classics group of ten professors pale into insignificance beside the demands of the same number of engineers.

Emphasis on professionalism is further promoted by the increasing practice of pointing work from the junior year onward toward some professional school. The modern university is full of prelaw, prebusiness, predentistry, preëngineering, and premedical students whose course of study is determined by their professional ambitions. In some institutions the professional schools themselves begin with the junior year. This, as I shall show later, would be a sound organization under certain circumstances. Unfortunately those circumstances do not obtain today.

We find, moreover, that outside professional schools and in departments of arts, literature, and science the atmosphere in which the student labors is highly professional. Students do graduate work in organic chemistry because industry engages a large number of Ph.D.'s in this field every year. Students study for the M.A. because it is becoming necessary for positions in secondary schools. In the Middle West 45 per cent of the graduates of colleges of liberal arts go into teaching. In some colleges this proportion rises to 90 per cent. These colleges have been forced to offer the Master's degree so that their students may teach in secondary schools. They must also offer professional courses in education because state laws and accrediting agencies require such training for the prospective teacher at all levels of the public schools. In the universities students study for the Ph.D. because it is almost impossible to secure a college or university post without it. Seventy-five per cent of them have no interest in research; at least, that percentage never does any more after the exertions of the dissertation. It is hardly an exaggeration to say that university departments exist to train people to teach in university departments.

The pursuit of knowledge for its own sake is being rapidly obscured in universities and may soon be extinguished. Every group in the community that is well enough organized to have an audible voice wants the university to spare it the necessity of training its own recruits. They want to get from the university a product as nearly finished as possible, which can make as large and as inexpensive a contribution as possible from the moment of graduation. This is a pardonable, perhaps even a laudable, desire. But the effect of it on the universities will be that soon everybody in a university will be there for the purpose of being trained for something.

You may ask, what of it? You may suggest, and with reason, that the surroundings of a university are better than those in which the young practitioner might otherwise learn to practice. You may point out that a desirable uniformity may be obtained by insisting on educational requirements through which all neophytes must pass. You may say that the legal profession, for example, is not to be trusted with the education of the young lawyer; and if you do, you will, I am afraid, be right. My answer is that the burdens imposed upon the universities by this arrangement are bad for them and bad for the professions, and that the hope of doing a better job of training young people in the practices of a profession by having the universities do it is quite illusory.

It is plain enough, I suppose, that it is bad for the universities to vocationalize them. I do not deny that the professional atmosphere has an electrical effect on some students. I have seen Big Men at Yale, football heroes and social luminaries, wake up in the Law School under the stimulus of the incentives and competition of professional work. The close connection between law-school grades and law-office jobs and the fact that it is the fashion to work in law school accomplish a good many miracles of this variety. Undergraduate study can make no such appeal: it has no apparent connection with anything; and the fashion of working at it would be difficult to start.

On the other hand, the vocational atmosphere is ruinous to attempts to lead the student to understand the subject. By hypothesis he is learning to practice the profession. You must, therefore, make clear to him at every step that the questions you are discussing have a direct bearing on his future experiences and on his success in meeting them. You must give him practical advice. A friend of mine recently took an hour to explain to his law-school class the economic and social background of the fellow-servant rule. At the end of the discussion one student inquired, "What's this got to do with the law?" There is a good deal to be said for the boy's position; he had come to the university under the impression that it would prepare him for the bar examinations and teach him the rules of the game. He felt that he was being cheated. Under these circumstances the temptation is irresistible to tell your students stirring anecdotes of your own days at the bar, to let them in on the tricks of the trade, and to avoid confusing their minds by requiring them to think about anything except what the courts will do. . . .

If there are permanent studies which every person who wishes to call himself educated should master; if those studies constitute our intellectual inheritance, then those studies should be the center of a general education. They cannot be ignored because they are difficult, or unpleasant, or because they are almost totally missing from our curriculum today. The child-centered school may be attractive to the child, and no doubt is useful as a place in which the little ones may release their inhibitions and hence behave better at home. But educators cannot permit the students to dictate the course of study unless they are prepared to confess that they are nothing but chaperons, supervising an aimless, trial-and-error process which is chiefly valuable because it keeps young people from doing something worse. The free elective system as Mr. Eliot introduced it at Harvard and as Progressive Education adapted it to lower age levels amounted to a denial that there was content to education. Since there was no content to education, we might as well let students follow their own bent. They would at least be interested and pleased and would be as well educated as if they had pursued a prescribed course of study. This overlooks the fact that the aim of education is to connect man with man, to connect the present with the past, and to advance the thinking of the race. If this is the aim of education, it cannot be left to the sporadic, spontaneous interests of children or even of undergraduates.[5]

Mr. Gladstone once remarked that it is difficult to discern the true dimensions of objects in that mirage which covers the studies of one's youth. Even at stages beyond general education, when the student because he has had a general education and because he is more mature might be given wider latitude in selecting the subjects interesting to him, this can be permitted only to a limited degree. If there are an intellectual tradition and an intellectual inheritance in the law, for example, law schools must see to it that they are transmitted to law students even if law students are more interested in the latest devices for evading the Sherman Antitrust Act.

It cannot be assumed that students at any age will always select the subjects that constitute education. If we permit them to avoid them, we cannot confer upon them insignia which certify to the public that they are in our opinion educated. In any field the permanent studies on which the whole development of the subject rests must be mastered if the student is to be educated.

The variations that should be encouraged fall not in the realm of content but in that of method. Allowances for individual differences should be provided for by abolishing all requirements except the examinations and permitting the student to take them whenever in his opinion he is ready to do so. The cultivation of independent thought and study, now almost wholly missing from our program, may thus be somewhat advanced. And this may be done without sacrificing the content of education to the obsessions of the hour or the caprices of the young.

If we are educators we must have a subject matter, and a rational, defensible one. If that subject matter is education, we cannot alter it to suit the whims of parents, students, or the public. Whewell, Master of Trinity College, Cambridge, one hundred years ago, said:

"Young persons may be so employed and so treated, that their caprice, their self-will, their individual tastes and propensities, are

---

[5] Plato, *Republic,* Book IX: " 'And it is plain,' I said, 'that this is the purpose of the law, which is the ally of all classes in the state, and this is the aim of our control of children, our not leaving them free before we have established, so to speak, a constitutional government within them and, by fostering the best element in them with the aid of the like in ourselves, have set up in its place a similar guardian and ruler in the child, and then, and then only we leave it free.' "

educed and developed; but this is not Education. It is not the Education of a Man; for what is educed is not what belongs to man as man, and connects man with man. It is not the Education of a man's Humanity, but the Indulgence of his Individuality."

In general education we are interested in drawing out the elements of our common human nature; we are interested in the attributes of the race, not the accidents of individuals. . . .

We have then for general education a course of study consisting of the greatest books of the Western world and the arts of reading, writing, thinking, and speaking, together with mathematics, the best exemplar of the processes of human reason. If our hope has been to frame a curriculum which educes the elements of our common human nature, this program should realize our hope. If we wish to prepare the young for intelligent action, this course of study should assist us; for they will have learned what has been done in the past, and what the greatest men have thought. They will have learned how to think themselves. If we wish to lay a basis for advanced study, that basis is provided. If we wish to secure true universities, we may look forward to them, because students and professors may acquire through this course of study a common stock of ideas and common methods of dealing with them. All the needs of general education in America seem to be satisfied by this curriculum.

What, then, are the objections to it? They cannot be educational objections; for this course of study appears to accomplish the aims of general education. One objection may be that the students will not like it, which is, as we have seen, irrelevant. But even if it were relevant, it is not true. Since the proposed curriculum is coherent and comprehensible, and since it is free from the triviality that now afflicts our program, students will respond to it if the teachers will give them a chance to do it.

It may be said that the course of study is too difficult. It is not too difficult for students who can read or who can be taught to do so. For ease of reading, as well as other qualities, *The Federalist,* an American classic, is superior to some recent treatises on government and public administration; Herodotus is more sprightly than most modern historians of the ancient world; and Plato and Aristotle are as intelligible as contemporary philosophers.

No, the students can do the work if the faculties will let them. Will the faculties let them? I doubt it. The professors of today have been brought up differently. Not all of them have read all the books they would have to teach. Not all of them are ready to change the habits of their lives. Meanwhile they are bringing up their successors in the way they were brought up, so that the next crop will have the habits they have had themselves. And the love of money, a misconception of democracy, a false notion of progress, a distorted idea of utility, and the anti-intellectualism to which all these lead conspire to confirm their conviction that no disturbing change is needed. The times call for the establishment of a new college or for an evangelistic movement in some old ones which shall have for its object the conversion of individuals and finally of the teaching profession to a true conception of general education. Unless some such demonstration or some such evangelistic movement can take place, we shall remain in our confusion; we shall have neither general education nor universities; and we shall continue to disappoint the hopes of our people. . . .

We see, then, that we may get order in the higher learning by removing from it the elements which disorder it today, and these are vocationalism and unqualified empiricism. If when these elements are removed we pursue the truth for its own sake in the light of some principle of order, such as metaphysics, we shall have a rational plan for a university. We shall be able to make a university a true center of learning; we shall be able to make it the home of creative thought.

We see, too, that in such a university the dilemmas of the higher learning are resolved. The dilemma of professionalism cannot obstruct us, because no distinction is made between the professional and non-professional disciplines. They are all studied in the free faculties and studied in the same way. Training in the techniques of the profession is left to the profession, or, if necessary, to technical institutes so organized as not to confuse the university.

For somewhat similar reasons the dilemma of isolation will also cease from troubling. Disciplines will not be isolated from one another; they will be united, and by a rational principle. Professors and students will all be pursuing the truth for its own sake; they will know what truths to pursue and why. Since all students will study under all the faculties, the education they acquire will not be piecemeal or miscellaneous; it will be as unified as the university itself.

Even the dilemma of anti-intellectualism is easier to deal with. Anti-intellectualism is so much a part of the temper of the times that it will be difficult to meet this dilemma as squarely or satisfactorily as we can meet the other two. The university that I have been describing is intellectual. It is wholly and completely so. As such, it is the only kind of university worth having. I believe that it will accomplish greater political and professional results than one that is devoted to current events or vocational training.

If the country is not prepared to believe these things, it can get what it wants through the technical and research institutes I have proposed. They are so planned as to draw off the empricism and vocationalism that have been strangling the universities and to leave them free to do their intellectual job.

If we can secure a real university in this country and a real program of general education upon which its work can rest, it may be that the character of our civilization may slowly change. It may be that we can outgrow the love of money,[6] that we can get a saner conception of democracy, and that we can even understand the purposes of education. It may be that we can abandon our false notions of progress and utility and that we can come to prefer intelligible organization to the chaos that we mistake for liberty. It is because these things may be that education is important. Upon education our country must pin its hopes of true progress, which involves scientific and technological advance, but under the direction of reason; of true prosperity, which includes external goods but does not overlook those of the soul; and of true liberty, which can exist only in society, and in a society rationally ordered.

---

[6] Aristotle, *Politics,* II, 7: "For it is not the possessions but the desires of mankind which require to be equalized, and this is impossible, unless a sufficient education is provided by the state."

6. Harry D. Gideonse on Hutchins and Flexner, 1937

Harry D. Gideonse was born in Rotterdam in 1901 and educated at Columbia College, where he received his B.S. in 1923. In 1928 he also received a diploma from the École des Hautes Études Internationales of the University of Geneva. He taught economics at Barnard and Columbia for a few years, served as the director of international students' work at Geneva, and then resumed his career as a teacher of economics. After teaching at Rutgers, Chicago, and Columbia, he became president of Brooklyn College in 1939. Gideonse was at Chicago when President Hutchins published his book, *The Higher Learning in America.* This polemical answer caught the attention of the educational world.

See Docs. 3 and 5, and *Current Biography,* 1940.

It is possible to agree with a great many of the specific criticisms of Flexner and Hutchins and still be thoroughly dissatisfied with their proposed solutions. They have failed to recognize the forces that led to present conditions, and to supply specific evidence of the direction in which reorientation should take place. In the writings of both these critics the question that presses is the question that is begged: How find a metaphysics, if there be one, which will remedy rather than intensify prevailing "confusion"? It may be true that no consistent philosophy or metaphysics "lies beneath the American university of today." It would be more significant to inquire how much more consistency a country's educational institutions can have than the society in which they exist. It would be an even greater contribution to suggest— if only for discussion—the specific character of the metaphysical principles which would bring "rational order" out of our free "chaos." The plea that the entire structure of higher education should be recast to accord with some set of metaphysical principles turns upon the nature and acceptability of those principles. To write volumes in support of the thesis that there should be a unifying philosophy, without specific indication of the type of unity or of philosophy, is to miss the essential problem underlying the modern dilemma.

If the higher learning is to be unified, is the unity to be voluntary or mandatory? If the unity is to be voluntary, must it not be developed within the community of scholars and based upon the multiplicity of contemporary data and methods of attaining insight? If the unity is

Harry D. Gideonse, *The Higher Learning in a Democracy* (New York, 1937), pp. 2–6, 8–10, 19–27, 30–34. Reprinted with the permission of Holt, Rinehart & Winston.

to spring from *agreement,* will it be the fruit of "the single-minded pursuit of the intellectual virtues"[1] or will it be derived from a new stress on human values? And if the unity is to be mandatory, rather than voluntary, who will choose the philosophy that is to be imposed from above? Is there not acute danger that the "clarity" of the unifying metaphysical principles will be achieved by sacrificing a multitude of contemporary methods of acquiring knowledge and insight?

American scholars and scientists are not unaware of these intellectual problems. Our best educational institutions are today experimenting with a wide variety of departures from traditional objectives and procedures. There is little or no mention of this vigorous self-criticism in *The Higher Learning in America.* Mr. Hutchins' own criticism of the confusion that has arisen as a result of the freedom of selection which President Eliot's generation used as the most effective weapon against the rigidity of the traditional college curriculum, is a college administrator's reflection of a broad movement that has been visible in our leading colleges since the war. With the abandonment of the classical kernel of the academic curriculum, we have witnessed a variety of efforts to devise a curriculum based upon a defensible discipline. The new plan in the college at the University of Chicago is one such attempt to substitute a twentieth-century *cosmos* for the *chaos* that has arisen as the unplanned result of our rebellion against the traditional curriculum. . . .

The heart of Mr. Hutchins' indictment of the higher learning in America lies in the charge of "confusion," "chaos," or "disorder." The essence of his proposal for change is a plea for a return to a rationally ordered unity to be achieved by restoring the primacy of "metaphysics" in the curriculum. . . .

He explicitly repudiates the Cartesian tradition. He completely neglects modern logic and modern philosophy. His only suggestion of a positive answer is in the form of constant reference to the writings of Plato, Aristotle, and Aquinas. It is true that he often refers favorably to Euclid, Galen, Galileo, and Newton, but in general he approves of the sciences only in so far as they carry on an ancient heritage: "Contemporary physical and biological research inherited the analytical procedures which, combined with observation, constitute a science; and to a great extent the heritage has been fruitful." By a process of elimination many readers and most reviewers have come to the conclusion

---

[1] [R. M. Hutchins, *The Higher Learning in America* (New Haven, 1936), p. 32.]

that the heritage in question is the Platonic-Aristotelian-Thomistic tradition. This is precisely the tradition from which modern science progressively freed itself. Is this the metaphysics which is to be used as the core of the higher education and the norm for the contemporary world? ...

In the light of this intellectual history Mr. Hutchins seems to many persons to have selected out of man's rich intellectual heritage one metaphysical tradition as the standard, and to have designed his program for higher education so as to inculcate this system of metaphysics. Those who do not accept this simplification of intellectual history may feel that all the major defects of Mr. Hutchins' proposals stem from his apparent selection of certain stages of human thinking as final, for the general description of his proposed college and university curriculum is determined by this selection. . . .

The dominant emphasis, the detailed criticisms, and the educational suggestions which Mr. Hutchins' books present originate from and make sense only within the framework of the traditional metaphysics of rational absolutism. It may well be that their author is changing his emphasis and perhaps to some degree his philosophical position. But until this is explicitly stated and the implications for specific problems are drawn, discussion must center around the larger published presentations of his views. No one would be more delighted than its author if Mr. Hutchins, recognizing in this essay the substance of his views, allays the apprehensions which his own pages have raised. But the fact remains that the misapprehensions—if misapprehensions they be—are responsible for the idea that the higher education in America is to forsake the path of science and humanistic concern for a democratic society and to return to the Ivory Tower of absolutistic metaphysics. There are even rumors—incredible as it may appear—that the faculty of the University of Chicago, nourished by Scholasticism, is to take the lead in charting this new course for the higher learning. This essay is contributed to the discussion with the purpose of correcting these misapprehensions and rumors. . . .

The university must seek to train men who will use learning in the service of the society about them. For such a goal the first requirement is the habit of deriving conclusions from the analysis of relevant data, and this habit is best achieved, perhaps uniquely achieved, by work on concrete problems. The danger that Mr. Hutchins professes to see in scientific specialization is well answered by Mr. Flexner: "It is fashionable to rail at specialization; but the truth is that specialization has brought us to the point we have reached, and more highly specialized intelligence will alone carry us further."[2]

Mr. Flexner proceeds to emphasize the generalizing intelligence as inevitably interwoven with the specialized pursuit of new truth, of new materials, of new data. Mr. Hutchins appears frequently to hold the position that the gathering of new data is carried on without reference to generalization. . . .

It is important to stress again that Mr. Hutchins nowhere specifies or illustrates the so-called "first principles" that are to be taught in the university. It is therefore impossible to discuss either their existence or their relevance to the higher learning. But it is possible to challenge some of his assertions and their implications.

Outstanding in his book and underlying his not always consistent pronouncements is the deprecation of facts as such. He regards "research in the sense of gathering data for the sake of gathering them" as having "no place in a university" (HL, 90). The obvious implication is that a great deal of activity of this sort is actually going on in universities. Since he does not state what he means by "facts," "data," and "information," and gives no examples, it is impossible to examine the validity of his criticisms. At any given moment there will always be a certain amount of misdirected research, but it may well be doubted whether even on the lowest level there is any appreciable amount of "gathering data *for the sake* of gathering them." The question might be raised whether in general it is possible to collect facts without having at least implicit hypotheses or generalizations in mind.

The same separation between facts and ideas, between particulars and generalizations implicit in Mr. Hutchins' critique of the universities leads him to draw a line between the university and the research institute, and between the university and the professional school. To him research appears to be altogether too often the mere piling up of data rather than the advancement of knowledge, and professional training too often a lapsing on the part of the university into gross vocationalism.[3] . . .

The University enjoys an enviable reputation as an institution not

---

[2] [Abraham Flexner, *Universities: American, English, German* (New York, 1930), pp. 17-18.]

[3] As to research institutes, which Mr. Hutchins separates from the university because they are fact-gathering institutions, see Mr. Flexner's strikingly different observations, *op. cit.,* pp. 31-35.

afraid to try the new. But this involves the correlative need to preserve such gains as have been made and not to give up known and tested practices until a reasonable chance exists that a superior practice is at hand to be tried. In education, as in everything else involving a change in social policy, the burden of proof is upon the innovator. It is he who must show that what now is, is defective, and that what might and can be contains a reasonable probability of advance.

Of the two functions of a university—the transmission of knowledge and its advancement—perhaps the most important is the latter, for unless knowledge is constantly broadened and refined it tends to become static and authoritarian and fails to keep pace with changing reality and emerging problems. From this standpoint a separation of the university in personnel and in administration from research and the professional schools contains a double danger: a segregated intellectual life on the one hand and an exaggerated vocationalism on the other.

The cross-fertilization of theory and practice is the very life of each. It can be achieved only by constant preoccupation with both the universal and the particular—and to isolate these functions in the formal organization of institutions of higher learning is to destroy our principal reliance for new knowledge and insight. . . .

Liberal education has always aimed at both theory and practice with the dominant concern of making the theory available for practice, and of correcting and fertilizing the theory by the practice. It is now proposed to truncate this process and to restrict the content of the higher learning to pure theory and a few facts chosen to illustrate it. At the college level the content proposed is directed away from laboratory concreteness, field work, and in general from exposure to "raw" experience. "Facts" appear to be foolish when ageless ideas are in the offing. Education is to Mr. Hutchins, in a word, sensitization to the abstract, to the universal, to the "intellectual," and the preference appears to rest upon the presumption that a person thus exposed to generality is more proficient in practice than others, once he turns his hands to industrial work or his mind to professional cares.

Fundamentally, the entire proposal is based upon an unproved assumption about the transfer of learning. It is taken for granted that participation in practice requires no special training, a brief apprenticeship under technicians will suffice to make a superior practitioner of the theoretical product of the higher learning. This easy faith arises out of a prejudgment as to the inferiority of the practical to the intellectual. Such a view involves a fallacy as to the transfer of training, indeed a most difficult transfer—that from theory to action. It is precisely the mutual cross-fertilization of theory and action that is the hardest task of all. If education does not achieve this, it fires wild, and it will more nearly achieve it if the aim is quite deliberately set.

Experience does not suggest that the accommodation of general ideas to specific facts and concrete action can be safely trusted to an educational afterthought. This is precisely the most common source of present failure. To know *in general* is as easy as Aristotle indicated; but to know the *when,* the *where,* the *wherefore,* the *whereunto,* and the *how much*—this, as Aristotle concluded, is the final test of a wise man. An education which does not recognize this, and specifically provide for it, makes not wise men, but educated fools. It might hide the shame engendered of its weakness by perpetuating a division of labor that will exempt its graduates from the test of life and action, assigning to them the task of passing on the "metaphysics" in education—and in so doing it might also contribute to the strength of the forces that are now undermining freedom of thought as the most effective attack upon freedom in general.

We must meet the present on its own terms. If there is confusion in our present situation, there is also unparalleled promise. In place of the metaphysical orientation of the classical academy, the theological orientation of the medieval university, and the literary orientation of the Renaissance university, modern higher education must put its main emphasis on the method of science. This does not mean that the activities of former systems of higher education are not to be included in the present system; it means that the intellectually distinctive characteristics of the modern world—scientific methods and results, and a philosophy co-operating with scientific and humanistic interests—should be the dominant quality of modern higher education. We can do full justice to the richness of man's intellectual and cultural heritage, and yet give science a high place in meeting the demands of active living in the modern world. This is a modern alternative to exclusively theological, metaphysical, or literary orientations. Science can be at once its own reward, and the highest award of living thought to the life of action.[4] . . .

The clamor for a rational order, for a comprehensive set of first principles with due subordination of historical and current empirical

---

[4] Schiller's picturesque characterization of science may be in point here: "To some she (science) is the sublime, heavenly Goddess; to others a diligent cow that provides them with butter."

material selected with an eye to illustration or confirmation of the metaphysics, is essentially a claim to intellectual dictatorship. Reason, however, is not necessarily a principle of order. It is analytical; it discriminates and distinguishes. Order historically is the fruit either of authority or of shared values. The clamor for rational order, therefore, boils down to a demand for submission to the particular metaphysical dogma that is advocated.

If philosophers are to contribute their share in the mastery of the ensuing perplexity as to what the knowledge means and what its potentialities might be, they will have to drop medieval claims to match the position of theology as the queen of the sciences. Essentially the integrative quality of medieval theology did not lie in its intellectual superstructure but in the common *faith* of those who elaborated the theology. Mr. Hutchins seems to hesitate here on the brink of a vital distinction. He stresses the role of theology in the medieval university but thinks it is not possible for our generation, which is "faithless" and takes "no stock in revelation." To our modern mind, however, metaphysical first principles require as much revelation as the medieval theology requires.

The integration of medieval society—such as it was—was essentially that of faith in common *values.* The disintegration of modern culture is not primarily the fruit of intellectual error but rather the inevitable result of an outlook that regards values as the concern of individuals, and, if anything, as an obstacle to academic achievement. Our basic problem is not that of improved *means* to unimproved *ends,* but rather that *means* are ever more available to *ends* ever more muddled and evanescent. Philosophy's most tempting opportunity lies in the clarification and statement of the values by which we live, and such a clarification of values will spring from a detailed and synthetic knowledge of the conditioning *means* rather than from sterile parroting of a discarded metaphysics. . . .

For several generations the idea has prevailed that there was something peculiarly strong-minded and scientific in discarding ethical considerations in the pursuit of knowledge; and the quality of traditional preachment helps to explain the tendency. In imitation of the physical sciences, mechanical theories prevailed even in the study of society, but in an increasingly plastic environment the old mechanical theories, which had their roots in the assumption of a fixed environment, lost their interests even in the explanation of the physical universe. In social matters, new habits of thought intimately involved in the new experience of continuous remodeling of man's environment once again focused attention upon the *ends* which the new *means* sought to implement. If reason is to serve us in our present confusion, it will be through the clarification of our *ends* in relation to ever more diversified and powerful *means*. If those who are at the frontiers of advancing knowledge have cavalierly disregarded their responsibilities in these matters, able and aggressive leadership faces a new responsibility.

To repeat, it is possible to agree with much of Mr. Hutchins' criticism of the American university of today and yet to reject his proposals for reconstruction. Unity imposed by authority is only another term for uniformity. While chaos and disorder have their disadvantages, they at least maintain a field that is widely open to new truth and new methods of gaining insight. The true scholar recognizes the need for integrating his own work with the body of knowledge pertaining to other fields and with the values of his society. He does not look for a verbal nostrum nor for a superimposed authority to introduce meaning, significance, and unity into his work.

Truth to finite man is never single, complete, and static. It is rather multiple, fractional, and evolving. The true scholar finds his unifying principles in the humanistic spirit and in the methods of science. It is not so much the tentative truths that he discovers as the developing methods for discovering and analyzing truths, that unite him with his associates into a community of scholars and of scientists. . . .

To describe the higher learning in America as if it were almost entirely vocational and provincial in the chronological sense is to overlook some of the highest achievement and some of the most seminal inquiry ever pursued under academic auspices. Critical scrutiny of abuses of academic privilege is essential to continued vitality—and even the best of our American institutions afford abundant opportunity—but to avoid the abuse by the advocacy of a monastic withdrawal to a community of scholars primarily concerned with the elaboration of a discarded metaphysics is to abandon the very essence of modern achievement. The contemporary scene is full of societies in which the logical development of first metaphysical principles with "due subordination" of observed facts, is diligently pursued. It is sad to reflect that a commendable concern for moral and intellectual integrity should be deflected by distortion of focus into a weapon against the very forces it seeks to strengthen.

7. John Dewey on Hutchins' Philosophy of Education, 1937

John Dewey (1859–1952) was born in Burlington, Vermont, and received his B.A. at the University of Vermont in 1879 and his Ph.D. at the Johns Hopkins in 1884. He taught psychology and philosophy at the University of Michigan and Minnesota up to 1894, when he became Professor of Philosophy at the University of Chicago and in 1902 the director of its school of education. From 1904 to his retirement he was professor of philosophy at Columbia University. His voluminous writings in philosophy, psychology, education, and politics won him world-wide renown, and he was acclaimed a major figure in the tradition of American pragmatism. More than any other writer, he molded the progressive movement in American education.

The literature by and about Dewey is so large as to preclude an adequate brief selection; Milton Halsey Thomas and Herbert W. Schneider, *A Bibliography of John Dewey, 1882–1939* (New York, 1939), alone contains 246 pages of references; Melvin C. Baker, *Foundations of John Dewey's Educational Theory* (New York, 1955), has more recent bibliographical references on educational writings; Paul A. Schilpp (ed.), *The Philosophy of John Dewey* (Evanston and Chicago, 1939), is also helpful.

THE EXISTING DISORDER

President Hutchins' book consists of two parts. One of them is a critical discussion of the plight of education in this country, with especial reference to colleges and universities. The other is a plan for the thorough remaking of education. This second part is again divided. It opens with an analysis of the meaning of general or liberal education, and is followed by an application of the conclusions reached to reconstruction of education in existing colleges and universities. The criticism of the present situation is trenchant. "The most striking fact about the higher learning in America is the confusion that besets it." The college of liberal arts is partly high school, partly university, partly general, partly special. The university consisting of graduate work for the master's and doctor's degree, and of a group of professional schools, is no better off. The universities are not only non-intellectual but they are anti-intellectual.

There then follows a diagnosis of the disease of "disunity, discord,

---

John Dewey, "President Hutchins' Proposals To Remake Higher Education," *The Social Frontier*, III (January, 1937), 103–4.

and disorder." Fundamentally, the ailment proceeds from too ready response of universities to immediate demands of the American public. This public is moved by love of money, and the higher learning responds to anything that promises to bring money to the college and university whether from donors, student-fees, or state legislatures. The result is that these institutions become public service-stations; and as there is no special tide in public opinion and sentiment, but only a criss-cross of currents, the kind of service that is to be rendered shifts with every change in public whim and interest. Love of money results in demand for large numbers of students, and the presence of large numbers renders training even more indiscriminate in order to meet the demands of unselected heterogeneous groups.

Another symptom of our quick response to immediate and often passing public desires is seen in the effect upon higher education of the popular notion of democracy. This notion, although confused, encourages the belief that everybody should have the same chance of getting higher education, and everybody should have just the kind of education he happens to want. As against this view, President Hutchins holds that the responsibility of the public for providing education ends properly at the sophomore year of college, and after that point education should be given only to those who have demonstrated special capacity. (Incidentally, the author attributes to the false popular idea of democracy the existing perverse system of control of higher institutions by boards of trustees.)

The third major cause of our educational disorder is the erroneous notion of progress. Everything is supposed to be getting better, the future will be better yet. Why not then break with the past? Since in fact the "progress" that has taken place is mainly in material things and techniques, information, more and more and more data, become the demand; and higher learning is swamped by an empiricism that drowns the intellect. Somewhat strangely, the natural sciences are regarded by Mr. Hutchins as the cause and the mirror of this empiricism.

THE REMEDY

One may venture to summarize the evils in relation to their source by saying that they are an excessive regard for practicality, and practicality of a very immediate sort. The essence of the remedy accordingly, is emancipation of higher learning from this practicality, and its devotion to the cultivation of intellectuality for its own sake.

Many readers will share my opinion that Mr. Hutchins has shrewdly pointed out many evils attending the aimlessness of our present educational scheme, and will join in his desire that higher institutions become "centers of creative thought." So strong will be their sympathies that they may overlook the essence of the remedy, namely, his conception of the nature of intellectuality or rationality. This conception is characterized by two dominant traits. The first, as I pointed out in an article in the December number of this journal, is belief in the existence of fixed and eternal authoritative principles as truths that are not to be questioned. "Real unity can be achieved only by a hierarchy of truths which shows us which are fundamental and which are subsidiary." The hierarchy must be already there, or else it could not show us. The other point is not so explicitly stated. But it does not require much reading between the lines to see the remedy proposed rests upon a belief that since evils have come from surrender to shifting currents of public sentiment, the remedy is to be found in the greatest possible aloofness of higher learning from contemporary social life. This conception is explicitly seen in the constant divorce set up between intellect and practice, and between intellect and "experience."

I shall not stop to inquire whether such a divorce, if it is established, will be conducive to creative intellectual work, inviting as is the topic. I content myself with pointing out that—admitting that many present ills come from surrender of educational institutions to immediate social pressures—the facts are open to another interpretation with respect to educational policy. The policy of aloofness amounts fundamentally to acceptance of a popular American slogan, "Safety first." It would seem, on the other hand, as if the facts stated about the evil effects of our love of money should invite attention on the part of institutions devoted to love of truth for its own sake to the economic institutions that have produced this overweening love, and to their social consequences in other matters than the temper of educational institutions; and attention to the means available for changing this state of things. The immediate effect of such attention would probably be withdrawal of donations of money. But for an institution supposedly devoted to truth, a policy of complete withdrawal, however safe, hardly seems the way out. I have given but one illustration. I hope it may suggest a principle widely applicable. Escape from present evil contemporary social tendencies may require something more than escape. It may demand study of social needs and social potentialities of enduring time span. President Hutchins' discussion is noteworthy for complete absence of any reference to this alternative method of educational reconstruction. It is conceivable that educational reconstruction cannot be accomplished without a social reconstruction in which higher education has a part to play.

AUTHORITY AND TRUTH

There are indications that Mr. Hutchins would not take kindly to labelling the other phase of this remedial plan "authoritarian." But any scheme based on the existence of ultimate first principles, with their dependent hierarchy of subsidiary principles, does not escape authoritarianism by calling the principles "truths." I would not intimate that the author has any sympathy with fascism. But basically his idea as to the proper course to be taken is akin to the distrust of freedom and the consequent appeal to *some* fixed authority that is now overrunning the world. There is implicit in every assertion of fixed and eternal first truths the necessity for some *human* authority to decide, in this world of conflicts, just what these truths are and how they shall be taught. This problem is conveniently ignored. Doubtless much may be said for selecting Aristotle and St. Thomas as competent promulgators of first truths. But it took the authority of a powerful ecclesiastic organization to secure their wide recognition. Others may prefer Hegel, or Karl Marx, or even Mussolini as the seers of first truths; and there are those who prefer Nazism. As far as I can see, President Hutchins has completely evaded the problem of who is to determine the definite truths that constitute the hierarchy.

In view of the emphasis given by our author to the subject of logic, it is pertinent to raise the question of how far institutions can become centers of creative thought, if in their management it is assumed that fundamental truths and the hierarchy of truth are already known. The assumption that merely by learning pre-existent truths, students will become even students, much less capable of independent creative thought, is one that demands considerable logical inquiry. President Hutchins' contempt for science as merely empirical perhaps accounts for his complete acceptance of the doctrine of formal discipline. But it is difficult to account for complete neglect of the place of the natural sciences in his educational scheme (apart from possible limitations of his own education) save on the score of a feeling, perhaps subconscious, that their recognition is so hostile to the whole scheme of prescribed antecedent first truths that it would be fatal to the educational plan he proposes to give them an important place. Considering, however, that their rise has already created a revolution in the old logic, and that they now afford the best existing patterns of controlled inquiry in search for truth, there will be others besides myself who will conclude that President Hutchins' policy of reform by withdrawal from everything that smacks of modernity and contemporaneousness is not after all the road to the kind of intellectuality that will remedy the evils he so vividly depicts.

The constant appeal of President Hutchins to Plato, Aristotle, and St. Thomas urgently calls for a very different interpretation from that which is given it. Their work is significant precisely because it does not represent withdrawal from the science and social affairs of their own times. On the contrary, each of them represents a genuine and profound attempt to discover and present in organized form the meaning of the science and the institutions that existed in their historic periods. The real conclusion to be drawn is that the task of higher learning at present is to accomplish a similar work for the confused and disordered conditions of our own day. The sciences have changed enormously since these men performed their task, both in logical method and in results. We live in a different social medium. It is astounding that anyone should suppose that a return to the conceptions and methods of these writers would do for the present situation what they did for the Greek and Medieval eras. The cure for surrender of higher learning to immediate and transitory pressures is not monastic seclusion. Higher learning can become intellectually vital only by coming to that close grip with our contemporary science and contemporary social affairs which Plato, Aristotle, and St. Thomas exemplify in their respective ways.

8. James Bryant Conant on the Meaning of General Education, 1945

James Bryant Conant was born in Boston in 1893 and educated at Harvard, where he received his A.B. in 1913 and his Ph.D. in chemistry in 1916. From 1916 to 1933 he taught at Harvard, winning a distinguished reputation in organic chemistry and occupying for the last five of these years the Emery professorship of organic chemistry. In 1933 he became president of Harvard, an office which he served for twenty years. During the Second World War he acted as chairman of the National Defense Research Committee and, briefly, as a member of the Atomic Energy Commission. A powerful advocate of federal aid to higher education, he was in good part responsible for the creation of the National Science Foundation in 1950. From 1953 to 1955 he was United States High Commissioner for Germany and after that for two years the ambassador to the Federal Republic of Germany. Upon his return to the United States, he surveyed American secondary education in behalf of the Carnegie Corporation. The first fruits of his inquiries were published as *The American High School Today* (New York, 1959) and *The Child, the Parent and the State* (Cambridge, Mass., 1959). During the Second World War, when it became apparent that American education needed revaluation, Conant called upon his faculty to consider the problems of general education and Harvard's policy toward them. In his prefatory remarks to the faculty report, he offered this explanation of the term "general education."

See Doc. 9, and *Current Biography,* 1951.

There will be some who open the book with an initial prejudice against the contents derived from the title. "General education," they may exclaim, "what's that? I'm interested only in liberal education—that's what the country needs." For the use of the current phrase "general education" instead of "liberal education," the writer is ready to take his share of blame. Shortly after the Committee had been appointed (in January, 1943, to be exact) I reported to the Board of Overseers of Harvard University as follows:

". . . I am taking the liberty of appointing a University Committee on 'The Objectives of a General Education in a Free Society.' This committee, composed of members of several faculties including Arts and Sciences and Education, I hope will consider the problem at both the school and the college level. For surely the most important aspect of this whole matter is the general education of the great majority of

General Education in a Free Society: Report of the Harvard Committee (Cambridge, Mass., 1945), pp. viii–ix. Reprinted with the permission of Harvard University Press.

each generation—not the comparatively small minority who attend our four-year colleges. . . .

"The heart of the problem of a general education is the continuance of the liberal and humane tradition. Neither the mere acquisition of information nor the development of special skills and talents can give the broad basis of understanding which is essential if our civilization is to be preserved. No one wishes to disparage the importance of being 'well-informed.' But even a good grounding in mathematics and the physical and biological sciences, combined with an ability to read and write several foreign languages, does not provide a sufficient educational background for citizens of a free nation. For such a program lacks contact with both man's emotional experience as an individual and his practical experience as a gregarious animal. It includes little of what was once known as 'the wisdom of the ages,' and might nowadays be described as our 'cultural pattern.' It includes no history, no art, no literature, no philosophy. Unless the educational process includes *at each level of maturity* some continuing contact with those fields in which value judgments are of prime importance, it must fall far short of the ideal. The student in high school, in college and in graduate school must be concerned, in part at least, with the words 'right' and 'wrong' in both the ethical and the mathematical sense. Unless he feels the import of those general ideas and aspirations which have been a deep moving force in the lives of men, he runs the risk of partial blindness.

"There is nothing new in such educational goals; what is new in this century in the United States is their application to a system of universal education. Formal education based on 'book learning' was once only the possession of a professional class; in recent times it became more widely valued because of social implications. The restricted nature of the circle possessing certain linguistic and historical knowledge greatly enhanced the prestige of this knowledge. 'Good taste' could be standardized in each generation by those who knew. But, today, we are concerned with a general education—a liberal education—not for the relatively few, but for a multitude."

Whether or not one wishes to equate the terms "liberal education" and "General education" at the college stage, the latter phrase has advantages when one examines in a comprehensive way the manifold activities of American schools and colleges. If the Committee had been concerned only with Harvard College, the title might have read "The

Objectives of a Liberal Education." A minor annoyance, to be sure, would have arisen quickly, for many specialists in various faculties would have been ready to testify eloquently to the fact that their specialty if properly taught was in and by itself a liberal education. No such claim has as yet been made in terms of a general education. But quite apart from this quarrel over the meaning of a much used and much abused adjective, any serious consideration of the problems of American schools would have been difficult for a university group designated as a committee on liberal education. The reasons lie deep in the history of American education in this century and are evidence of the cleavage between "educators" and "professors" to which I have referred already. Phrases become slogans and slogans fighting words in education no less than in theology.

9. *The Harvard Report on General Education, 1945*

The committee appointed by President Conant to survey the problems of general education in the United States and in Harvard College consisted of a dozen men, headed by Paul H. Buck, the dean of the Faculty of Arts and Sciences and professor of history, as chairman, and John H. Finley, Eliot Professor of Greek, as vice-chairman.

See Doc. 8.

It was remarked at the end of the previous chapter that a supreme need of American education is for a unifying purpose and idea. As recently as a century ago, no doubt existed about such a purpose; it was to train the Christian citizen. Nor was there doubt how this training was to be accomplished. The student's logical powers were to be formed by mathematics, his taste by the Greek and Latin classics, his speech by rhetoric, and his ideals by Christian ethics. College catalogues commonly began with a specific statement about the influence of such a training on the mind and character. The reasons why this enviable certainty both of goal and of means has largely disappeared have already been set forth. For some decades the mere excitement of enlarging the curriculum and making place for new subjects, new

General Education in a Free Society, pp. 43–58.

methods, and masses of new students seems quite pardonably to have absorbed the energies of schools and colleges. It is fashionable now to criticize the leading figures of that expansive time for failing to replace, or even to see the need of replacing, the unity which they destroyed. But such criticisms, if just in themselves, are hardly just historically. A great and necessary task of modernizing and broadening education waited to be done, and there is credit enough in its accomplishment. In recent times, however, the question of unity has become insistent. We are faced with a diversity of education which, if it has many virtues, nevertheless works against the good of society by helping to destroy the common ground of training and outlook on which any society depends.

It seems that a common ground between some, though not all, of the ideas underlying our educational practice is the sense of heritage. The word heritage is not here taken to mean mere retrospection. The purpose of all education is to help students live their own lives. The appeal to heritage is partly to the authority, partly to the clarification of the past about what is important in the present. All Catholic and many Protestant institutions thus appeal to the Christian view of man and history as providing both final meaning and immediate standards for life. As observed at the outset, it is less than a century since such was the common practice of American education generally, and certainly this impulse to mold students to a pattern sanctioned by the past can, in one form or another, never be absent from education. If it were, society would become discontinuous.

In this concern for heritage lies a close similarity between religious education and education in the great classic books. Exponents of the latter have, to be sure, described it as primarily a process of intellectual discipline in the joint arts of word and number, the so-called *trivium* (grammar, logic, rhetoric) and *quadrivium* (arithmetic, geometry, astronomy, music). But, since the very idea of this discipline goes back to antiquity and since the actual books by which it is carried out are in fact the great books of the Western tradition, it seems fairer, without denying the disciplinary value of such a curriculum, to think of it as primarily a process of opening before students the intellectual forces that have shaped the Western mind. There is a sense in which education in the great books can be looked at as a secular continuation of the spirit of Protestantism. As early Protestantism, rejecting the authority and philosophy of the medieval church, placed reliance on

each man's personal reading of the Scriptures, so this present movement, rejecting the unique authority of the Scriptures, places reliance
on the reading of those books which are taken to represent the fullest
revelation of the Western mind. But be this as it may, it is certain that,
like religious education, education in the great books is essentially an
introduction of students to their heritage.

Nor is the sense of heritage less important, though it may be less
obvious, a part of education for modern democratic life. To the degree
that the implications of democracy are drawn forth and expounded, to
that degree the long-standing impulse of education toward shaping
students to a received ideal is still pursued. Consider the teaching of
American history and of modern democratic life. However ostensibly
factual such teaching may be, it commonly carries with it a presup-
position which is not subject to scientific proof: namely, the presup-
position that democracy is meaningful and right. Moreover, since contemporary life is itself a product of history, to study it is to tread unconsciously, in the words of the hymn, where the saints have trod.
To know modern democracy is to know something at least of Jefferson, though you have not read him; to learn to respect freedom of
speech or the rights of the private conscience is not to be wholly ignorant of the *Areopagitica* or the *Antigone,* though you know nothing
about them. Whether, as philosophers of history argue, being conditioned by the present we inevitably judge the past by what we know
in the present (since otherwise the past would be unintelligible) or
whether human motives and choices do not in reality greatly change
with time, the fact remains that the past and the present are parts of
the same unrolling scene and, whether you enter early or late, you see
for the most part the still-unfinished progress of the same issues.

Here, then, in so far as our culture is adequately reflected in current
ideas on education, one point about it is clear: it depends in part on an
inherited view of man and society which it is the function, though not
the only function, of education to pass on. It is not and cannot be true
that all possible choices are open to us individually or collectively. We
are part of an organic process, which is the American, and, more
broadly, the Western evolution. Our standards of judgment, ways of
life, and form of government all bear the marks of this evolution,
which would accordingly influence us, though confusedly, even if it
were not understood. Ideally it should be understood at several degrees
of depth which complement rather than exclude each other. To study

the American present is to discern at best the aims and purposes of a free society animating its imperfections. To study the past is immensely to enrich the meaning of the present and at the same time to clarify it by the simplification of the writings and the issues which have been winnowed from history. To study either past or present is to confront, in some form or another, the philosophic and religious fact of man in history and to recognize the huge continuing influence alike on past and present of the stream of Jewish and Greek thought in Christianity. There is doubtless a sense in which religious education, education in the great books, and education in modern democracy may be mutually exclusive. But there is a far more important sense in which they work together to the same end, which is belief in the idea of man and society that we inherit, adapt, and pass on.

This idea is described in many ways, perhaps most commonly in recent times, as that of the dignity of man. To the belief in man's dignity must be added the recognition of his duty to his fellow men. Dignity does not rest on any man as a being separate from all other beings, which he in any case cannot be, but springs from his common humanity and exists positively as he makes the common good his own. This concept is essentially that of the Western tradition: the view of man as free and not as slave, an end in himself and not a means. It may have what many believe to be the limitations of humanism, which are those of pride and arise from making man the measure of all things. But it need not have these limitations, since it is equally compatible with a religious view of life. Thus it is similar to the position described at the end of the last chapter as cooperation without uniformity, agreement on the good of man at the level of performance without the necessity of agreement on ultimates. But two points have now been added. First, thus stated, the goal of education is not in conflict with but largely includes the goals of religious education, education in the Western tradition, and education in modern democracy. For these in turn have been seen to involve necessary elements in our common tradition, each to a great extent implied in the others as levels at which it can be understood. Certainly no fruitful way of stating the belief in the dignity and mutual obligation of man can present it as other than, at one and the same time, effective in the present, emerging from the past, and partaking of the nature not of fact but of faith. Second, it has become clear that the common ground between these various views —namely, the impulse to rear students to a received idea of the good—

is in fact necessary to education. It is impossible to escape the realization that our society, like any society, rests on common beliefs and that a major task of education is to perpetuate them.

This conclusion raises one of the most fundamental problems of education, indeed of society itself: how to reconcile this necessity for common belief with the equally obvious necessity for new and independent insights leading to change. We approach here the one previously mentioned concept of education which was not included under the idea of heritage: namely, the views associated with the names of James and Dewey and having to do with science, the scientific attitude, and pragmatism. This is hardly the place to try to summarize this body of thought or even to set forth in detail its application by Mr. Dewey to education. To do so would be virtually to retrace the educational controversies of the last forty years. But, at the risk of some injustice to Mr. Dewey's thought as a whole, a few points can be made about it. It puts trust in the scientific method of thought, the method which demands that you reach conclusions from tested data only, but that, since the data may be enlarged or the conclusions themselves combined with still other conclusions, you must hold them only tentatively. It emphasizes that full truth is not known and that we must be forever led by facts to revise our approximations of it. As a feeling of commitment and of allegiance marks the sense of heritage, so a tone of tough-mindedness and curiosity and a readiness for change mark this pragmatic attitude.

Here, then, is a concept of education, founded on obedience to fact and well disposed, even hospitable, to change, which appears at first sight the antithesis of any view based on the importance of heritage. Such hostility to tradition well reflects one side of the modern mind. It is impossible to contemplate the changes even of the last decades, much less the major groundswell of change since the Renaissance, without feeling that we face largely new conditions which call for new qualities of mind and outlook. Moreover, it is obviously no accident that this pragmatic philosophy has been worked out most fully in the United States. Yet, in spite of its seeming conflict with views of education based on heritage, strong doubt exists whether the questioning, innovating, experimental attitude of pragmatism is in fact something alien to the Western heritage, or whether it is not, in the broadest sense of the word, a part of it.

The rest of the present volume would hardly suffice for this sweeping subject. But it can be observed even here that we look back on antiquity not simply out of curiosity but because ancient thought is sympathetic to us. The Greek idea of an orderly universe, of political freedom under rationally constructed laws, and of the inner life itself as subject to the sway of reason, was certainly not achieved without skepticism, observation, or the test of experience. The ancient atomists and medical writers and, to a large extent, Socrates himself relied precisely on induction from observed facts. Socrates, the teacher and the gadfly of the Athenian city, impressed on his pupils and the public at large the duty of man to reflect on his beliefs and to criticize his presuppositions. Socrates was an individualist proclaiming that man should form his opinions by his own reasoning and not receive them by social indoctrination. And yet, it was this same Socrates who died in obedience to the judgment of the state, even though he believed this judgment to be wrong. Again, historical Christianity has been expressly and consistently concerned with the importance of this life on earth. The doctrine of the Incarnation, that God took the form of man and inhabited the earth, declares this concern. While perhaps for Greek thought, only the timeless realm had importance, in Christian thought the process of history is vested with absolute significance. If the ideal of democracy was rightly described above in the interwoven ideas of the dignity of man (that is, his existence as an independent moral agent) and his duty to his fellow men (that is, his testing by outward performance), the debt of these two ideas to the similarly interwoven commandments of the love of God and the love of neighbor is obvious.

These evidences of a consistent and characteristic appeal through Western history to the test of reason and experience are not adduced for the purpose of minimizing the huge creativeness of the modern scientific age or of glossing over its actual break from the past. In the well-known opening chapters of his *Science and the Modern World* in which he inquires into the origin of modern science, Mr. Whitehead pictures it as inspired by a revolt against abstract reasoning and a respect for unique fact. So considered, the first impulse of modern science was antirational or, better, antitheoretical, in the sense that it was a reaction against the most towering intellectual system which the West has known, namely, scholasticism. But be this question of origin as it may, there is no doubt that the modern mind received one of its characteristic bents in the empiricism, the passion for observation, and the distrust of abstract reasoning which have attended the origin and growth of science.

But there also seems no doubt that what happened was a shift, perhaps to some degree a restoration, of emphasis within the Western tradition itself rather than a complete change in its nature. It is a mistake to identify the older Western culture with traditionalism. Classical antiquity handed on a working system of truth which relied on both reason and experience and was designed to provide a norm for civilized life. Its import was heightened and vastly intensified by its confluence with Christianity. But when, in its rigid systematization in the late Middle Ages, it lost touch with experience and individual inquiry, it violated its own nature and provoked the modernist revolt. The seeming opposition that resulted between traditionalism and modernism has been a tragedy for Western thought. Modernism rightly affirms the importance of inquiry and of relevance to experience. But as scholasticism ran the danger of becoming a system without vitality, so modernism runs the danger of achieving vitality without pattern.

While, then, there are discontinuities between the classical and the modern components of our Western culture, there are also continuities. For instance, it would be wrong to construe the scientific outlook as inimical to human values. Even if it were true that science is concerned with means only, it would not follow that science ignores the intrinsic worth of man. For the values of human life cannot be achieved within a physical vacuum; they require for their fulfilment the existence of material conditions. To the extent that classical civilization failed to mitigate the evils of poverty, disease, squalor, and a generally low level of living among the masses, to that extent it failed to liberate man. Conversely, to the extent that science, especially in its medical and technological applications, has succeeded in dealing with these evils, it has contributed to the realization of human values. Thus science has implemented the humanism which classicism and Christianity have proclaimed.

Science has done more than provide the material basis of the good life; it has directly fostered the spiritual values of humanism. To explain, science is both the outcome and the source of the habit of forming objective, disinterested judgments based upon exact evidence. Such a habit is of particular value in the formation of citizens for a free society. It opposes to the arbitrariness of authority and "first principles" the direct and continuing appeal to things as they are. Thus it develops the qualities of the free man. It is no accident that John Locke, who set forth the political doctrine of the natural rights of man against established authority, should have been also the man who rejected the authority of innate ideas.

Students of antiquity and of the Middle Ages can therefore rightly affirm that decisive truths about the human mind and its relation to the world were laid hold of then, and yet agree that, when new application of these truths was made through a more scrupulous attention to fact, their whole implication and meaning were immensely enlarged. Modern civilization has seen this enlargement of meaning and possibility; yet it is not a new civilization but the organic development of an earlier civilization. The true task of education is therefore so to reconcile the sense of pattern and direction deriving from heritage with the sense of experiment and innovation deriving from science that they may exist fruitfully together, as in varying degrees they have never ceased to do throughout Western history.

Belief in the dignity and mutual obligation of man is the common ground between these contrasting but mutually necessary forces in our culture. As was pointed out earlier, this belief is the fruit at once of religion, of the Western tradition, and of the American tradition. It equally inspires the faith in human reason which is the basis for trust in the future of the democracy. And if it is not, strictly speaking, implied in all statements of the scientific method, there is no doubt that science has become its powerful instrument. In this tension between the opposite forces of heritage and change poised only in the faith in man, lies something like the old philosophic problem of the knowledge of the good. If you know the good, why do you seek it? If you are ignorant of the good, how do you recognize it when you find it? You must evidently at one and the same time both know it and be ignorant of it. Just so, the tradition which has come down to us regarding the nature of man and the good society must inevitably provide our standard of good. Yet an axiom of that tradition itself is the belief that no current form of the received ideal is final but that every generation, indeed every individual, must discover it in a fresh form. Education can therefore be wholly devoted neither to tradition nor to experiment, neither to the belief that the ideal in itself is enough nor to the view that means are valuable apart from the ideal. It must uphold at the same time tradition and experiment, the ideal and the means, subserving, like our culture itself, change within commitment.

GENERAL AND SPECIAL EDUCATION

In the previous section we have attempted to outline the unifying elements of our culture and therefore of American education as well. In the present section we shall take the next step of indicating in what ways these cultural strands may be woven into the fabric of education. Education is broadly divided into general and special education; our topic now is the difference and the relationship between the two. The term, general education, is somewhat vague and colorless; it does not mean some airy education in knowledge in general (if there be such knowledge), nor does it mean education for all in the sense of universal education. It is used to indicate that part of a student's whole education which looks first of all to his life as a responsible human being and citizen; while the term, special education, indicates that part which looks to the student's competence in some occupation. These two sides of life are not entirely separable, and it would be false to imagine education for the one as quite distinct from education for the other—more will be said on this point presently. Clearly, general education has somewhat the meaning of liberal education, except that, by applying to high school as well as to college, it envisages immensely greater numbers of students and thus escapes the invidium which, rightly or wrongly, attaches to liberal education in the minds of some people. But if one clings to the root meaning of liberal as that which befits or helps to make free men, then general and liberal education have identical goals. The one may be thought of as an earlier stage of the other, similar in nature but less advanced in degree.

The opposition to liberal education—both to the phrase and to the fact—stems largely from historical causes. The concept of liberal education first appeared in a slave-owning society, like that of Athens, in which the community was divided into free men and slaves, rulers and subjects. While the slaves carried on the specialized occupations of menial work, the freemen were primarily concerned with the rights and duties of citizenship. The training of the former was purely vocational; but as the freemen were not only a ruling class but also a leisure class, their education was exclusively in the liberal arts, without any utilitarian tinge. The freemen were trained in the reflective pursuit of the good life; their education was unspecialized as well as unvocational; its aim was to produce a rounded person with a full understanding of himself and of his place in society and in the cosmos.

Modern democratic society clearly does not regard labor as odious or disgraceful; on the contrary, in this country at least, it regards leisure with suspicion and expects its "gentlemen" to engage in work. Thus we attach no odium to vocational instruction. Moreover, in so far as we surely reject the idea of freemen who are free in so far as they have slaves or subjects, we are apt strongly to deprecate the liberal education which went with the structure of the aristocratic ideal. Herein our society runs the risk of committing a serious fallacy. Democracy is the view that not only the few but that all are free, in that everyone governs his own life and shares in the responsibility for the management of the community. This being the case, it follows that all human beings stand in need of an ampler and rounded education. The task of modern democracy is to preserve the ancient ideal of liberal education and to extend it as far as possible to all the members of the community. In short, we have been apt to confuse accidental with fundamental factors, in our suspicion of the classical ideal. To believe in the equality of human beings is to believe that the good life, and the education which trains the citizen for the good life, are equally the privilege of all. And these are the touchstones of the liberated man; first, is he free; that is to say, is he able to judge and plan for himself, so that he can truly govern himself? In order to do this, his must be a mind capable of self-criticism; he must lead that self-examined life which according to Socrates is alone worthy of a freeman. Thus he will possess inner freedom, as well as social freedom. Second, is he universal in his motives and sympathies? For the civilized man is a citizen of the entire universe; he has overcome provincialism, he is objective, and is a "spectator of all time and all existence." Surely these two are the very aims of democracy itself.

But the opposition to general education does not stem from causes located in the past alone. We are living in an age of specialism, in which the avenue to success for the student often lies in his choice of a specialized career, whether as a chemist, or an engineer, or a doctor, or a specialist in some form of business or of manual or technical work. Each of these specialties makes an increasing demand on the time and on the interest of the student. Specialism is the means for advancement in our mobile social structure; yet we must envisage the fact that a society controlled wholly by specialists is not a wisely ordered society. We cannot, however, turn away from specialism. The problem is how to save general education and its values within a system where specialism is necessary.

The very prevalence and power of the demand for special training makes doubly clear the need for a concurrent, balancing force in general education. Specialism enhances the centrifugal forces in society. The business of providing for the needs of society breeds a great diversity of special occupations; and a given specialist does not speak the language of the other specialists. In order to discharge his duties as a citizen adequately, a person must somehow be able to grasp the complexities of life as a whole. Even from the point of view of economic success, specialism has its peculiar limitations. Specializing in a vocation makes for inflexibility in a world of fluid possibilities. Business demands minds capable of adjusting themselves to varying situations and of managing complex human institutions. Given the pace of economic progress, techniques alter speedily; and even the work in which the student has been trained may no longer be useful when he is ready to earn a living, or soon after. Our conclusion, then, is that the aim of education should be to prepare an individual to become an expert both in some particular vocation or art and in the general art of the freeman and the citizen. Thus the two kinds of education once given separately to different social classes must be given together to all alike.

In this epoch in which almost all of us must be experts in some field in order to make a living, general education therefore assumes a peculiar importance. Since no one can become an expert in all fields, everyone is compelled to trust the judgment of other people pretty thoroughly in most areas of activity. I must trust the advice of my doctor, my plumber, my lawyer, my radio repairman, and so on. Therefore I am in peculiar need of a kind of sagacity by which to distinguish the expert from the quack, and the better from the worse expert. From this point of view, the aim of general education may be defined as that of providing the broad critical sense by which to recognize competence in any field. William James said that an educated person knows a good man when he sees one. There are standards and a style for every type of activity—manual, athletic, intellectual, or artistic; and the educated man should be one who can tell sound from shoddy work in a field outside his own. General education is especially required in a democracy where the public elects its leaders and officials; the ordinary citizen must be discerning enough so that he will not be deceived by appearances and will elect the candidate who is wise in his field.

Both kinds of education—special as well as general—contribute to the task of implementing the pervasive forces of our culture. Here we revert to what was said at the start of this chapter on the aims of education in our society. It was argued there that two complementary forces are at the root of our culture: on the one hand, an ideal of man and society distilled from the past but at the same time transcending the past as a standard of judgment valid in itself, and, on the other hand, the belief that no existent expressions of this ideal are final but that all alike call for perpetual scrutiny and change in the light of new knowledge. Specialism is usually the vehicle of this second force. It fosters the open-mindedness and love of investigation which are the wellspring of change, and it devotes itself to the means by which change is brought about. The fact may not always be obvious. There is a sterile specialism which hugs accepted knowledge and ends in the bleakest conservatism. Modern life also calls for many skills which, though specialized, are repetitive and certainly do not conduce to inquiry. These minister to change but unconsciously. Nevertheless, the previous statement is true in the sense that specialism is concerned primarily with knowledge in action, as it advances into new fields and into further applications.

Special education comprises a wider field than vocationalism; and correspondingly, general education extends beyond the limits of merely literary preoccupation. An example will make our point clearer. A scholar—let us say a scientist (whether student or teacher)—will, in the laudable aim of saving himself from narrowness, take a course in English literature, or perhaps read poetry and novels, or perhaps listen to good music and generally occupy himself with the fine arts. All this, while eminently fine and good, reveals a misapprehension. In his altogether unjustified humility, the scientist wrongly interpets the distinction between liberal and illiberal in terms of the distinction between the humanities and the sciences. Plato and Cicero would have been very much surprised to hear that geometry, astronomy, and the sciences of nature in general, are excluded from the humanities. There is also implied a more serious contempt for the liberal arts, harking back to the fallacy which identifies liberal education with the aristocratic ideal. The implication is that liberal education is something only genteel. A similar error is evident in the student's attitude towards his required courses outside his major field as something to "get over with," so that he may engage in the business of serious education, identified in his mind with the field of concentration.

Now, a general education is distinguished from special education, not by subject matter, but in terms of method and outlook, no matter what the field. Literature, when studied in a technical fashion, gives rise to the special science of philology; there is also the highly specialized historical approach to painting. Specialism is interchangeable, not with natural science, but with the method of science, the method which abstracts material from its context and handles it in complete isolation. The reward of scientific method is the utmost degree of precision and exactness. But, as we have seen, specialism as an educational force has its own limitations; it does not usually provide an insight into general relationships.

A further point is worth noting. The impact of specialism has been felt not only in those phases of education which are necessarily and rightly specialistic; it has affected also the whole structure of higher and even of secondary education. Teachers, themselves products of highly technical disciplines, tend to reproduce their knowledge in class. The result is that each subject, being taught by an expert, tends to be so presented as to attract potential experts. This complaint is perhaps more keenly felt in colleges and universities, which naturally look to scholarship. The undergraduate in a college receives his teaching from professors who, in their turn, have been trained in graduate schools. And the latter are dominated by the ideal of specialization. Learning now is diversified and parceled into a myriad of specialties. Correspondingly, colleges and universities are divided into large numbers of departments, with further specialization within the departments. As a result, a student in search of a general course is commonly frustrated. Even an elementary course is devised as an introduction to a specialism within a department; it is significant only as the beginning of a series of courses of advancing complexity. In short, such introductory courses are planned for the specialist, not for the student seeking a general education. The young chemist in the course in literature and the young writer in the course in chemistry find themselves in thoroughly uncomfortable positions so long as the purpose of these courses is primarily to train experts who will go on to higher courses rather than to give some basic understanding of science as it is revealed in chemistry or of the arts as they are revealed in literature.

It is most unfortunate if we envisage general education as something formless—that is to say, the taking of one course after another; and as something negative, namely, the study of what is not in a field of concentration. Just as we regard the courses in concentration as having definite relations to one another, so should we envisage general education as an organic whole whose parts join in expounding a ruling idea and in serving a common aim. And to do so means to abandon the view that all fields and all departments are equally valuable vehicles of general education. It also implies some prescription. At the least it means abandoning the usual attitude of regarding "distribution" as a sphere in which the student exercises a virtually untrammeled freedom of choice. It may be objected that we are proposing to limit the liberty of the student in the very name of liberal education. Such an objection would only indicate an ambiguity in the conception of liberal education. We must distinguish between liberalism in education and education in liberalism. The former, based as it is on the doctrine of individualism, expresses the view that the student should be free in his choice of courses. But education in liberalism is an altogether different matter; it is education which has a pattern of its own, namely, the pattern associated with the liberal outlook. In this view, there are truths which none can be free to ignore, if one is to have that wisdom through which life can become useful. These are the truths concerning the structure of the good life and concerning the factual conditions by which it may be achieved, truths comprising the goals of the free society.

Finally, the problem of general education is one of combining fixity of aim with diversity in application. It is not a question of providing a general education which will be uniform through the same classes of all schools and colleges all over the country, even were such a thing possible in our decentralized system. It is rather to adapt general education to the needs and intentions of different groups and, so far as possible, to carry its spirit into special education. The effectiveness of teaching has always largely depended on this willingness to adapt a central unvarying purpose to varying outlooks. Such adaptation is as much in the interest of the quick as of the slow, of the bookish as of the unbookish, and is the necessary protection of each. What is wanted, then, is a general education capable at once of taking on many different forms and yet of representing in all its forms the common knowledge and the common values on which a free society depends.

10. The President's Commission on Higher Education for Democracy, 1947

In 1946, with hundreds of thousands of veterans returning to college, it was clear that the facilities of higher education were being overstrained and that a major turning point in education loomed ahead. Accordingly, President Truman appointed a Presidential Commission on Higher Education in the summer of 1946, urging that "we should now re-examine our system of higher education in terms of its objectives, methods, and facilities; and in the light of the social role it has to play." A commission of 28 educators and laymen, headed by George F. Zook, president of the American Council on Education, went promptly to work and produced at the end of the following year a report consisting of six volumes: The first volume, *Establishing the Goals,* excerpted here, set the pattern for the others and summarized the Commission's conclusions. The other volumes were as follows: II, *Equalizing and Expanding Individual Opportunity;* III, *Organizing Higher Education;* IV, *Staffing Higher Education;* V, *Financing Higher Education;* VI, *Resource Data.*

See Doc. 11; in addition to the volumes of the Commission's report, see also Gail Kennedy (ed.), *Education for Democracy: The Debate over the Report of the President's Commission on Higher Education* (Boston, 1952); James Russell, *Federal Activities in Higher Education after the Second World War* (New York, 1951); Charles A. Quattlebaum, *Federal Aid to Students for Higher Education* (Washington, 1956); John S. Brubacher and Willis Rudy, *Higher Education in Transition* (New York, 1958), chap. xi.

The President's Commission on Higher Education has been charged with the task of defining the responsibilities of colleges and universities in American democracy and in international affairs—and, more specifically, with reexamining the objectives, methods, and facilities of higher education in the United States in the light of the social role it has to play.

The colleges and universities themselves had begun this process of reexamination and reappraisal before the outbreak of World War II. For many years they had been healthily dissatisfied with their own accomplishments, significant though these have been. Educational leaders were troubled by an uneasy sense of shortcoming. They felt that somehow the colleges had not kept pace with changing social conditions, that the programs of higher education would have to be

Higher Education for Democracy: A Report of the President's Commission on Higher Education. Vol. I, *Establishing the Goals* (New York, 1947), pp. 1–3, 5–8, 25–29, 32–39, 47–49. Reprinted with permission of Harper & Brothers.

repatterned if they were to prepare youth to live satisfyingly and effectively in contemporary society.

One factor contributing to this sense of inadequacy has been the steadily increasing number of young people who seek a college education. As the national economy became industrialized and more complex, as production increased and national resources multiplied, the American people came in ever greater numbers to feel the need of higher education for their children. More and more American youth attended colleges and universities, but resources and equipment and curriculum did not keep pace with the growing enrollment or with the increasing diversity of needs and interests among the students.

World War II brought a temporary falling off in enrollment, but with the war's end and the enactment of Public Laws 16 and 346, the "Veterans' Rehabilitation Act," and "The G.I. Bill of Rights," the acceleration has resumed. The increase in numbers is far beyond the capacity of higher education in teachers, in buildings, and in equipment. Moreover, the number of veterans availing themselves of veterans' educational benefits falls short of the numbers that records of military personnel show could benefit from higher education. Statistics reveal that a doubling of the 1947–48 enrollment in colleges and universities will be entirely possible within 10 to 15 years, if facilities and financial means are provided.

This tendency of the American people to seek higher education in ever greater numbers has grown concurrently with an increasingly critical need for such education. To this need several developments have contributed:

(*a*) Science and invention have diversified natural resources, have multiplied new devices and techniques of production. These have altered in radical ways the interpersonal and intergroup relations of Americans in their work, in their play, and in their duties as citizens. As a consequence, new skills and greater maturity are required of youth as they enter upon their adult roles. And the increasing complexity that technological progress has brought to our society has made a broader understanding of social processes and problems essential for effective living.

(*b*) The people of America are drawn from the peoples of the entire world. They live in contrasting regions. They are of different occupations, diverse faiths, divergent cultural backgrounds, and varied interests. The American Nation is not only a union of 48 different States;

it is also a union of an indefinite number of diverse groups of varying size. Of and among these diversities our free society seeks to create a dynamic unity. Where there is economic, cultural, or religious tension, we undertake to effect democratic reconciliation, so as to make of the national life one continuous process of interpersonal, intervocational, and intercultural cooperation.

(c) With World War II and its conclusion has come a fundamental shift in the orientation of American foreign policy. Owing to the inescapable pressure of events, the Nation's traditional isolationism has been displaced by a new sense of responsibility in world affairs. The need for maintaining our democracy at peace with the rest of the world has compelled our initiative in the formation of the United Nations, and America's role in this and other agencies of international cooperation requires of our citizens a knowledge of other peoples—of their political and economic systems, their social and cultural institutions— such as has not hitherto been so urgent.

(d) The coming of the atomic age, with its ambivalent promise of tremendous good or tremendous evil for mankind, has intensified the uncertainties of the future. It has deepened and broadened the responsibilities of higher education for anticipating and preparing for the social and economic changes that will come with the application of atomic energy to industrial uses. At the same time it has underscored the need for education and research for the self-protection of our democracy, for demonstrating the merits of our way of life to other peoples.

Thus American colleges and universities face the need both for improving the performance of their traditional tasks and for assuming the new tasks created for them by the new internal conditions and external relations under which the American people are striving to live and to grow as a free people.

THE ROLE OF EDUCATION

It is a commonplace of the democratic faith that education is indispensable to the maintenance and growth of freedom of thought, faith, enterprise, and association. Thus the social role of education in a democratic society is at once to insure equal liberty and equal opportunity to differing individuals and groups, and to enable the citizens to understand, appraise, and redirect forces, men, and events as these tend to strengthen or to weaken their liberties.

In performing this role, education will necessarily vary its means and methods to fit the diversity of its constituency, but it will achieve its ends more successfully if its programs and policies grow out of and are relevant to the characteristics and needs of contemporary society. Effective democratic education will deal directly with current problems.

This is not to say that education should neglect the past—only that it should not get lost in the past. No one would deny that a study of man's history can contribute immeasurably to understanding and managing the present. But to assume that all we need do is apply to present and future problems "eternal" truths revealed in earlier ages is likely to stifle creative imagination and intellectual daring. Such an assumption may blind us to new problems and the possible need for new solutions. It is wisdom in education to use the past selectively and critically, in order to illumine the pressing problems of the present.

At the same time education is the making of the future. Its role in a democratic society is that of critic and leader as well as servant; its task is not merely to meet the demands of the present but to alter those demands if necessary, so as to keep them always suited to democratic ideals. Perhaps its most important role is to serve as an instrument of social transition, and its responsibilities are defined in terms of the kind of civilization society hopes to build. If its adjustments to present needs are not to be mere fortuitous improvisations, those who formulate its policies and programs must have a vision of the Nation and the world we want—to give a sense of direction to their choices among alternatives.

What America needs today, then, is "a schooling better aware of its aims." Our colleges need to see clearly what it is they are trying to accomplish. The efforts of individual institutions, local communities, the several States, the educational foundations and associations, and the Federal Government will all be more effective if they are directed toward the same general ends.

In the future as in the past, American higher education will embody the principle of diversity in unity: each institution, State, or other agency will continue to make its own contribution in its own way. But educational leaders should try to agree on certain common objectives that can serve as a stimulus and guide to individual decision and action.

A TIME OF CRISIS

It is essential today that education come decisively to grips with the world-wide crisis of mankind. This is no careless or uncritical use of words. No thinking person doubts that we are living in a decisive moment of human history.

Atomic scientists are doing their utmost to make us realize how easily and quickly a world catastrophe may come. They know the fearful power for destruction possessed by the weapons their knowledge and skill have fashioned. They know that the scientific principles on which these weapons are based are no secret to the scientists of other nations, and that America's monopoly of the engineering processes involved in the manufacture of atom bombs is not likely to last many years. And to the horror of atomic weapons, biological and chemical instruments of destruction are now being added.

But disaster is not inevitable. The release of atomic energy that has brought man within sight of world devastation has just as truly brought him the promise of a brighter future. The potentialities of atomic power are as great for human betterment as for human annihilation. Man can choose which he will have.

The possibility of this choice is the supreme fact of our day, and it will necessarily influence the ordering of educational priorities. We have a big job of reeducation to do. Nothing less than a complete reorientation of our thinking will suffice if mankind is to survive and move on to higher levels.

In a real sense the future of our civilization depends on the direction education takes, not just in the distant future, but in the days immediately ahead.

This crisis is admittedly world-wide. All nations need reeducation to meet it. But this fact does not lessen the obligation of colleges and universities to undertake the task in the United States. On the contrary, our new position in international affairs increases the obligation. We can do something about the problem in our own country and in occupied areas, and hope that by so doing we will win the friendly cooperation of other nations.

The fundamental goal of the United States in its administration of occupied areas must be the reeducation of the populations to the individual responsibilities of democracy. Such reeducation calls for the immediate removal of authoritarian barriers to democratic education, and inculcation of democratic ideals and principles through the guidance, example, and wisdom of United States occupation forces. The primacy of the objective of reeducation, however, appears too often to have been lost sight of in the press of day-to-day administrative problems. Yet every contact by Americans with Germans or Japanese either strengthens or retards the achievement of the goal. Evidence reaching this Commission indicates that while many specific existing barriers to democratic reform have been removed, new obstacles are being created daily by inadequacies of educational personnel and policy. Cognizant of the great responsibility of American education to promote democratic ideals in occupied areas, the Commission recommends the formation of a special committee to appraise progress and offer advice to the Departments of State and National Defense on educational policy and administration in occupied areas.

The schools and colleges are not solely or even mainly to blame for the situation in which we find ourselves, or that the responsibility for resolving the crisis is not or can not be entirely theirs [*sic*]. But the scientific knowledge and technical skills that have made atomic and bacteriological warfare possible are the products of education and research, and higher education must share proportionately in the task of forging social and political defenses against obliteration. The indirect way toward some longer view and superficial curricular tinkering can no longer serve. The measures higher education takes will have to match in boldness and vision the magnitude of the problem.

In the light of this situation, the President's Commission on Higher Education has attempted to select, from among the principal goals for higher education, those which should come first in our time. They are to bring to all the people of the Nation:

Education for a fuller realization of democracy in every phase of living.

Education directly and explicitly for international understanding and cooperation.

Education for the application of creative imagination and trained intelligence to the solution of social problems and to the administration of public affairs.

Education is by far the biggest and the most hopeful of the Nation's enterprises. Long ago our people recognized that education for all is not only democracy's obligation but its necessity. Education is the foundation of democratic liberties. Without an educated citizenry alert to preserve and extend freedom, it would not long endure.

Accepting this truth, the United States has devoted many of its best minds and billions of its wealth to the development and maintenance of an extensive system of free public schools, and through the years the level of schooling attained by more and more of our people has steadily risen.

RECORD OF GROWTH

The expansion of the American education enterprise since the turn of the century has been phenomenal. The 700,000 enrollment in high schools in the school year 1900 was equal to only 11 percent of the youth of usual high-school age, 14 through 17 years old. This increased in 1940 to over 7,000,000 students representing 73 percent of the youth.

Almost as spectacular has been the increase in college attendance. In 1900 fewer than 250,000 students, only 4 percent of the population 18 through 21 years of age, were enrolled in institutions of higher education. By 1940 the enrollment had risen to 1,500,000 students, equal to a little less than 16 percent of the 18–21-year-olds. In 1947, enrollments jumped to the theretofore unprecedented peak of 2,354,000 although approximately 1,000,000 of the students were veterans, older than the usual college age because World War II had deferred their education. The situation in the fall of 1947 gives every indication that the school year 1948 will witness even larger enrollments. (See Chart 1, "Growth of College Population.")

This record of growth is encouraging, but we are forced to admit nonetheless that the educational attainments of the American people are still substantially below what is necessary, either for effective individual living or for the welfare of our society.

According to the U. S. Bureau of the Census, almost 17,000,000 men and women over 19 years of age in 1947 had stopped their schooling at the sixth grade or less. Of these, 9,000,000 had never attended school or had stopped their schooling before completing the fifth grade. In 1947, about 1,600,000 or 19 percent of our high-school-age boys and girls were not attending any kind of school, and over two-thirds of the 18- and 19-year-old youths were not in school.

These are disturbing facts. They represent a sobering failure to reach the educational goals implicit in the democratic creed, and they are indefensible in a society so richly endowed with material resources as our own. We cannot allow so many of our people to remain so ill equipped either as human beings or as citizens of a democracy.

Great as the total American expenditure for education may seem, we have not been devoting any really appreciable part of our vast wealth to higher education. As table 1 shows, even though in the last 15 years our annual budget for education has risen in number of dollars, it has actually declined in relation to our increasing economic productivity.

The $1,000,000,000 we have put into our colleges and universities in 1947 was less than one-half of 1 percent of the gross national product, which is the market value of all the goods and services produced in the country in that year.

BARRIERS TO EQUAL OPPORTUNITY

One of the gravest charges to which American society is subject is that of failing to provide a reasonable equality of educational oppor-

TABLE 1

DIRECT COST OF HIGHER EDUCATION AND ITS
RELATION TO THE GROSS NATIONAL PRODUCT

Fiscal year	Amount (in millions)[1]	Proportion of gross national product (percent)[2]
1932	$ 421	0.63
1940	522	.55
1947	1,005	.46

[1] Source: General and educational expenditures, not including capital expansion, as reported by U.S. Office of Education.
[2] Source of gross national product: U.S. Bureau of Foreign and Domestic Commerce.

tunity for its youth. For the great majority of our boys and girls, the kind and amount of education they may hope to attain depends, not on their own abilities, but on the family or community into which they happened to be born or, worse still, on the color of their skin or the religion of their parents.

Economic Barriers

The old, comfortable idea that "any boy can get a college education who has it in him" simply is not true. Low family income, together with the rising costs of education, constitutes an almost impassable barrier to college education for many young people. For some, in fact, the barrier is raised so early in life that it prevents them from attending high school even when free public high schools exist near their homes.

Despite the upward trend in average per capita income for the past century and more, the earnings of a large part of our population are still too low to provide anything but the barest necessities of physical life. It is a distressing fact that in 1945, when the total national income was far greater than in any previous period in our history, half of the children under 18 were growing up in families which had a cash income of $2,530 or less. The educational significance of these facts is heightened by the relationship that exists between income and birth rate. Fertility is highest in the families with lowest incomes.

In the elementary and secondary schools the effects of these economic conditions are overcome to a considerable extent, though not entirely, by the fact that education is free and at certain ages is compulsory. But this does not hold true at the college level. For a number of years the tendency has been for the college student to bear an increasing share of the cost of his own education. Even in State-supported institutions we have been moving away from the principle of free education to a much greater degree than is commonly supposed.

Under the pressure of rising costs and of a relative lessening of public support, the colleges and universities are having to depend more and more on tuition fees to meet their budgets. As a result, on the average, tuition rates rose about 30 percent from 1939 to 1947.

Nor are tuition costs the whole of it. There are not enough colleges and universities in the country, and they are not distributed evenly enough to bring them within reach of all young people. Relatively few students can attend college in their home communities. So to the expense of a college education for most youth must be added transportation and living costs—by no means a small item.

This economic factor explains in large part why the father's occupation has been found in many studies to rank so high as a determining factor in a young person's college expectancy. A farm laborer earns less than a banker or a doctor, for instance, and so is less able to afford the costs of higher education for his children. The children, moreover, have less inducement to seek a college education because of their family background. In some social circles a college education is often considered a luxury which can be done without, something desirable perhaps, "but not for the likes of us."

The importance of economic barriers to post-high school education lies in the fact that there is little if any relationship between the ability to benefit from a college education and the ability to pay for it. Studies discussed in the volume of this Commission's report, "Equalizing and Expanding Individual Opportunity," show that among children of equally high ability those with fathers in higher-income occupations had greater probability of attending college.

By allowing the opportunity for higher education to depend so largely on the individual's economic status, we are not only denying to millions of young people the chance in life to which they are entitled; we are also depriving the Nation of a vast amount of potential leadership and potential social competence which it sorely needs.

Barrier of a Restricted Curriculum

We shall be denying educational opportunity to many young people as long as we maintain the present orientation of higher education toward verbal skills and intellectual interests. Many young people have abilities of a different kind, and they cannot receive "education commensurate with their native capacities" in colleges and universities that recognize only one kind of educable intelligence.

Traditionally the colleges have sifted out as their special clientele persons possessing verbal aptitudes and a capacity for grasping abstractions. But many other aptitudes—such as social sensitivity and versatility, artistic ability, motor skill and dexterity, and mechanical aptitude and ingenunity—also should be cultivated in a society depending, as ours does, on the minute division of labor and at the same time upon the orchestration of an enormous variety of talents.

If the colleges are to educate the great body of American youth, they must provide programs for the development of other abilities than those involved in academic aptitude, and they cannot continue to concentrate on students with one type of intelligence to the neglect of youth with other talents.

Racial and Religious Barriers

The outstanding example of these barriers to equal opportunity, of course, is the disadvantages suffered by our Negro citizens. The low educational attainments of Negro adults reflect the cumulative effects of a long period of unequal opportunity. In 1940 the schooling of the Negro was significantly below that of whites at every level from the first grade through college. At the college level, the difference is marked; 11 percent of the white population 20 years of age and over had completed at least 1 year of college and almost 5 percent had finished 4 years; whereas for the nonwhites (over 95 percent of whom are Negroes) only a little more than 3 percent had completed at least 1 year of college and less than 1½ percent had completed a full course.

Gains Have Been Made. Noteworthy advances have been made toward eliminating the racial inequalities which in large measure are responsible for this low level of educational achievement by the Negroes. Between 1900 and 1940 the percentage of Negroes 5 to 20 years of age attending school rose from 31.0 percent to 64.4 percent. And the percentage of Negro youth 15 to 20 years old attending school increased

TABLE 5

PROPORTION OF YOUNG PERSONS ATTENDING
SCHOOL, BY AGE AND COLOR: APRIL 1947[1]

AGE	ATTENDING SCHOOL	
	White	Nonwhites (about 95 percent Negro)
	Percent	Percent
6 years of age...........	67.8	63.4
7 to 9 years of age.......	97.1	89.2
10 to 13 years of age......	98.2	93.7
14 to 17 years of age......	82.5	71.9
18 to 19 years of age......	28.2	24.2
20 to 24 years of age......	11.3	6.7

[1] Source: U.S. Bureau of the Census.

from 17.5 in 1900 to 33.8 in 1940. That differentials still persist, however, is shown in table 5.

Institutions which accept both Negro and non-Negro students do not maintain separate record systems for Negroes, and so data on enrollment of Negroes are restricted to those institutions—usually located in the South—which accept only Negro students. In recent years, since 1932, these institutions have almost tripled their enrollments whereas the institutions for whites or which are unsegregated only about doubled theirs (see table 6).

Inequalities Remain. But the numbers enrolled in school do not tell the whole story. Marked as has been the progress in Negro education in recent years, it cannot obscure the very great differences which still persist in educational opportunities afforded the Negro and the non-Negro.

In 17 states and the District of Columbia, segregation of the Negroes in education is established by law.[1] In the *Gaines* decision, the U. S. Supreme Court ruled that "if a State furnishes higher education to white residents, it is bound to furnish [within the State] substantially equal advantages to Negro students." Although segregation may not legally mean discrimination as to the quality of the facilities it usually does so in fact. The schools maintained for the Negroes are commonly much inferior to those for the whites. The Negro schools are financed at a pitifully low level, they are often housed in buildings wholly inadequate for the purpose, and many of the teachers are sorely in need

TABLE 6

ENROLLMENT OF INSTITUTIONS OF HIGHER EDUCATION
AND INDEX OF CHANGE[1]

| YEAR | ENROLLMENTS IN INSTITUTIONS ACCEPTING | | | |
| | Negroes only | | All other | |
	Number	Index of change (1932 = 100)	Number	Index of change (1932 = 100)
1932.	21,880	100	1,132,237	100
1936.	32,628	149	1,175,599	104
1940.	41,839	191	1,452,364	128
1947[2].	63,500	290	2,290,500	202

[1] Source is resident enrollment as reported by U.S. Office of Education.
[2] Estimated.

of more education themselves. Library facilities are generally poor or lacking altogether, and professional supervision is more a name than a reality.

These facts are supported strongly by a recent study in the District of Columbia. The District's Superintendent of Schools in his 1946–47 report to the Board of Education states that the student-teacher ratios in the schools for Negroes were significantly and consistently higher

---

[1] In the case of *Mendez v. Westminster School District,* the segregation of students of Mexican ancestry in the Westminster, Calif., school district, on the alleged grounds that because of their ancestry such students have language difficulties, was held illegal. The U.S. district court which heard the case held that segregation is unconstitutional under the Federal constitution. On appeal by the Westminster school district, the U.S. circuit court of appeals limited its affirmance of the district court's decision by holding that the specific statutes involved were illegal under the California law.

than those for non-Negroes—from the kindergartens through the teachers' colleges.

Segregation lessens the quality of education for the whites as well. To maintain two school systems side by side—duplicating even inadequately the buildings, equipment, and teaching personnel—means that neither can be of the quality that would be possible if all the available resources were devoted to one system, especially not when the States least able financially to support an adequate educational program for their youth are the very ones that are trying to carry a double load.

It must not be supposed that Negro youth living in States in which segregation is not legalized are given the same opportunities as white youth. In these areas economic and social discrimination of various sorts often operates to produce segregation in certain neighborhoods, which are frequently characterized by poorer school buildings, less equipment and less able teachers.

Equality of education opportunity is not achieved by the mere physical existence of schools; it involves also the quality of teaching and learning that takes place in them.

The Quota System. At the college level a different form of discrimination is commonly practiced. *Many colleges and universities, especially in their professional schools, maintain a selective quota system for admission, under which the chance to learn, and thereby to become more useful citizens, is denied to certain minorities, particularly to Negroes and Jews.*

This practice is a violation of a major American principle and is contributing to the growing tension in one of the crucial areas of our democracy.

The quota, or *numerus clausus,* is certainly un-American. It is European in origin and application, and we have lately witnessed on that continent the horrors to which, in its logical extension, it can lead. To insist that specialists in any field shall be limited by ethnic quotas is to assume that the Nation is composed of separate and self-sufficient ethnic groups and this assumption America has never made except in the case of its Negro population, where the result is one of the plainest inconsistencies with our national ideal.

The quota system denies the basic American belief that intelligence and ability are present in all ethnic groups, that men of all religious and racial origins should have equal opportunity to fit themselves for contributing to the common life.

Moreover, since the quota system is never applied to all groups in the Nation's population, but only to certain ones, we are forced to conclude that the arguments advanced to justify it are nothing more than rationalizations to cover either convenience or the disposition to discriminate. The quota system cannot be justified on any grounds compatible with democratic principles.

Consequences of Inequalities of Opportunity

These various barriers to educational opportunity involve grave consequences both for the individual and for society.

From the viewpoint of the individual they are denying to millions of young people what the democratic creed assumes to be their birthright: an equal chance with all others to make the most of their native abilities. From the viewpoint of society the barriers mean that far too few of our young people are getting enough preparation for assuming the personal, social, and civic responsibilities of adults living in a democratic society.

It is especially serious that not more of our most talented young people continue their schooling beyond high school in this day when the complexity of life and of our social problems means that we need desperately every bit of trained intelligence we can assemble. The present state of affairs is resulting in far too great a loss of talent—our most precious natural resource in a democracy.

In a country as vast as the United States, with all its regional differences in cultural patterns and economic resources, absolute equality of educational opportunity perhaps may not be reasonably expected. But today the differences that do exist are so great as to compel immediate action.

In communities where the birth rate is low, where the burden of caring for the nurture and education of the oncoming generation is relatively light, where the level of living is high, the advantages of education are extended to youth on more nearly equal terms. But in communities where the birth rate is high, where the economic structure is weak, where the level of living is low, where community and family resources contribute least to intellectual growth, there we support education in niggardly fashion, though at great effort.

If over the years we continue to draw the population reserves of the Nation from the most underprivileged areas and families and fail to make good the deficit by adequate educational opportunities, we shall be following a course that is sure to prove disastrous to the level of our culture and to the whole fabric of our democratic institutions.

We have proclaimed our faith in education as a means of equalizing the conditions of men. But there is grave danger that our present policy will make it an instrument for creating the very inequalities it was designed to prevent. If the ladder of educational opportunity rises high at the doors of some youth and scarcely rises at all at the doors of others, while at the same time formal education is made a prerequisite to occupational and social advance, then education may become the means, not of eliminating race and class distinctions, but of deepening and solidifying them.

It is obvious, then, that free and universal access to education, in terms of the interest, ability, and need of the student, must be a major goal in American education.

TOWARD EQUALIZING OPPORTUNITY

The American people should set as their ultimate goal an educational system in which at no level—high school, college, graduate school, or professional school—will a qualified individual in any part of the country encounter an insuperable economic barrier to the attainment of the kind of education suited to his aptitudes and interests.

This means that we shall aim at making higher education equally available to all young people, as we now do education in the elementary and high schools, to the extent that their capacity warrants a further social investment in their training.

Obviously this desirable realization of our ideal of equal educational opportunity cannot be attained immediately. But if we move toward it as fast as our economic resources permit, it should not lie too far in the future. Technological advances, that are already resulting in phenomenal increases in productivity per worker, promise us a degree of economic well-being that would have seemed wholly Utopian to our fathers. With wise management of our economy, we shall almost certainly be able to support education at all levels far more adequately in the future than we could in the past.

The Commission recommends that steps be taken to reach the following objectives without delay:

1. High school education must be improved and should be provided for all normal youth.

This is a minimum essential. We cannot safely permit any of our citizens for any reason other than incapacity, to stop short of a high school education or its equivalent. To achieve the purpose of such education, however, it must be improved in facilities and in the diversity of its curriculum. Better high school education is essential, both to raise the caliber of students entering college and to provide the best training possible for those who end their formal education with the twelfth grade.

2. The time has come to make education through the fourteenth grade available in the same way that high school education is now available.

This means that tuition-free education should be available in public institutions to all youth for the traditional freshman and sophomore years or for the traditional 2-year junior college course.

To achieve this, it will be necessary to develop much more extensively than at present such opportunities as are now provided in local communities by the 2-year junior college, community institute, community college, or institute of arts and sciences. The name used does not matter, though community college seems to describe these schools best; the important thing is that the services they perform be recognized and vastly extended.

Such institutions make post-high-school education available to a much larger percentage of young people than otherwise could afford it. Indeed, as discussed in the volume of this Commission's report, "Organizing Higher Education," such community colleges probably will have to carry a large part of the responsibility for expanding opportunities in higher education.

3. The time has come to provide financial assistance to competent students in the tenth through fourteenth grades who would not be able to continue without such assistance.

Tuition costs are not the major economic barrier to education, especially in college. Costs of supplies, board, and room, and other living needs are great. Even many high-school students are unable to continue in school because of these costs.

Arrangements must be made, therefore, to provide additional financial assistance for worthy students who need it if they are to remain in school. Only in this way can we counteract the effect of family incomes so low that even tuition-free schooling is a financial impossibility for their children. Only in this way can we make sure that all who are to participate in democracy are adequately prepared to do so.

4. The time has come to reverse the present tendency of increasing tuition and other student fees in the senior college beyond the four-teenth year, and in both graduate and professional schools, by lower-ing tuition costs in publicly controlled colleges and by aiding deserving students through inaugurating a program of scholarships and fellow-ships.

Only in this way can we be sure that economic and social barriers will not prevent the realization of the promise that lies in our most gifted youth. Only in this way can we be certain of developing for the common good all the potential leadership our society produces, no matter in what social or economic stratum it appears.

5. The time has come to expand considerably our program of adult education, and to make more of it the responsibility of our colleges and universities.

The crisis of the time and the rapidly changing conditions under which we live make it especially necessary that we provide a continu-ing and effective educational program for adults as well as youth. We can in this way, perhaps, make up some of the educational deficiencies of the past, and also in a measure counteract the pressures and distrac-tions of adult life that all too often make the end of formal schooling the end of education too.

6. The time has come to make public education at all levels equally accessible to all, without regard to race, creed, sex or national origin.

If education is to make the attainment of a more perfect democracy one of its major goals, it is imperative that it extend its benefits to all on equal terms. It must renounce the practices of discrimination and segregation in educational institutions as contrary to the spirit of de-mocracy. Educational leaders and institutions should take positive steps to overcome the conditions which at present obstruct free and equal access to educational opportunities. Educational programs everywhere should be aimed at undermining and eventually eliminating the atti-tudes that are responsible for discrimination and segregation—at cre-ating instead attitudes that will make education freely available to all.[2]

---

[2] The following Commission members wish to record their dissent from the Com-mission's pronouncements on "segregation," especially as these pronouncements are re-lated to education in the South. Arthur H. Compton, Douglas S. Freeman, Lewis W. Jones, Goodrich C. White. A fuller statement, indicating briefly the basis for this dis-sent, will appear in volume II of the Commission's report.

NUMBER WHO SHOULD RECEIVE HIGHER EDUCATION

Achieving these immediate objectives necessarily will require a tremendous expansion of our educational enterprise at the college level.

It will be noted that many of the Commission's projects focus upon the year 1960. There are several important reasons why the Commission has chosen to look this far ahead. First of all, in the President's letter of appointment, the Commission was asked to direct its energies toward the investigation of long-term policy issues in American higher education. The Commission itself selected the terminal date of 1960 since it was felt that manageable data could be procured for studies up to this point. The basic consideration of population data weighed heavily in the selection. Individuals who will be enrolled in colleges in 1960 through 1964 have already been born, and thus the Commission has a tangible figure with which to make its projections.

The Commission believes that in 1960 a minimum of 4,600,000 young people should be enrolled in nonprofit institutions for education beyond the traditional twelfth grade. Of this total number, 2,500,000 should be in the thirteenth and fourteenth grades (junior college level); 1,500,000 in the fifteenth and sixteenth grades (senior college level); and 600,000 in graduate and professional schools beyond the first degree.

In thus appraising future enrollment in institutions of post-high school education, this Commission has not sought to project the future on the basis of the past nor to predict annual enrollments over the period 1948 to 1960. It frankly recognizes that such a forecast would be subject to unpredictable world-wide social and economic conditions.

THE NEED FOR GENERAL EDUCATION

Present college programs are not contributing adequately to the quality of students' adult lives either as workers or citizens. This is true in large part because the unity of liberal education has been splintered by overspecialization.

For half a century and more the curriculum of the liberal arts college has been expanding and disintegrating to an astounding degree. The number of courses has so multiplied that no student could take all of them, or even a majority of them, in a lifetime. In one small midwestern college, for example, the number of courses offered increased from 67 in 1900 to 296 in 1930. During the same period the liberal arts college of one of the great private universities lengthened its list of courses from 960 to 1,897.

This tendency to diversify the content of what was once an integrated liberal education is in part the consequence of the expansion of the boundaries of knowledge. New advances in every direction have added more and more subjects to the liberal arts curriculum and have at the same time limited the area of knowledge a single course could cover. This development is at once the parent and the child of specialization.

Specialization is a hallmark of our society, and its advantages to mankind have been remarkable. But in the educational program it has become a source both of strength and of weakness. Filtering downward from the graduate and professional school levels, it has taken over the undergraduate years, too, and in the more extreme instances it has made of the liberal arts college little more than another vocational school, in which the aim of teaching is almost exclusively preparation for advanced study in one or another specialty.

This tendency has been fostered, if not produced, by the training of college teachers in the graduate school, where they are imbued with the single ideal of an ever-narrowing specialism.

The trend toward specialization has been reenforced by the movement toward democratization of higher education. The young people appearing in growing numbers on college campuses have brought with them widely diverse purposes, interests, capacities, and academic backgrounds. Some expect to enter one of the old-line professions; others want training in one of the numerous branches of agriculture, industry or commerce. Some consider college education a natural sequel to high school; others seek it as a road to higher social status.

The net result of the situation is that the college student is faced with a bewildering array of intensive courses from which to make up his individual program. To secure a reasonably comprehensive grasp of his major field, he must in some cases spend as much as half or more of his time in that one department. The other half he scatters among courses in other departments which, designed for future specialists in those fields, are so restricted in scope that the student can gain from them only a fragmentary view of the subject. He, therefore, leaves college unacquainted with some of the fundamental areas of human knowledge and without the integrated view of human experience that is essential both for personal balance and for social wisdom.

Today's college graduate may have gained technical or professional training in one field of work or another, but is only incidentally, if at all, made ready for performing his duties as a man, a parent, and a citizen. Too often he is "educated" in that he has acquired competence in some particular occupation, yet falls short of that human wholeness and civic conscience which the cooperative activities of citizenship require.

The failure to provide any core of unity in the essential diversity of higher education is a cause for grave concern. A society whose numbers lack a body of common experience and common knowledge is a society without a fundamental culture; it tends to disintegrate into a mere aggregation of individuals. Some community of values, ideas, and attitudes is essential as a cohesive force in this age of minute division of labor and intense conflict of special interests.

The crucial task of higher education today, therefore, is to provide a unified general education for American youth. Colleges must find the right relationship between specialized training on the one hand, aiming at a thousand different careers, and the transmission of a common cultural heritage toward a common citizenship on the other.

There have already been many efforts to define this relationship. Attempts to reach conclusions about the ends and means of general education have been a major part of debate and experimentation in higher education for at least two decades.

"General education" is the term that has come to be accepted for those phases of nonspecialized and nonvocational learning which should be the common experience of all educated men and women.

General education should give to the student the values, attitudes, knowledge, and skills that will equip him to live rightly and well in a free society. It should enable him to identify, interpret, select, and build into his own life those components of his cultural heritage that contribute richly to understanding and appreciation of the world in which he lives. It should therefore embrace ethical values, scientific generalizations, and aesthetic conceptions, as well as an understanding of the purposes and character of the political, economic, and social institutions that men have devised.

But the knowledge and understanding which general education aims to secure, whether drawn from the past or from a living present, are not to be regarded as ends in themselves. They are means to a more abundant personal life and a stronger, freer social order.

Thus conceived, general education is not sharply distinguished from liberal education; the two differ mainly in degree, not in kind. General education undertakes to redefine liberal education in terms of life's problems as men face them, to give it human orientation and social direction, to invest it with content that is directly relevant to the demands of contemporary society. General education is liberal education with its matter and method shifted from its original aristocratic intent to the service of democracy. General education seeks to extend to all men the benefits of an education that liberates.

This purpose calls for a unity in the program of studies that a uniform system of courses cannot supply. The unity must come, instead, from a consistency of aim that will infuse and harmonize all teaching and all campus activities.

11. *Hutchins on the President's Commission, 1948*

See Docs. 5 and 10.

I

. . . The Report of the President's Commission on Higher Education reflects the educational system with which it deals. It is big and booming. It is confused, confusing, and contradictory. It has something for everybody. It is generous, ignoble, bold, timid, naïve, and optimistic. It is filled with the spirit of universal brotherhood and the sense of American superiority. It has great faith in money. It has great faith in courses. It is anti-humanistic and anti-intellectual. It is confident that vices can be turned into virtues by making them larger. Its heart is in the right place; its head does not work very well.

Every cliché and every slogan of contemporary educational discussion appear once more. Much of the report reads like a Fourth-of-July oration in Pedaguese. It skirts the edge of illiteracy, and sometimes falls over the brink. And, when the battle has ended, the field is strewn with the corpses of the straw men the Commission has slain.

The cry is "more"; more money, more buildings, more professors,

Robert M. Hutchins, "Report of the President's Commission on Higher Education," *Educational Record*, XXIX (April, 1948), 107–22. Reprinted with the permission of The American Council on Education.

more students, more everything. The educational system is taken as given. It may be wasteful and shoddy. But let us expand it, even if that means that it will be more wasteful and shoddier, and all will be well.

If the Commission's purpose was to write a propaganda document, to praise American education and not to criticize it, the result is unconvincing. A good propaganda document should not promise what is obviously impossible and undesirable, as the Commission does when it proposes to double the output of doctors by 1960 and to double the staff of colleges by 1952. Only disillusionment can follow from a program which undertakes to make the American people intelligent, prosperous, and happy by the simple process of doubling the students, the professors, and the expenditures of higher educational institutions.

II

The Commission is right about many things. It is right in pointing out that higher education in the United States is free only in the sense that public colleges or universities charge low fees or none. Higher education is not free in the sense that students without money can avail themselves of it. The cost of living and the loss of earning power to their families prevent many young people from going to a free college. They are just as well qualified as those who go. Many of those who go do so because they can afford it. Many of those who do not go don't because they can't. The Commission properly insists that the economic conditions of a young person's parents should not determine his educational opportunities.

The Commission sees that the economic barriers to educational opportunity must be broken down by the federal government. Only the federal government has the money. Only the federal government can equalize educational opportunity among the states. Federal equalization without federal control can best be obtained by national scholarships and fellowships; students could use them to pay their way at any accredited institution, public or private.

The Commission attacks the economic barriers to education by advocating the wide extension of the junior college movement. These institutions, which the Commission prefers to call "community colleges," enable the student to live at home through the conventional sophomore year. The Commission favors making this college as free to the student as the high school is today. Although, as we shall see, the Commission has no clear idea of the purpose, organization, or activities of the community college, the Commission does understand that this unit can do much to equalize educational opportunity.

The Commission strongly condemns those barriers to educational opportunity which have been thrown up by racial and religious prejudice. These are indefensible, and have never been defended on their merits. The defense has been that colleges and universities would do more harm than good, or at least would do no good, to those whom they were trying to help, if they took a stand against discrimination which was much in advance of the communities in which they were located. Actually the horrid consequences predicted when the removal of discrimination is discussed in educational institutions never materialize when it is removed. If there were some unpleasantness, it could not be regarded as important. What is important is that institutions of higher learning should stand for something. If they will not stand for the Rights of Man, how can they expect anybody else to?

The Commission is on sound ground when it urges the extension of the educational opportunities open to adults. Many adults have had no education, including great numbers who have graduated from college. Education is a process which should go on through the whole of life. Many disciplines, and they are among the most important, will not give up their secrets except to those who have had experience with the issues which the disciplines raise. The education of youth is a waste of time if youth is to have no future. Unless we can educate those who control the world today, it seems most unlikely that youth can have a future.

The Commission is right on many other matters with which it deals more briefly. It is right on the value of technical aids to learning, though it exaggerates the educational possibilities of AM broadcasting. It is right on the place of intercollegiate athletics. It rightly attacks specialization, the narrow preparation of college teachers, and the limitations which professions place on their numbers in order to increase the prestige or value of their services. It rightly urges the support of basic research by industry, though it says, for reasons which are obscure, that half the support of basic research must in the future come from the federal government. It opposes secrecy in research and the control of research by the military. It is for academic freedom.

III

It is impossible to form a judgment on some sections of the report, because it is impossible to discover what the Commission's attitude is.

The most important of the issues which the Commission leaves unresolved is that of the organization of education. Yet, unless this question can be intelligently settled, the extension of the junior colleges will be of doubtful benefit to the country; much of the money which the Commission wishes to have spent on education will be wasted; and the system which results will be inferior to the one we have today.

Apparently because it does not wish to arouse the antagonism of vested interests, the Commission dodges the question of organization every time the question rears its head. The Commission does so even when its arguments seem to lead inevitably to an attack on the problem and a rational solution of it. The Commission says (III, 7), "The senior high school and the first two years of college, particularly the liberal arts college, are similar in purpose, and there is much duplication of content in their courses." It goes on (III, 12), "The present difficulty grows largely out of the fact that the academic work of the last 2 years of the high school and that of the first 2 years of the typical arts college are essentially identical in purpose." We then find (III, 17) that "many young people of ages 16, 17, 18, and 19 are well suited for residence on a college campus. In the school system developed on the 6-4-4 plan, the last unit embraces those ages. Liberal arts colleges may well parallel this last unit. . . . Furthermore there is a tendency at present to stretch out too long the period of pre-professional and professional study. Students ought much more generally than now to enter many fields of professional study when not older than 20. . . . Today the age of 20 falls in the middle of the arts college course." Later the Commission says (III, 70) in urging a great increase in the number of community colleges, "This development should be guided by a State-wide plan in which at least the following features should be found: (1) The larger municipalities will extend their public school programs to include the thirteenth and fourteenth years or grades, thus making possible further experimentation with the 6-4-4 plan."

Meanwhile we have learned (III, 18) that, "The present plan of building a curriculum for a bachelor's degree and then another often poorly related program for a master's degree is far inferior as a preparation for teaching than would be a unified 3-year program above the community college, or above the sophomore year of the liberal arts college."

From these quotations one might suppose that the Commission, recognizing the waste and incoherence of two-year units and two-year courses of study, would recommend a six-year elementary school, a four-year high school, a four-year college, and a three-year program to the master's degree. One might even suppose that the Commission would be forced to suggest the relocation or elimination of the bachelor's degree, since that degree obviously interferes with the construction of an intelligible curriculum to the master's. The Commission does none of these things. It assumes that the bachelor's degree must stay where it is. In general it assumes an 8-4-2-2-1 program to the master's; its pages are studded with references to "2-year curricula" in the senior high school, the junior college, and the senior college. We even hear (III, 5) that, "The two-year college—that is the thirteenth and fourteenth years of our educational system—is about as widely needed today as the 4-year high school was a few decades ago."

Far from being widely needed, the two-year college disrupts the educational system. As the Commission shows, it duplicates the high school; it cuts the college of liberal arts in half and makes it a two-year unit, too. The opportunity which the Commission had, and missed, was the opportunity to follow its own reasoning to the creation of a 6-4-4-3 system to the master's degree and to put the bachelor's degree, two-year units, and two-year curriculums, with the inefficiency, duplication, and aimlessness which they reflect and cause, to sleep forever.

IV

Some difficulties arise in discussing matters even more important than the organization of education because the Commission, through inadvertence, indecision, or a desire to please everybody, contradicts or qualifies its statements to such an extent that it is possible to prove almost anything from the report.

For example, we are told at the outset (I, 6) that "to assume that all we need to do is apply to present and future problems 'eternal' truths revealed in earlier ages is likely to stifle creative imagination and intellectual daring." A few pages farther on (I, 11–12) we learn that, "The everlasting moral essence of democracy lies in its fundamental principles, not in its means and methods of the moment."

The Commission appears indifferent to all considerations of quality in education; but it says (I, 44), "Simply to keep more of our youth in school for a longer period will not of itself, of course, achieve the personal and social ends we have in mind. The measure to which extended educational opportunities accomplish our purposes will depend on the kind of education provided."

The Commission seems to think that education should be infinitely diversified; but it says (I, 46), "Yet in the midst of all the necessary diversity we must somehow preserve and expand a central unity. We must make sure that every student includes the kind of learning and experience that is essential to fit free men to live in a free society."

These contradictions and qualifications illustrate one of the fundamental misconceptions upon which the report is based. This is the assumption that education can do everything and that education ought to do everything. Since education can do everything and ought to do everything, it can and should pursue conflicting purposes, for every purpose is as good as every other. Hence there can be no such thing as a contradiction in the report. I am reminded of a great educator I once knew who, when he was told that something he proposed was wrong and that he ought to do the opposite, would say, "We'll do that too!"

The fact that distresses the Commission most is that in 1945 half the children of America were growing up in families which had a cash income of $2,530 or less. The Commission is pained to learn that the birth rate is highest in the families with the lowest income. When we get to the second volume of the report (II, 11), we find the Commission saying in passing that, "All measures which will contribute to increasing the total national productivity thus become essential as indirect means toward lessening economic barriers to education." But the whole report is based upon the proposition that it is necessary to overcome the maldistribution in income by expenditures on education itself.

If the economic barriers to education arise because of the inequities in the economic system, and if the birth rate is highest in the families with the lowest incomes, the first consideration of the educational statesmen should be to remove the inequities in the economic system and to raise the income or lower the birth rate of the families with the lowest incomes and the highest birth rate. The Commission is a little sanctimonious about the birth rate. It says (I, 32), "No one would suggest that the proper remedy for this situation is a lower birth rate in any part of the country." But if we can raise the incomes of the families with the lowest incomes, we shall lower the birth rate of those families and hence lower the birth rate in the parts of the country in which those families live.

It may be said that there is no harm in the fact that the Commission takes the economic system for granted and tries to see what can be done to overcome the handicaps which it causes by direct assistance to students and institutions: the Commission was appointed to study education and not economics. The reply is that the Commission gives its powerful support to the omnibus fallacy, the doctrine that education, more education, more expensive education, will solve every problem and answer every prayer. The omnibus fallacy diverts the public mind from direct attack on the evil under consideration by proposing the easy, if costly, alternative, "Let education do it." In the case of the economic barriers to education it is clear that whatever is done by way of scholarship or grants-in-aid to institutions cannot go to the heart of the matter. But our people are likely to think that, if they make the vast educational expenditures recommended by the Commission, the problem is solved.

V

According to the omnibus fallacy there is nothing which education cannot do; and it can do everything equally well. Education, in this view, cannot decline a task because it is not qualified to perform it; education cannot suggest that another agency or institution could perform it better. In discussing the kind of higher education it wants, the Commission gets more and more inclusive until its summary "sentence" is this (II, 6), "One which is not only general and liberal, not only sufficiently vocational, not only for broad competence in citizenship and in the wise use of leisure, but also an integrated and meaningful combination of all these aims at successive levels of education in accordance with the potentialities of each." . . .

Education cannot do everything. It cannot do everything equally well. It cannot do some things as well as other social institutions can do them or could do them if these institutions were forced to discharge their responsibilities instead of leaving the educational system to struggle along with them by default. It may be that education could teach our people to build richly textured and gracious lives if it were free to concentrate on that task. It may be that our people can learn to make a living without asking higher education to teach them how. It seems altogether likely that the attempt on the part of education to do what it cannot do well will prevent it from doing what it can do well. One of the things education cannot do well is vocational training. That can best be conducted on the job. The rapid changes in technology and the mobility of our population makes vocational training given one day in one place a handicap the next day in another place. "Rarely does a college student expect necessarily to live in the State where he is attending college."

VI

Among the objectives of general education the Commission lists certain "basic outcomes." The student must be taught to be healthy: "What is needed is a course . . ." (I, 54). The student must be taught the knowledge and attitudes basic to a satisfying family life: "Such a general course would include . . ." (I, 56). The student must be taught to "get on well with people" (I, 53). The picture is one of the student coming to the college absolutely naked, with no past, no parents, no church, even without any Boy Scouts, being carefully swathed in layers of courses and sent out into the world, ready to cope with economic, political, domestic, social, or meteorological vicissitudes. I say it cannot be done; and I say that, if it is attempted, the educational system will fail in the attempt, and what is more important, it will fail in its proper task.

The Commission at the end of its list of eleven basic outcomes (How can an outcome be basic? And can eleven outcomes all be equally basic?) says, "Ability to think and to reason, within the limits set by one's mental capacity, should be the distinguishing mark of an educated person" (I, 57). With this I entirely agree. The distinguishing mark of the educated person is intellectual power. Hence, the primary aim of higher education is the development of intellectual power. Any other aim is secondary and can be tolerated only to the extent to which the attempt to achieve it does not interfere with the effort to achieve the primary aim. Such an aim as adjustment to the environment is not merely secondary, it is wrong: it would prevent education from putting forth its noblest effort, the effort to produce men like Socrates and Gandhi, who were not adjusted to their environment, who did not "get on well with people," and who died because they did not.

Although one would think that the proper task of higher education was to place the distinguishing mark of the educated person, intellectual power, upon those who pass through our colleges and universities, the Commission never misses a chance to communicate the news that our educational institutions are far too intellectual. This will certainly surprise the students, parents, administrators, and citizens who have had anything to do with our educational system. To the disinterested observer the American educational system looks like a gigantic playroom, designed to keep the young out of worse places until they can go to work.

The Commission solemnly warns the colleges and universities not to turn out a generation of impractical visionaries. Oh, for just one impractical visionary a year! The Commission deplores "the present orientation of higher education towards verbal skills and intellectual interests" (I, 32). It says that American schools and colleges are preoccupied with the training of the intellect. It even thinks that faculty meetings are too intellectual and recommends "deliberations which have some immediate results, such as the purchase of new movie projectors, or the issuance of a career guidebook for students" (IV, 40). It urges administrators to be irrational. "Administrators tend to think in terms of a logical approach to curriculum problems—formulating an over-all philosophy first, then stating broad objectives, appraising the present program in terms of those objectives, defining weaknesses, and discovering ways to eliminate them. Experience demonstrates that this approach is likely to be unproductive of the one essential change, a change in the thinking and teaching and research activities of individual faculty members" (IV, 41). And so we end up with a college in which neither the students, the faculty, nor the officers are supposed to think, or, at least, to look as though they were thinking.

VII

The report calls again and again for greater diversification in education. It says, "There is already a wide variety of purposes and programs in American colleges . . ." (This would appear to be an understatement.) ". . . but there is need for even greater diversification and experimentation to take account of different kinds and degrees of intellectual capacity, talent, and interest" (II, 7). The Commission believes that, "As we bring more and more students to the campus, we shall increase in proportion the tremendous variety of human and social needs the college programs must meet. We shall add to the already overwhelming diversity of aptitudes, interests, and levels of attainment that characterize the student body. And so we shall have to increase the diversification of curricular offerings and of teaching methods and materials to correspond" (I, 45–46).

Since American institutions of higher education are already so diversified that neither the faculty nor the students can talk with one another except about the weather, politics, and last Saturday's game, the Commission's advice is a little like telling a drowning man that he can improve his position by drinking a great deal of water. On the very next page the Commission says, in bold-face type, that the colleges are failing in large part "because the unity of liberal education has been splintered by overspecialization" (I, 47). This is one time when the Commission cannot have it both ways: either it must admit that it does not care about liberal education, or it must recognize that it is impossible to offer a program that includes everything that might interest everybody, from acrobatics to zymurgy, and have it add up to a liberal education. If you believe, as the Commission says it does, in bold-face type (I, 49), that, "The crucial task of higher education today, therefore, is to provide a unified general education for American youth," then you must find out what that education is; you must offer it to American youth; and you must not divert your mind or theirs from this crucial task until you are sure that it has been accomplished.

The Commission's program of infinite diversification rests on a non sequitur. Since men are different, the Commission holds their education must be different. Men *are* different; but they are also the same. As the Commission points out, education in this country has failed in large part because it has emphasized those respects in which men are different; that is what excessive specialization means. The purpose of liberal or general education is to bring out our common humanity, a consummation more urgently needed today than at any time within the last five hundred years. To confuse at every point, as the Commission does, the education of our common humanity, which is primary and fundamental, with the education of our individual differences, which is secondary and in many cases unnecessary, is to get bad education at every point.

VIII

As we have seen, the Commission's principal reason for demanding greater diversification is that it proposes to double the number of students beyond the twelfth grade by 1960. The basis for this proposal is the revelation, provided by the Army General Classification Test, that at least 49 percent of the college-age population of the country has the ability to complete the first two years of college work, and at least 32 percent has the ability to complete additional years of higher education. ". . . these percentage figures supply conservative yet conclusive evidence of the social advisability of increased numbers attending college" (II, 7).

These percentage figures supply some evidence that a larger proportion of the college-age population has the ability to complete certain years of college. They supply no evidence whatever of the social advisability of having them do so. The argument that they should do so is based on the proposition that they have as much ability as those who are in college now. To know whether it is socially desirable to have them go to college, we should have to know whether it is socially desirable for all those who are in college now to be there, a question on which the Commission offers no evidence, and we should have to know why those who are not in college are not there. For example, it does not seem self-evident that a young man of twenty should be in the junior year in college if he prefers to be somewhere else.

Every citizen of a free society is entitled to a liberal education. This is the education which develops his intellectual power and the humanity which he has in common with his fellow-men. The first object of American educators should be to determine what a liberal education is; the second should be to discover the organization of the curriculum and of the educational system which will permit the student to acquire a liberal education in the shortest period of time. Father Gannon of Fordham has suggested that through a six-year elementary school, a three-year high school, and a three-year college the student can get a liberal education by the time he is eighteen. There is plenty of evidence that the 6-4-4 plan permits the acquisition of liberal education by the age of nineteen or twenty.

This program requires the rigorous exclusion of triviality, frivolity, and duplication from the educational system. The student cannot get a liberal education by the age of eighteen or twenty if he has to be taught eleven basic outcomes; he cannot do it on the 8-4-2-2 plan. Nor can he do it if it is assumed that everything which might be useful or interesting to the citizen can and should be taught him in his youth. One of the reasons why the education of adults should be greatly expanded is that many things can be really learned only in adult life. Sir Richard Livingstone has taught us long since that for this reason the cultural level of a country cannot be automatically raised by the simple expedient of raising the school-leaving age.

Up to the point at which they have acquired a liberal education, then, we have an obligation to have all our youth, not 49 percent, but all, in college. Beyond that point education is a privilege, not a right. Its continuation beyond that point must chiefly depend on ability and interest. The Commission makes an appalling statement about interest: "Further, many individual young people offset their economic handicaps with cultural aspirations, ambition, and a driving thirst for knowledge that lead them to attempt to work their way through college if such a path is opened up to them. Yet such individual efforts will necessarily be the exception and are not palliatives to adverse conditions." (II, 11. Can the Commission mean that such efforts are mere palliatives?)

I am opposed to the prevailing superstition that it is a good thing for a boy to work his way through college; but the implication that cultural aspirations, ambition, and a driving thirst for knowledge are to be regarded as exceptional in our colleges has dreadful consequences; for these are precisely the qualifications for advanced study. Without them nobody should be admitted to it.

If everybody were in school or college until he had acquired a liberal education, and if beyond that only those were admitted who had the interest and ability that advanced study requires, we should have far more students up to the ages of eighteen or twenty and far fewer over those ages. The number of students we have should not be based on the number or on the ability of those we have now. It should be based on a clear definition of the purpose of each unit of the educational system.

IX

At the present time the omnibus is not going anywhere in particular, or rather, it is going off in all directions at once. The problem of higher education in America is not the problem of quantity. Whatever our shortcomings in this regard, we have a larger proportion of our young people in higher education than any country I can think of; and we certainly have more teachers and more square feet per student in bigger, newer buildings than any other nation in the world.

Neither the proportion of the population in school, nor the length of their schooling, nor the amount of money spent on it is an index to the educational requirements of a people, *unless* it is first established that the educational system under discussion is headed in the right direction. To increase the number of students, to prolong the period of their incarceration in schools, to spend twice the money, but spend it in the same way, when the system is headed in no direction, or in the wrong direction, or in all directions at once—these things will merely add to the embarrassments of the taxpayer; they will not promote the moral and intellectual development of our people.

What America needs, what the world needs, is a moral, intellectual, and spiritual revolution. Higher education in America fails unless it does what it can to initiate and carry through this revolution. This revolution will not be assisted by the infinite multiplication of trivial courses, of buildings, students, professors, salaries, or of colleges and universities. It will come only when the educators of America are willing to admit that the revolution must come and that they must make their contribution to it. It will come only when they are ready to forget their vested interests and try to see what the revolution will involve and how higher education should be related to it. The educators of America will be entitled to the support they demand when they can show that they know where they are going and why. The report of the President's Commission on Higher Education suggests that the time is still far off.

INDEX

PRINTED IN U.S.A.